THE BRITISH CONSTITUTION

Other books by J. Harvey

★

ELEMENTARY ECONOMICS

WORKBOOK FOR ELEMENTARY ECONOMICS

INTERMEDIATE ECONOMICS

MULTIPLE-CHOICE QUESTIONS FOR INTERMEDIATE
ECONOMICS

MODERN ECONOMICS

MODERN ECONOMICS STUDY GUIDE AND WORKBOOK
(with M. K. Johnson)

MODERN ECONOMICS STUDENTS' NOTEBOOK

INTRODUCTION TO MACRO-ECONOMICS
(with M. K. Johnson)

INTRODUCTION TO MACRO-ECONOMICS WORKBOOK
(with M. K. Johnson)

PRODUCING AND SPENDING (with M. Harvey)

HOW BRITAIN IS GOVERNED

HOW BRITAIN IS GOVERNED WORKBOOK
(with M. de la Cour)

GOVERNMENT AND PEOPLE (with M. Harvey)

THE
BRITISH CONSTITUTION

BY

J. HARVEY, B.Sc. (Econ.)

AND

L. BATHER, B.A., Ph.D.

FOURTH EDITION

M

Macmillan Education

First Published 1963
Reprinted 1964 (twice), 1965, 1966, 1967
Second Edition 1968
Reprinted 1969
Third Edition 1972
Reprinted 1974, 1976
Fourth Edition 1977
Reprinted 1978, 1980

Permission has been given for this book to be transcribed into Braille

Published by
MACMILLAN EDUCATION LTD
Houndmills Basingstoke Hampshire RG21 2XS
and London
Associated companies in Delhi Dublin
Hong Kong Johannesburg Lagos Melbourne
New York Singapore and Tokyo

ISBN 0 333 21470 6

Printed in Hong Kong by
China Translation & Printing Services Ltd

Contents

I INTRODUCTORY

II THE LEGISLATURE

IV THE JUDICIARY

V LOCAL GOVERNMENT

VI THE COMMONWEALTH

VII REFLECTIONS ON THE BRITISH CONSTITUTION

VIII INTERNATIONAL POLITICAL
INSTITUTIONS

List of Figures

TABLES

Preface

IN writing this book, our primary object has been to provide a textbook covering the British system of government. It has been designed particularly for students of 'British Constitution' in the General Certificate of Education, for those taking professional examinations such as the Diploma in Public Administration, and for undergraduates needing a broad survey of the field.

As far as possible, the book seeks to be analytical as well as historical, descriptive and factual. Subjects have usually been introduced historically, for 'the British system of parliamentary government is, of all political regimes, the most difficult to understand without constant reference to the history of the country' (Prof. A. Mathiot: *The British Political System*). In some places, as when dealing with parliamentary procedure and the organisation of the judiciary, considerable detail has been included in order to ensure precision. It is recognised, however, that this has tended to make those sections essentially factual. Nevertheless, it is trusted that compensation will be found where broad principles, such as the rule of law and the separation of powers, are discussed, and where the problems confronting our different political institutions, such as the House of Lords, the monarchy, and administrative tribunals, are analysed.

It is to be hoped that the ideas surveyed in such sections will stimulate the reader to further thought and research. To facilitate this, a book list is provided at the end of each chapter, although it is not claimed that this represents an exhaustive bibliography. Where more up-to-date knowledge of current trends is required, the reader should consult the *Political Quarterly*, the *Journal of Public Administration*, *Parliamentary Affairs*, periodicals such as *The Economist*, *New Society* and *The Listener*, and the more serious daily and Sunday newspapers. Up-to-date information on aspects of British government is also published from time to time by Her Majesty's Stationery Office. For reference to particular issues, both *Keesing's Archives* and *The Times* are well indexed. As regards statistics, *British Political Facts*, *1900–1967*, by D. E. Butler and J. Freeman (Macmillan) and the *Annual Abstract of Statistics* (H.M.S.O.) will be found particularly useful.

One brief word of apology. It has been necessary to analyse the British constitution chiefly in terms of England and Wales. While this makes no substantial difference to the argument, it has meant that details regarding Scotland and Northern Ireland tend to be somewhat summarily treated.

It is impossible to thank individually all who have contributed to this book. To some, however, we are particularly indebted. Civil servants in almost every government department have answered our many queries with unfailing care and patience; but, as usual, they must remain anonymous. Dr. Donald Southgate of The University of St. Andrews, read the typescript and offered many helpful suggestions — though naturally this must not be taken to imply that he subscribes to all the views expressed. And the one author who is married would like to express his gratitude to his wife, who not only typed and re-typed the manuscript, but, over a period of three years suffered reference books lying around, isolated the children, and accepted lonely evenings.

Preface to the Second Edition

CHANGES in the British constitution since 1963 can no longer be confined to bringing facts up to date. In this new edition, alterations have been made to allow for fresh interpretations of the Constitution, the development of old institutions and the introduction of new ones. This has necessitated the re-writing, in particular, of the sections on the House of Lords, the procedure of the House of Commons, the organisation of government departments, the Civil Service, administrative justice, local government, the Commonwealth, and on the concept of democracy.

Help in this revision has come from a wide variety of sources — teachers and students who have taken the trouble to make valuable suggestions, Press Officers of the various branches of the administration who have checked facts and answered queries, and the staff of the Battersea District Reference Library who have been unflagging in their zeal to provide books, pamphlets, and government publications.

But we owe a special debt of gratitude to a few upon whom our demands have been particularly heavy; Mr. D. Pring, Deputy Principal Clerk of the House of Commons; Mr. D. Howe, Central Conservative Office; Mr. W. Brown, Transport House; Mr. A. Macdonald, Secretary of the Council on Tribunals; and Mr. L. Evans, Local Government Information Officer. All have devoted much of their scarce time to reading the relevant sections of the book and making pertinent comments. Naturally the views expressed in the book are those of the authors and they are responsible for any blemishes which remain.

Preface to the Third Edition

SINCE 1968, considerable changes have taken place in the British constitution. As a result we have had to re-write to a considerable extent the chapters on the House of Lords, elections to the House of Commons, the Cabinet, Government Departments, the Civil Service, the Judiciary, Local Government, the Commonwealth, and the concept of democracy. Facts have also been brought up to date.

Preface to Fourth Edition

THIS Fourth Edition recognises the trend of most of the Examining Boards, for both G.C.E. 'A' level and for professional examinations, to move away from constitutional mechanics to an examination of the contemporary political scene. Thus, while the basic elements of the British system of government are retained, two new chapters on 'Voting Behaviour' and 'Power and Politics' have been added.

Apart from bringing facts up to date, there has been considerable re-writing of the chapters on the Civil Service, the Judiciary, Local Government and World Government.

The authors are indebted to those readers who have made comments. Many of their suggestions are reflected in this new edition.

I

INTRODUCTORY

I

What is a 'Constitution'?

'The good or bad fortune of a nation depends on three
factors: its Constitution, the way the Constitution is
made to work, and the respect it inspires.'

GEORGES BIDAULT

THE NEED OF GOVERNMENT

Man has discovered that, by associating closely with his fellow-
men, he can lead a fuller life. Co-operation enables him to provide
for his material needs more easily, to satisfy his spiritual desires
more completely and to develop his cultural aspirations more richly.
Hence, to take a few examples, we find him enjoying the society of
his family, his trade union, his savings group, his Church, his
record club — and his State.

That persons with like interests should merely associate is,
however, usually inadequate. The objectives of the association can
be pursued effectively only if it is organised in some definite way
to co-ordinate the work of its members, to reconcile their conflicting opinions, to provide leadership and inspiration and, often, to
afford protection from outside attack.

Consider any club, society or organisation to which you belong.
It may have a single leader with authority, but more likely the
governing body is a committee which includes the officials of the
club. This committee organises the work of the society; makes
those decisions which are necessary between the full meetings of its
members; suggests the adoption of certain rules which, while
limiting the powers of individual members, promote the well-
being of the club as a whole; takes action to reconcile opposing
interests, and may even punish members who break the rules; and,
where necessary, suggests and organises measures for the defence
of the club.

Government, then, even in the simplest social unit, is an essential activity. It springs from the fact that man, by his nature, prefers to live in close relationship with his fellows.

When we consider the wider association of men within a State, the necessity of government becomes even more obvious. As a minimum the community requires first, that there shall be internal law and order and secondly, that there shall be effective defence against outside attack. The former involves the making of rules, ensuring that these rules are obeyed and, where they are not, taking effective action against the offender. The second necessitates deciding upon defence measures and seeing that they are implemented. Even in the most elementary organisation of a State, the work of government is concerned with the exercise of legislative, executive and judicial powers, i.e. the power to suggest and make laws, the power to administer these laws, and the power to judge when the laws have been broken.

THE PROBLEM OF GOVERNMENT

There is, however, an important difference between the government of a club and the government of a State. In a small club or society, legislation is usually left in the hands of the total body of members, rules being introduced, amended or rescinded only at a general or special meeting. A State, on the other hand, is too large and complex today for all its adults to assemble to make rules. What happens, therefore, is that the people elect certain members and charge them with the task of suggesting and passing laws deemed necessary for the community. In practice, this delegation of authority leads to certain problems. First, it involves giving power to a relatively small body of men, a power which usually has to be considerable if the government is to carry out its functions efficiently. Secondly, it necessitates a somewhat indirect supervision by the people of the way in which authority is exercised. A football club, for example, finds it comparatively easy to arrange a special meeting when a particularly important decision has to be reached or when it is felt that officials may have overstepped the mark. Indeed, the rules usually specify both the circumstances in which such a meeting must be called and the procedure for calling it.

This is, in effect, the practice followed by those States which insist on a referendum to decide certain vital issues. But to adopt the procedure frequently would, at the least, be inconvenient and, at the worst, might lead to irreparable delay in taking decisive action. The result is that governments, in fulfilling their tasks, are allowed to exercise wide discretion, even to the extent of committing a country to war.

But how can the people effectively retain ultimate control? They can never be sure that a government will act in complete harmony with their wishes and, above all, there is always the more serious danger that the authority given may be exceeded. 'Power tends to corrupt and absolute power corrupts absolutely,' said Lord Acton.

A government may become dictatorial and remove the liberties of the people because it thinks it has superior knowledge and that, by doing so, it will benefit the people in the long run. 'Throughout history the most terrible form of tyranny has been forcing on one's fellow-creatures what one believes to be good for them' (Sir Carleton Allen: *Law and Orders*). As evidence of this we have only to consider how Cromwell's government developed — his peremptory dismissal of the House of Commons, his savage subjection of Ireland, and his disregard for the feelings of the people through his belief in his own righteousness — to see how far a good man may become detached from his early ideals. Alternatively, a weak government may take dictatorial measures in order to preserve its tottering authority. This is vividly portrayed in Shakespeare's *Macbeth*. In the early part of the play we are shown a man with a strong strain of nobility in his nature; yet, before long, in a vain attempt to maintain his newly achieved and uncertain power, he is prepared to terrorise his country with murder.

Such then are two ways in which a country can slide into tyranny. Even more serious is the situation where, from the outset, there is a determination by the rulers to abuse their authority in order to satisfy their lust for power. Reflect on Napoleon's character as portrayed by George Orwell in *Animal Farm*. Here is a complete survey of the methods of such a dictator — the playing on the hopes and aspirations of the animals (the people); the tolerance of the altruistic and theoretical mystic who, in the first instance, rallies the animals to a worthy cause; the removal of the instruments of propaganda from democratic control; the secret police; the introduction of arbitrary and ruthless justice; and the total disregard of original principles. The tragedy is that it has all happened in recent times. Consider how the German people allowed Hitler, a megalomaniac, to obtain power. Now that they see how completely he was prepared to disregard their sufferings, they realise that at some stage a move should have been made to stop him. But how, and when, and where? He controlled education, the Press, the radio, the police, the courts and the army — and all were used unscrupulously for his own ends. Could there not be some automatic check to prevent such a situation from arising?

THE OBJECTS OF A 'CONSTITUTION'

This then is the essence of successful government: while sufficient power must be granted to enable certain persons to carry on the affairs of State efficiently, there must be the assurance that such persons can be controlled or removed should they attempt to encroach further than is absolutely necessary upon the liberty of the individual. To achieve this objective, there must be agreed principles and rules determining the structure and powers of government. It is these principles and rules (whether written or unwritten, legal or non-legal) which form the constitution of the State. Hence the constitution lays down the political institutions that will be allowed to exist, the functions of those different institutions, and the distribution of powers among them.

In most countries the fundamental rules are contained in one document for which the word 'constitution' is reserved, but in Britain no such document exists. The rules governing our political institutions are found in written laws known as statutes or Acts of Parliament, in judicial decisions interpreting those statutes and the common law, and in conventions which, though unwritten, are equally binding (see Chapter 29).

The form the constitution takes will depend upon the nature of the country being governed — its history, geographical position, social structure, economic development, religious beliefs and racial composition. But since the constitution exists primarily to protect the rights of citizens and to limit the powers of those entrusted with authority, its character will ultimately be determined by what rights and powers are accepted by the community as being essential.

Only if it fulfils certain conditions can the constitution work satisfactorily. In the first place, it should be sufficiently flexible to allow for changing economic and social circumstances. Where the constitution does not bend, there is always a danger that it may break by revolution. Secondly, it should attract leaders of wisdom and experience to take part in government. Thirdly, these men must all desire to work according to the spirit of the constitution. Fourthly, the constitution should so satisfy the needs of the citizens as to enlist their loyalty. (The real weakness of French politics following World War II lay in the failure to comply with these last two conditions. Dominated by narrow and personal interests, the Fourth Republic produced only unstable governments and so, unmourned by the people, it passed away.) Lastly, the constitution should give protection to minorities, all of whom should have their say in determining their future. 'If all mankind minus one, were of one opinion', says John Stuart Mill, 'and only one person were of the contrary opinion, mankind would be no more justified in silencing that one person, than he, if he had the power, would be justified in silencing mankind' (*Essay on Liberty*). But since it would be impossible to achieve complete agreement on all matters, the only solution is for the will of the majority to prevail. This does not mean that majorities can ride roughshod over minorities. The success of a constitution often rests on how far it can reconcile opposing interests. The majority must make concessions and, except in most unusual circumstances, such as war, always allow other opinions full freedom of expression. People cannot opt out of a State in the same way as they can withdraw from a society or club and, when the majority's power becomes intolerable, minorities, by resisting the government, will cease to work the constitution.

SUGGESTED READING

Alan Bullock, *Hitler: a Study in Tyranny* (Odhams, 1956; Penguin Books).
F. A. Hayek, *The Road to Serfdom* (Routledge, 1944).
Aldous Huxley, *Brave New World* (Chatto, 1950; Penguin Books).
George Orwell, *Animal Farm* (Secker and Warburg, 1945; Penguin Books). *Nineteen Eighty-Four* (Secker and Warburg, 1949; Penguin Books).

2

Principles of the British Constitution: An Outline

'We Englishmen are Very Proud of our Constitution, Sir. It Was Bestowed Upon Us By Providence.'
CHARLES DICKENS: *Our Mutual Friend*

Before examining in detail the British system of government, it is helpful to consider some of the fundamental principles which have determined its broad structure.

THE DISTRIBUTION OF THE POWERS OF GOVERNMENT

When all three powers of government — legislative, executive and judicial — are concentrated in the same hands, a few men, or even one man, may enjoy absolute authority. Those responsible for executing policy can make their own laws, good or bad, and themselves determine whether the citizen has broken any of them.

The 18th-century theory of the separation of powers was based upon this observation. In its simplest form it asserts that, since united power means tyranny, legislative, executive and judicial powers should be not only distinguished but carefully separated and allocated to different institutions. Only if the rules of government are formulated according to this principle can the freedom of the individual be preserved.

Whereas in the United States this theory determined the form of the constitution, in Britain it has played no fundamental part. Only in the emphasis which is placed on the independence of the judiciary is there any approach to a distinct separation of power, and this really stems from the recognition in the Middle Ages that justice must be an end in itself, to be administered impartially in accordance with known rules. Separation, the British have discovered, can lead to deadlock and even to open conflict. Some connection between the three branches of government is therefore retained. Thus the Cabinet links the legislature and the executive; the Lord Chancellor, the judiciary and the executive; and the Lords of Appeal, sitting in the House of Lords, the legislature and the judiciary.

Yet while there is no strict separation of powers in the British constitution, the fundamental concept of the theory — that all powers should not be held in the same hands — is still recognised. The British have merely preferred to implement it in a somewhat different way — by developing a system of mutual checks and balances. Thus we find the legislative authority of Parliament divided between the House of Commons and the House of Lords, the power of the Cabinet counter-balanced by the criticism of Her Majesty's Opposition, and administration of the Civil Service examined by the legislature. In other fields, too, we have a division of authority. Local government supplements central government; the industrial activities of the State enjoy some degree of independence from the executive; the Government does not control the means by which opinion can be expressed. Although such forms of separation were not envisaged by the original theory, they play just as important a part in preventing tyranny as the separation between the legislature, executive and judiciary. At the same time they allow harmony to exist in place of deadlock and government to be effective instead of sterile. It is in such checks and balances that we shall see the effective working of the British constitution.

PARLIAMENTARY SOVEREIGNTY

While, therefore, all power does not rest in the same hands, the British people have, through their constitution, granted the supreme power to make laws to one body — Parliament. We therefore speak of the 'sovereignty of Parliament'.

Parliament is composed of three parts — the House of Commons, the House of Lords and the Queen — but no one part can make law on its own. Today the Queen's function is purely formal, while the powers of the House of Lords have been severely restricted. Hence the real legislative authority rests with the House of Commons, that part of Parliament elected at regular intervals by the citizens.

The essential nature of parliamentary sovereignty is epitomized in two dicta of the 18th-century constitutional lawyer, Sir William Blackstone. Quoting Sir Edward Coke, he says: 'The power and jurisdiction of parliament is so transcendent and absolute, that it cannot be confined, either for causes or persons, within any bounds.' To this he adds the observation, 'what the parliament doth, no authority upon earth can undo.' Let us examine the implication of these quotations a little more closely.

The first emphasises that Parliament can pass any law it likes. In essence this means that there is no difference between ordinary law and constitutional law. Here Britain differs from many other countries, such as the U.S.A., Australia, and South Africa, whose constitutions specify certain kinds of law which can only be enacted according to a special procedure. The British Parliament is completely unfettered in this way. It can pass any law it likes, even altering its own life, as with the Septennial Act in 1716, or prolonging it indefinitely, as on the outbreak of war in 1939.

Moreover, Parliament can repeal, modify or temporarily set aside any law. Thus it repealed the Trades Disputes Act in 1946 and amended the Parliament Act in 1949. This power extends to all kinds of law — common law, statute law and case law — even though such law guarantees fundamental rights. During the last war, footpaths across aerodromes were closed, the Habeas Corpus Act was suspended, and the freedom of the Press was restricted — all on the ultimate authority of Parliament. Indeed, Parliament can 'legalise illegality' or set aside decisions of the Courts. Between 1727 and 1828 it passed annual Indemnity Acts to protect those dissenters who had broken the Test Acts by accepting municipal office without having first partaken of the Sacrament, while in 1966 it passed the War Damage (Burmah Oil) Act in order to undo the decision of the Courts that the Burmah Oil Company could claim compensation for plant destroyed during the war.

Blackstone's second observation draws attention to Parliament's supreme authority. Since there is no difference between ordinary law and constitutional law, no arbiter is needed to judge whether Parliament should follow the special prodecure required for constitutional law. Thus, there is no Supreme Court (as in the U.S.A.) to declare an Act of Parliament *ultra vires*, i.e. null and void.

It may be asked how it is that various other bodies, such as local authorities and the Thames Water Authority, can legislate in Britain. The answer is that their legal powers are exercised only under the authority of Acts of Parliament, are limited by those Acts, and can be rescinded whenever Parliament so desires.

Finally, the supreme authority of Parliament covers not only its power to make law but also the conduct of its own business. Consequently no court can interfere with its proceedings. The separate Houses of Parliament are likewise the guardians of their own privileges and any person acting in a way which they consider a hindrance to their work can be summoned to appear before them (see Chapter 9).

In practice, however, certain limitations to the sovereignty of Parliament are evident.

First, any alteration to the Royal style and titles or to the succession to the throne requires the approval of those Commonwealth countries which are not republics.

Second, Parliament cannot bind its successors, though in practice treaties, obligations, and even changes in organisation are usually accepted.

Third, Parliament is unlikely to pass any law contrary to international law.

Fourth, through the two-party system, Parliament itself exercises its powers, as we shall see (page 172), largely according to the dictates of the Cabinet.

Fifth, and most important, Parliament enjoys only a *legal* sovereignty which exists, in the last resort, because the courts recognise it. So long as it submits to periodic elections, it is dependent upon the electorate, which holds *political* sovereignty.

THE RULE OF LAW (for detailed discussion see Chapter 23)

Human dignity demands that the individual shall have certain rights. On the one hand, he must have the protection of law and order so that he can go about his ways unmolested; on the other, he requires freedom and opportunities to plan his life with a reasonable degree of certainty. The degree to which individual freedom should be limited depends upon the prevailing philosophy of the people, but the western world puts the emphasis on the liberty of the individual and is always ready to examine critically any suggestion that the powers of government should be extended.

To make government acceptable, therefore, the constitution must provide the individual with guarantees against the disorder of anarchy and the oppression and caprice of tyranny. The idea of the 'rule of law' has been conceived to meet these elementary needs. It stresses the fundamental idea that the law is all-important; it provides the citizen with a shield of protection as he goes about his everyday life; it is a prepared line of defence against the arbitrary government. Thus, while the law can be invoked to maintain order, any exercise of power must be in accordance with the law.

In practice, discussion of the rule of law concentrates on the latter idea. This is largely due to Professor A. V. Dicey, whose writings at the end of the 19th century were inclined to reflect his *laissez-faire* philosophy. His definition of the rule of law (discussed in Chapter 23) has been subjected to severe criticism, particularly by Professor Sir Ivor Jennings, and the result is that the term has now lost some of its precision. Here, therefore, it is necessary to state the main principles inherent in it.

(1) The individual should be able, through his legal adviser, to ascertain the law fairly precisely so that he can plan his actions with some degree of certainty.

(2) Encroachment on the freedom of the individual must be lawful. Hence: (*a*) any act of the Government or its officials must be backed by law; (*b*) no authority can interfere arbitrarily in the individual's way of life; (*c*) a citizen can feel certain he will not be arrested unless he is charged with some definite breach of the law.

(3) Before the citizen can be punished, a breach of the law must be established in a lawful manner before an impartial tribunal.

(4) Justice must be regarded as an end in itself, interpreting the law as it stands and uninfluenced outside the law by the wishes of Parliament or the Government.

POLITICAL SOVEREIGNTY

But in some ways the abstract term 'rule of law' is misleading. The 'law' itself cannot rule in the sense that it is the ultimate authority. In Britain, as we have explained, this authority is legally Parliament, which consists of men and women, the representatives of the people. They can make either good law or bad law, law aimed at promoting democratic government or law which seeks to impose dictatorship. Whatever the type of law Parliament passed, it would (and the rule of law does not dispute this) be applied. Any suggestion, therefore, that the rule of law is some high principle which would curb a Parliament using its powers tyrannously is false. There is no absolute principle enshrined in the rule of law. In practice, the interpretation of it is subjective, resting on the objects and views of the people who comprise the law-making body.

What then are the safeguards protecting the British people against oppressive authority? If we are looking for automatic devices which will come into play as soon as some dangerous situation appears likely, the answer is simply 'none'. But there are certain rules, principles and institutions by which parliamentary government can be tested.

Obviously it must be asked: 'Is Parliament subject to the wishes of the electorate?' But this question involves many others. Are elections held at regular and fairly frequent intervals? Can the people choose between competing parties representing different shades of opinion? Do all adults over the age of eighteen years have the right to vote, none being specifically excluded by reason of race, religion or political adherence in order to maintain the ruling authority in power? Is voting by secret ballot? Does the Government submit to an adverse result at an election? If an affirmative answer can be given to each of these questions, then the will of the people must ultimately be obeyed by Parliament, and the laws of Parliament will take the form which the majority of electors are prepared to accept. It can be seen, therefore, that the legal sovereignty of Parliament is only tolerated because of the political sovereignty of the electorate.

Nevertheless, elections need be held only at five-year intervals and, in war time, not even then. Suppose an unscrupulous Government schemed to seize arbitrary power at the beginning of its term of office. How could the people become aware of this aim before it was too late? Here again a judgment can be based on the answers to pertinent questions. Is there an Opposition in Parliament and does it have opportunities to voice opinions critical of the ruling party? Is the Press free to criticise? Can parties, societies and groups critical of the Government still meet together without restriction? Are the courts of law free from outside interference, and impartial in judging between the citizen and the official? If to each of these questions the answer is 'yes' there is little need to fear; if, on the other hand, it is 'no', urgent action is vital.

Thus the rule of law has to be supplemented by other principles which ensure that the law-making authority is both a representative and responsible body:

(1) Parliament must be composed of persons who represent the wishes of the electorate.

(2) Persons should be permitted to form their own opinions and express them openly.

(3) Each citizen must be free to associate with other citizens.

(4) No groups within the community, such as officials, the police, civil servants or members of a particular party, must be given an unjustifiably privileged position by the law.

Without such principles the rule of law is meaningless, for it could afford no protection against arbitrary government. Interference with freedom of discussion and association, for example, would make elections a mere formality. But, in conjunction with such principles, the rule of law itself becomes of fundamental importance.

DIFFICULTIES IN INTERPRETING THESE PRINCIPLES

Unfortunately, the difficulties do not end here. It is extremely hard to control the law-making body, and there are many subtle ways by which a system of government can be undermined. Moreover, in practice it is not easy to interpret many of the phrases which are in use. It is a principle of the rule of law, for example, that no authority can interfere arbitrarily in the individual's way of life. But what is meant by 'arbitrarily'? Can the Government exercise its discretion, for example, in acquiring land for a road-widening scheme or for building a rocket range? Furthermore, it is specified that a citizen must be tried before an 'impartial tribunal'. Although this presents few difficulties in ordinary criminal and civil law, problems arise when the rules of an administrative body are in dispute. Who, for instance, should be appointed to tribunals which consider technical offences by farmers against Marketing Board regulations? Should they include technical experts and other farmers? If so, is there not a possibility that these may be prejudiced through having a personal interest in the efficiency of the Board's schemes? The growth of government activity during the 20th century has increased the number of such problems.

Many other phrases, left undefined, are little more than clichés. Thus, when it is said that Parliament must 'represent the wishes of the people', it has to be asked how such wishes can be discovered without continual recourse to the referendum? Is such a procedure practical? If not, does it make government impossible unless political leaders are given wide discretion to act over a period? Similarly, a consideration of the principle that no group should enjoy an 'unjustifiably privileged position before the law' immediately poses the question: 'Who decides what is justifiable?'

It becomes evident, therefore, that no adequate understanding of the constitution is possible through a bare description of its institutions. To show its strengths and weaknesses and to reveal inherent difficulties, some examination of the principles on which it is based is also essential. Moreover, since the British constitution is largely the result of a process of adaptation covering a period of over a thousand years, a historical background helps considerably.

Nevertheless, some insight into their system of government is highly desirable for all citizens. It has not been easy to construct for over fifty million people, of varied views and temperaments, a form of government which both follows the stipulated rules and acts with promptness and efficiency. That the British people have devised a constitution which, if not perfect, at least appears to them to work reasonably satisfactorily is not due to providence. Political sovereignty still rests with them only because they have always been watchful of their rights and willing to take decisive action whenever those rights seemed to be in danger. Government is not merely a science or an art. Ultimately, it is a way of living, a reflection of the people's philosophy. A Frenchman, Joseph de Maistre, writing in 1811, said: 'Every nation has the government it deserves.' If the citizens do not prize their liberties sufficiently to guard them jealously and with vigilance, democratic government will eventually pass away.

SUGGESTED READING

Sir Carleton K. Allen, *Law and Orders* (3rd Ed., Stevens, 1970), Chapter 1.
N. H. Brasher, *Studies in British Government* (2nd Ed., Macmillan, 1971), Chapter 12.
A. V. Dicey, *Introduction to the Law of the Constitution* (10th Ed., Macmillan, 1961).
E. C. S. Wade and G. G. Phillips, *Constitutional Law* (8th Ed., Longmans, 1970), Part I, Chapter 2. Part II, Chapters 1, 2 and 3.

II

THE LEGISLATURE

3

Parliament: Its Historical Development

'Parliament resembles an ancient family mansion which
has been lived in continuously for a period of centuries,
and served the needs of those who have dwelt therein
by constantly modifying and adding to its conveniences
from generation to generation.'

QUINTIN HOGG: *The Purpose of Parliament*

Although the history of Parliament shows a continuous development over the last 900 years, it can be divided quite naturally into
four main periods. The first, covering the Middle Ages, is concerned with Parliament's early growth. The second, dating from
1485, extends over the reigns of the Tudor and Stuart monarchs.
Here Parliament is mainly engaged in its struggle with the King
as to who should exercise the ultimate authority. The third, which
is largely one of consolidation, stretches over the 18th century or,
more precisely, from 1688 to 1832. It witnesses the beginning of
the party system in Parliament, the development of the principle
of ministerial responsibility, and the laying of the foundations of
the Cabinet system. The last period dates from 1832 and continues
up to the present day. During this period, the relationships between
the House of Commons and the House of Lords, and between
Parliament and the other institutions of government, are so modified as to ensure that the legal sovereignty of Parliament is exercised in conformity with the wishes of the people.

MEDIEVAL DEVELOPMENT

(1) *Early principles*

The British constitution has not been shaped to a preconceived
plan; it has simply evolved over the centuries by responding to
changing needs and circumstances. But its foundations are based

on two principles, accepted by the King and his subjects in Saxon times:

(1) in important matters, such as the making of laws and the imposition of taxes, the King should not act without first taking advice;

(2) in summoning such counsellors, the initiative should rest with the King.

The recognition of the first did much to preclude the possibility of despotic government; from it developed the idea of 'no taxation without representation' and, eventually, the theory of the legal supremacy of Parliament. The observance of the second placed the responsibility for suggesting policy squarely on the Government; Parliament's task is to watch, criticise and, whenever possible, to exercise control. Let us see how these two principles developed.

On important matters, the Saxon kings consulted with their 'wise men', the Witenagemot, and William I, through his feudal organisation, developed the practice. 'King William wore his crown', says the Saxon chronicler, 'every year he was in England; at Easter he wore it at Winchester, at Pentecost at Westminster, and at Christmas at Gloucester; and at these times all the men of England were with him — archbishops, bishops and abbots, earls, thegns and knights.' Some, however, it is revealed in Magna Carta, were sent individual writs to attend, while others were summoned collectively. Yet these conferences (later known as Great Councils) were little more than the formal implementation of the principle that the King should act with counsel. Sometimes, as with Henry II, the Sovereign summoned the customary Great Councils, but worked primarily through more select bodies, choosing counsellors chiefly according to the place of meeting and the business to be conducted. Nor was the Great Council, consisting chiefly of the largest landowners, a body representative of the whole kingdom.

(2) The arrival of the Commons

The expense of wars, however, pressed so heavily on successive kings that they were forced to seek fresh sources of revenue. Not only were additional aids levied on the barons, but the tax basis was extended to include a new class, the freemen of the county. The first method was illegal, and one of the barons' grievances in Magna Carta, 1215, was the King's levying of extraordinary feudal aids without consent. The second necessitated the introduction of the principle of representation.

A step in this direction had already been taken in 1188 when Henry II imposed a tax on movables, the 'Saladin tithe', to raise money for the Third Crusade. If a man disputed the assessment of his liability, the issue was decided by a jury of neighbours, chosen locally and probably from among his fellows. It was but a short step for representatives of these new taxpayers to be sent to the Great Council. In 1227, four knights from each county, elected in the shire court, went to Westminster. The position was consolidated in 1254 when Henry III, who was fighting the French in Gascony, demanded an aid through his regent. The great landowners, both lay and spiritual, promised help, but advised that any other aid would rest on a declaration by the King of his intention to observe the Great Charter of Liberties, and that additional taxes should be agreed to by those paying them. The bishops assembled the diocesan synods to persuade the clergy to grant an aid, while the sheriff of each shire was required to send to the Council two locally-elected 'discreet knights to consider together with the knights of the other counties whom we have summoned for the day, what aid they will be willing to grant us in our great need'. The sheriff had to explain the King's requirements to the knights and freemen, 'so that the said knights shall be able on the date fixed to answer exactly to our Council in the name of the counties.' Since this was merely a temporary meeting of the knights with the Council, it was not a parliament. Nevertheless, it is important, not only because the representatives of the shire had been summoned for *financial* reasons, but because it established a precedent for similar meetings.

But such representatives were not summoned regularly until the middle of the 14th century. To the so-called 'Model Parliament' of Edward I in 1295, individual writs were sent to the two archbishops, all nineteen bishops, the forty-eight greater abbots, seven earls and forty-one barons. The rest were summoned collectively. The bishops had to bring clergy from each diocese, while every sheriff had to arrange for two knights from each shire, two citizens of each city, and two burgesses of each borough to be elected. This meeting of the Great Council, however, was still not a parliament in the modern sense. It was not bicameral. It contained both proctors of the clergy and judges and ministers *ex-officio*. Above all, the representatives were called merely to report what they were prepared to do by way of taxation, not to discuss affairs of the realm. Nevertheless, the feudal Council was fast developing a more national character, representing the three great classes of the time — the clergy, the barons, and the commons — 'those who pray, those who fight, and those who work' (F. W. Maitland).

Since each class was expected to tax itself separately, it may seem strange that Parliament divided into two chambers instead of three or four. The bishops, however, soon began to disregard that clause in their writ of summons which required them to bring representatives of the clergy and the latter attended Parliament for no more than forty years. Instead they taxed themselves in their own Convocation, a practice which continued until 1664 when, in return for the right to vote for M.P.s, they agreed to submit to the same taxation as the laity. But how came the knights of the shire to align themselves with the citizens and burgesses in the Commons? They were probably small tenants-in-chief and thus, coming from the same class as the land-owning barons, they could easily have associated with them. The simple answer is that, in common with the citizens and burgesses, the knights were new arrivals on the political scene. All represented an inferior part of Parliament and were sent away together to the same ante-room after the King had made known his wishes.

From 1376, therefore, the Commons began regularly to elect a Speaker to present their petitions and to convey their answers to the King and the Lords.

(3) The increasing power of the Commons

Whereas the summons of the Lords to Parliament was based on their feudal claim to be the King's advisers, the Commons were called only because the King needed additional revenue. This placed the Commons in a strong position.

In the first place, since they represented those persons, notably the merchants, whose wealth was increasing most rapidly, the bulk of taxation eventually fell on them. Hence, they became the dominant partner in the common grant to the King, and their power was strengthened when they began to deliberate as a separate body. Soon they claimed to be the sole originators of taxation, and this was expressed in the formula appearing in 1395 that grants were made 'by the Commons, with the advice and consent of the Lords spiritual and temporal'. Their pre-eminence was confirmed in 1407, when Henry IV accepted that 'any grant *by the Commons granted* and by the Lords *assented to*' should be reported only by the Speaker of the Commons, a principle which is still enshrined in modern practice.

Secondly, the Commons used their power to obtain redress of grievances and eventually, with the Lords, to become legislators. When he summoned Parliament, it was usual for the King to explain, through his Chancellor or some other minister, why he wanted money, though he might ask for advice on other matters. His subjects, on the other hand, had grievances to be remedied. Individual petitions could usually be dealt with by judicial redress or administrative action, but others affected the whole community, and very soon the Commons began to present petitions corporately on national grievances. Whenever a King, such as Edward III, needed money on account of war, they were in a strong position, and eventually they claimed to make the provision of Supply conditional upon the granting of their petitions.

The presentation of such petitions eventually developed into the modern procedure of legislation. Parliament was not a popular assembly. Most members found it inconvenient to remain absent from home, and some boroughs even tried to be relieved of their obligation to send representatives. Hence, once the bargains had been concluded, the Commoners and most of the Lords dispersed, leaving it to the King and his permanent advisers to devise the means of implementing them. Often this necessitated a statute and, since this was not drawn up until Parliament had departed, the terms of the agreement were frequently modified to the advantage of the King. Naturally the Commons complained, and in 1414 Henry V agreed that henceforth 'nothing be enacted to the petitions of the Commons that be contrary to their asking, whereby they should be bound without their consent'. But the position was not secured until the procedure developed a stage further. This came about when individual bills, as distinct from common petitions, were sent to the King. Legislation by statute and not by petition eventually became the rule, though not until the 16th century was the procedure invariably adopted for public bills.

The Commons still had to correct the inferior position they occupied in legislating, and so a new formula was adopted whereby statutes were made 'by the advice and consent of the Lords Spiritual and Temporal and Commons'. By the middle of the 15th century, 'and by the authority of the same' had been added, thus signifying that the statute derived its authority from the whole Parliament. Henceforth the King could only affect a Commons' bill by refusing his consent. The Commons, on the other hand, could reject a royal bill, though there is no record until the 16th century of this happening.

(4) Growth in the political power of Parliament

Parliament's control of the purse strings was used to good effect. Supplies were granted for a limited period only, so that Parliament had to be called at fairly frequent intervals. Consequently its political power increased considerably during the 14th century, so much so that in 1399 Richard II was deposed by the Parliament he summoned. Henceforth English kings enjoyed their thrones only by the sanction of Parliament. From the middle of the 15th century, however, Parliament began to lose some of its power. Not only did it become dominated by warring nobles but, in reverting to granting taxes for life, it allowed the King to dispense with summoning Parliament annually, a practice which had been established under Henry V.

THE TUDOR AND STUART PERIOD

(1) The Tudors

Since Parliament had fallen apart during the Wars of the Roses, the strong government which was needed in the ensuing unsettled conditions could be provided only by the Sovereign. Thus, in the twenty-four years of his reign, Henry VII called only seven Parliaments. Henry VIII, however, decided to use Parliament as a positive instrument in achieving his policy. Thus it was by statute that the King secured the annulment of his marriage to Catherine of Aragon in 1533, and established himself as the supreme head of the Church of England in 1534.

Elizabeth continued the partnership between monarch and Parliament with even greater success. To obtain support for her policies, she secured the election of a number of Privy Councillors. Nor, unlike her predecessors, did she dissolve Parliament as soon as its particular business had been completed; Parliaments thus became more permanent, but with their powers still under her control. Disagreements did occur, and at times the Speaker was admonished when Elizabeth considered that Parliament had interfered in affairs outside its concern. On the rare occasions when Parliament proved particularly obstinate, an adroit compromise was used to settle the issue.

It was during the Tudor period that the outlines of parliamentary procedure were settled, a development made necessary partly to maintain orderly debate in a fairly large assembly and partly to protect Parliament against the encroachments of the administration. At the same time, both Houses began to keep their Journals, thus providing for posterity written records of day-to-day business. In 1547 the Commons obtained their first permanent home, St. Stephen's Chapel in the Palace of Westminister, and during the reign of Elizabeth the committee system was inaugurated.

(2) The Stuarts

Whereas the Tudor monarchs knew how to manage Parliament in order to obtain its consent to their wishes, the Stuarts showed no such finesse. Moreover, a crippling price inflation forced them to summon Parliament to grant money for their needs. A collision was therefore inevitable. On the one hand, the Commons, through their control over finance, had established certain rights which they deemed fundamental. On the other, it was an undisputed fact that the Sovereign possessed many common-law powers under the royal prerogative. These included the power to summon and dissolve Parliament, the right to suspend or dispense with laws, the maintenance of an army, the issue of Proclamations having the force of law, and the imposition of certain taxes. But James I wanted to go beyond these. His doctrine of 'divine right' placed him above the law and therefore beyond the authority of Parliament. The issue was simple: should government be by the King, or by the King-in-Parliament, as in Tudor times? The Civil War, which resulted because neither side would give way, settled once and for all the legal sovereignty of Parliament, although not until 1689 was this conclusively demonstrated.

The Commonwealth period represents a break in the main trend of England's constitutional growth. Government was by two independent bodies, the Protector and Parliament, the latter without an Upper House. But the experiment failed, and the restoration of the monarchy in 1660 was to a large extent a return

to the system which had worked so well in Tudor times —
government by the King through Parliament.

So eager had everyone become for such a restoration, that no
attempt was made to put into statute form the exact constitutional
relationship between the King and Parliament which the Civil
War had been fought to determine. Legally, the King's prerogative
powers were unaltered; nor had conventions as yet been established to indicate how they should be exercised henceforward.
Once again, therefore, the monarch came into conflict with
Parliament, and in 1688 James II, like his father before him, was
deposed. This time the Bill of Rights put into statute form many
of the limitations on the royal prerogative which had been
determined over the past hundred years.

THE 18TH CENTURY

The next two stages in the history of Parliament are concerned
almost exclusively with the development of the Cabinet system, the
reform of the House of Commons and the changes in the relationship between the Commons and the Lords. These are discussed in
detail in chapters 4, 5, 8 and 15.

During the 18th century the Sovereign began to summon
Parliament regularly and not merely on occasions to suit himself;
for one thing the Mutiny Act legalised a standing army for only a
year at a time. Parliament's life, too, was increased from three to
seven years by the Septennial Act in 1716. But the main task of the
Commons was to consolidate the victory of the previous century,
and this it had to do in the face of war against France from without
and party strife and a disputed succession from within. Moreover,
a method still had to be devised by which the legal power left with
the King could be exercised in harmony with the incontrovertible
supremacy of Parliament. The solution was to be found in the
appearance within Parliament of new institutions — parties, the
Prime Minister, and the Cabinet. Important developments had
taken place in all these before 1832, but not until the reform of
Parliament were they finally welded together into our present
system of parliamentary government.

Movements aimed at such reform began to appear at the end of
the 18th century, but they failed to gather momentum and
eventually perished in the reaction following the French Revolution. Nevertheless, one important advance was made. Largely

through the efforts of John Wilkes, the Commons permitted from 1771 the reporting of parliamentary debates, a step vital to democratic government.

1832 TO THE PRESENT DAY

The Reform Act, 1832, is important because it gave political sovereignty to the electorate. But this political sovereignty had to be reconciled with the supremacy of Parliament. How this was achieved will be studied in detail later on. In brief, it came about by extending the party system from Parliament to the country, linking parties with the Cabinet system of government, developing an Opposition to take over many of the traditional functions of Parliament, formalising the relationship between the Commons and the Lords, and modifying parliamentary procedure to secure effective government in the face of determined obstruction and to economise in time in order to cope with increased State activities.

SUGGESTED READING

Lord Campion, *An Introduction to the Procedure of the House of Commons* (3rd Ed., Macmillan, 1958), Chapter 1.

J. E. A. Jolliffe, *The Constitutional History of Medieval England* (4th Ed., A. & C. Black, 1961).

D. L. Keir, *The Constitutional History of Modern Britain* (9th Ed., A. & C. Black, 1969).

F. W. Maitland, *The Constitutional History of England* (C.U.P., 1908).

4

The House of Lords

And while the House of Peers withholds
Its legislative hand,
And noble statesmen do not itch
To interfere with matters which
They do not understand,
As bright will shine Great Britain's rays
As in King George's glorious days!

W. S. GILBERT: *Iolanthe*

I. HISTORY OF ITS RELATIONSHIP WITH THE HOUSE OF COMMONS

EARLY WEAKENING OF THE POWER OF THE HOUSE OF LORDS

By the middle of the 14th century, the feudal Magnum Concilium of the Normans, composed of the great landowners, had developed into a Parliament representing the three classes of the nation, barons, clergy and commons. The next step, as we have seen, was the division of this Parliament into two Houses, but not until the reign of Henry VIII did the term 'House of Lords' come into existence to describe the meetings of the lay and ecclesiastical peers. By this time a totally new conception of 'peerage' had developed. It consisted of the holders of titles whose heirs had successively received individual writs ('barons by writ or fee') and those barons created by patent by Richard II and later sovereigns.

From the 14th century onwards, the history of the House of Lords is chiefly a study of its gradual surrender of authority to the Commons. Exploiting its ability to make grants to the King, the Commons had, by 1395, established its right to be the exclusive originator of taxation. Yet for the rest of the Middle Ages the House of Lords was pre-eminent. The King's chief advisers were to be found in the Upper House and, through their social influence and personal connections, the peers could still exert considerable control over the Commons. Moreover, the House of Lords remained small in number; only forty-nine spiritual peers and thirty-six temporal peers sat in Henry VII's first Parliament.

The position of the Lords was weakened less by the Commons than by the King. After the Wars of the Roses the nobles were so depleted by death and exhausted by military combat that Henry VII, unlike his predecessors, had little cause to pay heed to their wishes. They were outnumbered by the spiritual peers, whom the King was able to influence since they owed both their position and their hopes of advancement to him.

Later Tudor monarchs continued the process of weakening the position of the House of Lords. They turned to the Privy Council rather than to the Upper House when they wanted advice or help, and looked to the House of Commons to give legal sanction to their actions. After the dissolution of the monasteries the temporal peers outnumbered the spiritual, but control of the Lords was still maintained through the new families which had been raised to the peerage — the Cecils, Cavendishes, Seymours, etc.

Under the Stuarts, harmony between the King and Commons came to an end and the Lords were again able to play a bigger role in the government of the country, seeing themselves for a time as mediators between the King and Commons. James I appreciated that his influence over the Upper House could be extended, and his income augmented, by the sale of titles (an earldom cost £20,000), so that in this way the number of temporal peers was doubled. The result was that the House lost prestige and tended to side with the King in his disputes with the Commons. Nevertheless, when in 1626 Charles I arrested those M.P.s who had arranged the impeachment of Buckingham, and again in 1642 when he tried to arrest the Five Members, the Lords supported the claim of the Commons to freedom from arrest. But when it came to taking up arms against the King, most of the peers embraced the royalist cause. It is hardly surprising, therefore, especially as opposition to the monarch had originated in the Commons, that a victorious 'Parliament' should, within a week of the King's execution, abolish the House of Lords as being 'useless and dangerous'.

The restoration of the monarchy in 1660 was followed by the reinstatement of the House of Lords, not by any statute or resolution of the Convention Parliament, but simply by its reassembling again. Yet the Civil War had strengthened the position of the

Commons and it was they who had decided to bring back Charles II. The powers of the Lords, however, were not inferior, and both played an equal part in law-making. In fact, later Stuarts were able to play off one House against the other, as Charles II did in his quarrel with the Commons over their proposal to exclude his brother James from the throne. But during this period the Lower House confirmed its ancient rights over taxation. In 1671 it passed a resolution denying the Lords the right to amend a tax, and a more comprehensive one followed in 1678 stressing its sole right to grant aids or supplies. This did not, however, affect the Lords' right to reject a money bill, a right which, at least in theory, was retained until 1860.

18TH-CENTURY HARMONY BETWEEN THE TWO HOUSES

Generally speaking, there was little difference of opinion between the Lords and Commons during the 18th century. The Union with Scotland, 1707, added sixteen representative Scottish peers to the Lords. This addition created difficulties for, being often poor, such peers were ardent place-hunters, throwing in their lot with the Government of the day. It frequently happened that, on English affairs, their solid vote held the balance, but on Scottish matters they were outvoted! The most serious issue of difference was over the Treaty of Utrecht, to which the Whigs, who held a majority in the Lords but not in the Commons, were opposed. The difficulty was resolved by taking advantage of the Sovereign's prerogative to create peers, twelve new peers being sufficient to secure approval for this treaty.

Thereafter, only Stanhope's Peerage Bill, which sought to limit the creation of new peers, met with strong opposition in the Lower House. The Lords retained their importance and managed to work in harmony with the Commons. Several factors contributed to this end. First, the 18th-century system of government was based essentially on the holding of property, and here both Lords and Commons represented the same interest, the great landowners. Secondly, the leading personalities of both parties were frequently peers, and the highest posts, including that of Prime Minister, were often filled from the Lords. Thirdly, as a result of the electoral system, many members of the House of Commons were nominees of the Lords. Hence, there was little difference in outlook between the persons who sat in the two Houses. Lastly, the patronage system enabled the Government to control both Houses. George III followed the policy of creating peers, and during his reign the House of Lords doubled in size to approximately 400 members, though these included many recommendations by Pitt and the 28 who were added in 1801 through the Act of Union with Ireland, 1800.

THE EFFECT OF THE REFORM ACT, 1832

With the turn of the century, there began a period in which the gulf between the Houses steadily widened. The Lords were against change. Roman Catholic emancipation was held up until 1829, first by the opposition of the King and then by the Lords. But the big clash came over the introduction of the Reform Bill in 1831 to which the Lords were violently opposed, since it took away the control which many of them could exercise over elections. Only after the threat to create sufficient peers to carry the Bill was it passed, but, for the first time, it showed that the peers had not enough power to resist a popular reform.

The Reform Bill, which became law in 1832, by giving the vote to the lower middle classes, and by sweeping away the foundations of the peers' power to nominate members, increased the possibility of strife. Henceforth legislation had to consider the interests of these new voters; and never again would the Lords control the composition of the Commons. But for a generation yet, country gentlemen continued to predominate in the Commons, while in the country at large there was still, in spite of the Industrial Revolution, little interest in social revolution. A few bills met with opposition. The University Tests Bill, which sought to open degrees to British subjects irrespective of religion, was rejected in 1834, while the Corn Laws were only repealed in 1846 through Wellington's loyalty to Peel.

By 1850, however, the Commons had become the real centre of political life, while the influence of the land-owner, still dominant in the Lords, was waning rapidly in the Lower House. This can be seen in the repeal of the Corn Laws, a step which served the interests of both manufacturers and workers in that it meant cheaper food. As the Houses drew apart, so the Lords began to oppose more measures, particularly reforms affecting the law, divorce, or the Church. Eight times up to 1858 they rejected a Commons bill permitting Jews to sit in that House, and until 1869 they opposed the abolition of imprisonment for debt. And although Lord Lyndhurst, in the debate on admitting Jews in 1858, declared that it was not the duty of the House to make 'a firm, determined, and persevering stand against the opinion of the other House of Parliament, when that opinion is backed by the opinion of the people', an important clash occurred over the Paper Duties Repeal Bill, 1860.

This bill sought to repeal the excise duty on paper in order that cheap books and journals might be made generally available. In rejecting it, the Lords were tactically strong, since their opposition to the repeal of a tax did not embarrass the Government financially. But strategically they were weak, especially with Gladstone as Chancellor of the Exchequer. He obtained a Select Committee to examine the precedents, and this found that the House of Lords had neither the right to amend a money bill nor the power to reject it on purely monetary grounds. Palmerston introduced resolutions in the House of Commons to this effect, and Gladstone secured the passage of his proposal by including it as part of the budget, the rejection of which would have challenged the whole of the Government's financial policy.

THE OPPOSITION OF THE LORDS TO LIBERAL POLICY

The Reform Act, 1867, by adding about a million voters, almost doubled the electorate. Its most important result, however, was to enfranchise the majority of the working class in the towns, and it is quite likely that the bill would have been opposed by the Lords had it not been introduced by a Conservative Government. The effect on the relationship between the two Houses was considerable. The House of Commons was still further removed from the influence of the landed aristocracy and, through the links which were being forged by the new organisation of the parties, became much more closely identified with the middle and working classes. As political power was now centred in the Commons, the Government found it desirable to have more of its leading ministers there, while it could afford to pay less regard to the possibility of opposition from the Lords. This applied particularly to the Liberals, many of whose measures were deemed to be radical. Indeed, in order that his proposal for dis-establishing the Irish Church could be presented more effectively in the Lords, Gladstone obtained the creation of twelve Liberal peers. The secret ballot was also opposed but eventually both measures found their way on to the statute book, the first in 1869 and the second in 1872.

With the death of Disraeli in 1881 the relationship between the two Houses deteriorated further. The Lords almost succeeded in forcing a dissolution over the Third Reform Bill, 1884, introduced in Gladstone's second ministry. It gave the vote to the rural workers and, though the Lords did not feel able to oppose the principle of the bill, they did manage to hold it up until it could be coupled with a measure to redistribute seats. But it was the dispute, beginning in 1886, over Home Rule for Ireland which made the situation impossible, for here a compromise was out of the question. The Conservatives were adamant against the measure and in the Lords they were overwhelmingly predominant. The result was a popular agitation against the Upper House in the course of which John Bright outlined plans for limiting its powers.

An open collision was averted only through the good offices of Queen Victoria, the ascendancy enjoyed by the Conservatives at the end of the century, and because the Lords were too subtle to force an open contest on any issue which could be formulated as privilege versus reform. During the period from 1892 to 1895, the only years when the Liberals were in power between 1886 and 1906, there was almost continual conflict with the Lords. The latter invoked the doctrine of the mandate, claiming the right to check what it considered to be radical or violent measures. This, however, was a purely bogus invention, for in practice the Lords used their power exclusively against the Liberals, whose government between 1892 and 1895 was reduced to a travesty. The Lords defeated the second Irish Home Rule Bill by 419 votes to 41, amended the District and Parish Councils Bill, and so mangled the Employers' Liability Bill that it was dropped by the government.

EVENTS LEADING TO THE PARLIAMENT ACT, 1911

Such tactics contributed largely to the defeat of the Liberals in 1895, and for the next eleven years the Conservatives enjoyed office. But the Lords made the mistake of thinking that they could follow a similar course in 1906, when a Liberal Government was returned with a majority in the Commons of 240 over all other parties. Mr. Balfour even went so far as to say that he would use the House of Lords to govern the country, as he considered that a Liberal House of Commons would bring ruin upon it. Between 1906 and 1910, 18 out of 210 Government bills failed to become law, either through outright rejection or violent amendment. Five of these were held to be of first-class importance — the Education Bill, 1906; the Plural Voting Abolition Bill, 1906; a Scottish land-owning Bill, 1907; the Licensing Bill, 1908; the Finance Bill (Budget), 1909.

It had become obvious that some stricter definition of the Lords' powers was needed, for, as Mr. Lloyd George said, 'the House of Lords is not the watchdog of the constitution; it is Mr. Balfour's poodle.' In 1907 the Prime Minister, Mr. Campbell-Bannerman, announced that 'a way must be found and a way will be found by which the will of the people, expressed through their elected representatives in this House, will be made to prevail', and this was followed by a House of Commons' resolution that the power of the Lords to alter or reject a bill should be 'so restricted by law that within the limits of a single Parliament the final decision of the Commons shall prevail'.

The rejection of the Finance Bill, 1909 (Lloyd George's 'People's Budget'), provided the Liberals with the opportunity they had been waiting for. The Lords' objection to the proposal to tax the profits derived by landlords from the increased value of land induced them to make the fatal mistake of forcing the issue on a matter which was bound to result in their defeat. Not only did it represent an open defiance of the long tradition that the Commons had primacy in matters of finance, but it made it impossible for the Government to carry out the administration of the country accord-ing to its declared policy. Mr. Asquith, the Prime Minister, reacted sharply. Within three days a resolution was passed by the Commons to the effect that the action of the Lords was 'a breach of the constitution and a usurpation of the rights of the Commons', and Parliament was dissolved. He followed this by drawing up a definite scheme for restricting the powers of the Upper House and when the electorate went to the polls in January, 1910, this, rather than the merits of the budget, was the real issue.

As a result of the election the Liberals lost 104 seats; but, with the backing of 82 Irish Home Rulers and 40 Labour members, they still retained a large majority. The Conservatives acknow-ledged that the Government now had popular support for its budget, but they would not recognise that there was a mandate for the Parliament Bill. Thus, though the budget was passed in April, 1910, it became clear that the willing consent of the Lords to a curtailment of their powers would never be obtained and that the King would have to be asked to create sufficient new peers to sway the House. This would have involved a much more drastic step than in 1832, for it was estimated that over 400 new creations would be necessary — a move which would have produced a substantial change in the character of the House. The Parliament Bill was introduced, but the death of King Edward VII in May stayed proceedings on it.

The opportunity was taken to try to settle the dispute through a conference of the Leaders of the parties in both Houses. But behind the bill lurked the spectre of Home Rule for Ireland, and no formula could be worked out which would overcome this difficulty. In November, 1910, the failure to reach agreement was announced and a new bill passed quickly through the Commons, to be just as quickly thrown out by the Lords.

A dissolution, requested immediately by Mr. Asquith on account of the danger of civil war in Ireland, was granted, and the Liberals went to the country on the Parliament Bill. Mr. Asquith had previously obtained an undertaking from King George V that he would accept the electorate's decision and create the necessary peers if the Lords still refused the measure, though this fact was not made public at the time. The general election of December, 1910, left the Commons much as before. After a little hesitation the Lords passed the bill, which became law on the 18th August, 1911.

THE PROVISIONS OF THE PARLIAMENT ACT, 1911

(1) A Money Bill became law within one month of being sent up to the House of Lords, with or without their agreement. It was to be left to the discretion of the Speaker to certify what was a 'Money Bill', but it must be one the main object of which was financial. In practice, Speakers have refrained from so certifying where any policy change is involved, and about half the Finance Bills since the Parliament Act have not been certified a 'Money Bill'.

(2) Other Public Bills could receive the Royal Assent without the agreement of the Lords. Such a Bill must have been passed by the Commons in three consecutive sessions (whether of

the same Parliament or not), and two years must have elapsed between the date of the second reading in the House of Commons in the first session and the third reading in the third session. This provision did not, however, apply to a bill extending the maximum duration of Parliament beyond five years or to a Provisional Order Confirmation Bill. It should also be noted that it did not include private bills.

(3) The maximum duration of Parliament was reduced from seven to five years, the idea being to ensure that a Commons which was over three years old, and thus possibly out of touch with the wishes of the electorate, should not be able to pass a bill in defiance of the Lords.

As regards a Money Bill, the Act really made legal only what the Commons had secured in 1860, when all budget proposals began to be embodied in a single bill. But for other bills it marked a fundamental constitutional change, making it possible to pass legislation without the consent of one House. On the other hand, it left several problems unsolved. Those likely to introduce radical legislation could see that the period of delay would be such as to prevent the effective administration of a measure before the Government responsible for it had to meet the electorate again. Yet it did not preclude rash experiments; by its provisions, even the House of Lords itself could be abolished after two years. Above all, it did not deal with the composition of the House, which still remained a Conservative bulwark. Even during the remaining years of Liberal office the Lords showed their failure to appreciate that the new policy was the result of the more democratic franchise. Conservative leaders were still willing to use the Lords to influence the government of the country. Two measures to end plural voting in 1913 and 1914 were destroyed by the Lords, while, because of their opposition, the Home Rule Act and Welsh Disestablishment Act had to be passed under the procedure of the Parliament Act and both were later suspended on the outbreak of war.

THE INTER-WAR YEARS

The period of violent controversy came to an end in 1914 with the outbreak of war. In the following thirty years there was less occasion for conflict because, apart from two brief periods, peacetime governments were controlled by the Conservatives. In those clashes which did occur, however, the House of Lords defended

Conservative interests. Thus in 1931 it threw out the second Labour Government's bill to raise the school-leaving age, while it did nothing to prevent the passing of the rather vicious Trades Disputes Act, 1927, which the Conservatives introduced following the General Strike. On the rare occasions when it did seriously amend a Conservative measure, it did so because it was likely to please an important section of the party, as, for instance, in 1933, when it deleted a clause which would have ended whipping for juvenile delinquency.

The subsidiary position of the Lords in the constitution was further emphasised in 1923 when the convention was established that the Prime Minister should sit in the House of Commons (see page 122), and this was underlined in 1963 when Lord Home became Prime Minister, for he renounced his peerage in order to sit in the Commons. Indeed, it is now regarded as essential that the ministers in charge of certain other important departments shall sit in the Commons, where they can be answerable to the elected representatives of the people (see page 241).

THE PARLIAMENT ACT, 1949

After World War II a Labour Government was returned to power with a huge majority and was committed to a heavy programme of highly controversial legislation. People were interested to see how the Lords would respond to this new political situation. Since 1911 the relations between the two Houses had been fairly harmonious, and the considerable economic and social changes of the 20th century had come about without interference. 1945 was the first occasion on which the Lords had been faced with a strong Labour Government, intent on carrying out a radical programme of extensive nationalisation and social reform. In 1924 and 1929 the party had been dependent on Liberal support, and its periods of office were too short to provide much evidence of how a Labour Government and a House of Lords containing many creations of this century would accommodate themselves to each other.

The Government met no determined opposition from the Lords. But the Labour leaders were not prepared to risk obstruction later, particularly over the intended nationalisation of the iron and steel industry. In order that this could be carried through quickly if the party were returned to power, a bill was introduced in 1947 to weaken further the delaying power of the Lords, and it was passed under the provisions of the 1911 Act. The Parliament Act, 1949, simply reduced the period of delay to one year spread over two sessions from the second reading in the first session to the third reading in the second. The other provisions of the 1911 Act remained unchanged. The new Act, therefore, lacked the importance of its predecessor, for it introduced no new principle. It merely made it harder for a reactionary Upper House to hamstring a radical government; but, since the events of 1945–51 seem to indicate that the peers have learned their place in the new, more democratic society, this is unlikely to happen.

II. FUNCTIONS OF THE HOUSE OF LORDS

While a few countries, such as New Zealand, Denmark, Israel, Lebanon and Ghana, do not have two chambers in their legislatures, the great majority of countries are bicameral.

One important function of a second chamber is to serve as a constitutional device by which states of unequal strength, or with fundamental differences of background, can be induced to join together in a federation (see page 538). In this case it is usual for the lower house of the federal legislature to be elected on a purely numerical basis, the position of the smaller states being safeguarded by giving them an equal, or more nearly equal, representation with the larger states in the upper chamber and by laying down a definite procedure, involving both houses, for altering any of their fundamental rights. Thus in Australia, while the House of Representatives is elected on a population basis, the Senate consists of sixty members, each of the six states sending ten representatives.

While this is a useful device in large or diverse countries, and has been adopted in the Commonwealth, where the common link through Britain has done much to promote federation, it does not explain the existence of a second chamber in Britain itself, which has a fairly homogeneous population and a unitary, not a federal, form of government. In this country, it is retained because it performs other valuable functions.

(1) Legislative

The wide scope of present-day government activity entails a large volume of legislation. Good law-making, however, is a lengthy process. Not only do the purposes of the Act have to be discussed to ensure that they are desirable, but attention has to be paid to detail in order that as many difficulties as possible may be foreseen, and ambiguities in the working of the Act removed. Unaided, the House of Commons could not complete the work involved, and no proposals for improving its procedure could overcome this difficulty. Its members already spend long periods in the Chamber, and could hardly remain there longer without neglecting their other duties. Hence a considerable part of the legislative process is still performed by the House of Lords.

All money bills originate in the House of Commons. So do bills concerning the major policies of the Government, especially those exciting party feeling, for it is essential that the principles of such legislation should be settled in the elected chamber. But non-controversial bills are often introduced in the Lords, enabling their main outlines to be thrashed out before they reach the Commons and thus saving time there. Some of these bills, such as the Crown Proceedings Act, 1947 (which made it possible for the citizen to sue the Crown for damages), and the Companies Act, 1948 (which contained 460 complicated clauses consolidating the law on companies), are important measures. In addition, the House of Lords, not being elected, is in a better position than the Commons to introduce legislation which, though desirable, might be avoided because it would cost the Government votes by alienating a certain section of opinion.

But the main legislative work performed by the House of Lords is in the revision of bills. This may be aimed at achieving concessions in Government policy, and the House still has the ultimate power to reject. More usually, however, the object is to make the bill more workable. Since there is no closure (see page 148) in the Lords, clauses can be debated adequately and details examined. Publicity given to the bill during its passage through the Commons, and discussions between the departments and interests concerned, may have revealed various practical defects which the Government might wish to put right. Moreover, there is always 'cleaning-up' to be done in the wording of a bill to make it legally sound. How the Lords can help a busy Government is illustrated by the fact that at the Report stage of the Local Government Bill, 1972, the Government introduced no less than 380 amendments in the Lords. Altogether the Upper House made over 600 changes to the Bill. The main difficulty now is that of ensuring that the House has sufficient time for the consideration of such major bills.

The Lords also relieves the burden of the Commons by undertaking an equal part of the work in considering private bills and delegated legislation, especially as regards Provisional Order Confirmation Bills and Special Procedure Orders (see chapters 11 and 21). Here it would be particularly difficult to hand over all the work to the Lower House for, apart from being overburdened already, M.P.s are reluctant to do work which brings no publicity and very little political reward.

(2) Deliberative

The Lords' debates are mainly concerned with general issues of policy. They are usually of a high standard, partly because the House can draw upon elder statesmen, ex-ministers, former Governors-General and life peers who are experts in particular fields, and partly because it has certain advantages over the Commons as a forum for debate. Whereas an M.P. may often speak simply to attract attention or to convince his constituents that he is working hard, a peer need only engage in debate when he feels he has something valuable to say. Nor is he bound to the same extent to follow the party line. The Whips may bring pressure by persuasion to bear on him at the division lobby, but he can speak more freely than his counterpart in the Lower House. In any case, there are a number of peers who do not accept a party whip, and these fulfil the role of the now extinct Independent Member of Parliament. Above all, the pressure of time is not so great as in the Commons. The House usually meets only on Mondays, Tuesdays, Wednesdays and Thursdays, from 2.30 p.m. to about 8 p.m. The Government does not claim priority for its business, and so it is relatively easy for a peer to raise any subject he likes. Debate is very free, the Lord Chancellor's duties as chairman hardly being required, and there is no closure. Hence a peer, unlike an M.P., can always be sure of having an opportunity to deliver the speech he has prepared.

Occasionally, it is true, debates in the Upper House tend to be somewhat repetitive, since the main arguments on much-publicised controversial issues have already been thrashed out thoroughly in the Commons. Generally, however, they further policy formation. Because they are conducted quite differently from the tightly-organised debates in the Commons, a wider range of opinions can be expressed. The Lords thus makes a valuable contribution to consultative government.

(3) Judicial

The original jurisdiction of the House of Lords is now of little importance. It still decides disputed claims to the peerage, and it may fine or commit to prison for breaches of its own privileges. But the last impeachment was in 1806, while the privilege of peers to be tried by the House of Lords was abolished by the Criminal Justice Act, 1948.

In appeal matters, however, it remains the supreme and final court in the United Kingdom, both for criminal and civil jurisdiction. This function is distinct from the others, for it could be exercised quite as effectively by a Supreme Court, and it therefore provides no real reason for retaining the Lords.

(4) Constitutional

In practice, the existence of an Upper Chamber helps the Prime Minister. It enables him to secure a position in Parliament for a person whom he wishes to include in his Government, and it affords him a gracious way of dropping from his Cabinet a minister who has outlived his usefulness. In addition, it provides a place of semi-retirement for elder statesmen no longer able to withstand the full rigours of political life in the Commons, and permits the introduction into the legislature of people who, while not desirous of participating in party politics, are yet prepared to offer the country the benefit of their wisdom, experience or expert knowledge from time to time.

But for some critics of the Constitution, the House of Lords has a deeper significance: it helps to balance the increasing weight of the Government. The necessity for this is underlined by: (a) the Government's dominance over the House of Commons through the party system; (b) Parliament's power to alter the constitution by the ordinary processes of legislation; (c) the single straight-voting system which may produce a Government with an absolute majority on a minority vote (see page 70). Such a Government could extend its powers to an unforeseen extent entirely by legal means.

The House of Lords cannot guarantee that this will never

happen, but its existence is one of the safeguards against it. By its criticism of bills, it can act as a check on the 'rash, hasty and undigested legislation of the House of Commons'. Through the publicity given to its debates, it can ensure that all aspects of Government policy are brought to the notice of the public. By its delaying powers, it can concentrate attention on fundamental issues and insist on time for further reflection on the desirability of particular legislation which, at the best, may only be the result of temporary democratic fervour and, at the worst, may represent an attempt by the Government to seize absolute authority. Usually, however, having made its point, the Lords does not persist in its opposition to the Commons. Thus in 1968, it at first rejected a Government Order imposing economic sanctions against Rhodesia, but when the Commons 'declined to think again' the Opposition spokesman in the Lords acknowledged that the House could not be the final arbiter of Government policy and the Order was then passed without a division.

On one recent occasion, however, the Lords did refuse to accept the wishes of the Commons on a constitutional matter. The Home Secretary is obliged to lay before Parliament the Boundary Commissioners' proposals to bring up to date the boundaries between parliamentary constituencies (see page 63). The Commissioners produced a Report which could have righted very unequal representation in time for the 1970 election but the Government, which feared the electoral consequences, argued that revision should be delayed until local government boundaries had been changed (see chapter 25) and to this end the Home Secretary introduced a Bill in 1969 whose effect would have been to retain all constituency boundaries, except in London. This Bill the Lords refused to pass except in a form so amended as to change its purpose, and the Home Secretary, forced by law to lay the Boundary Commissioners' proposals before Parliament, had to ask the Commons to reject them. In the event, therefore, the old constituencies were retained for the 1970 election, but the Lords' action did ensure that the Government's decision was subjected to the widest public discussion and criticism.

This does not mean that, in exercising its revising and delaying functions, the House of Lords should be able to hold up a controversial bill until the electorate can give their verdict on it at an ensuing general election. Any such suggestion emanates from too naïve an opinion of what can be achieved at the polls. Usually all the electorate can do is to choose between two or three alternative party programmes; they have no chance to disentangle their opinion on one particular part of them. Some authorities still think that the Lords could hold up a controversial measure which had received no discussion at the previous general election or which did not obviously follow from the party's record and policy; but modern political history provides no evidence that the Lords subscribes to this view.

The Upper House has lost much of its power during this century, primarily to the Government. But the position of the Commons is similarly weaker. Neither House can now prevent the Cabinet from carrying out its policy, but both, in a different way, can remind it that a return to office depends upon pleasing the electorate.

III. CRITICISMS OF THE HOUSE OF LORDS

CRITICISMS OF ITS COMPOSITION

Four main groups of persons are entitled to sit in the Lords: (i) hereditary peers; (ii) first generation and life peers chosen from people who have contributed to the national life in politics, the armed forces, administration, welfare, science, education and the arts; (iii) senior bishops and Lords of Appeal, who sit by virtue of their office; (iv) Scottish peers.

In some ways this membership suits its work. Not only can it draw upon the advice of the most eminent lawyers when carrying out such tasks as the tidying-up of bills, but it contains the leading figures in many walks of national life. Moreover, the strange mixture of people entitled to take part does, in practice, make for a good deliberative assembly. A hard core of politicians is supplemented by a wider group of experts who usually come along on those occasions when they have something valuable to contribute. Churchmen speak from time to time on moral and social problems and the Service chiefs on defence matters. Life peers appointed during 1971-4 included Sir Arthur Porritt, a surgeon and ex-Governor General of New Zealand; Sir Denis Greenhill, retired head of the Diplomatic Service; Sir Burke St. John Trend, previously Secretary of the Cabinet; Vic Feather, retired General Secretary of the Trades Union Congress; Sir Solly Zuckerman, former Chief Scientific Adviser to the Government; and Sir Leslie O'Brien, former Governor of the Bank of England. Such experts bring originality and specialist knowledge to the deliberations of the House but, since they are balanced by the politicians, they do not dominate the debates even on their own subjects.

Nevertheless, today political power based solely on birth is an anachronism. In the Middle Ages, peers had administrative, legal' and military responsibilities, and hence it was appropriate that they should have legislative powers. While duties and responsibilities continued to be closely aligned with the ownership of land, there was little opposition to the principle of an Upper House consisting almost entirely of hereditary peers. Even today, many peers are influential men, sitting on the boards of banks or firms, securing election to their local councils, holding offices in different societies and serving their immediate localities in other ways.

But heredity is no guarantee of fitness to govern. Hereditary peers are not only free from the necessity of considering the views of the electorate, but their upbringing and background may keep them out of touch with its aspirations. As regards education, for instance, they or their sons are generally educated at a few select public schools and the most fashionable Oxford and Cambridge colleges.

In any case, intelligence and worth are not confined to a narrow class in the community. Recent creations of life peers have not entirely satisfied those critics who point out that there are few working-class members, although the workers and their trade unions have attained great political importance and many problems of policy are of particular concern to them. Other critics argue that there should be more scientists now that science is playing an increasing part in our way of life, and legislation on such widely differing subjects as disarmament, fuel policy and transport planning, for instance, must be related to scientific progress.

As the Lords is at present composed, the Church of England, too, enjoys a privileged position. But this does not arouse much feeling, for the Non-conformists and Roman Catholics do not find any difficulty in getting their views expressed in Parliament.

In practice, although there are over 800 hereditary peers, comparatively few take a real part in its deliberations. It is the influx of life peers which has raised the average attendance of the Lords to nearly 300. The snag is that all hereditary peers, unless they have been 'granted' leave of absence, may still attend to vote upon controversial measures. Thus these 'backwoodsmen', with their strong Conservative bias, have the power to play a vital role.

CRITICISMS OF ITS POWERS

Today all parties recognise that a second Chamber in which the hereditary principle still predominates is indefensible. In the Inter-Party Conference on the Future of the House of Lords in 1948 it was agreed that heredity should not by itself constitute a qualification for admission and that a revised House should not ensure a permanent majority for one political party. But deadlock ensued over the powers of delay which should be given to a reformed House. The Conservatives would have settled for a minimum of 12 months from third reading in the Commons; the Labour Government would agree to no more than 9 months. In the end, the Parliament Act, 1949, as we have seen, provided for 12 months from second reading.

Not that this really satisfied the more radical members of the Labour Party. They considered even the one-year power of delay remaining with the Upper House excessive. Even though the Lords might not force the resignation of a Labour Government, it could disrupt the legislative programme. Before a bill is introduced, time has to be allowed for its preparation and drafting and for consultation with interested parties. When it is held up for a year, the processes may have to be repeated to cover possible changes in conditions and opinion. Even when the measure is eventually passed by the Lords, time must be allowed for setting up complicated administrative machinery and overcoming teething troubles. The result is that a Government may have to go to the polls before any real benefits of its policy can become apparent to the electorate.

IV. REFORM OF THE HOUSE OF LORDS

ATTITUDES TO REFORM

Yet until recently it has seemed that neither party wished or would be willing to find the time for a major revision of the Lords' composition and powers. Naturally the Conservative Party did not want to introduce reforms which would destroy the built-in Conservative bias of the Lords. If anything they considered its powers to delay highly controversial legislation to be inadequate. The Lords have no power at all over money bills, yet these may play a major part in the introduction of such fundamental changes as a swing from free trade to protection, or the inception and development of a Welfare State. In the case of other bills, the twelve-month delaying period is partly an illusion, for two-thirds of this period may be occupied in passing through the Commons. Nor can the Upper House prevent a Government from using its powers to act without legislation, as, for example, in releasing detainees in Northern Ireland or in cutting defence, 1975. Thus fundamental changes in economic and military policy can occur without the possibility of any brake being applied by the Lords. Indeed, a Government with a good majority in the House of Commons could, during its five years of office, push through measures completely transforming society.

Hence, while the Conservatives were in office only piecemeal and minor changes were introduced. Payment for peers (now £13.50 a day) was introduced in 1957 in order to encourage the attendance of those without private means. The Life Peerage Act, 1958, permits men and women life peers to be created on the advice of the Prime Minister (who consults with the leader of the Opposition where appropriate). And finally the Peerage Act, 1963, allows (a) peers and peeresses in their own right to disclaim their titles for life and stand for the House of Commons, (b) peeresses in their own right to sit in the House of Lords.

On the Labour side there were also good reasons for supposing future inaction. First, since the events of 1945–51, the Lords seemed to have adjusted themselves to their limited role in the constitution, criticising governments but not throwing down the gauntlet. Secondly, many in the Labour Party have shown no relish for a reformed Upper Chamber composed of influential and able persons. Without the backwoodsmen to lower its prestige, it would merit such respect that, even if it did not demand increased powers, no government would be happy at the prospect of being continually subject to its criticism. Thirdly, since abolition was out of the question for both practical and political reasons, there was the difficulty of deciding the lines upon which reform would actually take place. Selection of members, whether by some form of nomination or election, presents difficulties which tend to increase as the number to be selected grows larger.

In the case of nomination, the chief problem is to find an entirely impartial nominator. The Sovereign, the Speaker and the Prime Minister have all been suggested, but each has disadvantages. While today the monarchy is politically neutral, to give the Sovereign power to select members of the legislature could easily endanger the tradition of impartiality. In the same way, the task might involve the Speaker in a political wrangle. Nor could the choice be left to the Prime Minister. He would always be tempted to nominate such members as would ensure his future control of the Upper House and, where one party remained in control of the Commons for a long time, the Upper House could become just as politically unbalanced as it is today.

On the other hand, there is no simple system of election which could be employed. If the Lords were elected at the same time and on the same franchise as the Commons, it would merely reflect the Lower House. Indirect election by local government councils would increase the influence of party politics in local government. While this might stimulate more interest in local affairs, it could also distract councillors from their true functions. Election based on the constituent parts of the United Kingdom — England, Wales, Scotland and Northern Ireland — has no obvious merits and would unduly strengthen nationalist feeling. Forming the country into regions — London, the West Country, the Midlands, and so on — would produce such artificial divisions that they would probably evoke little loyalty or interest.

One compromise suggestion is that various important bodies — the trade unions, the professions, the Confederation of British Industry, the local authorities, the universities, the various Church denominations, and so on — should form themselves into a college to elect a certain number of representatives. Not only would this put selection on a systematic basis, but it would remove the decision from the whim of the Prime Minister of the day. In addition it would provide the experts necessary for the job of revising the Commons' work. Against such a scheme it may be argued that the persons so elected are likely to be fairly elderly, that, due to apathy (see page 572), the spokesmen of some bodies are not necessarily representative of the people for whom they would speak, and that persons elected in this way, unlike present members of the

House of Lords, may be too tempted to look over their shoulders at those who elect them to be an effective check on any proposal which has some popular support regardless of its merits.

RECENT DEVELOPMENTS

In the Queen's Speech, November, 1967, it was announced that 'legislation will be introduced to reduce the powers of the Lords and eliminate its hereditary basis thereby enabling it to develop within the framework of a modern Parliamentary system'. Following inter-party talks which reached a large measure of agreement, the Government embodied its ideas in a Parliament (No. 2) Bill, 1968.

This Bill proposed that the reformed House should be two-tiered. Only the first tier would have the right to vote. It would consist of about 230 peers, created for life by the Queen on the advice of the Prime Minister, so as to give the Government of the day a small majority (about 10 per cent) over the opposition parties combined. But it would not have a majority in the House as a whole for there would be a number of cross-benchers. In this way the independence of the House would be preserved, and the creation of a large number of new peers with every change of government avoided. Effective power of decision would reside with these voting peers, who would be responsible for the bulk of the legislative work and day-to-day business. They would be obliged to attend at least one-third of the sittings of the House each session, and would be paid.

The second tier would comprise non-voting peers, limited to attending and speaking. At first it would consist of the present hereditary peers and those other peers who do not wish to accept the attendance obligation of voting peers. Successors to the present hereditary peers would have no right to attend the House of Lords, and they would be replaced by representatives of the professions, scientists, industrialists, trade union leaders and other leading members of the community, together with retired parliamentarians who, although unable to attend regularly, could make valuable contributions from time to time.

As for powers, this reformed House would be able to delay an ordinary public bill for six months from the date of disagreement between the two Houses and would lose its power of final rejection of delegated legislation, though it could still ask the Commons to reconsider an order (see chapter 21).

While all parties agreed that a second *revising* chamber is desirable in the British parliamentary system, the fate of the Bill simply revealed once again how great is the problem of deciding upon its membership and particularly upon its powers. Although the two front benches looked on the Bill sympathetically, progress on it was so obstructed in the House of Commons by the opposition of an unusual combination of Labour left-wing and Conservative right-wing back-benchers that the Government eventually dropped the Bill rather than delay other important and urgent measures.

As far as the composition of such a reformed House was concerned, the main objections were to the increased power of patronage which the Bill would have given to the Prime Minister and to the arrangement whereby ultimate voting control could be exercised by independent 'cross-benchers' acting together. Many doubted whether it would have been possible to find sufficient active and able 'cross-benchers' to serve in a House with such limited powers, while others feared that such 'cross-benchers' could be gradually phased out (like the hereditary peers) by the greed of the parties for more peers of their own colour after each change of power.

But it was over the powers of the House that there was most difficulty in reaching a compromise. This is because there is not complete agreement on the role of a Second Chamber in the British constitution. Shall it have the right to delay legislation, or is it merely to be a revising body? The Labour Party insists that decisions must rest with the elected representatives of the people. It is undemocratic if what is decided at the elections is subject to the possibility of appeal elsewhere. Nevertheless its leaders agreed to a delay of 6 months for 'second thoughts'. The Conservatives, on the other hand, would like the Lords to be able to exercise a real delay over the controversial legislation of the Lower House. In short, they want it to have the power to say 'no', not merely 'think again'. Such a constitutional 'check', they say, is essential with our 'first-past-the-post' system of voting and the power which now rests with the Government through the high organisation of the party machine and party discipline. The proposed six-months' delay would be of little real value except as a deterrent to last-gasp contortions of a dying government. They consider, too, that the Lords must be given real powers if busy men of character and ability are to devote their time to its work, for there would be little point in engaging in 'wordy battles signifying nothing in the end'.

Whether Parliament will make a further attempt to reform the House of Lords remains to be seen. After the February, 1974 election, the Upper House could make its decisions in the knowledge that the Labour Government had no overall majority in the Commons and might well remain in office only a short time. Hence a number of clauses in Government measures were defeated in the Lords, including the Trade Union and Labour Relations Bill. As a result, Mr. Michael Foot, Secretary of State for Employment, declared that when Labour had a real majority it would have to deal with the 'comic old nobility' and make sure that the 'built-in majority there is never again allowed to repeat the monkey-tricks performed by their lordships in the past two weeks'. In contrast to this, however, it must be recognised that the life peers, who now form the majority of the regular attenders, have transformed the Lords into a respected and hard-working assembly.

Whatever firm proposals for reform may be made in the future, there seems little purpose in modernising the Upper Chamber and emasculating it at the same time.

SUGGESTED READING

B. Crick, *The Reform of Parliament* (Rev. Ed., Weidenfeld and Nicolson, 1968), Chapters 5 and 6.

Benjamin Disraeli, *Sybil; or The Two Nations* ('The World's Classics' series, O.U.P., 1926).

G. W. Keeton, *Government in Action in the United Kingdom* (Ernest Benn, 1970), Chapter 4.

Massereene and Ferrard, Viscount, *The Lords* (Leslie Frewin, 1973).

5

The House of Commons: An Elected Chamber

'Free elections are the essential basis of democracy.'
PROFESSOR A. MATHIOT: *The British Political System*

I. REFORM OF THE ELECTORAL SYSTEM

'Democracy,' writes George Bernard Shaw in *Maxims for Revolutionists*, 'substitutes election by the incompetent for appointment by the corrupt few.' Maybe there is an element of truth in his cynicism, but the remedy lies in endeavouring to make the electors less incompetent, for democracy cannot be said to be fully realised in a country until all adults enjoy the right to vote. Naturally this involves giving equal voting power to persons having unequal ability to think intelligently on matters of government, unequal willingness to equip themselves for exercising their political rights, and unequal responsibilities, both functional and financial, as citizens. But it ensures universal application of a principle which is fundamental to the rights of the individual — the opportunity to have a voice in determining how he shall be governed — and eliminates the possibility of political discrimination on account of income, language, nationality, colour, creed or sex.

Yet although the principle of representation has operated in Britain for over 700 years, universal adult suffrage was instituted only some thirty years ago. Nor did Britain lag far behind other countries, for only comparatively recently has the principle come to be recognised as an essential objective. Even in Ancient Greece, which cradled the political philosophy of democracy, only the freemen had the right to vote. Similarly in England, where a civil war was fought to decide the supremacy of Parliament, nothing was done to share the fruits of victory with the people. Indeed, when Colonel Rainsborough suggested that the new Parliament of

1647 should be based on adult suffrage, he was fiercely opposed by Cromwell, who thought that a franchise not based on property would lead to the majority confiscating the possessions of the minority. Cromwell's view prevailed, and for close on another 200 years only the landed interest was directly represented in Parliament, the vote being confined to approximately 3 adults out of every 100.

REPRESENTATION AND VOTING AT THE BEGINNING OF THE 19TH CENTURY

The first House of Commons of Henry VIII's reign consisted of 298 members, 74 for the counties and 224 for the cities and boroughs. This was considerably smaller than the Model Parliament of 1295, the decrease resulting from the attitude of many boroughs who regarded the sending of representatives as an onerous duty rather than a right to be defended. The downward trend was reversed by the Tudors. Henry VIII added the 24 members of Wales among his creation of 41, but the largest increases occurred during the reigns of Edward VI and Elizabeth, when boroughs were created partly to secure the election of 'placemen'. No addition to the English seats was made after 1677 (when the number stood at 513); but the Union with Scotland in 1707 added 45, and the Union with Ireland in 1800 a further 100 seats.

Thus in 1830 the House of Commons consisted of 658 members, representing 40 English counties, 179 boroughs, 24 cities, the Universities of Oxford and Cambridge, 12 Welsh counties and 12 Welsh boroughs, and the Scottish and Irish constituencies.

The most stable element was the counties, for only Monmouthshire, Cheshire and Durham had been added since the 13th century; moreover, the two knights sent by each county to Westminster by ancient right were fairly representative of the body of electors. But by the end of the 18th century the counties had fallen almost completely under various 'influences'. Sussex, for instance, provided two of eleven seats which were virtually controlled by the Duke of Newcastle. Often the seats were regarded as hereditary, and elections were rare because arrangements could be made to avoid the cost of fighting them.

It was the boroughs, however, returning two-thirds of the House of Commons, which really determined its political composition. Most of them had obtained the right to send two members to Parliament some 300 years previously, but in the meantime their size had changed considerably, in some cases almost beyond recognition. At the end of the 17th century, Locke wrote in *Civil Government*, 'We see the bare name of a town, of which there remains not so much as the ruins, where scarce so much housing as a sheep-cote or more inhabitants than a shepherd is to be found, sends as many representatives to the grand assembly of law-makers as a whole county, numerous in people and powerful in riches.' Matters grew worse; whereas the Industrial Revolution resulted in a shift of population to the Midlands and north of England and in the growth of large towns, the boroughs were concentrated in the

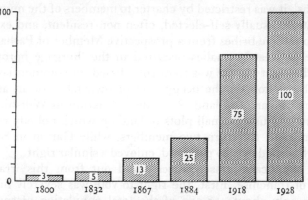

FIG. 1. *Number of persons having right to vote per 100 adults.*

south. Well over half of them were contained in Wiltshire and the ten counties bordering the sea south of the Wash and the Severn. Cornwall, with a population in 1831 of 300,000 returned 42 members, whereas Lancashire, having 1,300,000, returned only 14. Such large towns as Manchester, Birmingham, Leeds and Sheffield, returned no M.P.s.

The franchise was equally out of date. In the counties, the uniform qualification established in 1430 still remained. It was simply the ownership of *free* land or tenement to the value of 40s. a year. Elections took place at the county court and often extended over many days. No list was prepared. Those claiming the right to vote attended in person and merely swore on oath to the effect that they were qualified. Often this qualification had been obtained by the device of carving off a small portion of land, a 'faggot', from a larger freehold. Since there was no secret ballot, electors could be intimidated or bribed by rich patrons. It has been estimated that the average cost of winning a county seat in 1830 was £6,000.

The borough franchise, unlike the county, was irregular, depending largely on local custom. Some boroughs were fairly democratic. Thus, in the 'scot and lot boroughs', a liability to pay the local poor rate was accepted as the qualification to vote, while in the 'potwalloper' boroughs, all persons having a single room with a hearth in it were deemed to be able to 'boil their own pot' and so were enfranchised. The majority of boroughs, however, contained only a limited number of electors. Sometimes the franchise was enjoyed by all the hereditary freemen; in others, the 'close boroughs', it was restricted by charter to members of the municipal corporation, usually self-elected, often non-resident, and existing solely to receive bribes from a prospective Member of Parliament. But the greatest anomalies occurred in the 'burgage boroughs', where the right to vote was frequently based on common law and vested by custom in the occupation or ownership of an ancient tenement or parcel of land. At both Old Sarum in Wiltshire and Midhurst in Sussex, small plots of land on which nobody resided were sufficient to return two members, while Gatton in Surrey, although turned over to parkland, enjoyed a similar right.

Two significant consequences stand out from this irrational system of franchise. First, the right to vote was severely limited. In 1831 only about 435,000 of the total population of some 20 million people could vote. The ratio of voters to population also varied from place to place. Winchester, with a population of 9,000, had 60 voters, while Scotland, with a population of 2 million, had only 3,000. Secondly, seats came under the control of powerful patrons, often great landowners, who either actually owned the 'pocket' or 'rotten' boroughs, or were in a position to bribe or intimidate the electors. In 1793, approximately half the House of Commons was returned by 154 patrons, of whom 40 were peers. These patrons could either sell the seats to the highest bidder or look to their nominees for support in Parliament when they sought office or honours. No wonder the Younger Pitt exclaimed: 'This House is not representative of the people of Great Britain; it is the representative of nominal boroughs, of ruined and exterminated towns, of noble families, of wealthy individuals, of foreign potentates.'

Nevertheless, although the House of Commons was undemocratic, it cannot be completely condemned. Democracy was not then accepted as an ideal and indeed was often regarded with suspicion as being close to mob rule; even Burke considered that Parliament should not represent the people but rather 'property and intelligence'. Some people have defended the system on the grounds that such talented young men as the Younger Pitt and Charles James Fox were able to enter Parliament from rotten boroughs. It may be fairly said that Parliament did, to a large extent, succeed in governing according to the wishes of the people. The men who sat for the extinct boroughs had defied the Pope, stood up to a despotic King, and successfully fought wars against the Dutch in the 17th century and the French in the 18th century. And, when the demand grew strong, it sanctioned its own reform.

Towards the end of the century, however, various factors were beginning to undermine the structure of Parliament. George III, by using patronage against the Whigs, had united them in demanding the reform of the out-of-date electoral system which made this possible. Moreover, the House of Commons was becoming inefficient, manifest in the loss of the American colonies, and was falling out of touch with the wishes of the people, as the popular support for John Wilkes bore testimony. Above all, the old House of Commons had been successful only because, as an assembly of great landowners, it conformed to the general structure of an agrarian society. When the Industrial Revolution caused that society to pass away, its collapse was certain. The middle classes became increasingly dissatisfied with their exclusion from political power; the workers, suffering from the wretched conditions of both employment and home, began to realise that the reform of Parliament was a necessary step towards legislation for improving their lot. The growth of the popular Press, the repressions following the Napoleonic Wars and the weak and unstable governments of the 1820s, all encouraged them to intensify their demands.

THE REFORM ACT, 1832

The first attempts at reform in the 18th century failed to gather momentum through lack of organisation. They had the support of no political party, and merely represented the spontaneous and isolated efforts of a number of individuals. Although *The Gentlemen's Magazine* had reported parliamentary debates regularly since 1736, the first political society was not formed until 1769. This was 'The Society of the Supporters of the Bill of Rights' and it was founded to uphold John Wilkes and to press for parliamentary reform. In 1776, Wilkes moved in Parliament for a 'just and equal representation of the people in Parliament' and demands were made to limit bribery and corrupt practices at elections. Pitt himself was in sympathy with the movement, and in 1785 proposed a Reform Bill limiting the number of rotten boroughs, but this was heavily defeated. Further progress was halted by the excesses of the French Revolution and by the demands of the ensuing wars with France.

With the ending of the Napoleonic Wars, people once more began to take an interest in parliamentary affairs. Petitions for the reform of the House of Commons increased in frequency, but progress was hampered by lack of concerted effort. In 1830, however, Attwood founded the Birmingham Political Union, a peaceful political alliance of the town's middle and lower classes. The liaison produced mutual benefits: the middle classes provided the movement with organisation and direction, the workers gave it weight.

Although 1830 was a year of revolution throughout Europe, there was no violence on any appreciable scale in Britain. Instead, the people's attention was focused on parliamentary reform, and this became the dominant issue in the election which followed upon the death of George IV in July of that year. The Duke of Wellington's Government continued until November, when it was defeated, and Lord Grey, the Leader of the Whigs committed to reform, became Prime Minister. But it took eighteen months of political crises and the threat of revolution before his bill was passed into law.

The first Reform Bill was introduced in the Commons by Lord John Russell in March, 1831, but after being given a second reading by one vote, it was defeated in the committee stage and the Government was granted a dissolution. The election which followed is significant as being the first time a definite issue has been submitted to the electorate for a decision with members more or less committed to voting in the Commons according to the wishes of their constituents. The Whigs were returned with a majority of 136, being supported by the Non-conformists, professional classes, merchants and manufacturers, tradesmen in towns and the Whig aristocracy. Opposed to reform were the

Church, the law, the universities, most of the nobility, the landed interests, the Services and some bankers.

A new bill passed through all its stages in the Commons, but was rejected by the Lords in October. This challenge to the principle of representative government antagonised the country, and riots occurred in Bristol, Derby and Nottingham. A modified bill was then introduced, but in December even this was rejected by the Lords. Thereupon Lord Grey advised William IV to create some fifty peers to ensure the bill's passage. This the King refused to do, and so Grey resigned. Wellington, who personified reaction, tried to form a Tory Government to pass a measure just sufficient to forestall revolution. An even more intense agitation spread throughout the country. 'The Bill, the whole Bill, and nothing but the Bill' was the slogan, and Francis Place, leading the demonstrators, threatened 'no Bill, no taxes'. The Tories would not support Wellington, and within a week Grey was back, armed this time with a promise from the King to create the necessary peers. The Reform Bill, therefore, passed both Houses in May, 1832, the Tory peers absenting themselves as it went through the Lords.

The Reform Act, 1832, contained three main provisions. In the first place, it redistributed seats. 56 rotten boroughs were completely disenfranchised and 31 lost one member, thus allowing the transfer of 143 seats to the large towns in the north of England. Secondly, it widened the franchise, the main hope of the agitators. In the counties, to the traditional 40s. freeholders, it added £10 copyholders and £10 long leaseholders, and £50 short leaseholders and tenants at will occupying land or tenement at a minimum rental of £50 per annum. In the boroughs, the various customary rights to vote were abolished and replaced by a uniform requirement — the occupation of any premises of an annual value of £10. Although this qualification enfranchised the middle classes, in practice it sometimes took the vote from the artisan who had enjoyed it by virtue of the older qualifications. Lastly, the Act provided for the registration of electors, by which a qualification to vote entitled a person's name to be placed on the electoral register; only if it appeared there could he vote; and that is still the position today.

Judged by its immediate effects, the Act may seem rather insignificant. It did not achieve a democratic franchise; to an already small electorate, 217,000 voters were added, a 50% increase.

Indeed, the decrease in the value of money in the middle of the century, whereby the annual value of many houses was raised to £10, had a far greater effect. (This, together with the growth in the population, produced an electorate in 1866 of about a million.) Nor did it bring about complete equality in the geographical distribution of voting power. Many small boroughs in the south of England still retained at least one member and there 1 in 4 voted, whereas in the large manufacturing towns the proportion was only 1 in 45. Moreover, the old corruption continued, for while the electorate ceased to be in the pockets of borough-mongers, it was yet small enough to be bought. The 1841 Parliament was known as the 'Bribery Parliament', each vote costing on the average £1. Elections were still marked by intoxication and violence.

Constitutionally, however, the effects of the Reform Act were fundamental and far-reaching. The system of nomination was replaced by the principle of election. Members of Parliament remained aristocratic, with land and trade interests predominating, but they were no longer independent of the views of their constituents. Since ultimate sovereignty now rested with the electorate, parties were extended from Parliament to the country. On the other hand, the Sovereign lost the controlling voice in the composition of his ministry; within two years William IV was to discover this, for he was unable to retain Peel, a Tory, as his Prime Minister because the electorate had returned a Whig majority to the House of Commons. Instead, the Cabinet had to be chosen from the party having the support of the Commons and thus it became directly linked with the extended party system. Lastly, the vesting of political power in the electorate increased the importance of the representative body, the Commons, at the expense of the Lords.

While it took time for the main effects of the Reform Act to become evident, the immediate legislation following it signified the new principles which had been introduced with the spirit of reform. The Poor Law Amendment Act, 1834, and the Municipal Corporations Act, 1835, both proved that the Government and not the private member had become the mainspring of legislation. The latter Act also introduced the principle of elections in the municipal boroughs, while the Factory Act, the first government education grant, and the abolition of slavery in the British Empire, all in 1833, were measures conforming to the wishes of the common man.

THE REFORM ACT, 1867

The 1832 Reform Act did not introduce democracy — far from it, for only 5 out of every 100 adults had the vote. But it had shown that the ancient system could be successfully assaulted. Nevertheless, after the legislative zeal of the 1830s, Parliament's attention was concentrated on the repeal of the Corn Laws. The main political movement, the Chartists, achieved little and by the middle of the century was a spent force.

With the anti-Corn Law League's success in 1846, the radical forces led by John Bright could now devote their energies towards a further extension of the franchise. The Municipal Corporations Act had proved so successful in the boroughs that it was felt a similar measure should be applied to Parliament. Moreover, a further redistribution of the population had taken place through the rapid construction of railways between 1830 and 1860. People were also critical of the conduct of the Crimean War by the traditional political families, while later the success of the democratic forces in the American Civil War undermined the authority of the governing classes in Britain who had given their support to the South.

However, Palmerston, the Whig Prime Minister, did not really favour further reform, and it was not until after his death in 1865 that Lord John Russell was able to introduce a Reform Bill. Even though these proposals were moderate, the bill was defeated and the Conservatives took office. Disraeli, who was Chancellor of the Exchequer, persuaded his party to seize the chance of 'dishing the Whigs' and the result was that a more radical bill was introduced!

In the counties, this Reform Act of 1867 reduced the property qualification of the leaseholder and copyholder to £5 and introduced as an additional qualification the occupation of a tenement of a minimum rateable value of £12. This increased the county electorate by 50%, but as this did not include the agricultural labourer and voting was not yet secret, it still left the counties under the control of the aristocracy. In the boroughs, however, the working man was enfranchised, for the Act amended the voting qualification to include every male householder occupying for one year a separate dwelling-house and paying the poor rate, and lodgers who occupied for a qualifying period of one year lodgings to the annual unfurnished value of £10. Besides doubling the electorate to 2 million, the Act also carried out a further redistribution of seats, 45 boroughs with a population of less than 10,000 losing one member to the new large towns.

LATER 19TH-CENTURY REFORM

The objects of subsequent reform were the elimination of coercion and bribery at elections, improvement in the machinery for registering voters, and the simplification and extension of the franchise — measures which further undermined the influence of the old landed interests.

The first step forward was in 1868, when decisions on disputed elections were transferred from parliamentary committees, which were highly partisan in character, to the Court of Common Pleas (now the Queen's Bench Division of the High Court), where the judges could decide the question with complete objectivity. In 1879 jurisdiction was invested in two judges who must be unanimous in their decision for an election to be declared void.

But that further measures were necessary to prevent corruption at elections can be seen from Bright's description of what occurred in 1868. 'The corruption, bribery, compulsion, tumult of this General Election have probably never been exceeded — the whole country is disgraced and ought to be shocked, and no man who has no other remedy to offer can with any show of reason resist the ballot.' In fact, the secret ballot was introduced in 1872, though the move was violently opposed by the House of Lords on the grounds that politics should not be conducted in secret. The tenants at will, who became qualified by an Opposition amendment in 1832, had been compelled until now, on account of the insecurity of their tenure, to vote according to the wishes of their landlords. The secret ballot put an end to this intimidation. The Act also introduced the modern system of nomination; previously candidates were adopted at a public meeting and if no opponent came forward, the one person was automatically declared elected.

Yet other irregularities continued. Hence Gladstone's Corrupt Practices Act, 1883, required that election expenses should be proportional to the size of the constituency, and specified the objects on which money might be spent. In addition, corrupt practices were more closely defined, election agents were given the statutory duty of submitting accounts, and heavy penalties were imposed for a breach of the Act. Henceforth a man with moderate means could afford to fight an election. Expenditure on elections declined from £1 for every elector in 1880 to 3s. per head in 1885. Today it is approximately 3p per head. The Act was a notable success in checking malpractices, though it was the introduction of the mass vote in the following year which indirectly struck the real blow.

Although the 1832 Act had provided for the registration of voters, it established no machinery for the purpose, and registration was left to the political parties with the Overseers of the poor supervising. From 1878 onwards a series of Acts created registration authorities, who today are the Clerk of the Council in the case of county constituencies, and the Town Clerk in the boroughs. Until 1918, however, disputes as to a voter's qualifications were settled by revising barristers. Today the Registration Officers decide, although there is a right of appeal to the County Court.

THE REFORM ACT, 1884

The Reform Act, 1867, had produced an unstable situation. The urban working-class householder had been given the vote, but the labourer in the county district had not. In practice, the distinction between the county and urban areas was purely arbitrary, for what had become urban areas through industrialisation were still treated as though they were rural. Both parties therefore agreed that the household qualification should be extended to the counties, though the Conservatives were apprehensive for their county strongholds, fearing that the agricultural vote would be swamped by that of increasing industrial workers, such as miners. Hence, any change in the franchise had to be linked with the redistribution of seats, a policy agreed upon after the defeat in the House of Lords of the original Liberal bill. Consequently, two Acts were passed.

The Representation of the People Act, 1884 (Third Reform Act), made three changes:

(1) it extended to the counties the household and lodger franchise which had been conferred on the boroughs in 1867;

(2) it re-modelled the occupation qualification so that in both the counties and boroughs a person occupying *any* land or tenement of a clear annual value of £10 obtained the vote;

(3) it instituted a new domestic service qualification giving the vote to any servant, such as a gardener, living separate from his employer, but not to one living in, such as a butler.

The main effect of the Act was to enfranchise the working man in the county, particularly the agricultural labourer. The electorate was increased from 3 to 5 million.

The necessity of the Redistribution of Seats Act, 1885, arose because of the rapid influx of population from the rural to the new urban areas. For instance, Calne (Wiltshire), had one M.P. for a population of only 5,000 whereas Liverpool's three M.P.s represented over 450,000. The Act, therefore, introduced two main principles — equal electoral districts and single-member constituencies. As far as possible, there was to be one M.P. to every 50,000 of the population. To achieve this, 134 seats were taken from the boroughs, and the number of members was increased to 670. Boroughs with less than 15,000 inhabitants lost their M.P. and were made part of the county. Single-member constituencies were brought about by dividing the counties and larger boroughs into separate electoral districts each with its own distinctive name. However, 22 towns and some universities retained 2 members apiece, and double-member constituencies continued until 1950.

THE EXTENSION OF THE SUFFRAGE TO WOMEN

Women had to wait almost half a century longer before enjoying the same rights as men. In 1867, John Stuart Mill had tried to include women's suffrage in the Reform Bill, but it was not until the Women's Social and Political Union, led by Mrs. Emmeline Pankhurst, was founded in 1903 that their cause was taken seriously. After 1911, the 'suffragettes' began to draw attention to their aims by a series of illegal acts and by hunger strikes when in prison, and their campaign was brought to a halt only by the outbreak of war in 1914. Women then undertook jobs previously performed exclusively by men and in general proved so successful and responsible that, before the conclusion of hostilities, Mr. Lloyd George introduced a new bill.

The Representation of the People Act, 1918, carried our far-reaching reforms:

(1) It substituted a simple qualification to vote for the numerous qualifications which then existed; henceforth all that was

necessary was 6 months' residence or the occupation of business premises.

(2) The vote was given to a woman over 30 years of age, provided she or her husband was qualified to vote at local government elections.

(3) It removed the disqualification of receipt of poor relief.

(4) It provided that, at a general election, all elections were to be held on the same day and that no elector could vote in more than two constituencies.

(5) It introduced the requirement that a candidate shall deposit £150 with the Returning Officer, to be forfeited if he does not poll one-eighth of the total votes cast.

(6) It redistributed seats on the basis of one member to every 70,000 of the population.

In effect, the Act increased the electorate from 8 to 21 million, and the number rose to over 28 million when in 1928 women were given the vote on equal terms with men.

The Representation of the People Act, 1948 abolished the business premises qualification to vote and the university seats. Henceforth nobody could enjoy more than one vote. Changes in constituencies made necessary by shifts in the population were allowed for by the House of Commons (Redistribution of Seats) Act, 1944, which set up four Boundary Commissions to report regularly. In 1969 the voting age was reduced to 18 years.

We see, therefore, that over the last 130 years, there have been great changes in the electoral system. Representation of communities has been replaced by the representation of numbers, and the representation of property by that of citizens. Hence, a severely limited franchise has developed to one based on the egalitarian principle of one man, one vote. In addition, single-member constituencies have been introduced and corruption eliminated.

II. Procedure at Elections

WHEN ARE ELECTIONS HELD IN THE UNITED KINGDOM?

While universal adult suffrage is an essential to full democratic government, there must also be opportunities for the electorate to select representatives freely and at reasonable intervals. In the United Kingdom, both the House of Commons and the councils of local authorities are formed as a result of periodic elections by secret ballot.

Elections for the House of Commons are of two kinds, general elections and by-elections. General elections are held either when a Parliament has run its full term of five years or when it is dissolved by the Queen on the advice of the Prime Minister. The 1959 Parliament was the only one since 1832 to run its full term, although, owing to the exceptional conditions of war, the 1911 Parliament continued until 1918 and the 1935 Parliament until 1945.

Usually Parliament is dissolved at some moment during the last two years of its life when circumstances appear most favourable to the Government's chances of being re-elected. The choice of this moment now rests entirely with the Prime Minister, though naturally he consults the more important members of his party. No prime Minister likes to delay an election too far into Parliament's fifth year, for this exposes him to the possibility of having to hold it when circumstances are particularly unpropitious to the Government.

The legitimacy of this procedure is easily defended. The decision rests with the Prime Minister because the fortunes of his party are bound up with him; it comes from the Government side because that is where the British constitution lays the emphasis. The alternative would be to require that Parliament should complete its full five years. This would lead, however, to inflexibility, making it impossible to change a Government when there has been a reversal of public opinion. Apart from elections, our constitution provides no regular method of assessing public opinion; and this is as it should be. Public opinion polls, although improving in accuracy, are based on samples. More important, we could not reduce to some statistical ruling the decision as to when an election should be held. A Government may have to take measures which for a time may cause it to lose favour with the electorate. When it goes to the country, it is seeking confirmation of its policies, and it must be able to delay the appeal until those policies have had a chance to prove their worth.

With the tightness of modern party discipline, other reasons for a general election today are rare. If his majority is small, the Prime Minister may decide on an appeal to the country, either when he feels he could strengthen his position or when the physical strain of attending frequent divisions becomes too great. Or he may consider that upon a particularly vital issue the electorate should have a chance to express an opinion. But if he is defeated on a major issue in the House of Commons or a vote of censure is carried against him, the Prime Minister can either appeal to the electorate or recommend that the Leader of the Opposition be sent for to form a Government. In the latter case, the new Prime Minister would probably ask for a dissolution of Parliament so that his position could be confirmed. Lastly, a Prime Minister may recommend a dissolution when he feels that he is losing the support of his party, a situation which faced Mr. Attlee in 1951.

By-elections occur to fill odd vacancies arising through: the death or ill-health of a member; the acceptance of certain paid offices under the Crown; elevation to the peerage; expulsion by the House of Commons; vacation of the seat for private reasons, such as business commitments or disagreement with the party (although in the latter case it is possible to continue as an Independent). An M.P. cannot just resign; he has to be disqualified. Hence when he wishes to give up his seat for ill-health or private reasons, he applies for the post of Steward of the Chiltern Hundreds or Bailiff of the Manor of Northstead which, as paid offices under the Crown, automatically disqualify him. Once disqualified, he resigns the appointment.

PRESENT QUALIFICATIONS TO VOTE

In order to vote, a person must have his name on the electoral register of the constituency, a list compiled yearly by the Registration Officer. The qualification for inclusion is residence in the constituency on the qualifying date, but a person must be over 18 years of age and a British subject or a citizen of the Irish Republic. In the twelve Ulster constituencies, a person must have had 3 months' continual residence before the qualifying date. Certain persons are ineligible to vote. These include peers, aliens, prisoners serving sentences for felony of more than 12 months' imprisonment, and persons disqualified upon conviction of corrupt practices at elections.

ADOPTION AND NOMINATION OF CANDIDATES

To stand a chance of being elected to Parliament today, it is necessary to be nominated as the candidate of one of the main parties. Selection by the local Constituency Association of Party is the first step. In the Conservative Party, names may be submitted by party headquarters, personal sponsors or directly by personal application. Under Labour Party selection procedure, party headquarters cannot submit names (except for by-elections) although they do circulate a list from which Constituency Parties can invite applications if they wish, direct applications are not acceptable, and affiliated and party organisations can only submit one nomination each.

In a safe seat, the first list may contain nearly a hundred names and from this a short list of two to five persons is selected. This is done in the Conservative Party by a committee of ten to thirty members elected by the local executive; in the Labour Party the constituency executive recommends to the general management committee, which has the real power of deciding the short list. Persons so selected appear before the full executive of the constituency, if a Tory, and before the general management committee, if a Socialist. Both these bodies represent the parties' local branches, youth organisations, etc. and, in the Labour Party, the affiliated organisations as well. They vary in size from 50 to 200 members. Each applicant makes a speech of 10–15 minutes and is then questioned for a similar period. Ability to donate to party funds plays little part in the choice. Both the Conservative and Labour parties restrict the contributions of their candidates, though in the Labour Party a trade union or co-operative society may pay up to 80% of the cost of fighting the election if their sponsored nominee is the candidate. Conservative choices are cleared by the standing advisory committee of the Central Council, but they are rarely vetoed. This, however, is not so in the Labour Party, where the management committee's choice has to go before the National Executive, whose approval is far from formal. Actual adoption takes place at a general meeting of the constituency association.

The main advantage of this system of selection is that it gives freedom of choice to the constituency party and, in the case of Conservative candidates, there is no financial barrier or outside lobbying. But it means that, in safe seats, the M.P. is virtually chosen by a select few active party members, and the qualities looked for are not always those required for effective membership of the House of Commons. On the Labour side, too, the tendency can be for seats to go to the highest bidder, with some seats the sole possession of trade unions and co-operative societies.

The prospective candidate, as he is now termed, is usually selected long before an election is due. In the meantime, he is expected to 'nurse' the constituency, appearing at public functions and making addresses on political subjects.

Nominations can take place after the publication of the statutory notice of an election and not later than the eighth day after the Proclamation summoning a new Parliament. The candidate's name, address, occupation and party are filed with the Returning Officer by a proposer and seconder and eight additional 'assenting electors', and at the same time £150 is deposited.

THE ELECTION CAMPAIGN

Each candidate is required by law to appoint an agent (usually one is already employed as a full-time official to organise the constituency's political machine), and this agent is responsible for seeing that the election expenses do not exceed the prescribed maximum. This is £1,075, plus 6p. for each six electors in the counties and for each eight in the boroughs. Personal expenses do not form part of the legal limit, but any above £100 must be paid through the election agent. The limit was originally introduced to stop corruption, but it now serves to put poor and rich candidates and constituencies on an equal footing as regards finance. The difficulty is that the limit applies only to expenses which promote the *candidate* (as distinct from those which promote the party) and thus heavy expenditure can take place beforehand by the parties and by private sources. During the campaign, all centrally-produced posters and literature must be authorised by election agents and their cost included in expenses.

Locally, the campaign is waged through the Press, from loud-speaker cars in the street, by posters and election manifestos, at public meetings and by personal canvassing. On the average a constituency contains 60,000 electors, but only a small fraction of these will attend a meeting; approximately one half are canvassed in their homes by enthusiastic party supporters. Although by law the local constituency party has to be dissolved during an election, it is the organisation which has been built up that fights the campaign, and its headquarters are hired to the candidate for his committee rooms. The candidate is allowed the free use of schools

TABLE 1: General election results 1951-74

Party	1951			1955			1959			1964			1966			1970			Feb. 1974			Oct. 1974		
	Votes (mn.)	Seats	% of poll	Votes (mn.)	Seats	% of poll	Votes (mn.)	Seats	% of poll	Votes (mn.)	Seats	% of poll	Votes (mn.)	Seats	% of poll	Votes (mn.)	Seats	% of poll	Votes (mn.)	Seats	% of poll	Votes (mn.)	Seats	% of poll
Labour (and Co-operative)	13·9	295	49	12·4	277	46	12·2	258	44	12·2	317	44	13·1	363	48	12·1	287	43	11·7	301	37	11·5	319	39
Conservative and supporters	13·7	321	48	13·3	345	49	13·7	365	49	12·0	304	43	11·4	253	42	13·1	330	46	11·9	296	38	10·4	276	36
Liberal	0·7	6	3	0·7	6	3	1·6	6	6	3·1	9	11	2·3	12	9	2·1	6	7	6·1	14	19	5·3	13	18
Others (inc. Speaker)	0·2	3	1	0·3	2	1	0·3	1	1	0·4	—		0·5	2	1	0·9	7	3	1·7	24	6	1·9	27	7
TOTALS	28·6	625	100	26·8	630	100	27·9	630	100	27·7	630	100	27·3	630	100	28·3	630	100	31·3	635	100	29·2	635	100
Percentage voting	82·6			76·8			78·7			77·1			75·8			72·0			78·7			72·8		

Note: For figures of earlier elections refer to the Appendix of *The British General Election of 1966*, D. E. Butler and A. King (Macmillan).

for meetings and one free postal delivery, usually reserved for his manifesto. Nationally, the battle is waged through the great daily newspapers and at public meetings, and party political broadcasts on radio and television are given. The two big parties are allocated equal opportunities over the air, though the smaller parties consider that the time is unfairly apportioned.

To what extent does the election campaign influence the result? Both major parties have a solid core of supporters. But there are other voters who have been weighing up the respective performances of the government and alternative government throughout the previous Parliament. Some of these floating voters have not yet made up their minds, and it is chiefly at these that the parties direct their propaganda, with the major effort being made in the marginal constituencies. It has been estimated that in the two-and-a-half weeks before the election, it is possible to persuade only some 12% of the electors (*Studies in British Politics,* Ed. R. Rose). Most, therefore, have already made up their minds before the election campaign.

POLLING DAY

Polling takes place seventeen days after the dissolution of Parliament, excluding Sundays and holidays. On election day the effort of the parties is directed towards ensuring that their supporters go to the polls. Cars are used, and ardent workers check electors as they attend to vote so that absentees may be rounded up later.

At the polling station, the elector gives his name and address to a clerk, who checks it against the official list of those eligible to vote and ensures that no one votes twice. The elector is then handed a slip of paper on which the candidates' names and parties are printed. He then enters a booth, puts a 'X' against his preference and drops the folded slip into a sealed ballot box. All polling at a general election takes place on the same day, polling stations being open from 7 a.m. to 10 p.m. At the close, the sealed boxes are taken to the town hall, where the count is supervised by the Returning Officer. Absentee voters in the Forces or on business can vote by post, and about half a million do so. It seems that Conservative supporters make the most use of this concession, and in the election of February, 1974, D. E. Butler and Dennis Kavanagh calculated that the postal vote was probably worth about 12 seats to the

Conservative Party (see *The British General Election of February, 1974*). Most results are announced soon after midnight, though in some constituencies counting does not take place until the next morning. Expenses of Returning Officers are charged on the Consolidated Fund and amount to approximately £1 million. The cost of compiling the annual register is about £2 million which is shared between the Treasury and the local authorities about equally.

III. THE CASE FOR AND AGAINST SOME FORM OF PROPORTIONAL REPRESENTATION

The results of the present single-vote system have been criticised for not giving a true arithmetical reflection of the wishes of the electorate. First, as Table 1 on page 68 shows, the number of seats obtained by the different parties is not a true reflection of the votes cast for them; usually the winning party has more seats than its support justifies. In February, 1974, the Labour Party polled fewer votes than the Conservatives but had five more seats. Such a result occurs because many marginal constituencies are won by a slender majority. Secondly, it leaves a fairly large minority third party, the Liberals, almost unrepresented. Indeed, the critics of the system go further, claiming that the figures do not reveal the true measure of distortion because many people, for fear of wasting their vote, do not vote for the person they really want, and others do not vote at all.

Proposals for reform come chiefly from the Liberal Party. The major parties refrain from introducing an alternative system which would favour the growth of smaller parties at their expense. The Conservatives benefit directly in that they usually secure more seats than the number of votes polled for them would justify on a strictly arithmetical basis, while the Labour Party is sufficiently strong to ensure that a small swing of the floating vote in their favour would almost certainly give them a majority of seats. Such views, however, are purely subjective. Would any alternative method of voting effect a real improvement in the constitution?

Proposals for reform of the electoral system take many different forms.

(1) *The single transferable vote*

Under this system, often referred to as 'proportional representation', the single-member constituency is replaced by fewer constituencies, each returning many members. Voters mark each candidate in order of preference. (In Tasmania, where this system operates, there are seven M.P.s to a constituency and the voter has to put at least three in order of preference.) To be elected, a candidate has to obtain a 'quota' of votes. This quota is determined by applying this simple arithmetical formula:

$$\left(\frac{\text{total votes cast}}{\text{number of seats} + 1}\right) + 1$$

which gives the minimum votes which a candidate must obtain in order to ensure election. (If, for instance, a total of 100 votes were cast for two candidates in a one-seat constituency, 51 would be a quota.) Any candidate who receives the 'quota' of votes is declared elected. But the chances are that he will receive more than the quota; if so, these surplus votes could be considered as 'wasted' and, in fact, would be under our present system, since they would be in excess of those necessary to secure election. Hence all his second choices, as stated on the ballot paper, are counted and the surplus votes distributed proportionately among the other candidates according to those second choices. If another candidate now has the 'quota', he is similarly declared elected. Any surplus votes that the latter candidate has received would be transferred in the same way according to the third choices of the first candidate, since the surplus votes originally came from him. This process continues until the required number of candidates have the quota. If this does not occur through the distribution of second choices, then the candidate with the least number of votes is eliminated and his votes distributed among the other candidates according to his second choices, and so on.

It is claimed for this system that: the result corresponds as closely as possible to the wishes of the electorate; each appreciable minority receives fair representation; no vote is wasted, as a person can vote for a candidate he really wants; it improves the quality of candidates, because in the larger constituencies which would be formed there would be fewer safe seats; it gives original and able Independents more chance of succeeding at an election; it results in greater stability of Government policy by eliminating the 'swing of the pendulum' under the present two-party system.

Against the single transferable vote, however, there are weighty arguments. First, it raises technical difficulties. It is complicated, though this is really the concern of the Returning Officer. It takes longer, though this is justified if it produces a better government. It cannot give a *proportional* result in by-elections (where it simply becomes the 'alternative vote'), though this is hardly a reason for not using it in general elections. It would lead to difficulty in allotting the scarce debating time in Parliament were every party to have an opportunity of expressing its views.

Secondly, with the introduction of large constituencies, members would lose much of their personal contact with constituents. This argument is weakened because Britain, on the whole, is so densely populated that only in north Wales, the south-west of England, and the south and north of Scotland would candidates have to cover exceptionally large areas. In any case, under the present system of voting for a party rather than a person, the advantages of the single-member constituency are eliminated, since few electors ever see the candidate for whom they voted. On the other hand, when the qualities of the man are made to count, as they would be under P.R., the electors would be less apathetic over attending political meetings, and it could well be that a first-class member would be constantly re-elected and not turned out whenever his party lost favour. Moreover, with the multi-member constituency, a person would be able to contact a representative of the same political persuasion and not, as so often occurs today, have to seek the help of a member from the opposite party or one in another constituency.

Thirdly, it must be pointed out the single transferable vote would only 'accurately' reflect the opinion of the country *at a particular moment*. In effect, therefore, the logic of proportional representation also demands frequent elections — or at least a system of staggered re-elections so that there are annual tests of opinion.

But the main reason for opposing proportional representation is fundamental — it would strike at the heart of our constitutional system. Throughout its development, the British constitution has placed the emphasis on effective government. Parliament's task is to support a Government or allow it to be replaced. Hence the real purpose of a general election is not to get a new House of Commons but either to confirm the Government in power or to obtain a different one. The test of the poll will not be mathematical accuracy but whether the result reflects the 'swing' in the country. With our present method the electorate is faced with a straight choice and its decision determines the nature of the Government and the broad policies to be followed over the next five years. But this does not apply when the Government has to be formed from a coalition of many small parties. Quintin Hogg puts it thus: 'Honesty in politics depends on the electors choosing between teams and real issues, not on party groups driving bargains over the heads of the electors when a General Election has failed to produce an intelligible answer because the electors were never compelled to answer one intelligent question' (*The Purpose of Parliament*). Nothing in our constitution says that we should have an arithmetical reflection of public opinion in the House of Commons. The essence of the British pattern of parliamentary government is the interplay between Her Majesty's Government and Her Majesty's Opposition, the alternative Government. As Professor Wheare says, it is 'a front-bench constitution'.

Proportional representation may endanger this fundamental characteristic. Since it puts a premium on the insistence by small minorities on their own opinions instead of a willingness to make mutual concessions, it can lead to the existence of many parties. This may result in weak coalition Governments, which are maintained by narrow, sectional interests to the neglect of major, national issues, and in divided Oppositions, which are irresponsible because none of the parties can hope to secure an absolute majority and therefore need never contemplate accepting the duties of government.

The straight-voting system is not unfair between the two major parties. While it may accentuate swings, it does not create them. British electors generally seem to have confidence in a method which maintains the two-party system and produces strong governments. It suits their temperament, because its success rests on mutual give-and-take. In practice, minority views do not go unheeded. In the first place, to be successful in a general election, a party must modify its more extreme policies and show an ability to compromise in order to capture the floating vote (see page 109). Secondly, in Parliament, the Government does not ride roughshod over minorities but makes concessions where it can in order to secure as wide an agreement as possible for its policies. Admittedly the present system does not work perfectly, but the people understand it and find it basically acceptable. Tampering with it might produce harmful repercussions in some other part of the delicate machinery of the constitution. Nevertheless, in some countries, such as the Republic of Ireland and Tasmania, proportional representation has been introduced successfully. Indeed, where there are racial or religious minorities, some form of it may be necessary to guarantee their representation.

For this reason, the single transferable vote was introduced into Northern Ireland in 1973 for electing the Northern Ireland Assembly and the new District Councils, and it was used again in 1975 for electing the Convention (see page 284).

Recently, too, there seems to be an increasing recognition of the merits of the single transferable vote system. For instance, the Kilbrandon Report on the Constitution, 1973, unanimously recommended its use for the election of the proposed Scottish and Welsh Assemblies. Support for some form of proportional representation has also come from within the Conservative Party. It is argued that not only have frequent changes in government since World War II made it difficult to follow consistent economic policies, but that recent Labour governments have been able to force through radical socialist policies when they have commanded less than 40% of the votes. Generally, a mixed proportional system, described in (3) below, is advocated

(1) *P.R. in local elections.* For the following reasons, the case against P.R. in local government elections is not so strong:

    (i) The division of local politics into two parties may not always be a good arrangement. There is less need to formulate a strong policy for carrying out administrative functions, and the committee or conference table is more appropriate than the debating chamber. Indeed, most council chambers are arranged on a horseshoe pattern. Moreover, local government should foster the corporate life of the community and representation of all sections helps to achieve this. The probability is, too, that electors have a more personal link with local government than with parliamentary candidates. The system of election, therefore, should permit some persons to be elected on their personality rather than on their party attachment.

(ii) The technical snag of large constituencies does not apply since there already are many councillors for a relatively small area.

(iii) Straight voting may result in *all* the councillors of an authority coming from one party. Thus in 1971 all the councillors of the London Borough of Hackney were Labour.

(2) *The party list system*

An alternative form of proportional representation is the party list system, which is used in Sweden. Voters choose between lists of candidates submitted by the parties and seats are allocated between the parties in proportion to their votes. If, for instance, a party gained half the votes in a constituency, it would receive half the seats and nominate candidates from its list to fill them.

Although the system is simpler than the single transferable vote, it tends to eliminate personal voting for a candidate.

(3) *A mixed proportional system*

A mixed proportional system, similar to that of the Federal Republic of Germany, has the advantage of simplicity. It provides for an equal mixture of directly-elected constituency candidates (as in the United Kingdom today) and candidates elected proportionately from party lists in numbers sufficient to make the total seats for each party proportional to its share of the total vote.

It works as follows. The voter is given a ballot paper consisting of two sections. The first part contains the names of the candidates in that constituency (as in Britain) together with their party affiliations. The candidate first past the post is elected. The second part of the ballot paper is a list of the political parties competing in the election, and electors vote for the party they prefer. 'List' seats are then allocated so that, together with the members already directly elected, the total representation of each party will be in proportion to the votes it received on the second part of the ballot paper.

There are four important qualifications:

(*a*) there is no compulsion to vote on the first part for a candidate of the party for which the voter decides on the second part of the paper;

(b) proportional seats are allocated only among those parties which poll 5% of the total vote;

(c) it is possible for a party to win directly more seats on the first part of the ballot paper than their proportional votes on the second part entitle them to;

(d) seats are allocated from the list by a sophisticated system of distribution.

(4) The alternative vote

In this system, electors mark the candidates in order of preference. If no candidate receives an absolute majority over the rest, the bottom candidate is eliminated and his votes are distributed among the others according to his second choice. This continues until one candidate has an absolute majority.

(5) The second ballot

This system is somewhat similar to the above except that, where no candidate secures an absolute majority, the bottom candidate is struck out and a second poll is held in approximately ten days' time.

Both the last two systems are designed to prevent an M.P. being elected on a minority vote. Moreover, they allow an elector a larger measure of choice for, by voting in the first instance for his real preference, he need not fear his vote will be wasted. Nevertheless, both schemes have certain disadvantages. It is doubtful whether the usual high percentage of voters would trouble to poll a second time. Nor does either system ensure representation of minorities. Often the person who is least objectionable is elected, rather than the one who is positively wanted. In Britain, it would probably merely mean that the Liberal Party would gain extra seats. There would be less likelihood of one party's securing an absolute majority. This would reduce the electorate's power to choose a Government and possibly result in indecisive policies.

SUGGESTED READING

A. J. Allan, *The English Voter* (E.U.P., 1964).
J. Blondel, *Voters, Parties and Leaders* (Penguin, 1969).

D. E. Butler and D. Kavanagh, *The British General Election of February, 1974* (Macmillan, 1974).

G. D. H. Cole and R. Postgate, *The Common People* (4th Ed., Methuen, 1962), Chapters 7, 8, 9, 20, 23 and 25.

Charles Dickens, *Pickwick Papers*, Chapter 13.

E. Lakeman, *How Democracies Vote* (Faber and Faber, 1974).

E. and A. G. Porritt, *The Unreformed House of Commons* (C.U.P., 1930), 2 Vols.

R. M. Punnett, *British Government and Politics* (2nd Ed., Heinemann, 1971), Chapter 2.

R. Rose (Ed.), *Studies in British Politics* (2nd Ed., Macmillan, 1969).

R. Rose, *Influencing Votes* (Faber, 1967).

6

Voting Behaviour

'The candidate is at last face to face with real live people who smile, laugh, scowl, jeer, cheer or pointedly ignore him.'

NESTA WYN ELLIS: *Dear Elector*

I. THE ELECTORAL GEOGRAPHY OF BRITAIN

There is one common feature of the political geography of Britain. Although as many as 2,000 candidates may seek the voters' support, most seats fall to the two main parties. This supremacy, although still there, is less marked in Scotland and Wales, for while England (owing to its larger population) has five times as many Members of Parliament as her two smaller neighbours put together, these 'celtic fringes' to the north and west of Britain provided in October, 1974, 13 of the 22 Members drawn from outside the two main parties. Nationalists had an exceptionally good result at that election when Plaid Cymru won three constituencies and the Scottish Nationalists eight. Although this left the major parties still dominating the electoral scene, the nationalists had emerged as a serious electoral force and as one of the distinctive features of the electoral geography of Britain.

A difference of emphasis can be discerned in the appeal made in the two countries. Scottish Nationalists concentrate on allegations of economic deprivation said to be the consequence of government from a remote English capital and on the opportunity which North Sea oil now gives to the Scottish people. Welsh nationalists tend to give greater precedence to safeguarding the culture, language and traditions of Wales. In both countries, as well as appealing to patriotism and economic advantage, the nationalists can attract some of the idealism of the young—who now form a larger proportion of voters—and, like the Liberal Party, they can collect votes from electors who feel disillusioned with both the main parties.

Strong forces work against the further development of nationalism in British politics. Britain is geographically a small country and historically it has had a unitary rather than a federal form of government for a very long time. Not only is Britain fairly centralised—as evidenced by the readership of national newspapers—but there is considerable mobility of population which must encourage a broader interest and participation in British affairs. Many able and articulate Scotsmen and Welshmen, including numerous people who have special qualities of leadership to offer the community, go to live and work in England, especially in the capital, and there is also a significant movement of English people going to live and work in Wales and Scotland. Nor is there any discrimination, nor any language barrier. Less than 2% of the population speak Welsh or Gaelic and few of these cannot speak English well. Religion is not a dividing factor—as it is, for instance, between the north and south in Ireland—although there are distinctive religious traditions in the two countries. There are in fact a number of significant cultural differences between the parts of Britain, but cultural similarities tend to be much stronger and the political ideas and aims which appeal to most people are most powerfully articulated in the two great British parties, which also are helped by having the best share of attention in the media of communication. By providing common news, features and entertainment, the media in the main draws the people of Britain closer together in their tastes and outlook.

In 1975, however, the Government announced that it intended to establish separate parliamentary assemblies for Scotland and Wales. Although the Leader of the House, Mr. Edward Short, declared that Parliament at Westminster must retain its sovereignty and its responsibility for the overall management of the United Kingdom economy, the devolution of more power to Scotland and Wales may have a significant effect on the further development of nationalist politics (see page 466).

Because at a national level the two main parties are usually fairly evenly balanced, the presence of other Members can be of considerable political significance. In October, 1974, for instance, the Labour Party had 315 Members of Parliament and the Conservatives 271, but the political situation was complicated by the presence of 22 Members from other parties, together with 10 from Northern Ireland.

Although the two main parties tend to be well-balanced nationally, there may be wide differences in certain localities, often related to variations in local social background. For instance, an overwhelmingly strong Labour constituency such as Ebbw Vale, where the Conservatives won only 7·5% of the vote in October, 1974, can be contrasted with a strongly Conservative constituency such as Cheadle, where only 15·3% voted Labour. Thus while most voters live in constituencies where the two main parties are in strong competition with each other, others live in places where one party permanently dominates local politics. The Labour Party is stronger than the Conservative in Scotland, Wales, the North East and North West, whereas the Conservative tends to draw better support in the Midlands, London, the South East and the South West. Yet even within each of these regions, there are extreme differences between constituencies. There is then a markedly uneven spread of party support and we must now consider some of the reasons for this.

II. Social Influences on Voting Behaviour

THE CLASS STRUCTURE

(i) *What is social class?*

One of the difficulties in exploring any possible relationship between social class and voting behaviour is that the idea of class is such a vague one. Membership of a particular class may be said to be characterised by occupation, the source and size of income, education, parentage, speech, dress, one's interests in arts and sports and various other characteristics and attitudes. Indeed a person might consider himself to be a member of one class whilst a neutral observer thinks that in fact he belongs to another.

Attempts have been made to reach a more precise understanding. Advertisers, for instance, are interested because they wish to direct their sales campaigns towards the social groups that are most likely to buy the product. It would be useless to advertise Rolls-Royce cars in a magazine which turned out to be bought mainly by lower income groups. Anything which can be called an 'upper class' is too small to be of any electoral significance, but the business world usually divides the middle and working classes into different groups along the following lines.

Middle class

A Higher managerial or professional

B Lower managerial or administrative

C1 Skilled, clerical, supervisory non-manual or professional workers

Working class

C2 Skilled manual workers

D Semi-skilled and unskilled manual workers

E Casual workers, persons dependent on State welfare payments, pensioners

(ii) *Occupational class and party preference*

If class is defined in occupational terms, along the lines of those given above, then certain trends can be discerned. Surveys show that among the upper middle class, Conservative sympathies are very strong. The lower middle class, too, mainly give their support to the Conservatives, but not with such an overwhelming backing.

No similar clear distinction exists, however, between the divisions of the working class for in each division the Labour Party enjoys majority support. This is not surprising for a party in whose history and present-day organisation the working-class trade unions play such a part (see page 119). Nevertheless the working class is less firmly allied to the Labour Party than is the middle class to the Conservatives. Research has shown that nearly one-third of working-class trade unionists support the Conservatives at election time. Indeed, in view of the fact that about two-thirds of the population may be described as working class, it would be virtually impossible for the Conservative Party to win a general election if it had no appeal among working-class people.

(iii) *Subjective social class*

Although social class is not easily defined, people tend to identify themselves with a particular class. It has been discovered that persons who identify themselves with the middle class are likely to vote Conservative and there is a similar tendency, though not so strong, for those who identify with the working class to vote Labour.

Not only do people identify with a certain class, but they develop their own life-style and there is also a relationship between this and voting behaviour. Those people who have more consumer goods, and in particular those who own their own houses, are more likely to vote Conservative. This might be a stronger influence even than occupational background, for surveys have indicated that a majority of working-class people who own their own homes are likely to vote Conservative.

The survey by D. E. Butler and D. Kavanagh of the February 1974 election suggests that class-consciousness may be declining and that political attitudes are becoming less clearly defined along class lines. This could be because society has changed a good deal from the early days of the Labour Party, and there are now more affluence and different patterns of wage settlement and tax distribution. This trend is particularly marked in younger electors, among whom more from the middle class voted Labour and more from the working class voted Conservative (*The British General Election, February, 1974*).

ENVIRONMENTAL INFLUENCES

People are naturally influenced by the views of their parents, and those they regularly meet at work or in local pubs and shops. We have seen that although national support for the two main parties is fairly evenly balanced, there are many localities where one or other of the parties is overwhelmingly popular. Evidence suggests that, in these circumstances, some voters are influenced by the locally accepted view and by the arguments of the partisans of the dominant party, so that the normal voting pattern according to occupational class is modified. In particular it seems that working-class and lower-middle-class voters are less likely to vote Labour where most of their neighbours are Conservatives.

New housing patterns may intensify the effect of local popular opinion on voting behaviour. For instance, since World War I large numbers of working-class council estates have been built, and this concentration of one class in a locality has resulted in strong support for the Labour Party.

Group opinion may give an extra advantage to a particular party if people join together in any organisation which has a strong political viewpoint. An example of this is the trade union movement, which is actually represented in the structure of the

Labour Party, whose views, therefore, are easily diffused among the unions. Consequently membership of a trade union tends to encourage support for the Labour Party. Nevertheless the effect is hard to measure, for those who are inclined to vote Labour are also likely to be the very people who are most keen to join a trade union.

Similar measurement problems apply to the relationship between membership of church communities and voting intention. Anglicans tend to be more Conservative than Roman Catholics and Nonconformists, but this relationship is much weaker now than it was when religious questions were more politically important. Its strength varies in different places, Wales, for instance, being both traditionally Nonconformist and politically left-wing. Such voting tendencies, where they do exist, may be less a political legacy from the past than a reflection of social class groupings, for there is also a relationship between religion and social class, Anglicans tending to draw a greater proportion of their members from the middle classes than the other churches.

Some modern developments tend to weaken the force of group opinion on the individual. Nowadays, for instance, more young people leave home to pursue higher education at university or college. As a result, they meet people from more varied backgrounds and hear a greater diversity of opinion. What was regarded as the only acceptable viewpoint at home may command less support in this new environment, and consequently the student's viewpoint may either change or be reinforced under the influence of the new people he meets. Today more young people leave home to further their careers at work, and such change of environment may lead to a change of political opinion.

Technical developments may also lessen the impact of the environment on a person's political outlook. Thus the ownership of a car and a telephone encourages personal relationships outside the immediate locality. Other technical advances have transformed the newspaper industry and made radio and television possible. Through these 'media of communication', distant influences are brought right into the home.

THE MEDIA

In this chapter we are mainly concerned with the effect in the fairly short term of newspapers, radio and television on voting behaviour, rather than with any possible long-term effect on the formation of public opinion or upon the nature of the political system itself.

Although newspapers give intensive coverage to general elections, and although they are widely read, they appear to have little or no success in converting their readers from the support of one political party to another. There are many reasons for this. Many people, particularly the less educated and those in the lower income groups, read newspapers mainly for amusement and recreation. Editors realise that, to secure large sales, they must concentrate on features which provide for their readers' interests; serious political argument may not, therefore, obtain much space, for it often gets little attention from many readers.

Another consideration is that people do not normally buy newspapers whose views are unsympathetic to their own, and they are more likely to admire and remember reports and articles echoing their own political opinions. It seems likely that both voting behaviour and choice of newspaper—and probably the selection of what items to read in the newspaper—are the result of social and political attitudes which the reader had developed at some time in the past. This cuts across the simple relationship between occupational class and party support. Thus it has been shown that a majority of working-class readers of the three Conservative papers, the *Daily Telegraph*, the *Daily Mail* and the *Daily Express*, vote for the Conservative Party, and that a majority of the middle-class readers of the Labour papers, the *Sun* and the *Daily Mirror*, vote for the Labour Party.

In some ways, however, newspapers may have a significant effect. Together with radio and television, they publicise and dramatise the election campaign and create the impression of an exciting occasion. This helps to increase the turn-out of voters, and indeed the absence of a sustained Press and broadcasting campaign at local elections may be one explanation why fewer people vote at them. If the media do increase the poll, not only is this healthy for democracy, but it may even change the result, since in certain circumstances a higher turn-out may work to the advantage of one party.

Although newspapers are usually strongly partisan, only if the result is quite close can they have a chance of changing the course of events during the campaign. Such was the Labour landslide in

1945 that no effort by the Conservative Press would have mattered. The opportunity to influence is greatest at such times as 1964 or February, 1974 when the parties are running neck-and-neck. The strong backing given to Labour by the *Daily Mirror* and the *Sun* may have encouraged a number of Labour readers in marginal constituencies to vote, and so have helped the Socialist cause a little. More likely, the extra 8% of the working class who voted Labour were aroused from their usual apathy by the 3-day week enforced by the Heath government to combat the miners' strike. It has to be concluded that newspapers have little effect on voting intentions in the short run, while their contribution to the building up of attitudes over the longer period cannot be isolated from other influences. Indeed, the influence of the Press can hardly be distinguished from that of the other media.

Television is a persuasive medium which may bring political information in front of people who do not read about politics in the newspapers or go to political meetings. But although the existence of television may alter the nature of the campaign, it is hard to discern any effect on voting behaviour. Unlike the newspapers, television authorities are expected to adopt a detached and impartial attitude, so that there is little likelihood that their programmes will cause big swings of opinion during the campaign.

One instance in which television may possibly have had some effect is the publicity given to the Liberal Party. Since the mid-sixties, leading Liberals have received good coverage in news, current affairs and party broadcasts on both television and radio. This may have compensated the Party for the loss of their only newspapers, the *News Chronicle*, which closed down, and the *Guardian*, which moved gradually away to a general left-wing position—and for the penalising electoral system—so making it easier for the Liberal Party, despite these considerable disadvantages, to increase its vote greatly in the 1970s.

It is the more interested electors who are likely to pay most attention to the political information provided by the media, and since these are usually the most committed voters anyway, their voting intentions are unlikely to be altered, especially in the short term. There may be some effect on political attitudes in the long term, but it is unwise to reach too firm a conclusion when so many of the influences at work are intangible and indirect.

Parties themselves obviously consider the media to be important and they pay great attention to publicity both on television and in the Press during the campaign. This may help the party in many different ways; for instance, by successfully projecting the personalities of its most important politicians or by boosting the morale of party workers in the field who may in consequence be more effective in getting sympathisers to the polling booths.

EDUCATION

There is evidence of a relationship between the amount of education a person has had and his voting preferences, the tendency being for those who have had the least formal education to support the Labour Party. However, there is also a close link between education and social class in that young people with middle-class parents are more likely to choose a more extended education, and such education is more likely to lead to middle-class occupations and life styles. Another qualification that has to be made is that this link between education and voting behaviour does not apply to the same extent to the most educated middle-class voters. A survey in 1974 showed that primary school teachers tended to favour the Conservative Party while the more academically qualified university lecturers had a greater tendency to vote Labour.

AGE

Younger voters are more likely to support the Labour Party whilst older people tend to vote Conservative, especially among the middle class. The lowering of the voting age to 18, by increasing the number of young voters, might have been expected to work to the advantage of the Labour Party. But some qualifications have to be made; for instance, there is also a tendency for younger voters to be less likely to vote than their elders.

III. THE INFLUENCE OF PARTY POLICIES ON VOTING BEHAVIOUR

THE DEGREE OF IRRATIONALITY

It must be concluded that the electorate cannot simply be viewed as a body of people who rationally choose between the

policies of rival candidates on the basis of what is thoughtfully
deduced to be either best for the national interest or for each
elector's own economic self-interest. Indeed, the level of knowledge of many voters about some of the most important policies
and political personalities of the day is not nearly as high as
might be expected. In a survey made by Independent Television
in 1971, of 355 people who were questioned before and after
seeing a news or current affairs programme, it was discovered
that, although whether or not to join the Common Market had
been a dominant political issue for some years, one-fifth of those
questioned thought that the letters 'E.E.C.' stood for Eastern
Electricity Council. David Butler and Donald Stokes have
recorded that 'in 1963 we encountered respondents who were
unable to identify Harold Macmillan after he had been Prime
Minister seven years; one even believed that Mr. Attlee was still
at the head of government' (*Political Change in Britain*). Policy
issues then often play a less important part in determining how
votes are cast than party loyalties based on such factors as those
discussed above—social class, family tradition, age and so on.
But there is some evidence of a trend towards more thoughtful
voting. David Butler and Dennis Kavanagh in their book on the
February 1974 election came to the conclusion that voters were
'acting in an increasingly instrumental way, rationally considering
their self-interest rather than recording traditional loyalties' and
that 'class has become far less salient as a cue for voting and issues
such as Europe, trade union reform, and incomes policy have
transcended traditional Conservative–Labour divisions'.

THE SALIENT ISSUES

As well as a somewhat greater willingness to pay attention to
matters of policy on the part of the electorate, the size of the
floating vote increased in the mid-seventies. With some local
variations in degree of swing, general elections tend to be marked
by fairly small swings of votes to one party or the other throughout
the country. Under the British electoral system quite a small swing
of votes can produce a large turnover of seats, for a change of
1,000 votes is equivalent to a swing of only about 1% of votes in a
constituency. It is important then to identify what is the kind of
issue which might cause those relatively small national swings of
opinion which can lead to a change of government.

Two conditions must be met. First, voters must regard the issue as an important one in that it will have some effect on their own lives. Second, they must believe that the result of the election will make a real difference to how the issue is tackled because the two main parties have shown that they are genuinely divided over the best way to solve the problem.

Economic questions today often meet these two requirements since everyone prefers greater prosperity to stagnation or decline. Although such questions as the balance of payments are above the heads of most voters, movements in prices, incomes, national output and unemployment produce general feelings of stress or benefit which in turn may be reflected in feelings of hostility or gratitude towards the government of the day. Such questions, too, as the position of the trade unions or membership of the E.E.C. may evoke a response when they become recognised as relevant to the voter's economic well-being.

Welfare issues, such as house rents and mortgages, pensions and education, may also help to cause short-term movements of opinion. Not only do these determine the quality of life of the individual, but parties sometimes pursue distinctive policies towards them. Thus Conservative policy in the 1970s was considered more favourable than that of the Labour Party towards private housing and less favourable to including a large proportion of council houses in new building and to low rents for the mass of council tenants.

Policies, however, have to be understood and interpreted by the voter. Traditional supporters of a party will interpret the facts differently from its political opponents. Sympathisers tend to pay more attention to matters which favour their own party and to minimise the significance of facts favouring the other side. Nevertheless, evidence cannot always be ignored: rising prices in 1970 were a handicap to the Labour Government, and the 'three-day week' in February 1974 resulting from an unsuccessful Government confrontation with the National Union of Mineworkers, placed the Conservatives at a disadvantage.

Policies are often associated with the party Leader and his prominent colleagues, all the more so as journalists both in the popular Press and in broadcasting tend to personalise issues. Nowadays the Leader receives extensive television coverage and he usually dominates the party's election campaign, playing an important part in projecting the party's image. In modern times both the extension of government activity and the greater complexity of the political system have strengthened his decision-making role and it is rightly recognised that the quality of party leadership as a whole will be crucial to the ability of that party to deal successfully with important issues. The fact that Mr. Wilson was personally held in higher esteem than the Conservative leader in the mid-1960s was an electoral asset for Labour; yet, as we have seen, this is but one of many influences. In 1945 the Conservatives lost heavily despite Winston Churchill's high stature as a leader, while in 1970 the Conservatives won, although polls consistently showed that Mr. Heath had a less favourable image than Mr. Wilson. The appointment in 1975 of the first woman, Mrs. Thatcher, to lead a British political party gave a 'new look' to the Conservative Party after political troubles in the early 1970s. At a time of rising household prices, Mrs. Thatcher was portrayed both as a housewife who shared the concern of women voters over prices in the shops and also as a grocer's daughter sympathetic to the problems of retailers. Her selection as leader was accompanied by much speculation as to whether a woman leader would be an electoral asset or liability.

IV. Some Important Groups of Voters

(1) WORKING-CLASS CONSERVATIVES

One outstanding characteristic of the Labour Party is that, both by origin and in its present-day organisation, it has its roots in the working class, especially through the trade union movement. Why then do a third of working-class electors cast their vote for the Conservatives?

A partial explanation is that in Britain class is a relatively minor source of political conflict. Karl Marx, the 19th-century founder of international socialism, gave a theoretical basis on class lines to socialist thought. He argued that there were two classes, the capitalists who owned the land and the factories, and the proletariat, or working class, who had only their labour to sell. Marx believed that the capitalist system of production led inevitably to class struggles, out of which a communist system would eventually emerge.

In Britain, however, such ideological theories of class conflict are not widely held. Although at times the policies of a party may appear more attractive to one class rather than to another, this is often not the case, and success or failure in carrying out economic and social measures are recognised as benefiting or harming people generally, irrespective of class. Nor do other ideologies support political loyalty on class lines in the way, for instance, that religion does in those countries where the Catholic working-class vote is really important.

One explanation that has been given for the working-class Conservative vote is that it comes in part from a section of working people who adopt a 'deferential' attitude towards people with a higher status in society. These 'deferentials' are said to vote Conservative because they believe that the party includes in its ranks the politicians who by their birth, education, experience and outlook are the natural rulers of the country. Possibly the frequent practice of using the Union Jack at Conservative Party meetings is linked with a wish to appear to voters in this light.

Yet it may be doubted whether this contributes a great deal to explaining voting behaviour. Winston Churchill possessed all the characteristics of membership of a traditional ruling class, together with an immense personal popularity, but he was defeated heavily in 1945 and again narrowly in 1950. Nor did the fact that Sir Alec Douglas-Home was the fourteenth earl seem to carry much weight with leading Conservatives who encouraged him to resign as party leader in 1965, to be succeeded by Mr. Heath, whose more modest background is not markedly dissimilar to that of Mr. Wilson. Mr. Heath went on to win the 1970 election and when he in turn was rejected as party leader in February 1975, he was replaced by Mrs. Margaret Thatcher who was portrayed as a 'self-made' leader who had risen by effort and intellect from quite an ordinary home 'above the grocer's shop', whereas her rival, Mr. William Whitelaw, came from a traditional Tory landowning family. Against this, it may be pointed out that Mrs. Thatcher's first Shadow Cabinet included six old Etonians, two peers, a baronet and two peers' sons.

While not doubting the existence of the 'deferential' voter, the working-class Conservative vote must be attributed also to a combination of many causes already mentioned in this chapter—self-identification with the middle class, family tradition and all the various environmental influences, education, and assessments both of the successes and failures of party policies and of the personalities of party leaders. Moreover, class divisions are softening, and British society has become relatively homogeneous in comparison with Victorian times, with a good deal of social mobility, especially now that opportunities of secondary and further education have been so considerably extended. It is not really at all strange, therefore, that a sizeable portion of the large working class prefers the Conservative Party.

(2) THE LIBERALS

Well before World War II the Liberal Party ceased to be one of the two main parties, and Liberal voters know that under the present electoral system there is no likelihood of a Liberal Government being formed. Nevertheless, in February 1974, the Liberal vote rose to 19·3% of the total poll, and opinion polls suggested that this could have risen further to about a third of the electorate had the party any hope of winning a majority.

This support does not rest upon a class basis. Unlike the main parties, Liberal voters tend to come from a cross-section of society in terms of social class. Indeed the party has tried to attract voters with the claim that it is independent of both working-class trade union power and middle-class business power.

Some support is traditional, and comes from older people who grew up before about 1930 and were forming their political attitudes at a time when the Liberals could still be regarded as a major party. There still remains, too, some trace of middle-class nonconformist support, a relic of the political divisions about church schools early in the century. Yet traditional loyalties can explain only a small part of the Liberal vote, especially in view of the fact that Liberal successes in parliamentary and local elections are not at all restricted to areas where there is a strong surviving tradition.

The extent of support is influenced by the number of Liberal candidates. In the thirties, the Liberals undermined their position as a major party by not putting up candidates in a great many constituencies, thus forcing potential supporters either to abstain or to switch to the Labour or Conservative parties. The high Liberal vote in February, 1974, followed a decision to have 517 candidates, the most since 1929. Habitual Liberal voting does depend upon the regular putting up of candidates, and the failure to do this may be one reason why support for the party comes less from a stable than from a constantly-changing group of supporters. Even so, the magical 25% support, which Liberals have been encouraged to believe would make a Liberal government a possibility, still appears far distant. Indeed, in the October 1974 election, the Liberal vote declined.

Although the personality of the leader is a minor influence on voting, some votes have been gained by the favourable image projected by both Liberal leaders in the sixties and seventies, Mr. Grimond and Mr. Thorpe. Unlike leaders of smaller parties, both succeeded in gaining good personal publicity through the media of communication, and Mr. Thorpe sought to make the most of this by such tactics as a tour by hovercraft of West Country coastal constituencies prior to the October 1974 election.

Some votes are negative, won from electors who have become disenchanted with one major party and yet are hostile to the other. Especially if they consider it their civic duty to vote, such electors may well turn to the Liberals.

Other support may come from 'tactical' voting. Many seats in Britain are won with a minority of the total vote. Suppose there is a seat where the Labour Party expects to come third and the Conservatives are likely to win by a margin over the Liberal candidate. In these circumstances, a Labour supporter who wished to vote tactically would support the Liberal candidate in the hope that he will gain the seat and thus reduce by one the Conservative numbers in the House, thereby dividing and weakening the anti-Labour strength. On the other hand, where the Liberals occupy the third place, tactical voting would work to their disadvantage.

At any rate, whatever the motives, Liberal voting has remained much more politically interesting and important than might be expected from the simple fact that nowadays the party has only around a dozen M.P.s in the House of Commons.

(3) POLITICAL EXTREMISTS

George Orwell wrote that 'the gentleness of English civilisation is perhaps its most marked characteristic'. The attitude of the electorate towards political extremists bears out this observation.

Inside the three major parties, extremists have limited influence. A few members at the extremes may be regarded by some as doctrinaire and uncompromising, and some parliamentary candidates might take militancy as far as joining well-conducted public demonstrations. But for most there is a basic loyalty to the political system and a rejection of violent, arbitrary and undemocratic actions. Opponents of the Labour Party in the mid-seventies spoke with concern about a 'small group of power-hungry trade union leaders' on the extreme left-wing of the Party, but 'moderates', such as James Callaghan, were known to be the best vote-winners and were consequently given prominence in the 1974 general election campaigns.

By their support of the three main parties, the electorate have clearly shown that they are not looking for extremist politicians to represent them. Evidence of this is found in some of the rare cases of politicians breaking away from their parties and yet managing to retain much popular support, for this difficult feat has been achieved most noticeably by men who have been more moderate than the local party associations with whom they have quarrelled, such as Dick Taverne in Lincoln in March 1973 and February 1974. Even Enoch Powell, who broke with his party in February 1974, provides further evidence that people in general are not looking for an extremist. His more extreme statements, e.g. on race, and the advice to Conservative constituents to vote Labour in order to oppose Britain's membership of the Common Market, tended to weaken rather than strengthen his position. Much of his following is derived from his charisma and ability as a political speaker; even so, he was able to return as a backbencher to the House of Commons only through the support, not particularly spectacular, of a Northern Ireland constituency.

To the right of the main parties, the most striking and capable political leader in modern times has been Sir Oswald Mosley. Mosley resigned from the Labour government in 1930, and became leader of the British fascist movement. Yet, although fascism was popular on the Continent in the 1930s, it failed to win electoral support in Britain. Racial tension after the war helped Mosley's cause no more than had unemployment and poverty before. By the late 1950s, racialism was showing signs of becoming a political issue, and in 1958 there were some unpleasant riots in the Notting Hill district of Kensington, London. Even so, when Sir Oswald Mosley stood as a candidate in the North Kensington by-election a year later, he could not even save his deposit.

By the 1970s the prominent fringe party on the right was the National Front which in the February 1974 election put up 54 candidates who campaigned against immigration, preferential housing treatment for Ugandan Asians and the E.E.C. The time should have been propitious, because voters at that election were said to be disillusioned with the main parties, but even in areas of high immigration the National Front did not do well, and overall it was not able to attract more than 3% of the votes.

Fringe parties on the left have had even more disastrous results. Support for the Communist Party, the main continuous challenge on the far left, has steadily declined. This has been reflected in the number of candidates which has dropped from 58 in 1970, when all lost their deposits, to only 28 in October 1974. Their average vote has been rather less than 2% of the poll. In February 1974 the Communist candidate in Dunbartonshire Central was Mr. Jimmy Reid, well-known as a popular personality on radio and television after his success as leader of the work-in at the Upper Clyde Shipbuilding Yard. Mr. Reid's popularity among radical young people was shown by his election as Rector of Glasgow University. At the general election, however, the result was different. Even though the position of the trade unions was a main issue in February 1974 and even though the constituency was a favourable one, Mr. Reid could not push the Communist vote up beyond 14% of the total poll, leaving him in fourth place with only half as many votes as the Conservatives who came third behind Labour and Scottish Nationalist. Nor did the personality of the actress Vanessa Redgrave, who stood for the 'Workers' Revolutionary Party' at Newham, North-East in February 1974, help her to win more than 760 votes, a mere 1·7% of the poll. The seat was won with 24,200 votes by Mr. Reg. Prentice, who is generally regarded as a moderate among Labour Party leaders.

Thus have the electorate snubbed extremists even when they have been articulate, able and personally popular, and the political circumstances apparently favourable. Not even mass unemployment in the thirties, world war, the loss of Empire and big power status, inflation, immigration, I.R.A. bombings in England and a rise in violent crime, have turned voters from moderate and democratic traditions. This can be seen as a tribute to both the British people and to the flexibility of the

British Constitution which has shown its capacity for innovation in changed circumstances.

(4) THE ABSTAINERS

Cynics sometimes say that people are becoming disillusioned with politics and politicians; but if this were so, voters would show their discontent with the existing political system either by turning to extremists or by lapsing into apathy. Election results prove that neither of these disasters for democracy has happened.

It is true that the turn-out of only 72% of the electorate at the 1970 election was the lowest for a quarter of a century, but the turn-out of 79% at the next election, in February 1974, was the highest since 1951—although it was still behind the record post-war vote of 84% in 1950.

People abstain for different reasons. Sometimes it is a positive decision made by those who have some interest in politics but who either completely reject all the parties competing in their constituencies or who are temporarily disillusioned with the party they normally support. In either case a protest can be registered by staying at home on election day. Other voters respond in an entirely negative way to the election. Some do not vote because they are too lazy or too busy; thus housebound women with children are high abstainers. A number, especially those badly-informed or poorly-educated, have little interest in politics. Abstention among young voters and the very old largely falls in this category, for where the motivation is small, a decision as to whether to vote or not can be influenced by such minor matters as the weather. A third category of non-voters are not deliberate abstainers, but are unable to vote because the register is out of date, omitting those who have reached voting age or have moved into the constituency, while containing names of people who have died or moved away. Others may be too ill to vote, or away on holiday.

Although deliberate abstainers are a small proportion of the electorate, they are not politically insignificant because, together with those who are converted from one party to another, they form part of the floating vote. They have the biggest effect when the supporters of one party decline to vote in greater numbers than the supporters of their opponents. This differential turn-out gives one party an advantage of about 1%, but there is no consistency as to which party gains this advantage. Surveys have suggested that in 1964 and 1970 Labour supporters were more likely to have stayed at home, while in 1966 Conservatives seemed less likely to have turned out.

(5) THE ACTIVISTS

Voting in Britain is a voluntary act, but it is generally regarded as a civic duty, the widespread neglect of which would weaken democracy. Even in a safe constituency, votes which cannot sway the result give moral backing to a party. In any case, Press and broadcasting create such a feeling that a big and interesting event is taking place that all but a few people want to take part.

To sacrifice a few minutes every four or five years to voting is the minimum of democratic involvement; it is possible to play a more active role. Yet, just as, on one hand, a small percentage of voters abstain, so on the other, only a small percentage work directly on behalf of a candidate. Nevertheless, this 3% represents about a million people.

It is the possible abstainers who are the special target of the party workers rather than political opponents, for the latter are unlikely to be converted quickly and any attempt to achieve this may be counter-productive. Canvassing, therefore, will be concentrated on those areas known to have most supporters in an attempt to get as many of these as possible to the polling station. In safe constituencies, this work has less significance; indeed, in their book on the 1966 election, D. E. Butler and Anthony King remarked that in many safe seats canvassing was not even attempted. Liberal activists are especially important to the Party; because there is a higher turnover of support among Liberal voters, there is more need for Liberal canvassers to encourage potential supporters.

Activists of each party are not found uniformly in all areas; nor do they represent a social cross-section of party voters. Conservative associations tend to thrive in more middle-class areas, and Labour parties in more working-class districts. In both parties a higher proportion of party activists than of supporting electors come from the middle class; in the Conservative Party support is drawn especially from businessmen, and in the Labour Party particularly from such professions as teaching and journalism.

Politics is only part of life and a person's inclination towards political activism reflects not only his political allegiances but also his general social values. Ideas of leadership and serving the community have been prevalent among the middle class and this has possibly helped to produce a bias towards middle-class leadership within both main parties.

Party attitudes reflect a broad philosophy of life and the more strongly this is held, the greater is the desire likely to be to participate in political activity. Conservative supporters may be motivated by strong beliefs about free enterprise, the right to private property, individual freedom, law and order in national life, rewards for effort and skill and so on. On the Socialist side, activism may stem from enthusiasm for such ideals as the equality of all citizens, the removal of privileges, national planning for welfare and economic benefit, giving more scope to the working class in the nation's affairs, or a belief in the value of protest and dissent as a stimulus to beneficial change.

The importance of activists is that they supply a vigour which stems from their convictions. At election time people who feel strongly on such matters seek the satisfaction which can be derived from becoming more involved than the ordinary voter. They work to activate and mobilise the electorate, encourage political interest and spread political knowledge, and in a marginal seat this might even sway the result. Although political life would be an impossibility if all electors were activists, their attempt to influence voting behaviour is the very stuff of democracy.

SUGGESTED READING

D. Berry, *The Sociology of Grass Roots Politics* (Macmillan, 1970).

J. G. Blumler and D. McQuail, *Television in Politics* (Faber, 1968).

D. Butler and D. Stokes, *Political Change in Britain* (Macmillan, 1969).

D. Butler and D. Kavanagh, *The British General Election of February 1974* (Macmillan, 1975).

R. McKenzie and A. Silver, *Angels in Marble* (Heinemann, 1968).

R. M. Punnett, *British Government and Politics* (Heinemann, 1968), Chapters 1–4.

R. Rose, *Influencing Voters* (Faber, 1967).

R. Rose, *Studies in British Politics* (Macmillan, 1966), Chapters 1, 2 and 5.

C. Seymour-Ure, *The Press, Politics and the Public* (Methuen, 1968).

C. Seymour-Ure, *The Political Impact of Mass Media* (Constable, 1974).

7

The Member of Parliament

'Your representative owes you, not his industry only,
but his judgement; and he betrays, instead of serving
you, if he sacrifices it to your opinion.'
                    EDMUND BURKE: *Letter to his Constituents in
                    Bristol, 1774*

I. WHO BECOMES AN M.P.?

In order to stand for Parliament, a person must be a British
subject over 21 years of age and be nominated by 10 electors.
There is no residence qualification but, to prevent frivolous
nominations, £150 must be deposited with the Returning Officer.
Persons legally disqualified from membership of the House of
Commons include: members of the House of Lords; clergy of the
Church of England, the Church of Scotland and the Church of
Ireland, and Roman Catholic priests; undischarged bankrupts;
felons still serving sentence; persons convicted of corrupt practices
at elections (for 7 years); and those precluded by the House of
Commons Disqualification Act, 1957, such as some civil servants,
judges, ambassadors, members of the regular armed forces and the
police forces, paid members of the Boards of nationalised industries and government-appointed directors of commercial companies (e.g. British Petroleum), directors of the Bank of England,
Clerks of county councils, and Town Clerks.

Now that the university seats have been abolished, there is little
chance of any person successfully contesting a parliamentary
election without having a party label. In practice, however, mere
membership of a party is not sufficient; he must be adopted by the
local constituency association in the manner already described.

What sort of a man is the average parliamentary candidate?
He is probably a long-standing member of the party and has often
taken an active part in local politics. Frequently, before being
chosen as candidate for a safe seat, he has fought forlorn elections

in another constituency. The probability is that he is over thirty years of age, for the tenure of an M.P. being somewhat chancy, he will want to enjoy some financial independence, either through a profession or business, before standing for Parliament. There is an even chance that he will have been to a university, most likely to Oxford or Cambridge if a Conservative candidate, but 'Redbrick' if a Labour candidate. On the other hand, he may be the one out of every four Labour candidates who is sponsored either by a trade union or a co-operative society. Only about 4% of the candidates are women.

More difficult to answer is the question: 'What makes a person wish to become a Member of Parliament?' Most certainly it is not the financial rewards. While he may be awarded ministerial office or receive an honour, the days have long since passed when membership of the House of Commons could be used for monetary gain. A Member of Parliament today receives £5,750 per annum (plus subsistence supplements and an allowance of up to £3,200 for secretarial assistance) and also first-class railway travel between Parliament and his home and his constituency. But not until 1911 were M.P.s in this country first paid 'an allowance', as Mr. Lloyd George put it, and even today, although more members are entirely dependent on their parliamentary salary, the idea that they should be part-laymen still prevails. Moreover, most M.P.s are of sufficiently high calibre to command an equivalent salary outside politics. In any case, an M.P.'s life abounds with disadvantages. If his main source of income is work outside, then he will possibly suffer financially. Since he is constantly subject to the demands both of his party and his constituents, he has to sacrifice his home life, his recreations and even much of his cultural interests. And in the House itself, the facilities afforded M.P.s (in the way of office accommodation, secretarial assistance, etc.) are inferior to any other legislature in the civilised world.

In return for these disabilities, most M.P.s would admit that they enjoy the sense of power and prestige which membership of 'the most exclusive club in London' provides, though many would question whether the power was very real in view of the modern party machine. With some M.P.s, the desire to reform or to preserve what they consider to be essential ideas and institutions is stronger than in others. But, whatever their zeal, the vast majority believe in the ideas to which they subscribe or otherwise it is unlikely that they would pass the searching examination of the local selection committee. Most M.P.s have probably arrived in Parliament through their enthusiasm for politics. Some have politics in their blood, while others have been bitten by the 'political bug.' For both, the natural goal is to become a Member of Parliament.

But political life is too uncertain for many members to make it a whole-time career. In practice, therefore, they are usually laymen, drawn from all walks of life and sharing in the work of the nation — directors of companies, university dons, brokers, barristers, solicitors, doctors, journalists, trade-union leaders, farmers, teachers, and so on. Even when elected, most members continue with their outside interests if they can. The Commons gains from this arrangement. A House composed entirely of full-time politicians would lose its intimate contacts with the outside world, and lack breadth of view. At present such a variety of persons sit in Parliament that few subjects can be discussed without at least one M.P. having expert knowledge.

We need not worry unduly over why persons seek to sit in Parliament. Whether they become M.P.s from motives of power, prestige, vanity, missionary zeal or political interest, they still have to retain their seat in order to fulfil their political ambitions. Members, therefore, must have some ability and, above all, must pay attention to the wishes of the electorate or at least to those of their local party workers and the principal pressure groups in the constituency.

II. Duties of an M.P.

The duties of a minister are obviously arduous and exacting; but it should not be too readily assumed that the work of the back-bench M.P. is easy. The conscientious member will have a 14-hour working day, and maybe longer if he has outside business interests. Where he cannot afford a full-time secretary, he will have to share one. His duties are heavy because he has four main spheres of responsibility — his party, his constituency, the nation and himself.

(1) *His party*
'Damn your principles! Stick to your party,' exclaimed Disraeli, and this is the sentiment which usually prevails today. The M.P. is

in Parliament as a result of the support the party has given him, and it demands loyalty in return. Stability of government rests on the party system and, except on the few occasions when a free vote is allowed, the M.P. is expected to follow the party line. But he also has a responsibility to himself and his own conscience. If he feels he cannot accept party policy, then he must choose whether to give up his seat, sit as an Independent, or carry on in the hope that the party will recognise the nature of his convictions and respect them. Party headquarters are likely to be more tolerant than the local constituency of the member with individual ideas. The local party can summon him to explain his actions on any matter it chooses. Mr. Nigel Nicolson in 1956 had to account to Bournemouth East for his failure to support the Conservative Government's Suez policy; in 1960 Mr. Alfred Robens (now Lord Robens) had to explain to the Blyth Labour Party executive the implications of his appointment as labour relations consultant to Atomic Power Construction, Ltd. If the member can satisfy the local party, national headquarters will almost certainly overlook the matter. But the constituency may ask the member to resign; whether he does so or not, his parliamentary career is at an end, for he is never likely to be adopted again for that or any other constituency.

The party's interests must also be promoted by the member in his own constituency. The local association requires him to report at fairly regular intervals (sometimes as often as once a week) to explain the policy being followed by the party in Parliament. And, as we shall see in the next section, he must nurse the constituency in other ways.

(2) *His constituency*

A candidate having first-rate qualities and working indefatigably is unlikely to add more than a few hundred votes to his poll. Only in a marginal constituency, therefore, is the member's work really significant. Nevertheless, most M.P.s are careful to nurse their constituencies by holding regular political meetings, attending such local functions as flower shows, bazaars, school speech days and civic receptions, and receiving, perhaps entertaining, any constituents who come to Westminster. But, apart from these courtesies, a member can add to his local standing in two major ways.

First, as regards his constituents, the M.P. has a personal responsibility. The British constitution recognises that at times the individual may need protection from the bureaucrat, and the principal safeguard it has provided is the right of the citizen to approach his Member of Parliament, asking him to look into the matter on his behalf. The member is the representative in Parliament of all his constituents and not merely of his party supporters, and he must therefore be available to help each one in his personal difficulties. It has been estimated that an M.P. receives approximately thirty letters a day. In addition, many members attend the local party office on a regular evening each week for interviews. Many enquiries can be dealt with by his secretary, for only a letter is necessary. Others can be answered by providing the appropriate information or advice — and could often have been handled in the first instance by the local Citzens' Advice Bureau! But it may be a grievance which only an M.P. can handle effectively. Perhaps the usual channels have failed to secure satisfaction from a government department. Here a letter from the member may change the whole attitude of a bureaucrat. If this fails, a direct approach to the minister in charge of the particular department, either personally or by letter, may be tried. Since 1967, too, there has been an alternative course of action — reference to the Parliamentary Commissioner (see page 322).

Unless the M.P. is seeking notoriety the parliamentary question will be used only when all other methods have failed for, in spite of what has been said in its favour, it has serious limitations. Few topics are so simple that they can be probed or aired with any thoroughness in a two-minute bout with a minister. In any case, the minister and his department are on their dignity under public fire and so, instead of admitting a mistake, are likely to produce only a carefully worded reply. Nor, if the civil servant knows his job, will the supplementary question fare much better. But where a member, on whatever side of the House, feels a constituent has a genuine grievance he should not flinch from any form of action in Parliament to secure redress.

Secondly, where a special interest is important in his constituency (because, for instance, one industry or type of agriculture predominates) the member is expected to present its viewpoint forcibly in Parliament. There is, however, a limit to how far he can go, for the local problem must be seen in its national setting. One of the member's tasks may be to educate his constituents in this wider view, though this tends to be somewhat neglected in modern politics, where every vote counts. In any case, since issues are seldom clear-cut, the member can usually plead for his constituency in what he sincerely believes is also the national interest.

(3) The nation

Democracy is secured much more by the spirit than by the form of the constitution. Each M.P., therefore, whether on the Government or Opposition side, must observe the rules of the game and help Parliament to discharge its functions. He must serve on parliamentary committees, play his part in the financial procedure, watch legislation, and help to control the executive. In short, he must assist Parliament to fulfil its traditional functions (see page 171). Many of these duties are irksome and time-consuming, yet frequently do not secure the publicity they deserve. Much credit, therefore, must be given to those M.P.s who nevertheless discharge their responsibilities conscientiously and perform duties which may be neglected by their headline-seeking fellows. Fortunately, the former may be rewarded by being chosen as members of a parliamentary delegation to countries abroad, particularly in the Commonwealth.

But the member's responsibility to the nation has a wider implication. He has a duty to inform himself concerning the various problems he will be likely to vote upon. Apart from reading in the library and listening to debates, he attends study groups organised by the party where ministers and leading authorities address back-benchers on important issues. Should his deliberations ever force him to the conclusion that there is a divergence of interest between the nation and his constituency, he must always remember that he is a Member of the Parliament of the United Kingdom, 'a deliberate assembly of one nation with one interest, that of the whole, where not local purposes or prejudices ought to guide but the general good resulting from the general reason of the whole' (Edmund Burke). Indeed, there is really no mechanism by which an M.P. can ascertain the view of his constituents as a whole, rather than that of the party officials, the lobbyists and the letter-writers.

This is the generally accepted view. The member is not a mere delegate instructed by his constituents as to how he shall speak and vote in Parliament. Instead, he is a representative who, while giving full weight to their opinions, still forms and acts upon a personal judgment which is based on the argument and counter-argument put forward in the debates of the House. Burke's letter to his Bristol constituents is still the classical exposition: 'Government and legislation are matters of reason and judgment and not of inclination; and what sort of reason is that in which the determination precedes the discussion, in which one set of men deliberate, and another decide, and where those who form the conclusion are perhaps three hundred miles distant from those who hear the arguments.'

Yet how far are Burke's views applicable to modern practice? Usually local constituency associations expect their member to follow the party line. Should he not do so, he may even be unseated. Mr. Stanley Evans, Labour M.P. for Wednesbury, was forced to resign for failing to support the line taken by his party during the Suez crisis, 1956. On the other hand, at times local interests and national policy may diverge. In 1971 Sir John Eden, Conservative M.P. for Bournemouth West, was warned by his local association that he risked not being re-adopted if he supported the Government's proposals to amalgamate the County Borough of Bournemouth with Dorset County Council in the local government boundary changes. A member with views in advance of his constituents (consider the question of the abolition of capital punishment) may succeed in educating and leading them. Or a free vote may be declared to enable him to express an independent opinion. But, where neither is possible, it takes a very strong character to sacrifice a political career on a personal judgment which, after all, cannot be infallible.

(4) His own ideas and interests

On many subjects, the M.P. has his own particular views. He may think the betting laws are unreasonable, or he may consider that any relaxation would have bad moral effects. He may be in favour of blood sports, or he may wish to abolish them. He might want to make divorce easier, or his religion may lead him to oppose any such attempt. His attitude is often translated into definite action in Parliament. Indeed, it may be partly through an interest, such as a co-operative society or trade union, that he is there. In return for such help, he is expected to promote its cause through avenues open to him as an M.P. The most obvious method is to sponsor legislation by a private member's bill; but he can also serve by going into the appropriate division lobby when any bill affecting the interest comes before Parliament and by asking a parliamentary question from time to time. Where a member is connected with no particular interest, he soon finds that there are bodies eager for him to espouse their cause or simply to provide information. Thus many M.P.s are appointed directors or consultants of companies with the main task of collecting political intelligence covering early warning of future government policy.

III. OPPORTUNITIES OPEN TO AN M.P.

Because our method of government is based on the party system, parliamentary time is almost completely monopolised by the Government and Opposition (see chapter 9). The ordinary back-bencher is regarded primarily as a mere cog in the party machine, serving it, not by speeches in the House or by the initiation of legislation, but by his presence in the correct division lobby at the appropriate time. The ineffectiveness of the Government back-bencher is almost complete. Any criticism he makes of the Government is merely embarrassing; any speech he delivers in support will often be regarded as wasting precious Government time; any legislation he initiates (unless it is a government bill for which the Government has no time) is quite likely to be of a sectional nature, costly of votes where some of the party support comes from an interest opposing the measure.

Yet back-bench M.P.s are not without influence. Individual views can be aired in meetings of the parliamentary party. Opinions can be expressed to the Whips when Government proposals appear unpopular and, if such misgivings are general, they will be conveyed to the party leaders. Moreover, should a member wish to criticise the Government, initiate legislation or disseminate propaganda on behalf of his particular interest, he will still find opportunities available although they may be somewhat limited.

(1) *Opportunities to criticise policy*

These occur at question-time, by ballot on the motion for the adjournment at 10 p.m., and when the House is adjourned under

Standing Order 9 on an 'important matter that should have urgent consideration'. In theory, too, provided he catches the Speaker's eye, the back-bencher can speak in debate or raise matters on the Address in reply to the Speech from the Throne, on the adjournment motions before a recess, and in the debates on the Appropriation and Consolidated Fund Bills. In practice the private member finds little time available, for front-bench speakers occupy four to five hours of the day's debate. Moreover, the subjects are now largely agreed upon beforehand and a member is normally expected to keep to these arrangements. The same even applies, but to a lesser degree, to the debates on the Estimates. Here it is easier to catch the Speaker's eye and, if successful, a member may raise any question relating to an item.

(2) *Opportunities to initiate legislation*

Unless a private member's bill is comparatively non-controversial and can secure time by ballot on a Friday for a second reading, it stands little chance of becoming law (Chapter 11). Nevertheless although doomed from the start, the attempt does serve the purpose of airing the member's ideas or proposals.

(3) *Opportunities to disseminate propaganda*

Legislation is often necessary to fulfil the objects of an interest. In preparation for this, a member may try to build up a more sympathetic attitude by drawing attention over a number of years to the interest's case. The M.P. enjoys opportunities for propaganda both inside and outside Parliament. While a bill brought in under the 'Ten Minutes Rule' stands little chance of passing (see page 189), the procedure does allow the member to speak in support of his cause for ten minutes.

More time is allowed on the ten Fridays which are allotted by ballot in each session to private members' motions. Ballots are held for these periodically, about sixteen days before the given Friday and, if successful, the debate on his particular subject enables the member to assess the feeling of the House, perhaps before promoting a bill on a Friday later on. Minor opportunities to raise a matter of a sectional interest also occur at question time, and possibly on the Estimates debates.

Outside Parliament, there are numerous occasions when the position of the private member carries weight. The Press is only too willing to publish opinions from such a source, while the member is frequently asked to make speeches at public dinners and functions. Radio and television programmes, such as 'Any Questions', 'The World at One' and 'Panorama' provide an exceptionally wide audience.

SUGGESTED READING

A. Barker and M. Rush, *The Member of Parliament and his Information* (Allen and Unwin, 1970).
R. Butt, *The Power of Parliament* (Constable, 1967), Chapters 6–10, 12.
Nigel Nicolson, *People and Parliament* (Weidenfeld and Nicolson, 1958).
P. G. Richards, *Parliament and Conscience* (Allen and Unwin, 1971).
P. G Richards, *The Backbenchers* (Faber, 1972).

8

The Party System

I. THE NATURE OF PARTY GOVERNMENT

WHY GOVERNMENT ON THE BASIS OF PARTY?

For democracy to be real, the Government's policies must be
related to the wishes of the electorate. In Britain, this is secured by
a highly developed party system, with a general election taking the
form of a choice between different party programmes. The party
winning a majority of seats in the House of Commons chooses the
Government. In this sense, government is by party.

At first sight, this may appear somewhat unsatisfactory. It could
mean that: (*a*) a party, once it has obtained power, may act
viciously towards any persons holding contrary opinions; (*b*) a
large number of electors may be permanently governed according
to principles of which they disapprove; (*c*) able men in minority
parties can take no effective part in government.

Such difficulties might, it seems, be solved by choosing a
Government which cuts across party lines. This could take the form
of a Council of State, embodying the best brains of the country
irrespective of political attachments, or a coalition, containing the
leaders of all parties. But except in unusual circumstances, such
as war or times of extreme crisis, neither method is practicable.
Generally speaking, people are fairly uniform in what they demand
of the Government — security from outside attack, a higher
standard of living, and as much freedom in living their lives as is
compatible with the legitimate interests of others. No party could
hope to gain power in Britain if it did not subscribe to these

objectives. Where people differ is not in the ends but in the means to achieving those ends. Thus it is over the differences in the policy to be followed that the parties divide.

Party government is satisfactory provided certain conditions are fulfilled. First, the Government must submit periodically to a vote of confidence from the electorate. Secondly, the Government must consider the views and feelings of minorities and, wherever possible, moderate its policies accordingly. Thirdly, when it refers matters to the people, the Government must seek to win support by an appeal to reason, not to prejudice. The first condition ensures that, if the electorate changes its opinion, the Government can be replaced. The second encourages the minority to accept unpopular measures for the time being and to adopt constitutional methods to modify them. The third admits that emotion and other factors may influence elections, but it also implies that people are not unduly swayed by temporary feelings and the hysterical outbursts of politicians, or divided on such immutable matters as religion, race, region or history. The former would make them an easy prey to a would-be dictator; the latter would induce them to resort to force as the only means of realising their wishes.

In Britain, all three conditions apply. In fact, the effective operation of the party system is facilitated by the nature of the parties themselves. Because they cut across religion, race, region and, above all, economic status, we find Welsh Non-conformist trade unionists supporting both the Labour and the Conservative parties. Again, because the two major parties are roughly of similar strength, each has a reasonable chance of being elected to power and so acts responsibly. Above all, since the staunch following of each party is fairly equal, in order to win an election a party must capture the uncommitted voters. Such voters are inclined to change their party allegiance from one election to another and are therefore known as the 'floating vote'.

THE FLOATING VOTE

A phenomenon of British politics over the last hundred years has been the way in which the two major parties have held power alternately. Over the 90 years previous to the general election, 1959, when the Conservatives were returned to power for the third time running, no Government had survived more than two terms of office. So obvious has been this periodic reversal in the fortunes of the parties, that it is often referred to as the 'swing of the pendulum'.

It is possible for a reversal of political fortune to come about without a single elector changing the way he voted at the previous election. There are probably at least 10 million persons on the electoral register who did not record a vote then, consisting of about 7 million who did not attend the poll and 3 million new voters who have attained the age of 18 years in the meantime. If the Opposition can induce some of the former to vote for them and can capture the young voters, then it can win the election.

But amongst those who voted at the previous election, some are bound to change their support. What is surprising is the relatively small number who come into this category. Even when its fortunes are at a low ebb, each party can rely on a solid core of loyal voters, approximately equal in strength. Hence the result of an election is largely decided by those voters who have no fixed party allegiance. Of these, some may be Liberal in sympathy but are forced to choose between the two major parties. Others, and probably the majority, would waver even if a Liberal candidate stood. At the most, there are only about 4 million such voters, although their numbers may be increasing. Since World War II the combined share of the vote of the two major parties had never been less than 87% until the 1974 elections when it fell to 75%, the chief beneficiary being the Liberal Party. These electors do not necessarily possess the highest political discernment. If that were so, we should have expected the old university seats to have been filled first by one party and then the other, on the assumption that graduate voters could think more acutely on politics than other sections of the community. However, with the exception of a few Independents and Liberals, these constituencies consistently returned Conservative Members of Parliament.

On the contrary, the floating voters may change their support for a number of reasons. Not only is there little difference in ends, but basically the policies advocated by different parties to achieve those ends are similar too. Between the moderates of both parties there is much in common; indeed, the greatest difference often lies between the left and right wings of each party. This moderation is reflected in the leaders; Conservative leaders tend to be left of centre and Labour leaders slightly right of centre. Moreover, the elector knows from experience that a change of Government will not entail the loss of benefits already secured, for, with few exceptions, a party accepts the measures of its predecessor.

Persons can easily change their vote, therefore, out of perversity, selfishness or as a result of thoughtful reflection. During its term of office, a Government usually loses some of its vitality. The original proposals which brought it into power are implemented and then become commonplace. Unless an occasional injection of new ideas proves that it has retained its dynamism, the floating voters may turn to the Opposition party, which has been using every weapon to convince them that it could provide a more effective government. In this objective the Opposition is helped by the inherent British insistence on fair play which more or less says, 'we have seen what this particular party can do in power, now let us give the other a chance'.

Above all, personal considerations may cause a voter to 'float'. Although the two major parties are closely associated in voters' minds with class interests, they each draw considerable support from both the middle and working classes. The National Opinion Poll shows that at the general election of 1970 Labour secured 10% and 31% of the middle and lower middle-class votes respectively, and the Conservatives 35% and 33% of the skilled working and 'very poor' votes respectively. While parties are judged on national as well as personal and local interests, disillusionment may easily occur amongst those who voted 'out of class' if they feel that they are bearing an undue burden. The middle-class 'floaters' voted for the security of the Labour Party's Welfare State at the 1945 election; but they soon repented of the high rates of taxation it entailed. The working-class 'floaters' voted for the full employment policy at the same election; but they became alarmed at the thought of further nationalisation. Most troubled were the small business people (shopkeepers and owners of one-man or two-men service, haulage and contracting firms), higher office grades and senior professional people. Yet between 1945 and 1951, these accounted for a transfer of only half a million votes. On the other hand, over the same period, nearly two million working-class voters were captured by the Conservatives. There is thus a high proportion of floating voters found in each class, and consequently any Government action which may be interpreted as unduly favouring one particular class may produce a swing among such voters.

But it is the straight-voting system which makes the floating vote of such importance to the result of a general election. Unless the existing Government was returned with a very large majority at the previous election, a swing of only about 2% will replace the sitting member by one from the opposite party in about eighty constituencies. The effect of the floating vote is thus magnified.

The floating vote is not entirely an unmitigated blessing. Sometimes, as in 1964 and February 1974, the change of heart is too indecisive, and political stalemate ensues. Moreover, the resulting 'swing of the pendulum' can produce frequent changes of government and hence dislocation in the administration, and obstacles to long-term planning. But, by keeping each party on its toes, it ensures the successful functioning of the two-party system. The thought that it can so easily lose the next election prevents the Government from becoming too slack; the possibility of overthrowing the Government, not through a defeat in the House but at the polls, leads to responsible Opposition. Above all, the fact that the gaining of power depends upon winning the support of the floating voters, drawn from all age-groups, occupations and social classes, prevents both parties from becoming purely sectional in their appeal and insensitive to the views of minorities. 'The floating vote is as essential to political life in this country as the party system itself and serves to prevent party from degenerating into faction' (Quintin Hogg: *The Purpose of Parliament*).

II. DEVELOPMENT OF THE PARTY SYSTEM

A distinction must be made between 'parties' and 'the party system'. Very broadly, a party consists of a relatively permanent division of people into a group which, on a particular matter or matters connected with politics, is psychologically a whole. The 'party system', which forms the basis of our parliamentary government, is far more comprehensive and elaborate. In Britain, parties have a much longer history than the party system, for it was not until after the Reform Act, 1832, that they attained their full maturity by being integrated into the processes of government.

ORIGIN OF POLITICAL PARTIES

In politics, men can be broadly divided into two groups — those who are liberal in outlook and anxious to bring about changes, and those who are conservative by nature, emphasising the desirability of preserving continuity. Yet not until the 19th century did this natural division become the basis of party allegiance. Until then, parties were separated much more by historical influences than by any permanent political differences.

In England, political parties originated in the reign of Charles II. Previously, there had been some division in Parliament between the 'Church', those who preferred one national Established Church instead of diverse sects and who also supported the King and his Court, and the 'Puritans', those who attacked the Established Church, especially where it retained forms of Roman Catholicism. Both parties, however, wished to uphold the sovereignty of Parliament in face of the King's claim of divine right. It was only because its supporters shrank from revolution that the 'Church' rallied to the King's side when it came to a question of taking up arms. Henceforth, it became closely linked with the Cavaliers and later the 'Royalist' party which, under the leadership of Edward Hyde (Lord Clarendon), lived in exile in France during the Commonwealth period.

Once the sovereignty of Parliament had been finally established and the King had been restored to the throne, division had to be on other issues. After 1660 there were, on the one hand, the returned Cavalier gentry who were closely associated with the Church and, on the other, those landowners who, remembering past struggles, still jealously guarded the sovereignty of Parliament. With these were grouped others who had taken a prominent part in the overthrow of Charles I — the non-conformist middle class and the merchants and businessmen of the City of London and other large towns. Disputes arose on a variety of subjects. Thus, in 1678, a proposal was made by those who feared a Catholic king to present a bill which would exclude the future James II from the throne. 'Tories' was the name given to those who refused to concur in this proposal and they were accused of having secret leanings towards the Roman Church. The term was meant to be abusive, referring to the outlaws, Roman Catholic by religion, who lived in the middle 'bog' counties of Ireland, where they preyed on the Anglo-Irish gentry who had been given their confiscated estates. 'Whigs', the counter-term, was likewise derogatory. Originally a name given to the Covenanters of the western Lowlands and Argyllshire, it was later applied to all Presbyterian zealots and eventually transferred to those English politicians who were inclined to support Parliament against the King, press for the liberties of the people and advocate religious toleration for all except Roman Catholics.

After the 'Glorious Revolution', parties showed a marked development. Although Charles II had been able to form his favourite advisers into an inner group of ministers holding mixed views, similar experiments by William and Anne failed. In 1695, William excluded the Tories from his ministry and formed the Whig 'junto'. On the other hand, so that the war with France could be brought to an end, Anne was forced to dismiss Marlborough and Godolphin, and for the rest of her reign she had an almost wholly Tory ministry supported by a Tory majority in Parliament. Both Sovereigns in turn had discovered that mixed ministries were incompatible with active parties. Whigs and Tories were now taking a definite form. Each had its own pamphleteers; on the Whig side, Addison, Defoe, Steele and Locke, and on the Tory, Swift and Bolingbroke. Moreover, these pamphleteers could set out the principles of each party. Swift claimed that the Whigs wished to limit the prerogative still further, extend religious freedom to all Protestants, and to favour the monied interests as against the landed. On the other hand, according to Bolingbroke, the Tories stood for modification of the terms which settled the Revolution of 1688, the imposition of further disabilities on dissenters, the development of the 'squirearchy' system and a policy of non-interference in Europe.

Although both the Whig and Tory parties can trace their descent from the end of the 17th century, their basic traditions, prejudices and social background were transformed as they developed over the following 200 years. Nor, early on, was there anything resembling a two-party system. In the first place, people frowned on any attempt to separate men into two groups. They had not yet learned to distinguish between parties and sects, but simply remembered that they had suffered a great deal from such divisions in the past. Secondly, the principle of demarcation between the two parties differed. Whereas modern parties are grouped according to their particular methods of solving the problems of government, 18th-century parties were held together by historical, family and local ties rather than by political ideas. Thus the dominant factor uniting the Whigs until well past the middle of the century was their desire to preserve the Hanoverian succession. Thirdly, the parties had to face a number of difficulties which made discipline impossible. They consisted of family cliques within which individuals pursued personal ambitions; they had to contend with the King's use of patronage to cut across party divisions; they were not called upon to fight or organise an Opposition; they were not united by a definite policy. This brings us to the fourth difference. Unlike modern parties, which have a programme dealing specifically with all major points at issue, the 18th-century Whigs and Tories made no promises as to their particular policy if returned to power. In contrast, their main aim was quite simply to enjoy the spoils of office while they had the chance! Lastly, parties existed only in Parliament. There was no notion at the time that they should be extended to the country. When voters could be bought instead of being wooed by promises of political action, candidates had little need to consider the wishes of the electorate. In any case, few seats were ever contested and general elections as we know them today did not exist. Although by the beginning of the 19th century the Whigs were raising a fund to pay for future election campaigns, payments from it were chiefly in the nature of bribes.

As we have already seen, various influences combined to bring this system to an end. But one of the major factors was the development of closer-knit parties in Parliament. When, in George III's reign, patronage weapons were used against the Whigs, they demanded reform of the whole system. Their common purpose enabled Burke, the leading propagandist, to formulate the classical definition of a party, 'a body of men united, for promoting by their joint endeavours the national interest, upon some particular principle in which they are all agreed.' Parties with cohesion had now arrived in Parliament. But they were not large enough to be dominant. Until well past the turn of the century, the majority in every House of Commons was decided by 'independents' upon whom no minister (not even Pitt) could impose his policy in all matters.

THE EXTENSION OF PARTIES TO THE COUNTRY

Political parties did not extend to the people at large. There was a variety of groups, such as the Society of the Supporters of the Bill of Rights, the Yorkshire Association, and the Society for Promoting Constitutional Information, agitating for Parliament to effect particular reforms. But no liaison existed between societies in the country and the parties in Parliament, and the societies existed for specific and limited objects and not for the promotion of a political programme covering all aspects of the national life.

The growing awareness of political division can be seen in the establishment of the Carlton Club by the Tories in 1832 and of the Reform Club by the Whigs in 1836. Such factors as the development of the popular Press, improved communications between country districts, and the emergence of great Leaders like Peel, Disraeli and Gladstone, all combined to promote political organisation. But the real impetus sprang from the Reform Act, 1832. Although bribery continued, it was now impossible to buy sufficient electors to ensure a majority in Parliament. Thus it became necessary to organise support at the poll, and the parties in Parliament extended their activities to the country. Through a minor requirement of the Reform Act, a person's name had to be on the electoral register before he could vote. This was not always easy, especially where an illiterate person had to establish a voting qualification. Hence, through their two Clubs, both parties organised local 'registration societies', which compiled and revised electoral lists.

But the registration societies were not concerned with nominating candidates or conducting election campaigns. Moreover, the liaison between the central and local organisations was still imperfect. The vital change came about as a result of the Reform Act, 1867, which, amongst its provisions, gave certain cities, such as Birmingham, Manchester, Liverpool and Leeds, three members apiece, each voter being allowed two votes. If two or three of a party's candidates were to be returned, it meant that the really dependable votes would have to be carefully allocated so that some should not be wasted by over-support for one candidate. Such a system had already been started by the Tories, but it was so successfully developed by the Radicals in Birmingham that in the election of 1868 they won all three seats. The method was now applied to municipal affairs, enabling Joseph Chamberlain and Schnadhorst, the secretary of the Birmingham Association, to achieve complete control over local government. Consequently both parties extended the organisation throughout the country.

The registration societies thus developed into local party associations, carefully organised and associated with the central organisation for fighting elections. Linked together nationally by the formation of the National Union of Conservative and Constitutional Associations in 1867, and the National Liberal Federation in 1877, their development was further assisted by the Corrupt and Illegal Practices Prevention Act, 1883, which, by limiting expenditure, necessitated organising support from a great number of voluntary workers. The increased strength of the parties was reflected in a new type of Leader who depended less on personal loyalties and more on principles, policies and programmes. These Leaders, such as Gladstone and Disraeli, did not confine their election efforts to issuing addresses, but 'stumped the country' (although on a limited scale) to explain their policies personally.

The Labour Party really had its origins in the growth of the mass unions at the end of the 19th century, although it did not actually come into existence until 1900, when delegates of three socialist organisations, the Social Democratic Federation (1881), the Fabian Society (1883), and the Independent Labour Party (1893), together with delegates of some 64 trade unions, set up the Labour Representation Committee, renamed in 1906 'the Labour Party'. Whereas the socialist organisations believed in 'the common ownership of the means of production', the trade unions merely wished to secure increased working-class representation in Parliament in order to achieve benefits for their members. Until 1918 local organisation varied considerably, and membership of the Labour Party was only possible through an affiliated organisation. The conference of that year, however, adopted a constitution drawn up by Arthur Henderson and Sidney Webb by which local party associations of individual members could join. The Labour Party was thus transformed from a federation of affiliated societies to a national organisation with its own branches. There is now a local party association in every constituency, but the trade unions are still the dominant force in the movement, contributing over 5½ million members out of a total Labour-Party membership of approximately 6½ million.

III. Organisation of the Two Main Political Parties in Britain

Political parties exist because people wish to see the government of the country carried on according to a particular policy. Their main object, therefore, is to win elections. To do this, they have to provide an effective organisation at local and national levels, ensure that sufficient funds are available for an effective election campaign, and formulate a policy which will appeal to a majority of the electorate.

An outline of the organisation of the two main parties is given in Figures 2 and 3. Many of the differences between the two can be explained by the fact that, whereas the Conservative Party grew up within Parliament, the Labour Party was really founded as a pressure group to obtain parliamentary representation of a movement outside Parliament. But neither organisation has followed a formal pattern based on carefully-thought-out principles. Instead, both are the result of historical development and accident, the desire to broaden the basis of the party, and the need for greater efficiency.

The main difficulty is to organise support from the country without sacrificing flexibility of action within Parliament. A party consists of three main parts — the constituencies, the headquarters, and the parliamentary party which contains its leading spokesmen and is the centre of publicity. The Leader occupies a key position in harmonising the work of the three, but he can do this only if he is given the power to lead. Although there is a marked difference in his formal authority as regards the two parties, in practice the position in each is roughly similar. If the party is elected to power, he will be the Prime Minister, but even out of office he is such a figurehead that the party will suffer if attempts are made to undermine his authority.

The Conservative Party appears to allow much more power to its Leader in order to give him room to manoeuvre. He determines the party policy on important issues of the day and signs election manifestos. The Central Office works under his direction and the Chairman of the party is appointed by him. Nor is the Annual Conference a policy-forming body, for its views are not binding but are merely noted by him. Nevertheless, while there is usually little public criticism of his policy, his powers are exercised only by consent, and Leaders such as Neville Chamberlain have been driven from office, or, as with Sir Alec Douglas Home and Edward Heath, forced to step down.

Although the position of Leader of the Labour Party is formally quite different, much still depends on his leadership and his personality. He is elected by the Parliamentary Labour Party for a year at a time. But he is not the head of the Party; that position is occupied by the National Executive Committee, which consists of twenty-five persons and the Treasurer elected at the Annual Conference, together with the Leader and deputy-Leader, *ex officio* members. The Committee elects its own Chairman who serves for a year. The usual procedure is for the National Executive Committee to draw up policy proposals which are submitted for the approval or modification of the Annual Conference. The latter is the policy-forming body, though no proposal can be included in the party programme unless it has a two-thirds majority on a card vote. The trade unions' vote amounts to 80% of the total and the six largest unions account for 50%. Thus, together, the trade unions can veto any proposal, a power used in the past to over-ride the more radical local constituency organisations and the socialist societies.

Both parties maintain permanent headquarters to give help and professional advice to the local groups. The Conservative Central Office (C.C.O.) works directly under the Leader, but Transport House, the Labour Party's headquarters, is run by the Party's general secretary, who is selected by the National Executive and approved by the Annual Conference. At the local level, there are full-time election agents. The Conservative Party has one in nearly every constituency, but the Labour Party is not so well served, lack of funds necessitating a low salary.

As regards finance, the Conservative Party obtains considerable sums from industrial and commercial interests, In addition, constituency associations subscribe on a 'voluntary quota basis'. At one time, candidates bore a large part of their own election expenses and made sizeable contributions to the Party's funds. But in the selection of candidates, this tended to exclude the able person without money, and the 1948 Conference agreed that all election expenses should be the responsibility of the constituency association; candidates can contribute not more than £50 per annum to the funds of their association. In the Labour Party, affiliated trade unions, representing 5,600,000 members, pay a fee of 21p per year for each member. The total of these dues is about seven times the sum subscribed by the individual members of the local Labour Party organisations. Most trade unions have political funds to which those members who have not contracted out pay a due which varies in amount. These funds are used to promote policies and candidates. Over one-fifth of the members contract out. The minimum subscription for an individual member of a constituency party is 10p per month; 10p a year goes to Head Office for every membership card used. Sponsoring organisations may contribute to the constituency party's funds or to a proportion of a full-time agent's salary. They may also pay 80% of the legal maximum election expenses, and this is usually done when the candidate in the constituency is put up by a trade union or a co-operative society. [*Text continues on p. 126.*]

NOTES ON FIGS. 2 AND 3

THE CONSERVATIVE PARTY

CONSTITUENCY ASSOCIATION

The Conservative Party organisation emphasises the autonomy of the local constituency association, which consists of all persons who contribute regularly to the local party fund. There is a local association in each constituency which, for the purposes of organisation, is divided into wards or polling districts. It makes and amends its own rules and chooses its own officers. Its functions are: to raise election funds, through subscriptions, donations, dances, bazaars, etc.; to recruit members; to fight elections; to appoint an agent; to select prospective candidates, usually with the approval of the Standing Advisory Committee on Candidates of the National Union. The constituency associations are the real roots of the party. 'Those undertaking the strain of government need the sense of a powerful and dominant membership behind them' (Lord Woolton).

The constituency association works through an Executive Council consisting of the officials of the Association, representatives of the ward and polling district branches, the Young Conservatives and subscribing Conservative Clubs, and certain co-opted members. Each Executive Council has various sub-committees, such as Women, Young Conservatives, Education, Trade Unions and Local Government.

AREA COUNCILS

Constituencies are linked on a provincial level into twelve Areas, which are organised on the committee basis of the constituencies. Area functions are: to co-ordinate the resources of the area; to organise on the area level; and to advise the Central Office.

THE CENTRAL COUNCIL OF THE NATIONAL UNION

The Central Council is composed of the Leader and officers of the party, the parliamentary party, all adopted candidates and four representatives from each of the constituency associations, covering over 5,500

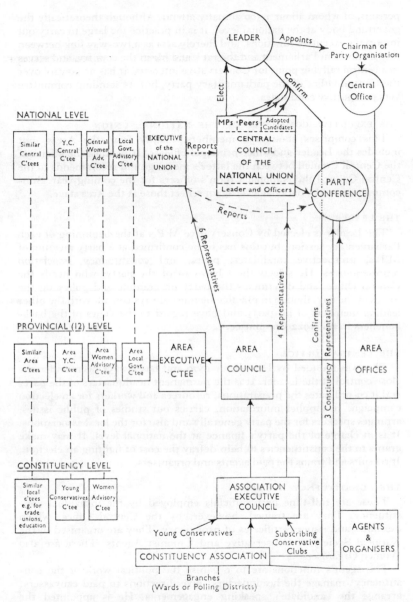

FIG. 2. *Organisation of the Conservative Party.*

persons, of whom about 3,500 actually attend. Although theoretically the
governing body at the national level, it is in practice too large to carry out
important executive functions, and merely acts as a two-way link between
the members in Parliament and the rank and file in the country, and serves
as a central rallying point for Conservative interests. It has no control over
the Central Office of the parliamentary party, but its standing committee
vets prospective candidates.

THE EXECUTIVE COMMITTEE OF THE NATIONAL UNION

This comprises about 150 members, mainly from the Areas, but
includes the Leader and other principal officers. It handles the affairs of
the Central Council between the latter's meetings and recommends to the
Central Council the National Union's officers for the coming year. Sub-
committees on the national level again reflect those at the Area stage.

THE LEADER

The Leader is elected by Conservative M.P.s at the beginning of each
Parliamentary session, but this has to be confirmed at a party meeting of
M.P.s, prospective candidates, peers, and constituency association
representatives. He selects the Chairman of the party, who heads the
Central Office, and determines the party programme and policy on the
issues of the day, though in practice he must always consult with the other
leading members of his party and have regard to the views of the back-
benchers in the 1922 Committee.

THE CENTRAL OFFICE

This was founded by Disraeli in 1870 and has always been under the
close control of the Leader. It is the permanent headquarters of the party
and it co-ordinates the preparations, resources and workers for an election
campaign. It supplies information, carries out studies of public issues,
arranges speakers for the party generally and also for the local associations.
It is in charge of the party's finance at the national level. It may make
grants to the constituencies to help defray the cost of fighting an election.
It recruits and trains the paid agents and organisers.

THE CONSTITUENCY AGENTS

These are full-time party officials employed by the individual constituency. They are trained, however, by the Central Office, which
examines and issues certificates of proficiency. They are organised in the
National Society of Conservative and Unionist Agents. There are also
Women Organisers.

The agent's functions are to organise the political work of the constituency; manage the headquarters; give directions to paid canvassers;
arrange the candidate's speaking engagements. He is appointed the
'Election Agent' for an election and is thus responsible for accounting for
the monies spent at the election. In practice, the agent is the link between
the member and the constituency association. He has probably a better
knowledge about the political issues which arouse interest locally than the

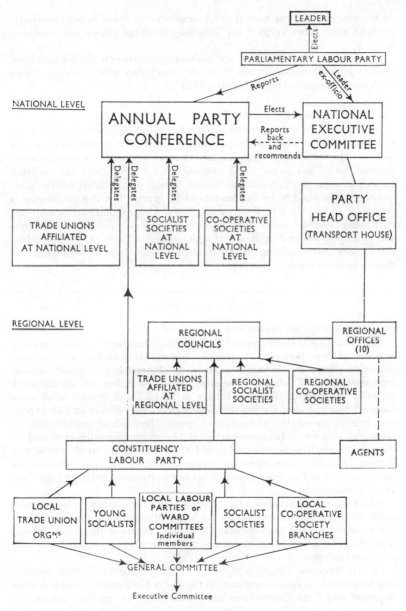

FIG. 3. *Organisation of the Labour Party.*

M.P., who most of the time is at Westminster or at his home elsewhere. A good agent also keeps local voluntary workers happy and enthusiastic.

Local agents receive help on special matters, such as women's activities, publicity, youth organisations, from the Area Office which is in the charge of an agent appointed by the Central Office.

THE ANNUAL PARTY CONFERENCE

The Annual Party Conference is attended by all members of the Central Conference of the National Union, together with the constituency agents and an additional three representatives from each of the constituency associations. Thus some 5,600 persons attend. Delegates representing various groups put forward resolutions which are debated by the conference and replied to by the leaders of the party. But the conference is only very indirectly a policy-forming body, for, although its resolutions may influence the Leader, they are not binding on him. The conference acts chiefly as a sounding board of opinion and a Party rally, applauding the Leader and renewing the enthusiasm of members as well as giving them a sense of unity.

THE LABOUR PARTY

CONSTITUENCY ORGANISATION

Since 1918 each Constituency Labour Party has been a federation of a number of organisations, It includes individual members of the constituency party, the Young Socialists, local branches of trade unions, representatives of socialist societies, local branches of co-operative societies and parties. Representatives of all affiliated groups serve on a General Management Committee which elects the officers and an executive committee of the constituency party. Individual membership is organised into wards (in town parties and borough constituencies) and, in the county constituencies, into Local Labour Parties (in small towns) and Polling District Committees (in villages). Individual members do not meet together at the constituency level but participate only through their Ward Committees, etc.

The Constituency Labour Party deals with headquarters, raises funds, fights elections, selects candidates for local authority elections, and nominates candidates for parliamentary elections. Its most important official is the Secretary, and where the constituency employs an agent he usually occupies both posts.

Eleven Regional Councils co-ordinate the resources of their regions and function in a similar manner to the Party Conference. Trade Union Regional and Area Committees are represented, as are the various Co-operative and Socialist organisations, Constituency Labour Parties, and The Women's Area Councils. A Regional Executive Committee is elected and they arrange educational and other activities on a regional basis, as well as co-ordinating the party work within the Region.

ANNUAL PARTY CONFERENCE

This is attended by just over 1,100 delegates drawn from the affiliated organisations. But delegates vote according to the number of due-paying members in the group they represent. In practice, therefore, this card-vote is dominated by the trade unions and in particular by the six largest trade unions. Members of Parliament, prospective candidates and members of the National Executive are *ex-officio* members of the conference.

The conference determines the Party's general policy, debating a proposed programme drawn up by the National Executive Committee. Especially where it is following a moderate policy, a Labour Cabinet may find itself at variance with resolutions carried by the conference. Since, however, extreme proposals usually come from the constituencies and socialist societies, the dominant trade-union block vote can be used to rescue the Government from embarrassment. Moreover, the National Executive and the parliamentary party have the main influence in drawing up any election manifesto.

NATIONAL EXECUTIVE COMMITTEE

The other main function of the Annual Party Conference is to elect the National Executive Committee. This consists of 28 members. Twelve are elected by trade unions, 7 by constituency parties and county federations, 1 by socialist and co-operative societies, and 5 are women elected by the whole Conference. The Leader and deputy-leader of the party are *ex-officio* members. The other member, the Treasurer of the party, is elected by the whole Party Conference.

The National Executive meets regularly. Its functions are to: interpret and implement Annual Party Conference decisions; manage the party finances; maintain liaison with the parliamentary party; supervise the local associations; and enforce discipline.

THE LEADER

The Leader is elected by the Parliamentary Labour Party for a year at a time, but it is customary to re-elect him. Although he exercises considerable influence, he does not occupy so dominant a position as his Conservative counterpart. He has no control over the officials of Transport House.

PARTY HEAD OFFICE — TRANSPORT HOUSE

This works under the supervision of the general secretary of the Labour Party, who is appointed by the National Executive Committee. It acts as the national headquarters of the party, dealing with party finance, research, international affairs, women's organisations, Press and publicity and gives general assistance to constituency parties in such matters as organisation, the provision of speakers, training election agents.

The Head Office has eleven regional offices (including London) to provide the full-time staff for the Regional Councils.

IV. DISCIPLINE WITHIN THE PARTIES

Fairly strict party discipline is an inevitable consequence of the two-party system. It is imposed at two levels — by the local constituency and by the parliamentary party.

Discipline by the constituency association is necessary to win elections. At a general election, the electorate chooses between the respective party programmes. But electors appreciate the seriousness of their choice, and the floating voters in particular are reluctant to vote for a party which is not united on important issues. (The Labour Party is probably at a serious disadvantage in that its more democratic organisation makes it easier to express individual views so that the Leader has to make constant efforts to prevent party splits.) It is necessary, therefore, to have a programme supported by all candidates, and the task of ensuring that the nominee will support it falls to the constituency association. The views of each applicant short-listed are examined, chiefly to verify that they conform to the orthodox policies of the party. Generally speaking, constituencies have little room for independent attitudes on party issues. Where the applicant is at all suspect, the central organisation, as we have seen, may play a decisive part, especially in the Labour Party.

Even when elected, the member is still subject to some control through the constituency association. Not only must he account periodically for his stewardship, but the association is vitally concerned with its member's relationship with the parliamentary party. The essence of the party system is that a Government can rely upon support in Parliament for fulfilling its election promises, while the Opposition can make a united attack upon these policies and present alternative proposals. This calls for loyal support in both debate and the division lobby, except where the issue cuts across party policy, e.g. the abolition of capital punishment or remaining in the Common Market, when a member may be allowed to vote as he thinks fit. Otherwise, where he disagrees with his party, the most he can usually do is to abstain, and even this may be taken as evidence of disloyalty. The local constituency party has the last word. Where a recalcitrant member refuses to resign, he is simply not re-nominated at the next election.

In Parliament, members of both Houses are formally linked through their respective parliamentary parties, the Parliamentary

Labour Party and the 1922 Committee, the back-bencher equivalent on the Conservative side. The parliamentary party determines details of policy, agrees on tactics and disciplines members to ensure support for the party line. Membership signifies acceptance of its rules, the chief of which is to obey the Whip. Its organisation, whether Conservative or Labour, follows the same broad lines. The party Leader is its head, being Prime Minister if the party is in power and Leader of the Opposition if it is not. For the discussion of particular issues of policy, groups or committees are formed and these keep the Leaders in touch with party sentiment.

The leaders of the party form the Cabinet if in power, if not, the 'shadow Cabinet'. In the Conservative Party, both are chosen by the Leader, but in the Labour Party the shadow Cabinet is a Parliamentary Committee consisting of 5 *ex-officio* members, 12 elected representatives of the Labour M.P.s and 1 elected representative of the Labour peers. Since the Cabinet must deliberate in secret, arrangements have to be made to keep the leaders in touch with the back-benchers of the party. With the Tories, ministers (other than a representative of the Whips' Office) are not allowed to attend meetings of the 1922 Committee, except by invitation (which may mean that they are to be sharply criticised). The Labour Party has a Liaison Committee and ministers also attend meetings of the P.L.P. It rests with the leaders whether they modify proposals in the light of the views expressed. Even if they do not, loyal support is still expected; indeed, this is required by the standing orders of the P.L.P.

Maintaining day-to-day discipline within the party is the responsibility of the Chief Whip and his 8 to 10 Assistant Whips, all Members of Parliament. The term was first used in 1769 by Burke, who borrowed it from the hunting-field, where one person has the task of whipping-in hounds straggling from the pack. Today the Whips occupy a key position in party organisation. On the Government side they are given posts carrying a salary, but elsewhere only the Opposition Chief Whip is paid. The Government Chief Whip is Parliamentary Secretary to the Treasury, sometimes referred to as 'Patronage Secretary', a relic of the 18th century when the Government disposed of offices and pensions as rewards for service. Some of the Assistant Government Whips hold such posts as Lords Commissioners of the Treasury and

Comptroller, Treasurer and Vice-Chamberlain of the Royal Household; junior Assistant Whips are now also paid.

The Whip's chief function is to ensure unity of voice on policy and support from members when political action is necessary. Thus he communicates to back-benchers the line which the leaders expect them to follow on a particular question, bringing pressure to bear on them to back it actively by their presence at the appropriate time. Members are grouped according to the geographical area of their constituencies and each group is under the charge of an Assistant Whip. Every week the Whip sends to the M.P.s of his party a notice giving the order of business for the following week, underlined according to its importance, once, twice or three times. Where a division is likely, the member is requested to attend, the notice often being underlined three times (a 'three-line whip'). This means that only if the member is out of the country on parliamentary business, is ill or has other exceptionally urgent reasons will the Whip countenance his absence. Before giving his sanction, the Whip will contact his opposite number in the other party to see whether any similar requests have been made; if they have, he can cover himself by 'pairing' the member. Members may arrange 'pairs' directly, but the pairing has to be registered with the Whip, sanction being automatic in the case of a one-line whip and unlikely, except in the most pressing circumstances, for a three-line whip. Here again we see the constitution working in a spirit of 'give and take' with mutual trust and understanding prevailing between the Government and Opposition. Pairing simplifies the work of all, minimising inconvenience to members and relieving the Whips of much uncertainty over their party's showing in a division. When a division takes place, the Whips usually act as 'tellers', marking off members as they pass through the division lobbies; a 'free' vote is indicated by the fact that they are not performing this task.

The Whips play an important part in helping the Government to complete its business while allowing the Opposition time for effective criticism. The time-table for the session is arranged under the direction of the Leader of the House and the Chief Government Whip. Moreover, if business is to proceed smoothly, there must be communication between the parties in Parliament over the weekly programme. Hence, the Whips meet to agree on the time to be allotted to Government business and to the Opposition for

criticism. The subjects and proposed time-table are then submitted to the Speaker for his approval. Even the order of debate is
largely arranged 'through the usual channels', the Whips submitting to the Speaker the names of their leading speakers.

Usually members are quite willing to accept the discipline
imposed by the Whips. Withdrawal of the Whip might mean
eventual expulsion from the party. But seldom is such drastic
action necessary, for the Whips, especially on the Government
side, have certain carrots to offer members. They make recommendations to the Prime Minister for the award of honours and
supply names for parliamentary delegations abroad. Moreover,
those seeking political advancement find it inadvisable to add to
the Whip's difficulties, for it is he who brings to the notice of the
Prime Minister those back-benchers worthy of consideration for
junior ministerial posts. In minor ways, too, the Whip may help a
member. Where an M.P. has been successful in the ballot for
promoting a private member's bill, the Whip can help him to
obtain a quorum on a Friday and, where he has no ready-made bill,
the Whip will see that the party provides one.

But the Whip is not solely concerned with getting awkward
members to accept the party's policy. He is the 'eyes and ears' of
the Leader, for it is through him that back-benchers express their
uneasiness over particular proposals and communicate their constituents' views. This function is particularly important to the
Conservative leaders when in office, since they do not attend full
meetings of the parliamentary party. A Whip is always present at
the regular meetings of the back-benchers' specialist party groups.
He also works in conjunction with the Parliamentary Private
Secretaries, for these see that their chief, the minister, does not
incur the displeasure of back-benchers and that he is on the front-
bench at the right moment to reply in debate or to answer
questions.

The Whip thus occupies a key position. Although not a member
of the Cabinet, he usually sits on the extreme right of the front-
bench. He must be able to get on well both with the members of
his own party and with his opposite number, showing tact and
firmness as the situation demands. Where members do not respond
to his directions, he can seek the backing of the Leader, secretary
of the party or other influential member, and, if necessary, of the
party machine. While the system undoubtedly stifles initiative in

the individual M.P., a large measure of discipline is necessary for the successful working of party parliamentary government. Moreover, even if more free votes were allowed, it would not mean that the M.P. was freed from pressure. Instead he would be open to the full force of organised pressure groups.

V. FUNCTIONS OF PARTIES

The fundamental features of a party are organisation and discipline — organisation of support in the country, discipline of members in Parliament. Having achieved these, its next task is to link the two, the electorate and Member of Parliament, through the national organisation.

But the process can be carried one stage further. Through the party organisation, the electorate is linked directly, not only with Parliament, but with the Government. This is what we mean by the 'party system'. At every stage in this process of integration, the parties fulfil functions essential to democratic government.

(1) *Parties organise public opinion on national matters*

Different people have different ideas, ranging from the sensible to the cranky. Often persons of similar mind group together to form societies, such as the R.S.P.C.A., the National Floral Society, the Royal Photographic Society, etc. But such bodies do not embrace all aspects of the national life.

Political parties, on the other hand, seek electoral success through formulating a programme which will attract as many supporters as possible. Therefore they crystallise many shades of opinion into a policy and unify numerous diverse elements into a whole, an achievement which can be seen in the different interests represented in each of the two major parties in Britain. A party, in its policy, lays plainly before the electorate the issues involved, and outlines its proposals with regard to them. Not only does this combat apathy by arousing the electorate's interest but, by the simple process of voting for the appropriate party, enables an effective choice to be made between the different policies.

(2) *Parties educate public opinion*

As the parties propagate their views, so the electorate is presented with argument and counter-argument and enabled to make a reasoned choice. Thus parties 'help to preserve the serious and objective approach to politics, the mistrust of generalisations and extremist points of view, and the respect for the freedom of the citizen regardless of his opinions, that have become outstanding characteristics of political life in Britain' (A. Mathiot: *The British Political System*). The electorate, for its part, likes to be reasoned with and treated responsibly by the party leaders. In 1970, Mr. Wilson's complacent, non-controversial campaign probably cost him the election.

(3) *Parties provide a permanent political connection between Parliament and the country*

Not until after 1832, when the parties in Parliament extended their organisation to the country, was it possible to reconcile the legal sovereignty of Parliament with the political sovereignty of the electorate. The later development of detailed party organisation and discipline completed the process. Today, people vote for a party policy rather than a man, and they know that, through the party system, the Government will be formed from that party which has a majority of seats in the House of Commons.

Nor is the elector impotent between elections. Apart from other means — the Press, lobbying, public meetings, radio, television, and demonstrations — by which opinions can be brought to bear upon the Government, representation can be made and views expressed through the local constituency organisation. Thus parties provide the link between government and the governed.

(4) *Parties give stability and cohesion in Parliament*

Were the legislature composed chiefly of Independents or of a number of small parties, no Government could be certain of support. But the party system provides a political connection in Parliament which enables policy to be put into effect. Party loyalty unites the majority in support of the Government and the remainder in opposition to it. Three important results follow. First, the party programme can be implemented, because the Government is assured of the necessary support in the parliamentary processes. Secondly, an effective Opposition is formed from the next largest party. Thirdly, *national* issues are dealt with in a balanced manner. All M.P.s have their particular interests and hobby-horses. One may be interested in foreign affairs, another in local government reform, a third in education. They may therefore tend to lose sight of the importance of other aspects of government activity. A Parliament consisting of mainly Independents could easily allow discussion of individual ideas to supplant consideration of the broad aspects of national policy. The essential of a party programme, on the other hand, is that it ranges over the whole field of national affairs. Thus, support of a party places personal enthusiasms in their proper perspective and strengthens the individual member in resisting pressure groups.

Nor must we forget that in Parliament it is such party arrangements as those 'behind the Speaker's chair' which make parliamentary procedure workable.

(5) *Parties give consistency to government*

The Cabinet system depends on the party system. The accepted Leader of the party commanding a majority in the House of Commons must become the Prime Minister. Since ministers are selected by him from among his own party, the Government is composed of persons having similar political views. This assists in the formulation of a consistent policy and makes it easier to agree on its timing.

(6) *Parties promote stability of government*

Not only do parties link like-minded men, but 'collective responsibility' requires that where an individual minister is unable to support a particular Cabinet decision, he must resign. Governments stand or fall together, but thanks to the party system, and to political advancement being tied to a party, they usually stand. Hence, particularly under a two-party system, a well-disciplined party holding a majority in the House of Commons can expect to enjoy continuity of office, and is thus able to accept responsibility for implementing a long-term policy. When we compare the weakness of 18th-century Cabinets, split by internal dissensions, with their 20th-century counterparts, we can appreciate how much the stability of present governments owes to the party system.

(7) *Parties provide the most effective means of changing a Government*

The main function of Parliament has always been to control the Government. Until the 19th century, however, the inadequacy of the methods available made this a difficult task. Parliament had to resort either to the obstruction of policy by refusing to grant Supply or, more directly, to the impeachment of individual ministers. Both methods were clumsy in the extreme, and, since they did little to provide for an alternative policy, negative in operation.

But the party system has instituted a more effective form of control. This is a political one — loss of office to the opposing party. Such a change of Government may result either from the reversal of the verdict of the electorate at a general election or by defeat on a matter of major importance in the Commons. Whatever the cause, the party system provides automatically a new Government, for on the Opposition front-bench sits the 'shadow Cabinet' armed with its own distinct policy.

DISADVANTAGES OF THE PARTY SYSTEM

Although for democratic government the party system is essential, indeed inevitable, its development has not been free from drawbacks. In the first place, it has led to the complete elimination from the House of Commons of the Independent, a member who is not bound to a particular party policy. His election campaign has to be fought without the backing of a party machine or the funds at its disposal. Indeed, both the major political parties will usually sponsor their own candidate in opposition to an Independent. It is thus almost impossible for him to be elected, particularly since the abolition of the university seats in 1948. A rare exception was Mr. Dick Taverne, who resigned as Labour M.P. for Lincoln in 1973. The local Labour Party, displeased with his support for entry into the E.E.C., had decided not to adopt him. But Mr. Taverne, standing for his own newly-formed Social Democratic Party, went on to win the seat, not only in the by-election, but also in the February 1974 general election. However, he was defeated by the Labour candidate in the next general election in October 1974.

Not only is the Independent seriously handicapped at an election, but he suffers from many disadvantages in Parliament. Since he does not take orders from the party Whip, he loses the assistance which the Whip can give through the party connection. Thus he does not receive the notices and information on parliamentary business which come from the Whip's office. Nor, in debate, has he a Central Office to help him in the preparation of his speeches or the moral support which comes from the party's followers behind with the timely 'hear, hear' when he scores a good point or loyal laughter at any joke made at the expense of the benches opposite. Should he be lucky in the ballot to debate a private member's bill, he has to frame and draft his own bill, find supporters for it, and arrange for a quorum to be present when it is being read.

No professional politician could nowadays afford to sit as an Independent. If he depends on his salary as an M.P., he is much more likely to keep his seat with the backing of a party. The reason why most M.P.s were Independents until the end of the first quarter of the 19th century was that they could afford to let politics be a purely part-time affair. More important, however, promotion to ministerial rank is open only to the party man; an M.P. with ambitions, therefore, has little political future as an Independent.

But the elimination of the Independent is to be regretted. Since he had to win an election entirely on his own merits, his ability was usually well above that of the average M.P. Moreover, the electorate was forced to consider the personal qualities of the man instead of merely looking at his party label. In Parliament, he could vote according to his convictions, untrammelled by party interests. Above all, when he did speak, he was not just reiterating the oft-repeated party view; hence he was listened to with respect. Similarly, when he introduced a bill, he could draw support from all sides of the House, for other M.P.s had no need to be suspicious of the existence of some obscure political advantage, as happens when a member of the opposite party sponsors a measure. Hence important legislation has been steered through Parliament by Independents, such as divorce reform by Sir Alan (A.P.) Herbert and revised pensions for civil servants by W. J. Brown.

The Independent M.P. disappeared because he did not fit into the pattern of the party system. To parties, the Independent represents a member 'who cannot be depended upon' (Lord Derby). The main business in Parliament is conducted on the basis of opposition between the two large political parties, each relying on the disciplined support of its members. The Independent does not submit to this discipline. Moreover, he remains outside the main struggle in Parliament because he can play no part in the formation of policy through party conferences and meetings of the parliamentary party.

Thus, although the passing of the Independent is a distinct loss, it was largely necessary to secure the advantages of the party system. Criticism of the Government is much more effective through an Opposition organised on party lines than by a number of unconnected Independents. Moreover, the back-bencher's views are not ignored. Although he is expected to support the official party line, he has opportunities behind the scenes to express his views and endeavour to modify policy. First, there are the party meetings. Second, and more important, are the parliamentary party's various committees and study groups which consider party policy on such subjects as defence, housing, local government, health, economic affairs and education. Third, there are the Standing Committees taking the Report Stage of Bills. Indeed, it might be argued that an M.P. has more effective influence through a party than by acting on his own as an Independent.

The second disadvantage of the party system largely reiterates what has been said above — it suppresses individuality in M.P.s. This tends to minimise the advantage of the single-member constituency and to undermine the argument, put forward so often in its favour, that it allows the electorate to know the individual member. However, the party M.P. cannot ignore the wishes of his constituents. Where he finds the party line unpopular, he must make representations to the Whips, who may pass them on to the party leaders.

Thirdly, as a result of the party system, certain subjects tend to be neglected. This may happen because some matters, such as new roads and local government reform, are not direct party issues. Or, like marriage law reform, the Sunday observance laws and gambling regulations, they may cut across party. Independents can bring up such matters, whereas parties tend to ignore them.

Lastly, there is always the danger of the party becoming all-important and overbearing, as has already happened with some constituency parties. The main hazard, however, is of a caucus developing outside Parliament which dictates to its members in the House of Commons. Fortunately, this has not taken place on any scale in the United Kingdom. When, in 1945, Professor Harold Laski, the Chairman of the National Executive of the Labour Party, did put forward certain pointed suggestions to Mr. Attlee as to the course the latter should follow, he was soundly rebuffed. In Australia, however, the Labour Party dictates who shall be members of the Cabinet of a Labour Government and may even go so far as to distribute the portfolios. The development of such a caucus system in Britain could do nothing but injury to our form of parliamentary government, for it would strike at the fundamental principle that the majority must show moderation and a willingness to compromise. Parliament is an assembly where the affairs of the nation are discussed and policies examined. Members attend it as representatives, not as delegates shackled to a given line of action. The caucus system, on the other hand, transfers policy decisions to the private party meeting, where extremists may easily win the day by a small majority. This then becomes the official party line to be steam-rollered through Parliament without amendment or compromise. In addition, the party leaders in Parliament are controlled so rigidly by orders from the caucus that they have little room for manoeuvre according to their appraisal of the situation at the moment.

Mr. Gaitskell, as Leader of the Opposition, faced this very situation in September, 1960. The Labour Party Conference of that month voted for unilateralist rejection of the H-bomb, a policy with which the P.L.P. did not agree. Mr. Gaitskell's refusal to be bound by the decision was possible because the Labour Party constitution leaves the question of control of the P.L.P. by Conference unsettled. His stand was vindicated the following year when the Conference reversed its previous policy.

VI. The British Two-Party System

Over the last 100 years there have, at any one time, been virtually only two parties of importance in the United Kingdom. Between 1874 and 1918 the Irish Nationalists mustered around ninety seats, which at times gave them the power to influence Government policy. Again, in 1923 and 1929, the Labour Party could enjoy office only with the support of the Liberals. But at other times, except on a few occasions when certain groups defected within the party (e.g. on the repeal of the Corn Laws and on Irish Home Rule), the Government of the day has been able to rely on its party majority to secure the support of the House of Commons. Indeed, at the end of the 19th century W. S. Gilbert could write in *Iolanthe*:

> *I often think it's comical*
> *How Nature always does contrive*
> *That every boy and every gal,*
> *That's born into the world alive,*

Is either a little Liberal,
Or else a little Conservative!

This certainly is not true of every democratic country. France
Italy, Demark and Israel, to take but a few examples, all have a
number of parties. There is no simple explanation of Gilbert's
observation. Influences, similar to those which gave rise to the
two-party system in Britain, can be found in other countries,
but have not produced the same results; while in other parts
of the world, notably the U.S.A., different factors have brought
about a two-party system. Nor is it possible to say which influences in Britain have been dominant; often the combined
effect of many factors has reduced political warfare to two main
parties.

In the first place, the two-party system follows the basic
division which exists between men. In the long run, social
improvements are bound to take place. Some people, the radicals,
wish to hurry ahead with them, whereas others, the conservatives,
prefer to let them come more gradually.

Secondly, religious, national and geographical differences have
never been sufficient to bring about sub-divisions of the two main
groups. Although the British people are predominantly Protestant,
they have usually been fairly tolerant of those of different faiths.
Moreover, the smallness of the country has hampered the formation of national and regional parties. Until recently the only
national party of any significance was the Irish one.

Thirdly, a new party finds difficulty in becoming established.
The British ability to compromise helps the major parties to absorb
sectional differences, while the floating vote, which could form the
basis of a new party, has concessions made to it. Thus, since
neither party appeals to a single class of voter, there is no definite,
distinct reason for a third (page 108). One of the difficulties facing
the Liberals today is to find a policy which is really different from
that of the other two parties. Again, practical obstacles prevent a
new party from gaining momentum. Lack of funds restricts the
number of seats that can be contested, so that no hope exists of
winning sufficient to form a Government. When there is no chance
of the party as a whole succeeding, voluntary workers, especially in
hopeless constituencies, tend to be discouraged. Nor are people
willing to vote for a party which is either on the decline or has not

yet proved itself. Once the rot sets in, it is difficult, as the Liberals discovered, to arrest.

Fourthly, once the two-party system is established, the Leaders do everything possible to prevent a fractious section of the party from breaking away. In this, they are strengthened by the innate British ability to compromise, and, above all, by the threat of dissolution or the power to ruin politically those who take part in a revolt which fails to gain impetus. Thus, on the Conservative side, the Suez rebels were soon re-absorbed into the Party, while Labour has almost always succeeded in closing its ranks before a general election.

But the main reason for the two-party system is that it follows the fundamental characteristic of the British constitution — the emphasis which is placed on the importance of the Government. The purpose of a general election is to confirm or get rid of the Government. This is the form of democracy which the British people prefer, for it allows them to exercise complete sovereignty every five years even though the composition of the legislature may not precisely reflect their different views. Each general election, therefore, re-emphasises the division of the country into two main groups, and a party which is too small to present itself as a possible alternative Government finds it difficult to muster support. This set-up is automatically carried over into the parliamentary scene, where the principal issues are resolved into a struggle between the Government and the Opposition. All major proposals originate from the Government front-bench; resistance to them comes almost entirely from the Opposition. Any third party feels that it is butting in on this main fight; and, in practice, it can do little to influence events. Should it continually support the Government or Opposition, it comes to be identified with it, and the electorate eventually feels that it can no longer be considered as a separate party. It is, therefore, ultimately absorbed into one of the two major parties. On the other hand, if a minor party changes its support, it stands the risk of being regarded as inconsistent and opportunist. Two alternatives remain; it can abstain or it can divide within itself. When it abstains frequently, it creates the impression that it has no policy of its own; if it divides, then it ceases to be a united party. Thus we find that even a rebel group (e.g. the Peelites, the Liberal Unionists and the National Liberals) soon becomes an appendage of another party. Consequently the tendency to recreate the two-party system is much stronger than the counter-tendency of parties to divide. Faced with the alternative of Government or Opposition in 1859, the various sundered wings of the Liberal Party quite deliberately decided to recreate the party system of 1832–46; they determined not only to turn out a Tory Government but to keep a Liberal one in. 'The two-party system is the natural concomitant of a political tradition in which government, as such, is the first consideration, and in which the views and preferences of voters or of members of Parliament are continuously limited to the simple alternative of "for" or "against" ' (L. S. Amery: *Thoughts on the Constitution*).

Lastly, the mechanics of the constitution discourage deviation from the two-party system. Our simple majority, straight-voting method acts against the formation of small parties, while in Parliament the seating and lobby arrangements compel members of third parties to take sides.

ADVANTAGES OF THE TWO-PARTY SYSTEM

The Greek idea of democracy did not envisage a party system. The government was to be formed on an arithmetical basis according to the wishes of the people as shown at an election. Control was to be fairly direct, a practicable possibility in view of the small number of citizens, the freemen, who could vote. Hence a system in which there was a Government and an alternative Government did not occur to them even as a theoretical idea; it was unnecessary, but in any case would probably have been opposed as being not fully representative.

Such a view does indicate certain deficiencies in the two-party system, deficiencies which in fact can be observed in British politics today. Persons with progressive ideas stand little chance of maintaining a party to represent them. Thus Mr. Desmond Donnelly's Democratic Party failed to survive after the 1970 election. Both major parties have a vested interest in maintaining the system, and if radical ideas cannot be embraced by one of these parties, those holding them are unlikely to progress far on their own. The two-party system therefore tends to conservatism. Moreover, the electors, confronted by the choice between two broad policies, are left with little opportunity for individual refinement. They cannot support home policy, for instance, but register disapproval of the conduct of foreign affairs.

But no political institution in itself is perfect. It must be considered in the light of its contributions to the general solution of the problem of government. The British apply a strictly empirical test: does it work in the constitution as a whole? If it does, it will be accepted in principle, though efforts will be made to improve it. Intuition and experience, not theory, have been the major influences in the development of the British constitutional system. Hence, the British people want the two-party system. That is one reason why, in re-building the bombed House of Commons, they preserved the existing lay-out; it explains, too, the lack of support for the introduction of proportional representation. To them, the system has real advantages, particularly when it is compared with the multi-party systems of other countries, such as France under the Fourth Republic.

In the first place, the two-party system gives stability to democratic government. Whereas dictatorships are stable because they rely on force, democratic governments, in appealing to reason, suffer from the defect that people may respond with a variety of opinions. Many parties do not inevitably produce instability, but there is always the likelihood that governments can be formed only with the support of minor parties. The position then is that the Government (a) never knows when it may be brought down by the passing whim of a minor party on a particular issue, (b) can never be certain of support for its policies when they are submitted to the legislature. Real government is therefore more easily attained under the two-party system, where one party is bound to have an absolute majority.

Secondly, the two-party system shows clearly where political responsibility lies. It puts the onus of government squarely on the shoulders of one party; it makes the duty of criticism just as unequivocally the responsibility of the other. The first gives real government; the second makes for constructive criticism because, should the Opposition succeed in ousting the Government, it has to accept the responsibility of carrying out its alternative policy.

Thirdly, the simple task of deciding between two parties not only simplifies matters for the electorate, but is truly democratic in that it allows the people to choose their Government. Where there are many parties, alignments take place after the result of the election is known and political bargains influence policy. But in Britain, the electorate, in voting for a party, not only chooses a

Government, but indicates the broad lines of policy which it wants them to follow. Hence 'the people participate in the exercise of power more directly than in many other countries where the electoral system produces a legislature far more accurately representative of public opinion than the British Parliament' (A. Mathiot: *The British Political System*). Thus, although the two-party system may be crude, it produces the kind of government which the British prefer, provided that the winning party makes concessions to minority opinion.

SUGGESTED READING

L. S. Amery, *Thoughts on the Constitution* (2nd Ed., O.U.P., 1964), Chapter 1.

N. Gash, *Politics in the Age of Peel* (Longmans, 1953).

A. J. Hanham, *Elections and Party Management; Politics in the time of Disraeli and Gladstone* (Longmans, 1959).

Quintin Hogg, *The Purpose of Parliament* (Blandford Press, 1947), Chapter 10.

Sir Ivor Jennings, *Party Politics. Vol I. Appeal to the People* (C.U.P., 1960); *Vol. II. The Growth of Parties* (C.U.P., 1961); *Vol. III. The Stuff of Politics* (C.U.P., 1962).

R. T. McKenzie, *British Political Parties* (2nd Ed., Heinemann, 1963).

Lord Morrison, *Government and Parliament* (3rd Ed., O.U.P., 1964), Chapters 6 and 7.

R. M. Punnett, *British Government and Politics* (2nd Ed., Heinemann, 1971), Chapters 3 and 4.

R. Rose, *The Problem of Party Government* (Macmillan, 1974).

G. K. Roberts, *Political Parties and Pressure Groups in Britain* (Weidenfeld and Nicolson, 1970).

B. Shrimsley, *The Candidate* (Secker and Warburg, 1968).

9

The Work of the House of Commons

'Democracy is a notoriously difficult system to work,
and not the least difficult part of it is to get a large
representative body to function efficiently.'

LORD CAMPION: *An Introduction to the Procedure
of the House of Commons*

I. ITS PROGRAMME OF BUSINESS

THE PARLIAMENTARY SESSION

Parliament is summoned and dissolved by the Queen. Dissolution must occur at the end of the statutory five years, but in practice usually takes place earlier, on the advice of the Prime Minister. The proclamation dissolving Parliament also orders the issue of writs for the election of a new House of Commons, and announces the date of its meeting.

The life of each Parliament is divided into sessions, which usually extend from November to November. The session of both Houses is ended together by prorogation and the new session is opened by the Queen in person when she makes her Speech from the Throne in the House of Lords or by Royal Commissioners on her behalf (as in 1959). Prorogation terminates all public business. Any public bills, except those going through under the Parliament Act, lapse if by then they have not completed all stages in both Houses, but private bills may be carried over by resolution to this effect before the end of the session. Wiping clean the slate for the start of a new session has certain advantages. It keeps the Government on its toes in order to complete its legislative programme, while at times it may be desirable to drop a bill and replace it with a better one later. But often bills, upon which much time has been spent, have not been completed by the adjournment for the summer recess in July. Consequently, Parliament has to reassemble for a short period in the autumn before prorogation to clear up outstanding business.

The session is interrupted in the summer by a long recess, and at Christmas, Easter and Whitsun by shorter recesses, the period of adjournment being decided by each House separately.

THE DAILY TIME-TABLE

The normal time-table of the House of Commons is regulated by its standing orders:

2.30 *Prayers*

2.35 *Preliminary business*

    Motions for new writs (to fill vacant seats)

    Unopposed private business

    Presentation of public petitions

    Questions to ministers

3.30   'Private notice' questions

    Requests for leave to move the adjournment of the House under S.O. [Standing Order] 9

    Any other preliminary business, e.g. ceremonial speeches, statements by ministers, personal explanations by ex-ministers of circumstances of resignation.

  Public business

    Presentation of public bills

    Motions for leave to bring in bills

    Public business — Orders of the Day

10.00 *Interruption of public business*

    Government Business Motions, exempting business from the 10 o'clock rule

    Business taken after 10 p.m., chiefly proceedings on statutory instruments

    Motion for the adjournment

10.30 *House adjourns*

Nevertheless, standing orders do provide for some variation of this time-table. Thus, the House can continue sitting after 10.30 p.m. to consider certain automatically 'exempted business' (page 153) or to deal with a heavy Government programme where a motion suspending standing orders has been carried. Late sittings, however, are not popular with members and, when they take place at times other than those above, usually indicate that arrangements 'through the usual channels' have broken down.

On Fridays, the House sits only from 11 a.m. to 4.30 p.m., thus allowing the M.P.s opportunity to visit their constituencies at the week-end.

II. RULES OF PROCEDURE

The formal procedure of the House of Commons is laid down in its standing orders, which are interpreted according to precedents established by the decisions of previous Speakers. But a House of 635 members could not maintain order and work effectively if it had to rely exclusively on its written procedure. In the final analysis, the success of a constitution depends on a universal desire to make it work and, as with any other co-operative effort, demands a spirit of give-and-take. Nowhere is this better illustrated than in the customs which have been established over the centuries. For instance, the opportunities to criticise afforded to the Opposition rest upon custom. And, while the rules of procedure thus reflect essential characteristics of the British constitution, they in their turn serve to maintain them.

In the first place, by ensuring that the Government can secure all the powers it needs to carry out its policy, they emphasise the importance of effective government. Standing orders limit the time spent each day on preliminary business, allocate the period from 3.30 p.m. to 10 p.m. on at least four days of the week to the full use of the Government and, by providing a 'closure', guarantee that the Government is not hamstrung by endless debate. In the last resort, the Government can use its majority to secure the suspension of standing orders to allow the continuation of business after 10.30 p.m. and the appropriation of the Fridays allotted to private members. A sitting on a Saturday or the recall of the House during a recess is possible with the concurrence of the Prime Minister and Speaker. But, because all sides make mutual concessions, such departures from the normal time-table do not occur frequently.

Secondly, the rules of procedure safeguard the principle that minorities, however small, must be given full opportunity to criticise the Government. Thus, standing orders allocate a regular time for questions, lay down conditions for adjourning the House on a matter for urgent consideration and guarantee the Opposition a minimum number of days on Supply. Again, interpretation of standing orders is left to the Speaker, who frequently has to decide whether minorities have had adequate time. Moreover, since it is he who ultimately determines the order of debate, the Government cannot exclude likely critics of its policy. Even so, as we shall see, the main opportunities available to the Opposition for criticising Government policy are not secured by formal rules but by generally accepted agreements.

Thirdly, the rules of procedure embody that spirit of fair play which is inherent in our constitution and is essential to a system of government by consent. In calling on members in debate, the Speaker sees that every party in turn has the chance to state its views. The rules which require notice of a question protect the Government from being caught unawares, while the formal orders of the day ensure that business is not slipped through when the attention of the Opposition is elsewhere. Similarly, the limitation of the Supply debates to twenty-nine days and the shortness of time for the traditional discussion of grievances before adjournment are to some extent mitigated by allowing the Opposition to choose the subjects on these occasions.

Fourthly, the procedure promotes moderation both in the conduct and language of members. The Speaker's authority is supported by all sides, and speeches must be directed to him and not to an individual member. With a Chamber small in size, no special place to speak from, and the regulation that speeches may not be read, rhetoric and declamation are discouraged and members are induced instead to concentrate on replying to the arguments of earlier speeches. Nor must a speaker use 'unparliamentary' language or refer to another member by name, a requirement which not only keeps personalities out of the discussion, but allows time for reflection while a substitute phrase is sought.

Lastly, attention must be drawn to the ceremonial procedure which affords dignity to the meetings of the House and symbolises fundamental relationships. Such regular customs as the summons by Black Rod to attend the House of Lords to hear the Queen open Parliament and the Speaker's procession to the Lords, serve to show the permanence of the House of Commons and to give continuity to its proceedings. Indeed, they do more. The ancient unity of the three institutions comprising Parliament is underlined when the Commons attend before the Queen in the House of Lords, while the harmony of purpose on fundamental issues deeply felt beneath all political squabbles, is expressed in such arrangements as the position of the Speaker and daily prayers.

III. GOVERNMENT BUSINESS

An average session of the House of Commons contains about 165 days when business is conducted. Yet slightly less than half of these are normally available to the Government. The others are taken up by private members' business, incidental business, and routine and financial business.

Private members' business consists of bills and motions considered during the time allocated to private members (see page 189). In all it occupies twenty-four days or more.

Incidental business accounts for a similar period. It includes opposed private business, debates under S.O. 9, votes of censure, adjournments moved by the Government for the purpose of hearing a ministerial statement on a subject not easily covered by a motion, debates on the annual reports of the nationalised industries, and matters, such as breach of privilege, for which the House must make time at the expense of the Government.

Routine and financial business includes a 6-day debate upon the Address in answer to the Queen's speech, motions for the adjournment of the House before the recesses (4 days), debates on the Estimates and on the Consolidated Fund Bills (29 days), discussion of the Budget and Finance Bill (15 days) and miscellaneous bills, such as the Annual Expiring Laws Continuance Act (about 5 days). In general, these are the main and regular occasions when the Opposition fulfils its function of challenging the Government.

The Government, therefore, has only an extremely limited time for its tasks of initiating policy and securing the necessary legislative authority from Parliament. Yet, for the following reasons, it is able to complete its work:

(1) *The present-day tendency is to restrict discussion to matters on the Order Paper*

Consideration of other items throws out the agreed time-table. Consequently, urgency motions under S.O. 9 are not frequent, while the 10 o'clock rule limits the day's debate.

(2) *If necessary, priority is given to Government business*

Standing orders automatically exempt certain business from the 10 o'clock rule (see page 153). In addition, specified subjects and all Government business during certain periods may always be exempted by vote of the House. At 10 p.m. a minister simply moves 'that the proceedings on ... (subject stated) ... be exempted at this day's sitting from the provisions of Standing Order 1' (which governs the sittings of the House).

(3) *Arrangements for debate are made 'behind the Speaker's chair'*

Every Thursday, arrangements for the following week's business are announced by the Leader of the House in reply to a question put to him by the Leader of the Opposition. Previously discussions have taken place ('behind the Speaker's chair') between the party leaders and Whips ('the usual channels') to allocate the available time to their mutual satisfaction. For instance, the Government may agree to a day's debate on a censure motion provided that the Opposition will allow the completion of specified Government business on another day. Such agreements afford an excellent example of customs which have developed to enable the constitution to work in the true spirit of democracy. The alternative to this constructive approach would be purely negative, with the Opposition trying to hamper the Government by obstruction and all-night sittings. On occasions when these do occur, it is usually because: (*a*) agreement behind the Speaker's chair has not been reached because the Opposition cannot accept the proposals of the Government Chief Whip; (*b*) the Opposition is fundamentally opposed to certain measures; (*c*) the Opposition hopes that, by a wearing-down process, it can induce the Government to compromise.

(4) *The order of debate is arranged beforehand and speeches are kept short*

To be successful in 'catching the Speaker's eye', it is usually necessary for some representation to have been made to him beforehand. Indeed, this is merely another aspect of arrangements 'behind the Speaker's chair'. When a subject for debate has been agreed upon, both the Government and the Opposition nominate their leading speakers. Back-benchers who wish to take part usually let the Speaker know beforehand.

(5) *The legislative programme is carefully planned by the Cabinet*

Special Cabinet committees are now appointed to plan business. Thus under the Labour Government of 1945, a Future Legislation

Committee settled which bills should go into each sessional programme so that the party's legislative proposals could be completed in the lifetime of the Parliament. In addition, there was a Legislation Committee to examine the actual bill which was to come up for Cabinet approval. Usually an effort is made to have as many bills as possible read a second time in the early part of the session so that they will not be delayed by the Supply debates.

(6) *Considerable use is made of 'delegated legislation'* (see page 401)

(7) *The parliamentary business of the week is regularly discussed at Cabinet meetings* (page 263)

(8) *Standing orders make specific provision to enable the Government to control the time spent in debating a subject*

(a) *'Simple closure'.* In the 18th and early 19th centuries, procedure was loose and anybody who wished to speak could do so before the debate was closed. Eventually the convention developed that the Speaker could call on leading members of the Government and Opposition to make closing speeches.

Filibustering by the Irish Nationalists at the end of the 19th century necessitated specific measures to tighten up procedure. In 1881, one sitting of the House lasted forty-one hours until closed by the Speaker on his own authority to preserve the repute of the House. Hence, for the Coercion Bill of that year, Mr. Gladstone and the Speaker had an 'emergency resolution' approved. This empowered the Speaker to put a closure motion on his own authority and, when passed, the question was put and the debate ended. This procedure was incorporated in standing orders in 1882, with the initiative transferred to M.P.s in 1887. It is now governed by S.O. 31, which allows an M.P. (in practice, usually a Government Whip or the M.P. in charge of a private member's bill) to move 'that the question be now put'. Provided the Speaker considers that there has been adequate discussion, the motion is put to the House. If it is carried, and those in favour number at least 100, the debate ends and a vote is taken on the matter under discussion. Thus the simple closure gives the Government a weapon to counter obstruction. The safeguard for minorities is that the motion requires the Speaker's approval, and it is not unusual for him to refuse. The rule also applies to Committees of the Whole House and to Standing Committees, provided that in the latter a quorum (one-third of total membership) supports the motion.

(b) *The 'guillotine'*. The 'guillotine' was introduced under the 'Urgency Rules' of 1881, which allowed for closing debate on a bill by compartments, provided the motion was carried by a majority of three to one. The latter requirement has now been replaced by a simple majority.

The guillotine is applied chiefly to those bills considered by the Government to be of special importance. A time-table is drawn up allotting a specific number of days to each of the remaining stages of the bill, although, in the case of the Committee and Report stages, a certain number of clauses are allotted to each day. At the end of the given period, the question is put on the clauses or any Government amendments. Thus, through the guillotine, the Government knows in advance when each stage of a bill will be completed. But it is a very drastic procedure, obviously disliked by the Opposition. Even the Government prefers not to use it, for a day is often lost in debating the motion. Hence an attempt is first made to agree on a time-table through the usual channels. If this fails and the guillotine has to be used in a Committee of the Whole House or on Report, S.O. 43 provides for a neutral Business Committee (consisting of the Chairman's panel and five others nominated by the Speaker) to divide the bill and allot days to each part.

(c) *Selection of amendments — S.O. 33*. Under an obsolete closure (often referred to as the 'kangaroo'), the Chair used to select the clauses of a bill to be debated after a motion to that effect had been passed.

Today the Speaker or the Chairman (in Committee of the Whole House or standing committee), can, without a motion, select the more important amendments for debate when an unreasonable time would be taken up if all were discussed.

The various forms of closure are thus essential weapons for ensuring completion of business. Indeed, the sanction they provide enhances the possibility of voluntary agreement. As Sir Ivor Jennings puts it: 'The closure, kangaroo and guillotine are the instruments for driving legislation through at a reasonable pace.' But they distort and stifle debate and prevent many members from expressing their views, while they do nothing to solve the problem of shortage of time, being merely a makeshift addition to the old procedure.

IV. Opportunities for Minorities to criticise the Government

The ancient principle of the British constitution — that the Government initiates policy and others oppose it — is reflected in standing orders. Minorities have few opportunities to initiate, but many to criticise. That part of the procedure, too, which is based on custom emphasises the importance of the front-benches. Few chances are available for the private member. On the Government side, he is loath to embarrass ministers even at question time. On the Opposition side, the tactics to be followed in attacking the Government are laid down by the party leaders, and back-benchers are not expected to deviate far from this line. Thus the party machine dominates. Through the arrangements behind the Speaker's chair, the recognised occasions for debating Government policy are allocated almost exclusively to the organised Opposition.

(1) *Opportunities available to the private member*

Standing orders afford the private member only four good opportunities for criticism.

(a) *Question-time*. Question-time, a development of the second half of the 19th century, is the real occasion when the procedure of the House of Commons allows the private member to assert that authority which he enjoyed before the development of the modern party system. Indeed, it is significant that, as the private member has become absorbed by the party machine, so the number of questions put down for answer in Parliament has increased (although procedure was tightened-up because the Irish Nationalists used questions for filibustering). Today the rules regarding questions are as follows:

(i) The time spent on questions is nearly one hour up to 3.30 p.m.

(ii) 48 hours' notice of a question must be given to the responsible minister. The only exception is where a member gives private notice to the Speaker, who may allow the question on grounds of urgency, in which case it is taken at 3.30 p.m. Ministers attend the House to answer questions on a rota basis, the Prime Minister answering questions on Tuesdays and Thursdays.

(iii) Members are limited to two oral questions a day. Questions requiring an oral answer are 'starred' on the order paper; the rest merely receive a written reply, circularised in the official report. In practice, the vast majority of questions look for an oral answer. They have better propaganda value, can be followed by a damaging supplementary and are answered more quickly and directly by the minister concerned. But many are not reached by 3.30 p.m. and for these a written answer has to suffice.

(iv) Questions must be interrogatory in form, seek information or press for action, involve some degree of ministerial responsibility, and conform to constitutional usage and parliamentary etiquette. No speeches are allowed. Where a member is dissatisfied with the answer to his question, he may ask a supplementary, or, if he is lucky in the weekly ballot, raise the matter on the adjournment at 10 p.m. On occasions he may request the adjournment of the House under S.O. 9 (see below).

Many people think the House is at its best at question-time. Certainly, in contrast with much other parliamentary business, the time spent gives full value. The importance of question-time lies in the opportunity it provides to counter-balance those bureaucratic tendencies found within any civil service. Devoting a definite part of parliamentary time to questioning ministers responsible for the work of departments does much to safeguard individual rights. Usually satisfaction is obtained without bringing the matter before the House, for the possibility that a question may be asked is a real sanction. A question starts the responsible minister delving into the detailed administration of his department, and the civil servant loathes this probing. As Professor Lowell says, questions turn 'a searchlight upon every corner of the public service.' Possibly they do this only at the loss of some initiative on the part of civil servants (see page 330).

Naturally, questions can be used as a weapon by the Opposition to embarrass the Government, especially where some fact damaging to its reputation can be discovered. Or they can be the means of requiring the Government to explain certain points of its policy where a full-scale debate would be premature. The Government, on the other hand, may not yet be ready to commit itself. Here the art of replying to questions is tested. What the minister must be prepared for is the insidious supplementary, 'following upon the minister's reply, is he aware that . . . ,' which always lurks behind the original question and may be put on the spur of the moment. The department does everything possible to brief the minister beforehand. It gives him the answer he reads out, adds notes on the questioner and his knowledge of the subject, anticipates possible supplementaries and provides replies to them. It has been said that the ideal answer to a question is 'brief, appears to answer the question completely, if challenged can be proved to be accurate in every word, gives no opening for awkward "supplementaries", and discloses really nothing'. Nevertheless, occasions can occur when supplementaries do not follow the expected course and the minister is left without a complete brief. Here only a minister who thoroughly understands his department and is quick in thought and repartee will come through with flying colours. But the House is quick to appreciate, and the Leader of the party to recognise, a minister who is consistently master of the situation when faced by hostile questioners and who appears to have a complete grasp of the work of his department. Only on exceptional grounds, such as defence considerations, will the House not frown severely on the failure of a minister to answer a question, and it is most unlikely that the matter will be allowed to drop.

Question-time also gives an M.P. the opportunity to raise special local problems affecting his constituency. In this he may be genuinely seeking information; or he may merely be taking advantage of his one real chance to advertise himself to his constituents.

One final use of questions should be noted. Occasionally a question may be used by the Government to make a public announcement or statement of policy in a somewhat informal way. Thus, on 23rd July 1975, Mr. R. Jenkins, the Home Secretary, in a written reply to a question, announced the higher London taxi fares and charges which would be permitted.

(b) *Adjournment of the House under S.O. 9.* After questions, and before the commencement of public business, any member may move the adjournment of the House for the purpose of discussing 'a specific and important matter that should have urgent consideration'. Since the amendment of the Standing Order in 1967, the Speaker is no longer bound by precedent but merely has to be satisfied that the matter is 'proper to be so discussed'. This means that it must be an important matter which comes within the administrative responsibility of a minister and is not likely to be shortly brought before the House by other means.

If the motion is accepted and is supported by at least forty members (or, if less, by a majority on division), the matter is debated the following day at the commencement of public business (3.30 p.m.) and is concluded after not more than three hours. Exceptionally, the Speaker may hold the debate on the same day at 7 p.m. (as formerly).

S.O. 9 was amended in order to extend its use, thus giving more opportunities to back-benchers. On 29th July, 1971, Mr. Wedgwood Benn was successful in moving the adjournment of the House on 'the Government's decision on the future of Upper Clyde Shipbuilders and its implications for those concerned, for Scotland, and for shipbuilding as a whole.'

(c) *The daily motion for the adjournment at 10 p.m.* Public business begins at 3.30 p.m. and continues until 10 p.m., when the '10 o'clock rule' applies. At that time, the Speaker calls 'order, order', and directs the minister in charge of the business being discussed to name a day for its resumption. Any unopposed business may then be taken, but it is not proceeded with if there is a single objection. This usually takes about five minutes. A member of the Government then proposes 'that this House do now adjourn'. This motion affords the opportunity to seek from ministers more detailed statements than could be obtained at question-time. Debates cover a variety of subjects, chosen on four days of the week by private members successful in the ballot, but on the other by members chosen by the Speaker. Ministers concerned have to be notified beforehand, while no matter concerning legislation can be discussed unless the Speaker permits. At the end of half an hour the Speaker adjourns the House without the question being put.

Certain business is automatically exempt from the 10 o'clock rule and this may force the House to sit late. Such business falls into two categories: (i) that exempt by standing orders, including most financial business and, until 11.30 p.m. or for an hour and a half (if later), 'prayers' against statutory instruments moved by private members who otherwise would have no opportunity, since they can exercise no control over the time of the House; (ii) that specifically exempted by vote of the House.

(d) *Adjournment for the recess.* The adjournment for a recess is secured by a Recess Adjournment Motion several days before the adjournment actually takes place, for this imposes less strain in maintaining a quorum than on the last day. Having secured this approval, the Government has attended to its own essential business. The adjournment debates take place on the last day, on the motion 'that this House do now adjourn' and are based on the long-established principle of 'grievances before adjournment'. Thus they cover a variety of subjects introduced by private members. The Speaker chooses the private members and allots a brief time to each topic. No matter concerning legislation can be raised unless the Speaker permits.

(2) *Opportunities available to the Opposition*

Apart from debates and discussions on the various stages of the Government's legislative measures (see chapter 10), the custom of the House provides additional time to the organised Opposition in formal debate.

(a) *The debate on the amendment to the Address on the Speech from the Throne.* At the opening of each Parliament, the Queen outlines the Government's programme for the coming session. In the amendment to the Address which follows, the Opposition chooses the particular proposals to be discussed.

(b) *Debates on subjects agreed upon between the Government and Opposition which are held from time to time, and votes of censure for which the Government will always find time.*

(c) *The Supply debates* (see page 206).

(d) *The debate following the budget speech and the stages of the Finance Bill incorporating the budget proposals.*

V. THE SPEAKER

'No institution expresses more faithfully the spirit of the Constitution,' says Professor Dicey, referring to the Speaker, and this will become evident as we survey the historical development of his position, the traditions surrounding his office, the nature of his functions, and the manner in which they are performed.

HISTORICAL DEVELOPMENT

The decision of the Commons to assemble separately necessitated appointing somebody to take the chair in debate, obtain a collective decision, and report that decision to the King and, at first, to the Lords. The first record of such a 'Speaker' was in 1377, when the office was filled by Sir Thomas Hungerford. But the Speaker was not always the Commons' nominee. As the necessity of having a political understanding with the Commons increased, so the Sovereign found it useful to have a person as Speaker who was in his confidence. Under Elizabeth, Speakers received an allowance and often held other high office, and in return were expected to steer the debate according to the Queen's wishes and to prevent discussion of those matters which she found distasteful. Even today, before presiding over a new Commons, the Speaker still submits himself for the approbation of the Queen.

Speakers were inclined to interpret their divided loyalty differently. In 1629, Speaker Finch reminded the Commons: 'I am not less the King's servant for being yours.' But as the Commons became more assertive of its rights, so the Speaker was increasingly called upon to act as its spokesman, and it soon became apparent that this was where his first loyalty lay. Hence, in 1642, when Charles I attempted to arrest the Five Members, Speaker Lenthall declared: 'Sire, I have neither eyes to see nor tongue to speak in this place, but as the House is pleased to direct me, whose servant I am here.' The position was not finally resolved until 1679 when Charles II, in an effort to save Danby from impeachment, tried to impose his own nominee as Speaker in place of the Commons' choice. In the end, both gave way and a third member was selected, but henceforth, the Sovereign lost the controlling voice, and today his approval of the Commons' selection is a pure formality.

Nevertheless, until well into the 19th century the Speaker still remained an active politician, even holding ministerial office and taking part in debate. Under Queen Anne, for instance, Harley was Speaker and a Secretary of State, while both Speaker Abbott in 1813 and Speaker Manners-Sutton in 1825 were prominent in opposing Roman Catholic relief. But the development of active parties increased the possibility that the Speaker's duties could be used to the advantage of one side. Hence, in order to place his impartiality above suspicion, Speaker Onslow (1727–61) resigned his office of Treasurer of the Navy; but not until Speaker Abercrombie (1835–9) was the principle recognised that the Speaker should not participate in debate. His famous successor, Shaw Lefèvre (1839–57), established that high standard of impartiality which now prevails both inside and outside the House. Today this neutrality is protected by charging his salary of £8,500 a year on the Consolidated Fund. (Other emoluments he enjoys are a residence in the Palace of Westminster and, on retirement, a peerage and pension, granted by the Queen at the request of the Commons as 'a signal mark of favour'.)

THE TRADITIONS OF THE OFFICE

The Speaker is always a sitting M.P., usually with long experience of the House. His fellow members, who elect him to the office, look for a person likely to act wisely and firmly (preferably with a sense of humour when tempers are on edge), and capable of maintaining the high standards of dignity and impartiality which the office demands. In practice, his election is usually a formality. While it is traditional when a Speaker retires for the majority party to nominate his successor, prior discussion takes place between the leaders of all parties in the hope that somebody generally acceptable may emerge. Even in the manner of election, efforts are made to show his impartiality and to preserve tradition. He is proposed by a back-bencher and, wherever possible, is elected without opposition, the proposer and seconder usually coming from different sides of the House. Moreover, since at one time the office involved conveying unpopular messages to an irate Sovereign, it was accepted only with reluctance, and today the mock ceremony is still performed of dragging the newly-elected Speaker to the Chair.

Custom also decrees that the Speaker, once appointed, holds office until he retires; hence, until recently, he has usually been returned unopposed in his constituency. This has the added effect of preserving his impartiality for, as a result, he has no need to issue an election address, to make political speeches or to undertake party propaganda. But the arrangement has certain disadvantages. Although he nominates a neighbouring M.P. to do his constituency work, the electors are virtually disenfranchised and the local party organisation is liable to fall apart during the period when there is no election to fight. In addition, if the Speaker represents a constituency where the parties are fairly evenly balanced, it means that the losing party, when he is first appointed, cannot attempt to regain the seat at subsequent elections. A proposal has therefore been put forward that the Speaker should represent a nominal constituency, St. Stephen's Westminster. So far nothing has come of this idea, largely because many feel that the Speaker, not being elected in the normal way, might lose status and thus some authority.

Other traditions connected with the Speaker do much to enhance the dignity of meetings of the House. He is attended by the Sergeant-at-Arms and the ceremony of the Speaker's procession marks the beginning and the closure of each sitting. Since the House is not constituted unless the Speaker is in the Chair, its symbol of authority, the Mace, is put under the Table when he is absent. The wig he wears not only adds to his impressiveness, but associates the impartiality of judicial proceedings with his office.

THE SPEAKER'S FUNCTIONS

The main function of the Speaker is to preside over meetings of the House in full session, a quasi-judicial task which can be fulfilled satisfactorily only by strict observance of his independence and impartiality. It is here that even minor traditions, such as the custom of bowing to him on entering or leaving the Chamber, play such an important part. But the over-riding reason why he succeeds in standing above party politics is the care taken by all members to preserve his position, a care which springs from the desire to make our institutions work. The Speaker is regarded as the referee in charge of the game, who sees that it proceeds smoothly and according to the rules. His decisions are rarely questioned and then only through the accepted procedure. Breach of the rules can be punished, even by 'sending a player off' or abandoning the game.

In presiding over the House, the Speaker has many tasks to perform. He must ensure that debate continues in an orderly manner. Members must address their remarks to the Chair and sit whenever the Speaker rises to his feet. Should the House appear to be getting a little out of hand, he calls for order. Any failure to respond to his authority by the House as a whole may lead to the adjournment or suspension of its sitting. Where an individual makes a remark which is out of order, he will be asked by the

Speaker to apologise or withdraw. Should he refuse to do so, he will be 'named' for disrespect to the authority of the Chair and be excluded from the rest of the sitting. Persistent disorderly conduct may result in a motion excluding him for a longer period.

His occupation of the Chair means that the Speaker has to enforce and interpret the rules of procedure according to standing orders and the precedents established by his predecessors. He has to refuse any motion appearing dilatory and make sure that a motion is in order before putting the question on it. He must also exercise a general censorship over notices, particularly of questions to ministers which may already have been asked earlier in the session. In the speeches of members, he checks what appears to be irrelevant to the motion or merely repetitive.

In deciding the order in which members shall speak, the Speaker has the sole authority although, as previously explained, 'catching the Speaker's eye' is usually achieved by a word in his ear beforehand. Any debate must, however, preserve the principle of free and fair discussion. Thus the Speaker gives particular attention to three points. First, he ensures that all parties have a fair share of the allotted time. (The strong tradition of the House that radical or dissident views shall be heard results in small parties having a larger share of time than their representation warrants.) Secondly, he sees that the individual member, especially the critical backbencher on the Government side, is protected from the party machine in asking questions and getting into debate from time to time. Thirdly, he safeguards the House from any undue encroachment by the Government, particularly when it is trying to complete a heavy legislative programme. Hence the decision to accept a closure motion rests with the Speaker, while, in order to prevent the possible exclusion of matters the Government finds embarrassing, his is the final authority for admitting amendments, questions, and the subjects to be debated on adjournment motions. In addition, the Speaker has the sole authority under the Parliament Act, 1911, for certifying whether a bill is a 'money bill'.

The Speaker plays a major part in procedure when the House has to reach a decision. He proposes and puts the necessary questions, decides whether the 'ayes' or 'noes' have it and, if the motion goes to a division, announces the result. Should the voting be equal, he has a casting vote, but this is always exercised so as to avoid change, thereby preserving his impartiality, allowing further consideration later and ensuring that the House does not finally pass or change anything except by a majority.

Apart from the above, the Speaker has a variety of duties. He issues warrants for the holding of by-elections, appoints the Examiners of private bills, appoints the Chairmen's Panel and from it selects the chairmen of standing committees, and allocates bills to the various standing committees (see page 164).

Outside Parliament, the Speaker is the Commons' representative and the guardian of its privileges. He attends official functions on behalf of the House and receives documents and messages addressed to it from foreign countries and legislatures. He lays claim to the privileges of the House at the opening of every Parliament. Important conferences concerning parliamentary institutions or procedure, such as reform of the electoral system, are often convened under the Speaker's chairmanship. Should any member complain of a breach of privilege, the Speaker decides whether a *prima facie* case has been established. Where a breach is found, he pronounces punishment (see below).

OFFICIALS OF THE HOUSE CONNECTED WITH THE SPEAKER

The Chairman of the Committee of Ways and Means, or Chairman of Committees as he is more usually called, has three main functions. First, he acts as deputy to the Speaker, taking over when the Speaker leaves the Chamber at meal times or is indisposed. Unlike the Speaker, however, he is appointed only for the term of Parliament. Secondly, he presides in place of the Speaker whenever the House goes into Committee. He then sits in one of the Clerk's chairs before the Table (see page 163). Third, he exercises oversight over all Private Business. There is also a *Deputy Chairman* who can undertake all the Chairman's duties. Neither takes an active part in political controversy.

The Sergeant-at-Arms is appointed by the Crown to attend upon the Speaker, to enforce the orders of the House, and to execute warrants issued by the Speaker.

The Clerk of the House of Commons (the Under-Clerk of Parliaments) and two *Clerk Assistants* are appointed by the Crown and are removable only on an Address from the House.

(In the House of Lords, there are the *Gentleman Usher of the Black Rod*, who enforces the orders of the House, and the *Clerk of Parliaments*.)

VI. PARLIAMENTARY PRIVILEGE

Parliamentary privilege can be regarded as an exception to the ordinary law of the land, for the determination of breach of privilege rests entirely with the House concerned, each House enjoying the right to punish offenders. However, neither House can create new privilege, and when there is a dispute as to the existence of privilege, it is decided by the courts. Thus in *Stockdale v. Hansard*, 1839, it was held that the Commons could not extend privilege to cover reports of its debates, which therefore had to be safeguarded from proceedings for defamation by the Parliamentary Papers Act, 1840.

The most important privileges of ancient Parliaments — freedom of speech, freedom of access to the royal person and the request for a favourable construction of its proceedings — came into being because both Houses, and particularly the House of Commons, found it necessary to uphold fundamental rights in their relationship with the Sovereign. From the precedents established, a body of unwritten law was formed conferring certain privileges on both Houses separately. (Here we describe those of the House of Commons, the Lords' being different only in matters of detail.) Even today these privileges are claimed by the Speaker at the Bar of the House of Lords whenever a new Parliament meets, the Lord Chancellor conferring them on behalf of Her Majesty.

Today, the most important privileges are:

(1) *Freedom from arrest*

This privilege was never claimed on criminal charges, but it was important before 1869, when persons could be imprisoned for debt. The privilege also extends to witnesses before the House or its committees and to the servants of the House.

(2) *Freedom of speech*

Originally this privilege was claimed to protect members against the Sovereign. Elizabeth I recognised it, but stipulated that certain subjects, such as foreign policy and the question of her marriage, should not be discussed, as they were no concern of the House. But the Stuarts challenged the privilege. In 1621, James I complained to the Speaker because the House criticised him and, when the House formally protested, tore the offending page from its

Journal. Charles I went further, arresting Sir John Eliot and other M.P.s in 1629 and attempting to arrest the Five Members on a charge of treason for the views they had expressed in 1642. The privilege was finally confirmed in the Bill of Rights, 1689. Its importance now lies in the immunity it confers from an action for slander on words spoken in Parliament, an immunity extended in 1840 to all papers printed by order of either House and to faithful reports.

(3) *Freedom of access to the Sovereign* as a body to present an address and (4) *a request for a favourable construction of its proceedings* are still specified with the other two in the Speaker's claim, but are now not important.

In addition the House enjoys:

(5) *The right to provide for its own constitution*

This includes: the issue of writs for filling casual vacancies; the power to expel or suspend members bringing discredit upon the House; decisions as to the qualifications of sitting members.

(6) *The right to regulate its own proceedings*

The House can discuss any business and in whatever order it chooses. To assert this right, the Outlawries Bill (any bill would do) is given a first reading at the commencement of every session *before* the debate on the Address, but no further action is taken upon it. The right was well illustrated in 1884 when the House refused to allow Mr. Bradlaugh, a declared atheist who had been elected for Northampton, to take the oath or, subsequently, affirm. The courts refused to declare the action of the Commons illegal, expressing the opinion that the Commons were the only judges of matters arising within the House.

(7) *The power to punish for breach of privilege or for contempt*

Breach of privilege is contempt of the High Court of Parliament and so, as with the courts, action can be taken by either House to maintain its dignity and efficiency. Contempt can occur when a non-member threatens or intimidates a Member of Parliament or when anybody is disobedient to, or interferes with the execution of, the orders of the House.

The House may either resolve forthwith that breach of privilege has occurred or it can refer the matter to the Committee of Privileges for their consideration. The House may punish by admonition or reprimand by the Speaker, non-members appearing at the bar of the House. Members may even be suspended or expelled. For serious breaches, or where the offender does not show contrition, fines and imprisonment until the end of the session may be imposed.

VII. Committees of the House

EARLY DEVELOPMENT OF THE COMMITTEE SYSTEM

While a body containing many members is suitable for discussing principles, it is inappropriate for the examination of detail. The usual course, therefore, is to form a committee of a few members which can discuss the details of proposals and report back to the full body with recommendations. With the exception of the Committees of the Whole House, this is the reason for the committee organisation of the House of Commons today.

But the first committees of the Commons were formed for a different purpose. Originally, important bills were committed to a single member, usually a Secretary or Privy Councillor, who could give some official indication of the Sovereign's attitude towards them. In order to extend her control over legislation, Elizabeth I instituted the device of forming those Privy Councillors who sat in the Commons into Select Committees to which bills were referred. These committees met at first in places outside the House, but later had their own committee chamber at Westminster.

Committees of the Whole House developed for two main reasons. On the one hand, James I was slack in maintaining the Tudors' method of control. Because there were insufficient Privy Councillors in the House to fill committees, ordinary members, although not nominated, began to attend and were often welcomed in order to complete the quorum of eight. On the other hand, the House aimed deliberately at enjoying greater freedom in debate, especially in matters affecting the King. It therefore began to form itself into a Committee of the Whole House in order to have the Speaker, the King's representative, out of the Chair. Increasing use was made of Committees of the Whole House, and by 1628 the five large standing committees, which had developed out of the original

Select Committees, had, with the exception of the Committee for Privileges and Elections, become Committees of the Whole House and were termed 'Grand Committees'. But not until Charles II's reign did Committees of the Whole House begin to take the committee stage of bills.

Until 1882, Committees of the Whole House considered all public bills not referred to select committees. In that year, the first standing committees were set up by Mr. Gladstone to help combat the Irish obstruction. The scheme met with opposition, and it was not until 1907 that the present system was established by standing orders.

THE PRESENT-DAY COMMITTEE SYSTEM

Today there are five main types of committee:

(1) *Committees of the Whole House*

A Committee of the Whole House is merely the ordinary House of Commons sitting as a committee. When the House goes into Committee, the Speaker leaves the Chair, the mace is placed under the Table by the Sergeant, and the proceedings are controlled by the Chairman of Ways and Means. Procedure is less formal and discussion of detail is facilitated by allowing members to speak more than once to the same question.

Any matter may be referred to a Committee of the Whole House but today its chief use is to consider important bills of wide interest. After the second reading of a bill, any M.P. can move that it shall be referred to a Committee of the Whole House or that a part of it shall be committed to such a committee and a part to a standing committee.

When the Government has only a narrow majority the tendency is to refer all its controversial bills to a Committee of the Whole House. This is because in a Standing Committee its absolute numerical majority would be proportionately smaller and absence through sickness of a Government member could result in defeat.

(2) *Standing Committees*

A standing committee considers and amends public bills. S.O. 40 requires that all public bills except (*a*) a bill for imposing taxation and Consolidated Fund and Appropriation Bills, and (*b*) bills for confirming Provisional Orders, shall be committed to a standing committee unless the House otherwise directs. The House generally 'otherwise directs' for bills of 'first-class constitutional importance', bills required to pass quickly, and small non-controversial bills which soon go through by agreement. Such bills usually go to a Committee of the Whole House, but they may be referred to a Select Committee or a Joint Committee.

Today the House appoints as many standing committees as are necessary, designated A, B, C, D and so on. A Scottish Standing Committee is composed of 30 members nominated from Scottish constituencies and up to 20 other members. (There is also a Scottish Grand Committee which consists of all the members of constituencies to whom are added 10–15 other members in order to reflect the composition of the House. This discusses the principles of bills relating exclusively to Scotland on second reading — though the bill is 'read a second time' by the House itself — and spends six days discussing the Scottish Estimates and two days on matters relating exclusively to Scotland.) Although Wales has no separate committee, a bill relating exclusively to Wales and Monmouthshire is sent to a committee which contains all the Welsh constituency members. (A Welsh Grand Committee, consisting of the 36 members for Wales and Monmouthshire and not more than 5 other nominated members, is also appointed by sessional order to consider any specific matters relating to Wales and Monmouthshire which may be referred to it by the House.)

Each standing committee has between 16 and 50 members nominated by the Committee of Selection. This bears in mind the relative standing of the parties in the House of Commons, the persons who have qualifications for the matter being examined and the desirability of giving due representation to different parts of the country. When members particularly wish to serve on a committee, they inform the Whip. The Committee of Selection may discharge members from a standing committee for non-attendance or at their own request, but once consideration of a bill has begun, it will only add more members on account of sickness.

Each standing committee has a chairman, appointed for each bill by the Speaker from the Chairmen's Panel. This Panel is a body of not less than ten M.P.s nominated by the Speaker at the beginning of the session. (It also settles points of committee procedure not covered by standing orders and forms the nucleus of the Business Committee. Members also act as temporary Chairmen for Committees of the Whole House.) The Chairman of a standing committee was given closure powers in 1907 and powers to select amendments in 1934. Standing committees work mainly during the morning. A quorum is one-third of total membership.

The system of standing committees has certain advantages. Details of a bill can be discussed fully, often by members having expert knowledge of the subject. Procedure is less formal than in the full House and less pressure is put on members by the Whips. On the other hand, their proceedings are rarely reported, so that the public does not know what is going on, while their lack of publicity often leads to difficulty in getting members to serve on them.

(3) *Select Committees*

Select Committees are appointed by the House to consider occasional bills, conduct enquiries, and exercise supervisory functions. Members, who are usually nominated at the same time as the Committee is appointed, must not exceed fifteen without leave of the House. Each Committee chooses its own chairman, by agreement where possible, but otherwise by nomination of the major party. To enable the Committee to fulfil its terms of reference, the House may invest it with special powers. Thus, the Committee may summon witnesses on the order of the chairman (reporting as a breach of privilege any wilful failure to attend), send for papers and records, appoint sub-committees, and sit outside the House in order to carry out local investigations.

Select Committees are of three kinds: (*a*) *sessional*, (*b*) *ad hoc*, (*c*) *specialist*.

(*a*) *Sessional committees* are set up by standing order or by order of the House at the beginning of every session to exercise supervisory functions.

Those provided for by standing orders are:

(i) The Public Accounts Committee (see page 208).

(ii) The Committee of Selection, which consists of 11 members (6 from the Government side), and nominates members of standing committees; nominates the 8 members of the Standing Orders Committee; allocates private bills to Private Bill Committees; appoints the members of Private Bill Committees.

(iii) The Standing Orders Committee, which includes the

Chairman of Ways and Means and Deputy Chairman, and deals entirely with private business (see page 192).

The remainder of the sessional committees are appointed by order of the House, and are:

(iv) The Expenditure Committee (see page 207).

(v) The Committee of Privileges, which consists of fifteen experienced men from all parties, investigates alleged breaches of privilege where the House cannot give an immediate decision.

(vi) The Public Petitions Committee, which considers public petitions presented orally by members to see whether they are in order.

(vii) The Publications and Debates Reports Committee, which assists the Speaker in arranging for the reporting and publishing of debates, helps in deciding the form of notice papers, and enquires into the expenditure on stationery and printing both for the House and the public services.

(viii) The House of Commons (Services) Committee, which is concerned with the whole field of House administration, including the dining arrangements.

(ix) The Statutory Intruments Committee (see page 409).

(x) The Select Committee on Nationalised Industries (see page 344).

(xi) The Committee for the Parliamentary Commissioner (see page 322).

(xii) The Select Committee on Race Relations, which investigates the working of the Race Relations Acts and questions related to immigration.

(b) *Ad hoc committees* are appointed to:

(i) *examine bills*. A Select Committee is only a preliminary committee on a bill, for, after it has reported, the bill goes to a Committee of the Whole House. The advantage of committing a bill to a Select Committee is that special instructions may be given by the House which could not be given to the usual committees, and evidence may be heard from outside.

(ii) *conduct enquiries*. A variety of subjects is covered, e.g. increases in the Civil List, revision of the procedure of the House. The Committee's report is presented to the House and, if necessary, a day is fixed for its consideration.

(c) *Specialist committees*. See pages 169–71.

(4) *Joint Committees*

From the middle of the 19th century, joint committees have been used regularly on (*a*) non-political matters of equal concern to both Houses, e.g. statute law revision; (*b*) private bills involving an important matter of principle.

A Joint Committee consists of a small Select Committee of each House sitting together. The numbers from each House are equal, but the chairman is usually a peer. Each part reports to its own House.

There is one sessional Joint Committee, the Joint Committee on Consolidation, etc. Bills, which consists of 14 members (7 from each House) to consider all Consolidation and Statute Law Revision Bills (see page 387).

(5) *Private Bills Committees*

The work of these committees is discussed in more detail in chapter 11. Briefly, they are of two kinds. (i) The Committee for Unopposed Bills, consisting of the Chairman of Ways and Means, the Deputy Chairman, and four other members selected from a panel appointed by the Committee of Selection. (ii) Committees for opposed bills, usually known as 'private bill groups', consisting of a chairman and three members, all nominated by the Committee of Selection. Members must declare that they have no personal or local interest in the bill. Since these committees take up much time (sitting from 11 a.m. to 4 p.m.) and bring little public recognition, members often dislike serving on them.

VIII. CRITICISM OF PROCEDURE

If the House of Commons is to carry out its primary function of criticising the Government — over policy, legislation, administration and expenditure — it must have the necessary opportunities and knowledge.

Opportunities are severely limited by the time available. The House normally meets for 8 hours a day on about 165 days of the year. A balance has to be struck, therefore, between the time required by the Government to secure its essential legislative powers and that demanded by the Opposition to criticise. Too much criticism may result in paralysis, too little may lead to tyranny. Private members must also have opportunities to propose legislation, debate their motions, and ask questions concerning the administration.

Furthermore, the extension of government activities (particularly since World War II) and their increasing technicality have resulted in Parliament being overworked and inadequately informed. Thus criticism cannot be fully effective, and the government has been able to increase its powers at the expense of the House of Commons. Debate is curtailed, statutory instruments replace legislation, and no real control is exercised over government expenditure.

But the solution to the problem of how to make the Commons more effective is not a simple one. There can be no blueprint of reform which will guarantee success. Whether the remedy takes the form of revising procedure to give the Commons more time or of providing it with new institutions to reinforce its examination of policy and the administration, success or failure can only be assessed in the light of experience. The House of Commons is only part of the Constitution and changes may have far-reaching repercussions elsewhere in the delicate mechanism of checks and balances. Consequently innovations are often introduced only on a temporary basis and, as with regular morning sittings on a Monday and Wednesday, may be dropped in the light of experience.

Reforms fall broadly under three headings.

(1) *To provide additional opportunities for the private member*

In recent years the government has refrained from appropriating any of the 20 Fridays reserved by S.O. 5 for private members. Indeed, since 1967, the government has encouraged and given facilities to private members introducing social legislation which it does not wish to commit its support to. More recently it has been made easier to secure the adjournment of the House under S.O. 9. In addition, four extra days (up to 7 p.m.) have been allocated for private members' motions.

On the other hand, proposals of the Select Committee on Procedure to allow the Speaker to limit the length of speeches in order that more members could speak have not been implemented — but the suggestion has imposed some moral obligation on members to conform.

(2) To secure better use of Parliamentary time

Select Committees on Procedure have made various proposals for making better use of the time of the House. Some of these have been accepted. Thus the Committee of Supply and the Committee of Ways and Means have been abolished, and since 1968 details of the Finance Bill (which gives effect to the budget) have been considered upstairs in a general Standing Committee of 50 M.P.s instead of on the floor of the House.

But morning sittings, introduced in order to avoid late-night sittings, proved a failure. They were inconvenient for most members, and debates lacked significance, first, because ministers, having their departments to attend to, were rarely present, and second, because divisions could not take place until the evening. Thus they were abandoned after a trial period of six months.

(3) To make parliamentary control more effective

Critics of the House of Commons are chiefly concerned with its loss of control, especially by the back-bencher. Debates tend to lack vitality, largely because differences are ironed out at committee meetings of the party. The Government, too, can limit debate by the closure. The aim therefore is to restore the former significance of debates by improving their quality and giving fuller opportunities for the discussion of broad principles. As regards the former, many would like to see a free vote allowed on more occasions and members provided with secretarial and research facilities so that they could prepare their speeches more effectively. Adequate facilities cannot be hoped for, however, until completion of the extensions to the Palace of Westminster.

Parliamentary control has been strengthened by the setting up of the Parliamentary Commissioner for Administration (see page 322) and *Specialist Select Committees*. The former provides machinery for the investigation of complaints against the administration; the latter provide the Commons with bodies which are expert on the work of particular departments.

Select Committees of the House of Commons, expert in their own fields, have existed for some time, e.g. the Public Accounts Committee, the Expenditure Committee, the Statutory Instruments Committee, and the Committee on Nationalised Industries. But committees dealing with the work and policies of a department (somewhat like the Congressional Committee in the U.S.A.) are a comparatively new departure. So far only a few have been set up, e.g. for education and science, agriculture, science and technology and Scottish affairs, and some of these have been dissolved. To be really effective, committees would have to cover the important and controversial fields of defence, foreign affairs, economic and financial policy, and so on.

Until 1966 such committees were opposed because it was felt that they would undermine ministerial responsibility. But today the doctrine of ministerial responsibility appears to be so elastic that this objection is hardly valid. It was also feared that a narrowness of outlook would result if some of Parliament's authority were transferred to the committees. This is unlikely, and in any case the Commons retains ultimate control. Indeed such committees should make departments more answerable to Parliament.

This would come about because committees can discuss detail much more effectively than the whole House. Not only can they summon officials and papers but, by concentrating on one department and collaborating with experts, members can build up specialised knowledge and become as well-informed as Ministers. Even departmental expenditure can be examined.

It was hoped that these new committees would leave the House extra time for debating broad principles so that more back-benchers could participate. In practice, however, the arrangement has run up against obstacles.

In the first place, although each specialist committee contains only about 16 M.P.s, there is a limit to the number of committees the House can form. In a busy session, existing committees require some 400 members to man them. Such a demand means that the number of members attending debates in the Chamber at any one time tends to be small.

Secondly, too rapid an expansion of committees would simply mean that there were not the clerks with sufficient experience to service them adequately.

Above all, the M.P. loses his importance when he begins to seem (and feel) over-specialised and out of the political mainstream. While the few who serve on such committees may be better informed when the department is under discussion, their work cannot be put to use unless time is set aside to debate their reports. In any case, the main political confrontations take place on the floor of the House, and ambitious M.P.s can make more impression on their leaders there than in a committee room.

These considerations, together with the opposition of certain Ministers and civil servants to those committees which showed determination in uncovering arguments about current policy formation and in investigating the efficiency of administration, have resulted in some waning of enthusiasm for specialist committees. Thus the arrangement must still be regarded as being in the experimental stage rather than part of established procedure.

IX. FUNCTIONS OF THE HOUSE OF COMMONS

The House of Commons, as we have seen, originated through the dire financial necessity of the King. This placed its members in a strong position and, when they were summoned, the grant of revenue was made conditional upon the redress of grievances. The King's policies could be examined, his administration criticised and his arbitrary use of power considerably curbed. Rights once extracted from a reluctant but needy monarch were jealously guarded and added to as new situations arose. Thus the Commons discovered that the King's grant of petitions had more permanence if drawn up in the form of a bill, and so it became a legislating body. Later the House made it absolutely necessary for Parliament to be summoned at least once a year.

The functions of the House of Commons today are basically the same as those exercised by its predecessors some 500 years ago. They are:

(1) to support, watch and criticise the Government;
(2) to hold debates in which the Government is given an opportunity to explain and justify its policies to the electorate, and which educate the people in the merits of alternative approaches to the leading issues of the day;
(3) to preserve the rights of the individual in his relationship with the administration;
(4) to control the raising and spending of money;
(5) to help make the law.

The reason why these functions have been preserved for so long lies in the continuation of the original relationship between the Government and Legislature. The Government is responsible for initiating and implementing policy; the Legislature controls that policy in so far as the powers at its disposal permit. And although the centre of executive power has shifted from the Sovereign to the Cabinet, the relative position of the Government and Commons has been preserved.

In practice, however, there has been some modification of the relationship. Until the Reform Act, 1832, the Sovereign might choose his own Government and policy. The Commons tended to represent a separate power, and its control was inclined to be negative in operation. After 1832, this was changed. Harmony between the executive and legislature was achieved by choosing the Government from the party having a majority of seats in the House of Commons. The subsequent development of highly organised parties has meant that, to a large extent, the Cabinet now controls the Commons.

Yet we must not under-estimate the influence which the House of Commons still exerts. Even a small group of members may rally public opinion and cause the Government to modify its policy. Neville Chamberlain resigned in 1940 because he saw that, in spite of the majority of eighty-one which he could still muster, his leadership no longer enjoyed the confidence of the House. In 1956 Eden reversed his Suez policy because, apart from the criticism of the Opposition, he sensed the misgivings of a number of his own supporters. Moreover, it is usually through the House of Commons that politicians become ministers. The House moulds and trains them, and a member has usually served a long apprenticeship there before he attains Cabinet rank. 'The Cabinet is consequently more than a government formed by the party with a majority in the House of Commons. It is a government actually composed of House of Commons men' (A. Mathiot). Because he has risen to power through the House, a minister is better able to command its confidence, but he must also remember that the same House which nurtured him can also end his political career.

In any case, the increased power of the Cabinet over the Commons is not nearly so undesirable as some writers infer. Since the Cabinet can virtually guarantee the acceptance of its policies by the legislature, it makes for effective government. At least every five years, too, a new legislature has to be elected, and a Government which has been inattentive to the wishes of the electorate will be turned out. Thus, the essential of democracy, ultimate rather than detailed control over the Government, is preserved. Moreover, indirect checks are exercised by back-benchers in meetings of the parliamentary party or its committees and by grumblings to the Whips.

If anything, the development of this close link between the executive and the legislature has added to the significance of the Commons' traditional functions of criticising the Government and protecting the rights of the individual. The safeguard was provided, through the party system, by the development of Her Majesty's Opposition, described by Professor Lowell as 'the greatest contribution of the nineteenth century to the art of government'. Specific opportunities were made available to the Opposition, both by standing order and by the custom of the House, for criticising the Government.

Thus today the functions of the House of Commons are performed through the interplay between the Government and Opposition. Through the challenge of the Opposition, debates take place which 'express the mind of the English people on all matters which come before it . . . teach the nation what it does not know . . .' and make 'us hear what otherwise we should not' (Walter Bagehot: *The English Constitution*). The House of Commons is 'the grand inquest of the nation', a kind of national Press conference where the Government can explain its plans and answer criticism of its policies. Even in the preservation of individual rights and the control of finance, the Opposition plays the leading part, although on occasions some Government back-benchers may feel so strongly that they act as 'parliamentarians' rather than as mere party followers, perhaps going so far as to embarrass the head of a department or to vote against the Government. Finally, while the Government almost exclusively initiates legislation, the Opposition performs the important tasks of criticising principles and examining details of bills.

Thus, in order to explain exactly how the House of Commons works today, and the atmosphere which prevails, the next chapter studies the position of the Opposition in the constitution.

SUGGESTED READING

N. H. Brasher, *Studies in British Government* (2nd Ed. Macmillan, 1971), Chapter 6.
Lord Campion, *An Introduction to the Procedure of the House of Commons* (3rd Ed., Macmillan, 1958), Chapters 3, 4, 5 and 7.
D. N. Chester and N. Bowring, *Questions in Parliament* (O.U.P., 1962).
B. Crick, *The Reform of Parliament* (Weidenfeld and Nicolson, 1968).
A. Hill and A. Whichelow, *What's wrong with Parliament?* (Penguin Books, 1964).
Sir Ivor Jennings, *Parliament* (2nd Ed., C.U.P., 1957), Chapters 3, 4 and 5.
A. Morris, *The Growth of Parliamentary Scrutiny by Committee* (Pergamon, 1970).
Reports of the Select Committee on Procedure, 1959 onwards, H.M.S.O.

IO

Her Majesty's Opposition

'I disapprove of what you say, but I will defend to the
death your right to say it.'
Saying attributed to Voltaire in
S. G. TALLENTYRE'S *The Friends of Voltaire*

WHY AN OPPOSITION?

If the people are to retain control over their government, those
set in authority must from time to time be made to account for
their stewardship. In order to secure this, some countries have
written devices into their constitutions, a referendum, for instance,
to be held on specific issues. The British, preferring flexibility,
attempt to curb excesses of authority by a system of checks and
balances. Thus the early power of the King was always subject to
some control by Parliament, while today, as we have seen, the
House of Lords can require an over-zealous Lower House to have
second thoughts. The problem of how to make the Government
behave is solved in a similar way — through the Opposition. Upon
Her Majesty's Opposition falls the main responsibility for ensuring
that the acts and policies of the Government are exposed to the
glare of publicity and subjected to constant challenge.

The vital nature of the Opposition's role is signified by the
official recognition given it. On the one hand, we have 'Her
Majesty's Government'; on the other 'Her Majesty's Opposition'.
Indeed, it could equally well be regarded as 'Her Majesty's
Alternative Government'. Again, when the Ministers of the Crown
Act, 1937, paid the Prime Minister a salary, his counterpart, the
Leader of the Opposition, was given one (now £9,500) to be
charged on the Consolidated Fund. The Act also defined the
Leader of the Opposition as 'that member of the House of
Commons who is for the time being the leader in that House of the
party in opposition to Her Majesty's Government having the

greatest numerical strength in the House', and provided that where any doubt exists the Speaker decides.

Yet the Opposition, which now plays so vital a part in the British system of government, came into being quite fortuitously. Tierney, a Whig leader of the 1820s, viewed its tasks in purely negative terms. 'The duty of the Opposition', he said, 'is to propose nothing, to oppose everything and to turn out the Government.' Its development into an institution fulfilling essential and positive functions was the result of the growth of well-organised parties, usually limited to two in number. Until the Reform Act, 1832, the responsibility for criticising the Government rested with the House of Commons. Afterwards, the Commons as a whole was, through the party system, largely controlled by the Government, and so the challenge to the Government had to come from the party not in power. Moreover, since this criticism was really directed to the next election, the Opposition party had to be constructive, presenting a reasoned policy as an alternative to the Government's. In this, Her Majesty's Opposition differs fundamentally from the opposition to government in many countries.

FUNCTIONS OF THE OPPOSITION

(1) *It secures continuous accountability for the way in which the Government's powers are exercised*

Democracy in Britain is based on the principle of consent. There is free voting and an appeal to reason; change results from argument, not force. Since opinions differ, however, it is quite impossible to apply completely the maxim that 'what touches all must be approved by all'. Majority rule must prevail, though the wishes of minorities should be heeded. In any case, policy is a matter of opinion which can rarely be expressed in simple terms of 'yes' or 'no'. It has to be hammered into shape, and in this process the Opposition shares. 'Policy', as Quintin Hogg observes, 'is the product not, as is generally supposed, simply of majority rule, but of government by discussion, of the interplay between the Opposition's reasoning and objection, and the Government majority in the lobbies' (*The Purpose of Parliament*).

The real object of the Opposition, however, is to secure power at the next election. Hence, it examines the Government's proposals, criticises its policies, probes into its administration, and verifies its replies. An effective Opposition should bring to the fore all possible objections to a proposed line of action. It should draw attention to any Government proposals which appear undesirable, especially those which are extreme or which may possibly open a way to arbitrary government. It must try to make the Government modify its policies in the interest of minorities, and seek out and spotlight any instance of the administration riding rough-shod over the rights of individuals. Its weapons in Parliament are debate and questions, and, outside, propaganda through the party organisation by means of public meetings, television, radio and the Press.

In carrying out the above tasks, the Opposition ensures that the Government does not become too slack and that it considers public opinion when exercising its powers. On the other hand, through debates and questions, the Government is afforded opportunities to justify its stewardship in the most convincing form — detailed answers to specific criticism. When pressed to a division, the Government can ascertain its support within the House; and in the reactions of the Press and of the various 'interests', it can assess public opinion. Thus the interplay between the Government and Opposition is the life-blood, not only of the House of Commons, but of British politics as a whole.

(2) *It accepts the responsibility of government when the electorate desires a change of policy*

Only on rare occasions are the tactics of the Opposition purely obstructive. It knows, quite rightly, that the electorate regards it as 'Her Majesty's Alternative Government'. Thus its criticism is loyal, constructive and responsible. It is loyal because it accepts the fundamental principles of the British constitution. As Professor A. B. Keith says: 'The Opposition seeks power to effect the changes it desires, but does not seek power by means which deny democracy.' In short, it agrees with the Government on the 'rules of the game'. It is constructive because, under the two-party system, it is the alternative Government, having to put its own policy into effect if it succeeds in ousting the Government. Hence today it even presents a 'shadow Cabinet', with the leading members on its front-bench earmarked for definite ministerial posts and meeting regularly to determine tactics and policies. It is responsible, not only through the existence of Privy Councillors in its ranks, but because it stands a reasonable chance of eventually securing power. This can come about in two ways: by defeat of the Government on a major issue or by success at the polls. The former is a remote chance, for it depends upon a party split. But the latter is a real possibility. The Prime Minister and the rest of the Government are members of the legislature and their arguments can be met with counter-arguments across the floor of the House in order to prove to the floating vote that the Opposition would make a better government. That the Opposition is responsible can easily be appreciated when Britain is compared with other countries In France under the Fourth Republic, for instance, two conditions precluded such an opposition. First, some parties, such as the Communist and Poujadist, could not hope to obtain power by constitutional methods and were thus willing to resort to revolution. Secondly, the parties were so numerous and so poorly disciplined that no one party or group could stand forth under a recognised leader and present itself as an alternative Government.

The British Opposition is responsible, therefore, because 'it criticises with the knowledge and expectation that it may be called upon to take over the administration' (Professor K. C. Wheare). And because it is responsible, not only may the electorate reward it in the future, but the Government may take it into its confidence in the present. On certain matters, such as foreign relations, defence policy, Commonwealth affairs, and legislation of a non-party character, the Prime Minister may occasionally consult with the Leader of the Opposition before finally committing himself, especially if the decision is likely to impose obligations on future governments. On the other hand, in times of supreme national crises, particularly those concerning foreign powers, the Opposition will signify the unity of the nation on a particular Government policy by openly identifying itself with it.

(3) *It co-operates with the Government in the actual business of Parliament*

Co-operation is possible because both the Government and Opposition recognise the intrinsic value of democratic government. The Opposition accepts that the Government has duties to perform and a programme to complete. The Government realises that the Opposition plays a definite and positive role in the constitution and is prepared to allow it time to fulfil it. Hence, it is the custom for the Opposition to choose the subjects to be debated on the reply to the Address from the Throne and Supply days, and to move a vote of censure when it so requests. Moreover, because time is short, even the day-to-day business is arranged 'behind the Speaker's Chair' by consultation between the two sides.

In law-making and the control of finance, the Opposition also has a responsibility. Legislation must be tolerable, workable and enforceable, and the efforts of the Opposition are directed to seeing that it is so. By its criticism, it can secure reconsideration of a bill which is hasty or ill-conceived, or modification of it in the interests of minorities. It provides members to assist in the onerous work carried on in the Standing and Private Bill Committees and plays a major part in examining delegated legislation. The traditional function of the Commons of controlling finance is now largely performed at the instance of the Opposition. It chooses the votes to be debated and its members serve on all Select Committees, including the Expenditure and Public Accounts Committees. Indeed, it is now a convention that the Chairman of the latter shall be chosen from the Opposition.

(4) *It manifests the vital principle of free speech in the British constitution*

The Opposition embodies the spirit and proclaims the existence of our free democracy. In Britain, any Government, through its control of Parliament, has far-reaching powers. At times, too, it may not always be possible to see clearly whether or not the Government is set on securing arbitrary authority. A dictatorship, however, would have to stamp out all criticism. In the United Kingdom, this would entail censorship of the Press and, above all, elimination of Her Majesty's Opposition. The importance of the Opposition, therefore, is that, to the people, it is an emblem of liberty which is easily recognised. Any restrictions on it would be interpreted as an encroachment by the Government on the traditional freedom of Englishmen. While the response in defence of liberty would, as in the past, be immediate, it is far more likely to be effective as a result of this built-in 'early-warning system'. When we look at the dictatorships, we realise that 'the test of a free country is to examine the status of the body that corresponds to Her Majesty's Opposition' (Sir Ivor Jennings: *Law and the Constitution*).

DRAWBACKS TO THE BRITISH SYSTEM OF OPPOSITION

While its virtues certainly outweigh its disadvantages, we must not be led to suppose that the British system of an official Opposition is an unqualified success.

In the first place, the Opposition sometimes slows up the government machine by repetitive criticism. But the effect of this must not be over-estimated. While debate and discussion are taking place, the machinery for the administration of the proposal is being prepared. Moreover, government by consent is a two-way traffic; when the public are assured that a measure has been fully debated and passed in a democratic way by the elected law-making authority, they too feel bound by 'the rules of the game' and even those who personally disagree with the policy rarely obstruct it.

Secondly, there are times when the Opposition's right to criticise may be exercised solely on the basis of party advantage. Thus, in recent years, Oppositions have frequently criticised the Government for doing precisely what they would do were they in office. As a result, no consistent economic policy to contain inflation has been followed. On the other hand, at times the Opposition is so keen to appear responsible that it is inclined to 'pull its punches', and criticism is not nearly so devastating as circumstances warrant. Nevertheless, since in most matters the Opposition does find some grounds for criticism, the effect is all the more impressive both at home and abroad when, on rare but important occasions, e.g. the unrest in Northern Ireland, it is able to identify itself completely with the Government's policy.

Lastly, the possibility always exists that foreign countries may base their policies on a misconstruction of the role played by the Opposition in the British constitution. The duty of the Opposition is to provide an outlet for all minority opinions and to make all possible criticism of Cabinet proposals so that the Government may justify them in reply. Objections may even be raised which the Opposition well knows would not carry much weight in its own policy should it replace the Government. But they have to be made, often in an extreme form. Such a procedure is open to the danger that some countries, either because they are still immature in their understanding of political science, or because their governments so despise democracy that they fail to appreciate how it works, imagine that all the views expressed by our Opposition are held by nearly a half of the electorate. Such an inaccurate assessment may induce them to rash action with disastrous results. Thus it is still a matter of conjecture whether Germany would have invaded Poland in 1939 had Hitler been certain that the British people were united in regarding this as cause for war, while the danger of the policy of 'brinkmanship' is that either side may under-estimate the resolution of the other.

SUGGESTED READING

R. Butt, *The Power of Parliament* (Constable, 1967), Chapter 11.

Quintin Hogg, *The Purpose of Parliament* (Blandford Press, 1947). Chapter 11.

Sir Ivor Jennings, *Parliament* (2nd Ed., C.U.P., 1969), Chapters 6 and 15; *Cabinet Government* (3rd Ed., C.U.P., 1969), Chapter 15.

R. M. Punnett, *Front-Bench Opposition* (Heinemann, 1973).

II

Making the Law

'At heart all Governments believe that the House is
only occupied when it is discussing Government-
sponsored legislation.'
Memorandum presented by the Clerk of the
House of Commons, Sir Edward Fellowes, to
the Select Committee on Procedure, 1959.

In chapter 3 we saw how legislation by bill developed from
petitions. Sometimes these petitions came from groups within
Parliament, sometimes from groups or individuals outside. From
the former source, public bills descended; from the latter, private
bills. Public bills alter the general law and are concerned with
national interests. Private bills, on the other hand, are concerned
with particular interests and are often limited to a special locality.
These two groups still form the main distinction between bills
today, for each has a separate procedure, but they can be sub-
divided:

  I. *Public bills*
      Government bills
        (i) Money bills
        (ii) Other bills
      Private Members' bills
 II. *Private legislation*
      Private bills
      Provisional Order Confirmation bills
      Special Procedure Orders

I. Public Bills

GOVERNMENT BILLS

While any bill except a money bill may be introduced in either
House, almost all major bills originate in the Commons. It is
convenient, therefore, to describe the progress of a bill through that

House, especially as there are only a few minor differences when a bill originates in the Lords.

(1) *The basis of Government legislation*

In a normal session, about 110 days are available for public legislation and all but ten of these are appropriated by the Government. Even so, the Government is pressed for time. Not only do certain annual bills (e.g. the Finance Bill, the Consolidated Fund and Appropriation Bills, and the Expiring Laws Continuance Bill) have to be passed so that the Government's work can continue, but unforeseen events and emergencies often necessitate legislation. This leaves only about sixty days for new legislation.

First place must be given to the legislation necessary to carrying out election pledges. But since the party programme covers many topics, and a Government with a good majority can anticipate five years of office, there is wide scope in determining the priority and timing of bills. Under the Labour Government of 1945, preliminary work was performed by a Future Legislation Committee of the Cabinet. This contained no departmental ministers in order to be as objective as possible in settling the priority of bills.

Nevertheless, every Government, in accordance with the spirit of the constitution, must give both Houses of Parliament a fair opportunity to examine its legislative proposals. On controversial issues, some obstruction is inevitable, and where the Government has only a small majority its difficulties will be increased. Rather than resort to excessive use of the closure, it will possibly temper its proposals in order to reduce opposition to them. In any case, it is always advantageous to widen the area of agreement. Often a 'Green Paper' sets out various alternatives for discussion. Interest and pressure groups make their views known, and all government departments concerned are consulted. The Government then usually issues a 'White Paper' containing its definite proposals for legislation. This is debated in Parliament, and, as far as possible, legislation takes note of the views expressed.

Apart from the party's main proposals, departments desire legislation on particular matters. Additional legislation and amendments to existing law will probably have been found necessary in the light of administrative experience. The initiative will probably come from the department's advisory committee, a group of civil servants and other experts who advise on the work of the department. Or the proposals may result from the findings of a recent Royal Commission. Interests may also request a department to promote legislation, but their proposals are unlikely to be espoused until they have been the subject of a private member's bill, propaganda in the Press, parliamentary lobbying and evidence before Royal Commissions, a process which may extend over many years. A number of department bills, however, will be introduced during each session, according to the time available, but exactly which ones will depend on the influence of the minister in the Government, the views of the appropriate policy committee of the Cabinet, the importance of the matter in the eyes of the Future Legislation Committee, and the degree of controversy the measure is likely to excite.

Governments today consult the interests concerned before sponsoring a bill. This not only implements the basic principle that government by the majority must bear in mind the wishes of minorities, but frequently speeds the bill's passage by minor modifications which reduce opposition. The interest can always make representations during the processes of a bill. The minister and M.P.s may be 'lobbied' and, if the minister will not relent, the interest's spokesman in Parliament may put down an amendment or seek concessions in the committee stage.

(2) Drafting

Since a bill has to be watertight legally, it must be carefully drafted by lawyers. Drafting of Government bills is performed by the Parliamentary Counsel's Office, a branch of the Treasury, and it is to this office that the department explains the proposals it wants embodied in a bill.

Drafting is a long and skilled process. Meetings are arranged between the draftsman and the department, and as many as twenty drafts may have to be prepared before the bill appears to be word perfect. Hence, the complete drafting of a bill may take up to four months, and even then amendments in the wording may be necessary in committee or in the House of Lords. The Parliamentary Counsel remains responsible for the bill while it is before Parliament, but amendments have to be moved by an M.P., who is usually the minister in charge.

When drafted, the bill goes before the Legislation Committee of the Cabinet, which examines its structure and details to ensure that it is generally acceptable as a workable measure.

A bill takes the form of a draft statute and consists of a long title, which covers its purposes and content; a short title, by which it is generally known; an enacting formula, sometimes preceded by a preamble, beginning 'Be it enacted by the Queen's Most Excellent Majesty . . . '; the clauses (which become sections in the Act), containing the main provisions and so arranged that the important principles come first; schedules containing lists of statutes affected; and details of machinery and procedure resulting from the main provisions. A Memorandum, which has now almost replaced the preamble, is often attached to explain the objects of the bill, but it is not technically a part of it.

(3) *Stages through which a bill passes*

(a) *Introduction and First Reading.* There are certain procedural differences between money bills, whose *main* object is to impose taxation or to authorise expenditure, and other bills. Money bills can be introduced only in the Commons, and until 1938 had to be approved by resolution of a Committee of the Whole House before being introduced. Today, however, the Government introduces its money bills under S.O. 91, proceeding as though the charge involved were merely subsidiary.

Few bills today are introduced by order of the House. The main exception is bills introduced under the 'Ten Minutes' Rule' by private members (see page 189). Instead, most bills, whether Government or private members', are introduced without a motion under S.O. 37 (1). A member, usually a minister, notifies the House that he intends to introduce a bill. On the appointed day, it appears on the Order Paper, the member's name is called by the Speaker, and the 'dummy' bill is presented to the Clerk at the Table, who reads the short title. This constitutes the first reading and a day is then fixed for the second reading. (The process of 'reading' a bill probably dates from the time before the invention of printing.)

Although the first reading is purely formal, it warns the House and the various interests affected. The Public Bill Office now arranges for the bill to be printed so that it can easily be studied. In addition, the bill is examined to see whether: (i) its main object is to impose a charge, when a special procedure applies (described below); (ii) it affects private rights, when it must be examined by Examiners (see page 192); (iii) its contents are covered by the long title; (iv) it is similar to a previous bill already decided upon by the House in the session.

(b) *Second Reading.* On the appointed day, the member in charge explains the background and purposes of the bill and the chief issues of policy involved, and concludes by moving that 'the bill be now read a second time'. A debate, which may take anything from a few minutes to two or even three days, then follows on the general principles of the bill, no discussion of detail being allowed. At the end of the debate the motion is put, 'That the Bill be now read a second time.' The traditional way of defeating the bill is either by postponement or by a 'reasoned amendment'. In the first case, the Opposition moves as an amendment, 'That the Bill be read a second time upon this day six (three after Whitsuntide) months.' In the second, the Opposition may move an amendment such as, 'That this House declines to give a second reading to a Bill which fails. . . .' (Similar amendments may be moved to the third reading.) If the amendment is defeated the Speaker declares forthwith that the bill is read a second (or a third) time. After the second reading amendments to the text may be received at the Table for consideration in committee.

As a result of a recommendation by the Select Committee on Procedure, it is now possible for a non-controversial bill to be referred to a Second Reading Committee (a standing committee of 30 to 80 members) to recommend whether or not it should be taken as read a second time. Ten days' notice of the intention has to be given on the Order Paper, and if a minimum of 20 M.P.s object by rising in their places, the Second Reading is taken by the Whole House.

In the case of money bills introduced under S.O. 91, a special procedure is necessary before they can go to committee. Whether the expenditure is a single payment or a permanent charge on the Consolidated Fund or is to appear in future Estimates, it must be recommended by the Crown, that is, by a minister (S.O. 89).

(c) *Committee stage.* The bill is now referred to a committee, usually a standing committee, whose task it is to examine the bill, clause by clause and, if need be, word by word. Amendments may be made, many being moved by the minister or member in charge of the bill both to improve it and to make it more acceptable. But the committee cannot amend the bill so that its main principles are destroyed, as these have already been agreed upon by the House in second reading. Nor can it admit irrelevant amendments. While a Government defeat in standing committee does not operate as a vote of no-confidence, such defeats are rare, for they lower the prestige of the Government.

(d) *Report stage.* If a bill is referred to a Committee of the Whole House and no amendments have been made, there is no debate when the bill is reported back. It simply proceeds, sometimes immediately, to the third reading.

All other bills are reported to the House. The Speaker is in the Chair and the more formal rules of debate apply. Thus a member can speak only once to the same question, unless he is in charge of the bill or moved the amendment. The committee's recommendations are either accepted or rejected, thus ensuring that the bill, in its final form, represents the opinion of the majority of the House and not merely that of the committee. But on the Report stage, the House can make further amendments, consider new matter that the committee did not cover and insert new clauses. The latter is often done at the instance of the minister in charge to meet those criticisms made in committee with which he is in sympathy. In practice, however, the Report stage often develops into a second Committee stage. The bill may be re-committed if there are many deviations from the committee's report. Furthermore, the Speaker can limit the time spent on the bill by selecting amendments.

(e) *Third Reading.* Usually the bill is read a third time immediately after the Report stage. This is the final debate. Since it is limited to the contents of the bill and only verbal amendments (grammatical corrections and any slips which do not change the intended sense), it does not usually take long.

(f) *'Another Place'.* As soon as the bill has completed its stages in the Commons, it is taken by a Clerk to the House of Lords, where it is delivered to one of the Clerks at the Table. (The reverse procedure applies to a bill originating in the Lords.)

The bill passes through the same stages in the Lords, although usually more quickly. Generally the Committee stage is taken by a Committee of the Whole House. Apart from money bills, it is legally possible for the Lords to reject or amend a bill, but in practice the position is very delicate (see page 42).

The amended bill is taken back to the Commons by a Clerk of the House of Lords. The Commons debates each amendment in turn, either accepting it, rejecting it or itself amending it. The bill is then returned to the Lords for further discussion. It may go to and fro between the Houses three of four times. If agreement is not possible, a conference may be held with the object of reaching a compromise. Otherwise the bill must either be dropped or the procedure of the Parliament Act invoked.

(g) *The Royal Assent.* A bill, if urgent, will be presented for the Royal Assent immediately, but usually bills are presented in batches before a long adjournment or at the end of the session. The Royal Assent is now purely formal, and is given by the commission issued under the Great Seal and sign manual. In order not to interrupt Common's business, the Royal Assent Act, 1967, allows the Speaker in the Commons and the Lord Chancellor in the Lords simply to report the Queen's approval for legislation. But the old ceremony can still be used and is likely to become an annual spectacle. Under this, the Speaker and Commons are summoned by Black Rod to the bar of the House of Lords where three Lords Commissioners sit before the Throne. As the title of each Act is read the Royal Assent is signified by the Clerk of the Parliaments in the Norman-French formulae, for money bills, 'La reyne remercie ses bons sujets, accepte leur bénévolence, et ainsi le veult,' and, for other bills, 'La reyne le veult.'

The stages through which a bill must pass often take a long time. But, except in the case of money bills, more than one stage can be taken on the same day and, in emergencies, all stages can be completed in a few hours, as with the Northern Ireland Act, 1972.

PRIVATE MEMBERS' BILLS

A private member's bill is a public bill introduced and piloted through the House by a private (unofficial) member. While in theory a member may introduce any bill he pleases, in practice he would meet opposition from the Whips if it were likely to cost the Government votes or if it cut across Government policy. The Government can also block a private member's bill involving expenditure by not giving the recommendation of a minister.

Hence bills introduced by private members are of comparatively minor importance. A member may have a particular subject dear to his heart — Mr. David Steel's Abortion Act, 1967, was of this nature — but he could be the representative in Parliament of an interest which expects him to further its cause by appropriate legislation and, if the member does not have a bill, it will provide him with one, or he may be merely a good party man, in which case the Whips are certain to be able to produce a bill on a minor administrative matter which the Government would like to see passed into law.

Private members' bills may be introduced in three ways:

(1) By *ordinary presentation under S.O. 37*. Any member has the right to have a bill *published* if he presents it at the commencement of public business on any day of the week when the House is sitting. Presentation is purely formal, and no debate on it is possible at the time.

(2) Under the *'Ten Minute Rule' procedure (S.O. 13)*. On a Tuesday or Wednesday after Questions, an M.P. can make a short speech in favour of a bill he wishes to present. If any one Member wishes to oppose the motion for leave to introduce the bill he too may make a short speech before a decision is taken, by vote if necessary. If leave is given, the bill is deemed to have been read a first time, and the M.P. in charge of the bill names a Friday for second reading. This procedure is popular amongst M.P.s who, being unsuccessful in the ballot for a Friday, have little chance of time for debating their bills. At least it ensures some publicity, and at a time when the Chamber and the Press Gallery tend to be quite full. Opinion can sometimes be tested on controversial matters by putting them to the vote. If the motion is defeated, however, the bill cannot be introduced and cannot therefore be printed. There is always a chance, too, that the bill can be made so uncontroversial that an M.P. may be able to get it through on the nod at 4 o'clock on a Friday after other private members' bills or, if the business on the other bills ends early, after a short debate.

(3) *Under the ballot procedure [S.O. 6(4)]*. The main difficulty facing private members is in obtaining time to have bills debated. Early in each session a ballot is held for priority on a Friday. About three-quarters of all members enter their names and a small number (20 in recent sessions) are chosen by lot. After about three weeks the successful members present their bills and name one of the allotted Fridays for their second reading. About twelve Fridays are reserved each session for private members' bills (six for second reading and six for later stages). The first six members have the chance of a full Friday's second reading debate and, if it is at all controversial, it is likely to take up most or all of the time available.

The remaining bills put down for that day must either be given a second reading on the nod, i.e. without any discussion, or be deferred if even a single member shouts 'object'. Many bills are deferred for this reason from one private member's Friday to another throughout the session, without ever being debated at all.

Even when a member has priority for a bill on a Friday, he can still run into difficulties. He has to draft his own bill, though since 1971 the first ten members in the ballot can be reimbursed up to £200 for drafting expenses. He has to cope with the complications of parliamentary procedure. Moreover, if the bill offends Government policy, the Whips will be put on against it. Above all, it may be 'talked out' without a decision if 100 Members are not present to vote for a closure. In any case he has to secure the attendance of members to vote for his bill, just when they want to visit their homes or constituencies. When the bill is not first on the Order Paper for the day, opposing interests may debate the previous bill at length so as to leave insufficient time for the following bill.

In view of the above difficulties, it is not surprising that of an average of about 80 bills introduced by all methods by private members in a full session, only about 15 get on the statute book.

II. PRIVATE LEGISLATION

In addition to passing public bills concerned with the community at large, Parliament can confer particular powers or benefits on a person or body of persons, companies and, especially, on local authorities, public utility corporations and the nationalised industries. Thus a local authority can seek powers not covered by an existing Act of Parliament, while a public utility corporation can ask for powers to make bye-laws or to acquire land compulsorily from private persons. This is known as Private Legislation, and in its procedure Parliament endeavours to hold the balance between competing interests. Although desirable, the powers sought may be far-reaching, granting a privileged position to one group of persons and interfering with the rights of others. Consequently, in its Standing Orders (Private Business), Parliament has laid down a detailed and elaborate procedure so as to secure that private legislation does not unreasonably harm either the national interest or private interests.

PRIVATE BILLS

A private bill is a bill for the particular interest or benefit of any person or persons. The range of subjects for which it may be introduced is very wide. Mr. Anthony Wedgwood Benn, for instance, promoted (unsuccessfully) a bill to renounce his succession to the peerage so that he could continue to sit in the Commons after his father's death, while Luton municipal borough used the procedure unsuccessfully to try to obtain county borough status.

Not until 1798 was a clear distinction made by Parliament between public and private bills. As we have seen, early legislation was based on petitions for the redress of grievances presented either on behalf of the community or for a private person. Indeed, measures redressing the grievances of a person often contained enactments which were public in nature, since they applied to everybody. As legislation by statute was adopted, a distinction developed between bills of a general nature and those which were 'personal' in character, but it was not until the 18th century that the latter were specifically subjected to different processes. This was the period of the rapid increase in such bodies as the turnpike trusts and canal companies, all of which enjoyed special administrative powers. But because the misuse of such powers by the sovereigns of the 16th and 17th centuries was still fresh in Parliament's memory, a special procedure was laid down to limit these powers precisely.

Although in the middle of the 19th century private bills numbered 600 to 700 in each session, today they do not exceed fifty and most of them are promoted by local authorities. The decrease has occurred because: (i) the era of land enclosure and canal and railway development has now passed, while modern inventions, such as electricity, the wireless and the aeroplane, have less territorial claims; (ii) more general Acts have been passed to permit local authorities to carry out certain schemes if they so wish, e.g. the provision of libraries; (iii) Parliament today recognises the necessity of administrative powers, and has permitted the private bill to be superseded in many cases by Provisional Order Bills and Special Procedure Orders.

Stages through which a bill passes

(a) *Petition, Preliminary Advertisement and Examination.* Every bill is founded upon a petition signed by the 'Promoters of the

Bill'. (In practice, the bill is conducted through the House by Parliamentary Agents, known as 'The Agents of the Bill' or 'The Agents for the Promoters'. Similarly, Parliamentary Agents are employed to oppose the bill on behalf of interests, and they also watch all bills which come before Parliament so as to alert the interest should it be adversely affected.)

Unless the bills are personal bills introduced in the House of Lords, or are late bills introduced by special leave of the House, the Petition, a copy of the bill and other relevant documents must be presented in the Private Bill Office by 27th November in each year. Where works are being constructed, or land is being compulsorily acquired, plans have to be deposited with the Clerk of the County Council of the Town Clerk of the County Borough by 20th November. Standing orders also require that advertisement of the bill and its purposes shall be published twice in local newspapers by 11th December, and in the London Gazette. The government department most closely affected must also be notified, and by 5th December owners or occupiers of land affected by compulsory purchase must be informed. Where opponents of the bill do not consider that standing orders have been complied with, they can, by 17th December, deposit memorials against the bill addressed to the Examiners.

Examination begins on or after 18th December. It is conducted by two Examiners, one appointed by the Speaker and the other by the House of Lords. They see that standing orders governing the preliminaries have been complied with. Any adverse report is referred to the Committee on Standing Orders, who decide whether or not to dispense with standing orders, and report their decision to the House. By 8th January bills are divided between the two Houses by the Chairman of Ways and Means and the Lord Chairman of Committees, conferring together, and opponents of the bill have until 30th January to present the petitions upon which their opposition is founded.

(b) *First Reading*. If the Examiner endorses the petition 'Standing Orders complied with', the bill is presented, laid on the Table of the appropriate House, deemed to have been read a first time and ordered to be read a second time. This stage is purely formal.

(c) *Second Reading*. Between first and second readings there must be at least 4 and not more than 7 clear days, arranged for by the Agents for the bill. If the bill is 'unopposed', it can be taken after prayers as 'Unopposed private business'. If it is opposed, the Chairman of Ways and Means selects a night for it to be debated at 7 p.m. as Opposed Private Business. Most bills go through this stage without opposition, but a few each session have to be debated, either the Government or interests objecting.

Unlike a public bill, the second reading of a private bill does not determine its desirability but merely that, given the facts stated in the Preamble to be true, the bill is not objectionable to the Government. Occasionally a matter of principle is involved. For instance, the Whips may have to be put on to defeat the bill if the Government thinks that it goes beyond the scope of a private measure and should be a public one. More often, however, opposition comes from interests who want to air grievances or delay the bill. On their behalf M.P.s oppose it from the floor of the House — but strictly on national grounds!

(d) *Committee stage.* After second reading, the bill is referred to the Committee of Selection, whose subsequent action depends upon whether the bill is opposed or unopposed. Unopposed bills go to the Committee for Unopposed Bills, where the proceedings are brief and informal. The Committee's main duty is to see that all standing orders have been complied with and public rights not unduly infringed. Opposed bills are formed into groups and re- ferred to a Private Bills Committee consisting of four members of the House of Commons or five of the Lords. This is the really important stage.

A Private Bill Committee is more like a court of law than a committee of the House. The battle is between the Promoters, who have to make out the case for the bill, and the opponents; both are usually represented by counsel. The Committee acts as referee and jury. The proceedings are semi-judicial, with evidence being heard on oath from witnesses subject to cross-examination. The first task of the Committee is to determine whether the bill is in the public interest, for second reading has merely indicated that the House considers there is a case worth examining. Any government department affected may state its case. The Committee bases its decision on the weight of evidence, the public interest in general, and the standing orders of the House. Its decisions are embodied in legislative form, either by finding the Preamble not proved (which amounts to a rejection), or by finding it proved and allow- ing it to proceed, with or without amendment. The Committee calls in the parties and the clauses are agreed to, amended or rejected. The final bill is reported to the House.

Obviously, the above procedure is expensive. Not only is there the cost of the preliminaries and the fees of counsel, but the House charges fees to the Promoters and opponents. Hence it is usual for discussions to take place before the committee stage so that amendments to clauses can be made to meet the objections of both the Government and private interests. So successful are these preliminary negotiations that, although originally most bills are opposed, by the time they reach the Committee about half go through without opposition.

(e) *Consideration stage.* An amended bill has to lie on the Table of the House for three clear days before it can be considered, but unamended bills are ordered to be read a third time forthwith. The House can amend a bill, provided such an amendment could have been proposed in committee; but usually the bill goes through without amendment or debate.

(f) *Third Reading.* This stage is very similar to that of a public bill. Only verbal amendments are possible and the House finally approves all the alterations made since second reading.

(g) *House of Lord's amendments and the Royal Assent.* A bill is reported to the House of Lords (or to the Commons if it originated in the Lords). Any amendments follow the same procedure as with a public bill.

The Royal Assent is formal and is given in the same form as for a public bill, but the Act is printed in a separate volume of statutes.

Bills originating in the House of Lords go through the same processes, with a few minor differences.

The private-bill procedure has certain advantages. In the first place, it does not make a heavy demand on Parliament, for only the few members concerned with Examination and Committee have to devote much time to it. Secondly, the quasi-judicial procedure is free from political influences. Thirdly, the cost, though heavy, does encourage concessions, so that a wide basis of agreement is usually possible.

PROVISIONAL ORDER CONFIRMATION BILLS

Many progressive local authorities promoted private bills in order to extend general powers granted by Parliament. But in doing so they were involved in heavy expense. Hence, from 1870, the 'Provisional Order' system was introduced to provide a simpler, shorter and cheaper procedure. It allowed most government departments to issue local authorities with Provisional Orders. In scope, these are practically private bills, but they are termed 'provisional' since they cannot be acted upon until they have received Parliament's approval, given in a 'Provisional Order Confirmation Bill'. The procedure is as follows.

A local authority (the 'Applicants') applies for the issue of a Provisional Order to a government department (the 'Promoters'). The purpose of the Provisional Order has to be advertised locally and in the London Gazette, and a preliminary local enquiry is conducted by the department concerned. If the findings are satisfactory, a Provisional Order is made. Orders are then usually assembled in batches, and a bill covering them is introduced by the minister as a public bill but at the time of Private Business. Between first and second readings the bill is referred to Examiners who report whether standing orders have been complied with. If their report is satisfactory, the bill is ordered to be read a second time on the following day.

The committee stage of the bill is similar to that of a private bill. Bills are divided into 'Opposed' and 'Unopposed', the majority coming into the latter category. Even where a bill is opposed, the chances of its being defeated are slight, since a government department is unlikely to make a Provisional Order to which Parliament will object. Nevertheless, with all Orders the task of protecting the individual from unjustifiable encroachment by a local authority is shifted to a department, with Parliament preserving the possibility of appeal to its own authority (see chapter 21).

For Scotland, the Secretary of State for Scotland has wide powers of issuing Provisional Orders under the Private Legislation Procedure (Scotland) Act, 1936. Today this system, somewhat simpler than its counterpart just described, is used almost exclusively in Scotland for private legislation.

SPECIAL PROCEDURE ORDERS

The Provisional Order procedure has been largely supplemented by the Special Procedure Order system. This was introduced in 1945 and is now governed by the Statutory Orders (Special Procedure) Act, 1965. It aims at quicker and cheaper preliminary approval of those departmental Orders which give effect to decisions of national policy but which might affect private rights, e.g. the amalgamation of two water undertakings or the compulsory acquisition of land for planning purposes. Since 1962, however, these Orders have not been used for minister's statutory powers to amend local Acts, Provisional Orders (which are subject to greater scrutiny) having replaced them. The persons affected by a Special Procedure Order have to be notified and, if necessary, a local inquiry is held. The Order is then laid before Parliament by the minister for 21 days, during which it is subject to objection by petition. Any such petition is referred to the Chairman of Ways and Means and to the Lord Chairman of Committees who consider such Orders jointly.

The Chairmen report to the House whether petitions against the Order have been presented and, if so, whether they comply with the Act and with Standing Orders. They also state whether the petition is a general objection against the main purpose of the Order or only a petition for amendment.

There then follows a period of 21 days in which either House can annul the Order. Then, if no valid petition has been received, it automatically comes into operation.

If there is a petition against the Order, and the Order has not been annulled by either House, the Order is referred to a Joint Committee, though, in the case of a general objection, the House may decide its fate. The Joint Committee reports back to the House, recommending that the Order be accepted, not approved or amended, as the case may be. The minister has to decide whether to accept amendments, withdraw the Order, or confirm it in the form of a public bill.

SUGGESTED READING

Lord Campion, *An Introduction to the Procedure of the House of Commons* (3rd Ed., Macmillan, 1958), Chapters 6 and 9.

Sir Ivor Jennings, *Parliament* (2nd Ed., C.U.P., 1969), Chapters 8, 11, 13 and 14.

12

The Control of Finance

'This country produced no Voltaire or Rousseau or
Montesquieu whose writings provided inspiration and
philosophical basis for the great movements towards
freedom in France and in many other countries. The
same end was achieved in England through the pursuit
of strictly practical financial aims.'

PAUL EINZIG: *The Control of the Purse*

INTRODUCTION

There can be found no clearer expression of the relationship
between the executive and the legislature in the British constitution
than in the field of public finance. On the one hand, the Government
proposes; on the other, Parliament criticises. The Government's
proposals cover the raising of the necessary revenue and the
ways in which the revenue shall be spent. Parliament's criticisms
range over the nature of the taxes which are levied, the desirability
of the purposes for which revenue is raised, and the possibility of
any wastefulness in the expenditure.

The financial control, now exercised exclusively by the House of
Commons, came about in three stages. The first covers the period
down to the middle of the 17th century. The Commons was
originally summoned to grant supplies to the King in his hour of
need. By skilful exploitation of this power, the House was able to
establish and extend its own authority and to secure redress of
grievances. If the King was not prepared to grant its requests, his
alternative was to prorogue Parliament and manage without the
aids he sought or to impose taxes on his own authority.

The latter practice, followed by many early Kings, violated the
fundamental principle that Parliament alone could grant Supply,
and Magna Carta protested against it. But as the power of Parliament
increased, monarchs generally refrained from infringing its
exclusive right to levy additional taxes. Thus James I was able to
manage without Parliament by raising money by such dubious

methods as selling titles, granting monopolies, creating boroughs, and reviving forgotten laws in order to impose heavy fines. Charles I, however, was prepared to provoke a clash, claiming that he could impose taxes by virtue of his prerogative. The protest framed in the Petition of Right was largely ineffective; it was the deliberate stand made by John Hampden over the payment of Ship Money which really forced the issue. The Civil War decided conclusively that sole authority in the field of taxation rested with Parliament, and the principle was reiterated in statute form in the Bill of Rights, 1689.

Until the middle of the 17th century, however, the House, when granting finance, merely passed a bill of 'aids and supplies' for the Crown in exchange for the King's promise to redress grievances. Thus, while the Commons empowered the King to levy taxes, it had no control over the proceeds of those taxes and so could exert no positive influence on the details of the King's policy. Hence, the second stage of financial control begins with the adoption of the procedure of appropriation, that is, the allocation by the Commons of supplies to various items of expenditure. In 1665 the House of Commons appropriated the proceeds of a tax to the war with Holland and, from William III's reign onwards, appropriation became the regular practice. As the expenses of government increased, so the King had to rely increasingly on supplies granted by Parliament. Thus parliamentary control became more effective and, when George III surrendered his revenue from Crown lands, the whole of the national revenue was provided by Parliament, to whom the Government now had to apply for all its funds.

In the third stage, the House of Commons achieved exclusive control over finance. The Commons had always claimed some priority over the Lords in the field of finance. Thus, during the reign of Charles I, the enacting formula for bills of aids and supplies was introduced — the Commons granted a tax, 'by and with the advice and consent of the Lords.' Moreover, resolutions in 1671 and 1678 insisted that the Lords had no right to alter aids and supplies, and claimed that bills granting them should originate in the Commons. Nevertheless, the Lords still retained the power to reject, a right recognised in the dispute over the Paper Duties Repeal Bill, 1860. Thereafter the Commons ensured that the power would not really be exercised by including all its financial proposals for the year in one bill. When the Lords did reject the budget in

1909, the Parliament Act completely deprived it of the right to touch a money bill. Indeed, the privilege of the Commons goes further, for now discussion of financial business must first take place there and its proposals are embodied in statutes without amendment by the Upper Chamber.

PRESENT-DAY PRINCIPLES

The early principles of financial procedure — that the Government first requests supplies which are then granted by the Commons after redress of grievances — are still embodied in modern practice. Indeed, many are now prescribed in the standing orders of the House: (i) any proposal to spend money can only be initiated by a minister of the Crown (S.O. 89); (ii) twenty-nine days are allotted for the business of granting Supply (S.O. 18).

There are good reasons, apart from continuity, for following the traditional practice. The insistence on a minister recommending expenditure ensures that the same persons who propose to spend must also suggest how the money is to be raised. Again, the allocation of a specific number of days for considering Supply guarantees that all members have an opportunity to criticise policy. (On questions of finance the Government may be subject to attack even from its own back-benchers.) Finally, it is through its financial procedure that the Commons exercises its ultimate authority over the Government. By authorising the greater part of expenditure and the largest single item of revenue (the income tax) for only one year at a time, the House ensures that policy has to be justified at least once a year, while by its refusal to grant Supply it could make it impossible for a Government which had lost the confidence of the House to continue the administration.

TABLE 2: *Financial procedure—Session November, 1974 to October, 1975*

Month	
1974 November	Preparation of Estimates by departments.
	Beginning of parliamentary session. Estimates for financial year ending 31st March, 1976 and for four years ahead submitted by departments to Treasury at least by the middle of December. Provisionally approved within a month.
December	Consolidated Fund (No. 3) Act, 1974 passed to authorise withdrawals from the Consolidated Fund for the Supplementary Estimates. (It does not *appropriate*.)

1975 February   House commences consideration of Estimates and
                votes sums to be expended (chiefly for Service
                Departments).
      March   Resolution for a Consolidated Fund (No. 1) Bill,
                which:
                (i) Grants supplies for the first 5 months of the
                    financial year 1975–6 by:
                    (a) Civil 'votes on account';
                    (b) Votes for pay and wages, etc. of the
                        Navy, Army and Air Force for the
                        coming financial year. (These are
                        usually large enough to cover all ex-
                        penditure until August by 'virement',
                        and so no votes on account are required
                        for Defence.)
                (ii) Condones Excess Expenditure in the financial
                     year 1973–4.
                (iii) Approves Supplementary Estimates for year
                      1974–5.
                Consolidated Fund (No. 1) Bill passed.
                Budget submitted to the House of Commons.
                Budget Resolutions adopted; these have the tem-
                porary force of law and form the basis of the
                Finance Act, 1975, passed in August.
                House continues consideration of the Estimates.
      August   Consolidated Fund Act, usually known as the
                Appropriation Act, 1975, passed. It *appropriates*
                money previously authorised:
                (i) Appropriates Excess Expenditure 1973–4;
                (ii) Appropriates Supplementary Estimates 1974–5
                (iii) Appropriates grants for financial year 1975–6
                      and authorises the issue of money from
                      the Consolidated Fund;
                (iv) Authorises virement between the Votes for
                     Defence.
                Finance Act passed.

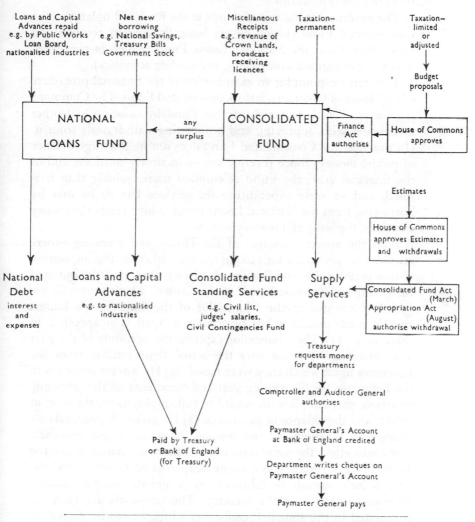

Loans and Capital
Advances repaid
e.g. by Public Works
Loan Board,
nationalised industries

Net new
borrowing
e.g. National Savings,
Treasury Bills
Government Stock

Miscellaneous
Receipts
e.g. revenue of
Crown Lands,
broadcast
receiving
licences

Taxation—
permanent

Taxation—
limited
or
adjusted

Budget
proposals

NATIONAL

LOANS FUND

any
surplus

CONSOLIDATED

FUND

Finance
Act
authorises

House of Commons
approves

Estimates

House of Commons
approves Estimates
and withdrawals

National
Debt
interest
and
expenses

Loans and Capital
Advances
e.g. to nationalised
industries

Consolidated Fund
Standing Services
e.g. Civil list,
judges' salaries,
Civil Contingencies Fund

Supply
Services

Consolidated Fund Act
(March)
Appropriation Act
(August)
authorise withdrawal

Treasury
requests money
for departments

Comptroller and Auditor General
authorises

Paymaster General's Account
at Bank of England credited

Paid by Treasury
or Bank of England
(for Treasury)

Department writes cheques on
Paymaster General's Account

Paymaster General pays

NOTES 1 House of Commons examines each year (a) tax adjustments (b) Supply Services
2 Any surplus of the Consolidated Fund is transferred to the National Loans Fund

FIG. 4. *The process of government revenue and expenditure.*

OUTLINE OF PROCEDURE

The government has two accounts at the Bank of England — the Consolidated Fund (which covers basically current receipts and expenditure) and the National Loans Fund (which is concerned with the government's borrowing and lending activities).

The starting-point for an examination of the financial procedure of the House of Commons is the Consolidated Fund. The Commons is concerned with replenishing this Fund by taxation and other means and with approving and authorising withdrawals from it. (In practice, the Consolidated Fund does not hold a large balance of public money. Since revenue comes in slowly until the end of the financial year, the Fund is emptied more quickly than it is filled, and so early expenditure on services has to be met by borrowing from the National Loans Fund, which raises the money chiefly by the issue of Treasury Bills.)

Both the ancient practice of the House and standing orders require that proposals for raising money, either by the imposition of new taxes or the modification of existing ones, must be initiated by a minister acting on behalf of the Crown. These proposals are mainly contained in the Chancellor of the Exchequer's budget speech, made usually at the beginning of April. The speech is in three parts. (1) The Chancellor explains the accounts of the past year, showing how and why the actual figures differ from the Estimates upon which they were based. (2) He directs attention to the Estimates for the coming year and comments on the economic situation, particularly with regard to full employment, the level of prices, and the balance of payments. (3) He gives his proposals for changes in taxation and the reasons for them. These proposals come into effect the same day, unless otherwise stated. Since the Budget is now regarded as a major weapon of economic policy, the Chancellor's speech is followed by a debate on the general economic situation of the country. The proposals are then incorporated in the annual Finance Act which has to be passed by 5th August.

Expenditure from the Consolidated Fund is of two kinds.

(1) *Consolidated Fund Services*

Payments on these services do not require annual parliamentary approval and are therefore known as 'charges on the Consolidated

Fund'. They are chiefly for services which it is considered should be removed from possible political controversy, e.g. the Civil List, salaries of the Speaker, the Leader of Her Majesty's Opposition, High Court judges and the Comptroller and Auditor General. Charges on the Consolidated Fund can be amended only by a new Act of Parliament, unlike payments for the Supply services, which can be terminated simply by omitting them from the Appropriation Act.

(2) Supply Services

With these services, supplies are granted by Parliament only for the current financial year and are based on the 'Estimates'.

The *Estimates* are detailed statements of the expected sums of money which the spending departments will require during the coming year and a few years ahead. They are prepared by the department and passed to the Treasury for examination by December. In their final form, they are submitted to the House of Commons in the following February or March, being presented in two groups — (1) Defence, (2) Civil and Revenue Departments. The last group is divided into ten classes. Each class is divided into votes, each vote into heads, and each head into items. The House of Commons has twenty-nine days to debate the Estimates, Supplementary Estimates and Excess Votes. The annual Appropriation Bill is introduced after the last Supply day towards the end of July and then passes, with one (all-night) second reading debate and a formal committee stage and third reading, within a few days. It authorises the withdrawal of the necessary money from the Consolidated Fund.

The financial procedure of the House of Commons is complicated by the fact that, while the session usually extends from November to November, the financial year runs from 1st April to 31st March. Thus the House has not considered all the Estimates by 1st April when money to cover the new financial year is required. Consequently, '*Votes on Account*' have to be voted before 31st March to provide sums sufficient to tide over the Civil and Revenue Departments until August, when supplies for the year will be granted in the Appropriation Act. [A vote on account is not necessary for Defence since 'virement' (that is, transfer) between votes is authorised. Hence, so long as one vote has been approved, the money can be used to meet expenditure on other votes until these have been approved in August.] The amounts authorised by votes on account are deducted from the annual appropriation grant.

In addition, during the previous financial year a department may have overspent the supplies granted to it on a particular vote. Such excess expenditure is first considered by the Public Accounts Committee and then passed by the House as an 'Excess Vote', being finally sanctioned in the Consolidated Fund Act of the March following the financial year in which the overspending occurred.

Since the Estimates are drawn up five to six months before the financial year to which they apply, a department may easily underestimate. *Supplementary Estimates* are usually authorised in the March Consolidated Fund Bill, but the money is appropriated in the main Appropriation Act of the following financial year. Supplementary Estimates may also be needed for new or unforeseen expenditure. If this occurs before July, it can be provided for in the Appropriation Act, but otherwise an additional Consolidated Fund Bill is required. In the meantime supplies must be obtained until this bill is passed. These can be authorised in a variety of ways: (*a*) by the Treasury using sums already authorised by a Consolidated Fund Act (Public Accounts and Charges Act, 1891); (*b*) by drawing from the Civil Contingencies Fund, created to provide for temporary unforeseen expenditure; (*c*) by virement (between votes in the case of Defence, and between heads in the case of Civil and Revenue Departments), with the Treasury's approval and provided the service falls within an existing vote and savings can be made on other heads. Expenditure on items can be transferred at the department's discretion.

Expenditure is voted by the House and the necessary withdrawals authorised in the Consolidated Fund Acts. The Act passed in March deals chiefly with the votes on account; that passed in August is the main Act and, since it deals with the appropriations, is known as the Consolidated Fund (Appropriation) Act. There may be a later Act to cover Supplementary Estimates.

THE HOUSE OF COMMONS' CONTROL OVER EXPENDITURE

If supervision of expenditure is to be effective, it must ensure that spending is: (1) desirable; (2) economic, in the sense that it is not wasteful; (3) in accordance with the authority given. How far does the control of the Commons conform to these principles?

(1) *Desirability of expenditure*

The extent to which expenditure is desirable is largely a matter of opinion. This is expressed by the electorate when they vote for a particular party, for most of its proposals will involve spending. The Cabinet decides when these measures shall be introduced, and they will then be debated in Parliament. In approving them, Parliament automatically accepts the expenditure involved.

Where policy can be implemented without legislation, there is still an opportunity for general criticism by the House of Commons in the Estimates debates. Indeed, in the early stages of a controversial measure, policy may well be debated twice — once during the passage of the bill and again in the debates when the necessary Estimates have to be voted.

(2) *Economy*

The original intention of the Estimates was to enable Parliament to see that Government expenditure was not wasteful. Thus the Estimates give detailed information. Not only are they broken down into votes, heads and items, but, for purposes of comparison, the previous year's Estimates are also given. Before being submitted to Parliament, they are carefully scrutinised by the Treasury. Any increase over the current year has to be justified, either on the grounds of increased costs or through a change in Government policy. These powers of scrutiny are derived not from the Crown, but through Parliament, and in this respect, therefore, the Treasury can be regarded as supplementing the work of Parliament. The Treasury can criticise and even disallow any item if it considers expenditure on it to be excessive or unjustified. This may easily lead to a dispute with the department concerned, and if it cannot be settled at a lower level the Cabinet may have to decide. Moreover, the Estimates of a department are subject to the Chancellor of the Exchequer's budget decisions and his proposals may involve a reduction of expenditure, as occurred with the defence cuts announced in December 1974. In effect, Treasury control of expenditure is generally efficient but it may fail to identify waste, e.g. over-charging the Ministry of Aviation on contracts by Ferranti (1963) and Bristol-Siddeley (1967).

But what of direct control by the House of Commons? In February the Estimates are submitted to the House of Commons and discussion on them is spread over twenty-nine days. In addition to being less formal than the debates of the House, the selection of the votes to be discussed is left to the Opposition, which chooses according to the departments it wishes to criticise, and to the specialist critics, such as ex-ministers, at its disposal.

Yet, although the Estimates are presented in detail, economy in spending on the various items is not really discussed. The reasons for this are:

(a) A body of 635 members is too large a body for effective discussion of details of expenditure.

(b) The twenty-nine days which, in addition to discussion of the main Estimates, have to cover excess votes, Supplementary Estimates and the reports of the Public Accounts and Expenditure Committees, give too short a time for adequate examination. The result is that many votes are not considered at all. The position is aggravated by the fact that, over the years, the Supply days have come to be used not for truly financial purposes but as a means of controlling the administration. The Opposition chooses the votes to be debated, its motive in doing so being political. Consequently Government back-benchers experience difficulty in having their own preferences discussed when these have no political significance.

(c) The Estimates are too complicated for the average M.P., usually a layman in accounting matters, to understand.

(d) The House starts its deliberations too late to make any parliamentary check really effective.

(e) Since both parties are intent on securing electoral support, usually neither will suggest economy by curtailing a service, as this would probably be unpopular politically. A past Chancellor of the Exchequer, Mr. Austen Chamberlain, has said: 'It is quite true that one section of members calls for economy here, and another section calls for economy there, and so on over the whole sphere, but at any given point there is always a majority for spending more, not less.'

(f) Much of the expenditure is by nature automatic, e.g. central government grants to local authorities, grants in aid to such bodies as the University Grants Committee, old age pensions which are dependent on the number of retired persons; over such expenditure, Parliament has very little control.

(g) It does not identify failures sufficiently early to prevent further wasteful expenditure (e.g. the cancellation of the TSR2 supersonic bomber in 1965 meant a loss of approximately £200 million).

While, therefore, the Commons can discover where the money goes, it cannot suggest where economies should be made, and stop the money going there. Its defects prevent it from examining details of expenditure; and so it merely criticises the policy underlying the Estimates.

All the same, its discussions are of value. First, they force the Government to justify its policy on matters deliberately chosen by the Opposition, although often the debate is merely a repetition of arguments heard many times before. Secondly, the debates draw the public's attention to the main political issues of the day. Thirdly, they provide the private member, if there is time, with an opportunity to get into debate. Although he is expected to follow the main line of discussion, he can often use an item as the excuse for a short speech on his own pet hobby-horse.

Thus the House of Commons has to rely largely on the Treasury's watchfulness to ensure economy. But Treasury control is no real substitute for parliamentary control. Hence, beginning in 1912, the Commons appointed a standing select committee, the Estimates Committee, to examine the Estimates. In 1971 this committee was re-styled the *Expenditure Committee* with powers to scrutinise all public expenditure rather than merely the Supply Estimates. Unlike its predecessor, it can consider policy behind the Estimates. In particular it can investigate closely long-term projections of public expenditure and, where justified, press strongly for reductions before taxpayer's money is finally committed.

The Committee consists of 49 members organised into eight functional sub-committees for Industry, Transport, Agriculture, Education, Housing, Law, Defence and Foreign Affairs. It can invite Ministers to give evidence before it, appoint outside experts to supply technical information, send for persons, papers and records, hold meetings outside Westminster, and admit the public during the examination of witnesses.

Since it will also have a better call on staff, this new Expenditure Committee should prove far more effective than the old Estimates Committee (provided of course that the House of Commons provides time for considering its reports). Indeed it has been suggested that the Committee might be so developed that there would be no need to extend the Specialist Committees.

(3) *In accordance with the authority given*

At the end of the financial year, each department must show that it has spent no money beyond that authorised for the purpose by the Appropriation Act. Parliament's check is two-fold: first, it watches the issue of money to the department; secondly, it submits the department to a searching audit.

Any expenditure by a department necessitates the withdrawal of sums from the Exchequer Account at the Bank of England. The department applies to the Treasury for sums to be placed at its disposal, outlining the reasons for its request. When the application has been approved by the Comptroller and Auditor General, the money is transferred to the accounts of the department. These are kept by the Paymaster-General who, acting as cashier for the Government, makes the actual payments from his cash balance as and when requested by the department and debits its accounts accordingly.

In order to ensure a thorough audit on its behalf, Parliament requires that the spending accounts are kept in the same form as the Estimates, and has set up its own institutions, the Comptroller and Auditor General and the Public Accounts Committee.

The Comptroller and Auditor General, first appointed by Mr. Gladstone in 1866, is an officer of the House of Commons, having his salary charged on the Consolidated Fund and being removable only by Address of both Houses of Parliament. He has two main functions: (1) to control the issue of money from the Consolidated Fund by checking that the Treasury's demands are in accordance with the sums authorised by Parliament in the Appropriation Act; (2) to audit the accounts of the departments to ensure that money has been spent only on the purposes for which it was voted by Parliament. Since he is an officer of the House of Commons, he reports direct to that House, and his report forms the basis for the work of the Public Accounts Committee. This is possible because the Comptroller and Auditor General now goes beyond a mere audit, being encouraged by the Public Accounts Committee to draw attention to any unnecessarily extravagant or irregular items in the accounts of a department.

The Public Accounts Committee was first set up by Mr. Gladstone in 1861. It consists of fifteen M.P.s, most of whom have an interest in public finance. They are so chosen as to reflect the size of the parties in the House of Commons and, by convention, their Chairman is a member of the Opposition, often an ex-holder of the offices of Financial or Economic Secretary to the Treasury. The existing Financial Secretary to the Treasury and the Chairman of the Estimates Committee are also regular members. In the work of this Committee, the Comptroller and Auditor General performs a leading role, conferring with the Chairman before a meeting and always being present or represented when evidence is taken. Close contact is also maintained with the Treasury. Since it is an expert committee, party politics do not enter into its deliberations. Its duties are:

(1) to examine the Appropriation Accounts in order to ensure that no sums have been expended on purposes not authorised by Parliament or in excess of any authorisation;

(2) to report on any excess vote presented and, in the case of the Defence Estimates, on the application of surpluses on certain votes to cover deficiencies on other votes;

(3) to consider the reports of the Comptroller and Auditor General;

(4) to report to Parliament on the above matters;

(5) to make recommendations from time to time for the improvement of the form and method of the national accounts.

In carrying out its functions, the Committee has power to send for persons, papers and records. The Permanent Secretary of a department, in his role of Accounting Officer, may be summoned before it, and, as Lord Morrison points out, he can always remind a minister of this possibility should he be asked to spend money for any purpose for which his statutory authority is at all doubtful. Although strictly it is an audit check, and takes place after the expenditure has been incurred, its investigations have a far-reaching effect, for 'the effectiveness of the Committee is to be measured not by the attention its reports receive in Parliament, but by the attention which they receive in the departments' (Sir Ivor Jennings: *Parliament*).

Through the collaboration of the Treasury, the Comptroller and Auditor General, and the Public Accounts Committee, the House of Commons ensures most effectively that the departments spend only in accordance with the authority given them.

SUGGESTED READING

Lord Campion, *An Introduction to the Procedure of the House of Commons* (3rd Ed., Macmillan, 1958), Chapter 8.
Paul Einzig, *The Control of the Purse* (Secker and Warburg, 1959).
Sir Ivor Jennings, *Parliament* (2nd Ed., C.U.P., 1969), Chapter 9.

III

THE EXECUTIVE

I3

The Monarchy

'When the people cheer the Queen and sing her praises,
they are also cheering our free democracy.'
LORD MORRISON: *Government and Parliament*

I. INTRODUCTION: THE LAW RELATING TO
THE MONARCHY

No other institution illustrates more clearly the peculiar way in
which the British constitution has developed than the 'monarchy'.
While continuity is evinced in the fact that Queen Elizabeth II can
point to direct descent from King Egbert, adaptation is shown in
the way the Sovereign's functions have been moulded over the
centuries by changing circumstances.

Originally, occupation of the throne of England was enjoyed by
virtue of military might, underwritten by formal election in the
Witenagemot. Hence, William I based his claim to rule the whole of
England on the grounds that he had been elected and crowned at
Westminster, asserting that he had been the legal King of England
since the death of Edward the Confessor. Eventually the right to
reign was put on a common-law basis, making the succession to the
throne hereditary and women eligible.

The law relating to the monarch has been developed both by
convention and statute. Conventions have been concerned chiefly
with the Sovereign's common-law powers. But occasionally
statutes have been necessary to modify or supplement the law
where circumstances have changed. The more important of such
modifications are:

(1) No monarch may be a Roman Catholic or married to a
Roman Catholic (Bill of Rights, 1689).

(2) The title and succession to the throne is derived from the
Act of Settlement, 1701.

(3) The duration of Parliament is independent of the death of
the Sovereign (Representation of the People Act, 1867).

(4) The holding of office under the Crown is not affected by the death of the Sovereign (Demise of the Crown Act, 1901).

(5) Where the Sovereign is under 18 years of age, the royal functions are to be exercised by a Regent, who is the next person over 21 years in line of succession, or 18 years if the heir-apparent. But the Duke of Edinburgh will be Regent if one is necessary for a child of Queen Elizabeth II.

In the event of illness (not amounting to total incapacity) or absence from the United Kingdom, the Sovereign may appoint Counsellors of State to exercise such of the royal functions as may be conferred on them by letters patent. Such Counsellors must be the wife or husband of the Sovereign, the four persons next in line of succession to the Crown not disqualified from being Regent, and Queen Elizabeth, the Queen Mother (Regency Acts 1937–53).

(6) *The Civil List*. Originally, the King paid all the expenses of government out of his feudal revenue, but this soon became insufficient and Parliament had to sanction new taxes (see page 20). Although Parliament had fought the Stuarts' attempt to raise Supply by the sale of monopolies and illegal taxation, it recognised after the Restoration the necessity of finding the King new sources of revenue to cover the expenses of government. Much of his feudal revenue had disappeared, while the functions of government had increased. Hence, Charles II was granted the proceeds of the duties on spirits, cider and beer for life, and these became part of his regular income, or what came to be known during the reign of William III as the 'Civil List'.

But this still remained insufficient for the purposes of government, especially as a standing army and navy had to be paid for. The difference was mostly made up by annual Supply grants for particular services, and soon these Supply grants exceeded in total the Civil List. Even so, George III could not pay the expenses of that part of government which the Civil List was expected to cover, and so he surrendered the rents from royal estates and his hereditary excise duties in exchange for a larger Civil List. This unsatisfactory situation was brought to an end in 1830 when a Select Committee recommended that 'all expenditure not directly affecting the dignity and state of the Crown and the personal comfort of Their Majesties' should be removed from the Civil List.

Today, therefore, the Civil List covers only the personal income of the Sovereign, together with the expenses of the Royal Household and any allowance which Parliament may make for other members of the Royal Family. The other costs of government are either charged on the Consolidated Fund or voted annually. The Civil List is considered by a Select Committee on the accession of the Sovereign, and its recommendation is embodied in a statute. The Civil List Act, 1972, granted the Queen a Civil List of £980,000 and the Duke of Edinburgh £60,000. Such sums are charged directly on the Consolidated Fund in order to avoid an annual review.

While statutes have been concerned mainly with changes of a technical nature, conventions have come into being to modify the functions of the monarch in accordance with political developments. Such conventions are of fundamental constitutional importance and are concerned chiefly with the exercise of the royal prerogative, since basically this still rests on the common law. Other conventions, however, govern the functions fulfilled by the Queen as Head of State and Head of the Commonwealth (see below).

II. THE PREROGATIVE

DEVELOPMENT OF THE PREROGATIVE

An early king had three main functions: he was a figure of sacred significance, embodying in his person the prosperity of his people; he was a war-lord; he was a law-giver. All three can be discerned in the demand of the Israelites to Samuel: 'Nay; but we will have a king over us; that we also may be like all the nations; and that our king may judge us, and go out before us, and fight our battles' (I Samuel, Ch. 8, vv. 19, 20). His mystical significance arose largely through superstition, but his other two functions resulted from the continual challenge to his authority both without and within the realm. Consequently his position rested on his military power in defence of the State and his ability to ensure law and order internally. Government, therefore, was the responsibility of the king.

In England, this responsibility became manifest under the Normans, and the country was organised to fulfil it. As part of his feudal system, William I developed the idea that the holding of land entailed the acceptance of certain responsibilities. His authority for government, therefore, rested not only on his military power but also upon the moral obligations resulting from his ownership of all the land in England. It was thus a personal authority, evidence of which can still be found in all three branches of our constitution — the Queen approves legislation, all the ministers of the Crown are 'Her Majesty's Ministers', and justice is administered by 'Her Majesty's Judges'.

In order to fulfil his general function of government, it was necessary that the King should exercise more detailed powers of initiating and controlling policy. As a result of the stability which the Normans brought to English affairs, these powers were in use continuously and thus became accepted as part of the common law, being referred to in course of time as 'the Prerogative'. In the first place, therefore, the prerogative was based, as Blackstone says, 'on that special pre-eminence which the King hath, over and above all other persons, and out of the ordinary course of the common law, in right of his regal dignity.'

Although these powers conferred on the Sovereign were naturally ill-defined, from the beginning there were recognised limitations: decisions on grave and important matters could be taken only after consultation with the great men of the realm; taxation could be levied only with the consent of the Common Council; justice had to be equally available to all persons and administered in a legal manner. Such limitations were observed by the Norman kings, but later monarchs tended to ignore them.

Before the development of Parliament's authority, little could be done to check the King's abuse of power. Theoretically, since the prerogative was recognised as having legal validity, the King's powers could be tested and defined in the Courts. In practice, however, this process was unsatisfactory, since the independence of the judiciary was not established until the early 18th century. Thus, as late as the reigns of James I and Charles I, the courts, in interpreting the law, consistently found in the King's favour whenever his use of prerogative powers was challenged. The chief remedy, therefore, lay in petitioning the King. Where this proved ineffective, the ultimate sanction was direct action bordering on revolution. It was such an extreme course that the barons took in 1215 when John was forced to seal Magna Carta, a constitutional document giving greater definition to the King's powers.

The growth in the power of Parliament and the development of the process of legislating by statute provided another weapon for curtailing the Sovereign's prerogative. Not only was it possible to criticise the use of his powers but, Parliament claimed, it could, if it chose, limit them by statute. The acceptance of such a thesis would obviously end any 'absolute' prerogative which the King might have enjoyed. While the Tudor monarchs were careful not to force the issue, and retreated skilfully whenever Parliament could not be cajoled into submission, the Stuarts preferred to challenge Parliament's claim directly. It was not denied that the common law was inferior to statute law passed by Parliament. What the King claimed was that his prerogative powers did not rest on the common law, but were part of the Sovereign's 'divine right' and as such could not be restricted. Such a contention could not be resolved by legal processes. It had now become a political issue as to whether Parliament or the King should be the ultimate authority in matters of government, and it took a Civil War to decide the dispute. But the nature of the Restoration was such that little attempt was made to formalise the King's position. This did not come about until the indiscretions of James II forced the Glorious Revolution of 1688. Certain of the King's prerogative powers were then limited by the Bill of Rights, 1689, while William and Mary, in accepting the throne, had to consent to govern 'according to the Statutes in Parliament agreed on'. It was thus conclusively shown that the prerogative powers retained by the King were based, not on divine right, but on popular consent, and could therefore be limited, either directly or indirectly, by Act of Parliament. The prerogative as it exists today is thus 'the residue of discretionary or arbitrary authority, which at any given time is legally left in the hands of the Crown' (Professor A. V. Dicey).

Even after the Bill of Rights, the King still enjoyed many prerogative powers, and the manner in which he interpreted them depended largely on his own personality. William III chose mixed ministries; Queen Anne vetoed the Scotch Militia Bill in 1707; George III held up Catholic emancipation. But the position was radically changed by the Reform Act, 1832. Now the electorate was sovereign. Any attempt by the King, therefore, to take an active part in politics could quite easily bring him into conflict with the electorate, thereby endangering the continuation of the monarchy.

Consequently, the Sovereign, in exercising his prerogative powers, has had to observe two main rules. (a) In choosing his ministers, he must act impartially and follow the conventions dictated by the party system (see page 58). (*b*) Wherever possible, he must act on the advice of a responsible minister, usually the Prime Minister. Observance of these rules shields the Sovereign from any political consequences of his action, for when Parliament wishes to criticise the particular use of a prerogative power it is the responsible minister who is attacked. Such was Lord Esher's advice to George V in 1913: 'The Sovereign cannot act un-constitutionally so long as he acts on the advice of a minister supported by a majority in the House of Commons. Ministerial responsibility is the safeguard of the monarchy. Without it, the throne could not stand for long amid the gusts of political conflict and the storm of political passion' (Esher Papers, quoted Sir Ivor Jennings: *Cabinet Government*).

In order to strengthen this idea that the Sovereign is above politics, a distinction is often drawn between the Crown and the monarchy. The Crown is regarded as an impersonal, legal concept representing the total of all the powers, including the prerogative, exercised by the executive, that is, by ministers and their depart-ments. The monarch is a person who is not accountable for the exercise of his powers, since Ministers of the Crown are respon-sible. (The distinction is parallel to that between the Crown Lands, owned by the State, and the personal estates of the Queen, such as Sandringham and Balmoral.)

In practice, however, the doctrine is not completely acceptable except by contending that a minister can be held responsible for every action of the Sovereign. As early as 1834, Sir Robert Peel considered this to be the position. Although he had been in Italy when Lord Melbourne's Government was dismissed by William IV, he shielded the King by declaring to a hostile House of Com-mons: 'I am, by my acceptance of office, responsible for the re-moval of the late Government.' In this instance, Lord Melbourne did not make an issue of the King's action (see page 223), but a similar move by the Queen today would most certainly lead to her being attacked by the House even though the minister she had ap-pointed accepted responsibility. Indeed, it could be argued that, even if a subsequent election endorsed her action, she would by her conduct have forfeited the confidence of one party, thereby under-mining her position should that party be returned to power in the future. Similarly, in those circumstances where the Sovereign has to appoint a Prime Minister without advice, a breach of established conventions could be construed as partisan action and attacked in Parliament. The truth is that it is not in the distinction between the Crown and the monarchy that the Sovereign's position is maintained, but by her observance of the two broad rules stated above. This is the course which a Sovereign must follow in order to be a 'constitutional monarch', although it is only since the example set by George V that the rules have been scrupulously observed.

METHODS OF EXPRESSING THE ROYAL WILL

While in certain circumstances, such as the appointment of a Prime Minister or the request that a Secretary of State should hand over his seals of office, the monarch may act without written record, it is usually necessary to secure written authority. The recognised procedure for obtaining the appropriate instrument ensures that somewhere a minister must be consulted and thereby accepts responsibility. These written instruments are:

(1) *Orders in Council*, made 'by and with the advice of the Privy Council', for such matters as altering the government of a colony or commanding the issue of writs for the calling of a new Parliament. Orders are signed by the Clerk of the Council and the Seal is affixed. While the Councillors present need not include a minister, application has to be made by a minister to the Lord President for the making of the Order.

(2) *Proclamations*, announcing such matters as the declaration of war or peace and the prorogation, dissolution or summoning of Parliament. These decisions of the Council bear the Great Seal of the Realm, which is affixed by the Lord Chancellor.

(3) *Letters Patent*, covering such purposes as the authorisation for the opening of Parliament, the conferment of judgeships and peerages, the assent to bills by Commissioners. Here the Great Seal is affixed by the Lord Chancellor under the authority of a Sign Manual Warrant which has been duly counter-signed by a minister.

(4) *Sign Manual Warrant*, by which the Royal pleasure is signified for particular proposals, e.g. the commissioning of an officer, the grant of charters to towns, instructions to the governor of a colony, the commissioning of Counsellors of State to act during the monarch's absence or illness, the appointment of certain officials. The Warrant has to be

counter-signed by the responsible minister, the Home Secretary, for instance, on the appointment of a stipendiary magistrate or on the grant of pardon, and two Lords of the Treasury on the appointment of the Paymaster-General.

THE MOST IMPORTANT USES OF THE PREROGATIVE TODAY

A study of the occasions when use is made of the prerogative today will show the extent to which these legal powers still remain and, above all, the limitations which the monarch must observe.

(1) *The appointment of a Prime Minister*

In any constitution, somebody must take the first step in forming a Government; in Germany, this duty is performed by the President; in Britain, it is the function of the monarch. Normally the Sovereign's action is automatic and bound by convention. (*a*) If a party has both a majority and a recognised Leader in the House of Commons, that Leader must become the Prime Minister. (*b*) If the Government is defeated and the Prime Minister resigns, the monarch must send forthwith for the Leader of the Opposition.

In exercising this function, the Sovereign has to make what is essentially a personal decision, and there are occasions when the above conventions do not cover the situation. The first occurs when the Prime Minister dies in office and there is no recognised Leader of the party to succeed him. During World War II, George VI took precautions against this eventuality, and in response to his request Mr. Churchill recommended two successors, Mr. Eden, followed by Sir John Anderson, if both he and Eden were killed together.

The second occasion can arise when the Prime Minister wishes to hand over the reins to another person. The monarch may ask his advice as to his successor, but this course has not always been followed. Thus, Mr. Gladstone was not consulted when he resigned on account of ill-health in 1894. Queen Victoria chose Lord Rosebery, although Mr. Gladstone said that had he been asked he would have recommended Lord Spencer. That the choice does rest with the Sovereign was made clear in 1957 when Sir Anthony Eden tendered his resignation on account of ill-health. It was generally thought that Eden would be succeeded by Mr. R. A. Butler, who had presided over Cabinet meetings in his absence.

Whether Eden was asked to give the Queen advice is not known. If he was, it was either not definite or was not accepted, for there was some delay in announcing his successor. The Queen made her own enquiries, and eventually sent for Mr. Harold Macmillan.

A parallel situation occurred in 1963 when Mr. Harold Macmillan resigned on account of ill-health for there was no obvious acceptable successor. On this occasion the outgoing Prime Minister's views were considered to be so important that the Queen travelled to his sick bed to ascertain them. She accepted Mr. Macmillan's advice in sending for Lord Home to form an administration.

Neither of these first two situations is likely to occur in the future for both major parties have now adopted a formal procedure for selecting their Leader.

But with the third, a confused political situation, the monarch may have to make a personal choice. For instance, a general election may result in there being no one strong and united party with a majority in the House of Commons. Or complications in a national crisis could cause the resignation of the Government.

In both instances, the Sovereign has a Prime Minister to give advice. The monarch, in the first case, would either let the existing Prime Minister meet the new Parliament or, on his resignation, send for the person most likely to succeed in forming a Government. But there is a third alternative, and this applies particularly to the second case — the formation of a coalition Government. Here the Sovereign can use much influence, as the events of 1931 show. The then Labour Government could not agree on the measures to be taken to meet the prevailing economic difficulties. Had George V accepted a narrow definition of his powers, he would have waited for Mr. Ramsay MacDonald's resignation, and then sent for Mr. Baldwin, the Leader of the Opposition. Instead he consulted with the leaders of all three parties (Liberals included) and used his influence to persuade Mr. MacDonald to form a coalition National Government.

When the Sovereign has to exercise a personal decision, as on the three occasions described above, he can consult with whom he chooses. Where the Prime Minister resigns, the Sovereign probably would, but need not, ask his advice. Should this be inconclusive, he may go elsewhere. Thus, in 1957, Elizabeth II summoned Sir Winston Churchill, the 'elder statesman' of the Conservative Party, and Lord Salisbury, the Conservative Leader in the Lords, to ascertain the views of the Party which still had the support of the House of Commons. Advice may also be sought from selected Privy Councillors. But the main source of help will most likely be the Private Secretary, who, in the words of John Wheeler-Bennett, is 'the eyes and ears of his Sovereign'. It was largely through the meetings between Lord Stamfordham, Private Secretary to George V, and Mr. Amery and Mr. Bridgeman, that the King summoned Mr. Baldwin, and not Lord Curzon, in 1923. Sir Alan Lascelles consulted with Lord Salisbury and Sir John Anderson regarding the action George VI should take if, as a result of the election of 1951, the stalemate between the parties should be repeated.

(2) The appointment of ministers

At one time, ministers were selected by and personally responsible to the Sovereign. As parties in Parliament developed, however, the King's influence declined, and after 1832 it became clear that responsibility for the formation of the Government rested with the Prime Minister. Nevertheless, the practice has remained of submitting a list of proposed appointments to the Sovereign and discussing it with him. At times, it appears, Queen Victoria was forthright in her refusal to accept as ministers certain persons, such as Sir Charles Dilke and Mr. Labouchere, both of whom held views which she considered to be offensive to the Royal Family. But where the person to whom she objected had a strong political following, or was insisted upon by the Prime Minister, the Queen had to give way. Even today the Sovereign has some influence in appointments. When in 1945 Mr. Attlee informed George VI that he proposed to make Dr. Hugh Dalton his Foreign Secretary, the King, exercising his constitutional right to advise, suggested that Mr. Ernest Bevin would be a better choice. Mr. Attlee, after consultation with a number of colleagues and the Chief Whip, decided on Mr. Bevin. But in no case can the Sovereign now insist; if the Prime Minister feels strongly about an appointment, his will must prevail.

(3) The dismissal of a Government

Dismissal of a Government is effected by dismissing the Prime Minister, the principle of collective responsibility requiring that all ministers resign in sympathy. In fact, there has been no definite dismissal of the Government since 1783, when George III replaced

Fox and Lord North by Pitt. But Lord Melbourne's replacement by Peel in 1834 was tantamount to a dismissal, for the Liberals had a majority in the Commons and were returned to power when Peel had to seek a dissolution. Two facts alone saved William IV from being involved in a dangerous situation. The first was that he had acted on a hint inadvertently dropped by Lord Melbourne himself; the second was that the vital changes produced by the Reform Act had not yet been fully comprehended. Since then, no Sovereign has dismissed a ministry, for it is obvious that such action could be construed as interference in party politics.

Dismissal by the Sovereign could not be justified on the grounds that the Government appeared to be out of favour with the majority of the people. In the first place, the Sovereign is no better qualified to judge the position than is the Prime Minister, whose task it is to assess the support for his policies. Secondly, it is necessary to take a long view. A Government is elected for five years and some time during that period it may have to take unpopular measures; but it can always hope for a return to favour before it has to seek re-election. It may well be, for example, that Mr. Macmillan's Government was somewhat unpopular during 1957, but when he did go to the polls in October, 1959, he was returned with an increased majority.

Could the Sovereign use his prerogative, however, to dismiss a Government which was acting in an unconstitutional manner? The difficulty lies in defining what is 'unconstitutional'. In the past, when a fundamental change in the working of the constitution has been proposed, the monarch has been able to insist on a dissolution so that the wishes of the electorate can be ascertained. But what if a radical Government interprets such action as unfair discrimination, and is supported at the ensuing election? The Sovereign would then be in a difficult position. Hence Sir Ivor Jennings considers that the monarch's function is merely to see that the constitution functions in the normal manner. 'It functions in the normal manner so long as the electors are asked to decide between competing parties at intervals of reasonable length. She would be justified in refusing to assent to a policy which subverted the democratic basis of the Constitution, by unnecessary or indefinite prolongations of the life of Parliament, by a gerrymandering of the constituencies in the interests of one party, or by fundamental modification of the electoral system to the same end' (*Cabinet*

Government). Even in such circumstances, however, the Sovereign should act only with the greatest caution and in a manner which could reasonably be expected to receive the support of the electorate.

(4) *The dissolution of Parliament*

Although Parliament is dissolved by the Queen, she cannot act without advice. Dissolution involves both an Order in Council, made at a Privy Council meeting summoned by the Lord President, and a Proclamation, for which the Lord Chancellor in affixing the Great Seal accepts responsibility. Advice is tendered by the Prime Minister, and if this advice is not forthcoming, the Sovereign can only resort to dismissal of the Government. The Prime Minister may consult with his Cabinet colleagues, but he is not bound to do so and, as we shall see, the virtual placing of this prerogative at his disposal greatly strengthens his power and enhances his position in the party.

Some doubt appears to exist as to whether the Sovereign is bound to accept the advice of the Prime Minister on dissolution. It is obvious from the correspondence between Queen Victoria and her ministers that both thought she possessed the constitutional right to refuse in certain circumstances. Succeeding monarchs have also taken the same line but, since the requisite circumstances have never materialised, no dissolution has been refused by the Sovereign for over a century.

Nevertheless, in those Commonwealth countries where the Governor-General acts on behalf of the Sovereign the situation has arisen. In 1926 Mr. Mackenzie King, the Liberal Prime Minister of Canada, asked Lord Byng for a dissolution to strengthen his position in Parliament. There had already been an election some nine months previously, when the Conservatives had been the single largest party, but the Liberals, governing with the support of the smaller parties, had taken office. Lord Byng, assured by Mr. Meighen, the Conservative leader, that he could form a Government, refused to dissolve. Within a week, however, the Conservatives were defeated and Mr. Meighen was granted a dissolution. Again, in 1939, General Hertzog was refused a dissolution by Sir Patrick Duncan when his policy of neutrality in the war was rejected by the South African Parliament. In this case, General Smuts was able to form a stable Government.

The difference in the two cases underlines the assessment of the Sovereign's position made in 1950 by Sir Alan Lascelles, Private Secretary to George VI. As Mr. Attlee had secured only a narrow majority in the February election, the King was seeking guidance as to his position should a further dissolution be requested. Sir Alan Lascelles considered that no Sovereign could refuse unless three conditions were fulfilled: '(1) the existing Parliament was still vital, viable, and capable of doing its job; (2) a General Election would be detrimental to the national economy; (3) he could rely on finding another Prime Minister who could carry on his Government, for a reasonable period, with a working majority in the House of Commons.' If the first two conditions did not apply, the Prime Minister could justly claim that he had the right to present an issue to the electorate and it was for them, and not the Sovereign, to judge his action. Where the third condition was not fulfilled, the monarch would be placed in a dangerous position by his refusal. Whereas all three conditions applied in the instance of Sir Patrick Duncan's refusal, the third did not in the case of Lord Byng's. Mr. Mackenzie King was justifiably bitter at the Governor-General's action, and if the same course of events took place in Britain, a radical Prime Minister might seek to curtail the Sovereign's prerogative powers by statute. Since, however, all three conditions are unlikely to exist at the same time, it seems that, to all intents and purposes, the Sovereign is limited to the constitutional right of 'warning' the Prime Minister when a dissolution is advised.

(5) *The creation of peers*

Both hereditary and life peers are created by the Sovereign on the advice of the Prime Minister to: (a) reward or honour persons for public services; (b) give a particular party more representation in the House of Lords; (c) allow persons with special qualifications to take part in the deliberations of the Chamber; (d) find a place in Parliament for a person whom the Prime Minister wishes to include in his ministry; (e) resolve a deadlock between the Upper and Lower Chambers.

The use of the prerogative for the last purpose has in the past been of primary constitutional importance. Although it was only actually employed in this way in 1711, when Queen Anne created 12 Tory peers to pass the Treaty of Utrecht, the threat of its use in 1832 and 1911 was sufficient to cause the Lords to give way.

The present position seems to be that the Sovereign cannot refuse to create peers when advised to do so, but that when it is to pass a controversial measure he may insist on the Prime Minister first going to the country. With the passing of the Parliament Act, 1949, it is unlikely that any future use will have to be made of this prerogative power to compel the House of Lords.

(6) *The veto of legislation*

Although this prerogative was last exercised by Queen Anne, George III and George IV managed to delay Catholic emancipation by letting it be known that they would not agree to the bill. But no monarch today would revive this power. If a measure were considered 'unconstitutional', the only course open to the Sovereign would be the dismissal of the Government.

(7) *The prerogative of mercy*

In exercising this power, the Sovereign is advised by the Home Secretary, who makes the decision. Sometimes, however, the monarch does let his personal views be known. Twice, for instance, George VI discussed death sentences with Mr. Herbert Morrison. On each occasion the King was over-ruled, and it seems that such specific discussions are rather exceptional.

(8) *The grant of patronage and honours*

Although the Sovereign is responsible for a wide variety of appointments of public officials, high Churchmen and judges, he acts only on the advice of a minister, usually the Prime Minister. He can, however, expect to be consulted on the proposed appointments and may exert some influence. All important posts are in the Prime Minister's hands. These include: permanent secretaries and under-secretaries of State and other senior civil servants; all bishops, deans and canons; the higher judges, such as the Lords of Appeal, the Lord Justices, the heads of the three Divisions of the High Court and the Judicial Committee of the Privy Council; the Governors of the B.B.C. and the Civil Service Commissioners. Usually the Prime Minister would consult with the departmental head, the Archbishop of Canterbury or the Lord Chancellor, as the case may be. All other appointments for which the Sovereign is responsible, e.g. members of the diplomatic corps, colonial officials, commissioned officers in the Army and Air Force, rest directly with the respective minister, though he would normally confer with the Prime Minister. The one exception is the office of Governor-General, which is now filled on the advice of the Prime Minister of the country concerned.

Responsibility for recommending titles and honours also falls on the Prime Minister, but here again he would often seek the views of other persons, notably the Leader of the Opposition. Occasionally, too, the Sovereign may suggest a name. In order to eliminate any sale of honours, names of persons selected for political services must first be vetted by a committee of three Privy Councillors who are not members of the Government.

Certain honours — the Order of the Garter, the Order of Merit and the Royal Victorian Order — are reserved for the Sovereign's own conferment, and George VI in particular safeguarded this practice.

(9) *Miscellaneous prerogative powers*

Bagehot, writing in 1867, said: 'It would very much surprise people if they were only told how many things the Queen could do without consulting Parliament' (*The English Constitution*). And though prerogative powers exercised by ministers may be replaced by statutory powers, many still remain. These include: the whole conduct of foreign affairs; the declaration of war, peace or neutrality; the concluding of treaties; the changing of the constitution of most colonies; the grant of pardon; the creation of corporations; and the appointment of members of Royal Commissions. All are exercised by, or on the advice of, a responsible minister.

THE IMPORTANCE OF THE PREROGATIVE TODAY

The prerogative today is, as we have seen, merely a survival from the Middle Ages of those common-law powers of the Sovereign not superseded by statute. Since the monarch no longer exercises these powers in person, it is pertinent to ask why they have not been formally transferred by statute to the Prime Minister or to the appropriate responsible minister.

The real reason is that we have never taken the trouble to do so. The British people have no wish to formalise their constitution but prefer that it should be flexible to meet changing needs and conditions. Hence, prerogative powers have been replaced by statutes only piecemeal and, where they have remained, conventions have developed to regulate their use. So long as these conventions work satisfactorily, there is little demand for a more rigorous definition.

But there is a more positive reason why the prerogative is retained; its abolition would destroy many of the advantages which follow from it.

The first advantage is emphasised in Lord Hewart's definition of the prerogative — 'such powers as are exercisable by the executive Government without express authority from Parliament.' These powers, exercised by ministers may be attacked in Parliament, because of the way in which they have been used, but the House cannot insist on being consulted in advance. There are circumstances when the prerogative may be a valuable alternative authority for action when reference to Parliament would be inappropriate. (1) Certain matters, such as the dissolution of Parliament, the conferment of titles and honours, and the grant of pardon, cannot be wisely discussed in a deliberative assembly, especially one so large as the House of Commons. (2) Quick action may be needed to meet unforeseen circumstances. Proclamations are used to declare war and peace, and the provisions of the Emergency Powers (Defence) Act, 1939, were implemented in detail by Orders in Council. (3) Legislation is an unsuitable process for matters which are of little public importance or which would require lengthy amending statutes from time to time. Thus the constitutions of colonies are altered by Orders in Council. (4) Whenever it is desirable to keep certain matters out of party politics, they are best dealt with in ways unlikely to give rise to heated parliamentary discussion. For this reason, the Governors of the B.B.C. and the Civil Service Commissioners are appointed by Order in Council.

The second advantage of the prerogative is that it gives elasticity to the constitution, permitting it to keep in step with changing needs. If powers were defined by statute, this could come about only by frequent recourse to amending statutes. Exactly the same ends have been achieved through the prerogative, however, by gradual, and sometimes imperceptible, adaptation. Consider how the possibility of creating peers provided a safety-valve for the constitution both in 1832 and 1911. By ensuring that political power rested with the electorate, it may well have prevented a revolution. And how subtle is the use of the power to create peers today, enabling the Prime Minister to find a place in the legislature for somebody from outside whom he wants in his ministry, or allowing him to soften the blow when an elder statesman has to be dropped! Similarly, the convention, developed in the 20th century, that the Prime Minister must come from the House of Commons, reflects the dominance of that Chamber in the affairs of Parliament.

Thirdly, the prerogative permits a discretion in the exercise of powers which a hard and fast law could not achieve. Thus no law could legislate for every occasion when it might be advantageous to form a coalition Government, for the step depends on a delicate assessment of the conditions prevailing at the particular time. Similarly, the prerogative of mercy allows further consideration of the circumstances of a particular case outside the narrow confines of the courts of law.

Fourthly, the retention of the prerogative helps to preserve a monarchy with definite and important functions in our constitution. While it is only in the initial stages of forming a Government that the Sovereign today has an individual responsibility, the fact that he still possesses personal prerogatives does ensure that he is consulted. In an emergency, too, there is a psychological advantage in having certain actions, such as the conscription of persons and property, carried out in the name of the Sovereign rather than through such impersonal ideas as 'the State' or 'the Government'.

Lastly, such prerogative powers as the dismissal of a minister and the dissolution of Parliament can be held in reserve by the Prime Minister as sanctions for maintaining his authority.

III. Functions of the Monarchy Today

The prerogative powers of the Sovereign have, as we have seen, been gradually whittled away over the centuries, and even those remaining are, wherever possible, exercised only on the responsibility of a minister. But the decline in the importance of these executive functions has not been matched by a corresponding decrease in the part played by the monarch in the British constitution. While the monarchies of nearly every other country in the world have fallen, the position of the Sovereign in Britain today is stronger than ever. Success in war has prevented catastrophic changes in government. But, in consolidating their position, the wisdom of monarchs over the last century has been fundamental. Not only have they accepted 'constitutional monarchy', but they have developed new responsibilities. Thus the British people remain convinced that the monarchy is still the most effective means of fulfilling certain functions. 'Notwithstanding the fact that the Crown has lost its original great powers it can be said, certainly of the present century, that as those powers passed and the Monarchy became strictly constitutional, the Monarch has become increasingly popular in the hearts and minds of the British people' (Lord Morrison: *Government and Parliament*). What part then does the Sovereign play in the constitution today?

(1) *In the exercise of her remaining prerogative powers, the Queen fulfils essential executive functions*

Occasionally, as we have seen, the Queen may have to act on her own initiative, chiefly in the preliminary steps to forming a government. The retiring Prime Minister will almost certainly be among those consulted, but his advice, although weighty, cannot be binding. In the end, the decision is that of the monarch, and of the monarch alone. But she must strive to avoid any semblance of political bias.

In all other cases, the Queen ultimately acts on the advice of a minister, usually the Prime Minister, and the circumstances are unlikely to arise when the Sovereign could dismiss a Government or refuse a dissolution. Hence the position today is basically the same as in 1913 when it was stated by Mr. Asquith in a memorandum to George V. 'We have now a well-established tradition of two hundred years, that, in the last resort, the occupant of the Throne accepts and acts on the advice of his ministers. The Sovereign may have lost something of his personal power and authority, but the Crown has been thereby removed from the storms and vicissitudes of party politics, and the monarchy rests upon a solid foundation which is buttressed both by long tradition and by the general conviction that its personal status is an invaluable safeguard for the continuity of our national life.'

(2) *In discussing with ministers the advice they offer, the Queen can present views free from political bias*

While the Queen acts on advice, she does not have to give automatic endorsement to the decisions of ministers. Bagehot affords the Sovereign three rights — 'the right to be consulted, the right to encourage, the right to warn. And a king of great sense and sagacity would want no others.' Obviously, the Prime Minister must explain why he wishes the prerogative to be exercised for such matters as the summoning, proroguing and dissolving of Parliament, the creation of peers, the award of titles and honours, and the granting of mercy. But the right to be consulted is not confined to the prerogative powers; it covers all aspects of Government policy. Thus we find George VI remonstrating with Mr. Chamberlain in 1938 because he had not been kept informed of the difference of opinion between the Prime Minister and his Foreign Secretary, Mr. Eden, over suggested further appeasement of the dictators. Later, he wrote to Mr. Attlee regarding the Supplies and Services Bill, 1947: 'In view of the fact that the Bill has been the subject of so many different interpretations and that it is now on the Statute Book, a personal account by you of its purpose and scope would be of the greatest value to me.' The monarch may even cause issues to be considered further. In 1943, for instance, George VI arranged for General Smuts and Sir Winston Churchill to have dinner with him because Smuts had expressed some misgivings over the strategic wisdom of operation 'Overlord', the invasion of western Europe.

The need to refer matters to the Sovereign not only reminds ministers of the importance of their actions, but affords the Queen an opportunity to add her own observations. Because her position has many advantages, the Queen's advice may have particular value. Her reign may have extended over a number of Governments, as with the present Queen Elizabeth who has now had six Prime Ministers. To some degree, therefore, the transitory nature of Governments is counterbalanced by the continuity of the Sovereign. 'Ministers come and go, but the King remains, always at the centre of public affairs, always participating vigilantly in the work of government from a standpoint detached from any consideration but the welfare of his peoples as a whole. He is the continuous element in the constitution, one of the main safeguards of its democratic character, and the repository of a knowledge of affairs that before long comes to transcend that of any individual statesman' (*The Times*, 18th May, 1943). Bagehot, in *The English Constitution*, imagines the King saying: 'Have you referred to the transactions which happened during such and such an administration, I think about fourteen years ago? They afford an instructive example of the bad results which are sure to attend the policy which you propose. You did not at that time take so prominent a part in public life as you now do, and it is possible you do not fully remember all the events. I should recommend you to recur to them, and to discuss them with your older colleagues who took part in them. It is unwise to recommence a policy which so lately worked so ill.'

The Queen receives information from a rich variety of sources. Every day she studies Cabinet papers and Foreign Office despatches. She sees the Cabinet agenda in advance, and memoranda regarding the policy of particular departments. Each week, while Parliament is sitting, the Prime Minister attends on the Queen at about 6.30 on a Tuesday evening, the day before the regular Cabinet meeting. He is usually with her for over an hour, discussing matters which have arisen out of the week's Cabinet papers. She has thus a regular opportunity to encourage and warn. When she requires information, it is usually to the Prime Minister that she turns, though her Private Secretary may conduct enquiries on her behalf. Communications from the independent members of the Commonwealth come direct to her from their capitals or through their High Commissioners in London. New Governors-General, Governors of colonies and British ambassadors abroad have audiences with the Queen when appointed and maintain personal contact with her. Foreign ambassadors to London are received by her. She also presides at Privy Council meetings. In her contacts with all these officials she gleans information which can prove valuable to her in advising ministers.

Apart from experience, weight is given to the Queen's views through her record of impartiality. Moreover, since she has no political axe to grind, she is more likely to appraise policy objectively. As Sir Ivor Jennings points out, she is not a politician or controlled by politicians and is thus 'the nearest approach to the ordinary man provided by the British constitutional machine' (*Cabinet Government*). And the ordinary man, recognising that her views are unclouded by political bias, is glad that she is present to advise. His attitude is summoned up by Nevil Shute in *The Far Country*: 'It is a great thing to have a King, a leader, to prevent the politicians and the bureaucrats from growing stupid.'

Since the advice of the Queen emanates from such an exalted

position, it will be given due consideration. But the Queen cannot push her action further, and if the responsible minister insists, she must give way. Any other action, apart from embroiling her in party politics, would be undesirable. Her rather artificial upbringing means that the Queen may be in no better position to judge an issue than the responsible minister whose whole career has been spent in assessing the impact of policy on the electorate. Moreover, while the Queen is shielded from responsibility, she may be influenced by contacts who are frankly irresponsible. Above all, the requirement that the Queen should act impartially may be only a counsel of perfection. Some critics consider that on account of education, social position, friendships and contacts, and general upbringing, the Sovereign will have marked personal prejudices which make complete impartiality and objectivity impossible. The Sovereign's interpretation of the prerogative powers, especially those used in times of political crisis, and the advice given are thus likely to have a conservative bias.

The extent to which a minister bows to the wishes of the Sovereign will depend on his personality, and on how strongly he feels on the subject. But once the matter has been decided, the Queen must, in the words of Prince Albert, 'support the government with a majority in the House of Commons frankly, honourably and with all her might.' The position can be summed up by a further quotation from Mr. Asquith's memorandum to George V: 'In the last resort the occupant of the throne accepts and acts on the advice of his ministers. . . . He is entitled and bound to give his ministers all relevant information which comes to him; to point out objections which seem to him valid against the course which they advise; to suggest (if he thinks fit) an alternative policy. Such intimations are received by ministers with the utmost respect and more deference than if they proceeded from any other quarter. But, in the end, the Sovereign always acts upon the advice which ministers, after (if need be) reconsideration, feel it their duty to offer. They give that advice well knowing that they can, and probably will, be called upon to account for it by Parliament.'

(3) *By placing herself above party politics, the Queen is a unifying force in the constitution*

The British constitution operates chiefly through the party system. At times, however, the divisions created by parties are either inadequate or inopportune. No one party may have an absolute majority over all other parties, or a crisis may make it desirable that party differences should be moderated for the time being. In each case, the Sovereign can appeal to the party leaders to co-operate in overcoming the difficulties. Thus it was largely through the personal intervention of George V in 1931 that the coalition Government was formed.

The Sovereign may also use her influence to secure agreement or compromise on particular issues, though she should act only with the Prime Minister's consent. Agreement on the Reform Act, 1884, resulted largely from the active part played by Queen Victoria, who saw leaders on both sides, while George V made positive moves in 1914 to compromise on the question of home rule for Ireland.

From individuals, too, the prestige of the monarch evokes a special response. Lord Trenchard agreed to accept the post of Commissioner of the Metropolitan Police when he learned that it was the wish of George V. Similarly, at the outbreak of war, appeals to enlist are made in the name of the Sovereign.

(4) *Through her personal contacts with the heads of other nations the Queen may be able, on occasions, to influence international relationships*

Personal qualities, apart from the position as Head of State, have led to the Sovereign, at least during this century, being held in high esteem abroad. Hence, on a number of occasions, monarchs have secured, either directly or indirectly, a friendly and favourable response from other nations. The Entente Cordiale between France and Britain is often regarded as the outcome of Edward VII's official visit to Paris in 1903. Similarly, it was largely through the impression created by George VI in his private audience with General Orbay, the leader of the Turkish military mission to London in 1939, that the Franco-British treaty of alliance with Turkey was signed, while the strong personal friendship which existed between George VI and President Franklin Roosevelt did much indirectly to help Britain before the entry of America into World War II.

Nevertheless, before taking a leading role in international affairs, the Sovereign must obtain the consent of the Prime Minister. On a number of occasions during the critical first ten years of his reign, George VI refrained from making a direct approach to the heads of foreign governments as the Prime Minister considered that the time was inopportune in view of other negotiations in progress.

(5) *In fulfilling her ceremonial duties, the Queen gives dignity and interest to government*

The Queen is the ceremonial Head of State, opening Parliament, receiving and entertaining other Heads of States, and performing a variety of official duties both at home and in the Commonwealth. On such occasions, government stands above party, dignified and glamorous. In fact, Bagehot considered that the monarchy made government intelligible to the people, since it concentrated their attention 'on one person doing interesting actions'. Although the development of popular education and the Press has enabled the electorate to gain a more complete insight into how government works, it still remains true that 'the State' is personified most clearly in the minds of the people by the Sovereign, a sentiment which is expressed in the National Anthem. Moreover, by her hereditary position and the ancient origin of her ceremonial duties, the Queen symbolises the continuity of the State over the centuries. Evidence of the deep respect for government which the monarchy evokes was afforded by the care taken in the first televising of the opening of Parliament in 1958 lest people, in witnessing Her Majesty read the Speech from the Throne, falsely identified the Queen with the policies of the Conservative Government.

(6) *As Head of State and the leading example in its religious, moral and family life, the Queen unites the nation*

The Queen is 'everything to everybody', a mystical emblem uniting the nation. 'The importance of the Queen in the life of her many peoples resides not at all in what she does, but entirely in what she is. She is the embodiment of their tradition and their future, the focus of their aspiration, the symbol of their unity, their universal representative . . . In all that she touches the Queen represents the whole in relation to the part. Where she lends her name to any specialist activity, she intimates symbolically that the entire community takes an interest in it' (Dermot Morrah: *The Work of the Queen*). In the many functions which the Queen now attends, both in the world of work and the field of sport, she touches everybody. Her presence at a gathering not only signifies the importance of the activity in the national life but enables all her subjects, both great and small, to share in it, especially when it is televised. Thus the Coronation was a national celebration, while the regular Christmas broadcast draws together a Commonwealth family. But it means that the duties of the Queen have increased considerably and today are extremely demanding. Hence, proposals for dropping certain functions more appropriate to a former age have been put forward, and debutantes' presentations have already ended, while Court garden parties have been curtailed.

(7) *As Head of the Commonwealth, she strengthens the bonds which link the member nations*

The simple test of Commonwealth membership today is recognition of the Queen as 'Head of the Commonwealth'. The Queen thus has a unifying effect on the Commonwealth, for only the Sovereign, standing above politics, can bring together the separate units under a common person.

In many ways, the British monarchy performs functions similar to those of such Presidents as the German and Italian. There are drawbacks to a hereditary monarch — he may have little appeal to the people or his sons may be of dubious character. Both George III and Queen Victoria, when she retired from public life after the death of Prince Albert in 1861, became very unpopular. Upbringing and contacts, too, create difficulties as regards impartiality of action. Moreover, to some people, the institution represents an outmoded view of a hierarchical society with the monarchy at the apex.

Even so, these possibilities are outweighed by certain advantages the monarch enjoys. Being hereditary, the monarchy has enhanced glamour and draws strength from its continuity. Furthermore, the avoidance of elections eliminates the political bargaining which used to occur in France in obtaining a new President. Above all, the monarchy, being free from past political connections, has a record of impartiality. This leads to a more general acceptance of the Queen as the symbolic Head of State and of the Commonwealth, and adds significance and value to any advice given or action taken on those rare occasions when they are essential. In comparison, the

President of the U.S.A. has had almost half the electorate vote against him.

SUGGESTED READING

Walter Bagehot, *The English Constitution* (Kegan Paul, 1872), Introduction to Second Edition and Chapters 2 and 3.

F. W. G. Benemy, *The Queen Reigns: She does not Rule* (Harrap, 1963).

N. H. Brasher, *Studies in British Government* (2nd Ed. Macmillan, 1971), Chapter 1.

C.O.I. Reference Pamphlet No. 118, *The Monarchy in Britain* (H.M.S.O. 1973).

A. V. Dicey, *Introduction to the Law of the Constitution* (10th Ed., Macmillan, 1961), Chapters 14 and 15.

Sir Ivor Jennings, *Cabinet Government* (3rd Ed., C.U.P., 1969), Chapters 2, 3, 12, 13 and 14.

K. Martin, *The Crown and the Establishment* (Hutchinson, 1962).

Lord Morrison, *Government and Parliament* (3rd Ed., O.U.P., 1964), Chapter 5.

Sir Harold Nicolson, *King George V: His Life and Reign* (Constable, 1952).

Sir Charles Petrie, *The Modern British Monarchy* (Eyre and Spottiswoode, 1961).

John W. Wheeler-Bennett, *King George VI: His Life and Reign* (Macmillan, 1958).

14

The Prime Minister

'Nowhere in the wide world does so great a substance cast so small a shadow; nowhere is there a man who has so much power, with so little to show for it in the way of formal title or prerogative.'

w. e. GLADSTONE: *Gleanings of Past Years*

I. ORIGIN OF THE OFFICE

From the beginning of the 18th century, successive ministries usually had one or more dominant personalities — for instance, Stanhope and Sunderland (1717), Townshend (1721), Walpole (1722–42), Pelham (1744), Newcastle and Pitt (1756) and Lord North (1770–82). This came about because George I ceased to attend Cabinet meetings and one of the members had to preside. But this person was not a Prime Minister in the modern sense. His position depended on the King, not on the electorate. With the possible exception of Walpole, he did not lead a united ministry. Any pre-eminence he enjoyed was solely through his personality, for he had none of the powers and sanctions enjoyed by a present-day Prime Minister. Nor was he necessarily the First Lord of the Treasury; like the elder Pitt, he could be a Secretary of State.

Even Walpole, who was so dominant that in 1741 the peers framed a protest against the development of the office, did not perform the functions or enjoy the position of a modern Premier. Although he exercised some influence over the selection of ministers, the actual choice still rested with the King. Moreover, the ministry was not formed *en bloc*, but piecemeal. Any unity within it was secured solely by his personality, his skilful use of intrigue, and the strict discipline he imposed, for ministers who did not agree with his policies were either dismissed at his instigation or compelled to resign. Only in being First Lord of the Treasury and in living at 10 Downing Street did he resemble a modern Prime Minister. When he fell from office in 1742, his colleagues did not resign with him, and a further forty years elapsed before another minister, the younger Pitt, wielded equal authority.

Our modern Prime Minister is essentially a product of the 1832 Reform Act. He enjoys his position, not by royal favour, but because he is the accepted Leader of the majority party in the House of Commons, a fact which Peel discovered in 1834. Peel was quick to appreciate the new situation, and saw that, to form a Government, his party had to be supported by the electorate. Hence his Tamworth Manifesto in 1835 heralded more progressive ideas, designed to appeal to the voters, and the old Tory party received the new name of 'Conservative'. So successful was he that in 1841 his party was returned to power, thus justifying his refusal two years previously to head a minority Government when Queen Victoria refused to dismiss her Ladies of the Bedchamber (see page 258). The first Prime Minister in the present-day sense of the term was thus Sir Robert Peel.

II. Functions of the Prime Minister

The whole position of the Prime Minister is based, not on statute, but on convention. Although Disraeli signed the Treaty of Berlin in 1878 as 'Prime Minister of England', and Letters Patent in 1905 included the Prime Minister in the official order of precedence, it was the Chequers Estate Act, 1917, which first mentioned him in a statute by accepting Chequers as an official country residence for 'the person holding the office popularly known as Prime Minister'. Official recognition was complete when the Ministers of the Crown Act, 1937, granted him a salary (now £20,000 a year) and a pension on retirement; but no attempt has been made by statute to say who shall be Prime Minister or what he shall do. That he has immense powers and enjoys considerable personal prestige can be seen from the following description of his functions.

(1) *He is the Leader of his party in the country and in Parliament*

In the final analysis, the Prime Minister owes his position to his party. Hence, in carrying out his duties, he cannot afford to forget his political connections. He must use his powers of leadership to preserve his party against splits, working out compromise solutions when necessary. Both Peel and Gladstone failed here, the former over the repeal of the Corn Laws, the latter over home rule for Ireland. Moreover, to be successful in the next election, the Prime Minister must keep in touch with public opinion and induce his party to accept modifications of policy where desirable.

But while the Prime Minister cannot afford to neglect his party, it would find difficulty in discarding him. As its Leader, he has fought a successful election battle, proving himself both as a tactician and as a popular personality. Since voters choose a Prime Minister and a Government rather than a House of Commons, modern elections have developed into a battle not only between the opposing parties but between the two party Leaders. The Prime Minister has toured the country, spoken on the radio and appeared on television. Such advertisement means that, to most people, he is the symbol of his party, and so any rival starts at a disadvantage.

(2) *He is responsible for the formation of the ministry*

Her Majesty's ministers are now appointed on the advice of the Prime Minister. About a hundred offices have to be filled, and he controls them all. To refuse the offer of even the humblest post might jeopardise the whole of one's political career. Thus, when Sir Robert Horne, a successful President of the Board of Trade and Chancellor of the Exchequer, refused Mr. Baldwin's offer of the Ministry of Labour in 1924, he closed the door to future office. On the other hand, certain ministers, such as Anthony Eden, Harold Wilson and Iain Macleod, have won their way back into favour after resigning. Such ministers are usually of high standing in the party. Often, too, a resignation arising out of the doctrine of collective responsibility may be regarded as reflecting an honest and thoughtful politician.

In completing his ministry, the Prime Minister may select from a wide field. For the more important posts, he has a personal knowledge of the leading members of his party. In filling the minor offices, however, he usually considers the views of both the minister in charge and the Chief Whip. But, provided Parliament raises no objection to the distribution of portfolios, he has a free hand.

Nevertheless, the Prime Minister is subject to certain technical and political limitations. (a) While no statute requires that a minister should be an M.P. or a peer, there is a well-established convention to that effect. Ministers should be available to explain policy or answer questions in Parliament. Thus when Mr. Alun

Gwynne Jones became Minister for Disarmament in 1964, he was given a peerage so that he could sit in the Lords, while Mr. Frank Cousins, who became Minister of Technology, was elected M.P. for Nuneaton after the sitting member had vacated his seat. Nevertheless, such appointments are rare, ministers usually having had experience as politicians. (b) The Ministers of the Crown Act, 1964, limits the maximum number of ministers and Parliamentary Secretaries who can sit in the House of Commons to 91, thereby ensuring indirectly that there is a nucleus of ministers in the Lords. (c) Where the head of a department is in the House of Lords, his immediate deputy must be in the Commons, although the converse does not always follow. (d) Certain offices are invariably filled by members of the House of Commons, either because they have considerable political significance or because most of the discussion of their work is carried on there. Such posts include those of Chancellor of the Exchequer, Home Secretary and the Secretaries of State for Social Services, Education and Science, Trade and Industry, the Environment, and Employment. (e) The Lord Chancellor, the Attorney-General and the Solicitor-General must be lawyers. (f) When the Government is not a coalition, ministers must usually be members of his party, though Mr. Alun Gwynne Jones (mentioned above) was a leading member of the Liberal Party's policy-making groups. (g) All the leading party members expect departments and the Prime Minister is bound to consider their influence. This requires tact and skill for, if offence is given, he may be laying up for himself future difficulties. Moreover unless the different wings of the party are represented in the ministry, a party split may develop. Some Prime Ministers can act with more independence than others. Whereas Mr. MacDonald had preliminary consultations with his principal colleagues, Mr. Churchill merely summoned individuals to his country house and told them the offices they would hold. (h) In order that the Government shall not grow out of touch with its own back-benchers, younger members of the party must be given posts, if only minor ones. (i) The views of the Sovereign may have to be taken into account (see page 222). (j) Above all, ministers must have the essential personal qualities of competence and honesty.

Competence in a minister covers a variety of attributes. He must exercise powers of judgment in his department. He should recognise if a proposal raises new issues of Government policy, has political implications affecting the party as a whole, is likely to have important repercussions on other departments, or will meet with opposition in Parliament or from other members of the party. If so, it should be referred to the Prime Minister. Even if the matter can be determined within his department, the decision taken must follow the general trend of Government policy. This means that the minister must extract the salient points of memoranda presented to him quickly and accurately. But arriving at a decision may be only half the task; he will probably have to justify his decision in Parliament. Thus he needs to be an able speaker who can persuade Parliament to endorse his action. A Prime Minister will not look too kindly on a minister whom he has to rescue frequently in the House of Commons. In addition, the minister must have administrative ability. Since he personally will have little time for a detailed study of many problems, he must be able to choose able subordinates to whom he can safely delegate work. This calls for wide knowledge of human nature; a weak minister is liable to choose 'yes-men' and to leave too much to officials. Finally, much of a minister's time will be taken up in committee work, often as chairman. He must, therefore, be skilled in this kind of work — a skill which has probably been already gained by experience in standing committees or in minor office.

An incompetent minister soon becomes an embarrassment to the Prime Minister. Parliament, in its public examination of the work of departments, will harass any minister that it senses is not in complete control. The Press, too, may open a campaign of criticism against him and, if he fails to stand up to it confidently, the Prime Minister will soon be seeking an excuse to relieve him of his post.

While the Prime Minister, in filling offices, will naturally consider a colleague's experience in a previous Government, he should also look to the future, to his own retirement, and train possible successors in a variety of posts. Although transferring a minister from one department to another may prevent him having a thorough knowledge of any of them, it does not present a major difficulty. A first-rate man can usually turn the attributes mentioned above to the administration of widely differing departments. Above all, what is lost in knowledge of detail is more than compensated for by an increase in breadth of view, enabling a minister to comprehend the wider implications of decisions within his own department.

As regards integrity, it is not sufficient that the minister be honest; it is vital that he should appear to be so. In order to remove any suspicion that his official position may be used for personal gain, any directorships held by him, except those of an honorary nature in philanthropic undertakings and private companies, must be resigned. It is also expected that he will not write for the Press on anything connected with public policy which involves use of knowledge gained in office. This rule is observed strictly while holding a post; out of office, ex-ministers do publish articles and memoirs.

(3) *He dismisses ministers as circumstances require*

Any dismissal of a minister calls for delicate handling. Wherever possible, a Prime Minister would tactfully invite resignation and, if it was to facilitate a Cabinet re-shuffle or to make way for a younger man, the suggestion might well be accompanied by the offer of a peerage. At times resignation may be advised because the minister has been responsible for an action embarrassing to the Government, as with Dr. Hugh Dalton (1947). Resignations may also occur because of a fundamental disagreement with Cabinet policy, as with Mr. Frank Cousins (1966) and Lord Longford (1968). After such resignations, it is usual to publish the correspondence and, in disagreement over policy, the minister generally has the opportunity to explain his position to the House.

Nevertheless, a Prime Minister 'must be a good butcher'. Mr. Macmillan showed the strength of the Prime Minister's powers in 1962 when, in order to bring in new men and new ideas, he made overnight 24 governmental changes involving the removal of 7 ministers. Seventy back-benchers held a protest meeting, but Mr. Macmillan remained in office until he was taken ill a year later. Such ruthless dismissal, however, is rare and a Prime Minister does his best to avoid it. Where it involves a leading party member with political ambitions, there is always the danger that he will lead a troublesome breakaway group which, by disrupting the party's unity, damages the Government's standing in the eyes of the electorate. Thus Mr. E. Heffer, who was dismissed by Mr. Wilson in 1975, became a leading Left-wing critic of the Labour Government's policy.

(4) *He selects the Cabinet*

Between 16 and 24 ministers will be chosen by the Prime

Minister to form his Cabinet. Certain key offices are always included, partly on account of their importance in national affairs and partly because they will be filled by the leading members of the party.

The actual number depends upon the particular organisation of departments preferred by the Prime Ministers. Thus Mr. Wilson tended to favour many separate departments, but this still meant that even with a Cabinet of 23 some dozen heads of departments had to be excluded. On the other hand, Mr. Heath grouped a number of ministries under a single department (see page 270), thereby allowing him to reduce his Cabinet to 17. Subordinate ministers still receive Cabinet agenda and serve on its committees. Flexibility is provided for by having ministers without portfolio in charge of special subjects which are going to figure prominently in government policy. Thus Mr. Harold Lever, Chancellor of the Duchy of Lancaster, deals with special financial problems and sits on most Cabinet committees.

In addition to possessing administrative ability, members of the Cabinet must be able to work together. This welding of the individual ministers into a team is entirely the task of the Prime Minister, his success depending on his own personality, his powers of leadership, and the accuracy of his original estimate of the various individuals.

Even with modern party organisation, the decision as to which ministers shall be included in the Cabinet rests entirely with the Prime Minister and, as L. S. Amery says: 'Few dictators, indeed, enjoy such a measure of autocratic power as is enjoyed by a British Prime Minister while in process of making up his Cabinet.'

(5) He is chairman of the Cabinet

Although the Prime Minister controls procedure at Cabinet meetings, he is not a chairman in the usual sense of the term. The functions of such a chairman are to preserve order, to keep members to the point at issue, to see that everybody has a fair chance of stating his view and, at the end of the discussion, to put the motion to the vote. He must, therefore, show strength of character, judgment and impartiality. But while the Prime Minister has to perform the duties and possess the qualities of an ordinary chairman, he differs from him in many vital respects. In the first place, he has selected the members of the 'committee' himself and has not been elected by them as is usually the case, apart from parliamentary and government appointed committees. His superior position is brought home to ministers before the actual Cabinet meeting, for they are kept waiting in the hallway at 10 Downing Street until invited into the Cabinet Room by the Prime Minister or the Secretary of the Cabinet. Secondly, he chooses the items on the agenda and decides in which order they shall be taken. Thirdly, his views are dominant in Cabinet decisions. At Cabinet meetings, the minister responsible for the business under discussion usually puts forward his own observations and then other members add their comments. But the Prime Minister cannot be merely receptive. The general control of policy is in his hands and, after listening to the discussion, he must form his own opinion. As far as possible the decision should be a united one. Hence the Prime Minister sums up the sense of the meeting, and only on rare occasions is it necessary to resort to 'counting voices', as Lord Morrison puts it. Where differences appear irreconcilable, his ability to give a lead is vital. He may, for instance, have private discussions with the main contestants or suggest that the matter be referred to a committee for further examination before coming to a decision. But where squabbles between departments or rivalries between members persist, he is bound to take sides. Here tact is required in explaining why he prefers a certain line of action. To the minister whose claims, he feels, are going too far, he would stress the need of a co-ordinated policy and, in the last resort, appeal for party unity. Forcing the resignation of a Cabinet minister can lead to a dangerous 'party within a party' situation, as Mr. Attlee discovered in 1951 when Mr. Aneurin Bevan resigned over the imposition of the National Health Service charges.

(6) *He directs and co-ordinates policy*

The broad framework of policy is formulated by the party executive and usually endorsed by the party conference. But the exact interpretation of that policy and its timing rests with the Cabinet and, above all, with the Prime Minister. It is he who largely decides the precise lines which foreign, defence and economic policies follow. Hence he is always available to give ministers experienced help when a quick decision is required, for instance, on a private member's motion, an amendment to a bill or on defence problems. Or a minister may seek his opinion when he is initiating a policy which may have political consequences. Where necessary, a minister who comes under attack will be defended by the Prime Minister.

This overall supervision by the Prime Minister has two important results. First, he has to speak frequently in Parliament and answer questions on matters of general importance. Secondly, it enables him to play a major part in co-ordinating policy. Although he cannot control departments in detail, his general direction ensures that individual decisions are in harmony with the broad outlines agreed upon by the Cabinet.

(7) *He is the leader of the House of Commons, controlling its business and acting as its spokesman*

At one time, the Prime Minister, unless a peer, was the official Leader of the House, responsible for arranging the general programme of the session and the more detailed business for the week. Now, to relieve him of much of this burden, the day-to-day management is delegated to another minister who, as Leader of the House, arranges business through the usual channels. Nevertheless, the Prime Minister, as Leader of his party, still retains the ultimate responsibility for managing his majority so that Government business is completed to time and, as far as possible, in accordance with the wishes of the Opposition.

Whenever the House wishes to express its views on those national issues which over-ride party divisions, e.g. events concerning the Royal Family or the death of a distinguished statesman, the Prime Minister acts as its spokeman. On such occasions, the Leader of the Opposition usually underlines the unity of the House by adding his own observations.

(8) *He communicates the Government's decisions to the Sovereign*

The Sovereign has, as we have seen, a constitutional right to be informed and consulted on matters of government, and so most Prime Ministers have a regular weekly audience.

On certain occasions, too, the Prime Minister acts as personal adviser to the Sovereign and the Royal Family, for example, on the constitutional implications of marriage proposals, changes in names or the Royal title, or invitations to visit Commonwealth and foreign countries.

(9) *He is responsible for a wide variety of appointments and exercises considerable patronage*

This function is the result of the Prime Minister having largely taken over the prerogative powers of the Sovereign (see page 226).

(10) *He meets with Commonwealth Prime Ministers at periodic conferences and with the heads of other governments at 'summit talks'*

Conferences of Commonwealth Prime Ministers are now held regularly (see page 519). More occasionally, heads of government of the great nations meet together to discuss subjects of top-level importance. In such talks, the Prime Minister may commit Britain to far-reaching decisions.

III. Importance of the Prime Minister

The Prime Minister is the outstanding figure in the British constitution, the duties and powers of his office giving him a personal prestige which is limited only by his own personality and the extent to which he enjoys the support of his party.

His functions, important in themselves, have added significance in that, being based almost wholly on convention, they can largely be interpreted as he sees fit. As Lord Oxford and Asquith said in 1921: 'The office of Prime Minister is what its holder chooses to make it.' As leader of the majority party, he is chosen by the electorate, to whom he can appeal at any time to confirm his position. Since he controls the composition of the ministry, members of the Government are to a large extent subservient to him. In the Cabinet he occupies a dominant position, selecting the items for discussion, presiding at its meetings, giving a lead on policy and arbitrating between ministers. Opportunities to determine policy also arise when he gives a decision in an emergency, advises ministers or takes a hand in co-ordinating the Government's programme. Moreover, his management of the House of Commons almost completely guarantees the acceptance of that policy, while the fact that no other minister communicates with the Sovereign, except with his prior knowledge, places him in a strong position when offering advice.

Moreover, the tendency is for his powers to increase. Morley described the Prime Minister as 'the key-stone of the Cabinet arch'. Sir Ivor Jennings considers this description inadequate, saying that he should be regarded rather as 'the key-stone of the Constitution'. The exceptional authority which the Prime Minister now enjoys has a variety of causes.

The most important is the reliance which the Prime Minister can now place on his leadership being accepted both by the foremost party members and the rank and file. The former are usually in the Government; the latter are subject to the discipline of the party machine. Apart from the formal rules of the party, however, the Prime Minister enjoys formidable sanctions in securing united support. His patronage powers can be used to reward faithful followers; the political appointments for which he is responsible are the steps in the ladder to higher office. If the carrot does not suffice, he can wield the big stick. Ministers who cannot fall in with his policy will be asked to resign. If all else fails, the parliamentary party can be reminded of the possibility of dissolution. Fighting an election today is an arduous and costly operation. Having won his seat, a member does not usually wish to risk it again until Parliament is nearing the end of its statutory life. Thus the weapon of dissolution strengthens the executive relative to the legislature — and some writers, such as Christopher Hollis, assert that we now have cabinet government instead of parliamentary government. Moreover, since the decision to dissolve now rests with the Prime Minister, an election represents a personal appeal by him to the people. Nor need he wait for defeat in the House; when murmurings are heard within his party, he can ask for a dissolution at the most propitious moment. Rebels seeking support for an alternative policy are therefore at a serious disadvantage.

Recent developments in science and international affairs have also increased the Prime Minister's importance. Radio and television bring him more frequently than any other politician into the homes of the people, who therefore see in his personality the embodiment of the party and, in times of emergency, the trustee of the national cause. Summit conferences tend to replace the traditional methods of diplomacy through the Foreign Office, for the Prime Minister has had to assume the leading role in foreign policy.

Lastly, the creation of the Cabinet Office and the development of Cabinet committees have extended the Prime Minister's authority. Not only is the important administrative work of the Cabinet Office carried on under his direction, but he sits on the leading Cabinet committees, which gives him a breadth of knowledge and opportunities to influence recommendations available to no other minister.

Of course, it is the personality and character of the Prime Minister which will determine how he interprets the scope of his functions, the methods by which he fulfils them, and the success he achieves. He is always dependent on the support of his party, and so he would be unlikely to pursue a policy which carried a high risk of provoking a major party split. Thus Mr. Wilson dropped his anti-strike legislation in 1969 because of trade union and left-wing opposition. He must handle his Cabinet with tact, acting as chairman in the first instance so that every member can share in deciding policy, and only later playing a more decisive role as leader when he feels that a decision should be reached more in line with his own views. With most Prime Ministers, in fact, it is possible to trace personal policies — the repeal of the Corn Laws, 1846, by Peel; the appeasement policy at Munich, 1938, by Neville Chamberlain; the war strategy, 1940–5, by Winston Churchill; the invasion of Suez, 1956, by Eden; the compulsory prices and incomes 'freeze' of 1966 by Wilson; Common Market entry, 1971, by Heath. Once he has announced his policy, his followers rarely fail to support him and, given this solid party backing, 'a Prime Minister wields an authority that a Roman Emperor might envy or a modern dictator strive in vain to emulate' (Sir Ivor Jennings: *Cabinet Government*).

SUGGESTED READING

F. W. G. Benemy, *The Elected Monarch* (Harrap, 1965).

R. Butt, *The Power of Parliament* (Constable, 1967), Chapter 17.

Byrum E. Carter, *The Office of the Prime Minister* (Faber and Faber, 1955).

B. Crick, *The Reform of Parliament* (Weidenfeld and Nicolson, 1964), Chapter 2.

M. Edelman, *The Prime Minister's Daughter* (Hamish Hamilton, 1964).

Sir Ivor Jennings, *Cabinet Government* (3rd Ed., C.U.P., 1969), Chapters 2, 3, 5, 8, 9, 13 and 14.

J. P. Mackintosh, *The Government and Politics of Britain* (Hutchinson, 1970), Chapters 5–8.

15

The Cabinet

'The Cabinet is the core of the British constitutional system. It is the supreme directing authority. It integrates what would otherwise be a heterogeneous collection of authorities exercising a vast variety of functions. It provides unity to the British system of government.'

SIR IVOR JENNINGS: *Cabinet Government*

I. HISTORICAL DEVELOPMENT

THE PRIVY COUNCIL AND ITS WEAKNESSES

In chapter 4 it was shown how medieval kings consulted periodically with the Great Council, the Magnum Concilium, on important matters of State, especially those affecting taxation. As the business of the realm increased, the King had to appoint a smaller Council which was in permanent session. This contained the leading officials, such as the Justiciar, the Lord Chancellor, the Lord Treasurer, the Lord Keeper of the Privy Seal and the leading judges. It was known originally as the Curia Regis and developed later into the Privy Council.

By the 13th century the Privy Council was a definite body, having paid members who took an oath to give the King good advice, though he was not usually present at their deliberations. Its composition was decided solely by the King. It was not a large body, consisting in 1404, for instance, of nineteen persons. Though the King could consult with this Privy Council concerning the exercise of the royal power, it did not preclude him from meeting with the Great Council as a whole or contacting unofficial persons, such as nobles, bishops and court favourites. In practice, therefore, the scope of the Privy Council's activities varied with the strength and character of the King. Thus during the period when Henry III, Richard II and Henry VI reigned as minors, the Council virtually governed the country, but under Henry VII it was merely used to register the King's decisions.

The Proclamations of the Council became the means of communicating the royal will to the nation, the Council also taking the necessary administrative measures. But, in addition to executive functions, the Council soon acquired judicial powers in both civil and criminal cases. Original civil jurisdiction arose from people petitioning the King in Council as an alternative to the King in Parliament. By the early 15th century, cases going to the Council were automatically referred to the Chancellor, the King's chief legal adviser, and he developed a system of law alongside the common law, known as 'equity' (see page 358). Although it was admitted that the Council had authority for certain offences, such as neglect of duties by J.P.s, riots, and bribery of jurors, its criminal jurisdiction was, from the beginning of the 14th century, continually being opposed by the statutes of Parliament.

The Privy Council reached the zenith of its power under the Tudors, who turned it into an efficient engine of government with legislative, executive and judicial functions. It issued ordinances, controlled the administration of those ordinances and, with extended jurisdiction, punished those who did not obey them. Its Court of Star Chamber became particularly notorious for its investigation of political offences and its use of torture as a means of extracting confessions. But, as Parliament became bolder in its opposition to the King, so the power of the Privy Council declined. The Court of Star Chamber was abolished in 1641, while during the Civil War and the Commonwealth period, the Privy Council ceased to exist. When it was restored in 1660, its powers were considerably reduced.

The Privy Council today consists of some 300 members and contains all Cabinet ministers past and present, the Archbishop of Canterbury, the Speaker of the House of Commons, the Lords of Appeal, the Lord Chief Justice, retired High Court judges, high-ranking ambassadors, and other persons prominent in public life, both at home and in the Commonwealth. But it meets as a body only when the Sovereign dies or announces his intention to marry. Usually the business which remains to it is conducted by four to six members (a quorum is three) summoned by the Clerk of the Council. These members are usually Cabinet ministers who meet in the Queen's presence, and the Clerk gives authority to the proceedings by signing the minutes. Its functions are:

(1) Carrying out the formal business of receiving oaths of office, appointing and removing holders of certain Crown appointments, receiving homage from bishops.

(2) Giving effect, without deliberation, to Cabinet decisions, by Proclamation or by Orders in Council (see page 402).

(3) Providing members for standing committees, which represent the survival of the Council's old advisory function and today deal with matters relating to Jersey and Guernsey, the Universities of Oxford and Cambridge, and the charters of municipal corporations.

The most important surviving committee is the Judicial Committee of the Privy Council. The Act abolishing the Council's judicial powers in 1641 applied only to England, and it retained its authority to consider appeals from the King's subjects overseas. The Judicial Committee of the Privy Council was formally constituted in 1833. It has appellate jurisdiction from the Courts of the Channel Islands and the Isle of Man, from the overseas dependencies, and on certain legal issues arising in those independent members of the Commonwealth who have retained the right. (The present tendency, however, is for members to keep appeals within their own judicial system.) It also hears appeals from the Prize Courts, the Ecclesiastical Courts and the Disciplinary Committees of the General Medical Council. The Judicial Committee is composed of the Lord Chancellor, the Lord President of the Council, the Lords of Appeal in Ordinary and other Privy Councillors who have held high judicial office in Britain or the Commonwealth. In practice, it is the Lords of Appeal in Ordinary who man the committee. About 30 appeals are heard each year.

(4) Establishing special committees, containing three to five members, to consider particular problems. Thus in 1957, committees of Privy Councillors enquired into telephone tapping, and studied the problem of reducing the burden on ministers. While the alternative, a Select Committee of the House of Commons, would also have an intimate knowledge of government, the Privy Council committee has the advantage of being more compact, not having to represent a cross-section of the House.

THE 17TH-CENTURY CABINET

Under the Stuarts, the Privy Council was too large to be an efficient advisory or executive body, having increased to over fifty members. Moreover, containing critics and even traitors, it was unacceptable as a policy-forming body. Hence, both James I and Charles I sought advice either from a small body or, more frequently, from a single person, such as Strafford or Laud. The Council itself formed committees to deal with such matters as foreign affairs, the army and navy, complaints and grievances, and trade and plantations, but so clumsy was the procedure for referring matters to the appropriate committee and acting on its advice that the committee system proved unworkable.

The most important attempt to overcome the weakness of the large size of the Council was promoted by Charles II, who consulted with only a small group of members rather than with the whole body. This group was known as the Cabinet or Cabal, the former because it met in the King's closet, the latter from the initials of the men composing it — Clifford, Arlington, Buckingham, Ashley and Lauderdale. It was not a true committee of the Privy Council, for it was selected entirely by the King; nor did it resemble our present Cabinet. Its members were linked to the King rather than to each other and shared his confidence unequally. They distrusted and disliked one another and were therefore ineffective as a combination. Nor were they departmental heads assembling to discuss policy as a whole, but were called together by the King merely to consider such problems as he chose to submit to them. Moreover, by being present at their deliberations, he could hear conflicting opinions — quite different from the modern practice, where the Cabinet's advice carries weight, politically and psychologically, by being tendered as a whole. Above all, the Cabal did not represent a permanent body which would be consulted by the King on all problems and at all times, for he could, and did, confer with other persons.

The Cabal was justly unpopular. Not only did it tend to increase the personal influence of the monarch, since policy was formulated in secret outside the main body of the Council, but the uncertainty as to who actually tendered advice made it impossible for Parliament to fix responsibility for mis-government. Attempts were made, therefore, to restore the Privy Council to its former eminence, but these came to nothing.

DEVELOPMENT OF THE MODERN CABINET

The Cabinet first began to acquire an authority of its own when George I ceased to attend its meetings, for then decisions were conveyed to the King by one of the ministers present. The practice was continued by George II and accepted by George III, and, as a result, the personal influence of the monarch diminished and a dominant minister emerged.

But there seems to have been no continuous link between the Cabal and the modern Cabinet. At the beginning of the 18th century, the King chose the nominal or formal Cabinet from the great officers of State, many of whom had no departmental duties. But such a large body lacked solidarity and secrecy. Hence a small inner Cabinet, the 'efficient Cabinet', developed, consisting of the political officers of the Household, those who actually carried on government. Walpole, for instance, would usually prepare the ground for policy decisions by discussing the matter over dinner with the minister responsible. The efficient Cabinet would then be called and a united policy decided upon. The next step of summoning the nominal Cabinet was merely to obtain formal consent to the decisions already agreed upon.

It was then the task of the leading minister to persuade the King to accept this advice. Persuasion and subtlety would first be used, but often the King's views had to be over-ruled. The extent to which this happened was largely determined by the respective personalities of the monarch and his leading minister. Walpole resigned in 1717 when Townshend was dismissed, and was such a nuisance in opposition that he had to be recalled with Townshend in office. Similarly, when Pelham resigned in 1745 because George II would not have the elder Pitt in his ministry, the King had to give way, while Newcastle would only form a Government in 1757 on condition that Pitt served him as Secretary of State. Finally, the failure in 1807 of George III to extort a promise from the Grenville ministry that no further concessions would be made to the Roman Catholics gave rise to the doctrine that the Crown must not fetter its advisers by exacting pledges as to their future action.

Only gradually did the Cabinet develop its essential role as the link between the Crown and Parliament. The prevailing doctrine of the 18th century was the separation of powers, which held that the executive should be independent of the legislature. In terms of everyday government, this meant that the Crown was responsible for policy and administration, which Parliament could control directly by legislation or indirectly by refusing to grant Supply. Neither method, however, provided a really effective means of forcing the Government to follow a policy acceptable to Parliament. That came about only as the party system developed and the King admitted that, in choosing his ministers, he should accept the leaders of the majority party in the House of Commons and follow the policy which they advised.

This the 18th-century Sovereigns had to learn by experience. There was no party system in the modern sense of the term. Support for a Government in Parliament rested on family political groupings, patronage and the goodwill of the 'independents'. Such a situation could not produce with any consistency the characteristics of our modern Cabinet — submission to the authority of a Prime Minister, the ultimate supremacy of the Cabinet's view over the Sovereign's, political unanimity and collective responsibility. Most Prime Ministers were orignally chosen because of their acceptability to the King, though their survival depended on skilful management of the House of Commons. The Sovereign changed his advisers as the need arose. Only in 1714 did the whole of the ministry go at the same time, and this did not happen again until 1782. Moreover, since ministries usually contained men of both parties, there was no need for them to resign collectively if defeated in Parliament. In 1719 Stanhope's Peerage Bill was defeated through the opposition of Walpole, but it did not lead to the resignation of Stanhope, the leader of the Government. Again, in 1733 Walpole had to withdraw his Excise Bill, a Government financial measure, and in 1739 he had to declare war on Spain against his wishes, but he did not resign on either occasion.

Towards the end of the century, however, the Commons began to exercise more authority in controlling the Government. Thus in 1780 we have Dunning's motion, 'that the influence of the Crown has increased, is increasing, and ought to be diminished,' while the Economical Reforms of 1782 removed many opportunities for patronage When, a few years later, George III withdrew from active politics, Pitt was left supreme and the Cabinet system developed apace.

But it was the Reform Act, 1832, which dealt the final blow to the King's power, and set in motion those forces which made the

Cabinet the instrument by which the people could retain control over policy. The development of parties meant that from now on the choice of Prime Minister and Government rested with the electorate, not the Sovereign (see page 58). To determine the relationship between the Cabinet and these parties and between the Cabinet and Parliament, conventions evolved. Such conventions developed at different times and have been modified as conditions have changed. A consideration of them will reveal the main features of the present-day Cabinet system.

II. Main Conventions governing the Cabinet System

The functioning of the Cabinet system is determined almost entirely by convention. Indeed, until 1937, when the Ministers of the Crown Act provided for the payment of salaries to those ministers who were members of the Cabinet, it was entirely unknown to the law. Even in Parliament, Cabinet ministers are legally only on an equal footing with other members, a fact underlined in 1857 when the Commons would not approve priority for them when passing over to the Lords. In practice, however, ministers do enjoy some privileges by custom. Thus the front bench to the right of the Speaker is reserved for them, and in debate they find it much easier to catch the Speaker's eye.

The rules regulating the Cabinet system and its relationship to the Sovereign, the Prime Minister, Parliament, parties and the electorate, are the most fundamental conventions in the British constitution, for it is through them that the political sovereignty of the electorate is implemented. Here we merely describe how they normally operate; why they are followed and their advantages over written law are discussed in Chapter 29.

(1) *The composition of the Cabinet is decided by the Prime Minister*

Subject to minor qualifications, the Prime Minister has a completely free hand in selecting his Cabinet (see pages 240–4). Some ministers without portfolio are included and, if he chooses, the Prime Minister can create new departments. In 1970 Mr. Heath did this in order to reduce the Cabinet to seventeen (compared with Mr. Wilson's twenty-three).

(2) *The Cabinet is chosen from the majority party in the House of Commons*

The Leader of the party having a majority of seats in the House of Commons must be sent for by the Sovereign to form the Government. Two possible exceptions to this rule occur where: (*a*) the existence of an important third party results in no one party having an absolute majority; (*b*) abnormal circumstances make it desirable to form a coalition Government. But such conditions rarely apply. A third party may emerge as a result of a party split or in response to new political needs, but it finds difficulty in growing to a size sufficient to upset the two-party system. On the other hand, coalitions are disliked, since they fail to produce strong and decisive government.

It is this convention which solves the problem of how to secure co-operation between the legislature and the executive, a problem which led to the breakdown of government under the Stuarts. Later monarchs recognised the necessity of having a ministry not faced with a hostile House of Commons, and either selected ministers who were likely to receive support there or, as with George III, chose those who would follow his policy and then packed the House with sufficient members to uphold that policy. But the Reform Act, 1832, by transferring sovereignty to the electorate, made the adoption of this convention essential. The choice of the ministry could no longer rest with the monarch. Had he pressed the issue, the King might easily have become involved in party politics, with a loss of influence and dignity when he eventually had to climb down. As early as 1834 the situation was brought home to William IV. The King had seized on a hint by Lord Melbourne to secure his resignation and had replaced him with his own choice, Sir Robert Peel, the Tory Leader. At the election which followed, however, the Tories were defeated and Peel, since he could not obtain the necessary support for his Government, was forced to resign in favour of Lord Melbourne.

(3) *A Government defeated on a major issue in the House of Commons must either resign or ask for a dissolution of Parliament*

In 1841 it was proved that no Government can continue in office when faced by a hostile House of Commons. Two years previously Lord Melbourne had tendered his resignation when he lost the support of the Radicals and the Irish. Peel, however, declined office because the Queen would not change her Ladies of the Bedchamber, who were Whig in sympathy. Lord Melbourne therefore continued in office, although subject to frequent adverse votes in the House of Commons. The climax came in 1841, when a resolution was moved by Peel 'that Her Majesty's ministers do not sufficiently possess the confidence of the House of Commons to enable them to carry through the House measures which they deem of essential importance to the public welfare, and their continuance in office, under such circumstances, is at variance with the spirit of the constitution'. As a result, the Whigs asked for a dissolution, and at the general election which followed they were defeated; but it was not until a no-confidence amendment to the Address was carried against them that they resigned.

Today, strict party discipline makes a Government defeat in the House of Commons unlikely. Failure of party members to support Cabinet decisions in the division lobby will lead either to the resignation of the Government or to a dissolution. Thus they cannot afford to forget Bagehot's warning that the Cabinet is 'a committee which can dissolve the assembly which appointed it; it is . . . a committee with a power to appeal. Though appointed by one parliament, it can appeal if it chooses to the next' (*The English Constitution*). Members, as already pointed out, will not risk losing their seats other than on the most exceptional grounds. Hence, once formed, it is the Cabinet which now controls the Commons, rather than the House controlling the Government, and Cabinet policy is almost automatically ratified by Parliament.

(4) *A Government defeated at the polls resigns immediately*

At one time a Government, although defeated at a general election, went through the procedure of meeting Parliament and waiting for a formal vote of 'no confidence'. Disraeli, however, established the practice in 1868 of resigning immediately an election had been conceded.

The situation is somewhat different when no party is returned with an absolute majority, for it may not be known which way the minority parties will vote. In this case, the Government meets Parliament and awaits the result of an amendment to the Address.

(5) *All ministers are collectively responsible for Cabinet decisions*

Except when a minister explains the reasons for his resignation,

Parliament hears nothing of the Cabinet's current deliberations. These remain secret, and only decisions as a whole are reported to the House when policy is announced. Any leakage of divergent views held by ministers would, as during Queen Victoria's reign, seriously weaken the Government. In its decisions, 'the Cabinet is a unity to the House'. While a minister can speak against any proposal in a Cabinet meeting, he must either support the policy decided upon or resign. Recent resignations of this nature are Frank Cousins (Prices and Incomes Bill, 1966) and Lord Longford (education cuts, 1968). But such resignations are infrequent. Ministers come from the same party and, at least initially, are fairly homogeneous in their political views. In any case, a former minister is unlikely to cross the floor of the House and join the Opposition. His disagreement with the Government is usually over only one issue, and his basic political outlook remains unchanged.

Thus the Cabinet stands or falls together. Where the policy of a particular minister is under attack, it is the government as a whole which is being attacked. Thus the defeat of a minister on any major issue represents a defeat for the Government. However, today, unlike the 19th century, such defeats do not occur. The use of rigid party discipline ensures that the Government can always obtain a majority vote. Nevertheless, criticism may be so severe and wide-spread that the Government may modify its policy. If the minister identified with it feels that his prestige with the party has been badly damaged, he may resign, e.g. Sir Samuel Hoare (1935) over the proposals to partition Abyssinia.

In practice, therefore, all that collective responsibility means today is that every member of the Government must be prepared to support all Cabinet decisions both inside and outside the House. That this aspect of collective responsibility is still real today was seen in the case of Mr. Frank Cousins while Minister of Technology. He was constantly under attack from the Opposition for his known hostility to the Government's wages policy. Mr. Rees-Mogg (*The Sunday Times*, October 3, 1965) summed up the situation as follows: 'He must, if he is to remain in the Cabinet, give public support to the Cabinet's wages policy. He cannot remain in the Cabinet but not of it; that is an affront to the British constitution, and the British constitution will win in the end.' It did!

It should be noted, however, that resignation may not come immediately. The minister may remain for a time in the Cabinet hoping to convert its views, as with Mr. Cousins. Or disagreements over policy may not be pursued. Thus while in 1974 both Mr. Michael Foot (Secretary of State for Employment) and Mr. Eric Heffer (Minister of State for Industry) openly disagreed with the Government's decision to continue to supply arms to the new anti-Communist regime in Chile, neither resigned. Nevertheless, when a year later Mr. Heffer spoke against the E.E.C. contrary to the agreed guideline, he was dismissed. The open split in the Cabinet on whether to remain in the E.E.C. must be regarded as a unique occasion.

Collective responsibility does not apply to a minister's responsibility for his permanent officials or for his personal mistakes. Thus only Sir Thomas Dugdale resigned over Crichel Down (1954), Dr. Hugh Dalton through inadvertent budget disclosures (1947), Mr. John Profumo over lying to the House of Commons (1963), and Lord Lambton and Lord Jellicoe (1973) over their involvement with prostitutes.

III. Importance of the Cabinet in the Constitution

While the Cabinet has important policy-forming and co-ordinating functions, it is not merely an executive organ of government. It is the device which gives coherence to the whole of the British constitution and represents an alternative to the separation of powers as a basis of organising democratic government. Through the Cabinet, the executive power is directly related to the legislature and so to the electorate.

Until the development of the Cabinet system, there was always difficulty in ensuring that ministers acted in harmony with the wishes of Parliament. The Sovereign was responsible for deciding policy and, so long as he could manage without seeking funds from the Commons, he was subject to little restraint. The only sanctions available to the Commons were the ability to withhold Supply and, to a lesser extent, the impeachment of responsible ministers.

Both methods, however, were negative, leading to deadlock and sterile government. Tudor monarchs realised it was better to forestall criticism. Leading statesmen were therefore encouraged to seek election to the House of Commons so that they could explain policy and report back to the Sovereign the views expressed there.

The Stuarts were less skilful, and collisions between the executive and legislature brought about the breakdown of government.

After 1688, the liaison between the Government and Parliament became closer. By the arrangements made for the Civil List in 1697, the House of Commons ensured that, for a large part of his revenue, the King would in future have to make periodic application to Parliament. Policy thus became subject to continual examination, and henceforth Sovereigns recognised the desirability of choosing ministers acceptable to the Commons. This was achieved by linking the ministry with the party system which was developing in Parliament. Herein lies the essence of the Cabinet — it is an executive body deriving its authority from the legislature by being appointed from among those persons whose views there are in the majority. Bagehot explains it as follows: 'A Cabinet is a combining committee — a *hyphen* which joins, a *buckle* which fastens the legislative part of the state to the executive part of the state. In its origin it belongs to the one, in its function it belongs to the other' (*The English Constitution*).

When, in 1832, political sovereignty passed to the electorate, the Cabinet system was taken one stage further, for now the executive was linked, not only with the legislature but, through the extension of parties outside Parliament, to the electorate. Because of the two-party system, a general election today is virtually a plebiscite to decide which set of persons shall manage the country's affairs. Such an arrangement goes a long way towards achieving democratic and effective government. It is democratic for two reasons: (*a*) the electorate can vote for a definite Government following a policy announced in broad outline at the election; (*b*) the people retain the right to criticise that Government through their representatives in Parliament, chiefly on the Opposition side. It is effective because the Government is drawn from the party having a majority of seats in the House of Commons.

Some commentators fear that the executive is becoming too powerful. The Cabinet, through the party machine, tends nowadays to control the House of Commons rather than itself being subject to the sovereignty of Parliament. It disciplines the House by the threat of dissolution. It has virtual control over legislation. It makes all financial proposals and, by its demands on parliamentary time, prevents the Commons from discussing them adequately. It has secured increasing opportunities for delegated legislation. It has so added to the number of ministerial offices that today the Government alone (including the Parliamentary Private Secretaries and certain offices of the Royal Household which are political appointments) represents over a hundred seats in the Commons. It can interfere directly in 20% of national production through its supervision over the State industries.

Such developments, it can be argued, are essential to the modern Welfare State. The traditional theory of the sovereignty of Parliament has no special virtue in itself but was significant only in its conflict with absolute monarchy. Today the Cabinet should not be viewed in isolation as an organ opposed to Parliament, but rather the two must be regarded as complementary in the functioning of the constitution.

IV. FUNCTIONS OF THE CABINET

We now turn to an examination of the work for which the Cabinet is responsible. Although its functions tend to overlap, it is convenient to sub-divide them under the following headings:

(1) *It decides on the major policy to be followed in both home and foreign affairs*

The policies advanced by the parties at an election represent a reflection of their prevailing philosophies rather than programmes to be implemented in detail. A party can expect to see a certain line followed if it is returned to power, but it should not fetter the Government. The Cabinet has a duty, not only to the party, but to the whole nation, and so it must be given considerable freedom to act for what it considers is the national well-being. If people think that party interests have been allowed to dominate, the floating vote may turn against the Government at the next election. (The failure of the Labour Government to stand up to the trade unions probably contributed considerably to its loss of support in the election of 1970).

In any case, it is the Cabinet which decides the moment when each issue shall be submitted to Parliament and draws up the legislative programme which the Government aims to complete during its present term of office. Where a measure may temporarily cost it some popularity, e.g. the removal of subsidies on school meals and welfare milk in 1970, the Cabinet is likely to act early so that the general benefits of the policy can be appreciated before it has to seek re-election. The same applies to measures which cannot come into full operation before extensive administrative machinery has been established. In fact, during the last years of a Parliament, only those bills which excite little controversy are usually introduced.

(2) It fills in the details of policy

Apart from the working reports of the various committees of the Labour Party, the parties do not examine proposals in great administrative detail. This is left to the Government when the party gains office. For a number of reasons, there may be a considerable difference between what the election programme seemed to signify and the detailed scheme actually introduced. In the first place, the Government may have to modify its plans in the light of prevailing conditions. Thus, additional finance may impose limits. Secondly, the Government must ensure co-ordination between all the departments concerned with a project, directly or indirectly, and this may again prevent it going too far in one direction. Above all, in implementing proposals, the Government consults with the interests concerned, something not allowed for in the party programme.

(3) It co-ordinates the policies of different departments

If the administration is to work smoothly and policy is to be implemented successfully, there must be careful co-ordination between the departments affected. A proposal to raise the school-leaving age, for example, would affect not only the Department of Education and Science, but also the Department of Employment, the Ministry of Defence, the Department of Health and Social Security, and the Home office, to mention merely a few.

While a large measure of co-ordination may be achieved at lower levels by the departments concerned, the broad aspects have to be decided at Cabinet level (see page 267). This will apply both in planning policy and later when the scheme is in operation. If it is to be successful, therefore, the Cabinet must contain a number of heads of departments (see page 269).

(4) It takes decisions on unforeseen major problems

New problems are continually arising, both at home and abroad, which call for Government decisions. Apart from parliamentary business, which is a standing item on the agenda, and changes in the economy, which have to be discussed regularly, matters often reach Cabinet level by attracting the attention of the Press or being the subject of embarrassing questions in Parliament. Above all, in foreign affairs, urgent decisions frequently have to be taken. A revolution in the Middle East or an outbreak of violence in an African country would have to come before the Cabinet. Thus foreign matters form another standing item of business.

(5) *It formulates plans for the future*

Since the State has a continuous existence, plans have to be laid now for anything up to fifty years ahead. Thus measures have to be taken to provide for future changes in the population before the end of the century, to develop atomic energy in co-ordination with other industries providing power, to plan new methods of defence, and to apply scientific advance to production. It must be admitted that, to some extent, long-term planning is made more difficult by the Cabinet's being composed of frequently-changing party politicians.

Thus the Cabinet is the real policy-forming body in the British constitution. It provides the dynamic impulses vital to progressive government or, as Professor H. Laski puts it, 'the Cabinet pushes a stream of tendency through affairs.' Without it, policy would be stagnant; the only alternative would be to introduce committees to run departments, on the pattern adopted in the U.S.A. and in our own local government.

V. How the Cabinet Works

Although meetings of the Cabinet may be held anywhere and at any time, they usually take place each Wednesday in the Cabinet Room at 10 Downing Street. Circumstances may make it necessary for them to be held more frequently. Thus the burden of decision-making imposed by the war and the heavy reconstruction pro-gramme of the Labour Government led to the Cabinet meeting twice weekly from 1939 to 1951. Emergency meetings may also be summoned.

The agenda is under the control of the Prime Minister, who decides what shall be included and arranges the order of business. Urgent matters may be added by him or by other ministers with his consent. Usually discussion of an item begins by the Prime Minister calling upon the minister principally concerned to state the views of the department. If there is general agreement, a conclusion is soon reached. But criticism and alternatives may be put forward. Ministers are included in the Cabinet not so much for their departmental ability as for their capacity to consider policy as a whole. Thus, while on most matters discussion is confined chiefly to ministers immediately concerned, on those issues likely to evoke party controversy or to excite public opinion, every member of the Cabinet may state his point of view. Particular attention will be given to the opinion of the chairman of any Cabinet committee which has previously considered the matter. But it is the attitude of the Prime Minister which is of fundamental importance. Any person having special knowledge may be summoned. Service chiefs frequently attend and sometimes civil servants, on the special authorisation of the Prime Minister.

Secrecy of the proceedings of Cabinet meetings, essential to collective responsibility, is secured by the Privy Councillor's oath, which is taken by all ministers. But information about what occurs can be gathered from various sources. Communications are released to the Press, books are written by ex-Cabinet ministers, and political controversies always seem to produce inspired reports of what has taken place at Cabinet meetings. Moreover, where disagreement has led to a minister's resignation, it is usual for him to be given the opportunity in Parliament of explaining his position and his speech may well provide further information.

In order to avoid upsetting the solidarity of the Cabinet, decisions are not reached by voting for or against a proposal. Instead, the Prime Minister uses his influence to arrive at a common decision, expressing 'the sense of the meeting' in such terms as, 'Gentlemen, we are agreed that. . . .' Where this is not possible, it may be necessary to 'collect voices' by asking the individual members to express their views. This procedure is carried out as informally as possible; the Secretary keeps count of the numbers and the Prime Minister announces the majority view.

A Cabinet meeting usually lasts approximately two hours, an exceedingly short period of time considering the importance of its work. The reasons for its ability to complete its business so quickly are: (a) only those matters of such importance or political significance that they cannot be decided personally by a minister are brought before the Cabinet; (b) much of the ground is cleared before Cabinet discussion takes place through interdepartmental meetings and informal talks between ministers concerned; (c) the minister may confer beforehand with the Prime Minister and modify the proposal in the light of his advice; (*d*) departments anticipate and remove difficulties; (*e*) Cabinet papers, consisting of memoranda, summaries of arguments and the minister's recommendations are circulated by the Cabinet Office, if possible at least two days before the Cabinet meets; (*f*) where a subject has to be examined in some detail, it is usually considered beforehand by a Cabinet committee whose chairman will endeavour to make firm proposals; (*g*) the atmosphere of co-operation and quiet discussion as opposed to formal speeches is conducive to arriving at quick decisions; (*h*) the dominant position of the Prime Minister enables him to give a strong lead; (*i*) on major issues of policy, the Prime Minister may have had personal consultation with four or five of his leading colleagues, sometimes referred to as 'the inner Cabinet'; (*j*) improved organisation and methods have been developed to cope with the growth and complexity of Government business (see below).

VI. Development of the Cabinet during the 20th Century

The organisation of the Cabinet system has not been based on any carefully thought-out principles, nor could it follow any foreign pattern or learn from a previous experiment. Instead, improvements came gradually over a long period as experience was gained, circumstances changed, and fresh needs arose.

During the 19th century, the time-lag between new requirements and Cabinet development in response to them was not serious. The work of the State was comparatively light and Government could proceed at a fairly leisurely pace. But, with the turn of the century, the increased tempo of economic and political life, the end of the *laissez-faire* philosophy, the beginning of the Welfare State, and the demands of two major wars, all contributed to a more critical attitude towards Cabinet organisation. Four main criticisms emerged:

(1) *The procedure was too slack*

If the Cabinet were to complete its work effectively in the comparatively short period of time available, it was obvious that there would have to be a more formal organisation of its meetings: careful preliminary work should precede discussion by the full

Cabinet; more thought should be given to the preparation of the agenda; and formal minutes kept. Previously little had been committed to writing on the grounds of secrecy, but at times the resulting confusion was such that ministers had to ask their secretaries to contact their opposite numbers in other departments to ascertain the actual decision which the Cabinet had reached!

(2) *It failed to formulate and direct an effective long-term policy*

The Cabinet is the major policy-forming body. Not only must it decide on important day-to-day problems, but it should lay down consistent and co-ordinated plans for the future. For three major reasons, however, Cabinet organisation had proved particularly unsatisfactory as regards this general thinking: (*a*) Governments are ephemeral, changing at the behest of the electorate; (*b*) the Cabinet tends to be too large for an effective policy-forming body; (*c*) since its members are also departmental heads, Cabinet policy can easily develop into a mere collection of departmental policies, with no clear distinction between planning and administration. Christopher Hollis condemns it outright: 'The traditional system demanded that the heads of all the important departments form the Cabinet, and government policy be settled by Cabinet decision. No system could be devised from which a coherent planned policy is less likely to emerge and, like the American Constitution, the Cabinet system has only worked, so far as it has worked at all, in periods when the great need was to prevent the government from doing things' (*Can Parliament survive?*).

(3) *No provision was made for the full and effective use of expert advice*

Ministers, being essentially laymen, base their decisions on the advice of experts. Certain matters, however, such as defence and economic policy, are continuously being discussed by the Cabinet and this calls for direct contact between the Cabinet and the experts.

(4) *Departmental co-ordination was inefficient*

If the Government is to follow a consistent policy, the departments must be co-ordinated to ensure that their work does not overlap, that they do not encroach on each other's responsibilities or even follow contradictory policies, and that differences between them are resolved. When the Cabinet became the chief organ of co-ordination in the 19th century, there were only about a dozen departments. But today the functions of government are far more extensive and complex, and the number of departments has increased. Thus, not only had the brief meetings of the Cabinet proved inadequate for the full consideration of policy, but it was impossible to include all ministerial heads.

ATTEMPTS TO OVERCOME THESE WEAKNESSES

(1) *The establishment of a permanent secretariat*

The informal consideration of Cabinet business broke down under the stress of World War I. Consequently, in 1916, Mr. Lloyd George took over the existing secretariat of the Committee of Imperial Defence. The system proved so valuable that, despite opposition, it was decided to retain it permanently. Today the Cabinet Office performs the following functions for the Cabinet and its committees: (*a*) it circulates Cabinet Papers, consisting of concise statements by the departments, memoranda, documents and recommendations as to action on matters coming up for discussion; (*b*) it prepares agendas; (*c*) it summons persons to attend meetings; (*d*) it records the essential points of discussion and the conclusions reached; (*e*) it circulates these decisions to the departments affected; (*f*) it reports periodically on the implementation of decisions; (*g*) it promotes measures to remove friction between the departments.

The present tendency is for the Cabinet Office to develop into a 'Prime Minister's Office', through which the Prime Minister keeps himself informed. Thus, the Cabinet Secretary is not only secretary at Cabinet meetings but also the Prime Minister's chief official adviser. Moreover, there is now a central policy section whose task is to consider how policies in particular departments fit in with the government's basic strategy. While it works for Ministers collectively, it is under the supervision of the Prime Minister and serves to strengthen his hand in dealing with and co-ordinating departments by providing him with the necessary expert advice. Apart from the Secretariat, the Central Statistical Office has been brought under the Cabinet Office so as to keep its findings free from the influence of any one department.

(2) *A reduction in the size of the Cabinet*

That a large Cabinet cannot direct general policy efficiently became obvious in World War I, but it was not until 1916, when Mr. Lloyd George formed a small War Cabinet, that British war policy was completely directed by a single body. This Cabinet consisted of five members, all of whom, except the Chancellor of the Exchequer, were free from departmental responsibilities.

In order that there shall be a proper distinction between day-to-day administration and long-term general planning, many authorities, including the Haldane Committee on the Machinery of Government, 1918, and the late Mr. L. S. Amery, have advocated some form of smaller Cabinet in peace-time. This Cabinet would consist chiefly of co-ordinating ministers appointed on a functional basis to cover such matters as defence and foreign policy; environmental services; economic affairs; the social services. Departmental heads would attend its meetings only when their particular advice was required. The advantages claimed for this smaller Cabinet are: (a) members, freed from departmental duties, would see national problems as a whole and be mentally fresh to formulate and direct a national policy; (b) it would sit more frequently and thus be always available for taking important decisions; (c) the Prime Minister could more easily act as the supreme driving force; (d) each Cabinet minister would be able to direct the policies of departments under his supervision in the light of broad Cabinet decisions, co-ordinating their work and settling any disputes which might arise between them.

Such a proposal, however, raises difficulties. In the first place, it is not always possible to separate policy and administration. As Lord Morrison says: 'A Cabinet without departmental Ministers would be deficient in that day-to-day administrative experience which makes a real contribution to collective decisions' (*Government and Parliament*). Secondly, the arrangement could easily blur departmental responsibility to Parliament. Thirdly, such a small Cabinet might give rise to jealousy among those leading ministers not included, while, in excluding the brilliant young minister, it would deprive him of vital experience. Lastly, the restriction of policy-planning to six super-ministers would keep out many prominent members of the party enjoying the confidence of a particular section. The Cabinet has not only to formulate policy; it must give a political lead to its party, to Parliament and to the country as a whole. Where it concentrates almost exclusively on policy, it can easily lose touch with public opinion. For these reasons, nothing has come of the proposal, and post-war Cabinets have numbered about 20.

Mr. Wilson's 1969 Cabinet consisted of 23, mostly departmental heads. He attempted to get over the difficulty of size by forming a special kind of Cabinet committee, a 'Parliamentary Committee', consisting of the nine senior members of the government. This met twice a week to consider all issues of real political importance. These issues were not referred to it by the Cabinet, but were instigated by the Prime Minister and considered after full briefing by the Cabinet Secretariat. The Committee's decisions were reported to the full Cabinet (which met only once a fortnight), but they were unlikely to be challenged there since the other members knew that the nine senior ministers had been over the ground and had reached agreement. Thus Cabinet meetings merely provided an opportunity for co-ordination and keeping busy departmental ministers in touch.

Mr. Heath was able to limit his Cabinet to 17 members by amalgamating ministries under one department, e.g. the Department of the Environment (Housing and Local Government, Public Building and Works, Transport) and the Department of Trade and Industry (Trade and Technology). In 1975 Mr. Wilson had returned to his larger cabinet with 24 members.

(3) *The formation of committees containing experts*

The realisation that the Cabinet was not making full and continuous use of expert advice led to attempts to form specialised committees to undertake long-term planning in two fields, defence and economic affairs.

A Committee of Imperial Defence was constituted in 1904 from the Naval and Military Committee set up towards the end of the previous century to study strategy and co-ordination. By the outbreak of World War I, this Committee had reviewed every aspect of defence, embodying its plans in a 'Defence Book' which was virtually a blue-print of the action to be taken in the event of war. In theory, the Committee was merely a planning agency; in practice, since its plans were based on an alliance with France, it may be said to have committed the Government indirectly to a particular policy.

During World War II, the Committee of Imperial Defence was absorbed in the War Cabinet, and it was not re-constituted at the conclusion of hostilities. Instead, its responsibilities for defence problems and their implications for foreign and economic policy are performed on behalf of the Cabinet by the Committee on Defence and Overseas Policy which sits under the chairmanship of the Prime Minister.

Long-term economic planning met with less success. Whereas, in defence, everything can be sacrificed to the over-riding need to win the war, economic affairs permit more latitude in deciding priorities, so that the choice becomes political rather than objective. This applies, for example, to the nationalisation of industry, the use of monetary policy, forms of taxation and the redistribution of the national income. In any case, economic changes are difficult to forecast. Nevertheless, some economic research was thought desirable, and so Mr. Baldwin set up in 1928 a Committee for Civil Research with himself as chairman. But, since the Committee could only carry out research on subjects referred to it by the Prime Minister, it found it impossible to formulate a comprehensive long-term economic policy.

Since then we have had a succession of semi-independent advisory bodies which have become increasingly important as the government has assumed greater responsibilities for regulating the economy. These bodies include the Economic Advisory Council (1930), an Economic Planning Board (1947), the National Economic Development Council (1962), the National Incomes Commission (1962), and the National Board for Prices and Incomes (1965).

More recently, the task of advising on long-term economic policy has been made the responsibility of the Treasury or a separate department, e.g. the Department of Economic Affairs, 1964. The position today, however, is that while we still have the National Economic Development Council as a semi-independent body, responsibility for long-term economic planning has reverted to the Treasury.

Mention should also be made of the appointment of individual experts to advise the Prime Minister and Cabinet on their particular subjects. Thus, in 1964, Mr. Wilson appointed Dr. T. Balogh to advise on economic policy and Sir Solly Zuckerman to be Scientific Adviser to the Cabinet, both having direct access to the Prime Minister. Other Cabinet advisers included Dr. N. Kaldor (taxation) and Professor P. M. S. Blackett (technology). In 1970, Mr. Heath appointed Lord Rothschild as head of the Central Policy Review Staff (the 'Think Tank'). This was continued by

Mr. Wilson, and it is now an integral part of the Cabinet Office with the task of advising collectively on major issues of policy.

(4) *The systematic organisation of Cabinet committees*

With the growth in the number of departments, the problem of co-ordinating policy has increased. As we have seen, the Cabinet would be too large for directing policy if it were to include all departmental heads. On the other hand, the views of those ministers not included must be brought to bear on Cabinet decisions.

The Cabinet plays the major role in co-ordinating policy, but its burden can be eased by preliminary work. At the lower level, this is performed by inter-departmental committees and by the Treasury, exercising its control over departmental expenditure. Within the Cabinet, the Prime Minister exerts an important influence. Even so, a more formal organisation has been found necessary.

Sir Winston Churchill's Cabinet of 1951 contained a number of peers who were entrusted with the supervision of certain related ministries. Thus Lord Woolton, the Lord President of the Council, was made responsible for concerting the policy of the Ministries of Agriculture and Food; Lord Leathers was given a new office — the Secretary of State for the Co-ordination of Transport, Fuel and Power; and Lord Cherwell, the Paymaster-General, was placed in charge of research and scientific policy. The system was attacked by the Labour Opposition on the grounds that it tended to blur ministerial responsibility and prevented the Commons from exercising effective control, since the 'Overlords' sat in the House of Lords. The experiment ended in 1953, the main preparatory co-ordinating work reverting to Cabinet committees.

Cabinet committees were first organised on a really systematic basis during the war to meet the heavy demands then made on the Cabinet. When he took over in 1945, Mr. Attlee decided, in view of the extensive programme confronting the Labour Government, to develop this committee organisation and to enlarge the Secretariat to cope with the additional work of servicing these committees. From this time there have been both standing and special committees. Standing committees cover such subjects as defence, economic policy, home and social affairs, immigration, future legislation, agriculture, European affairs and industrial relations. There are at any one time about 20 numbered committees set up to deal on an *ad hoc* basis with issues which may be swiftly disposed of or which may in fact be very important and of a less temporary nature, e.g. the troubles of Northern Ireland.

Careful thought was given to the composition of each committee, especially to the key position of chairman, whose task it is to co-ordinate the views of the many departments concerned. In addition to being able to give a lead, therefore, the chairman must be a good conciliator, enjoying the confidence of all the committee's members and holding himself available to give advice. Hence, he was chosen by the Prime Minister (where the Premier himself did not take the chair) usually from those members of the Cabinet without departments (see above). Occasionally departmental ministers and even Parliamentary Secretaries are appointed. The rest of the committee is chosen according to its work. Where it is concerned with general matters, it contains the leading members of the Cabinet together with those ministers interested but not in the Cabinet. For specialised subjects, ministers directly concerned form the body of the committee, though often other ministers are added to contribute a detached view. Extensive use is made of ministers outside the Cabinet, thereby easing the burden of work and giving them opportunities to share in discussions on policy. Experts, too, may be present.

Meetings follow a pattern similar to those of the Cabinet, taking place as circumstances require, usually once or twice a week but sometimes fortnightly. Committees are serviced by the Cabinet Secretariat and their papers and conclusions are circulated to all ministers. Their terms of reference are carefully defined, the degree of executive authority which they are given varying. Thus one committee might be authorised to decide a matter on behalf of the Cabinet, while another would have to report back recommendations to the Cabinet. Frequently it is left to the chairman to decide whether or not to refer back. Any member who disagrees with the recommendations of his Committee can take the matter to the full Cabinet, though this rarely occurs.

The use of committees relieves the Cabinet of much work, reduces the demands upon its members, and allows more detailed examination of a subject. Frequently the committees divide into sub-committees, while there are many committees or working parties of civil servants and Service officers to sort out and present facts in an orderly way for a department and even to make recommendations to a committee. Where, as most frequently occurs, the committee agrees on policy recommendations, the Cabinet can usually adopt them without further discussion. But even if the committee fails to reach agreement, the exchange of views at least helps to prepare the way for a compromise. Nevertheless, there is always the danger of too many committees developing and of the functions and membership of the standing committees becoming outdated. Hence the Cabinet Office examines the organisation at least once a year and reports to the Prime Minister.

This development of the committee system of the Cabinet since World War II has meant that the full Cabinet of 20 or so members can no longer be regarded as a body which sits down to discuss exhaustively alternative policies. The majority of decisions are taken by the Prime Minister (either alone or in consultation with his most trusted colleagues) and by the various Cabinet committees (the most important of which are chaired by the Prime Minister). The Cabinet must therefore be regarded as an umbrella term to cover these policy-making groups. Instead of being a decision-making body, the full Cabinet is an instrument for co-ordinating the implementation of the decisions of the various committees in order to give coherence to Government work. But in its deliberations, the possible political repercussions of these decisions would loom large.

SUGGESTED READING

A. Aspinall, *The Cabinet Council 1783–1835* (Raleigh Lecture, O.U.P., 1952).

Walter Bagehot, *The English Constitution* (Kegan Paul, 1872), Chapters 1, 7, 8 and 9.

A. H. Birch, *Representative and Responsible Government* (Allen and Unwin, 1964), Chapters 10 and 11.

N. H. Brasher, *Studies in British Government* (2nd Ed., Macmillan, 1971), Chapter 2.

H. Daalder, *Cabinet Reform in Britain, 1914–1963* (O.U.P., 1964).

M. Edelman, *The Minister* (Hamish Hamilton, 1961).

W. Feinburgh, *No Love for Johnny* (Hutchinson, 1959).

Sir Ivor Jennings, *Cabinet Government* (3rd Ed., C.U.P., 1969).

J. P. Mackintosh, *The British Cabinet* (Stevens, 1968).

Lord Morrison, *Government and Parliament* (3rd Ed., O.U.P., 1964), Chapters 1, 2, 3, 4 and 13.

C. P. Snow, *The Corridors of Power* (Macmillan, 1964).

H. Wilson, *The Labour Government 1964–1970* (Weidenfeld and Nicolson, 1971).

16

Government Departments

'The student of political science will recognise that administrators are more or less bound to multiply.'
C. NORTHCOTE PARKINSON: *Parkinson's Law*

I. ORGANISATION OF GOVERNMENT WORK

Administering the services for which the Government is responsible are nearly thirty departments, organised so that each is primarily concerned with a particular field of State activity. Most departments have a minister of their own in control, though some, such as H.M. Stationery Office, the Central Office of Information, and the Department of the Government Actuary, all of which come under the Treasury, are in charge of ministers having other duties. One or two have no minister; thus the Exchequer and Audit Department is under the control of the Comptroller and Auditor General, an officer of Parliament.

The major functions of government are usually performed by departments under a Secretary of State. The title is derived from the King's secretary who, by the reign of Henry III, was relieving the Chancellor of much of his administrative work. Today there are Secretaries of State for the Home Department, Foreign and Commonwealth Affairs, Scotland, Wales, Social Services, Industry, Trade, Defence, Employment, the Environment, Education and Science, Energy, Prices and Consumer Protection and Northern Ireland. The Treasury is under the Chancellor of the Exchequer.

In 1970, when Mr. Heath unified various ministries, ministers were appointed to assist the Secretary of State. Thus, in the Department of the Environment, there is a Minister for Planning and Local Government, a Minister for Housing and Construction, and a Minister for Transport. Each of these Ministers (whose status is that of a Minister in charge of a department not represented in the Cabinet) has full charge of his functional wing of the department.

When the work is particularly heavy or involved, or when it entails frequent visits abroad, Ministers of State, who act as deputy ministers, may be appointed. This practice has grown in recent years and now there are Ministers of State in most government departments.

Junior ministers, usually having the title of Parliamentary Secretary or, where the minister in charge is a Secretary of State, Parliamentary Under-Secretary of State, help their senior ministers both in the department and in Parliament. The Treasury is an exception, for there the Parliamentary Secretary is the Government Chief Whip and some of the Junior Lords act as assistant Whips.

The political head relates the policy of his department to that of the Cabinet and acts as the link between the departments and Parliament. Under his direction, the permanent officials provide the expert technical information and advice, help to form policy and put that policy into effect. The minister is responsible to Parliament for all that takes place in his department (see chapter 17).

The whole history of State activity is reflected in the development and expansion of the government departments. During the 19th century, the era of *laissez-faire*, they remained few in number, though separate offices were set up for the Colonies, War, and India, and Boards were established for Local Government, Agriculture, and Education. During the present century, however, many new departments have been created to deal with social welfare, economic planning, scientific development, and the nationalised industries. Thus we now have departments for Employment, Health and Social Security, Trade, Industry, Prices and Consumer Protection and the Environment. The final decision as to how the activities of the State shall be organised rests with the Prime Minister. He can create new departments and abolish or amalgamate old ones, according to changes in their importance.

II. Brief Notes on the more Important Departments

Although it suffers from some over-simplification where the work of departments overlaps, the most useful classification is on a functional basis.

(1) Defence

The Ministry of Defence. A Minister 'for the Co-ordination of Defence' was appointed in 1936, but no separate department was created until 1947.

But in 1964, with the object of improving central control of defence policy, the government departments concerned with the formulation of defence policy and the control and administration of the three fighting Services were completely reorganised.

The Ministry of Defence, the Admiralty, the War Office and the Air Ministry were merged to form a unified Ministry of Defence under a Secretary of State for Defence. The offices of First Lord of the Admiralty, Secretary of State for War and Secretary of State for Air were abolished. The Board of Admiralty and the Army and Air Councils were replaced by a single Defence Council which deals mainly with major defence policy. The Defence Committee of the Cabinet has been replaced by a Committee on Defence and Overseas Policy.

There are three Parliamentary Under-Secretaries of State—for the Royal Navy, the Army, and the Royal Air Force respectively.

The Ministry of Defence also administers the Meteorological Office.

(2) Control

(a) *The Home Office.* The Home Office was created in 1782 when a redistribution of the functions of the two Secretaries of State divided them into Home and Foreign. Its head, the Home Secretary, is the most important of the Secretaries of State, undertaking those administrative duties not specifically assigned to another minister. He is in close touch with the Sovereign, receiving and submitting addresses and petitions to her.

The Home Secretary is also responsible for: the maintenance of internal law and order; the efficiency of police forces and the direct control of the Metropolitan Police; the treatment of offenders in prisons, remand homes, approved schools and on probation; the introduction of legislation on criminal justice; the efficiency of fire services and civil defence; public morals and safety; general questions of broadcasting policy; seeing that the law regarding parliamentary and local elections is observed; immigration and the naturalisation of aliens; race relations; advising the Sovereign on the exercise of the prerogative of mercy; supervising the control of firearms, explosives and dangerous drugs; deciding general policies on the law of liquor licensing, shops, music and dancing.

In Scotland, the Secretary of State for Scotland performs many of the above functions.

(b) *The Lord Chancellor's Departments.* The Lord Chancellor performs a number of functions. He is Speaker of the House of Lords, Custodian of the Great Seal, controls the machinery of the courts, appoints magistrates and advises on most other judicial appointments, reviews proceedings of Army and Air Force courts-martial where necessary, appoints chairmen of certain administrative tribunals and supervises the Judge Advocate General's Department, the Land Registry, the Public Trustee Office, the Public Record Office and other offices mainly concerned with legal practice and procedure. (See also Chapter 19.)

(c) *Law Officers' Department.* The Law Officers, the Attorney-General and his deputy the Solicitor-General, are always members of the House of Commons. They are the principal legal advisers to the Queen in her private capacity, to the Government and to the departments. In important cases, they appear in court on behalf of the Crown. The Attorney-General supervises the work of the Director of Public Prosecutions.

(3) *External relations*

(a) *The Foreign and Commonwealth Office.* The Foreign Office first became a separate department in 1782. It has responsibilities for drawing up treaties, representing the United Kingdom at the United Nations and other international bodies, protecting British subjects and their interests abroad, and explaining British policy to foreign peoples. It also deals with questions of nationality, the issue of passports, and the privileges of foreign diplomatic representatives. The Foreign Secretary is the U.K. representative in the Council of Ministers of the European Community.

(b) The *Ministry of Overseas Development* is responsible for

Britain's policy of financial and technical assistance to developing countries.

(4) Finance

(a) *The Treasury*, see following section.

(b) *The Revenue Departments*. Although the Revenue Departments are subordinate to the Treasury, they have statutory functions and a legal personality of their own.

  (i) *The Board of Customs and Excise*. Customs and excise duties were collected by private contractors until 1643, when Commissioners were appointed. The department is also concerned with preventing revenue evasion and the detection of smuggling. In carrying out its main duties, it gives considerable help to other departments, e.g. in enforcing restrictions on the importation of certain goods, administering the currency regulations and compiling statistics of the United Kingdom's overseas trade.

  (ii) *The Board of Inland Revenue*. The Board is responsible for the collection of direct taxes and advises the Chancellor of the Exchequer regarding them. It also values real property for such purposes as compulsory purchase, local rates and estate duty.

(c) *The Paymaster-General's Office*. The Paymaster-General is the banker for government departments (other than the revenue departments), sums authorised by Parliament being transferred to his account at the Bank of England from the Exchequer Account. The departments pay by orders (similar to cheques) drawn on the account of the Paymaster-General's Office.

The department also pays the pensions of such public officials as civil servants, teachers and Service officers.

(5) Social services

(a) *The Department of Health and Social Security*. This department was created in 1968. It administers the National Health Service and supervises the work of local authorities connected with public health, mental illness, socially deprived families, children in care and the care of the aged and handicapped.

It also deals with war pensions and administers the social services provided for by the Family Allowances Acts, the National Insurance Acts and the National Insurance (Industrial Injuries)

Acts. Often reciprocal social benefit arrangements are made with other countries. Within the Department there is a Supplementary Benefits Commission which determines awards of non-contributory benefits and Family Income Supplements.

(b) *The Department of Education and Science*. Responsibility for schools in Great Britain is shared between the Department of Education and Science (England), the Welsh Education Office and the Scottish Education Department. The Secretary of State for Education and Science is, however, responsible for the universities, civil science and support for the arts throughout Great Britain.

The Department works in close touch with local education authorities. Its relations with the universities are conducted through the Universities Grants Committee, and its responsibilities for civil science are discharged through the research councils, e.g. the Science Research Council, the Medical Research Council, the Agricultural Research Council and the Natural Environment Research Council.

(c) *The Department of the Environment*. This Department was created in 1970 by the amalgamation of the Ministries of Housing and Local Government, of Public Buildings and Works and of Transport.

Assisting the Secretary of State there is a Minister for Planning and Local Government, a Minister for Housing and Construction and a Minister for Transport. Each Minister has the status of a Minister in charge of a Department not represented in the Cabinet and, by delegation from the Secretary of State, he is in full charge of his functional wing.

Except in Scotland and Wales, this new Department is responsible for the whole range of functions which affect people's living environment. It is therefore concerned with the supervision of local authorities, regional policy, the protection of the coast and countryside, the preservation of historic towns and monuments, the control of air, water and noise pollution, the planning of land, the construction industries (including housing policy) and transport (including public programmes of support for and development of the means of transport). Through its Property Services Agency it manages government property.

(6) *Economic affairs*

(a) *The Department of Trade.* This Department is responsible for general overseas trade policy (including statistics), commercial relations (including those with the European Economic Community) and tariffs. It sponsors the work of the British Overseas Trade Board in export services and promotions, overseas finance and planning. The Export Credits Guarantee Department is responsible to the Secretary of State for Trade.

The Department is also responsible for matters arising from company legislation, the insolvency service, the work of the Patent Office, supervision of the insurance industry, civil aviation, marine and shipping policy, tourism and the newspaper and film industries.

(b) *The Department of Employment.* This Department replaced the Ministry of Labour in 1968. It is concerned with conditions of labour and employment. This involves it in such wide activities as operating Employment Exchanges, directing the Youth Employment Service, providing schemes for vocational training, supervising (through the Inspectorate of Factories) safety, health and welfare measures for industrial workers, collecting and publishing statistics on labour, promoting good industrial relations and generally co-operating with other departments to secure full employment.

The Secretary of State for Employment appoints the members of the independent Manpower Services Commission, Health and Safety Commission and the Conciliation and Arbitration Service.

In addition, the Department acts as agent for other departments in connection with social security benefits and the issue of passports, and participates in the International Labour Office.

(c) *The Ministry of Agriculture, Fisheries and Food.* The Board of Agriculture and Fisheries, created in 1889, was converted into a Ministry in 1919. It is responsible generally for the efficiency of agriculture, horticulture and fishing in England and Wales, working in conjunction with the Department of Agriculture for Scotland and with that for Northern Ireland. Advisory services are provided and active efforts are made to promote improvements through subsidies, grants for farm buildings and guaranteed prices. The control of diseases in animals and plants is also one of its functions.

The Ministry has a general responsibility for food supplies, home-produced and imported, and watches over the manufacture and storage of food. It conducts the National Food Survey and takes part in the work of international bodies such as the Food and Agriculture Organisation. The Royal Botanic Gardens, Kew, and the Ordnance Survey Department come under its administration.

(d) *The Department of Industry.* This department is responsible for general industrial policy, both national and regional. It provides technical services to industry as a whole, and exercises government policy regarding aerospace and industrial research and development.

The Secretary of State for Industry is also responsible to Parliament for the Post Office Corporation.

(e) *The Department of Energy.* This department is responsible for the development of government policies regarding all forms of energy—the nationalised coal, gas and electricity industries, the Atomic Energy Authority, the nuclear power industry and off-shore gas and oil resources. It deals with the oil-producing countries, co-ordinates energy conservation policy and encourages the development of new sources of energy.

(f) *The Department of Prices and Consumer Protection.* This department is responsible for consumer affairs covering protection, consumer credit, standards and weights and measures. It also supervises the work of the Price Commission, and deals with prices in the shops.

The Department carries out government policy regarding monopolies, mergers and restrictive practices and the Office of Fair Trading.

(7) *Miscellaneous*

The Department of the Procurator-General and Treasury Solicitor. The Treasury Solicitor provides a legal service for government departments, preparing cases for prosecution, representing them in court, advising on the law and conveyancing real property. He is also Procurator-General (Queen's Proctor), which entails duties in connection with the operation of the divorce laws.

(8) *Scotland*

In 1885 it was recognised that Scotland needed a system of administration separate from that of England and Wales, and so a Secretary for Scotland was appointed, becoming a Secretary of

State in 1926. He is assisted by two Ministers of State and two Parliamentary Under-Secretaries, but their functions are discharged by five main administrative departments—the Scottish Home and Health Department, the Scottish Development Department, the Scottish Economic Planning Department, the Scottish Education Department and the Department of Agriculture and Fisheries for Scotland, with a small 'Scottish office' in London. There are also separate departments for legal and minor matters.

(9) *Wales*

In the Cabinet there is a Secretary of State for Wales (an office created by Mr. Wilson in October 1964). He is assisted by two Parliamentary Under-Secretaries, and is responsible for housing, town and country planning, new towns, local government, schools, roads and certain health services in Wales. The Welsh Office is centred in Cardiff.

(10) *Northern Ireland*

The Government of Ireland Act, 1920, enacted a constitution for Northern Ireland which, while preserving the supreme authority of the U.K. Parliament and reserving certain matters to that Parliament, provided Northern Ireland with its own legislature and executive to deal with domestic transferred affairs. In normal times, administrative functions are exercised by the Governor. He appoints ministers to a number of departments, chiefly the Ministries of Finance, Home Affairs, Development, Insurance, Education, Agriculture, Commerce and Health and Social Services.

Following years of civil unrest, however, a Northern Ireland Office was set up, and in 1972 direct rule from Westminster was introduced. Laws were passed by Order in Council, and the Secretary of State for Northern Ireland became fully responsible for the government of Northern Ireland, including constitutional development, law and order and security. He is assisted by two Ministers of State and two Parliamentary Under-Secretaries who are in charge of the various Northern Ireland departments.

In 1973 a new type of constitution for Northern Ireland was introduced. It provided, among other things, for the devolution of powers to a legislative Assembly and a power-sharing Executive.

But it failed to win sufficient support from all sections of the Northern Ireland community, and was brought to an end in May, 1974.

In July, 1974, the Northern Ireland Act was introduced, providing for the election of a constitutional convention to consider what arrangements for the government of Northern Ireland would be likely to command most widespread acceptance throughout the community. In the meantime, direct rule continues.

III. THE TREASURY

Even before the Norman Conquest, the Treasurer was an important official of the Royal Household, but it was not until the 12th century that the Exchequer was created to help him with the collection of revenue and the keeping of accounts. The Exchequer officials sat at a table chequered like a chess-board (a device for counting often used before the general adoption of Arabic numerals in the 16th century), and it was from the type of table that the department drew its name. Any disputes regarding taxation were decided by the Exchequer officials and so there developed the Court of the Exchequer (see page 352).

In 1612 the office of Lord High Treasurer was put into commission, Lords Commissioners becoming responsible for the work. The special position of the Treasury in the field of finance vested in the Commissioners important powers. Not only could they exert considerable influence over all the other departments but, in the days of patronage, it was they who largely controlled appointments. Hence, during the 18th century, the First Lord of the Treasury was able to become the leading minister. This past history of the Treasury can still be observed in the post of Parliamentary Secretary to the Treasury who, as Chief Government Whip, is still sometimes referred to as the 'Patronage Secretary'.

Even when patronage as a system ceased, the power of the Treasury was not diminished. On the contrary, the tendency has been for it to extend its influence and to add to its functions. The demand for more financial rectitude was largely met by making the Treasury the supervisory body; while in order to promote the unification of the Civil Service, the Treasury became, until 1969, the single employer. But it was the 20th century need to plan and

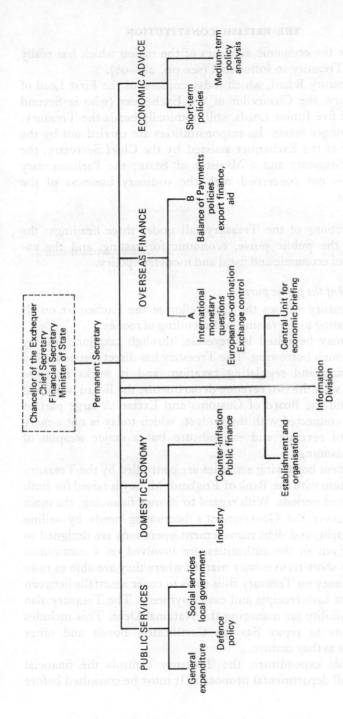

FIG. 5. *Organisation of the Treasury.*

co-ordinate the economic activities of the nation which has really made the Treasury so influential (see pp. 288–90).

The Treasury Board, which today consists of the First Lord of the Treasury, the Chancellor of the Exchequer (who is Second Lord), and five Junior Lords, still nominally heads the Treasury, but it no longer meets. Its responsibilities are carried out by the Chancellor of the Exchequer assisted by the Chief Secretary, the Financial Secretary and a Minister of State; the Parliamentary Secretary is not concerned with the ordinary business of the department.

The functions of the Treasury fall under three headings: the control of the public purse, economic forecasting, and the co-ordination of economic and fiscal and monetary policy.

(1) *Control of the public purse*

The Treasury advises the Chancellor of the Exchequer on all matters relating to the raising and spending of money.

Money may be raised by revenue, through taxation, and by capital, through borrowing. The Treasury has direct responsibility for proposing and regulating taxation, and it works in close association with the two revenue departments, the Board of Inland Revenue and the Board of Customs and Excise. A large part of its work is connected with the budget, which today is not a mere balancing of revenue and expenditure but a major weapon of economic planning.

Government borrowing activities are controlled by the Treasury in consultation with the Bank of England. Money is raised for both long and short periods. With regard to its own financing, the main aim is to cover the Government's borrowing needs by selling long-term debt, and debt management operations are designed to this end. Even so the authorities are involved on a continuous basis in the short-term money market where they are able to raise 3-month money on Treasury Bills so as to cover shortfalls between Government cash receipts and cash payments. The Treasury also has responsibility for managing the National Debt. This includes arrangements to repay Savings Certificates, Bonds and other dated stocks as they mature.

As regards expenditure, the Treasury controls the financial aspects of all departmental proposals. It must be consulted before any project involving a substantial increase in expenditure can be considered by the Cabinet. Discussions often take place before its formal sanction is needed so that the Treasury can indicate, after studying the financial details of the scheme, whether it will recommend the necessary money. The Chancellor will be especially careful if the proposal involves expenditure well into the future.

Treasury control over the recurrent annual expenditure of the departments was described in chapter 12. In examining the Estimates, the Treasury has two objects. First, it has to co-ordinate the demands of the various departments and relate them to the total income available. The Chancellor has already had the responsibility of deciding on economic grounds what the Government's total expenditure shall be. If the sum of all the departments' Estimates comes to more than this, the Treasury will instruct the departments to limit their expenditure to a given allocation. In the last resort, of course, disagreements may have to be decided by the Cabinet, though a determined Chancellor will usually have the final say, as Mr. Aneurin Bevan discovered in 1951 when charges on the health service were imposed by Mr. Gaitskell. Secondly, it seeks to ensure that policies are carried out in the most economical way. Although the Treasury lacks the expert technical knowledge of a department in its own particular field, it can compare expenditure in previous years, and its main duty is to ensure that the departments' spending proposals can be defended against criticism from outside. Over Estimates covering what is virtually automatic expenditure, e.g. retirement pensions and family allowances, the Treasury can do little more than examine the administrative efficiency of the arrangements for payment. Similarly, in the case of charges on the Consolidated Fund, for which no Estimates have to be submitted, the Treasury has practically no control.

Once approved, the expenditure is made by the department concerned, and responsibility for its legality rests with its account-ing officer, usually the Permanent Secretary. Nevertheless, the Treasury exercises limited control over expenditure as it takes place throughout the year. Where the department wishes to exceed its appropriation on a particular item, the Treasury can authorise virement. Moreover, transfers from the Exchequer Fund to the Paymaster-General's account out of which the de-partments are paid have to be sanctioned by the Treasury.

With the third stage of control, the audit of accounts, the

Treasury is less concerned. Two Treasury Officers of Account assist the departments in accountancy matters and advise on the form of all published government accounts. One of them attends permanently as a witness before the Public Accounts Committee on behalf of the Treasury. He also prepares Treasury Minutes on the views of the Committee regarding the propriety of proposals for expenditure. The main audit of accounts, however, is by the Comptroller and Auditor General who presides over the Exchequer and Audit Department which is independent of the Treasury.

Extravagance resulting from ineffective supervision of expenditure, therefore, is unlikely. Indeed, it is sometimes alleged that the Treasury's rules regarding finance may be too strict, producing a cramping effect on departmental initiative.

The Treasury also exercises a general control over the current and capital expenditure of local authorities and over the capital expenditure of the public corporations.

(2) *Economic forecasting*

It has now been recognised that full employment can be achieved only if the Government accepts responsibility for regulating the economy. Saving, consumption and investment must be so influenced by the authorities that total monetary demand is sufficient to provide full employment but not so large that it leads to inflation.

The task of assessing the way in which the national economy is likely to develop in the short- and medium-term is now the responsibility of the Treasury. In particular, it has to take into account the current employment situation, world economic prospects and the future balance of payments position.

Since 1969 when the Department of Economic Affairs was wound up, the Treasury has also been responsible for the formulation of long-term plans for the development of the economy.

(3) *The co-ordination of economic and fiscal and monetary policy*

Having made its forecasts, the Treasury has to relate them to the various objectives of economic policy — full employment, price stability, a reasonable rate of growth, a balanced regional development — and formulate advice on the policies to be pursued, having regard to the priorities decided upon by the government of the day.

The economic objectives referred to above are largely secured by fiscal and monetary policies. While the final decision on the various measures to be taken rests with the Cabinet (and in particular the Prime Minister and Chancellor of the Exchequer), the Treasury provides the expert advice and implements decisions.

The major single weapon for controlling the economy is the budget. The present-day approach emphasises the full employment of resources rather than the simple process of raising sufficient revenue to cover proposed expenditure. If resources are idle, the Chancellor of the Exchequer can provide for a budget deficit which will place more spending power in the hands of consumers, thus stimulating demand and encouraging production. On the other hand, if monetary demand is in excess of what is necessary to purchase the full employment output at current prices, the surplus purchasing power can be mopped up by means of a budget surplus. In addition, the Chancellor can use individual taxes, not merely to raise revenue, but to influence demand, e.g. through the variation of purchase tax and of excise taxes.

Changes in the bank rate are also used to control the economy. The process of decision-making before the rate is raised or lowered is so secret that it is not known how far proposals have originated with the Treasury and how far with the Bank of England. But major pronouncements on monetary policy are made by the Chancellor of the Exchequer. By Section 4 of the Bank of England Nationalisation Act, 1946, the Treasury can give directions to the Bank of England. It may also request the joint stock banks to restrict the granting of credit. This is done by a letter to the Governor of the Bank of England, who then approaches the Committee of the London Clearing Banks.

The pressure on consumer demand may also be regulated by varying the deposit requirement and the period of repayment for hire purchase transactions. The necessary orders are actually issued by the Department of Prices and Consumer Protection, but guidance is given by the Treasury, and in fact changes are sometimes announced by the Chancellor of the Exchequer.

In its management of the National Debt, the Treasury can also influence the economy. Thus a movement from short- to long-term debt would reduce liquidity in the economy and tend to curb expansion.

In the past, physical controls on investment have been applied by the Treasury through a Capital Issues Committee, and even today exchange control regulations still limit the amount of money which can be transferred abroad. Overseas financial transactions, so important to a country dependent on international trade, are also a major responsibility of the Treasury. It operates the Exchange Equalisation Account so as to prevent the value of the pound sterling from fluctuating violently, and represents the government on international bodies, such as the International Monetary Fund, the World Bank, and the Commonwealth Liaison Committee (through which consultations take place with Commonwealth countries on economic matters).

SUGGESTED READING

S. H. Beer, *Treasury Control* (2nd Ed., O.U.P., 1957).

Central Office of Information, *Britain: an official handbook* (H.M.S.O., 1975), Section 2.

For the Royal Institute of Public Administration. Different books on Government Departments in the *New Whitehall Series* (Allen and Unwin, 1955 onwards).

17

The Civil Service

'In England we all criticise the Civil Service. For most
of us, this is like talk about the weather; a good way to
open conversation because you can be pretty certain
that the other man will also have something to say on
the subject.'

Professor W. J. M. Mackenzie — Foreword to
C. H. Sisson's book, *The Spirit of British Administration*

I. DEVELOPMENT

EARLY HISTORY

Under Saxon and Norman monarchs, there was no clear distinction between the King's personal and official business. It was
natural, therefore, that, as the affairs of State increased, certain
administrative matters should be delegated to persons holding
offices which were primarily concerned with the King's own needs,
such as the Steward, Chamberlain, Marshal, Treasurer and
Secretary. In time, many of these officials concentrated increasingly
on State business, and progressed from fulfilling purely administrative tasks to positions exercising considerable political influence.
As their work increased, clerks were employed to record decisions,
assemble information, keep accounts, write despatches, and draw
up charters. Originally these clerks, who can be regarded as the
first civil servants, were recruited from the clergy, but as the laity
became more proficient in reading and writing, so they entered the
King's service. Such a person was Geoffrey Chaucer, who held
several offices in the 14th century, such as Comptroller of Customs
in the Port of London, Clerk of Works in the Royal Palace, and
Commissioner to maintain the banks of the Thames. In those days
there was little difference between political and administrative
offices, since both were dependent on the royal favour; thus the

official fortunes of Chaucer fluctuated with those of his patron, John of Gaunt.

By the 13th century these officials had so grown in number that there were too many of them to follow the King's court on its travels around the country, and Westminster became the seat of business. With the extension of central power under the Tudors, there was a large increase in the number of civil servants, and Whitehall developed as the centre of administration.

THE CIVIL SERVICE IN THE 18TH CENTURY

By the end of the 18th century a miscellany of some seventy-five offices existed, some important and others very minor, employing over 16,000 officials. But in its basis of recruitment, financial probity, organisation, and standards of efficiency, the administration was very different from our modern Civil Service.

Appointment to office was by patronage and not on grounds of efficiency. Since there was no proper audit of accounts, posts were frequently sources of considerable profit and so could be used by the ruling party to reward supporters. Even the pamphleteers, such as Defoe (Accountant to the Commissioners for the duty on glass), Addison (a Commissioner of Excise), and Steele (a Commissioner of Stamps), received their offices in return for political services, while later, it was alleged, the Exchequer List was filled with descendants of Walpole and Townshend. The system was even applied to the appointment of subordinate officials and clerks, control coming under the head of the department.

The result of the patronage system was that persons sought political power in order to enjoy the spoils of office. Sinecures were created to provide opportunities for further patronage, and corruption was widespread. Departmental funds were held in private banking accounts and the interest transferred to the owner. Fees were charged for services to members of the public, the Secretary of the Admiralty, for instance, exacting a levy when granting commissions. Posts not used as political rewards were often sold and offices 'farmed out' to deputies. Thus in 1786 the Comptroller of the Navy estimated that he received an average of 300 guineas annually from premiums on the appointment of clerks, while the Paymaster-General of the Forces appointed a deputy-Paymaster at a salary of £1,000. It is said that this practice even extended down to the charwomen!

Financial irregularities were facilitated by the lack of co-ordination in the collection of revenue and the failure to carry out an effective audit of expenditure. The two Auditors of Imprest, instituted in the days of Elizabeth, merely enjoyed the fees and left the work to deputies. The result was that the accounts were in hopeless confusion and the collection of revenue was usually in arrears.

In its organisation, too, the administration was equally inefficient. No attempt was made to co-ordinate the work of the Service. Each minister was directly responsible to the King and, since officials owed responsibility only to their immediate superiors, the Civil Service was split up into a number of autonomous bodies, each having its own organisation, pay and conditions of service, and its independent treasury. No one had a general supervisory power to ensure that there was some relationship between the size of a department and the work it had to do. Hence some departments were overworked at the same time as others were overstaffed. Moreover, the division into departments was often completely out of date, some offices even being survivals from the Middle Ages. Thus, there were two departments of the Foreign Office, one for northern and the other for southern Europe, and so it was possible for two strong-minded Foreign secretaries to be pursuing independent policies. The War Office was even divided into seven sub-departments dealing with separate matters and completely unco-ordinated. Commenting on it, Professor K. Smellie says: 'No more confusing or dislocated system could well have been devised' (*A Hundred Years of English Government*).

Nor could organisation of the work within the department stand up to any logical test. Rarely was there an attempt to classify duties so that persons could be appointed to posts appropriate to their ability. Instead, a young man entering a department had to spend his first years performing dull copying. Promotion was based on seniority, not merit, a rule which deterred able men from entering the Service and tempted young persons to join before their education was complete. Many methods were completely obsolete. Latin, and Roman numerals, were still used for keeping accounts; these were translated into Arabic numerals for totalling and then re-entered in Roman. Until 1826, receipts were recorded by means of tally sticks. Indeed, the burning of the 'foils' in 1834 started the blaze which destroyed the Houses of Parliament!

Criticisms of such a Service began to grow towards the end of the century. The Whigs, who had used patronage to maintain themselves in power for over fifty years, now found George III employing it against them. Hence, led by Burke, they began to demand reform. In 1780 a 'Commission of Enquiry into the administration of public business' was set up and this directed its criticism in particular to the administration of finance. From 1782 onwards a number of reforms took place. A blow at patronage was struck in 1782 when customs, excise, and postal officials (who formed one-sixth of the electorate), were dis-enfranchised. It was also required that outstanding accounts should be settled, and that henceforth all monies should be paid into the Bank of England, the Consolidated Fund being instituted by Pitt in 1787. Persons supervising finance in the Forces were more strictly controlled, and Commissioners of Audit replaced the old Auditors of Imprest.

THE NORTHCOTE-TREVELYAN REPORT, 1854

Further reform, however, was delayed by the shock which the French Revolution gave to the ruling classes in Britain, and even Burke joined with them in defending traditional institutions. But the cost of the war with France focused attention on the way in which public monies were being spent. A Select Committee on Finance was appointed in 1797, and from then on gradual improvements took place in the administration. Many sinecures were abolished and the appointment of deputies ended. Officials were forbidden to have a financial interest in Government contracts. In 1802 the practice was inaugurated of preparing an annual survey of the nation's finances. Other improvements, such as the use of the English language and Arabic numerals, were introduced in 1823 to simplify the keeping of accounts.

But such reform as was achieved came only slowly. Above all, for a number of reasons, little attempt was made to deal with methods of recruitment. First, in the 19th century, Governments undertook comparatively little work and so the need for a large and efficient administration was not felt. Secondly, the Service as it existed suited the class structure of the period in that it was filled by middle-class people frequently bound together by family ties. Thirdly, although the method of entry was undesirable, progress upwards usually depended on ability; good men, therefore, could reach the top. Indeed, Sir Charles Trevelyan, one of its most forceful critics, was Assistant Secretary to the Treasury, Lastly, the patronage system was a useful weapon by which Governments could control the House of Commons at a time when there were no well-disciplined parties. Hence the Patronage Secretary not only filled places himself in the Treasury from a list of nominees, but watched the distribution of offices in other departments in order to ensure that party considerations were placed first. In 1834, of over a hundred sinecure offices which still remained, one half was filled by Members of Parliament.

As the century progressed, however, the administration was subjected to increasing attack. Bentham, the leader of the Utilitarians, advocated entry by examination, and a little later John Stuart Mill was writing along similar lines. Although the reforming zeal of the 1830s passed over the Civil Service, the growth of State regulation which followed (e.g. the Poor Law Board, 1847, the General Board of Health, 1848, and the Education Department, 1856) foreshadowed the future need for increased efficiency. Moreover, in the 1830s the examination system of Oxford and Cambridge had been overhauled, degrees being awarded by merit, not influence, and divided into classes. Such examinations proved that ability could be tested. Indeed, the universities were among the foremost in demanding reform. Benjamin Jowett, Master of Balliol, was a man of exceptional influence, and he had personal links with such energetic reformers as Macaulay, Trevelyan, and Northcote. Eventually Parliament began to demand reduction in the cost of civil administration and, as a result of evidence given before a Select Committee, Trevelyan and Northcote were asked to prepare a report on the reorganisation of the permanent Civil Service.

Their four recommendations have formed the corner-stones of the present-day Civil Service, although they were considered radical at the time. They advocated that:

(1) recruitment should be by competitive examination;
(2) promotion should be according to merit and not seniority;
(3) the organisation should be improved by distinguishing between 'intellectual' and routine mechanical work such as copying, so that the more able civil servants could concentrate entirely on the former;
(4) there should be a single integrated Service, recruited as a whole.

The immediate response from those in authority was mostly one of hostility. The Government still valued its powers of patronage, many people had a vested interest in maintaining the existing system, and class prejudice was stirred. Thus, Queen Victoria expressed her fear that examinations would fill the public offices with 'low people without the breeding or feelings of a gentleman'. Officials within the Service were offended by its critics, and they mostly opposed the suggested reforms, Trollope caricaturing its authors in *The Three Clerks*.

Change, however, was inevitable. The introduction of open competitive examinations for the Indian Civil Service in 1853 produced better recruits than those entering the British Civil Service. Both the universities and schools were strongly in favour of the proposals, which they considered would stimulate educational advance, especially as the report recommended examinations in subjects outside the staple of classics and mathematics. Moreover, many middle-class parents hoped that a reformed Civil Service would provide an attractive career for their sons.

Nevertheless, it is quite likely that the proposals would have been shelved had it not been for the energy of the reformers and, above all, for the outbreak of the Crimean War and the tale of hopeless muddle, maladministration, inadequate supplies, and appalling conditions, which were revealed in the despatches of W. H. Russell, the correspondent of *The Times*. Henceforth there was less willingness to tolerate a Service which, in the words of the report, had attracted only 'the unambitious and the indolent and incapable'.

Therefore, in May, 1855, the Civil Service Commission was set up by Order in Council (so as to avoid parliamentary discussion). From now onwards, an independent body, not the separate departments, determined the standard of entrants. But open competitive examinations were not yet introduced for the Commission tested only candidates already nominated by the departments. Nevertheless, after 1859, it was possible to insist on a higher quality of entrant, since it was then laid down that officers could not qualify for superannuation unless awarded the certificate which the Commissioners gave to candidates who complied with their rules regarding age, ability, knowledge, health, and character.

LATER 19TH-CENTURY DEVELOPMENTS

Many defects, however, still remained. There was no recruitment by open competitive examination; little attempt was made at classification into grades; dreary mechanical copying was the lot of the new entrant; organisation was still on a departmental basis with different rates of pay, hours, and conditions of service; no machinery had been created to exercise an overall control.

Reform came slowly, usually after investigations by Commissions and Select Committees. By the end of the century, patronage had been replaced by competitive examinations, the Treasury had been given powers to approve rules for testing candidates, the Service was divided into First and Second Divisions (each divided into grades) and departmentalism was gradually weakening, as shown by the growth of the first associations and trade unions.

The problem of mechanical copying and the dead-end jobs which this created was largely solved by the invention of the Remington typewriter in 1873, this being first used in the Civil Service by the Board of Inland Revenue in the 1880s. Other departments were slow to adopt typewriters, partly because they were operated by women, whose entry aroused considerable hostility. The position was not altered until World War I when not only had girl typists to be fully accepted, but women were required to replace men in the other divisions of the Service. Henceforth, in the Home Civil Service, women competed on equal terms with men, often occupying positions of responsibility.

20TH-CENTURY DEVELOPMENTS

Major developments since World War I have been towards the more unified organisation made necessary by the expansion of government responsibilities. Treasury control was extended in 1919 through an Establishments Department. At the same time, Whitley Councils, consisting of representatives of the State and the employees' associations, were introduced to negotiate on wage claims and working conditions.

It was largely the report of a committee of the National Whitley Council which brought about the major re-organisation of 1921. This divided the Service into a hierarchy of four main classes —

administrative, executive, clerical, and writing assistant — broadly the structure which lasted until 1971.

Since this broad organisation was set up some fifty years ago, however, there have been vast changes in the work of government and these have had their impact on the civil service:

(1) The expansion of State activities, chiefly in the field of the social services, has led to a considerable increase in the size of the civil service.

(2) Many new government activities have necessitated recruiting scientists, specialists and other persons with professional skills, e.g. architects, valuers.

(3) The work of administration has changed with the development of statistical techniques, computers, organisation and methods analysis, etc. Civil servants, especially those at the top, now require managerial expertise.

(4) Full employment, by reducing the relative 'fringe benefits' enjoyed by civil servants compared with their counterparts in the private sector, has made it more difficult to attract sufficient entrants of the required standard. Not only did this necessitate an examination of the methods of recruitment, but it had to be made possible for able recruits to work their way up — something which tended to be frustrated by the rigid division of the three Treasury classes.

The Fulton Report, 1968

Such considerations led to the setting-up of the Fulton Committee in 1966 to study 'the structure, recruitment and management, including training, of the Civil Service'.

Its main recommendations were:

(1) responsibility for the civil service should be transferred from the Treasury to a new Civil Service Department;

(2) classes should be abolished and replaced by a unified grading structure;

(3) a Civil Service College should be set up to provide training courses in management and a wide range of short courses;

(4) greater mobility between departments and interchange between the public and private sectors;

(5) more opportunities for specialists to reach the top policy-making posts;

(6) candidates should be examined in subjects relevant to government.

All these recommendations, except the last, were accepted by the government, and have now been implemented. They are discussed in more detail in the appropriate sections of this chapter.

The Civil Service Department

In 1968 a new Civil Service Department was set up under the control of the prime minister, whose titles henceforth included that of 'Minister for the Civil Service'. The day-to-day work of the Department, however, was delegated to the Lord Privy Seal, assisted by a Parliamentary Secretary. The Department's Permanent Secretary is the official Head of the Home Civil Service.

The *Civil Service Commission* was absorbed into the new Department. It is responsible for the recruitment and selection of permanent civil servants, but specific and formal arrangements have been made to ensure its independence and impartiality, e.g. it is still appointed by Order in Council.

The Fulton Committee considered that a new Department should take over the civil service functions of the Treasury for two main reasons:

(a) the expanded role of central management which was envisaged would, with all its other functions, place too great a concentration of power in one department;

(b) central management required its own expertise and should not be staffed by those whose main training and experience had been in techniques of government finance and the control of expenditure.

Certainly the Department has wide management functions. These cover:

(1) the size and deployment of manpower, including grading standards in individual departments;

(2) personnel management, training and promotion, including running the Civil Service College and other training centres;

(3) the pay and conditions of service of all civil servants;

(4) responsibility for the development and application of modern administrative and managerial techniques;

(5) the provision of a central management consultancy for other departments to deal with organisation and methods, computers and operational research.

II. ORGANISATION AND FUNCTIONS

The term 'Civil Service' is restricted to staffs of the various government departments and of the Diplomatic Service. Civil servants are defined as 'servants of the Crown, other than holders of political or judicial offices, who are employed in a civil capacity and whose remuneration is paid wholly and directly out of moneys voted by Parliament' (Royal Commission on the Civil Service, 1953–5).

The government departments in which some 700,000 civil servants work differ in size and in the number, type and complexity of their functions. Hence each department decides on its own internal organisation and it may have regional and local offices. But there are common features. Most departments are organised on a functional basis, following a pattern similar to that of the Civil Service Department (Figure 6) in their relationship with the minister, division of work and the use of higher officials. This arrangement of work allows civil servants to specialise in particular duties and is the one usually adopted by any large organisation.

THE ADMINISTRATION GROUP

In 1971, civil servants formerly belonging to the old Treasury administrative, executive and clerical classes were combined to form a single 'Administration Group' (263,000 in size, 1974). The move followed the recommendation of the Fulton Committee who considered that a single group would allow the skills and experience of staff to be used more flexibly and ensure that the way to the higher levels of the Service was open to the most able people irrespective of how they joined.

The Administrative Group consists of ten grades from Clerical Assistant to Assistant Secretary. There are four main points of entry, depending on age and educational attainments.

(1) Clerical Assistant, for persons under 20 years of age with two G.C.E. 'O' level passes, including English.

(2) Clerical Officer, for persons under 20 years of age with five G.C.E. 'O' level passes, including English.

(3) Executive Officer, for persons 17½ to 28 years of age who have one of the following:

(a) four G.C.E. passes, including English at 'O' level and

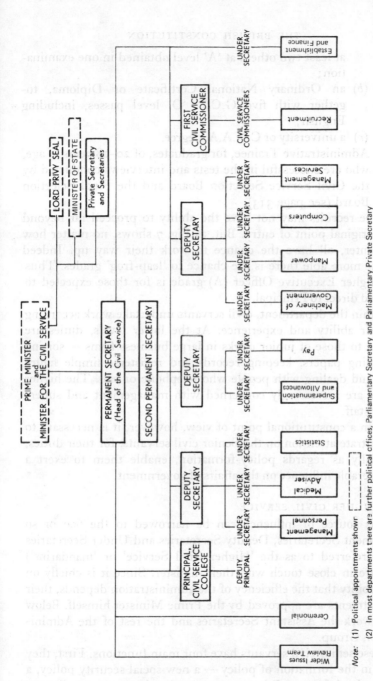

Fig. 6. Organisation of the Civil Service Department.

Note: (1) Political appointments shown

(2) In most departments there are further political offices, Parliamentary Secretary and Parliamentary Private Secretary

(3) The work of each division is further sub-divided under Assistant Secretaries and again under Principals

at least two others at 'A' level obtained in one examination;

(b) an Ordinary National Certificate or Diploma, together with five G.C.E. 'O' level passes, including English;

(c) a university or C.N.A.A. degree.

(4) Administrative Trainee, for graduates, of 20–28 years of age, who are successful in the tests and interviews conducted by the Civil Service Selection Board and the Final Selection Board (see page 313).

Some recruits may not have the ability to proceed far beyond their original point of entry. But, as Fig. 7 shows, no matter how they enter, all have the chance to work their way up. Indeed for the more able there is the chance to 'leap-frog' grades. Thus the Higher Executive Officer (A) grade is for those expected to proceed direct to Principal.

Within the department, civil servants undertake work according to their ability and experience. At the lower levels, duties are similar to those of junior clerks in large business firms — sorting and filing papers, keeping records and registers, simple figure work and dealing with people who telephone or call. The higher grades are increasingly concerned with management and supervising staff.

From a constitutional point of view, however, it is necessary to concentrate attention on the Senior civil servants, for their duties, especially as regards policy-formation, enable them to exert a considerable influence on the affairs of government.

THE HIGHER CIVIL SERVICE

This source of influence can be narrowed to the 600 or so Permanent Secretaries, Deputy Secretaries and Under Secretaries (often referred to as the 'Higher Civil Service' or 'mandarins') who are in close touch with their minister. Since it is chiefly on their ability that the efficiency of the administration depends, their appointments are approved by the Prime Minister himself. Below them work the Assistant Secretaries and the rest of the Administration Group.

These senior civil servants have four main functions. First, they assist in the formation of policy — a new social security policy, a change in defence policy, or a new national transport policy, to

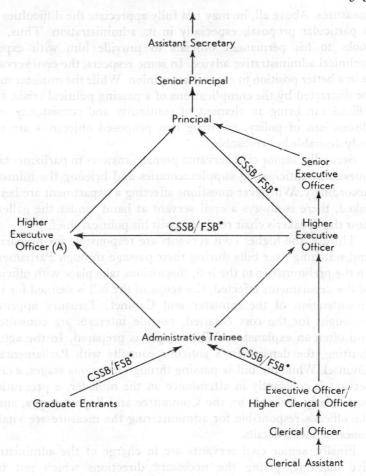

Assistant Secretary

Senior Principal

Principal

Senior Executive Officer

CSSB/FSB*

Higher Executive Officer (A)

CSSB/FSB*

Higher Executive Officer

Administrative Trainee

CSSB/FSB*

CSSB/FSB*

Graduate Entrants

Executive Officer/ Higher Clerical Officer

Clerical Officer

Clerical Assistant

* Civil Service Selection Board
and Final Selection Board

FIG. 7. *Administration group grades and promotion opportunities.*

quote examples from the Fulton Report. Having assembled and
interpreted all the data required, they are in a position to advise.
While the political head, the minister, is ultimately responsible to
the Cabinet and Parliament for his department, he must depend
considerably on the accumulated experience and wisdom of his
senior civil servants. The minister has neither the time to study
detailed facts and figures nor a complete knowledge of earlier

measures. Above all, he may not fully appreciate the difficulties of a particular proposal, especially in its administration. Thus, he looks to his permanent officials to provide him with expert technical administrative advice. In some respects, the civil servant is in a better position to express an opinion. While the minister may be distracted by the complications of a passing political crisis, the official can bring an element of continuity and consistency into discussions of policy, ensuring that proposed objectives are not only desirable but realisable.

Secondly, senior civil servants prepare answers to parliamentary questions, anticipating supplementaries and briefing the minister accordingly. Whenever questions affecting a department are being asked, there is always a civil servant at hand 'under the gallery' near the Speaker's chair ready to assist his political chief.

Thirdly, the higher civil servants are responsible for preparing and watching over bills during their passage through Parliament. In the preliminaries to the bill, discussions take place with officials of the departments affected, the scope of the bill is defined for the consideration of the minister and Cabinet, Treasury approval is sought for the cost entailed, outside interests are consulted, and often an explanatory White Paper is prepared. In the actual drafting, the department's solicitor consults with Parliamentary Counsel. While the bill is passing through it various stages, a civil servant is constantly in attendance on the minister, a precaution particularly desirable on the Committee and Report stages, since the officials responsible for administering the measure are vitally concerned with details.

Finally, senior civil servants are in charge of the administrative machine, giving the necessary directions which put the Government's decisions into effect. To quote from the Fulton Report: 'New policy may require the creation of a new administrative framework. There are major programmes to be managed and controlled, such as the planning and engineering of motorways from their initial location and design to the finished construction; the design of Polaris installations and other military works; the management of international programmes like Concorde; the vast range of scientific research and development and of Government procurement; the central responsibility for the nationalised industries and for the state of the economy.' In the case of new Acts of Parliament, rules, orders and regulations must be drawn up to fill in the details of the measure and laid before the House as statutory instruments. These may involve further discussions with the interests concerned, while both the Press and such bodies as local authorities must be kept adequately informed of new steps or changes. Moreover, although broad political policy rests with the Cabinet and the minister, administration of that policy involves its application to individual cases. Since only the most important matters can be considered by the minister, many decisions have to be left to civil servants. Thus, in order to achieve consistency, the higher civil servants must formulate a code of principles upon which those below them can base their judgments. This 'administrative policy' is established partly by initial directives and partly empirically by decisions on individual cases. Early on, many cases have to be referred to the top officials for a decision which, once given, creates a precedent for future action. Similarly, when any change takes place in Government policy, the higher civil servants take the necessary action to guide the administrators below them. In these ways, therefore, the actual administration considerably affects political measures, and the higher civil servant must use his judgment as to when he can act without reference to his minister. Any mistake may lead to serious repercussions in Parliament.

As can be seen from Figure 6, the minister has his own 'private office' consisting of a principal private secretary and a small group of clerks and shorthand typists. This office sees that the minister is always briefed, and looks after his appointments, telephone calls and correspondence. Thus he remains in close and continuous contact with the civil servants at the top of the department.

SCIENTIFIC CIVIL SERVICE

Before World War II, scientists were recruited as required by each department. The needs of the war, however, revealed that the Government had failed in peace-time to attract an adequate number of graduate scientists. As a result, departmental appointment was replaced by a Scientific Civil Service. Following the Fulton Report's recommendations in favour of greater flexibility of staff and a better career structure, the classes of the Scientific Civil Service were merged into the Science Category, with a new structure of five grades from scientific assistant to principal scientific officer, with possibilities of promotion from the bottom to the top. Scientists work both inside the departments and in the experimental establishments controlled by ministries in such fields as defence, transport, power, technology and agriculture. In the departments, the Chief Scientific Officer identifies problems where research is desirable, arranges for them to be studied by the appropriate research establishment and sees that the results are applied.

THE DIPLOMATIC SERVICE

The Diplomatic Service is a separate, self-contained Service formed in January, 1965, by the amalgamation of the former Foreign Service, Commonwealth Service and Trade Commissioner Service. The Foreign Service, which dated from 1943, was itself an amalgamation of the old Diplomatic, Consular and Commercial Diplomatic Services. The 6,300 members of the Diplomatic Service are divided into ten grades. They serve in the Foreign and Commonwealth Office in London, and in High Commissions, Embassies, Consulates, and delegations to international organisations abroad.

PROFESSIONAL AND OTHER CLASSES

Apart from those employed on general duties, there are in the Civil Service large numbers of specialists and members of various professions, including architects, economists, engineers, lawyers, psychologists, statisticians, veterinary officers, etc. For some of these posts candidates are expected to have had several years' experience in their chosen profession before entering the Civil Service.

In addition, several departments retain their own special departmental classes employed on duties such as those undertaken by Officers of Customs and Excise, Inspectors of Taxes, and Prison Officers.

III. MINISTERIAL RESPONSIBILITY

THE POSITION OF THE MINISTER

A minister has various forms of responsibility. He is usually an M.P. and, like any other M.P., he must visit his constituents, attend to their needs and strike a balance between national and local interests. As a leading member of his party, he will have to attend party committees, assist in the formation of party policy, and explain the policy of his department, especially to those who are critical of it. Indeed, the Party Conference provides an annual forum for this.

Ministerial responsibility, as usually defined, covers both collective responsibility for Cabinet decisions and the individual responsibility which the minister bears for the work of his department. Thus, unless he resigns, a minister is expected to support the Cabinet and to see that relevant decisions are applied fully by the officials under him. In Parliament, he answers for his department, defending the policy it follows and the acts of its civil servants. Obviously, he must exercise some control over both policy and officials, though, as this can hardly be direct or in detail, much has to be left to the Permanent Secretary.

The relationship between the minister and his Permanent Secretary has been compared by Lord Beveridge with that between husband and wife in the Victorian household. 'The Minister is the head of the household; all public acts (including correspondence) are done in his name, and he alone speaks and votes for the household. Formally he takes all important decisions, just as the husband decides where the family shall live, and where the boys shall be educated. But he does, or should do, all this on advice, and usually finds it very uncomfortable to disregard the advice. Though head of the household, he is not really in regular charge of it. His business is mainly to fight for it outside; he must not be always at home. The business of the Permanent Secretary is to mind the house; to keep all its members in order; to prevent them from quarrelling and to make them do their work; to see that the Minister, before he goes out to his daily toil in Cabinet or Parliament, is properly equipped with all necessary information; in the language of metaphor, that he has all his buttons on and his hat brushed. Like the Victorian wife, the Permanent Secretary has no public life; is quite unknown outside the house; wields power by influence rather than directly. Like the Victorian husband, the Minister is responsible for the acts and mistakes of the Permanent Secretary, and is expected to stand up for him in public and shield him from attack' (Introduction to T. A. Critchley: *The Civil Service Today*).

The minister accepts responsibility for all the actions of his department, irrespective of whether they involve fundamental issues of policy or are merely matters of administrative detail. But, as Professor Lowell says: 'The head of a department sits in the House of Commons quite as much in order to control the House as in order that the House may control him.' Having a champion in Parliament, and one who is supported by the Cabinet, relieves the Civil Service of all political functions, including that of defending itself in the Commons. Where the House decides that what has been done is unacceptable, it is the minister who resigns, while the civil servant is sheltered behind a cloak of anonymity.

In practice, however, ministers rarely resign even when quite serious errors are made in their departments. Thus in 1971 the Vehicle and General Insurance Company became bankrupt leaving some one million motorists uninsured. The Department of Trade and Industry was criticised for not investigating the company adequately, but although one Under-Secretary in the Department was found by the report to have been negligent, the issue of ministerial responsibility did not arise. In most instances, a Prime Minister and the parliamentary party will stand by ministers under attack, although the exposure of the failings of a minister's department at question-time is a valuable form of control because it will reflect upon his political standing. The determining factor in what forces a minister's resignation appears to be, not the volume of criticism in Parliament, but the feeling in the party. If this is running against him, he may decide to resign (as Sir Thomas Dugdale did over Crichel Down in 1954).

The importance of the principle of ministerial responsibility, however, still remains. It lies in the fact that where it is desired to attack policy, criticism can be directed to the minister responsible for the department concerned. While there is effective government, responsibility for government (or misgovernment) rests squarely with the appropriate minister. The doctrine of ministerial responsibility thus gives direction to the work of the Opposition and significance to the probing of M.P.s at question-time. It is the device by which the Government is forced to explain its actions and to listen to expressions of opinion.

THE INFLUENCE OF OFFICIALS ON POLICY

When the minister first takes office, he knows the broad Cabinet policy concerning the work of his department. But this policy will have to be translated into practice, and here the minister plays a special role. As a politician, his instinct and experience should tell him what the electorate and the Commons will accept. Indeed, so much of his time will be taken up by the political aspects of the department's work that he will have to leave most of the details of administration to his permanent officials. Yet this is both reasonable and desirable. Having time to meditate on policy and principles, he is enabled to exert a real influence on his Cabinet colleagues.

Nevertheless, even in the formation of policy, a minister usually consults with his experts in the department. As we have seen, this has advantages. To some extent, the minister, through his political background, is a victim of circumstance, his whole career depending upon his ability to overcome every passing political crisis. He may, therefore, be tempted to discount the future, especially as he knows that it is largely the short-term results which sway the electorate. The civil servant, on the other hand, is not subject to election and simply serves each Government loyally. But he can give mature advice, emphasising the probable long-term effects of policy and the value of consistency, continuity and certainty in government. Yet the civil servant also has his limitations, for he does not share the Cabinet's concern with broad overall policy, and he is not in such close touch with the political world as the minister. The two men, each with different backgrounds and outlook, are therefore complementary, both making a distinct contribution to the formation of policy.

Constitutionally, the minister is paramount and, in theory, he is not even bound to seek advice from his officials. In practice, however, he would almost always do so, and his top civil servants must then consider his policy in detail, raise possible objections, and submit alternatives. As a result of such informed criticism, the minister may modify his plans, but in the last resort the decision rests with him. Once his mind is made up, the official must help him in every possible way. Harmony between the minister and his civil servant is essential to the smooth working of the constitution and, although the day-to-day administration is hidden from the public view, there is every indication that this is the normal relationship. Thus Lord Butler has paid tribute to the 'modern-minded officials' with whose aid he was able to bring into the work of the Home Office a 'spirit of reform and zeal for progress'.

The relationship between minister and civil servant, however, depends considerably on their respective personalities. Some ministers come to their office with a clear idea of what they want to achieve and how they intend to do it. Little time is wasted in making plain their intentions to the leading officials, and they do not hesitate to refer a matter back to the civil servant when they feel that the administrative details submitted are below requirements. Winston Churchill at the Admiralty, and Aneurin Bevan at the Ministry of Health, possessed to a high degree energy, ability, and determination. Generally speaking, officials prefer to serve under men who can give such a lead and whose enthusiasm is felt right through the department.

The personality of the civil servant is also important. Just as the Member of Parliament is influenced by his experiences in the House of Commons, so the official is moulded by the traditions and atmosphere of the Service in which he has probably spent his whole working life. Hence he accepts his anonymity, and always endeavours to act within what he believes to be the minister's policy. Moreover, he is trained in a habit of mind which encourages thorough consideration of a problem before arriving at a conclusion. Nevertheless, he will have his own sympathies, and if his personality is strong he may press them vigorously. At times, where he does not see eye to eye with his political chief, it may even be that the official view prevails. Thus Sir Harold Scott has recorded how his advice as Prison Commissioner helped to persuade one minister to continue with a liberal policy in the treatment of offenders. On the other hand, Lord Vansittart, Ambassador to Germany, could not influence Chamberlain's appeasement policy.

But a distinction has to be drawn between exercising influence and wielding political power. The civil servant is a knowledgeable and efficient administrator, and hence he could hardly avoid influencing departmental policy. On the other hand, he must subjugate his own views and keep to the broad lines of Cabinet policy, knowing that his minister will have to defend this in Parliament. Thus one year he may loyally assist a minister to nationalise an industry and the next help his successor to hand it back to private enterprise.

This may, however, be a mere counsel of perfection. While it is not doubted that the civil servant endeavours to be politically impartial, some critics think that his private sympathies do play an unsuspected part. Higher civil servants are still largely recruited from the middle stratum of our society. In any case, entrants having a working-class background soon associate in clubs and residential districts with middle-class people and, as H. E. Dale shows in *The Higher Civil Service*, generally adopt their style of life. Moreover, in the 19th century the State merely fulfilled regulatory duties, and thus the qualities required from civil servants were basically the static ones of diligence and honesty. Nowadays the State undertakes progressive social and economic functions and these can be fully successful only if the officials responsible for them are dynamic and enthusiastic. There is evidence of occasional tension. Mrs. Barbara Castle, Secretary of State for Employment and Productivity in Mr. Wilson's second Government, said that she had to keep pushing hard when her policy was not welcomed by the Department. From the other side of the political fence, Mr. Nicholas Ridley, Under-Secretary of State at the Department of Trade and Industry from 1970 to 1972, likened the Civil Service to an enormous steel spring which could be pulled out of its natural position by great exertion, but which eventually pulled the minister back by its sheer persistence. According to Mr. Ridley, civil servants met the Conservative Government's plan for a more commercial and independent role for nationalised industries with 'procrastination, inactivity and sabotage'. Yet the constitutional position is probably unchanged from that of earlier years. Just as the Munich policy in 1938 and the Suez invasion of 1956 were carried through despite the hostility of the Foreign Office, there seems no reason to think that strong ministers today cannot dictate any feasible policies and take the political consequences for their success or failure, although the degree of success may well be affected by the energy and enthusiasm of their officials.

IV. Problems of Civil Service organisation

Certain failings of the administrative machine are largely the result of the British system of democracy. Unlike a private business, where the primary aim is to make profits, government objectives can change with different Parliaments. Thus any long-term planning is subject to political swings. Slowness and caution in decision-making are also the result of political checks, such as questions in Parliament, Opposition criticism and the views of pressure groups, provided by the constitution.

Nevertheless, while recognising these constraints, constant

attention must still be paid to the suitability of the civil service, especially as society is constantly changing and the State is frequently accepting new functions.

'The requirements of the Civil Service', says E. N. Gladden, 'are that it shall be impartially selected, administratively competent, politically neutral and imbued with the spirit of service to the community.' Generally speaking, it does comply with these criteria, and the Fulton Committee recognised 'its capacity for improvisation, its integrity and impartiality, and its strong sense of public service.'

On the other hand, the Committee's Report commenced with the words: 'The Home Civil Service today is still fundamentally the product of the nineteenth century philosophy of the Northcote-Trevelyan Report. The tasks it faces are those of the second half of the twentieth century.' Only one member, Lord Simey, dissented, he being of the opinion that, though the Service had nineteenth century foundations, it had so evolved that 'the main characteristics it displays today are mid-twentieth century developments.'

The Fulton Committee detailed six main criticisms:

(1) The Civil Service is based on the 'philosophy of the amateur', the view being that the all-rounder can apply administrative techniques in any sphere irrespective of its subject-matter.

(2) The division of the staff into classes impeded work by the restrictions it imposed, e.g. in allocating personnel to new tasks.

(3) Specialists tend to be excluded from higher management.

(4) Administrators lack managerial expertise both because they are not trained in management techniques and because they regard themselves primarily as advisers on policy.

(5) Contact between officials and the rest of the community is inadequate.

(6) Insufficient attention was paid to planning the careers of officials.

How the service is responding to these criticisms can be considered under the headings of recruitment, training and promotion.

(1) *Recruitment*

Until World War II, civil servants were recruited through open

competitive examinations conducted by the Civil Service Commission. The method was originally introduced to eliminate
patronage and secure recruits of high ability. A shortage of applicants, however, has led to the gradual dropping of exams for the
lower grades, who now enter on the basis of G.C.E. results and an
interview (see page 300).

But it was recognised that an examination, even at honours
degree level, could hardly assess all the qualities which should be
looked for in future administrators. Success in an examination
demands ability, learning, persistence, powers of discerning what
is relevant and important, composure and a cultural background,
all of which are vital to the work the examinee will be called upon to
perform. But personal qualities, such as a pleasant and confident
manner, patience and an even temper, quickness of thought and
fluency in speech are equally desirable. Above all, a high degree of
attainment in an examination based on academic subjects does not
always imply a similar level of administrative ability, or even of
practical common-sense. Hence, for the old administrative class,
the written examination was supplemented by other forms of
assessment designed to obtain a greater insight into candidates'
potentialities.

Today there is no examination in formal degree subjects;
candidates seeking entry to the civil service at Administrative
Trainee level must simply have an honours degree, the class being
unspecified. The selection procedure is then as follows:

(1) A written qualifying examination, lasting a day and a half.
This consists of an English summary, general papers and
objectively marked tests.

(2) Candidates who qualify in the written examination are
invited to the Civil Service Selection Board. Here the two-
day procedure consists of a series of tests, exercises and
interviews designed to assess the candidate's administrative
capacity for constructive thinking and administrative
potential. The Board's written report decides whether the
candidate is invited to the Final Selection Board.

(3) The Final Selection Board interviews the candidate and
awards a final mark based on his overall performance which
decides whether he is successful or not.

The procedure is thorough and revealing. Nevertheless,
possible defects must be recognised. Since there are no really

objective tests for assessing *personality*, success or failure depends largely on the subjective judgments of the interviewers. Certain candidates, too, may have initial advantages, either of home background or type of school, or through having been to an older university. Should a bias develop towards this type of entrant, three undesirable effects could follow. First, it might help to perpetuate class divisions in the country and to create a wide gulf between senior civil servants and the man in the street, so that the official is out of touch with the ordinary person's thinking and aspirations. Secondly, the recruitment of men who conform too closely to a commonly accepted pattern leads to the entry of only one type of candidate. Not only does the clash of different personalities stimulate ideas but, since the Service offers a wide variety of work, there is room for many kinds of people who should be tested with reference to particular posts. Thirdly, it might deprive the Service of men capable of outstanding work; a person who might make an excellent civil servant in a few years' time could be overlooked simply because he was in digs when at the university and had not gained the experience in discussion enjoyed by his residential contemporaries.

But any method of selection is bound to have some faults. Persons who conduct the interviews are highly qualified and experienced. They can be alive to any deficiencies in a candidate's background and concentrate on assessing potential. The procedure has been tested by experience and is the best yet devised for choosing likely top administrators. In any case, now that persons from the executive grade can compete up to the age of 32 years, many of the above objections lose much of their force.

We have to ask, too, whether the system of selection means that future senior civil servants are drawn from a narrow section of the community. A few years ago there were indications of a predominant upper middle-class background. In 1965, 76 per cent of the old administrative class entrants came from Oxford or Cambridge universities, and 53 per cent from Public and Independent schools. In 1970, the figures were 55 per cent and 25 per cent respectively. There is thus some evidence of a trend towards an intake from a wider social background.

A further possible criticism of the examination is that it reflects the failure of the Civil Service to approach public administration as a science. This was one of the main points made by the Fulton

Committee: 'As a body, civil servants today have to be equipped to tackle the political, scientific, social, economic and technical problems of our time. They have to be aware of interests and opinions throughout the country and of many developments abroad. They have to keep up with the rapid growth of new knowledge and acquire new techniques to apply it. In short the Civil Service is no place for the amateur. It must be staffed by men and women who are truly professional.' Yet, in recruiting graduates as future administrators, no account is taken, either in their degree qualification or in the entrance examination, of the relevance of their knowledge to the job they are being recruited to do. The Committee therefore recommended that preference should be given to candidates with qualifications in relevant subjects, such as government, economics and law.

On the other hand, there are strong arguments for seeking people of high quality from all academic disciplines. First, most students choose their first degree courses without any particular employment in mind. It is doubtful, therefore, whether taking certain degree courses provides a sufficiently clear indication of what the Committee calls a 'positive and practical interest in contemporary problems', or, on the other hand, a lack of it. Secondly, defining what is 'relevant' would create theoretical and practical difficulties. Thirdly, requiring 'relevant' subjects would unnecessarily limit the field, putting the Civil Service at a marked disadvantage in recruitment. It is therefore argued that the Service should simply seek recruits with the essential qualities for administrators — outstanding intellect, analytical ability and powers of literary expression.

A minority of the Fulton Committee agreed with the latter view and drew attention to the fact that big industrial employers were not much interested in a man's degree subject unless they wanted him for scientific research. In any case, senior civil servants have a problem of 'communicating with non-experts in the form of Ministers and Committees of the House of Commons which is fundamentally different from anything industry has experienced.' The minority report went on to observe: 'It has recently been pointed out that specialisation without a broad basis of foundation knowledge has profound disadvantages. It is true that modern economic and political organisation needs high specialism, but it also needs more general qualities of judgment and decisiveness, and the ability to understand how the reshaping of values may be embodied in and implemented by public policy. In effect, both specialists and generalists are required, and the problems become one of relationships and responsibilities, rather than the exclusion of one in favour of the other.'

In the event, the government did not accept the majority recommendation, preferring to place the emphasis on 'relevant' training after selection.

One other question has to be answered: how successful is the Civil Service in attracting recruits of the right calibre? The high standards demanded for the senior grades are possessed only by an exceptionally small proportion of the community. Before the war, the security offered by the State ensured a good supply, but today full employment has meant that administrative ability is in great demand by industry and the professions. Further, in laying down salary scales, the needs of the Service have to be balanced against the cost to the community, and salaries tend to compare unfavourably with posts of similar responsibility outside. There have been suggestions of some falling-off in quality but, apart from the Diplomatic Service, there is no conclusive evidence to support this. Indeed, in 1972 the Civil Service Commission reported that 'for the first time in many years we found ourselves largely in a buyer's market'.

It is in the professional and specialist fields that the situation is most serious. Here, especially for the higher grades, there is strong competition with the private sector. As a result many vacancies had to be left unfilled for scientific and experimental officers, electronics and light engineering specialists, economists, statisticians, actuaries, architects, valuers, quantity surveyors and civil engineers.

Difficulties have also been encountered in recruiting suitable candidates for the executive and clerical grades. The field for the latter in particular has been narrowed rather than widened by post-war developments in education. A much higher percentage of young people now remain at school beyond the age of 16 years, and many who would previously have entered the Service at the clerical level now continue their studies and obtain 'A' level or degree qualifications. This tends to reduce the numbers wishing to enter the clerical grade and to swell those applying for the executive.

(2) *Training*

The method of recruiting civil servants on the basis of a 'liberal' education pre-supposes that the new entrant will from the start be given training in the special arts of government. In addition, as he progresses towards the higher management grades, he must be equipped with the same skills and techniques as his counterpart in the private sector if he is to cope satisfactorily with the economic, industrial and social tasks which have been accepted by the modern State.

Since World War II, training of civil servants has received increasing attention. Such training is undertaken both by the departments and centrally by the Civil Service Department.

Departments run courses covering the background of government, basic skills, relations with the public, and the specialised knowledge essential to their own management staff. These courses are co-ordinated by the Management Personnel (Training) Division of the Civil Service Department.

The value of external courses in bringing the official into contact with the public generally and with his counterparts in the private sector in particular is also recognised by the departments. Thus staff under 18 years of age attend day release classes, while others are given time off or financial assistance to obtain recognised professional or educational qualifications or to attend courses at such places as the Imperial Defence College, the Administrative Staff college, Henley, or the major business schools. Some senior civil servants may be given sabbatical or study leave to conduct research abroad.

The Civil Service Department has introduced a greatly expanded training programme. Following the recommendation of the Fulton Report, a Civil Service College was established at Sunningdale in 1970, with off-shoots in London and Edinburgh. Training is directed mainly towards achieving that managerial expertise which the Fulton Committee considered to be lacking. There are now three basic courses:

(1) A 4-week introductory course in Quantitative Analysis and Structure of Government for Administrative Trainees.

(2) A 12-week course in Government and Organisation taken in the third year of service.

(3) A 28-week course devoted mainly to Economic and Social Administration, normally taken in the fifth year of service.

There are also courses in senior management (Assistant Secretary and Senior Principal Scientific Officer level) and seminars are held in which Under-Secretaries meet with executives from leading multi-national firms.

In its courses the Civil Service College receives assistance from university lecturers, local government experts, management consultants and industrialists. Some courses admit students from outside the Service.

(3) *Promotion*

The system of advancement influences efficiency not only by its effect on morale but because it reduces the likelihood of square pegs being forced into round holes. In practice, however, the public service encounters difficulties in determining the basis of promotion, assessing an official's suitability for advancement, and in arranging a steady rate of promotion.

Promotion may be based either on seniority or on merit. Especially where it is difficult to assess merit objectively, there is support for giving weight to seniority. An official repeatedly over-looked might develop a sense of grievance and, losing hope of advancement, settle down for the rest of his career in a comfortable niche. On the other hand, seniority as a criterion assumes that all are fit for promotion, that all can be absorbed into the available opportunities, and that the intake of the Service has been regular. None of these requirements does in fact hold good, and so efficiency demands that merit should play the dominant part.

But this necessitates an accurate means of assessing an official's qualities. While examinations are the most objective method, they cannot test adequately personality, powers of leadership, discernment, and breadth of view. Hence, only where specialised knowledge is paramount are they really satisfactory. On the other hand, the regular reports made on each official can only be subjective and may lack uniformity — and this in spite of the new methods of preparing 'pen portraits' of civil servants introduced in 1972. In practice, therefore, the final decision on promotions rests with the head of the department, who is advised by a departmental promotion board, consisting of the principal establishment officer and other senior officials. Its members may have personal knowledge of an officer, or work through an interviewing panel; in any case, they would refer to the written personal records.

It should also be noted that the unified grading structure which was introduced following the Fulton Report has opened a 'road to the top' for all civil servants, permitting staff to be deployed in such a way that use is made of their abilities and aptitudes as they become apparent, even when this entails 'leap-frogging' grades. This more flexible career structure also allows specialists, such as scientists and engineers, to be more easily promoted outside their present field into management.

V. CONTROL OF THE CIVIL SERVICE

Generally speaking, the Civil Service gets a 'bad Press'. Nobody likes paying taxes, and it is natural to tilt at those who are responsible for spending the revenue and who receive a large proportion of it in salaries. But more fundamental issues are involved. No profit motive measures a civil servant's efficiency, and the public often feel that there is something in the jibe that officials 'like the fountains in Trafalgar Square, play from ten to four'. Above all, people want an assurance that the far-reaching powers of ordering the lives of individuals which officials exercise are properly limited and controlled.

One of the most frequent complaints made of the Civil Service is that it is 'bureaucratic'. This loosely-used word is intended to imply a love of the administrative machine and office routine for their own sake; in short, actions are restricted by 'red tape'. Such complaints are naturally made by persons who have had to wait for the decision of a government department.

Yet the delay may not be the result of a bureaucratic attitude or of inefficiency in office procedure. Even though a department is well organised, speedy action may not always be possible. If a well-informed decision is to be given, problems may have to be considered by various offices within the department, and they may even cut across different departments. Hence a file, containing the observations of officials concerned, is prepared on each case. This system makes it possible to deal relatively speedily with a large number of cases simultaneously. While at first sight it might appear to be quicker if a civil servant phoned or dropped in on a colleague to discuss a problem, in practice it would merely interrupt the flow of work.

Some delay is also caused because the civil servant must ensure that his decision is in harmony with the minister's views by following the policy of the department and being justifiable in Parliament. Where no new principle is involved, it must be consistent with decisions on previous cases. If this were not so, different individuals would nurse grievances and express them through their M.P.s. There is thus no exact parallel with decision-making in private organisations, although similar problems exist in any large body.

A more sinister charge against bureaucracy is that it provides a cloak for petty despotism. Fears of this kind are associated with the increase in the power of the executive, particularly through delegated legislation and administrative justice (see chapters 21 and 22). Yet since Parliament requires and authorises the official to fulfil these duties, he cannot justifiably be blamed for doing so. What must happen, however, is that politicians and lawyers, with the help of the Civil Service, determine the conditions and safeguards under which these powers are exercised.

The main danger arises when the official develops an inordinate belief that he knows best, and uses his powers to implement his views irrespective of the opinions of members of the public. Individuals affected are at a disadvantage because of the anonymity of the civil servant. While this is necessary to help him maintain his impartiality, it strengthens the impression that the official is outside public control. 'You say that you are directed by Mr. Secretary — but well I know it is a man called Read,' quotes Sir Charles Jeffries from a letter sent to the Colonial Office. An individual can easily begin to doubt, therefore, whether an official's decision really corresponds to that which might have been taken by the minister.

The Crichel Down episode showed that it is possible for a group of officials to decide matters without proper consideration of the rights of the individual. Farmland at Crichel Down was compulsorily acquired for military purposes in 1937. After the war, when it was no longer required, it was returned to the Ministry of Agriculture. At first its former owner tried to buy it back, but when he discovered that it was not being sold, he sought permission of the authorities to farm the land himself. His requests, however, were ignored, the officials preferring to let it go to another farmer whom they had already chosen. As a result of letters by the local M.P. to the Minister and other forms of pressure, the Government was forced to hold a public enquiry. Although there was never any suggestion of corruption, such a sad tale of inefficiency and double-dealing was revealed that the Minister of Agriculture, Sir Thomas Dugdale, was forced to resign. Today, as the case demonstrated, the preservation of the rights of the individual depends upon the Civil Service being, not only efficient, but 'human' in its approach.

Thus, in order to protect the public, there must be adequate control of the administration, both external and internal. The most important external restraint is that imposed by Parliament. The Civil Service functions as a part of government and, in the last resort, there is no better safeguard than the awareness of the official that his actions may well lead to his minister being challenged in the Commons. A serious error may give rise to a political crisis, culminating in the minister's resignation. A wise minister, there-fore, seeks to ensure that his officials can act only within prescribed limits. Other external controls exist in a vigorous free Press and the wide variety of 'interests' which organise public opinion.

Within the Service, the most important form of control is that exercised by the Civil Service Department. Not only does it emphasise recruiting persons of integrity but, by insisting on improved organisation, lessens the possibility that, through sheer inefficiency, human problems are ignored when reaching decisions. Above all, the high tradition of the Service commands honesty, integrity and loyalty. This was referred to by Sir David Maxwell Fyfe, then Home Secretary, in the Crichel Down debate. 'There has been no attempt on the part of the Civil Service to cover up the faults that have been disclosed. . . . The Service, as a service, is as shocked by the errors brought to light as anyone else. Their pride in their Service, and its reputation and tradition for fair dealing and unfailing rectitude, makes them as determined as anybody that these errors should not recur.'

This tradition of honesty and integrity is all the more important now that civil servants have become less isolated from the rest of the community and are indeed constantly involved in dealings with the public over planning and government policy. That the experience and knowledge of civil servants has a high commercial value was underlined by the trial in 1973 of George Pottinger, a departmental head at the Scottish Office, who was sentenced to five years' imprisonment for corruptly accepting gifts from an architect, John Poulson. Lapses of this kind are rare, but it is important to ensure that rules and safeguards regarding relations with the public do meet present requirements. One such rule is that within two years of retiring, a civil servant needs the approval of the Government of the day before taking a place in a firm with which he has had dealings. When, in 1974, Sir William Armstrong retired early as Head of the Home Civil Service to become Chairman of the Midland Bank, some M.P.s thought it wrong that he should have been given this permission. Although this particular appointment was not itself a cause for any concern, they feared that if this practice became more common, the situation could arise where less scrupulous officials might seek to prepare the way for a plum job in a private firm later. On the other hand, it can be argued that it is in the public interest that able civil servants retiring at 60 should be able to contribute to the efficiency of private enterprises and that the traditions of the Service and the safeguards that exist are sufficient to prevent abuse.

THE PARLIAMENTARY COMMISSIONER FOR ADMINISTRATION

Nevertheless, the Crichel Down affair did suggest that some new constitutional safeguard might be desirable to counterbalance the powers entrusted to officials. An M.P. has neither the facilities to see whether officials are meeting his enquiries with bamboozlement, nor sufficient opportunities in a busy House of Commons to press his point if he is dissatisfied.

Consequently, in 1966 the Government added a further safeguard against officialdom by appointing a Parliamentary Commissioner for Administration with functions similar to those of the Ombudsman in Scandinavian countries and of the Parliamentary Commissioner in New Zealand.

He investigates complaints of personal injustice or of maladministration by the central government brought by M.P.s at the instance of individuals or companies. The Commissioner can call for written or oral evidence, and has the power to compel production of documents. But his functions do not tend to undermine the traditional position of the House of Commons as a redresser of grievances. Rather they serve to strengthen it for the Commissioner can only act on a complaint brought by an M.P. (unlike his counterpart in New Zealand who may act on complaints brought directly by the public or on his own initiative).

Since 1973 the Parliamentary Commissioner has also acted as Health Service Commissioner for England, Wales and Scotland and can investigate such matters as inadequate food, difficulties over the provision of ambulances or using patients without their consent in clinical trials. On such matters anyone can write direct to the Commissioner, but he only investigates complaints if a satisfactory reply cannot be given after they have first been brought to the attention of the authority concerned. Another responsibility of the Parliamentary Commissioner is to sit on two independent Commissions for Local Administration, one each for England and Wales, set up under the Local Government Act, 1974, to consider complaints about local government submitted through a councillor. He does not himself handle local complaints, but he is able to give other members the benefit of his experience, particularly in cases involving both central and local administration.

Channelling complaints through an M.P. prevents an avalanche, safeguards the primacy of Parliament and perhaps at times enables an M.P. to suggest an alternative action when a constituent raises a matter which is not in fact within the jurisdiction of the Parliamentary Commissioner. On the other hand, in other countries, the right of direct approach has been one of the reasons for the success of the system because citizens felt they had a personal contact with somebody at the highest level who could have dealings with officials on their behalf.

As far as the general public is concerned, one of the main weaknesses of the arrangements is the absence of any procedure to ensure that the Commissioner's work gets adequate publicity, although there is a Select Committee for the Parliamentary Commissioner to whom he submits his reports, and the Committee can decide what points it wishes to bring to the notice of the House. Reports on particular cases by the Commissioners for Local Administrations must be made available for public inspection and comment by the Press.

Not many big blunders have been uncovered. In 1973, for instance, 571 complaints were referred by M.P.s to the Ombudsman. Of these, 285 were outside his jurisdiction. But 88 cases of maladministration, leading to 'some measures of injustice', were found in government departments, 39 of them involving the Inland Revenue. Most, however, were the result of some sort of human error, sometimes a simple mistake in arithmetic, sometimes more far-reaching. One of the cases that did attract public attention was the Commissioner's strong criticism in 1967 of the Foreign Office for excluding 12 British survivors from Sachsenhausen concentration camp from compensation payments out of a fund provided by the West German Government, on the grounds that they had been detained in a special camp and cell block outside the main Sachsenhausen perimeter. The Commissioner found that the decision had been based on 'partial and largely irrelevant information and evidence'. His special report on this case was debated in Parliament, the Foreign Secretary was persuaded to change his mind and compensation was paid.

Mostly the Commissioner's work has been less spectacular than this, but routine enquiries are important to the individuals concerned, such as those in 1973 leading to the backdating of some war pensions, in one case to 1940, with the payment of £2,384 arrears.

As well as pursuing enquiries which may result in citizens being given cash compensation, the Commissioner's work encourages civil servants to follow the proper procedures. Some critics fear that civil servants may in fact be inhibited and bureaucratic weaknesses may be worsened rather than removed. Thus Mr. Graham Page, Minister of Local Government, said in 1971: 'I get very annoyed when I get from a civil servant a report carefully putting both sides of the case and finishing up with the remark, "the Minister may think very carefully about this, as it is probably P.C.A. (Parliamentary Commissioner Action)". When I see my civil servants saying this, I know they have been looking over their shoulders all the time and not having the guts to take a decision'. Similar fears were expressed about the extension of the watchdog powers into local government. For instance, the Society of Education Officers complained that education committees would have to devote much more time to the minutiae of administration, resulting in serious delays.

A quite different criticism of the Commissioner is that he is a 'paper tiger', or as Lord Butler has put it, 'a sop to public criticism of the Government's abuse of power'. A case concerning a wrongly-sited supermarket investigated in 1972–3 suggests that more protection still needs to be given to the citizen. While the inspector was compiling his report, the building of this supermarket was allowed to continue, so that the cost of compensation for re-building it in the correct position, which would have been about £50,000 at the outset, rose eventually to £250,000. Despite this high figure, the Inspector said that Oxfordshire County Council had made a gross error, injuriously affecting the amenity of those who lived opposite and the position of the building should therefore be set back. When the residents heard that the Minister was 'disposed to accept the Inspector's recommendation', they thought they had won, but the Council's continued opposition to re-siting was in the end effective. The Commissioner thought that some residents had suffered an injustice and that they had cause to feel aggrieved over the Department's failure 'to give them an opportunity to put their own views further before the Department's change of mind'. Nevertheless, although costs incurred in making the objections were reimbursed, the residents received no compensation for their 'unnecessary loss of amenity'.

It may be concluded that although payments are frequently made to citizens following errors discovered by the Commissioner, satisfaction with the outcome of his investigations depends on the interest and support given by Parliament, for while the 'Ombudsman' can penetrate into departments in a way not open to an M.P., he cannot be given any actual power to reverse any decision which he believes to be wrong, for this would endow him with executive powers which would be virtually dictatorial, or at least quite alien to the British traditions of representative and responsible government. Nevertheless, remedial action does follow when his investigations show that such action is desirable.

SUGGESTED READING

C. K. Allen, *Law and Orders* (3rd Ed., Stevens, 1965), Chapter 10.
N. H. Brasher, *Studies in British Government* (2nd Ed. Macmillan, 1971), Chapters 4 and 5.
R. D. Brown, *The Battle of Crichel Down* (Bodley Head, 1955).
R. G. S. Brown, *The Administrative Process in Britain* (Methuen, 1970).
Report by Justice, *The Citizen and the Administration* (Stevens, 1961).
Report of the Committee on the Civil Service (the Fulton Committee), Cmnd. 3638, H.M.S.O., 1968.
F. Stacey, *The British Ombudsman* (O.U.P., 1971).
K. C. Wheare, *Maladministration and its Remedies* (Stevens, 1973).

18

The Public Corporation

> 'And the beast which I saw was like unto a leopard, and his feet were as the feet of a bear, and his mouth as the mouth of a lion: and the dragon gave him his power, and his seat, and great authority.'
>
> *Revelation*, Ch. 13, v. 2

I. DEVELOPMENT OF THE PUBLIC CORPORATION

Government, as we have seen, comes into being to provide certain goods and services for the people. But the problem then arises as to the form of organisation to be created, not only to perform these duties, but also to secure means by which citizens can ascertain that their servants are efficient and do not exceed their authority. In the last two chapters we have considered one method of organisation, the government department. Later we shall look at another, the local authority. Here we examine a third, the public corporation.

ACCOUNTABILITY AND THE GOVERNMENT DEPARTMENT

The great merit of the government department form of organisation is that it achieves a high degree of public accountability. Its main features may be briefly recapitulated. At its head is a minister who takes full responsibility for all the acts of officials under him. Ultimate control is political; the minister is a member of the Government and at each general election the electorate has an opportunity to pass a verdict on how the Government has discharged its responsibilities. Between elections, control is exercised through its representatives in Parliament — at question time, in debate, and by the investigations of the Expenditure and Public Accounts Committees. The non-political control is exercised chiefly by the Treasury, which keeps a close check on the finance of each department.

Thus both the policy and day-to-day operations of a department are subject to scrutiny. Where a person is aggrieved by even a minor administrative decision, he can seek the help of his M.P. Should satisfaction not be obtained, the matter can be so pursued that eventually it may have to be considered by the Cabinet. Complaints which reveal serious maladministration may even bring about the downfall of the minister, the bearer of ultimate responsibility.

MINOR REASONS FOR ALTERNATIVE FORMS OF CONTROL

Nevertheless, the government department form of organisation cannot be used in all cases.

First, the service, although basically of a regional nature, may have national implications. Were it purely regional it could be administered by the local authority; because of its national importance, a compromise must be found. Consequently, for the administration of the ports and docks of London and Liverpool, there have been created the Port of London Authority and the Mersey Docks and Harbour Board, over which the Minister responsible for transport exerts a remote control by appointing a small proportion of the Board's members.

Secondly, where the work would be the responsibility of many local authorities, greater unity of purpose may be achieved by having a single body, e.g. the National Parks Commission (1949).

Thirdly, in the administration of certain services, many decisions of a judicial nature may have to be given. Cases must be determined impartially and on the evidence presented — and persons affected should feel that these two principles have been applied. Would a civil servant be able to inspire confidence in his impartiality? Or would not many persons, aggrieved by a decision, feel that he was merely the servant of a minister who favoured a certain policy? To overcome such distrust, a special body (the War Damage Commission) was set up to assess compensation for damage suffered during World War II.

Fourthly, it may be vital to ensure that there is complete political neutrality in the administration of the service, an objective virtually impossible to achieve if the service is directly controlled by a ministry and subject to continual attack from the Opposition. Hence we have such independent bodies as the British Broadcasting

Corporation, the Civil Service Commission, and the University Grants Committee.

Fifthly, in the administration of certain large trusts, a small measure of government control is thought desirable to protect property in which the public have a wide interest. Thus the Church Commissioners, who administer endowment income of approximately £25 million per annum, have to submit an annual report to Parliament.

DEVELOPMENT OF STATE ENTERPRISE AFTER 1945

The special bodies set up for the above reasons were comparatively small and uncontroversial, and little thought was given to general principles in determining their composition. In recent years, however, the State has undertaken the provision of goods and services which were formerly almost wholly within the province of private enterprise. Here the form of organisation has excited much more interest. For four main reasons, the government department was considered to be unsuitable. First, the vast extension in government responsibilities would have meant either an increase in the number of government departments or overloading existing departments with different functions. Secondly, a separate functional authority to deal with a particular activity is the more efficient means of organising work which would otherwise be the responsibility of many different departments (e.g. coal) and of concentrating expert knowledge in a particular field (e.g. electricity). Thirdly, the vast extension of State activities meant that Parliament had become, on account of lack of time and the deficiency of experts, an unsuitable body for exercising detailed control. Fourthly, and most important, there were inherent deficiencies in the government department as a means of providing these particular goods and services.

Private enterprise secures economic efficiency through the 'profit motive'. Where demand is estimated accurately, the reward is profit; where it is not, the penalty is loss, and possible bankruptcy. But complications arise where the State assumes responsibility. Inaccurate estimate of demand involves no personal loss; the taxpayer meets the bill when the Army over-estimates its requirement of boots, the London ratepayer supports the financial failure of the Festival Pleasure Gardens. Moreover, eschewing the profit motive makes it difficult to experiment in demand. Hence arbitrary decisions have to be made as to whether the local authority shall build houses or flats and provide central heating, washing machines and lifts. On the supply side, too, the absence of competition removes a spur to efficiency for, where a good is provided by a State monopoly, the consumer can do little to influence the producer by way of varying his demand. Hence price tends to be decided by costs of production.

While, therefore, the automatic operation of the profit motive makes for economic efficiency and public accountability under private enterprise, the use of this weapon is denied when the State provides the goods and services. Indeed, as we shall now see, there is a conflict of principle between efficiency and accountability.

THE GOVERNMENT DEPARTMENT AND ECONOMIC EFFICIENCY

The government department was developed when the emphasis was on checking abuse of power. Thus, while it secures a large degree of accountability, certain features of its organisation are incompatible with economic efficiency.

(1) *The influence of its political connections*

The minister in charge of a department is a politician. Two important results follow. First, he will always be conscious that the department may affect the political fortunes of his party. Since resistance to the demands of vested interests may well cost votes, it takes strength of character to refuse them. Such demands would come, not only from pressure groups representing workers, employers and consumers, but also from Members of Parliament who themselves are being lobbied. Quintin Hogg puts it as follows: 'When he [the M.P.] is in, every pressure is brought to bear on him to prefer sectional to the national interests' (*The Purpose of Parliament*). For example, it would obviously be in the interests of iron and steel manufacturers to have subsidised ('uneconomic') freight rates for the transportation of their raw materials and finished products. Suppose there were a Minister of Railways; then pressure for reduced rates might be brought to bear on him through M.P.s representing constituencies where iron and steel is produced. There is thus a *prima facie* case for organising the service in some other way.

Secondly, since he fills a political post, the minister may frequently be changed, either by promotion or through a replacement of the Government. Such discontinuity of the man in control may hinder the steady pursuit of long-term industrial and commercial objectives.

(2) *The method of its accountability*

Government departments are highly accountable even on matters of detail. With public utilities, individual complaints are likely to be frequent, for, unlike the earlier departments, the public are in close touch with them as consumers. The opportunities available for the examination of a department in Parliament are therefore inappropriate in their case. First, the minister may become so immersed in small details of administration that he finds it a physical impossibility to devote adequate time to developing policy. Secondly, questions in Parliament are inclined to be critical and restrictive, rather than encouraging and constructive. Often they are the instrument of political opposition or the medium of complaint by dispossessed interests. Even where the member is genuinely seeking information, only an expert may have the technical knowledge to appreciate the issues involved. The M.P.'s enquiries, therefore, are often irrelevant and ill-informed, and merely serve to hamper the expert and clog the machine.

Moreover, such continual accountability to Parliament encourages over-cautious decisions by civil servants. When planning for the future, bringing out a new product or developing other sources of supply, the argument might proceed as follows: 'If we pursue a bold policy (which nevertheless involves some risk of failure), it is unlikely, even if it succeeds, that we shall receive full credit in Parliament. On the other hand, if the policy fails, much political capital will be made out of it. Let us, therefore, not lay ourselves open to such a risk of criticism, but rather follow a safer, if less imaginative, policy.'

(3) *The mental attitude of the civil servant*

The criticism of the Civil Service goes even further than this 'play-for-safety' attitude. Many people consider that our method of recruitment attracts entrants whose first consideration is security, and that subsequent training does nothing to alter this. Moreover, not only is the civil servant by nature unsuited to activities where a dynamic approach is essential, but the methods in which he is trained would never allow him to sell a product in competition with other producers. Since it is necessary to have consistency in the work of a government department, action must be based on thorough investigation and precedent, a procedure which would seriously hamper the operations of a public utility where quick decisions are often required.

(4) *The nature of control over staff and finance*

Control over staffing is by nature rigid and restrictive. If a department were responsible for a public utility, its staff would be part of the Civil Service, recruited, trained and promoted according to the centralised policy of the Civil Service Department. Moreover, in spite of the fact that the old treasury classes have now been abolished, fairly rigid grading would still mean that little allowance could be made for variations in skill between employees or in the supply of workers in different localities. Pay of civil servants, too, still tends to be lower than the private sector, and this could make it difficult to attract the best man.

The Treasury's control of finance is similarly narrow, unlike the approach of the businessman, who takes a long-term view when incurring expenses. Certain firms have rented grouse moors to entertain their clients! Others have deliberately lost money on the swings in order to gain on the roundabouts. Such practices, however, would not be allowed to a public utility by the Treasury. Apart from insisting on the saving of 'candle-ends', it would require the minimum outlay on expenses and the balancing of receipts and expenditure on each separate item.

DEVELOPMENT OF THE 'QUASI-GOVERNMENT' BODY

The conclusion to be arrived at, therefore, is that while a department can adequately perform functions of government, it is far from suitable for running economic enterprises, since a high degree of public accountability can only be achieved by sacrificing enterprise and efficiency. The solution to the problem has been sought in the development of special bodies, variously termed Commissions, Boards, Authorities and Corporations. Such authorities existed even under Henry VIII, in whose reign, for instance, Commissioners of Sewers were appointed. Later, in the 18th century, somewhat similar organisations were established, since central control by the Privy Council had largely disappeared during the Civil War. Thus there were Turnpike Trusts for roads and Improvement Commissioners for lighting, paving, etc. Nevertheless, until the 20th century, additional services were more usually provided either by the new local authorities or by government departments. Where 'quasi-government' bodies were created, reasons other that economic efficiency were paramount as, for example, with the Civil Service Commission in 1855.

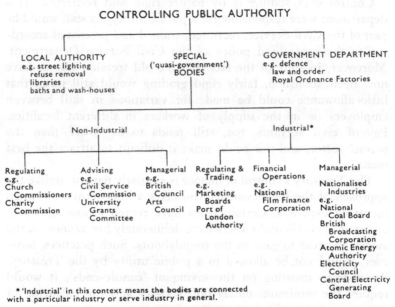

* 'Industrial' in this context means the bodies are connected with a particular industry or serve industry in general.

FIG. 8. *Forms of public organisation for the supervision or provision of goods and services.*

However, as the State began to interfere increasingly in the economic field, special bodies had to be created so frequently that today they number over 200. But, being established for separate reasons and varying in importance, their structure is often individual in character and their financial autonomy of differing degree. Yet all have two features in common: (a) they are appointed and not elected; (b) they are subject to some form of public control, even though this may be only slight. Thus, with the Port of London Authority, the Minister in charge of transport merely appoints two out of the eighteen members, while the Church Commissioners only have to submit an annual report to Parliament. On the other hand, with the nationalised industries, the minister may appoint the whole of the Board and give directions on general policy. Figure 8 shows how these special bodies fit into the pattern of government authorities.

II. Organisation of the Nationalised Industries

The rest of this chapter will deal almost exclusively with the large corporations which run the nationalised industries, for they deserve detailed attention. In the first place, they supervise basic industries, far exceeding in importance the earlier subjects of quasi-government control. Secondly, the majority of these industries were previously organised under a private enterprise system. Lastly, and most important constitutionally, they represent the latest attempt in this type of government control, their common features demonstrating that they have been organised on carefully thought-out principles.

These general features are:

(1) The Boards are 'bodies corporate'. This means that they have a legal identity and therefore, like a company, have a life of their own, can own property, and sue and be sued in the courts.

(2) The assets of the industry are vested in the Board.

(3) The nationalising Act usually gives the Board instructions as to its general responsibilities. Thus the National Coal Board is charged with:

(a) working and getting the coal in Britain;

(b) securing the efficient development of the coal-mining industry;

(c) making supplies of coal available, of such qualities and sizes, in such quantities and at such prices, as may seem to them best calculated to further the public interest in all respects, including the avoidance of any undue or unreasonable preference or advantage.

(4) A minister is given an overall control of the Board. He exercises, as it were, the shareholders' rights in a company, the 'shareholders' of a Board being the public. It is the minister, therefore, who appoints the Board's members, although the nationalising Act usually specifies their general qualifications.

These Acts also impose on him specific duties (see page 339), and in addition authorise him to give the Board general directions on matters which *appear to him to affect the national interest*. Thus the minister has a far greater control over the post-war Boards than over the earlier ones, the aim being to allow freedom in day-to-day administration but some subordination on general policy.

(5) The Boards are free from Treasury control over staffing and finance. They engage their own staff, arranging pay and conditions of service directly through employees' trade unions or associations. As regards finance, they must pay their way, taking one year with another, free from State subsidy. (For economic reasons, many Boards could not raise funds on the market and so they have had to rely on the Treasury for capital. In fact, in 1957 the Treasury was made responsible for supplying them with most of their funds in order to control borrowing.)

(6) To avoid parliamentary questioning on matters of detail and to ensure some direct representation by consumers, Consumer Councils have been established for the coal, electricity, gas and transport industries. They consist of 20 to 30 unpaid members appointed, except for air transport, by the minister. Nominations are made by bodies whom the minister selects as being representative of consumers, e.g. local authorities, women's organisations, professional associations, trade unions and trade associations. All Councils are organised on a regional basis, except in the coal industry, which has two national councils, one for industrial and the other for domestic consumers. Consumer Councils: (*a*) deal with complaints and suggestions from consumers (although they are also expected to act on their own initiative); (*b*) advise both the Boards and the minister of the general views of consumers. Unfortunately, either through ignorance, the remoteness of the offices, or lack of confidence, little use has been made of these Councils. As a result, ministers have incurred odium in Parliament by refusing to answer questions on detail, questions which really should have been dealt with through Consumer Councils.

Thus the public corporations are organised with the aim of securing the best of both worlds: on the one hand, the world of energetic dynamic endeavour found in the private enterprise system; on the other, the world of accountability to the public, to whom they belong and whom they serve.

Nationalisation of industry has led to economic problems. How shall we ensure the sovereignty of the consumer? How and when shall we award wage increases? What pricing policy shall be adopted? How shall profits be allocated between employees, consumers, future development and revenue for the State? How can we ensure efficient operation? What priority shall they enjoy for their capital requirements? Many of these problems are still far from solved, though discussion of them lies outside the scope of this book. But the method of organisation through the public corporation raises constitutional problems, which are indeed often related to these economic questions. If, for instance, a centralised organisation is too unwieldy on economic grounds, the management perhaps having grown out of touch, then a new organisation must be devised and this may present constitutional problems. What, for example, shall be the relationship between the central Board and its new off-shoots? What over-riding powers shall the Board enjoy?

Constitutional problems fall under two main headings, internal and external. Internal problems are concerned chiefly with establishing an organisation for the Board which is best suited to achieving efficiency. External problems arise mainly through the need to secure accountability without impairing that efficiency although this is an objective impossible to achieve completely.

III. CONSTITUTIONAL PROBLEMS: INTERNAL

(1) *How shall the Board be organised?*

The Board can be organised either on a functional or a regional basis, or on a combination of both. The Transport Commission was originally organised functionally, having six separate executives, for railways, London transport, road haulage, docks and inland waterways, road passenger transport, and hotels, but within this board structure the London Transport Executive was basically regional, while the Railway Executive was divided into six regions. Both electricity and gas, on the other hand, were divided regionally into twelve Areas. Each form of organisation has its advantages. The functional type leads to healthy competition between the different kinds of service and secures maximum economies of specialisation. Thus competition between the railways and road transport could lead to greater efficiency, while the Railway Executive could order standardised equipment in bulk for all the separate regions. The difficulty is, however, that functions may be so large and diverse that they cannot be combined effectively as a single undertaking. Consequently in 1962 the Transport Commission was replaced by four separate Boards — for British Railways, London Transport, British Transport Docks, British Waterways — each directly responsible to the Minister responsible for transport. Regional organisation permits better co-ordination of the various functions, facilitates variations according to different localities, yet still allows for healthy rivalry between areas.

In general, because of the problem of size and the need of de-centralisation, the tendency has been towards a regional organisation, e.g. for electricity, gas, and in 1954, for the railways. But the one actually adopted must depend on the nature of the service. Thus the Electricity Act, 1957, set up a functional authority, the Central Electricity Generating Board, to generate and deliver electricity in bulk, and in 1973 the Gas Corporation was established, a single body which, for technological and financial reasons, is better suited than the earlier regional organisations to run an industry transformed by the discovery of natural gas.

(2) *How centralised shall be the organisation?*

When the National Coal Board was created, the Act set up a *National* Coal Board, consisting of a chairman and seven full-time and four part-time members. But the Board itself was left to determine the rest of the coal industry's organisation. In practice it created eight Divisional Boards to control districts corresponding roughly to the main coal-bearing regions. In 1969 these Divisions were abolished and replaced by 17 Areas, each under an Area Director. He is directly and personally responsible to the Board for supervising and co-ordinating the work of the collieries within the Area. The day-to-day work of running the collieries is under the direction of colliery managers.

It seems, however, that the problem of the size of the operating unit was under-estimated. There was much criticism of the highly centralised nature of the Coal Board which, it was alleged, was leaving too little power to direct operations to the Divisional and Area Managements. Hence subsequent nationalising Acts allowed more de-centralisation. The Electricity Act, 1957, gave some independence of status to the twelve Area Electricity Boards, and each is financially autonomous. The Gas Council, established in 1948, was originally a central representative body for the industry, composed of the chairmen of each of the twelve Area Boards with an independent Chairman and deputy-Chairman appointed by the Minister, but from 1965 the Council was allowed to manufacture and supply the Boards with gas and, as we have seen, the creation of a single Gas Corporation in 1973 showed that technological advantages may be decisive in determining the structure.

(3) *What shall be the constitution and qualifications of the governing Board?*

In private enterprise, the shareholders appoint a Board of Directors, and the success of the Board is measured by a simple test — the scale of profits made. This shows a marked difference from public enterprise. The Board of a public corporation is not concerned with making a profit; in fact, as it often enjoys a monopoly in supplying a necessity, obtaining profits should present no great difficulty. Usually, therefore, the only criterion laid down for its financial policy is that it shall make ends meet over a period of time (e.g. five years). The main task of the Board is to satisfy a public need, and in doing so it has much wider responsibilities than a Board of Directors. It must be answerable to the consumers, its employees, the taxpayer, the Government and the nation as a whole. Such a consideration influences the choice of the Board — the number of its members, their qualifications, the method of appointment and the conditions of service.

In specifying the qualifications of a Board's members, the various nationalising Acts are merely platitudinous. The minister is required to appoint 'persons *appearing to him* to be qualified as having had experience of, and having shown capacity in, industrial, commercial and financial matters, applied science, administration or the organisation of workers'. Thus the minister is the sole judge of a person's fitness, while the qualifications cover almost any kind of experience! However, there are certain general considerations. First, appointments must be based on fitness for the task, and not be rewards for political services. Any suggestion of 'jobs for the boys' would make the Board a continuous political target both inside and outside Parliament. Secondly, members must be chosen for their ability to work as a team. Thirdly, certain members must be included who are concerned primarily with general policy in addition to those who head particular departments (such as finance, production, marketing, scientific development and staff), or represent important interests (such as employees' trade unions and consumers). A Board which was merely the meeting-place of diverse functional and sectional interests could not agree on a coherent, progressive policy. There are thus grounds for including a number of part-time members, men who can bring breadth of vision and see their own particular industry in relation to the wider needs of the nation. Such part-time members might even advise the minister on the appointment of full-time members, for these are likely to come increasingly from within the industry. The main difficulty with part-time members, however, is the suspicion that they may not be able to divorce their private interests and policies from those of the Board, a disadvantage revealed by the Parker Tribunal which investigated the alleged bank rate leak in 1957.

Since the minister exercises the ordinary shareholder's right, the appointment of Board members is left to him. (There are a few exceptions, notably the Court of the Bank of England, and the B.B.C., where, to avoid any suggestion of political bias, the choice rests with Her Majesty. In practice, this means that the Prime Minister has the main responsibility.) The minister usually consults interests beforehand and staggers appointments in order to give the Board continuity. It is better, too, if the size of the Board is flexible. Where the number is determined by the minister, he can add to the Board as different tasks arise and particular experience is required, appoint men of unusual ability as they become available and, if necessary, swamp the Board with men who subscribe to his views should it at any time be hostile to his policy.

But conditions of service must be acceptable if men of the high calibre required are to be attracted from industry. Salaries, for instance, must be considerably higher than those received by senior civil servants, especially as Board members do not enjoy pension rights or the same security of tenure. Moreover, Board members must feel free from the vicissitudes of politics, though this does not mean that they are immune from dismissal (see page 340).

(4) *What shall be the exact position of the staff?*

The Civil Service is chiefly recruited by open competition, conditions of service being uniformly applied according to the relevant grade. This would be impossible with the nationalised industries. Not only are employees mainly technicians with varying degrees of skill, but the Board must be free to adjust terms of service according to local differences. Area and Regional Boards, therefore, are usually made the employing authority.

The position of the trade unions raises another difficulty. It is felt that the Government should be a model employer; hence the unions have been given a special position in the nationalised industries, the Boards being required to establish joint negotiating machinery and other bodies for consultation on health, safety, and the organisation and conduct of operations. However, problems of labour relations have not yet been solved. Trade unions have been able to exploit their strong bargaining position. Most of the nationalised industries are basic to the economy, while few are concerned directly with export markets, where increased costs would undermine their competitive position. Hence, serious disputes have occurred, as for instance, in transport, the Post Office and coal-mining, particularly when the government has sought to set an example to private industry by limiting wage increases in the public sector.

IV. CONSTITUTIONAL PROBLEMS: EXTERNAL

The need to secure accountability without lowering efficiency raises the following questions:

(1) *What shall be the exact relationship of the minister with the Board?*

The post-war Boards have been subjected by Parliament to far greater ministerial control. This has been necessary to regulate the rate of capital development of these large industries; to make known the wishes of the Treasury, which guarantees most of their capital; to see that rationalisation schemes are carried through; to achieve some parliamentary control over those which are monopolies; to prevent the Board from becoming complacent and unenterprising; to see that decisions are in harmony with Government policy.

Ministerial control is exercised in three main ways. First, the minister can appoint and remove Board members, a task which imposes a heavy burden. The Secretary of State for Energy, for instance, is responsible for over 200 appointments in the National Coal Board, the Gas Council and the twelve Area Boards, the Central Electricity Generating Board, the Electricity Council and the twelve Area Electricity Boards. Much advice must therefore come from other persons. Power to dismiss a Board member is necessary if the minister is to exercise the rights of ordinary shareholders. Hence he can usually terminate the appointment of a member who becomes *in his opinion* 'unfit to continue in office or incapable of performing his duties'. But what this phrase means exactly is not clear. Obviously a member can be dismissed where he is physically or mentally incapable, and on moral grounds. A Chairman of the Yorkshire Electricity Board was dismissed after he had been given a prison sentence for wilfully exceeding the building licences granted for the Board's headquarters. But should a member be subject to removal simply because the minister doubts his ability, dislikes his policy or objects to his personality? On the first two grounds, the reply would probably be 'yes', but as regards the third it would be subject to many qualifications. That the exact position is open to doubt even in the minds of Board members was shown in 1949 when Mr. Strachey dismissed two members of the Overseas Food Corporation. One of them, Mr. Wakefield, refused to go, claiming that not just he, but the whole Board was responsible for policy. Again, in 1970, Mr. Christopher Chataway (Minister of Posts and Telecommunications) dismissed Lord Hall as Chairman of the Post Office Corporation. Lord Hall protested vigorously, and strikes followed in the Post Office.

Secondly, the minister has powers of direction and approval on certain matters *specified in detail* in the nationalising Acts. In general, these powers are designed to give the minister control in matters which affect national planning or the interests of consumers and employees. He can therefore: require periodic evidence, either in the annual reports and accounts or through information and statistics as requested, that the industry has performed satisfactorily; stipulate the form of accounts and the auditors; veto investment and borrowing programmes; approve research and development schemes; examine training and education proposals; act on the recommendation of Consumer Councils; supervise safety arrangements.

Thirdly, the nationalising Acts give the minister power to issue 'general directions' to the Board on matters affecting the national interest.

Fulfilling the above responsibilities is no easy task. Indeed, it is doubtful whether, in such large undertakings, the mere issue of a few directives by a minister would ever be sufficient to put matters right. In any case, certain dangers exist.

(a) An excessive use of his powers would destroy the raison d'être of the Boards. Some safeguard could be provided by requiring that certain matters, such as an application to increase prices, should be referred automatically to an external tribunal, with the minister interfering only after the tribunal had given an opinion. But it must not be assumed that the minister has completely unrestrained powers. Not only must he consult with Government colleagues but both the Chancellor of the Exchequer, who sanctions investment, and the Select Committee on the Nationalised Industries, exercise forms of control.

(b) The minister might interpret his powers narrowly. If his intervention comes too late, he fails to represent the community's interests, and avoids some accountability to Parliament. Mr. John Strachey, for instance, accepted no responsibility in 1949 for the failure of the Overseas Food Corporation's plans in Tanganyika (the 'groundnuts scheme'), although many critics thought that he acted far too tardily.

(c) The minister may become immersed in details of administration to the exclusion of national policy, resulting in a duplication of work between his department and the Board.

(d) Since Parliament often does not know where the minister's control begins and ends, it finds it difficult to allocate blame. Such divided responsibility, therefore, would enable a weak minister to shelter behind the Board to avoid criticism (see page 342).

(e) The minister, being a politician, may so use his influence that the operations of the Board favour interests supporting him politically.

(2) *What shall be the relationship between the minister and Parliament?*

The minister is expected to have a split personality. On the one hand, he represents the shareholders, exercising their rights and accounting to Parliament for his stewardship. On the other, he is the spokesman for the Board in Parliament, explaining and defending its policy. It is as though the Chairman of the Board of Directors and the leader of a critical group of shareholders of a limited company were one and the same person. While it is essential for the Board to have a spokesman, the minister need not, provided criticism is objective, rush to the Board's defence on all occasions. In any case, the good minister will largely forestall criticism by explaining policy in advance.

(3) *Has Parliament adequate opportunities for securing accountability of the Boards?*

Boards were created in order that the nationalised industries should be free from restrictive Treasury control and nagging interference by Parliament. Thus, they fix their own terms for employing labour and are free from submitting estimates of expenditure. While the minister appoints professional auditors, the Boards are not subject to the 'efficiency audit' of the Comptroller and Auditor General. Nor is Parliament free to ask questions on their day-to-day administration.

But there must be adequate opportunities for Parliament to discuss other matters concerning them. These occur, as with government departments, in question-time and debates.

The weapon with the sharpest edge is the parliamentary question, but since questions may not be asked on details of administration, they have to be confined to those matters where the minister has specified duties under the nationalising Act or where the Board has borrowed from the Treasury. Yet difficulties arise. Even on these limited topics, so many questions could be put down that Parliament would have insufficient time to deal with them adequately. Hence M.P.s may eschew the publicity of the parliamentary question and make direct enquiries of the Board first. More important, the minister may often refuse to answer on the grounds that he is not responsible. He can do so either because there is no clear distinction between policy and day-to-day administration or because he has chosen to influence the Board's policy informally by prior consultations instead of through clear-cut directives. The latter practice drew strong comment from the Select Committee on the Nationalised Industries in their report on the Air Corporations in 1959. They considered that the minister was managing to exercise control over the Air Corporations beyond his statutory authority, thereby leading to a diminution in the authority of the Boards and in their feeling of responsibility. Such informal control has serious constitutional implications, for it represents an extension of executive power over which Parliament has little control. It seems important, therefore, that the minister should make more use of definite directives in his dealings with the Board which would include them in its annual report.

While debate in Parliament is a more cumbersome weapon, it affords numerous opportunities to examine the workings of the Board in more detail. Broadly speaking, such debates can arise on occasions similar to those for examining a government department, viz.: (a) on the 10 o'clock adjournment, where the Speaker and not the minister decides whether the subject-matter is admissible; (b) on the reply to the Address on the Speech from the Throne, where the scope is unlimited; (c) on Supply days, when the Opposition could propose a reduction of the minister's salary on the appropriate vote; (d) where a bill is introduced to amend the original statute; (e) on the second reading of any private bill introduced by a Board; (f) where a minister seeks parliamentary approval of a statutory instrument made under a nationalising Act; (g) on a private member's motion; (h) on the day set aside for discussing the Board's annual report in the House of Commons.

While this is a formidable list, the aggregate time available from these opportunities is far too short for adequate discussion of each Board. The main debate should take place on the annual report, but here only one day is allowed. When time could be allocated on other occasions, it is often dissipated in reiterating old political arguments or by concentrating attention on only a few Boards. The debate itself may take place twelve months after the end of the period under review, while the reports themselves often vary in quality, contain too many details for the average M.P., and concentrate on window-dressing rather than major problems and objective self-criticism.

(4) *Is Parliament a suitable body for ensuring a Board's efficiency?*

With the removal of the profit motive, the public has to rely mainly on Parliament to see that public corporations are run efficiently. Unfortunately, there are many difficulties.

First, there is the one just referred to — the inadequacy of the time available.

Secondly, a Board's policy can be discussed objectively only if Parliament keeps it above party politics. This has been achieved with certain Boards, such as the Civil Service Commission which excites little public interest), the Atomic Energy Authority (which is highly technical), and the B.B.C. (where common consent keeps it free from politics). But nationalisation remains a party issue, and the industries concerned are often attacked because of the emotions which they still arouse. In such circumstances, debates can add little to an understanding of a Board's problems.

Thirdly, Parliament, having developed as a political body, is not designed for the task of supervising industrial enterprises. It is too large to examine efficiency properly and is without the experts who alone can assess technical matters.

In suggesting how to improve public control, few critics go as far as Mr. Christopher Hollis, who advocates the formation of a Third Chamber which would concentrate on the discussion of economic issues. Most feel that Parliament itself is capable of arranging for the desired degree of supervision, and steps have already been taken. In controlling government departments, the House of Commons had to make use of committees, chiefly the Expenditure Committee and the Public Accounts Committee. A similar pattern has been followed for the public corporations. Since 1955, a Select Committee on the Nationalised Industries has been appointed to examine the reports and accounts of the Boards and to investigate aspects of their work. But is a Select Committee, consisting chiefly of amateurs, competent to investigate in detail the activities of these large business undertakings? If the Committee merely exercises a general control, is there not a danger of dividing the minister's responsibility? On the other hand, if it is backed by a high-powered Comptroller at the head of an expert staff of auditors and accountants carrying out detailed supervision, will not it threaten the autonomy of the Boards, destroy their initiative, and cause them to adopt a 'play-for-safety' attitude? The difficulty lies in establishing the right balance of control. Too little could result in inefficiency; too much would mean that a government department might as well have been established in the first place. Any new controls should be complementary to those already existing. The reports of the Select Committee indicate that it is still feeling its way. What is essential is that Parliament knows how the important functions of these Boards and their vast spending (especially on investment) are being conducted.

Lord Morrison, who opposed the idea of a Select Committee, made three proposals in his *Government and Parliament*. First, control could be exercised through periodic committees of enquiry, similar to those which examine the B.B.C. every five years. Already there have been such committees for nationalised industries — the Fleck Committee on coal, and the Clow and Herbert Committees on electricity. Under a distinguished chairman, they could examine the organisation, policy and methods of the Boards, and make proposals. Secondly, the British Institute of Management could provide a panel of able industrial consultants which would be drawn upon by the Boards. Thirdly, the Boards themselves might *collectively* create their own industrial efficiency unit to which problems could be referred.

CONCLUSIONS

Accountability to Parliament should be on broad issues of policy only. Supervision of day-to-day administration can probably best be achieved through the development of alternative opportunities and institutions. This could take the form of:

(1) *Discussing the annual reports more effectively*. The preparation of a report serves as a constant reminder to the Board that it is accountable. Unlike the short statements made by the chairman of a limited company to its shareholders, these reports are full and informative, suitable for consideration both by Parliament and the public. Much more use could be made of the information they contain as the basis of objective discussion.

(2) *Improving the Consumer Councils*. Apart from their responsibility to the nation at large, the nationalised industries must be accountable to the consumer. Ways must be found of estimating his wants and explaining policy to him, especially as he is denied the use of his chief weapon, the withdrawal of his custom, by the monopolistic position so often enjoyed by the Boards.

At one time, it was hoped that consumers' interests would be protected through the Consumer Councils, but in practice the public has made little use of them. Many people are ignorant of their existence, while others do not submit their complaints, either because of the remoteness which results from their centralised organisation, or simply through lack of confidence. Complaining, many feel, would be a waste of time, an impression which is not surprising when it is remembered that the Council depends on the Board for its funds and often has as chairman a member of the Area Board! But, in comparison with the Board and its employees, consumers are so poorly organised that these Councils must be made more effective. Greater publicity should be given to their functions, and decentralisation carried out by establishing local offices to which all complaints concerning, say, fuel and power, could be taken.

(3) *Developing information services.* Some Boards have already established machinery to secure a closer link with consumers. The chairman holds Press conferences to explain new proposals and development plans. Popular versions of the annual report are issued to consumers and employees. Public relations departments have been created to let the consumer feel that the Board is endeavouring to meet his wishes. Letters received or appearing in newspapers on the Board's activities are analysed, and items of policy are explained through advertising, booklets and the Press. Other ideas which could be tried are market research techniques (on the lines of the B.B.C.'s audience research department), and close co-operation between the Board and the information division of the appropriate government department. The importance of these services is that where they prove effective fewer letters will be written by M.P.s to the Boards, and more time will be available for the discussion of broad policy.

Finally, in certain circumstances, two important forms of accountability can be invoked. First, ever-watchful organised interests can give publicity to objectionable proposals. In this way, the British Electricity Authority was prevented from taking cables across National Trust property. Secondly, the courts can grant injunctions to prevent possible infringement of private rights and can punish and order restitution for illegal acts.

SUGGESTED READING

R. Kelf-Cohen, *Nationalisation in Britain* (2nd Ed., Macmillan, 1961).
Lord Morrison, *Socialisation and Transport* (Constable, 1933); *Government and Parliament* (3rd Ed., O.U.P., 1964), Chapter 12.
W. A. Robson, *Nationalised Industry and Public Ownership* (2nd Ed., Allen and Unwin, 1962).

IV

THE JUDICIARY

19

The Judiciary

'The place of justice is a hallowed place.'

FRANCIS BACON: *Essays*

I. HISTORICAL BACKGROUND

INTRODUCTION

If democratic government is to be effective and enduring, it is essential that the laws passed by the elected representatives of the citizens shall be applied and upheld. There must, therefore, be courts of law, commanding the confidence of the people by their expeditious, efficient, firm and impartial dispensation of justice. Without such justice, the law would be held to ridicule, and eventually order would degenerate into anarchy.

The functions of these courts are:

(1) to declare the law where Parliament has not been sufficiently explicit;

(2) to prevent any tendency towards arbitrary government by applying the law, impartially and independent of any outside interference, where the citizen is in conflict with the authorities;

(3) to determine the exact penalty to be suffered by persons breaking the law;

(4) to decide disputes between citizens;

(5) to restrain any persons who interfere illegally with the rights of others;

(6) to provide the means whereby, as far as possible, an offended person can obtain redress for grievances suffered.

Our present judicial system, like so many institutions of British government, has its origins at least as early as Saxon times. Throughout its history, there have run two fundamental principles. The first, recognising the essential importance of justice, requires that it be administered by the State as one of the functions of government. The second, emphasising that justice must be an end in itself, stipulates that the judiciary must be kept separate from the other two branches of government, the legislature and the executive.

Although accepted, neither principle was fully implemented while the judiciary was still in the early stages of its growth. The application of the first was the result of the strong government and flair for organisation which came with the Normans. Previously, the central jurisdiction of the Saxon kings had, owing to difficulties of communication, been supplemented by local justice, administered in the shire, hundred and manorial courts. What the Normans did was to incorporate these local courts into their feudal organisation, so that by the 12th century a strong centralised system of justice in England and Wales had evolved. The manorial courts were, except by the consent of the parties concerned, limited to trying matters affecting the serfs. But the King's Court had wide jurisdiction. Not only did it punish and settle disputes between persons who held land directly from the Sovereign, but it could hear appeals from any freeman who chose to exercise his traditional right to petition the King when aggrieved by the justice of a local court.

Three further developments increased central control. Even in Saxon times, certain important crimes, such as housebreaking, sheltering outlaws, ambush, and the neglect of summons to the army, were reserved for the special jurisdiction of the King or his officials. Such offences were termed 'pleas of the Crown', and they were so extended by the Norman kings that by Henry II's reign all major crimes represented a breach of the King's peace and could not, therefore, be tried by local courts. The second and third developments were initiated by Henry II. In order to extend the King's influence over civil cases, he started the practice of serving a 'writ' when he wished to interfere with the jurisdiction of local courts. This removed the case to the King's Court where, it soon became evident to litigants, better justice was being offered. Hence the local courts lost much of their business. More important, however, was the appointment of travelling 'justices in eyre', who were later to develop into assize judges. This did much to reduce the difficulties facing the parties to a suit, for formerly both they and their witnesses had to travel to Westminster. But, above all, by carrying to all parts of the kingdom the practices and judicial decisions of the King's Court at Westminster, it established the principle that justice should be national in character and uniform in its application. This advance, however, was achieved only at the expense of the local courts; the shire and hundred courts decayed, while the manorial courts in effect passed away as serfdom came to an end. As a result, poor persons were often inconvenienced in settling small cases.

The second principle, that justice should be kept separate from the other functions of government, was not put fully into practice until much later. Saxon and Norman kings were personally responsible for the administration of justice. (Even today, we still speak of the Queen's judges, the Queen's courts and Her Majesty's prisons.) Nevertheless, by the 14th century, the government's judicial functions were being distinguished from its other activities, with the term, 'the King's Court' applied to the former, and 'the King's Council' to the latter.

Yet judicial and administrative functions continued to overlap for many centuries. The Court of Star Chamber provides the best known example. It originated as a small group of Privy Councillors, strengthened by a few judges, who sat as a Court to try important offenders and cases not specifically assigned to the regular courts. Eventually it was known as the Court of Star Chamber, taking its name from the stars worked on the roof of the special chamber of the King's palace where it met. There was initially little that was irregular about its work, proceedings being heard in public and recorded. Its downfall came about because, as part of the Privy Council, it also had administrative duties. Hence, Royal Proclamations were issued by the full body and breaches of them tried by Star Chamber, convictions being secured without a jury and heavy penalties imposed. This arbitrary procedure increased under Elizabeth I and James I, and by 1641 it had so aroused the opposition of the House of Commons that the Long Parliament abolished the Court and severely curtailed the judicial powers of the Council. But this step did not secure the independence of the judiciary, for the Stuart kings continued to remove unsympathetic judges, a practice which was not brought to an end until 1701, when the Act of Settlement made judges irremovable except by an Address by both Houses of Parliament.

THE MEDIEVAL JUDICIAL SYSTEM

(1) *The Common Law courts*

Under the early Norman kings, there was no judicial *system*. The administration of justice was one of the functions of the King in his Great Council (the Magnum Concilium), although in practice it was performed by permanent officials of the Continual Council (the Curia Regis). But because it travelled from place to place, the King's Court proved inconvenient for those seeking justice. Moreover, as the volume of work increased, it became inadequate. The result was specialisation; by the 14th century, its judicial functions had been taken over by three Common Law courts.

The *Court of the Exchequer* developed first. The Exchequer was a department of the Curia Regis concerned with the accounts of the Royal Household. Where disputes arose over the collection of taxes and the conduct of Exchequer officials, it gave a summary ruling. Soon its jurisdiction was extended to matters only indirectly concerned with the revenue, such as obtaining judgment against a debtor on the grounds that his failure to settle made it impossible for the plaintiff to pay what was due to the King. Hence, in the 13th century, royal officials, the Barons of the Exchequer, were appointed to try such disputes. So began the Court of the Exchequer which lasted until 1873.

The *Court of Common Pleas* resulted from the increase of pleas between subject and subject. To hear such cases, Henry II appointed in 1178 five justices to travel with, and sit permanently in, the Curia Regis, and only where they could not arrive at a decision was the case remitted to the King's full Court. Eventually there emerged a separate court, the Court of Common Pleas. One of the grievances of the barons in Magna Carta was that this court followed the King from place to place, and so John conceded that it should be permanently situated in Westminster.

The *Court of King's Bench* developed from that part of the King's jurisdiction which was concerned with specially important cases. These were marked 'coram rege' (to be heard before the King in person), and included matters affecting the King himself, complaints against certain great persons who were privileged to be tried only before the King, and appeals from inferior courts, including cases referred by the Court of Common Pleas. Eventually the justices dealing with these cases became separated from the Curia Regis and, as the Court of King's Bench, they too eventually began to sit regularly in Westminster Hall.

(2) *Assize courts*

Originally the word 'assize' meant a sitting of the King's Council, but during the 12th century it became applied to one of its decrees. Many of these decrees, such as the Assize of Northampton 1176, dealt with, and laid down procedures for settling, disputes over land. Actions were to be initiated by a royal 'writ of assize' and heard either at Westminster or in the locality where they originated by the justices in eyre under a 'commission of assize'. Eventually, therefore, such justices became known as 'justices of assize'.

In time, the work of the justices of assize was extended to other types of case. At the end of the 13th century, provision was made by which civil cases could, in order to save the expense and inconvenience of travelling to Westminster, be heard by a justice of assize, and the system was later adopted for criminal cases. Equally important was the practice of drawing the justices of assize from the judges of the Common Law courts at Westminster, for this resulted in the same principles of law being constructed and applied throughout the kingdom. Thus the common law was created.

(3) *The Court of Chancery*

As trade and commerce increased, Common Law courts, which were chiefly concerned with land disputes, proved inadequate. The judges were conservative, refusing to recognise new causes of action unless they followed from established legal rules. Consequently, for new types of offences, there was often no remedy; though the 'law' was administered, justice, in its true sense, was denied. Moreover, during the 15th century, judges and juries were often intimidated by powerful persons. Since, however, it was still recognised that a reserve of justice remained with the King and his Great Council, those persons who felt that justice would be denied them in the Common Law courts could petition the King. In practice, the King's Council had little time to consider petitions, and the petitioner was either told to seek his remedy at common law or his request was passed to the King's chief adviser, the Lord Chancellor, and upon his report the Council made a decree. By the end of the 15th century, not only were petitions being sent direct to the Chancellor, but he himself was making the decree. There was thus established a Court of Chancery to supplement the work of the Common Law courts.

Nevertheless, the Court of Chancery frequently came into conflict with the other three courts. It was not until the 17th century, when James I intervened in the dispute between Lord Chief Justice Coke and Lord Ellesmere, the Lord Chancellor, that it was finally established that, where they disagreed, the final decision rested with the Chancellor.

(4) Other superior courts

The *Court of Admiralty* was established in the middle of the 14th century. After the Battle of Sluys, 1340, England held such a commanding position at sea that Edward III was able to require that disputes on maritime matters, such as punishment of and payment for acts of piracy, should be tried before the Admiral of the Fleet. Eventually the work was delegated to lawyers, chiefly specialists in Roman law, the law most commonly used by international merchants. During the 17th century, the Common Law courts successfully regained a share of this profitable jurisdiction, the Court of King's Bench dealing with the criminal and many civil matters, while the Court of Admiralty was concerned chiefly with piracy, prize, salvage and wrecks.

Ecclesiastical courts had jurisdiction over wills and matrimonial affairs, as these affected the work of the Church. Wills had to be proved before the bishop, and while Church doctrine would not permit a divorce, it could award a decree, the equivalent of a separation. Until the middle of the 19th century, divorce could only be obtained by Act of Parliament, but it began to be felt that spiritual matters and clerical discipline only should be left to the Church. Hence, in 1857, two new Courts were established within the ordinary legal system, the Court of Probate and the Court for Divorce and Matrimonial Causes.

(5) Local courts

Because of the decline of the local courts, the King found that, for minor criminal offences, his own Court and the justices of assize had to be supplemented by some form of local justice. Until 1215, coroners (instituted in the 12th century to act as a royal check on the sheriff) and sheriffs both heard pleas of the Crown, but the practice was ended when the barons protested against it in Magna Carta.

More important was the institution of *Justices of the Peace* in 1327, when Edward III appointed qualified men in each county to act as conservators of the peace. One of their duties was to hold alleged criminals in gaol until they could be tried by an Assize judge. In 1360 the justices were given powers to try felonies and trespasses, and a little later they were directed 'to keep their sessions in every quarter of the year at least'. Eventually they acquired administrative duties which became very important under the Tudors.

For civil cases, however, no satisfactory institutions replaced the local courts. Included in the terms of a charter given to a town there might be permission to establish a court, while in Tudor times various local 'Courts of Requests' were set up to deal with minor cases. The latter lasted only a century, and the problem remained unsolved until 1846, when the present system of County Courts was established.

REORGANISATION OF THE JUDICIAL SYSTEM

The existence of so many different courts could only result in overlapping of function and diversity of procedure. Therefore, the Judicature Acts, 1873–5, carried out a complete reform. It set up a Supreme Court of Judicature consisting of the High Court of Justice and the Court of Appeal.

This basic organisation lasted until the 1970's when changes were made in two stages:

(*a*) The Probate, Divorce and Admiralty Division of the High Court was renamed the 'Family Division', its admiralty work being transferred to a new Admiralty Court of the Queen's Bench Division (Administration of Justice Act, 1970).

(*b*) Crown Courts replaced Assizes and Quarter Sessions to try criminal cases (Courts Act, 1971).

The *High Court* is now organised in three Divisions — Queen's Bench, Chancery, and Family — the work being distributed between them according to convenience and tradition. In practice,

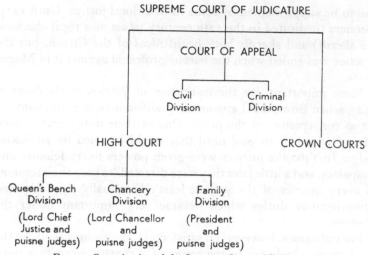

FIG. 9. *Organisation of the Supreme Court of Judicature.*

judges specialise in the work of one particular Division, though they may sit in any. They are appointed by the Crown from barristers of at least ten years' standing. Appointment by the Crown means, in the case of Presidents of Divisions, that they are nominated by the Prime Minister, who is advised by the Lord Chancellor. Puisne judges (those High Court judges who are not President of a Division) are nominated by the Lord Chancellor. Their independence, however, is guaranteed; not only are they irremovable, but their salaries are charged on the Consolidated Fund. At present (1975), there are 75 puisne judges distributed among the three divisions according to the volume of work.

The *Court of Appeal* succeeded the former appeal courts and now has two Divisions—civil and criminal. Its full-time judges, Lord Justices of Appeal, must be barristers of at least fifteen years' standing or have had previous experience as judges of the High Court. The House of Lords was retained as the final court of appeal.

Recent specialised legislation has necessitated the setting-up of another court—the Restrictive Practices Court, 1956 (see page 365).

II. The Law administered by the Courts

English law has largely been built up as the courts themselves developed. Today it comes from the following sources:

(1) *The common law*

The common law originated in the ancient customs and practices which were brought over by the tribes from north-west Europe who settled in England some 1,500 years ago. These customs were not written down, like Acts of Parliament, so there is no one authoritative text which contains the whole of such law. (The same idea persists today in common law rights, e.g. to footpaths, which are legally enforceable if they can be shown to have persisted from 'when the memory of man runneth not to the contrary'.) But what was generally recognised as the custom of the realm was the form of law administered by the old Common Law courts.

The real step towards systematisation of the common law occurred when Henry II instituted his justices in eyre, for they had to meet together to formulate rules of law which could be applied uniformly throughout the country. Thus, divergent local customs were replaced by a unified system of common law decisions; and even today the same rules guide judges in their decisions when there is doubt over the interpretation of a statute.

Today the common law can be found in: (*a*) the legal treatises of jurists, such as Glanville and Blackstone, which, while not authoritative in the strict legal sense, may weigh heavily with judges; (*b*) the successive decisions of the courts, for when the common law is in dispute it is they which have to define its scope.

(2) *Case law*

While the decisions of the higher courts are not absolutely binding upon future judgments, they are quoted as authoritative pronouncements when cases arise involving a similar point of law. Hence, in both the way they apply common law rules and in the decisions they give in particular cases, the judges are, in a sense, making law. The practice of following previous rules and decisions maintains consistency and continuity, essential qualities of justice, for they guard against the human failings of judges and enable a person to foresee the legal consequences of his actions. Both are necessary if there is to be an effective rule of law. On the other hand, they tend to make the law conservative, past decisions and the views of judges being somewhat rigid in face of changing economic conditions and variations in social philosophy. Nevertheless, some flexibility has been provided for by the House of Lords' decision in 1966 that its previous decisions are not irretrievably binding.

(3) *Rules of equity*

In matters which were outside the concern of the Common Law courts, or where the strict application of the law would prevent true justice being applied, plaintiffs came to the Lord Chancellor. A person, for instance, who feared an injury could, under the common law, only wait for it to happen and then claim damages. But such an award would not compensate for an irreparable injury, and so he might apply instead to the Court of Chancery for an 'injunction' to prevent the injury taking place. As successive Chancellors settled disputes according to the decisions of their predecessors, there grew up a body of rules known as 'equity', which later became even more rigid than the common law, whose narrowness the procedure had been framed to circumvent.

(4) *Statutes*

Sometimes both the common law and equity failed to deal with a subject, entirely new rules being required for the purpose. Hence, a statute had to be made, originally in the form of pronouncements by the King, but later through royal ordinances in response to petitions from Parliament. Eventually Parliament became the principal legislating authority.

Acts of Parliament are supreme over both the judiciary and all other forms of law, thus upholding the principle of parliamentary sovereignty. Today the bulk of law is in statute form, and its volume has increased as the State has added to its responsibilities in our social and economic life.

(5) *Other law*

The courts also have duties regarding both the law and custom of Parliament and international law. The first concerns breaches of parliamentary privilege. While each House decides itself whether or not there has been a breach, the courts define the limits of privilege and will allow no additions to it. The second, international law, is usually enacted by the subscribing countries in

their own Parliaments so that a breach of it can be punished in
their own courts.

CIVIL AND CRIMINAL LAW

The real distinction between civil and criminal law is not
between the nature of the acts, but between the legal proceedings
brought. If the object is to seek compensation, then the plaintiff
must bring a civil action; if it is to punish the accused, the procedure must be criminal. Generally speaking, however, criminal
proceedings have their origin in the old 'pleas of the Crown'
and exist where the accused person is alleged to have offended
against society as a whole and not merely against a single individual.
Stealing and such road offences as dangerous driving, for example,
set a bad example to everybody. Hence the State takes proceedings
against the person involved, either through the police or the
Director of Public Prosecutions. In a civil action, on the other
hand, proceedings against the defendant must be initiated by the
person claiming that he has suffered injury of body, property,
or reputation, or by his representative if he has died. If successful,
he receives any damages awarded, whereas fines imposed in
criminal proceedings are paid into public funds. In some cases,
such as assault and libel, either kind of proceedings may be
brought, the plaintiff choosing whether he wishes to punish the
accused or obtain compensation.

All cases, whether civil or criminal, are divided according to
their importance. Broadly, the less important go to the lower
courts, the more important to the higher.

III. CIVIL JURISDICTION

The organisation of civil jurisdiction is shown in Figure 10;
with two minor exceptions, cases go either to the County Court or
to the High Court. The first exception covers certain cases which
are dealt with by Courts of Summary Jurisdiction, such as applications for matrimonial and affiliation orders and for permission to
marry by persons under eighteen years of age where the parents
refuse consent. The second concerns a special court set up to deal
with legislation in the economic field, the Restrictive Practices
Court.

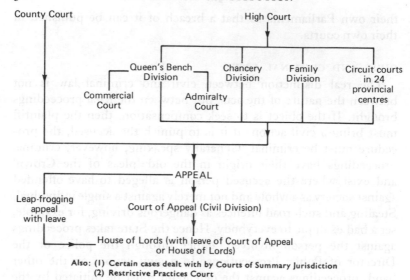

County Court   High Court

Queen's Bench Division
Commercial Court

Chancery Division
Admiralty Court

Family Division

Circuit courts in 24 provincial centres

APPEAL

Leap-frogging appeal with leave

Court of Appeal (Civil Division)

House of Lords (with leave of Court of Appeal or House of Lords)

Also: (1) Certain cases dealt with by Courts of Summary Jurisdiction
(2) Restrictive Practices Court

FIG. 10. *Organisation of civil jurisdiction.*

THE COUNTY COURT

The County Courts, set up in 1846, have nothing to do with the counties, but were simply named after the courts for small causes which had virtually passed away. In all, there are nearly 375 such courts strategically placed for easy reach throughout England and Wales.

Under the Courts Act, 1971, all judges of the Supreme Court and all circuit judges and Recorders have power to sit in the County Courts. But each County Court must have one or more circuit judges appointed and assigned to it by the Lord Chancellor, and the regular sittings of the Court are usually taken by these judges. Each is responsible for a circuit which contains a number of courts according to the work involved. A court has to be held at least once a month. The registrar, who is a solicitor and head of the Court's office staff, may hear cases when the amount in dispute is not greater than £75 (but over this with the consent of the parties) and his decisions can be reviewed by the judge. He also makes enquiries for the judge and can act as an arbitrator.

The jurisdiction of the County Courts is both local and limited. They deal with actions founded on contract or tort (civil wrong) where the claim does not exceed £750; equity cases up to £5,000 in value affecting trusts, mortgages and dissolution of partnerships;

admiralty matters up to £1,000 (except salvage cases, where the limit is a £3,500 value of the property saved); most bankruptcy proceedings outside London (where they are heard by the Chancery Division); actions concerning land (which includes houses and other buildings) where the rateable value does not exceed £400. Cases outside these limits may be tried in the County Court by consent of the parties. All these limits may, however, be amended from time to time by Order in Council. The County Court also deals with matters arising out of social legislation, such as the adoption of children, the guardianship of infants, the validity of hire purchase agreements, disputes under Rent Acts and the determination of the extent to which farms have been improved by tenants. Since 1968 all undefended divorce cases (about 90 per cent) have been tried in certain County Courts designated as Divorce County Courts. Complaints of racial discrimination are also heard by specially designated Courts.

The County Court, therefore, covers a variety of cases. While both barristers and solicitors may appear on behalf of clients, the judge may well have to decide the merits of a case from the different stories put forward by laymen. Thus, the present tendency for more cases to go to the County Court rather than the High Court indicates the general confidence in his judgments.

A large increase in the work of County Courts is likely to result from two changes in the law. The first is the Supply of Goods (Implied Terms) Act, 1973. This places responsibility on the retailer for any defective goods sold by him. This should encourage dissatisfied customers, previously unsure of their rights, to take County Court action. The second is that consumers with small claims (maximum £75) arising from faulty goods can apply to the County Court for *informal arbitration* by a judge or registrar.

THE HIGH COURT

Except for a few cases which are exclusive to the County Court, a civil action may commence either in the High Court or County Court. In general, small cases go to the County Court and the larger to the High Court, but usually the plaintiff decides. Where the claim is above the monetary limit, the case must go to the High Court unless both parties agree otherwise, but even if it is within the County Court limits the plaintiff may start a High Court action. Such proceedings are usual for test cases where an authoritative decision is required, or where the plaintiff thinks that the issue of a High Court writ will intimidate the defendant into not fighting the case. Judges, however, discourage High Court actions where County Court procedure would be appropriate. If the amount involved is less than £750, they may remit the case to the County Court or allow costs only on the County Court scale if continued in the High Court.

A High Court case goes to one of three Divisions.

(1) *The Queen's Bench Division*

This succeeded the three old Common Law courts and is thus responsible for both criminal and civil cases. Its President is the Lord Chief Justice and he is assisted by puisne judges.

In civil cases, the Queen's Bench Division deals with actions founded upon contract and tort. These may be heard either at the Law Courts in the Strand or at twenty-four principal cities or towns in England and Wales where High Court judges sit. The location chosen depends upon convenience, the nature of the action, and whether any special arrangements, as for divorce, are applicable. Often it is more convenient for all witnesses to travel to London rather than to journey across the country to a 'High Court' town, while London barristers usually prefer to have a case dealt with there since they may have others down for hearing. Furthermore, when specialised knowledge is required, as in actions involving commercial law or income tax, the judges who specialise in these cases may be found only in London. After a writ has been applied for, the master (in London) or the district registrar (in provincial towns) decides where the case shall be heard. In practice, the issue of a writ is usually the means whereby the defendant agrees to terms with the plaintiff. Only a small proportion of actions come to court, and less than 2% of all cases are fought to a conclusion. Disputants, it seems, have a high preference for settlement rather than involving themselves in the high cost of fighting a case to judgement. Settlement is also encouraged by the system whereby a defendant pays what he considers is a reasonable sum into court, for if a successful plaintiff is awarded less than this he cannot obtain costs.

Either party may insist on trial by jury in cases involving claims for defamation, malicious prosecution, false imprisonment, fraud, and seduction. Other cases are tried by jury only if the Court agrees to the application of one of the parties. Today, the use of juries is declining and they are now summoned for only about 4% of cases.

While a judge of the Queen's Bench Division may be called upon to hear many different types of case, some specialise. Commercial cases are heard in the *Commercial Court* established formally in 1971. Here, in addition to having a judge experienced in this type of work, there are procedural advantages which expedite decisions.

The *Admiralty Court* (which was transferred to the Queen's Bench Division in 1971) is highly specialised in maritime law. Nearly all the work is done in London, though some small cases may be heard in certain County Courts. There is no jury, but, where they are needed to act as nautical assessors, the judge sits with two Brethren of Trinity House. The volume of work is not large, amounting to about 400 writs a year with about a tenth reaching trial. The chief subjects of contention are salvage, towage, collisions, the building and repairing of ships, and goods supplied to foreign ships. Costs are small relative to the sums of money involved, and the Court keeps abreast of its work quite comfortably.

One important function still performed by the Queen's Bench Division is the supervision of inferior courts and tribunals through prerogative orders and the protection of the liberty of the individual by the issue of writs of Habeas Corpus. There are three types of order — prohibition, certiorari and mandamus — all of which were originally writs used by the King under his prerogative when he thought that an official was abusing his authority or neglecting his duties. Today an order can be issued upon the application of a private person. An order of prohibition commands an inferior tribunal to proceed no further with a case when the judge considers that it is exceeding its jurisdiction. But where a decision has already been given or when it is desired to remove the case from an inferior to a higher court, an order of certiorari applies, quashing the original decision and ordering the matter to be dealt with elsewhere. An order of mandamus is issued to compel a court or public authority to fulfil the duties laid upon it by law. Habeas Corpus still remains a writ, and is normally issued by a Divisional Court. If no such court is sitting, the application may be made to a single judge of the Queen's Bench.

(2) The Chancery Division

Although this Division is nominally headed by the Lord Chancellor, he is too busy to preside. His deputy, the Master of the Rolls, used to perform his duties, but today most of his time is occupied in presiding over the Court of Appeal, and so the bulk of the work falls to a Chancery judge who is appointed Vice-Chancellor by the Lord Chancellor and the other puisne judges. All chancery cases are tried in London.

When the Chancery Division was formed in 1873, it had various matters assigned to it. Over some, those formerly belonging to the old Court of Chancery, it has exclusive jurisdiction. Such cases include the administration of the estates of deceased persons, the execution of trusts, the dissolution of partnerships, and the redemption or foreclosure of mortgages. Bankruptcy jurisdiction was added in 1921 as being particularly suitable to investigation by the inquisitorial method. In many of the above matters there may be no real dispute, applicants merely wishing the Court to give a ruling.

With other cases, jurisdiction is held concurrently with the Queen's Bench. The main type is breach of contract. Here the plaintiff can choose the Division which he feels will be most suited to his case. In the earliest days of equity, the Lord Chancellor always investigated a case himself, uncovering facts and examining persons in reaching a decision, using the inquisitorial method. No juries were used. The Common Law courts, on the other hand, developed a formal method of cross-examination which is still in use today. Hence the atmosphere differs in the two types of court, and a plaintiff may well prefer the Queen's Bench procedure, even though juries are seldom used.

(3) Family Division

When the judicial system was reorganised in 1873, the Court of Probate and the Court of Divorce and Matrimonial Causes (page 332) were rather illogically lumped together in the same Division as the Court of Admiralty. The only reason for combining 'wills, wives and wrecks' was that all three had a Roman law basis. In 1971, however, admiralty work was transferred to the Queen's Bench Division, and the Division was re-named the 'Family Division', dealing with all domestic and matrimonial matters, guardianship (the latter being transferred from the Chancery Division) and probate.

Most of the work is concerned with divorce, despite the transfer in 1969 of undefended cases to certain Divorce County Courts. Judges of the Division hear defended cases in the 'Divorce Court' in London, but outside the capital, 42 towns have a Commissioner to decide matrimonial matters. These Commissioners have the same powers and pay as High Court judges.

Probate means the official proving of a will. When the deceased has left a will, the Court decides on its validity. If there is no will, or no executors are named, the Court appoints an administrator by letters of administration to wind up the estate. Usually there is no dispute, and the work is performed by officials either at the Law Courts in the Strand or at a local District Probate Registry. Where cases are contested, estates of less than £1,000 may be dealt with by the County Court; of the larger estates, only about 100 are contested each year.

RESTRICTIVE PRACTICES COURT

The Restrictive Trade Practices Act, 1956, set up a Registrar of Restrictive Trading Agreements and a Restrictive Practices Court. Restrictive pacts and, since 1964, all minimum resale price requirements, have to be registered with the Registrar, who refers to the Court any agreements which, unless justified by any of seven closely-defined tests, are contrary to 'the public interest'.

The Court is described as a superior court of record, and is thus parallel to the High Court rather than to a special tribunal. It consists of 5 judges (3 from the High Court, 1 from the Court of Session in Scotland, and 1 from the Supreme Court of Northern Ireland) and not more than 10 lay members. A quorum consists of 1 judge and 2 lay members, the decision being given on a majority basis.

APPEALS

(1) *The Court of Appeal*

Appeals from both the County Courts and the High Court go to the Court of Appeal except where the trial judge certifies that the case should 'leap-frog' direct to the House of Lords because it concerns a matter of public importance involving an Act or statutory instrument. This is to save the waste of going through the Appeal Court when the judge is bound by an existing decision which he feels to be wrong.

The civil work of the Court of Appeal is performed by the Master of the Rolls and fourteen Lord Justices of Appeal, who are either ex-judges of the High Court or barristers of at least fifteen years' standing. In addition there are *ex-officio* members, the Lord Chancellor (who is the President), any ex-Lord Chancellor or Lord of Appeal in Ordinary, the Lord Chief Justice and the President of the Family Division. An odd number of judges, with a minimum of three, hear an appeal, and the decision is by a majority. The Court now sits in four divisions, additional judges being drawn from the High Court if required.

(2) The House of Lords

The early Parliaments were essentially judicial in character, and today we still speak of 'the High Court of Parliament'. When the Commons began to meet separately from the Lords, the judicial work of Parliament was left to the Upper House, which today is still the final court of appeal for England and Wales and Northern Ireland and, for civil causes, Scotland. No appeal is possible unless either the Court of Appeal or the House of Lords gives leave, usually only granted when an important point of law is involved. By convention, lay peers do not sit on appeals, and the work is done by the Lord Chancellor, the ten Lords of Appeal in Ordinary (the Law Lords), ex-Lord Chancellors, and such other peers who have held high judicial office. A quorum is three. Although they hear arguments separately from the House as an Appellate Committee (which may sit simultaneously in two divisions), their judgment is delivered when sitting as the House of Lords. Technically, it takes the form of a motion, each judge making a speech, which may be printed instead of read aloud, expressing his concurrence or dissent.

CRITICISM OF CIVIL JURISDICTION

The system of civil justice must allow plaintiffs adequate opportunity to present their claims, but also protect defendants against unwarranted demands. Hence the costs of presenting a case should not be excessive, unreasonable delay in obtaining justice should be avoided, courts should be so constructed that they hold a fair balance between opposing parties, and a correct decision must be reached in the light of the evidence presented.

In general, civil jurisdiction in Britain meets these requirements, more so in the County Courts than in the High Court.

Unlike the County Courts, High Court organisation and procedure have been built on ancient foundations. Although this continuity has created a high standard of justice in which litigants have confidence, it has also produced defects of organisation involving delay and costs which some plaintiffs find prohibitive. The main points of criticism are:

(1) *Delay in hearing cases*

At any given moment, civil actions are being heard in the Queen's Bench Division, concerning matters which occurred some two years previously. While it takes some time to prepare a case, the fact remains that the pace of the preliminary work is often regulated by the knowledge that the court will be unable to deal with it for many months. However, with recent increases in the number of judges, the length of time should shorten, especially for civil cases outside London.

More vexing to litigants, however, is the uncertainty surrounding the actual day on which a case will be heard. Even after a provisional day has been fixed, it may be put back because previous cases have taken longer than was estimated or the judge is required for criminal appeal on the Court of Appeal. Even when an action appears on the list for a particular day, witnesses have to attend early so that it can be dealt with immediately should the previous case be disposed of quickly. However, this case may take longer than expected, so that witnesses must hang around until their own case is heard. The difficulty lies in devising a system of allocating a definite day which does not involve wasting the valuable time of judges. Nobody can estimate exactly how long a case will take; it may collapse in a few minutes or it may drag on for weeks. Attempts in recent years to fix trial dates have improved matters without being fully successful.

(2) *The high costs of litigation*

Costs of litigation cover the facilities provided by the court and the work of preparing and presenting the case. Generally speaking, they are paid by the unsuccessful party but, since the court reduces them to a reasonable minimum by 'taxing', some usually have to be borne by the successful litigant. In any case, since the work involves employing highly skilled persons, High Court costs are bound to be heavy. There is thus point to the remark of Lord Justice Darling that 'the law, like the Ritz Hotel, is open to all'.

Even so costs tend to be higher than is necessary. It has already been shown how uncertainty of the exact time for hearing a case involves witnesses standing by for long periods. Moreover, when cases are heard in London, there is the added expense of bringing witnesses to the capital and providing for them throughout the case. Although London may be the most accessible centre for assembling counsel, solicitors and witnesses, certain costs could be avoided if there were more local jurisdiction. The difficulty might have been overcome by giving County Courts increased powers, a solution which proved effective in clearing up the backlog of divorce cases, for it was virtually the County Court judges who were appointed Commissioners. Now, with the abolition of assizes, each of the 24 regions has a High Court judge in addition to its own pattern of County Courts.

The strict division of work between solicitors and barristers may involve extra cost. A solicitor is engaged directly by the client to carry out some legal administrative work or to give advice on a particular point of law. Although occasionally he specialises in one branch of the law, more usually he acts in a general capacity. When further advice is required, the solicitor, but not the client, takes the opinion of counsel, a barrister who specialises in the type of subject in dispute. A barrister belongs to one of the four Inns of Court and, through historical accident, is regarded as being superior to a solicitor. Only a barrister can appear in the High Court; hence, although the solicitor prepares the 'brief', a barrister must be engaged to present it. This arrangement has advantages. It promotes specialised knowledge and skills through division of labour, gives the client two different attitudes of mind to his problem and enables judges to acquire a thorough knowledge of the merits of a few selected advocates. But it may well involve avoidable expense, for the solicitor who prepared the brief could often present the case in court quite adequately and, moreover, from a few notes rather than from a full and expensive brief. Furthermore, if the barrister is a Q.C., he has to employ a 'junior'.

Extra costs are also incurred when appeals are lodged, especially as all appeals must be heard in London. There seems to be no reason why other large centres of population, such as Manchester, Birmingham and Newcastle, should not be used, except that

London probably suits the attorneys better! Moreover, the right of further appeal from the Court of Appeal to the House of Lords is in some respects illogical, for the judges sitting there are really no better. A case has to end somewhere, and it would save much expense if the parties knew from the outset that it could go no further than the Court of Appeal.

The high cost and delays of litigation have had two important results. In the first place, certain institutions, such as insurance companies, have attempted to by-pass the courts of law by stipulating in their contracts that disputes over a claim shall go to arbitration. Here proceedings are quicker, in private and can be arranged to suit the needs and convenience of the parties concerned. The atmosphere is friendly and the arbitrator is usually an expert. Written evidence is accepted. Secondly, because high costs might prevent a poor person from seeking and obtaining justice, a scehme of legal aid, run by the Law Society under rules laid down by the Lord Chancellor, was instituted in 1949. Applicants have to satisfy a committee of solicitors and barristers that they have a suitable case for legal action and that they come within the income limits for free legal aid. While they may be required to meet a part of the costs, most of the Legal Aid Fund comes from Exchequer grants. Legal advice is also included, but for the advice to be extended, the applicant has to show that there is merit in his case. In addition there exists a voluntary advice scheme without a means test. Here a solicitor will give a thirty-minute initial interview for a relatively small fee and provide an estimate of likely future costs. It is worth noting that most barristers have joined the legal aid panels, and most solicitors the legal aid and advice panels.

There are, however, certain inherent dangers in free legal aid. Expensive actions, where both parties have been in receipt of legal aid, have been fought on comparatively trivial issues. Moreover, in practice, it leaves the middle-income groups at a disadvantage in litigation for, unlike the rich, they cannot afford it, while, unlike the poor, they are not helped. They may therefore settle on unfavourable terms rather than go to law. Lastly, the scheme does not apply to administrative tribunals where legal representation may be just as essential.

IV. Criminal Jurisdiction

Like civil actions, criminal cases are divided according to their importance. Broadly speaking, the lesser cases, those which can be tried summarily, go to the Courts of Summary Jurisdiction, where there is no jury, while major cases, those dealing with indictable offences, go to Crown Courts, where they are heard before a judge and jury.

MAGISTRATES' COURTS

Magistrates' Courts (also known as Petty Sessions) are courts of summary jurisdiction where minor offences can be tried without jury. They are of four main types:

(1) *Magistrates' Court*

A bench of magistrates consists of two to seven Justices of the Peace. While each county is divided into petty sessions divisions (with each division represented by a number of J.P.s), boroughs, since they have separate justices, form one division. The number of courts held in each division in a month varies from place to place, some districts having only one, while in others there is a sitting almost every day.

(2) *Stipendiary Magistrate's Court*

Because the pressure of work has made it difficult to find sufficient lay justices, a few counties and large boroughs in the provinces have a full-time paid magistrate. He is appointed by the Crown on the advice of the Lord Chancellor from barristers or solicitors of at least seven years' standing. A stipendiary magistrate sitting alone exercises the powers of a bench, but lay magistrates may attend with him.

(3) *Metropolitan Stipendiary Court*

In inner London there is a unified system of magistrates' courts in which either a metropolitan stipendiary magistrate or justices may sit. Since the 19th century, the bulk of summary jurisdiction has been administered in the metropolis by stipendiary magistrates who sit alone. Up to thirty-six may be appointed by the Crown on the advice of the Lord Chancellor, but they are required to retire at the age of seventy. Eventually it is intended to integrate these with magistrates' courts in the rest of Greater London.

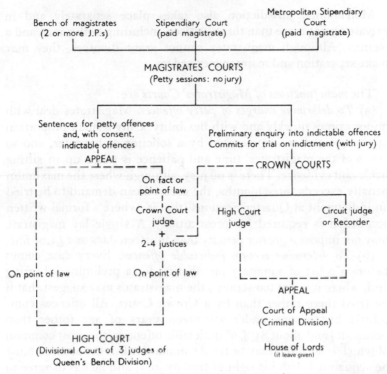

FIG. 11. *Organisation of criminal justice.*

(4) *Juvenile and Matrimonial Courts*

Juvenile and domestic proceedings form special branches of magistrates' work. A juvenile court hears cases (except homicide) concerning children (under 14 years of age) or young persons (14 to 17 years), and is composed of no more than three magistrates, one of whom should be a woman, drawn from a special panel. Cases are heard either in a different room or building from adult courts or on different days. Proceedings are in private, though the Press may attend provided no details are reported which might identify the offender. Informality is the keynote (uniforms are not worn by the police officers), for the emphasis is on reform and rehabilitation rather than deterrence through severe punishment. Indeed, criminal proceedings are not usually brought when other procedures, including committal to the care of the local authority, will suffice.

Matrimonial jurisdiction also takes place separately and in private by not more than three justices, including both a man and a woman. Although magistrates cannot grant divorces, they may make separation and maintenance orders.

The *main functions of Magistrates' Courts* are:

(a) *To determine charges of petty offences.* Magistrates deal with minor crimes quickly and with flexibility. Only a small proportion of the accused are represented by a solicitor or barrister, and so much of the magistrates' time and patience is taken up in sifting irrelevant evidence. There is no jury, although where the maximum penalty exceeds three months, the accused can demand to be tried on indictment at Quarter Sessions (that is, where a formal written accusation is required for prosecution). A single lay magistrate may not impose a greater penalty than fourteen days or a £1.00 fine.

(b) *To determine certain indictable offences.* Every case comes before a court of summary jurisdiction for a preliminary hearing and, where it is not too serious, the magistrates may suggest that it be tried there rather than by a Crown Court. All offences committed by persons under seventeen years of age (other than homicide) and about 85% of indictable offences (the most common of which is stealing) may be tried summarily. But the accused must be acquainted with his right of trial by jury, and he has to agree to summary trial. In practice, most persons elect to do so. While it is probably easier to secure an acquittal before a jury, magistrates are limited to a maximum penalty of six months for each offence (two may run consecutively) or £400, or both, and so an accused person who expects to be convicted will probably prefer the lesser court. The police may prosecute on a less serious charge, such as larceny instead of house-breaking, which must be tried on indictment, so that time and trouble can be saved by dealing with the case in petty sessions. Nevertheless, if, after hearing the case, a magistrates' court finds that the accused's record is so bad that the maximum sentence it can impose is inadequate, it may remit to a Crown Court for sentence.

(c) *To conduct preliminary enquiries into indictable offences.* The court decides whether there are grounds for sending the accused for trial. The prosecution submits written statements; only if requested are witnesses called by the accused. Even then their evidence is reported by the Press only if the defence asks for publicity

(Criminal Justice Administration Act, 1967). If satisfied, the court commits to a Crown Court.

In addition to trying criminal cases, magistrates decide certain civil matters, such as making maintenance orders on the application of wives, granting affiliation orders against the father of an illegitimate child, judging disputes over wages between a worker and his employer and the recovery of rates. They also perform administrative duties, in particular licensing public houses, bookmakers, and betting offices. Out of session, a J.P. may declare warrants for arrest and search, and take declarations on oath.

CROWN COURTS

Following the recommendations of a Royal Commission under the chairmanship of Lord Beeching, the *Courts Act, 1971* carried out important reforms of the organisation of criminal jurisdiction.

(1) Crown Courts replaced all courts of Assize and of Quarter Sessions. The Central Criminal Court (Old Bailey) retained its name but became a Crown Court.

(2) Existing local courts, such as the Mayor's and City of London Court, the Lancaster and Durham Palatine Courts, the Bristol Tolzey Court and the Norwich Guildhall Court, were abolished.

(3) All civil work of the Assizes was transferred to the High Court. This may now sit in any part of the country to deal with civil business, at places and times to be determined by the Lord Chancellor. The object is to give greater flexibility outside London.

(4) The Lord Chancellor's Office took over the responsibility from local authorities of providing and running the Crown Courts (which are now financed by the central government), and also became responsible for summoning jurors. (Magistrates' Courts are still provided for by local authorities—who obtain a grant of about 80% of their costs — under the supervision of the Home Secretary, but it is now being advocated that they should also be brought under the supervision of the Lord Chancellor and financed from central funds.)

England and Wales is divided into six regions, each having a number of Crown Courts placed strategically in towns throughout the region. There is a Circuit Administrator for each region to ensure that the days and places at which the courts sit are arranged as efficiently as possible.

Crown Courts may be presided over by:

(1) a High Court judge;

(2) a Circuit judge, appointed by the Queen on the advice of the Lord Chancellor from barristers of ten years' standing or solicitors with five years' experience as a Recorder, with a retirement age of 72 years (possibly extended to 75), and removable by the Lord Chancellor for incapacity or misbehaviour;

(3) A Recorder, who is a part-time Crown Court judge, and must be a barrister or solicitor of ten years' standing, with a retirement age of 72 years.

All existing county court judges, the Recorders of London, Liverpool and Manchester, and whole-time chairmen and deputy-chairmen of Quarter Sessions in Greater London and certain other places became Circuit court judges.

Up to four justices of the peace can sit with the judge in certain cases (the lower class) as specified by the Lord Chief Justice.

Within each region, towns having Crown Courts are divided into first, second and third tier. First-tier centres are served by High Court judges who deal with both civil and criminal cases. Second-tier centres, served by both High Court and Circuit judges, deal only with criminal cases. Third-tier centres, served only by Circuit judges and Recorders deal only with criminal cases, mainly those of the lesser class. They may sit with J.P.s.

When a person is committed for trial at the Crown Court, the magistrates may specify the most convenient location. The Lord Chief Justice has also made rules based on a four-fold classification of the type of case. (1) The most serious cases, such as treason, murder and genocide, must be tried by a High Court judge. (2) Other serious offences, such as manslaughter, rape and sedition, will be tried by a High Court judge unless released to a Circuit judge or Recorder. (3) Lesser indictable offences can be tried by a High Court judge, Circuit judge or Recorder. (4) Those cases which could have been tried summarily by magistrates, such as burglary, robbery, forgery and death by dangerous driving, will normally be tried by a Circuit judge or Recorder. Where a lesser case is of particular public interest, however, it may go to a High Court judge.

Solicitors can appear in Crown Courts at the discretion of the Lord Chancellor. He specifies the places or types of case, paying regard to the shortage of counsel in the area and to the solicitors' existing rights of audience in some places.

Delay in hearing cases was the major factor in instituting these reforms. In London, for instance, because of the increase in crime, it was taking over four months after committal to hear a trial. It is hoped that the new arrangements, together with an increase in the number of courts, will make the administration of criminal justice speedier, more convenient and less costly.

APPEALS

An appeal from a Magistrates' Court is either to a Divisional Court of the Queen's Bench Division or to a Crown Court sitting as a court of appeal. On a point of law, it goes to the former, which consists of three judges of the Queen's Bench. Since, however, the costs are often greater than the fine imposed, such appeals are uncommon. But sometimes the prosecution, such as a local authority, may wish to have the authoritative ruling of a higher court when a case has been dismissed. If the appeal is successful, the Divisional Court sends the case back to the magistrates with directions to convict.

Appeal to the Crown Court may be on a matter of fact, or on a point of law, or on both. Generally, it cannot be used by the prosecution to appeal against an acquittal, nor can the accused person appeal, except against the sentence imposed, if he pleaded guilty. Appeals are heard without a jury by a High Court judge, a Circuit judge or a Recorder sitting with two to four justices.

An appeal from a Crown Court is to the Criminal Division of the Court of Appeal, which is presided over by the Lord Chief Justice or a Lord Justice of Appeal. Queen's Bench judges sit with the Judges of Appeal. A quorum is three. The prosecution cannot appeal against an acquittal, but the convicted person may appeal either on a point of fact, or on a question of law, or on both, and, with leave of the Court, against sentence. By the Criminal Appeal Act, 1964, the Court may order a re-trial for a convicted person where additional evidence is brought forward after the original trial.

Where the Queen's Bench Divisional Court, the Court of Appeal, or the House of Lords itself certifies that a case involves a point of law 'of general public importance', an appeal may be taken to the House of Lords. In criminal cases, such appeals are rare.

PROCEDURE IN CRIMINAL CASES

If justice is to be administered impartially, and the rule of law is to be effective, an accused person must be tried according to a standard procedure.

An arrested person must be questioned according to the 'Judge's Rules' and, if charged, brought before a court within twenty-four hours. If this is not done, he may apply for a writ of Habeas Corpus through his legal adviser, to whom he must be given full access. When charged, he must be cautioned before making a statement and thereafter given full facilities to prepare his defence.

A prosecution may take place at the instance of a private person, the police (by far the most numerous), the Director of Public Prosecutions (see later), and government departments and local authorities, all of whom have legal departments to prosecute for such offences as income tax and customs duty evasion. The prosecution must prepare and present the case against the defendant and establish the charge.

Practically all criminal cases come before the magistrates, either to be tried summarily or for preliminary enquiry. The method of obtaining an appearance varies with the nature and circumstances of the offence. In many cases the police have already detained the accused under their powers of arrest. Otherwise a person is usually summoned to attend at a given time; if this summons is disregarded, the magistrates may issue a warrant for arrest. For small summary charges, such as minor motoring offences, where the accused writes to the court apologising and pleading guilty, the magistrates may excuse the attendance of the defendant and fine him in his absence.

Unless the offence can be tried only on indictment, the case may, with the consent of the accused, be disposed of summarily. If it is referred to a higher court, the prisoner may ask for bail, which is usually granted unless there is good cause to the contrary. Before the trial, the indictment (a document stating the details of the offence), is prepared.

In a Crown Court, the nature of the charge is read out to the defendant, who pleads either 'Guilty' or 'Not Guilty'. If he pleads

'Not Guilty', the prosecution, usually through a barrister but possibly through a solicitor, opens the case by describing the allegations and showing how it proposes to substantiate them. Since statements must be supported by evidence, witnesses are called and cross-examined in order to elicit the facts upon which the case is based. The defence may cross-examine these witnesses.

When the prosecution has completed its case, it is the turn of the defence. It may submit that there is no case to answer and, if the judge upholds the submission, the jury bring in a formal verdict of 'not guilty'. If not, counsel for the defence opens his case, calling witnesses to give evidence on behalf of the accused. If the prosecution wishes, it may cross-examine these witnesses. The accused need not give evidence on his own behalf, but if he does not go into the witness box it may look as though he fears cross-examination. After witnesses have given their evidence, the counsel for the defence makes his closing speech, followed by the closing speech for the prosecution. Where the defence has called no witnesses other than the accused, it has the final word.

After the summing-up by the Judge or Recorder, the jury retire to consider their verdict. In England and Wales, they have to reach a verdict on at least a 10-2 majority. If this cannot be achieved, a re-trial is ordered with another jury. If he is found guilty, the prisoner may address the court for mitigation of sentence. This is passed by the judge, the maximum penalty usually having been laid down by Parliament. There is no appeal against an acquittal. Where the Court of Appeal reverses a conviction, the prosecution may appeal, provided it obtains the necessary permission.

AN APPRAISAL OF THE ADMINISTRATION OF CRIMINAL JUSTICE

The administration of criminal justice in England and Wales has four main qualities: it is expeditious, certain, cheap, and impartial. Within twenty-four hours of his arrest, the accused person is brought before a court, either to be dealt with summarily or for a preliminary hearing prior to standing trial at the Crown Court. Any appeal against a conviction will be heard promptly, and the appeal procedure is quickly exhausted. Certainty is ensured by conducting the trial according to a given procedure. This affords adequate opportunities to both sides, but protects the accused by laying the onus of proof on the prosecution. Moreover, neither the cost of maintaining the courts nor that of conducting the prosecution or defence is excessive. If a person cannot pay for his own defence and it is desirable in the interests of justice, the justices can grant a certificate giving legal aid to the accused for a summary hearing and defence aid for the cost of a trial. Finally, the procedure of a criminal prosecution recognises the gravity of depriving a man of his fundamental right to liberty. Decisions, except in the case of stipendiary magistrates, are taken by more than one person (in summary hearings, by at least two justices; on indictment, by a jury).

Since the evidence must point to a person's guilt beyond any reasonable doubt, the benefit of uncertainty is given to the accused. The judge sees that the court is conducted impartially and according to the prescribed procedure. In short, our system of criminal jurisdiction preserves the balance between the rights of the individual and the protection of the community. Any error of judgment is on the side of the accused.

This does not mean, however, that the procedure of criminal trials is without its critics. One difficulty is that Crown Court cases take a long time in comparison with hearings before magistrates. Solutions proposed, especially as regards the growing number of motoring offences, are more fixed penalties for guilty pleas by post, removing the right for trial by indictment for certain offences and, where the case does go to trial, the admission of written evidence of facts to save them being proved. The police, too, tend to be critical of the jury system, claiming that it makes it far too difficult for them to obtain the conviction of a person whom they know to be guilty (but see also p. 381).

The qualities of British justice emanate from two important principles. One is that changes should come through the development of existing institutions rather than by innovation. Almost without exception, our institutions and procedure are the response to the practical requirements of everyday life rather than the implementation of theoretical ideas. They are thus in touch with the needs of the people who, by close contact with them over a long period of time, have seen how they work and gained confidence in them. Moreover, the ancient custom surrounding the courts not only helps to preserve their dignity and engender respect, but is a constant reminder of the continuity of justice. Similarly, the strong traditions of the legal profession have contributed to its high standards of efficiency and incorruptibility.

The second principle springs from the Englishman's long-held belief that his essential liberties can be guaranteed only if justice is regarded as an end in itself. Hence, judges must be free of any political interference, and in disputes between the authorities and the individual the same procedure is applied as in cases between one person and another.

Nevertheless, the acceptance of these principles also gives rise to certain weaknesses. Emphasising continuity has led to the preservation of outmoded institutions, while establishing the independence of the judiciary has encouraged a somewhat exclusive attitude on the part of judges. Consequently they have been reluctant to accept criticism or suggestions for reform of themselves, the institutions in which they work, and the law which they administer. The most important defects today concern the following institutions.

(1) *Justices of the Peace*

Justices of the Peace date from the 14th century and number nearly 20,000 in England and Wales. They are appointed and removed by the Crown on the advice of the Lord Chancellor, who himself is advised by a local advisory committee. The composition of these committees is secret and in the hands of the Lord Chancellor, although in the counties it comes under the chairmanship of the Lord Lieutenant of the County. There are no legal qualifications for becoming a J.P. except residence within fifteen miles of the area. In practice, political parties are dominant on the local advisory committee and bargains are made between them, though most persons appointed do have a record of public service. Since parties are active in the life of the community, however, it is difficult to see how they could be excluded. What is essential is that advisory committees should recommend justices from a broad cross-section of the community and should provide a balance of political viewpoint. Today some are even advertising in order to obtain more candidates.

Because the work is unpaid and courts usually sit during the morning, much use has to be made of retired persons and persons of independent means. Thus J.P.s tend to be old and conservatively-minded persons of middle- and upper-class backgrounds. Only one-fifth of justices are weekly wage-earners, and only one-third are women. Recent reforms, however, may improve matters. J.P.s now have to retire at 70 years of age, the minimum number of attendances has been reduced to 18 a year, and compensation is given for loss of earnings.

Other criticisms of J.P.s are that they are too ready to accept the evidence of the police (for whom they have a part responsibility, see page 458), that they rely too heavily on the guidance of their professionally-qualified clerk, that different benches are not uniform in their punishments, and that, although they are fair, they may be over-influenced by local attitudes. The recent introduction of compulsory training, however, should do something to meet these criticisms.

Now that England has ceased to be a rural and de-centralised country, are Justices of the Peace out-dated? Would it not be better to replace them completely by paid magistrates who, by being controlled centrally, could bring about greater uniformity in the administration of justice? Such an alternative may eventually prove obligatory, for the number of suitable persons able to give up their time is rapidly falling. Yet, although the system is a survival from the 14th century, such a change would represent on balance a loss rather than a gain. Trial by J.P.s still has certain advantages:

(a) More than one person is responsible for deciding a case;
(b) As laymen, J.Ps are closely connected with the wider aspects of everyday life. Most benches are broad-minded and approach their work with humanitarianism, common sense and understanding. J.P.s are, like the accused, not professional lawyers. They therefore discourage any legal technicalities and seek to have the issues presented in simple terms which the accused will readily understand. In sentencing, their views often compare favourably with the narrow professional attitudes of some full-time judges;
(c) Because the intimate atmosphere of the court encourages witnesses to speak freely, justices can usually discover the truth;
(d) As members of the local community, their knowledge of local conditions can improve the administration of justice;
(e) Service as a J.P. provides an opportunity for people to share in government—an essential of democracy;
(f) Trial by J.P.s is cheap, both to the accused and the State.

Finally, in this discussion of J.P.s, it is worth noting a suggestion

that the Magistrates' Courts should be linked with the High
Court and Crown Courts as part of a unified judiciary, all under
the control of the Lord Chancellor's office. This would leave the
Home Office to deal with the police, prisons and probation
service.

(2) Juries

A person is qualified to be a juror if he or she is a British subject
of 18 and under 65 years of age and has resided in the U.K. for five
years continuously since the age of 13. Property qualifications
were abolished in 1974. People sentenced to five years or more in
jail are disqualified from jury service for life, while imprisonment
for more than three months during the preceding 10 years dis-
qualifies. Jury service is obligatory, but many classes of persons,
such as peers, M.P.s, judges, J.P.s, barristers, solicitors, doctors,
dentists, H.M. Forces and clergymen, are exempt. A judge has
power to dismiss any person from serving as juror whom he feels
has inadequate command of English. Since 1949, travelling expenses, subsistence allowances and compensation for loss of
earnings can be claimed.

Criticisms of the jury system are:

(a) In cases involving highly technical matters (such as fraud),
    juries are likely to be out of their depth. A far more satis-
    factory arrangement would be on the pattern of Admiralty
    cases, where the judge sits with assessors.

(b) Inexperienced laymen are not capable of marshalling argu-
    ment and counter-argument based on evidence which may
    spread over many weeks, especially as they have no in-
    struction apart from the judge's last-minute summing-up.

(c) Juries are not accustomed to retain the spoken word in their
    memories, and are not often found to be taking notes.

(d) They may be actuated by prejudices, either consciously held
    or ones of which they are completely unaware. Lord Chief
    Justice Parker told of a juryman who had said 'I don't like
    the police and I'll never convict anyone'. In the Angry
    Brigade terrorist trial in 1972, the dangerous principle was
    put forward that persons of Conservative political views should
    not contribute to a verdict on persons who were opposed
    to existing constitutional institutions, whereas in 1971 an
    Old Bailey judge refused to allow nine coloured defendants

to be tried by an all-black jury after a defending counsel had told him 'You cannot guarantee in a society in which racial prejudice and racial discrimination is rife, that a white jury will not have on it persons who start off with prejudice against the defendants because they are black.' In 1974 Judge Anwyl Davies said that a jury at St. Albans Crown Court had found nine people guilty in a pornography trial despite the fact that the defendants had purposely selected an all-male jury of a younger age group in order to improve the chances of acquittal.

(e) Discrepancies may arise when a jury is responsible for assessing damages. The judge may direct that if they find for the plaintiff, 'considerable' damages should be awarded; but the interpretation of what is 'considerable' rests largely on the composition of the jury and their own standards of living.

Yet the public have faith in the jury system. In the past, it has proved a safeguard against oppression, especially when the interpretation of such terms as sedition and public mischief has been indefinite. Lord Devlin considers that its existence has helped to preserve the independence of judges and to ensure that the criminal law conforms to the ordinary man's idea of what is fair and just; if it did not, the jury would not be a party to its enforcement. In his words: 'Trial by jury is more than an instrument of justice, and more than one wheel of the constitution. It is the lamp that shows that freedom lives'. When the jury does err, it is usually in the right direction, on the side of the accused. Moreover, the ending of the property qualification has meant that juries today are more than ever a representative cross-section of society. As such, they tend to reflect current sentiment on such matters as 'reasonable force', 'an offensive weapon' and 'obscene material', which defy precise legal definition. Finally, through the centuries, juries have provided ordinary persons with an opportunity for active participation in the affairs of government.

One difficulty of the jury system is that the necessary strict rules of secrecy mean that we know little about what actually goes on in the jury room. Rather than advocate abolishing juries, it might be better to take up the suggestion made in 1973 by Sir Robert Mark, Commissioner of the Metropolitan Police, that a careful and detailed study be made 'to provide us with the material upon which we could evaluate trial by jury'.

(3) Judges

Judges are appointed by the Crown on the advice of either the Prime Minister or the Lord Chancellor, the former being responsible for the Lord Justices of Appeal, the Lord Chief Justice, the Master of the Rolls and the President of the Family Division, and the latter for puisne judges, Circuit judges and Recorders. The last two can be removed by him for incapacity or misbehaviour. Until recent years some political manoeuvring entered into the appointments, although once on the bench judges usually succeed in excluding their political views. In any case, the independence of judges can only be ensured by their remaining outside active party politics. Thus in 1968 Lord Avonside, a Scottish Court of Session judge, resigned from Mr. Heath's Scottish Constitutional Committee, set up to consider the Conservative Party's proposal for a Scottish Assembly, because the appointment had political implications. Fortunately, the ambitions of lawyers usually end with their appointment to a judgeship, for this is regarded as the peak of a career.

The main criticism of judges is their fundamental conservatism. They tend to regard themselves as a race apart and the only competent authorities to pronounce on reform, although little initiative comes from them in this direction. It is also doubtful whether they are in touch with modern social tendencies, for they are drawn almost exclusively from a high social class and indeed are often the sons of judges. In training, too, they are dominated by common law principles established when *laissez-faire* was the accepted philosophy. Hence many judges, such as Lord Hewart (*The New Despotism*), have failed to appreciate the changes necessitated by the modern Welfare State. Nevertheless, their isolation has served to strengthen their independence.

Moreover, is legal training alone sufficient experience for a judge in passing sentence? Without some knowledge of psychology, there is always the danger of the sentence being quite inappropriate, emphasis being placed on the deterrent effect of punishment rather than on the possibility of reform. Often the judge follows the customary sentence, learned while serving as a barrister. Starting in 1968, however, the Lord Chancellor instituted a week's course each year on sentencing for recently appointed judges. Nor does the age to which judges sit help towards a progressive attitude. Only in 1959 was a retiring age of 75 years instituted (compare the

limit of 65 years for university dons). As W. S. Gilbert observes in
Trial by Jury:

> *Though all my law is fudge,*
> *Yet I'll never, never budge,*
> *But I'll live and die a Judge!*

(4) *Coroners' Courts*

Coroners were first appointed during the 12th century to check
the King's revenues, chiefly those arising through fines. This
involved investigating deaths through violence, since the property
of a convicted murderer was forfeited, while objects (such as
horses, oxen, carts, and boats) causing other deaths were confiscated. Eventually the chief function of coroners became the holding
of inquests into sudden deaths.

A coroner must be either a barrister, solicitor or doctor, and is
usually part-time. He can order a post-mortem when the cause of
death is unknown and, at any inquest which follows, carry out a
fact-finding investigation into the cause of death. There may be a
jury of seven to eleven persons, but they are not drawn from the
ordinary jury list. Although the coroner's court is a court of law, it
does not decide a definite issue between two persons, nor do the
ordinary rules of evidence apply. Yet the coroner may commit a
person on a charge of homicide. The procedure, therefore, may
put the accused at a serious disadvantage when he comes to trial,
for evidence can have been published which would have been
inadmissible in the form presented, and he may not have been
legally represented at the time. Consequently, when the police are
likely to charge a person with homicide, the inquest is usually
adjourned until after the trial; but cases do occur of the coroner
committing while police investigations are still proceeding.

V. SCOTLAND

Scotland has retained her own judicial organisation.

On the *civil side*, the *Sheriff Court* corresponds roughly to the
County Courts in England, though its jurisdiction is not subject to
any pecuniary limits. Scotland is divided into twelve Sheriffdoms,
each with a Sheriff and a number of Sheriffs-Substitute, the latter
performing the ordinary work of the Court. Appeal may be made

to the Sheriff, or, if the value of the cause exceeds £50, directly to
the Inner House of the Quarter Sessions. Actions not exceeding £5
in value may be tried in a Justice of the Peace civil court.

The supreme civil court, having jurisdiction over the whole
country, is the *Court of Session*. This was established in 1532 and
consists of fifteen judges. Five sit as judges of the Outer House, a
court of first instance. The remainder (the Inner House) sit in two
divisions presided over by the Lord President and the Lord
Justice-Clerk respectively. From the Inner House an appeal may
lie to the House of Lords.

While minor *criminal cases*, e.g. breach of the peace and petty
offences, are tried by summary procedure in *police courts* in burghs
and in *Justice of the Peace courts* in counties, the bulk of the criminal
work is done by the *Sheriff Court*. The Sheriff sits alone for cases
which can be dealt with summarily, but for the more serious
charges, which are prosecuted on an indictment, the Court sits
under solemn procedure, that is, the Sheriff with a jury.

Appeal lies to the *High Court of Justiciary*, which is also the
highest criminal court of first instance. It consists of the Lord
Justice General (who is also the Lord President of the Court of
Session), the Lord Justice Clerk, and fourteen Lords Commissioner
of Justiciary who are also judges of the Court of Session. The seat
of the court is in Edinburgh, but judges also go on circuit. Appeals
against conviction are heard by three or more of its judges, but
there is no further appeal to the House of Lords.

VI. SHOULD WE HAVE A MINISTER OF JUSTICE?

THE CASE FOR A MINISTER OF JUSTICE

To what extent does the administration of justice keep in step
with changing needs and conditions? The answer is to be found in
an examination of more specific questions. Is there any provision
for periodic overhaul of the judiciary? Who exercises a general
supervision over the administration of the courts? Who is responsible to Parliament for answering questions relating to the law and
its administration? Who is responsible for scrutinising, consolidating, and codifying existing law and piloting through Parliament
the necessary legislation? Each will be considered in turn.

Although the organisation of justice should be subject to

periodic review, it is doubtful if this can be safely left to the members of the judiciary. Not only have they proved conservative in their outlook and almost barren of constructive suggestions, but any proposals which were forthcoming needed Government backing to be adopted. In practice, reform comes about in two main stages: (a) consideration of specific problems by an authoritative outside body, such as an official committee or a royal commission; (b) legislation putting into effect any recommendations acceptable to the Government. It is argued that both stages require the directing influence of a responsible minister who could take the initiative in obtaining Cabinet support for setting up the enquiring body, and in securing time for consequent legislation. What is necessary, therefore, is a minister *wholly* concerned with justice, supervising the periodical review of such judicial matters as the organisation and functions of magistrates, the composition of juries, the procedure of the courts, and legal education.

While interference in individual cases is not proposed, some overall control of the courts is desirable in the interests of efficiency and uniformity in administering justice. Hence, a general control should be exercised over the staffs of the courts, and suggestions made which would improve their day-to-day administrative work. Guiding principles must be laid down to assist judges and magistrates in inflicting punishments, and the responsible minister could also recommend for the appointment of judges and magistrates, even making the appointment himself for minor posts. At present the Lord Chancellor performs most of these tasks.

Some confusion also exists as to the responsibility for answering questions in Parliament regarding the law. A minister cannot be held responsible for a matter over which he exercises no control. Thus, while the Home Secretary must deal with any questions regarding the Metropolitan Police, he may decline to answer for the provincial police forces on the grounds that complaints should be made to the local police authority, since the supervision which he exercises is derived only indirectly from the financial help given by the central government. Indeed, while there are three ministers connected with justice — the Home Secretary and the Attorney-General in the Commons and the Lord Chancellor in the Lords — it is, in practice, impossible to define the limits of their responsibilities. Moreover, difficulties arise because nobody in the Commons fulfils the duties of a Parliamentary Secretary to the

Lord Chancellor. Hence, because the Lord Chancellor is responsible for the organisation of the higher courts, parts of criminal procedure and everything relating to civil law and its administration, there is really no means by which M.P.s can obtain answers to these questions in the Lower House.

Legislation requires periodic examination to see where it can be improved. This involves bringing it up to date, clarifying where it is obscure, consolidating Acts on the same subject into a single statute, and codifying statutes and case law in order to simplify it and to reduce the number of statutes.

Here the Lord Chancellor has a definite responsibility for it is he who appoints the members of the Law Commission for England and Wales. This permanent body, established in 1965, consists of five high-standing lawyers. Its duty is to scrutinise the law with a view to its systematic development and reform, including the possibility of codification, the removal of anomalies and the repeal of obsolete or unnecessary laws. The Commission submits to the Lord Chancellor programmes of reform (in its first six months it chose seventeen subjects) which it considers should be examined by itself or other bodies. These other bodies may be a Royal Commission, but are more likely to be the existing Law Reform Committee and the Criminal Law Revision Committee consisting of judges appointed by the Lord Chancellor and Home Secretary respectively to examine particular aspects of civil and criminal law.

The Commission is also responsible for the preparation of Consolidation and Statute Law Revision Bills. Procedure for passing such bills has been simplified. The Lord Chancellor lays before Parliament a memorandum of the amendments he intends to include in a Consolidation Bill so that interested persons can make representations. The bill then goes to a Joint Committee of both Houses. If, as a result of their report, the Lord Chancellor and Speaker agree that the usual legislative procedure is not called for, Parliament passes or rejects the bill without amendment. Usually such bills get an unopposed second reading.

Inadequacies in the machinery for reforming the judiciary and difficulties in obtaining information in the House of Commons are the result, say the critics, of the division of function between the Lord Chancellor and the Home Secretary. Hence, they argue, a single 'Minister of Justice' at the head of a department should be appointed and given an undivided responsibility for the administrative aspects of the judicial system.

Not that this is a new recommendation. As early as 1874 a Commission on the administration of the courts suggested that a reorganised Home Office might fulfil the duties of a Minister of Justice. Lord Haldane, too, frequently advocated the development. The Machinery of Government Committee, 1918, of which he was chairman, recommended that the Home Secretary should become the Minister of Justice. He would transfer work not concerned with legal administration to other departments, and take over the general administrative duties performed by the Lord Chancellor. The latter would then be free to concentrate on his judicial work and his responsibility as legal adviser to the Government.

OBJECTIONS TO THE PROPOSAL

The main argument against having a Minister of Justice is that it would violate the theory of the separation of powers. The term in itself represents a contradiction and sounds sinister to many people, who fear that the minister will eventually *control* justice. Critics consider that justice might become an instrument of government oppression and regulation, and recall the arbitrary government of the Stuart period, point to the sequence of events in Germany and Russia before the war, and express their forebodings as to the part being played by the Minister of Justice in South Africa at the present time. (Probably such views are exaggerated. Even were Britain to create such a minister, he would be unable to interfere with the process of justice in the courts, while important judicial appointments would still be made by the Prime Minister and the Lord Chancellor.)

Secondly, in his present position the Lord Chancellor fulfils the important function of securing harmony between the Government and judiciary without the subjection of the latter. Although a member of the executive, his legal standing keeps him aloof. Thus he is able, at one and the same time, to represent the legal profession and to bring it in touch with the problems facing the Government.

Thirdly, if a Minister of Justice had no legal training, the office would eventually be merely another department competed for by rising politicians. Not only would this lead to judicial matters becoming involved in politics, but the person appointed would have little legal knowledge and lack that continuity and direct contact with the legal profession which is so invaluable to the Lord Chancellor in making appointments to the bench. Since he would have insufficient personal knowledge of contemporary members of the bar, a Minister of Justice would have to rely on civil servants for advice. However, there is little reason why a layman should not be appointed for carrying out other tasks.

Lastly, while periodic reform is desirable, many lawyers emphasise the importance to the efficient administration of justice of stability and certainty of procedure. But such an opinion, coming from the legal profession, is more likely a reflection of conservatism.

CONCLUSIONS

The balance of argument probably lies with the appointment of a new Minister of Justice. In practice, however, such a minister is unlikely to be a great improvement on present arrangements especially if (as is now frequently advocated), the Lord Chancellor takes over the administration of magistrates' courts in addition to that of Crown Courts. A responsible minister could certainly answer questions in Parliament, but any measures for reform would still have to obtain Cabinet approval and parliamentary time. Yet, since reform of the law has no political significance, it could easily be overlooked; only if the new minister had considerable influence in the Cabinet would he fare any better than the present Lord Chancellor or Home Secretary in obtaining legislative time. In any case, up to the present, reform of administrative processes and of the law have usually followed the recommendations of royal commissions, etc. The merit of this method is that these bodies, having heard the views of all parties, can express an opinion which is generally recognised as being independent. Hence when the proposals are subsequently acted upon, Parliament usually concurs. In the administration of justice, it is vitally important that changes not only are but shall seem to be free from the politics of the minister who introduced them. Some suspicion would always lurk around a Minister of Justice — and this probably explains why such an office has not yet been created in Britain.

SUGGESTED READING

Peter Archer, *The Queen's Courts* (Penguin, 1968).

Henry Cecil, *Brothers in Law* (Michael Joseph, 1955); *Friends at Court* (Michael Joseph, 1956).

Charles Dickens, *Bleak House* (Macmillan).

R. M. Jackson, *The Machinery of Justice in England* (6th Ed., C.U.P., 1972).

Report of the Royal Commission on Assizes and Quarter Sessions, 1969 (Cmnd. 4153, H.M.S.O.).

20

The Separation of Powers

> 'When your time comes to sit in my Chair,
> Remember your Father's habits and rules.
> Sit on all four legs, fair and square,
> And never be tempted by one-legged stools!'
> RUDYARD KIPLING: *My Father's Chair*

THE THEORY OF THE SEPARATION OF POWERS

The theory of the separation of powers is closely associated with the name of the French political philosopher, Montesquieu, who lived from 1689 to 1755. This was a period when absolute monarchs reigned on the continent of Europe, and during the early part of Montesquieu's life the most despotic Sovereign of them all, Louis XIV, was still on the French throne. It is not surprising, therefore, that when Montesquieu visited England in 1729, he should have been struck by the high degree of political liberty enjoyed there. Indeed, so profound was his impression that he was induced to undertake a major study of the reasons for this preservation of individual freedom, and the result was his *Esprit des Lois*, 1748, a book which was widely acclaimed within two years of its publication.

Montesquieu observed that the powers of government were of three kinds — legislative, executive and judicial. Tyranny results when all three powers are accumulated in the same hands, for then a Government seeking to act despotically can pass such laws as it chooses, administer them without regard to the rights of the individual, and judge corruptly any opposition to them. Thus, in order to preserve political liberty, the constitution should ensure that the legislature, executive and judiciary are independent of each other. This did not mean that the three powers would never touch at any point, or that one could never act without the consent of the others. What Montesquieu had in mind was that each would impose restraints which would prevent the abuse of power.

England owed her political liberties, he considered, to the arrangement of her constitution in this way.

Subsequent political thinkers developed Montesquieu's analysis, but tended to emphasise the complete separation of powers. The theory exerted a dominating influence towards the end of the century when countries, newly released from oppressive governments, were seeking to ensure the preservation of their political liberties. Its practical application is evident in the constitution of the United States of America, drawn up by the Founding Fathers in 1787. Articles I, II and III begin by defining the position of the three branches of government:

> 'Article I. All legislative Powers herein granted shall be vested in a Congress of the United States, which shall consist of a Senate and a House of Representatives.
>
> Article II. The executive Power shall be vested in a President of the United States of America.
>
> Article III. The judicial Power of the United States shall be vested in one supreme Court, and in such inferior Courts as the Congress may from time to time ordain and establish.'

It then proceeds to specify the functions and relationship of these three 'Powers'. Although provision is made for resolving deadlocks between them, formally they are quite separate. Compare the following with the pattern of Britain's government:

(1) The President is separately elected for a fixed term of office of four years. His party, however, may not necessarily enjoy a majority in either House. Such a situation frequently occurs in the House of Representatives, for this has a life of only two years, and the new House, elected in the middle of the President's term of office, may indicate a swing of opinion away from his party.

(2) The President's powers are defined. While he can recommend bills to Congress, he cannot initiate them or compel their passage through either House. But he may veto legislation, in which case it can only become law by a two-thirds majority in each House. Similarly, any treaty negotiated by the President requires the consent of two-thirds of the Senate.

(3) The President appoints his own heads of the chief departments (about twelve). Like the President, the members of his Cabinet cannot sit in Congress. But since they are

responsible to him and not to Congress, they cannot be
removed by an adverse vote.

(4) The legislature consists of the Senate, which is an undying
House, and the House of Representatives, which is elected
for a fixed term of two years.

(5) The Federal Supreme Court is not only independent of the
President and Congress, but also has the power to declare
laws *ultra vires*, and acts of the executive invalid, if they
offend the constitution.

EVIDENCE OF THE OVER-LAP OF POWERS IN THE BRITISH
CONSTITUTION

To what extent has Montesquieu's doctrine been of influence in
Britain? Do persons or institutions perform functions or exercise
control in more than one branch of government?

Between the *legislature and the judiciary*, there is an obvious
over-lapping of powers. The Queen not only assents to bills, but
all judicial work is carried out in her name. But whereas the
Queen's duties are purely formal, the Lord Chancellor's functions
in the House of Lords are real. He occupies the Woolsack during
the legislative sittings of the House and presides when it hears
appeals. In addition, the Judicial Committee of the Privy Council,
the Court of Appeal and the Chancery Division of the High Court
all sit under his presidency, while he recommends the appointment
of judges (except the Presidents of Divisions), magistrates, etc.

The House of Lords, too, is not only a legislative body but the
highest court of appeal. While the convention has been established
that only the Law Lords can take part in its judicial proceedings,
the Lords of Appeal themselves may sit both as judges and as
legislators. And though the House of Commons contains no judges,
it does count among its members the Government's law officers,
the Attorney-General and the Solicitor-General, who give the
Government legal advice and represent it in the courts.

The most important exceptions to the separation of legislative
and judicial powers are, however, to be found in the judicial nature
of certain functions performed by each House. Both consider
private bills, where the vital part of the procedure is fundamentally
judicial, and both can try and punish for breach of privilege. But
since party considerations rarely enter into these matters, decisions
are reached impartially. Nevertheless, there is a danger. The

House of Commons in matters of privilege is judge in its own cause and, via 'contempt' (punishable without any specific privilege being breached), has an opportunity for arbitrary extension of privilege. Impeachment, in which the Commons prosecute before the Lords, is now obsolete, but still legal. Finally, the practical effect of the supremacy of Parliament is to permit the legislature, where it does not approve of judicial decisions, to amend existing law.

A similar breakdown in the separation of powers is obvious in the relationship between the *executive and the judiciary*. Not only does the Lord Chancellor both sit in the legislature and perform judicial functions, but he is a leading member of the Cabinet. The Home Secretary, too, is acting in a legal capacity when he advises the monarch on the exercise of the prerogative of mercy, for he does this on his own responsibility and not as a result of collective decisions by the Cabinet. In addition, he has executive duties connected with the courts, such as confirming the appointment of justices' clerks, sending out circulars on sentences, and being responsible for prisons, borstal institutions, the probation service, and the release of persons from Broadmoor and similar institutions.

Although the Lords of Appeal in Ordinary sit on the Judicial Committee of the Privy Council, which is theoretically part of an executive body, their work is concerned with hearing appeals and has no concern with policy. On the other hand, some tasks performed by judges, such as the administration of estates and the winding-up of companies, are of an administrative nature, while, at the lower level, Justices of the Peace carry out both judicial and administrative duties.

Two comparatively recent developments, the growth of delegated legislation and of administrative tribunals, call for such special notice that chapters 21 and 22 are devoted to them. Through them, the administration has been given powers to make legislation and to decide disputes in individual cases.

Encroachment of the *executive on the legislature* can be observed in the functions which the Queen exercises in both, and in the growth of delegated legislation just referred to. But the most important exception to the doctrine is the whole practice of Cabinet government. Ministers, by convention, must be members of the legislature; indeed, the most important offices are filled from the House of Commons, the Chamber having by far the greater legislative authority. Even in the House of Lords, however, the position of the Lord Chancellor is particularly notable, for he not only sits in the Cabinet, giving it the benefit of his legal advice, but in the Chamber he can move out of the Chair and stand to one side of the Woolsack in order to speak on behalf of Government policy.

As early as 1867, Bagehot drew attention to the fact that, while Parliament has the supreme legal right over making law, the time-table of the House of Commons, the more important Chamber, is dominated by the executive. Whereas back-benchers have only limited opportunities for legislation, the Government can ensure, through its party majority and the Whips, that it will have time to pass the bills forming its legislative programme. At all stages, therefore, the legislative functions of Parliament are exercised under the leadership of the executive.

HOW FAR HAS THE BRITISH PATTERN OF GOVERNMENT BEEN INFLUENCED BY THE IDEA OF SEPARATION?

Clearly, then, there is no strict separation of powers in the British constitution today. Nor was there when Montesquieu wrote, for the truth is that to some extent he misinterpreted the British system. Indeed, separation could hardly be expected in a constitution which was never planned but simply developed from a position where the King held ultimate responsibility for the exercise of all legislative, executive and judicial powers.

Yet the idea has not been completely foreign to the British view of constitutional needs. From earliest times, it was recognised that the King's powers should not be used arbitrarily. On important matters of State, for instance, he was expected to consult and thus to share responsibility with the wise men of the realm, while Magna Carta itself reaffirmed the principle that all the King's acts should conform to the common law of the land.

Indeed, the rule of law is fundamentally an application of the theory of the separation of powers. Justice is regarded as an end in itself, to be determined according to the law and not dictated by the executive. To achieve this, the independence of judges is guaranteed by their high salaries, the traditions of the legal profession and, above all, their irremovability. Never again can a Lord Chief Justice be dismissed simply because his decisions are disliked by the King, as happened to Sir Edward Coke in 1617. Nor do the occasions on which powers overlap lessen the importance of the judiciary's separation. Strange as it may seem, the Lord Chancellor finds it possible to keep his different functions distinct. He has been trained as and remains a lawyer, and the tradition of legal neutrality is so deeply ingrained in him that, when he sits as a judge, nobody would suggest that he is influenced by his activities as a politician. Similarly, at the other end of the judicial scale, the few administrative duties of J.P.s do not affect their impartiality in judicial proceedings. Moreover, as regards administrative tribunals, constant watch is maintained to see that their procedure conforms as closely as possible with the concept of 'natural justice' (see chapter 22). These points are important, for without the independence of the judiciary the rule of law would have no practical significance.

But, apart from the judiciary, the British have no strict separation of powers. Nor have they ever demanded such a severance. Indeed, in the 17th century, when the King and Parliament had attempted to go their different ways, only civil war could decide their respective powers. A complete separation of powers makes action slow and difficult, if not impossible. Suppose, for instance, that the judiciary could block every administrative measure or that the executive could never act on its own discretion but had to refer every matter to Parliament. The resulting deadlock would cause a breakdown of government. At times the American constitution has been saved from the effects of its rigidity only by elastic interpretation by the Supreme Court.

Nevertheless, although the doctrine has not been strictly implemented, it has influenced the development of our constitution. That there should be some separation is implicit in the requirements that a Member of Parliament should resign his seat on being promoted to a judgeship or on accepting certain offices of profit under the Crown, and that civil servants cannot sit in the House of Commons. But in place of the rigid separation of powers into three compartments, the British have preferred to have many divisions each providing mutual checks and balances on the other. This arrangement allows flexibility, promotes co-operation on a basis of understanding, and permits that ebb and flow of authority between the different institutions that makes efficient government possible.

The arrangement can be best seen in the close link between the legislature and the executive. In contrast to the separation of powers, Bagehot was able to declare: 'The efficient secret of the English Constitution may be described as the close union, the nearly complete fusion, of the executive and legislative powers'. Yet even in the House of Commons there is a balancing of the legislature against the executive. The Government consists of the leaders of the majority party and through the Whips is able to ensure that the House supports its policy. On the other hand, it cannot ignore the House; it must avoid splits amongst its supporters and, more important, appreciate the likely effect of its policies on the electorate. Here, because the House wields the ultimate power of removing the Government, we see clearly the balances and checks being worked out. While supporters of the Government may be instructed as to their attendance in the appropriate division lobby, the Whip must also inform the Cabinet of their reactions. As regards the electorate, it hears the criticism of Government by the official Opposition.

The result is that Governments are responsive to the feelings of Parliament, although the balance may still be weighted too heavily in favour of the executive. What is important, however, is that the system avoids, on the one hand, the disadvantage of complete separation — the possibility of a collapse of government — and, on the other, the disadvantage of complete fusion — the risk of tyranny. Moreover, the flexibility of the British constitution is such that, where added power is given to one branch of government, a counterbalance is usually found. Examples abound: the Cabinet's growth in power has been matched by 'Her Majesty's Opposition'; the increase in the size and importance of the Civil Service has been counterbalanced by an invigorated question-time and the appointment of a Parliamentary Commissioner: the new public corporations are watched by a newly-established Select Committee of the House of Commons. And, as we shall see, even with delegated legislation and administrative justice, two instances where Montesquieu's doctrine is quite evidently violated, similar checks are being developed.

Finally, the separation of power has been achieved in ways other than those envisaged by the original theory:

(1) Executive power is not in the hands of one strong man, but is shared with about twenty ministers.

(2) The legislative power is split between the House of Commons and the House of Lords, and although the former is by

far the more influential, the Upper Chamber does permit second thoughts on measures, enables legislation to be criticised by persons who do not have to toe a party line and, in the last resort, could still act as a first check on a revolutionary Government.

(3) The House of Commons is itself divided into two parts by the distinction between Government and Opposition. Criticism of the Government is thus ensured and because the parties are large and fairly equally balanced, rather than small and numerous, the check is all the more effective.

(4) The elected Chamber consists not of a few but of 635 members. Each represents a different district and, though subject to strong party discipline at Westminster, is still expected to advocate his constituency's interests. There is thus a balance between the different localities of the country.

(5) There is separation between central and local government. While all local powers are derived from Parliament, our system of local government is very different from a mere decentralisation of power through regional offices. Councils are directly elected by local people, raise their own rates, appoint their own officials, and enjoy considerable discretion in administering their services. Hence, their loyalties and responsibilities are directed towards the local electorate rather than to Whitehall. Moreover, this balance between central control and local independence makes it less likely that bureaucrats will neglect the interests of remote areas or introduce schemes which will not work under varying local conditions.

(6) Division of power between the executive and the State's industrial activities ensures that political and industrial functions are not entirely in the same hands. Public corporations, and not government departments, were specifically set up to administer the nationalised industries in order to avoid political interference.

(7) Industrial power is held by both the State and private enterprise. This facilitates flexibility of decision in different parts of the country and, by encouraging competition among alternative producers, promotes 'consumer's sovereignty'. Complete State monopoly of production would not only add greatly to the power of the executive, but deny the citizen that

freedom of economic choice which is almost as important as the political preference expressed through the ballot box.

(8) In the economy of the country, the Government exercises its planning functions to secure full employment, stability of prices in general, and improved living standards, but it leaves individuals free to make their own economic decisions such as what shall be produced, where they shall work, whether to do over-time, etc. Economic, as well as political freedom, is an aspect of democracy.

(9) Most important of all, there is separation between the Government and the expression of opinion. Despotism would result, as it does in present-day dictatorships, were the Government the sole source of influencing opinion. In Britain, different views are expressed openly and assessed freely. The Press, for instance, covers a wide variety of political outlooks, and even where a newspaper has a broad sympathy with a particular party, it is still likely to have its own individual approach to many problems. Nor does the Government control the B.B.C. or the I.T.A., and both are under a legal obligation to maintain strict political neutrality. Finally, no attempt is made to influence the political views of young persons either in State schools or in universities. The University Grants Committee is as independent as the judiciary.

Thus the exercise of power is widely diffused throughout the community by various forms of separation which are no less significant in preventing the growth of tyranny than the separation between the legislature, executive and judiciary.

Nevertheless, while no open attempt to concentrate power in the hands of one group is likely, some critics fear that the executive may extend its authority gradually, unplanned and unobserved, by means of delegated legislation and administrative justice. It is to a consideration of these that we now turn.

SUGGESTED READING

Sir Carleton K. Allen, *Law and Orders* (3rd Ed., Stevens, 1965), Chapter 1.

Sir Ivor Jennings, *The Law and the Constitution* (4th Ed., University of London, 1955), Chapter 1, Section 3, Appendix I.

E. C. S. Wade and G. G. Phillips, *Constitutional Law* (8th Ed., Longmans, 1970), Part II, Chapter 1.

21

Delegated Legislation

'Whether administrative power is legitimate authority
or bureaucratic abuse depends less on its scale than on
the conditions in which it is being employed.'

E. STRAUSS: *The Ruling Servants*

HISTORY OF DELEGATED LEGISLATION

Law-making, according to the theory of the separation of
powers, should be a function exercised only by the legislature. In
practice, however, the British Parliament confers powers on
numerous administrative authorities to make what is virtually
their own law. Ministers, for instance, are empowered to issue
rules, orders and regulations, while local authorities, public corporations and semi-private bodies like the National Trust, are
allowed to frame their own bye-laws.

Such 'delegated legislation', as it is termed, is not new. As early
as the 14th century the King was exercising delegated powers.
Thus, an Act of 1385 provided that the Staple (wool, wool fells,
leather, tin and lead) should be held in times and places ordered by
the King's Council with the authority of Parliament. Under the
Tudors, the practice increased, and the Statute of Sewers, 1531,
extended the right 'to make, constitute and ordain laws, ordinances
and decrees' to Commissioners of Sewers, a new statutory body
responsible for sewers and drainage.

Nevertheless, the Stuart attempt to rule England by administrative law — proclamations of the Privy Council enforced by the
Court of Star Chamber — made Parliament, in the following
century, reluctant to delegate powers. Instead, statutes tended to
fill in as much administrative detail as possible.

Delegated legislation did not really begin to grow until the
19th century. The 1830s inaugurated a period of reform, necessitated by the Industrial Revolution, which had led to a concentration of population in filthy and over-crowded manufacturing

towns. Legislation was introduced to deal with factory conditions, the poor law, municipal government, and public health. At the same time, Parliament was faced with the problem of authorising the development of water supplies and the railways and, somewhat later, gas and electricity services. It was obviously impossible to legislate in detail for all these matters, and hence powers had to be delegated to the ministers, bodies and officials responsible for administering the schemes. Moreover, during the 19th century the Civil Service was reformed and greatly expanded, and such zealous leaders as Chadwick, Southwood Smith, John Simon, and Sir Robert Morant sought regulating powers for effective administration.

From the beginning of the 20th century it became more generally recognised that the State should assume responsibility for rendering certain services and undertaking overall planning in the interests of the community. But the increase in government activities meant that Parliament could legislate for them only in broad terms, and powers to fill in the details had to be delegated. Moreover, this change in outlook coincided with two wars on an unprecedented scale.

REASONS FOR DELEGATED LEGISLATION

Delegated legislation, therefore, has developed out of necessity — the demands of the State and modern emergencies making it indispensable.

The functions of the State are now so extensive, that if Parliament attempted to enact statutes in detail the legislative machinery would break down. Such long and complicated public and private bills would have to be passed that there would be little time left for debating policy, answering questions, controlling finance, and carrying out Parliament's many other duties. Moreover, delegated legislation often provides a more appropriate means of regulating these new services than an Act of Parliament. In the first place, delegation helps in dealing with the technical nature of many of the schemes. Not only is it unsafe to presume that Parliament contains the necessary experts but, more important, it is as a body suitable only for the discussion of general principles. Technical details are best thrashed out by the departments in consultation with the experts and the interests concerned. Secondly, delegation meets the need for flexibility in the application of statutes. Parliament cannot foresee all contingencies, but it would be cumbersome if a new bill had to be introduced every time circumstances altered. Rules, orders and regulations, however, can be easily and quickly modified in the light of experience and to meet new developments. The problems of road transport, for example, are constantly changing as a result of higher incomes, faster cars and major road alterations, and it is convenient if the minister can make adjustments as required and according to local needs. Closely related is a third advantage, that delegation not only permits experiments to be made (for example, in new methods of traffic control or different parking systems), but it enables the minister to apply generally those ideas which prove successful. Lastly, unlike bills, which are often drafted in a hurry, delegated legislation can be carefully considered. Moreover, since there is less need for compression than in a statute, the rules can often be worded more completely and more precisely, thereby enabling the parent Act to be shorter and clearer.

The reasons for delegated legislation are somewhat different in time of war, for then the State assumes responsibilities for planning on a far greater scale. Extensive powers must be given to officials to implement the broad wishes of Parliament and, above all, to act in emergencies. Even in peace-time some provision must be made for quick action to meet an emergency where there is insufficient time for prior consideration by Parliament. This was the purpose of the Emergency Powers Act, 1964, which provides that a Proclamation might declare a state of emergency if it appears that events such as industrial action, abnormal weather conditions, natural disasters, stoppage of essential supplies from abroad, and major breakdowns of plant and machinery threaten to deprive the community of the essentials of life. Such a Proclamation would last a month (but might be renewed), during which period regulations (lasting only for seven days unless approved by both Houses) could be made.

FORMS OF DELEGATED LEGISLATION

Delegated legislation may take four main forms, but since these have already been fully discussed elsewhere, we shall bring them together here in outline only.

(1) *Orders in Council*

Orders in Council are of two kinds. Prerogative Orders and

Proclamations are issued by virtue of the prerogative powers of the Crown, and are independent of any statutory authority. Such Orders may be used, for example, to change the form of government of a dependent territory, or to regulate commerce and trade in times of war. Today, however, Orders in Council are, in practice, issued under the authority of a statute. Thus, the Emergency Powers (Defence) Act, 1939, passed on the outbreak of war, provided for the minister to act by Order in Council. Although Orders are subject to ratification by the Privy Council, this is usually a formality, and so there is really little difference between them and ministerial orders.

(2) *Rules, orders and regulations*

Instead of being empowered to act by Order in Council, as above, a minister may issue rules, orders and regulations under the authority of a statute. Both forms are now known as 'statutory instruments'. But there are vast differences in the scope of such rules, orders and regulations. At one extreme, an order may be simply concerned with the lay-out of a form. At the other, the minister may make such regulations as appear to him 'necessary and expedient' for achieving a specified object, a permission which is almost akin to giving him a blank cheque and which should obviously be subject to some degree of parliamentary control.

(3) *Provisional and Special Procedure Orders*

As we have seen in chapter 11, these have been instituted to relieve Parliament's burden of private bill legislation and to reduce applicants' costs.

(4) *Bye-laws*

Local authorities, public corporations, municipal and public utility undertakings, and certain semi-private bodies, such as the Port of London Authority, have power to draw up their own bye-laws for fulfilling their responsibilities. Although these bye-laws, as the name implies, can be enforced in the courts, the purposes for which permission is given do not usually excite much controversy.

CRITICISMS OF DELEGATED LEGISLATION

During the 19th century few objections were raised to delegated legislation, and the need for it eventually became recognised. But the form it took did evoke criticism, which became more pronounced when ministers interpreted widely the powers given to them by the Defence of the Realm Act, 1914, 'for securing the public safety and the defence of the Realm.' The courts in particular began to voice the opinion that a greater degree of definition was required, and that controls should be imposed on the almost unrestrained authority that the administration was exercising. The impact of Lord Justice Hewart's book, *The New Despotism* (1929), brought the whole problem to the fore, and the Lord Chancellor appointed the Committee on Ministers' Powers to consider the powers exercised by departments through delegated legislation and to report what safeguards were desirable to secure the constitutional principles of the sovereignty of Parliament and the supremacy of the law.

When it reported in 1932, the Committee upheld the principle of delegated legislation as an inevitable consequence of the needs of modern government. But it considered that there were serious practical defects, especially when powers were given to a minister to make orders of an 'exceptional' nature, dealing with matters of principle, imposing taxation, amending statutes and limiting the control of the courts. However, few positive results followed from the Committee's recommendations.

Certain objections to delegated legislation are based merely on an outdated *laissez-faire* philosophy. The practice, it is argued, facilitates violations of such principles as the sanctity of private property and the minimum of restraint upon the individual's freedom of action. But these principles are no longer held in their rigid form. The more constructive critics, however, accept delegated legislation in principle, but believe that in practice it violates fundamental requirements of the rule of law, the separation of powers, and the sovereignty of Parliament, as they still apply in our constitution today.

The rule of law (chapters 2 and 23) implies among other things that: (1) a citizen should be able to ascertain fairly easily what the law is on a particular matter; (2) in any possible breach of the law in its application to him by an official, a person should have the right of appeal to the courts. Both requirements, however, are infringed by modern delegated legislation.

As regards (1), rules, orders and regulations have become so numerous that the citizen is submerged by them. Not only that, but they are complicated by sub-delegation, regulations being made under the statute, orders under the regulations, and directives under the order. The confusion is added to by the language in which they are expressed, with references back to previous instruments making the order itself practically incomprehensible. Professor Sir Carleton Allen quotes Order No. 1216 of 1943. 'The Control of Tins, Cans, Kegs, Drums and Packaging Pails (No. 5) Order, 1942 (*a*), as varied by the Control of Tin Cans, Kegs, Drums and Packaging Pails (No. 6) Order 1942 (*b*), the Control of Tins, Cans, Kegs, Drums and Packaging Pails (No. 7) Order, 1942 (*c*), the Control of Tins, Cans, Kegs, Drums and Packaging Pails (No. 8) Order, 1942 (*d*), and the Control of Tins, Cans, Kegs, Drums and Packaging Pails (No. 9) Order, 1942 (*e*), is hereby further varied in the Third Schedule thereto . . . by substituting for the reference 2A therein the reference "2A(1)" and by deleting therefrom the reference 2B.' 'What contribution', he asks, 'was made to our jurisprudence by this Order of 169 words?' (*Law and Orders*). Finally, when we see from the above example how quickly such orders can be changed, could any solicitor really give firm advice to his client? In short, we have 'the comedy of control'. The most serious result, which was particularly evident during the war, is that even well-intentioned people give up the attempt to keep abreast of the various regulations, while the courts make obvious their reluctance to punish unwitting offenders, though normally ignorance of the law is not a valid plea. Such a situation brings the whole system of law into disrepute. Indeed, some critics go even further, asserting that the confusion encourages administrators to take the risk of over-stepping the law, knowing that it will be a long time before their action is challenged. Nor, when we remember that wireless licences were collected illegally for twenty years, should we dismiss such an accusation too lightly.

Maxim (2), that disputes as to the legality of orders should be decided by the courts, is also undermined by special provisions relating to certain delegated legislation. Here there is a close connection with the part that the theory of the separation of powers is still held to play in our constitution. Justice must be an end in itself, and disputes as to the intents of Acts of Parliament should be decided in the ordinary courts. But granting the minister permission to make such orders 'as he thinks fit', or inserting that the minister's confirmation 'shall be conclusive evidence that the provisions of the Act have been complied with', renders judicial review difficult, if not impossible. The attitude of the Government is understandable. Having had the desirability of the policy decided in Parliament, it does not want rearguard action by referring details to Parliament or submitting every dispute to the courts. Nevertheless, such an attitude must be carefully watched, for it carries with it the threat of arbitrary power.

The sovereignty of Parliament refers to the legal supremacy of its statutes and its unlimited legislative powers. In day-to-day practice, too, it covers the control exercised by the Commons over the executive by its supervision of the raising and spending of money. Here again, delegated legislation often strikes indirectly at the foundations of the principle. Not only is power given to the minister to alter taxes within limits (e.g. the 25% 'regulator' for value added tax), but legislation is left in such a skeleton form that the right to issue orders concerning general policy may be granted. Admittedly, it is often difficult to draw a clear line between matters of principle and detail, since the former are often closely related to the way in which the Act is put into operation, but, nevertheless, there is a tendency to give too wide a discretion. It thus becomes almost impossible to ascertain the limits which the Act really did intend to impose, thereby rendering it difficult for the courts to declare the orders of a minister *ultra vires*. Indeed, a statute may go further, giving the minister power to amend the parent Act or any other Act. Once again, the practice can be defended on the grounds that complicated legislation on the matter already exists, and that only in this way can the parent Act be brought fully into operation. Town and country planning schemes, for instance, may well conflict with several operative Private Acts. Yet the dangers inherent in the provision are obvious and, of all the exceptional powers, this one has been criticised the most.

In any case, some degree of sovereignty is sacrificed simply through the volume of present-day legislation, M.P.s being too busy to appreciate fully what they are conferring. When powers are scattered throughout the various sections of the bill, they may, unless interests draw attention to them, slip through unnoticed.

CONTROLS OVER DELEGATED LEGISLATION

(1) *Control by Parliament*

In deciding how to control delegated legislation, Parliament is faced with the problem of achieving adequate supervision without destroying the motive for delegation — the desire to relieve members of the necessity of discussing the details and technical aspects of new schemes. Ultimate control is retained by Parliament, for it can always revoke any authority it has given. Such action, however, would be basically negative; Parliament's aim must be not to destroy a minister's power to make orders, but to ensure that it is not excessive and that the orders themselves are not obnoxious.

Apart from Provisional and Special Procedure Orders, for which a particular procedure is laid down, Parliament exercises control by general supervision of the executive and by consideration of the actual orders. As regards the first, bills conferring delegated powers must pass through all the specified stages to become law. If, therefore, the minister is allowed to make regulations 'as he thinks fit' and, in this way, Parliament and the courts are partly disarmed, the fault rests largely with members, and the minister cannot be blamed for using the powers given him. The Government can, of course, influence Parliament through the party Whips, but even so, if Opposition members stir up sufficient adverse publicity in the Press, the provision may be abandoned. Questions, adjournment debates and the Supply days may also be used to criticise the exercise of powers, and a minister may drop a particular order rather than incur political odium on a comparatively trivial issue.

Consideration of the orders themselves generally takes place when they are before the House. Here there are four degrees of supervision. First, the order may require an affirmative resolution before it can come into effect or the draft may have to be similarly approved before the Order can be made. This is the most efficient form of control, for not only does it ensure that the order is expressly considered, but time has to be found by the Government for doing so. Thus it is reserved for statutory orders which are particularly worthy of attention, such as those modifying an Act or imposing a tax. Even so, the time found by the Government to secure the approval of the House is usually late at night, so that an order must be very controversial to arouse effective opposition.

Secondly, the order may take effect unless it is negatived by a motion praying for its annulment, which, by the Statutory Instruments Act, must occur within forty days. This is the most common procedure, but it encounters certain snags. (*a*) Since time for a negative resolution has to be found by the member moving it, the prayer is usually taken as exempted business after 10 p.m. when it may be difficult to maintain a quorum or even be subject to the closure. The latter arises because negative resolutions may be used for obstruction, and after 1950 the House was involved in numerous all-night sittings. Hence, in 1953, following the recommendations of a Select Committee, it was agreed that if discussion of them under exempted business was going on after 11.30 p.m., the Speaker could, at his discretion, put the question, or, if he thought further debate desirable, adjourn the House until the next time for exempted business. Since December, 1967, this has applied also to affirmative resolutions. (*b*) The order cannot be amended by the House, for this might result in lengthy debate on details, the avoidance of which is the whole object of delegation. But the minister may subsequently reconsider the order.

Thirdly, regulations may be laid before the House for its information with no specified action to follow. Such regulations will rarely be controversial. But even if a member does object, the necessary time is difficult to find, for the motion does not come within the scope of exempted business, and private members' time on Fridays is limited. Thus, the only practical action is to raise the matter without a motion on the adjournment or on the appropriate Supply vote or during the debate on the Consolidated Fund Bill.

Lastly, certain rules do not have to be laid before the House. These are concerned merely with matters of machinery, such as the nature of a form or the interval for making returns to a department.

But, although procedures are thus laid down, parliamentary control suffers from three main weaknesses: (*a*) the volume of orders is so bulky that members cannot ensure that some objectionable ones are not overlooked; (*b*) not all orders receive the publicity they deserve; (*c*) finding time in Parliament for objecting to an order is difficult. Nevertheless, steps have been taken in recent years to improve matters, notably by the appointment, since 1944, of a Statutory Instruments Committee, and the passing of the Statutory Instruments Act, 1946.

The *Select Committee on Statutory Instruments*, often referred to as the Scrutiny Committee, is appointed by the House of Commons in each session to consider every statutory rule or order laid before Parliament which requires confirmation or is subject to annulment. It is assisted by Speaker's Counsel. Orders which it thinks call for special attention are brought to the notice of the House, but only about 1% have to be dealt with in this way and the number is tending to diminish. However, the Committee is not unimportant. Admittedly its terms of reference are limited, for it cannot comment on departmental policy or on the merits of a particular instrument, subjects which are still left to the initiative of the individual member. But its mere existence has a salutary effect, for a department does not welcome Parliament's attention being drawn to one of its instruments. From time to time government departments are required to justify to the Committee the case for making a proposed Order and to give evidence to the Committee on the matter. Moreover, the Committee has made useful suggestions concerning the consolidation, drafting and clarity of language of statutory instruments and the means of giving them publicity. In the House of Lords, there is a Special Orders Committee, set up in 1925, which examines all instruments subject to affirmative resolution.

The *Statutory Instruments Act, 1946*, resulted from a recommendation of the Statutory Instruments Committee. It provides for the numbering, printing, publication, citation and laying before the House of statutory instruments.

Attention must also be called to other means of securing publicity. Sometimes the Act requires periodic reports to be made to the House. Certain M.P.s, too, try to keep abreast of statutory instruments. Moreover, interests are on the alert regarding orders which affect them. Indeed, today it is usual for the department concerned to consult those interests particularly affected by a proposed statutory instrument, and this may even be a statutory requirement (see page 555). Again, an order which is particularly obnoxious may receive such publicity in the Press that it has to be withdrawn. Such was the fate of an order made under the Road Traffic Act, 1937, to permit the testing of a car's brakes while the owner was absent.

Unfortunately, all methods of challenging an order are weakened by the shortage of parliamentary time. Even when the Statutory Instruments Committee brings an order to the notice of the House, the problem of securing an opportunity for adequate discussion remains. More use might be made of the positive affirmation to a statutory instrument as the most effective means of control, but nothing can be done until a reform of parliamentary procedure makes the extra time available.

(2) *Control by the courts*

Any person may ask the courts to rule that an executive action is *ultra vires*. Such a complaint may be founded on: an injunction; orders of prohibition, certiorari or mandamus; a declaratory judgment; a special procedure provided for in the main Act such as appeal to the High Court.

The main principle regarding delegated legislation is that where an order is not made according to the prescribed procedure or exceeds the powers conferred by the Act, it can be declared *ultra vires*. Hence, only the scope of the powers can be examined by the courts, except in the case of bye-laws, which may be declared invalid because they are unreasonable. Two examples of such judicial review may be quoted. In *R. v. the Minister of Health* (*ex parte Davis*), *1929*, the Court prohibited the minister from confirming orders of the Derby Town Council for compulsorily acquiring land. The Housing and Town Planning Act, 1925 (replaced by the Housing Act, 1957), authorised such purchases for slum clearance and improvement, but the Council was in fact selling or leasing the land at a profit without restricting the use to which it should be put. It was held that this did not come within the Act and, had the minister confirmed the orders, he would have exceeded his jurisdiction. Similarly, in *Mixnam's Properties Ltd. v. Chertsey Urban District Council* it was held that although the Caravan Sites and Control of Development Act, 1960, gave local authorities wide powers to impose conditions as to the use of the site, these powers must be exercised in accordance with the intention of the Act and thus do not extend to conditions relating to agreements for letting caravans to individual dwellers.

But provisions in the parent statute may make it difficult to challenge the legality of an order. The minister may be empowered to make such regulations 'as appear to him necessary'. Or the Act may say that confirmation of an order by a minister 'shall be conclusive evidence of compliance with the Act' or that orders 'shall have effect as if enacted in this Act' — phrases which, in recent years, have fortunately fallen into disuse. Nor can the courts challenge a purely administrative discretion. But they can investigate decisions which are of a judicial nature, quashing them if the rules of natural justice have not been observed. In practice, the distinction between what is administrative and what is judicial is not a clear one, and of recent years the courts have shown a greater tendency to interpret minister's actions in a way which makes them subject to review. In *Ridge v. Baldwin, 1964*, for instance, the Brighton Watch Committee had dismissed their Chief Constable following serious criticism of him by the judge when he was tried and acquitted on charges of conspiracy. In doing so the Watch Committee ignored the requirement of a formal enquiry laid down by the Police Act, 1919, contending that the dismissal was a purely administrative action. It was held that the regulations could not be disregarded and that in any case the failure to give the Chief Constable a hearing was a breach of the rules of natural justice.

Thus, although the power of the courts is a valuable check on the administration and should be excluded only in exceptional circumstances, it is a limited one, being confined merely to ensuring that orders are legal under the parent Act. Consequently the real control must rest with Parliament, which should define the powers it grants and scrutinise orders carefully.

SUGGESTED READING

Sir Carleton K. Allen, *Law and Orders* (3rd Ed., Stevens, 1965).
Lord Hewart, *The New Despotism* (Rev. Ed., E. Benn, 1945).
G. W. Keeton, *Government in Action in the United Kingdom* (E. Benn, 1970), Chapter 9.
H. W. R. Wade, *Administrative Law* (3rd Ed., O.U.P., 1971), Chapters 3, 4 and 9.

22

Administrative Justice

'Administration must not only be efficient in the sense that the objectives of policy are securely attained without delay. It must also satisfy the general body of citizens that it is proceeding with reasonable regard to the balance between the public interest which it promotes and the private interest which it disturbs.'

Report of the Committee on Administrative Tribunals and Enquiries, 1957.

INTRODUCTION

Until the beginning of the 20th century the functions of the State were chiefly concerned with control, and seldom did individual rights conflict with the responsibilities of public authorities. Where there was a clash, as for instance in the construction of the railways, the issue could usually be decided by Parliament or in the ordinary courts.

Today, however, our governing bodies act in the interests of the community as a whole, and powers have been granted them so that they can perform their duties. To take but a few examples, they can compulsorily acquire suitable sites for building schools and hospitals and buy land to construct new roads. Private building may be restricted in the interests of planning, and the price of necessities, such as housing, controlled to prevent exploitation of shortages. But this extension of State activities has increased the likelihood of disputes, not only between the citizen and government (e.g. compulsory purchase order for planning purposes), but also between individuals (e.g. control of the rents of furnished dwellings). For reasons which will be considered later, such disputes are not referred to the ordinary courts of law, but are decided either by specially-constituted tribunals or according to a specified procedure. What is important is that the administrative tribunals making 'quasi-judicial' decisions are so constituted that the rights of the individual are given full consideration when they conflict with the wider interests of the community.

FORMS OF ADMINISTRATIVE JUSTICE

Today there are over 2,000 special tribunals, for not only are there over 100 different types of adjudicating authority, but most of them have local off-shoots, such as the 300-odd National Insurance appeal panels. In constitution, they have the following points in common:

(*a*) in order that a majority decision can be reached, they consist of an odd number of members;

(*b*) where a legal chairman or member is required, he is appointed by the Lord Chancellor, but other members are usually appointed by the appropriate minister;

(*c*) members usually hold office for a specified period.

Nevertheless, these bodies do not form a coherent system, having simply been appointed as the need arose. Nor, since they differ so considerably, is classification easy. But the following distinctions can be made:

(1) *Bodies dealing with disputes in which a government department or public authority is interested*

These bodies are mostly appellate; that is, they hear and usually decide appeals from the decisions or proposed decisions of departments and departmental offices. The decision may be made either by a tribunal (e.g. local valuation courts for rating, general and special commissioners of inland revenue for income tax, and appeal tribunals for pensions), or by the responsible minister after an *ad hoc* enquiry. The procedure for the latter is usually governed by the Acquisition of Land (Authorisation Procedure) Act, 1946, and takes the following form. After the acquiring authority has advertised and served notice on the owners of property to be compulsorily purchased, any person may object within twenty-one days. The minister then holds a local enquiry, usually in public, and upon the report of the person in charge he confirms or rejects the acquisition proposals. The only appeal from the minister's decision is to the High Court, on the grounds that the order is *ultra vires* or that the prescribed procedure or the rules of natural justice have not been followed.

Tribunals have been set up to cover disputes arising out of most aspects of Government policy. The main fields are the social services (e.g. claims for pensions), land (e.g. disputed possession orders for inefficient husbandry), and economic control (e.g. the fixing of railway charges).

(2) *Tribunals dealing with disputes between individual and individual*

These are mostly regulatory tribunals; that is, they are concerned not with appeals from departmental decisions but with 'disputes' between private persons and interests which result from attempts by the government to regulate a particular aspect of the economy (e.g. rents, road and air transport) or the functioning of a particular service (e.g. the National Health Service). Often specialised knowledge is required by the tribunal as, for example, with the rent tribunals, which fix fair rents for furnished premises.

(3) *Domestic tribunals enforcing professional discipline*

Examples are the General Medical Council (doctors) and the Disciplinary Committee of the Law Society (solicitors). Such tribunals do not concern the ordinary public, and their constitution and procedure are left to the respective professional associations.

REASONS FOR THE ESTABLISHMENT OF ADMINISTRATIVE TRIBUNALS

Generally speaking, where decisions of a judicial nature have to be made in administering a public service, Parliament has preferred that they should be given by specially constituted tribunals rather than by the courts, in spite of the latters' fine tradition of impartiality and wisdom. The reasons for this are:

(1) *The type of case is different from that normally heard in a court of law*

Tribunals are concerned with administrative considerations as much as judicial decisions, having to reconcile the rights of the individual with the implementation of the policy of a democratically elected government. In many respects the judges are out of touch with this new requirement, as Lord Hewart's outburst in *The New Despotism* reveals.

(2) *The number of cases to be decided would grossly overburden the courts*

Many disputes, such as those over 'fair' rents and national

insurance claims, are comparatively trivial and do not warrant the services of a highly-paid judge. Moreover, being so numerous, they could be decided by the courts only if many additional judges were created, chiefly in the County Courts. Such a move takes time, and would thus result in a delay in hearing disputes. In any case, since it is doubtful whether there are sufficient persons available of the high quality required, the result, a lowering of standards, would be detrimental to the administration of justice as a whole.

(3) *The procedure of tribunals is more appropriate to the type of dispute*

A court of law is formal, its procedure being bound by strict rules. But though this form of approach may assist justice, it is not necessarily appropriate for deciding a claim to insurance benefit or fixing a fair rent for a furnished room. The merits of such cases can best be examined in the more intimate atmosphere of special tribunals, to which people feel they have access without the need of legal representation and where witnesses can be encouraged to speak freely. Moreover a tribunal, unlike a court of law where the procedure tends to be moulded by the established ideas of trial and evidence, can work out its own procedure — inspecting furnished premises or farmland, for instance, in order to arrive at its decisions.

(4) *Tribunals are quicker and cheaper*

A lengthy, costly hearing, with no certainty of success at the end, would tend to deter applicants on comparatively minor matters, such as seeking a reduction in rent. Moreover, with many disputes, such as those arising under the National Insurance Acts, costs in a court of law would be disproportionate to the sums involved. In contrast, tribunals, by specialising in a particular type of case, are able to elicit the pertinent facts quickly and to decide without delay. Together with the possibility of dispensing with legal representation, this makes for cheapness in comparison with the courts.

(5) *Appeal procedure is shorter, quicker and cheaper*

Decisions of a court of law may be appealed against in a higher court, involving considerable cost and delay. Such a procedure might ruin an administrative scheme, and so, as we shall see, appeals from tribunals to the courts are rarely possible.

(6) Technical knowledge may be necessary for a decision

A tribunal can contain experts chosen to deal with questions of a highly technical nature. Thus, persons with practical farming experience serve on the Agricultural Land Tribunal, which can give a landlord possession where a tenant farms inefficiently, and surveyors and lawyers serve on the Lands Tribunal, which decides compensation appeals when land is compulsorily acquired.

(7) The attitude of the judges may obstruct public service functions

Many left-wing theorists believe that the courts are not suitable for dealing with disputes arising out of modern socialist planning. First, judges are held to be biased against administrative law, which plays such a large part in these cases. Secondly, in finding the 'intent' of a statute, they are hidebound by the canons of common law, principles formulated in an age dominated by the *laissez-faire* philosophy, which assumes the rightness of capitalism and limits the State's function to public control.

In practice, however, the charge of reactionary obstruction has not been well substantiated — and the practice of appointing lawyers as chairmen of tribunals rather refutes it.

(8) Flexibility of decisions is desirable

Courts of law are rigidly bound in their decisions by precedent. This does make for consistency and therefore for certainty. Hence some tribunals, e.g. the National Insurance Commissioners, have developed a formidable body of precedent, and other tribunals, e.g. the Rent Assessment Committees (in London), seem to be in the process of doing so.

But extending the arguments of previous cases to decisions on administrative duties is not always desirable. With planning, for example, consideration has to be given to local conditions. Similarly, in public health and housing, standards are rising rapidly and decisions must keep abreast.

CRITICISMS OF ADMINISTRATIVE TRIBUNALS

Criticism of administrative tribunals is broadly of two kinds. The first, which comes chiefly from the legal profession, holds that they offend two cardinal principles — the separation of powers and the rule of law.

Justice, according to the British interpretation of the separation of powers, should be regarded as an end in itself, to be administered impartially by a completely independent authority. The very term 'administrative justice' thus violates this principle. Lord Hewart considered that 'administrative lawlessness' would be more appropriate. The Milk Marketing Board, as first established under the Agricultural Marketing Acts, 1931-3 (since amended), illustrates the point. The Board was given authority to make regulations regarding contracts, prices and contributions by registered producers. It had executive powers to call for information and returns, to impose levies, and to inspect farms, in order to ensure that its regulations were being observed. Above all, for a breach of the regulations or failure to supply information, the Board had the judicial powers to fine a farmer, or to revoke his licence. Thus legislative, executive and judicial powers were invested in one authority. Moreover, in carrying out its judicial functions, the Board was highly arbitrary. Sitting in London, it could summon a farmer from any part of the country to attend its hearings, which did not have to be in public. Nor was the Board bound by any rules of evidence, although the defendant had the right to be represented. Appeal was to an arbitrator appointed, where the parties failed to agree, by the minister — his choice usually falling on a civil servant. Lastly, the Board included members who had voted in favour of the marketing scheme and were thus financially interested in its success. Such extensive powers must be related to the fact that, while a producer had to join the scheme once a majority had voted in favour, revocation of his licence by the Board would ruin him.

Dicey's 'rule of law' is broken by administrative tribunals because they neither form part of the 'ordinary courts of the land' nor conduct their procedure in the 'ordinary legal manner'. This view however, is dependent on Dicey's exposition of the rule of law, which is no longer generally accepted (chapter 23).

The second kind of critic recognises that administrative tribunals are indispensable but observes defects in their working, especially as they strive to attain the correct balance between private rights and public advantage. Tribunals are not regarded as being incompatible with the principle of the separation of powers, for a distinction is still drawn between purely administrative decisions and those which must be classed as judicial because they affect the rights of individuals. Nor is the rule of law discarded, for its basic ideas are still held to be essential. In particular, it is held that tribunals must observe the 'rules of natural justice': (a) whoever makes the decisions should be independent of the parties to the dispute; (b) each side must have an opportunity to present its case adequately; (c) decisions should be made by the application of known principles or laws so that, as far as possible, they are predictable and the citizen knows where he stands.

Indeed, it was partly the failure to observe such rules which was so disturbing in the Crichel Down case, 1952/4. As a result, the Government appointed a committee under the chairmanship of Sir Oliver Franks to consider the composition and procedure of tribunals. (Thus such cases as Crichel Down, where no tribunal was involved, were outside its terms of reference!) Starting from the assumption that 'openness, fairness and impartiality' should characterise the methods of arriving at decisions, it concluded that many criticisms of tribunals were well founded. Most of its recommendations have been implemented, either under the Tribunals and Inquiries Act, 1958, or simply by administrative action, the latter covering in particular compulsory acquisition, slum clearance and planning appeals. What follows surveys the position with regard to tribunals.

(1) *Composition*

The composition of a tribunal has to be related to the kind of work it does. Two examples may be given. The Transport Tribunal has five members—a lawyer president, two experienced in business and two in financial matters. War Pension tribunals have a barrister or solicitor as chairman and contain medical members as well as ex-Servicemen. Some members of tribunals serve on a voluntary basis, but most are paid fees, together with travelling expenses. Full-time chairmen receive salaries on a scale equivalent to that of Circuit judges.

But there was no guarantee that a tribunal would contain members with legal qualifications, and this sometimes had serious disadvantages. Although technically qualified, members found it difficult to elicit facts, especially from awkward witnesses. Decisions were obviously based on insufficient evidence. Members, too, were occasionally suspected of bias — appeals against income tax assessments, for instance, are heard by Special Commissioners

of Income Tax, civil servants employed by the Board of Inland
Revenue. The tendency had been growing of appointing chairmen
with legal qualifications, and the Government accepted the Franks
Committee's recommendations that this should normally be the
case. Other suggestions — that chairmen should not be appointed
by the minister concerned but by the Lord Chancellor, and that
members should be appointed by a newly created Council on
Tribunals — were not, however, accepted, although the government did concede that for an important group of tribunals the
Minister should select a Chairman from a panel appointed by the
Lord Chancellor.

(2) *Procedure*

Any one who appears before a court of law is protected by
carefully formulated rules of procedure. No such standard code
applies to tribunals. Sometimes the details of procedure are laid
down strictly in a statutory instrument and may be modelled on the
ordinary courts, but other tribunals have considerable discretion
in deciding their own procedure. Thus, the Transport Tribunal
has a formal code of procedure and, since it adjudicates on matters
of considerable importance to industry, eminent counsel are often
briefed to appear before it. Rent tribunals, on the other hand, are
conducted much more informally, so much so that in 1949 the
Lord Chief Justice, Lord Goddard, made scathing comments on
the Paddington Rent Tribunal for arriving at decisions without
hearing any evidence at all.

A rigid procedure would make it impossible to secure the
informal atmosphere desirable for hearing certain kinds of cases.
Moreover, if all meetings were held in public, personal matters
might be disclosed to neighbours, as for instance before a Supplementary Benefits Appeal Tribunal. Nevertheless, there should be
some assurance that both sides will be given identical facilities for
stating their case and that facts will be sifted, and evidence
weighed, impartially. The Government, therefore, accepted several
important recommendations by the Franks Committee. Indeed,
some tribunals were already following these rules, the most
important of which are: (*a*) the citizen should be made fully aware
of his right to apply to a tribunal and notified in good time of the
case he has to meet; (*b*) except where intimate personal details
might be disclosed, hearings should be in public; (*c*) where

possible, an applicant should also be informed of departmental policy before an enquiry, so that he can estimate which of his arguments might carry the most weight; (*d*) legal representation should be allowed in all tribunals; (*e*) reasons for decisions should be given fully, and these should be sent to the parties concerned together with rights of appeal. Most important of all, the government agreed that there should be statutory rules of procedure for tribunals and that, in formulating these rules, the Council of Tribunals should be consulted. These rules have now been established for all the main tribunals.

(3) *Appeals*

Sometimes there is no formal appeal procedure against certain administrative decisions. In such cases, all that can be done is to complain to the administering authority, contact an M.P., or seek publicity in the Press. But even where appeals are possible, they may be to one of a variety of authorities. For example, there are: the County Court (against a local authority's order for the demolition of insanitary houses); a special tribunal (on a claim for National Insurance benefit); the minister, which in practice means a civil servant (against an acquisition order); the Court of Appeal (on a point of law relating to a decision of the Lands Tribunal).

The Franks Committee recommended that, generally speaking, there should be a straight appeal to an appellate tribunal, with a further appeal on a point of law to the courts. Final appellate tribunals should publish selected decisions and circulate them to lower tribunals. As a result, the Tribunals and Inquiries Act, 1958, extended the right of appeal on a point of law to the High Court (and thence to the Court of Appeal).

CONTROL OF ADMINISTRATIVE TRIBUNALS

Although tribunals possess the great merits of cheapness, flexibility, informality, and the capability of sifting technical evidence, some formal control over them is desirable. This is all the more essential since their work is mostly routine and therefore fails to attract in the Press the publicity which surrounds the courts. Hence control is exercised by the courts and the Council on Tribunals.

(1) The Courts

Apart from special provisions for appeal outlined above, the decisions of administrative tribunals are subject to review by the courts.

Administrative tribunals must act within the limits of their jurisdiction and within the prescribed procedure. If they do not, they can be prevented from adjudicating by an order of prohibition, or the case may be removed to the Queen's Bench Division of the High Court and any decision previously given quashed by an order of certiorari. Moreover, since they are giving quasi-judicial decisions, they are, as inferior courts, subject to the control of the High Court. Although proceedings need not be conducted as in a court of law (*Local Government Board v. Arlidge, 1915*), tribunals must observe the rules of natural justice or their judgment will be set aside.

Indeed this now applies to all cases where officials have power to make decisions affecting the rights of individuals. The exercise of such powers is not a purely administrative function (as it was held in *Franklin v. Minister of Town and Country Planning, 1948*). The official must act judicially in accordance with the rules of natural justice, and the Courts can interfere if they consider that this has not be done (*Ridge v. Baldwin, 1964*).

Now that 'conclusive evidence' and 'as if enacted in this Act' clauses have virtually ceased being used, the powers of the Courts to review cases have been increased, for such clauses almost eliminated the possibility of judicial supervision. Moreover, the Tribunals and Enquiries Act, 1958, provided that where an Act stated that a ministerial decision 'shall be final and not subject to appeal in any court of law', it should not prevent review by the High Court by way of *certiorari* or *mandamus*.

(2) The Council on Tribunals

As a result of a recommendation of the Franks Committee, a Council on Tribunals was established to keep the constitution and working of tribunals and enquiries under constant review. The Council, which has a special Scottish Committee, is appointed jointly by the Lord Chancellor and the Secretary of State for Scotland.

Legally, the Council's powers are of an advisory nature only. In practice, it has been shown that the supervision it exercises can have far-reaching effects.

First, it consults with government departments about rules of procedure for tribunals and inquiries, and about proposals for the establishment of new tribunals. Thus the Council can exert a direct influence on the future development of the tribunal and inquiry system — as was shown by the Chalkpit Case, 1959, as follows.

The Franks Committee had made recommendations for improving procedure at public enquiries and for challenging decisions in the High Court on the grounds of jurisdiction or procedure. These recommendations were accepted and the Town and Country Planning Act, 1959, gave the Lord Chancellor power to make rules for regulating the procedure for *all* statutory enquiries. But the Chalkpit case revealed a gap in the law. The Minister of Agriculture, contrary to the report of his inspector at a public enquiry, proceeded to grant permission for chalk-digging on land in Essex. It was held that the people affected could not appeal because they had no legal right infringed. The Council on Tribunals called the Lord Chancellor's attention to this defect. Hence, in 1962, he made rules of procedure for enquiries on compulsory acquisition by local authorities and on planning appeals.

Secondly, the Council considers complaints from members of the public who think that the procedure has not given them a fair hearing. If necessary the complaint is discussed with the department concerned and, in the last resort, the Council can make and publish a special report to the Lord Chancellor and the Secretary of State for Scotland. With regard to this aspect of the Council's work, *The Times* described the Council as the 'trailblazer' for the Parliamentary Commissioner.

(3) *The Parliamentary Commissioner for Administration*

Alternatively, complaints of personal injustice can be taken up by M.P.s with the Parliamentary Commissioner (see page 322).

Not all the recommendations of the Franks Committee were accepted by the Government. The appointment of inspectors has not been transferred from ministers to the Lord Chancellor, since it was thought that this might throw too much work upon him. Service departments still hold a privileged position in acquiring land. Nor did the Government agree to suggestions for the extension of legal aid and the award of costs to tribunals. But more regularity has now been brought into the proceedings of tribunals, thereby going a long way towards meeting the most important criticisms.

SUGGESTED READING

Report of the Committee on Administrative Tribunals and Enquiries, 1957 (Cmd. 218, H.M.S.O.).

H. J. Elcoch, *Administrative Justice* (Longmans, 1969).

R. M. Jackson, *The Machinery of Justice in England* (6th Ed., C.U.P., 1972), Chapter 6.

H. Street, *Justice in the Welfare State* (Stevens, 1968).

G. W. Keeton, *Trial by Tribunal* (Museum Press, 1960).

H. W. R. Wade, *Administrative Law* (3rd Ed., O.U.P., 1971), Chapters 5, 6 and 7.

23

The Rule of Law

'Ancient Right unnoticed as the breath we draw —
Leave to live by no man's leave, underneath the Law.'
RUDYARD KIPLING: *The Old Issue*

THE BROAD MEANING OF THE RULE OF LAW

The problem of government which the constitution seeks to solve is, as we have seen, how to give sufficient power to the country's rulers to allow them to govern efficiently and yet be assured that they will not encroach unreasonably on the fundamental liberties of the individual by seizing more power than was intended, or interfering arbitrarily in his way of life. The granting of sufficient power is achieved through 'parliamentary sovereignty' — the legal right that Parliament enjoys of passing any law it likes. Individual liberty is said to be protected by the 'rule of law' — the restriction of government action to that authorised by law. As indicated in chapter 2, however, there are obstacles to the full acceptance of this theory, and it is these which must now be examined.

The law has two purposes. On the one hand, it restricts the actions of individuals. On the other, it protects the individual by defining the powers granted to those in authority. Both ideas were recognised in Greek and Roman times. St. Paul, for instance, while submitting to the law, stood firmly on the rights which the law afforded him. 'Is it lawful for you to scourge a man that is a Roman, and uncondemned?' he demanded of the centurion (*Acts*, ch. 22, v. 25). Later, before the Jewish Council, he rebukes Ananias: 'God shall smite thee, thou whited wall: for sittest thou to judge me after the law, and commandest me to be smitten contrary to the law?' (*Acts*, ch. 23, v. 3).

Englishmen, too, have always put a large measure of faith in the law, expecting it to be applied, but demanding that it shall be as binding on the authorities as on the individual. The general complaint of the barons at Runnymede was the failure of John to observe the ancient customs of the realm (what today would be referred to as the 'common law'), and the real significance of Magna Carta is that it embodied the idea of a law which was supreme over the King himself. The Petition of Right, 1628, followed the same line of thought, being a petition to the King to observe the existing law of the land, which was as binding on him as on his subjects. In 1763 the idea was tested before the courts. John Wilkes, a Member of Parliament and publisher of the 'North Briton', was arrested on a general warrant (that is, one not specifically describing the place to be searched or the persons or things to be seized) because he had attacked the King's speech. His award of £1,000 damages against the Home Secretary for wrongful arrest demonstrated that Government officials were not shielded from the ordinary law of the land.

Thus our constitution has grown up recognising a rule of law. When the man in the street, aggrieved by some act of his neighbour, says, 'I'll have the law on you,' he is merely expressing his faith that the Law 'rules' and, in doing so, endorses a sentiment which goes back at least a thousand years. Or, as George Orwell puts it, in England 'the totalitarian idea that there is no such thing as law, there is only power, has never taken root' (*England Your England*).

DICEY'S 'RULE OF LAW'

Towards the end of the 19th century Professor A. V. Dicey, developing this idea, spoke of the 'rule of law'. He considered it to be *the* fundamental principle of the British constitution, and in order to give it precision, he resolved it into three distinct propositions.

(1) '*No man is punishable or can be lawfully made to suffer in body or goods, except for a distinct breach of the law established in the ordinary legal manner before the ordinary courts of the land.*'

This emphasises the supremacy of the law, and that penalties can only be imposed by the judiciary in a prescribed manner. Every citizen has the right to personal liberty unless: (*a*) he has broken the law; (*b*) this breach has been proved according to the procedure which the law stipulates; (*c*) the proof has been established in the *ordinary courts of the land*. All three conditions must apply at one and the same time.

While these requirements seem fairly commonplace today, we

need only look back a comparatively short period in our history to see that they have not always applied. Under James I, Sir Walter Raleigh was imprisoned in the Tower of London without any definite charge being preferred against him. In 1627 the judges of the King's Bench themselves upheld that it was sufficient return to a writ of Habeas Corpus to certify that the prisoner was detained by 'special order of the King'. No wonder then that the second clause of the Petition of Right declared that all arbitrary imprisonment without cause shown was illegal. Similarly, during the same period, extraordinary tribunals outside the ordinary courts of the land were in existence. These were the Court of Star Chamber and the Court of High Commission, both of which were under the authority of the King. Although these Courts had just been abolished, the Grand Remonstrance, 1641, put on record its protest against the injustices perpetrated by them.

Much was done in the later Stuart period to secure the liberty of the subject. The Petition of Right's declaration against arbitrary imprisonment and the abolition of the two prerogative Courts were the first steps. In 1679 the Habeas Corpus Act provided a further safeguard, for it laid down a specific procedure which could be followed by a detained person. Finally, by the Act of Settlement, 1701, judges were removed from the control of the executive.

(2) *'Not only is no man above the law, but every man, whatever his rank or condition, is subject to the ordinary law of the realm and amenable to the jurisdiction of the ordinary tribunals.'*

Here Dicey draws attention to the fact that, not only does the law make no distinction between different classes of persons, but it applies as much to the official as to the ordinary person, both having to obey it. Moreover, any dispute between the private person and the official is decided in the ordinary courts of law, unlike France whose system of 'droit administratif' decides such a case in an *administrative* court.

(3) *'With us, the law of the constitution, the rules which in foreign countries naturally form part of a constitutional code, are not the source, but the consequence, of the rights of individuals as defined and enforced by the Courts.'*

Dicey means by this that our freedom is not preserved by any general principles embodied in the constitution, like the 'Declaration of Rights' in America. With us, the rights of the individual transcend the constitution, existing before it and not being guaranteed by it. What these rights do depend on is the law of the land. Freedom of the person, freedom of speech, freedom of public meeting have not had to be declared; they exist simply because they do not offend the law, though it is quite usual to speak of them as 'common law' rights. Because the right to personal liberty was being set aside by the Stuarts, Parliament had to provide the means, through habeas corpus, by which the individual could vindicate it, and followed this later by allowing him to sue for damages upon wrongful arrest or false imprisonment and for assault where illegal restraint is alleged to have been imposed. The freedoms of speech and of public meeting are not thwarted by the laws concerning libel, slander, sedition, blasphemy and unlawful assembly, for these merely aim to stop abuse of them. Moreover, disputes between the private person and the official have been decided in the courts, which have simply extended the principles of law (that is, have implemented the 'rule of law') to determine the respective rights of the citizen and the Crown.

Hence, the constitution is the result of the ordinary law of the land, for its general principles have evolved from the rights of individuals as upheld by the courts in specific cases. This is in marked contrast with many a written constitution in which the rights of the individual are declared. But such rights are no less secure in Britain. In fact, as Dicey points out, at the height of the Revolution in 1791, when the French constitution proclaimed liberty of conscience, freedom of the Press and the right of public meeting, the people of France found them to be extremely precarious.

CRITICISM OF DICEY'S EXPOSITION

There has been some controversy as to whether the 'rule of law' ought to be accepted as an essential principle of the British constitution. The chief critic was Sir W. Ivor Jennings (*The Law and the Constitution*), who attacked Dicey's views on two main grounds.

(1) *The analysis over-stresses the importance of individual rights*

Although Dicey's *Law of the Constitution* is a scholarly work, its interpretation tends to be subjective. A *laissez-faire* philosophy still prevailed when the first edition was published in 1885. Dicey himself was a Liberal, and also a lawyer steeped in the principles of the common law. The whole background of his thinking, therefore, tended to emphasise the importance of the individual, the holder of certain unalienable rights which the Government should not infringe. His exposition would have placed less stress on individual rights had he allowed for the possibility of a new political philosophy which considered that the State should undertake public service functions, and not merely those of public control.

A planned economy and a 'Welfare State' necessitate the grant of discretionary powers to government officials. A tenant, for instance, in the interests of efficient husbandry, may be dispossessed of his land, while, in order to build schools and hospitals, construct new roads, clear slums, and plan the lay-out of towns, houses and shops may be compulsorily acquired from the owners and then demolished. Government officials, moreover, come into much more frequent contact with the individual, and persons are naturally prone to question the decision of the authorities when they feel it has affected them adversely. To settle these disputes it has been necessary, as we saw in chapter 22, for Parliament to establish a complex system of administrative tribunals outside the system of the ordinary courts and following a different procedure. As regards the second proposition in particular, Jennings takes Dicey to task for failing to recognise that administrative law, although relatively insignificant in comparison with the comprehensive system of 'droit administratif' in France, did exist and had existed for many centuries in England. In Henry VIII's reign, the Statute of Sewers had permitted various Commissioners for Sewers to make rules and to try offenders in their own courts. Even before Dicey was writing, these powers were beginning to increase, such bodies as railway companies and municipal authorities exercising the right to make their own bye-laws and regulations. The Public Health Act, 1875, for example, gave the urban and rural sanitary authorities many powers to coerce, provisions which had considerable significance for the age of the 'public service' State which it inaugurated.

(2) *The assertion of the third proposition that the constitution depends on the law is unjustified*

If we were to ask the question, 'On what does democracy depend in the British constitution?' Dicey would reply that it rests on the rule of law, since this means that the courts will apply remedies to ensure that no authority can continue to exceed the powers granted to it by the law. Sir Ivor Jennings disputes this, arguing as follows. Obviously, the rule of law does not mean simply that there is law and order, for this existed, for example, under Louis XIV, an absolute monarch. The courts merely enforce the law as it exists, but there is no guarantee that it will be 'good' law. In Britain, because Parliament is sovereign, it can make any laws it likes. Extensive powers can be granted to the Government to order the individual's way of life and to appropriate his property. This was done, in fact, in both World Wars, by the Defence of the Realm Act, 1914, and the Emergency Powers Act, 1939. Parliament could even strike a mortal blow at democracy by abolishing free elections. Moreover, where it does not like the way the courts interpret its statutes, it can pass further legislation. No rule of law can restrain Parliament, and hence there would be more justification in regarding the supremacy of Parliament as *the* fundamental principle of the constitution. In any case, Dicey's propositions encounter so many difficulties that any attempt to give a precise definition to the term 'rule of law' is undermined. The most we can do is to indicate certain notions which it implies. These are that governmental powers must be distributed and determined by reasonably precise laws, and that in matters of government there must be liberty and equality for all citizens. In essence, however, this represents little difference from an analysis of 'democracy'. Neither the 'rule of law' nor the 'separation of powers' guarantees democracy; they are simply the concomitants of it. Dicey's argument gets nowhere, since the way in which he attempts to separate the law and the constitution is quite impossible.

THE RULE OF LAW TODAY

Dicey's analysis of the rule of law failed, Jennings considers, because he was subjective in his approach, his propositions merely formulating a 'rule of policy for Whigs'. Yet we cannot take this criticism as the last word. Jennings too was writing in a special period, the first edition of *The Law and the Constitution* appearing in 1933, before the real meaning and consequences of government by dictatorship had been fully appreciated. His criticism of Dicey's first two propositions shows that there are difficulties in trying to give too much precision to the rule of law. On the other hand, vagueness is no proof of non-existence. To accept Jennings' views in their entirety is almost equivalent to saying that the principle of the rule of law has had no great practical effect on the development of our institutions and that it has similarly little influence on the constitution today.

But this is not so. Modifications may have to be made to Dicey's propositions to allow for the development of the modern State, but the basic ideas which they express have been, and still are, very real in their influence on government. As regards the first proposition, ordinary civil and criminal law procedure continues to follow a pattern consistent with his description, and it would be intolerable if it were otherwise. In these matters, no person is allowed to act arbitrarily, and punishment can only follow a breach of the law established in a prescribed manner in accepted courts of law. Personal liberty is protected by the writ of habeas corpus, by the possibility of seeking damages for false imprisonment or of prosecuting for illegal restraint, and by the right to ask an appeal court to set aside a judgment which has not been arrived at according to the prescribed procedure and the rules of 'natural justice' — open hearing before known judges, equal opportunities for each side to state its case, the application of established principles in reaching a decision.

But while civil and criminal law are administered in the same spirit as they were in Dicey's day, the acceptance of government planning and the Welfare State has led to departures from Dicey's proposition. Criticisms of delegated legislation were made in chapter 21. The essence of Dicey's rule of law is certainty for the individual, but the number, complexity and frequency of change of orders and regulations make it difficult for the individual to know exactly what the law is and thus to plan his actions so as not to break it. Special tribunals have also been developed and the discretionary powers of government departments extended in order to assist the administration of the public service State (see chapter 22).

Yet these developments do not invalidate Dicey's first proposition. In fact, they make its recognition even more essential, compelling it to be used as a yard-stick of their ultimate desirability. Thus it was the spirit expressed by the rule of law which led to the passing of the Statutory Instruments Act, 1946, and the setting up of the Franks Committee, 1955. It was this same spirit which allows and requires the Courts, when examining the actions of the executive, to look further than mere superficial legality and to decide whether the procedure has been carried out fairly and, indeed, as in the Enfield School affair, 1967, with due propriety of motive. Concern for the maintenance of the rule of law also lies behind the watch which is kept on Parliament's grant of discretionary powers in order to ensure that the parent Act lays down the general lines upon which they shall be exercised so that the courts can restrain any attempts to exceed them.

In the same way, there are exceptions to Dicey's second proposition. There can be no complete equality before the law while rich persons are able to engage a better counsel than poor persons, though here again the Legal Aid scheme has done something to remedy this defect. Nor is everybody amenable to the ordinary courts. Both Houses of Parliament punish for breach of privilege. Foreign diplomats are exempt from the English courts. Separate callings, such as the Law, Church, and Armed Forces, have their own procedures. Moreover, such officials as the police, health inspectors, and local authority welfare officers, have rights not possessed by other persons. These raise no constitutional difficulties, and Dicey was merely emphasising that they were liable to the courts for any excess use of their power, though, as Jennings observes, this is but 'a small point on which to base a doctrine called by the magnificent name of the "rule of law" '.

Nevertheless, although the rule of law may not exist in the form of Dicey's static doctrine, the term gives expression to a concept which is generally accepted by people irrespective of personal political views. The idea is best defined in the following conditions:

(1) *The freedom of the individual must be restrained only under the authority of the law*

The Government and its officials are no more free to act outside the law than anyone else. Parliament can change the law, but this does not violate the principle, provided that the individual, through his legal adviser, can be reasonably aware of what the law is. He can then plan his conduct accordingly and seek to modify the law if he so wishes.

Moreover, a distinction must be drawn between arbitrary and discretionary powers. The former are a complete violation of the rule of law, for those administering the law are then also responsible for making it and punishing breaches of it. Discretionary powers are, however, necessary to some degree in all societies and, in the modern State, are vital. Thus, if Parliament entrusts a minister with the task of providing for the defence of the country, it must allow him discretion in acquiring land for rocket sites, training areas, etc. The result may be that individuals cannot make plans with complete certainty, but should the Government be unable to promise them defence against enemy attack, they have no guarantee in any case of what may lie ahead. The essential meaning of the rule of law is maintained if discretionary powers are felt to be reasonable, to be clearly defined as to the manner in which they shall be exercised, and to give due consideration to the rights of the individuals likely to be affected. Thus Parliament must have adequate control over delegated legislation (for the courts can invalidate only those acts which are *ultra vires*), and individuals must receive fair compensation when their property suffers through the use of discretionary powers.

(2) *Justice must be regarded as an end in itself*

In the ordinary courts, it is clearly recognised that decisions must be given in accordance with the law and not the needs of policy. To this end, judges have been made independent of politicians and administrators. Recently, however, there has been controversy over the application of some politically controversial legislation under the rule of law. A leading trade union, the Amalgamated Union of Engineering Workers, refused to recognise any institutions set up under the Industrial Relations Act, 1971, including the Industrial Relations Court, by whom in 1973 it was fined £75,000 for contempt in not complying with the Court's order to end a strike at a small factory. When the Union failed to pay the fine, the Court sequestrated £75,000 from its political fund and this led 182 M.P.s to sign a motion urging the dismissal of Sir John Donaldson, President of the National Industrial Relations Court, a motion which was denounced by the Lord Chancellor, Lord Hailsham, in a speech at the Junior Carlton Club, as a threat to the rule of law. If M.P.s who are displeased with judicial decisions attack the judge and seek his dismissal, support for the rule of law may well be undermined. On the other hand, the Lord Chancellor's speech appealing 'to the voters of this country to note the identity of the members concerned, to note the party to which they belong, to sound the alarm', was thought by some to be couched in words not well chosen to give the impression of a politically neutral and constitutionally independent judiciary.

Moreover at the time of this refusal to accept a court ruling, various Labour-controlled local authorities threatened to refuse to accept the Conservative Government's Housing Finance Act, 1972, which increased rents on Council dwellings, but introduced a system of rent rebates for poorer tenants. While other rebellious councils gradually and reluctantly accepted the law, eleven councillors of Clay Cross, Derbyshire, persisted in refusing to levy higher rents and also broke the Government's pay code by giving unlawful pay rises to its labour force. As a result, the Government had to appoint a Housing Commissioner to run housing in Clay Cross, the councillors were taken to court, surcharged and fined and disqualified from holding office. At the Labour Party conference in October 1973, a resolution was passed calling upon a future Labour government to remove retrospectively 'all penalties, financial or otherwise' from councillors who had failed to carry out the law. However, when Mr. Wilson became Prime Minister, he told the House of Commons that the law of the land must be obeyed until it is repealed and announced that there would be no retrospective legislation to remove financial penalties. Mr. Wedgwood Benn has argued that one of the principles of parliamentary democracy is the 'supremacy of conscience over the law'. If this were interpreted to mean that citizens, individually or collectively, can ignore the laws of a democratically-elected Parliament on grounds of conscience and that a future government of a different political persuasion may then remove from them the penalties already imposed by the law, then the independence of the courts and respect for the law might well be undermined, and against this background followers of the Opposition might well be encouraged to flout the law in the expectation of a future indemnity. Under the British constitution, it is understood that Parliament may repeal any law but that the rule of law requires that Parliament should not tamper with the way the courts apply existing law.

Through the principle of parliamentary sovereignty, a democratically-elected Parliament makes the laws; according to the principle of the rule of law, the courts are free, impartial and unfettered in applying them to particular cases. As Sir John

Donaldson explained, Parliament writes the music; the courts, whether they like it or not, have to play it. Sir John argued that it is fundamental that the two roles should not be confused: 'The independence of the courts and a realisation that they have nothing to do with making, repealing or amending the laws they administer, lies at the heart of the rule of law and British Parliamentary democracy'.

Furthermore a strict watch must be kept on administrative tribunals. While they need not follow the exact procedure of the ordinary courts, they must inspire confidence in their impartiality by having neutral judges and observing the rules of natural justice. Generally they work well and, as we saw in chapter 22, reforms have been made to secure greater adherence to these principles.

One final question concerns Dicey's third proposition. Is there any justification for his assertion that the constitution is the result of the protection given by the law to the rights of individuals? Or is Jennings' opinion correct, that our constitution is not dependent on the rule of law but on the prevailing political philosophy of the British people? Here again, we consider that the weight of argument still rests with Dicey. Jennings is right in that, in the final analysis, the attitude of the British people is the ultimate guardian of their freedom. No institutional arrangements, such as Parliament or elections, can guarantee it, for unless citizens are prepared to resist, unscrupulous Governments can amend the law to abolish Parliament and elections. The rule of law itself is valueless if the laws made are not consonant with what the people really want. As Judge Learned Hand, the American lawyer, says: 'Liberty lies in the hearts of men and women; when it dies there, no constitution, no law, no court can save it' (*The Spirit of Liberty*).

But Jennings' weakness rests in his failure to stress that a part of the philosophy of the British people is fundamental and enduring. When we reflect on what every man really holds dear — the right to plan and live his own life free from undue interference — the change to the public service State which Jennings emphasises can be regarded simply as progress towards this main aim and, in any case, merely as marginal. At heart the British, indeed all peoples of the free world, feel deeply regarding the importance of the individual. This is a principle which goes far back into their history. It is central to the Christian religion, upon which they have been nurtured. It is implicit in the maintenance of human dignity, to which they firmly adhere. It is essential to their concept of civilisation, for a civilised man must be able to cultivate some independence of spirit and be secure in the freedom to observe, read, think and speak.

The true philosophy, Lord Lindsay considers, is illustrated in Colonel Rainsborough's observance in 1647: 'I think the poorest he that is in England hath a life to live as the richest he.' Upon this Lord Lindsay's comment is: 'That seems to me the authentic note of democracy. The poorest has his own life *to live*, not to be managed or drilled or used by other people. His life is his and he has to live it. None can divest him of that responsibility' (*The Essentials of Democracy*).

So long as men accept this as the aim of democracy, they will cherish certain fundamental rights, and it is upon these that the constitution will be built. Neither the rule of law, nor any other principle of the constitution — free elections, the supremacy of Parliament, the separation of powers, the right to criticise the Government — can, on its own, guarantee the preservation of democracy against arbitrary government. But, in conjunction with these, the rule of law, by its insistence on governmental powers being defined, affords that certainty to the individual which is essential if he is to be free to lead and plan his own life.

SUGGESTED READING

A. V. Dicey, *Introduction to the Law of the Constitution* (10th Ed., Macmillan, 1961), Introduction by E. C. S. Wade, Part II, Chapters 4, 10 and 14.

Lord Hewart, *The New Despotism* (Rev. Ed., E. Benn, 1945), Chapter 2.

Sir Ivor Jennings, *The Law and the Constitution* (4th Ed., University of London, 1955), Chapter 2, Section 1, Appendix II.

E. C. S. Wade and G. G. Phillips, *Constitutional Law* (8th Ed., Longmans 1970), Part II, Chapter 3.

D. C. M. Yardley, *Introduction to British Constitutional Law* (Butterworth, 1969).

V

LOCAL GOVERNMENT

24

The Functions of Local Authorities

'As I see it, when you come to the bottom, all this local
government, it's just working together — us ordinary
people, against the troubles that afflict all of us —
poverty, ignorance, sickness, isolation, — madness!'
WINIFRED HOLTBY: *South Riding*

I. REASONS FOR LOCAL GOVERNMENT

At first sight, it may seem odd that local government has been
preserved in the United Kingdom. Not only is the country
relatively small and homogeneous, but certain aspects of the constitution suggest that further provision for local administration is
superfluous. Parliament alone has legal sovereignty, and within its
walls the main political dramas are enacted, fundamental decisions
are taken, and political leaders receive publicity and recognition.
On the other hand, parties are organised on a local basis and people
vote for a member who represents quite a small constituency and
can be relied upon to put forward in Parliament the views and
difficulties of his locality.

Moreover, the Government has at its disposal a highly efficient
administrative machine which is quite capable of applying its
decisions to every town and village throughout the land. Centralisation facilitates co-ordination, permits large-scale economies,
secures uniformity of standards, and provides buoyant sources of
income which make it easier to develop services. In the last thirty
years, the central government has assumed control over health,
poor relief and many municipal public utility undertakings. Why,
therefore, do we continue with the additional paraphernalia of local
administration? Would anything be lost if the whole apparatus of
local government were to be scrapped next week?

There are in fact numerous advantages in retaining a system of
local government. In the first place, local government is more

than local administration. Local councils are elected by people locally and are directly accountable to them for their actions. In contrast, where there is merely local administration, e.g. gas and electricity boards, health and water authorities, a decentralised post office and social security services, control comes from above through Parliament, ministers and the courts of law.

Secondly, councillors being accountable to a local electorate have to be responsive to local needs. In itself, local control of affairs permits variation in government according to differences in local needs, character and circumstances. A rural area will probably want different kinds of schools from a large, densely-populated town. Town and country planning cannot be uniformly applied. The requirements of a police force differ from one part of the country to another. Such functions, therefore, are largely left for local administration. Each area, too, has its own special difficulties. Local schools may be housed in ancient, dingy buildings and find difficulty in attracting teachers; congestion on the town's roads may seriously lessen the efficiency of local industry and lead to deaths and injuries through accidents; a jungle of over-crowded houses in squalid streets may increase juvenile crime and social discontent. In solving such problems, it is desirable to enlist the help of local leaders to allow the people most affected a chance to choose between alternative proposals. 'The very object of having a local representation', says J. S. Mill, 'is in order that those who have any interest in common which they do not share with the general body of their countrymen may manage that joint interest by themselves' (*Representative Government*). If such local responsibility were to be replaced by administration from Whitehall, individuality of approach would give way to uniformity, and adaptability be superseded by rigidity. Could we expect Parliament, which has so many matters to discuss already, to debate whether a swimming-pool should be built in Cardiff, how fast slum clearance should proceed in London, or what scheme should be adopted for the relief of traffic in Oxford? To what extent, too, could we expect a government department to experiment? Would it exhibit the same initiative as Manchester, for example, which, when faced with a serious smog problem, pioneered the development of a smokeless zone? However, hostility need not develop between the two forms of government. While Parliament still decides overall policy, the minister will act as a counsellor, prompting, encouraging and co-ordinating the work of the local authorities.

Thirdly, direct responsibility for the government of a locality can harness powerful forces on behalf of the community. Local interests see a constant and direct relation between the efforts and sacrifices they make and the benefits enjoyed. Civic consciousness is aroused, a tradition built up and local pride fostered. Moreover, the raising of a large proportion of the funds locally encourages true economy, though at times some smaller authorities tend to be parsimonious with a consequent reduction in the services provided.

Fourthly, local government produces continuity of policy. The party conflict in local politics is still not nearly so acute as it is for Parliament, chiefly because local authorities are much more concerned with administrative matters than with broad political theories. Hence, councillors of whatever shade of opinion find it easy to serve together on committees in order to secure the efficient working of local services.

Fifthly, local administration is valuable in itself since it provides people with extra opportunities for taking an active part in the government of the country. Such wide and direct participation is essential to preserve democracy and to eliminate the risk of the nation being governed by a relatively small group of professional politicians or administrators. It is through local government that many M.P.s learn their first political lessons and, while there are other training grounds, such as trade unions, these tend to be somewhat narrow and specialised. The councillor, on the other hand, has to seek election from the general public, to be readily available to give advice and receive complaints from the rate-payers, and to share responsibility for making decisions on a wide variety of matters. Officials, too, are usually local men or women, primarily concerned with local needs and not with departmental policy. Their first loyalty is to the local people, not to the central department employing them, as would most likely be the case if they were civil servants. The public, above all, feel a more intimate contact with their own local administration. How a colony should be administered may be of little concern to them; but they are interested in the type of schools their children go to, how often their refuse is collected, and the state of repair of their roads and pavements. Moreover, having had the opportunity to vote on such matters, they are happier about the administrative measures which follow. In any case, they can take the matter up with a councillor who, as a local man, will, they feel, appreciate their point of view. Failing that, the local Press is only too ready to publish a letter airing a grievance. Local officials are more likely to avoid the frustration which results from the bureaucracy of a central government department. They tend to be more permanent, and so become better known through constant contact with the public. Decisions are arrived at locally, thereby avoiding delay and the impersonal process of long letter-writing. Thus interest and confidence in government is promoted.

Lastly, it is healthy to have a division of power between the central government and local authorities (see chapter 24). Although tension between the two does occur from time to time, this often serves the purpose of reminding Westminster that it is not sufficient to command but that continual consideration must be given to the feelings of even small groups of people.

Not that all these possible advantages are necessarily enjoyed. There is much public indifference, the percentage of the poll at local elections being only half what it is for Parliament. Local government, too, has its own form of bureaucracy in which the councillors, as committee members, themselves share, and here the remedy is less effective than the simple process of seeing the M.P. who represents the constituency. Sometimes local councillors are more extreme and intolerant of the wishes of minorities than national parties. Moreover, in the larger authorities, contact between the electors and their representatives and officials can sometimes be almost as remote as in central affairs, with the result that responsibility has to be enforced almost entirely through the party system. Nor must we overlook that local government may suffer from incompetence and, more rarely, from corruption.

II. Development of the Structure of English Local Government

To a foreigner, particularly a Frenchman or German, our system of local government would probably seem the least satisfactory part of our constitution, In many ways, since there has never been any complete re-planning, it is, unlike his own pattern, untidy and irregular. English local government is, to a large extent, still largely based on areas which were determined in Saxon times. Thus local loyalties were established before transport developments made reform possible. Hence, in making changes, Parliament has been restricted by having to take account of the views and interests of existing authorities. A strong local spirit makes boundary reform difficult, while a council which has taxed itself to provide a full range of services resents amalgamation with a backward neighbour. Outside interests, too, have had to be considered. The many variations which still exist in State-aided schools are partly the result of the concessions which have had to be made to the wishes of the various religious denominations. Finally, timid governments have recoiled from the task of reform, either because they felt it was too big an undertaking, or because it offered little political reward. Free from the possibility of invasion, there has been no necessity for efficient organisation on a regional basis, while the absence of any dictatorial form of government has excluded the ruthless imposition of reform.

THE LAYING OF THE FOUNDATIONS

Before the Norman conquest, England was divided into shires (under an Ealdorman), each shire into a Hundred (under a shire-reeve), or Wapentake in the north of the country, and each Hundred into Tuns or Parishes (under a reeve). The parish became closely linked with the manorial system, and it was the custom for the inhabitants of each parish to meet together in the church vestry for local business, which was mostly concerned with agriculture or fortifications. But the Norman kings were always mindful to curb the growth of local power, and so the importance of the ealdorman and sheriff declined, especially as the influence of the courts at Westminster was extended throughout the country by the justices in eyre.

Moreover, the new Justices of the Peace, established in 1327, soon acquired administrative as well as judicial functions. Their work was increased by the upheaval of the Black Death, 1349, and it was arranged that they should co-operate with the local parishes in such matters as the maintenance of bridges and footpaths, the care of straying animals, and the supervision of vagrants. Under the Tudors, the importance of the J.P. increased. An Act of 1555 made him responsible for supervising the work of the parishes with regard to bridges and highways. The parish vestries had to appoint an Overseer of Highways, and each parishioner was required to do four days' work a year on the roads. (Eventually the custom grew up by which people paid a rate so that labour could be hired to do the work). Moreover, when the Poor Law of 1601 provided for the relief of the poor, the parish was made the responsible unit. It had to raise and collect a poor rate and appoint an Overseer of the poor, all these responsibilities being supervised by a J.P.

In the meantime, the boroughs had developed a more comprehensive system of local government. Certain of them, anxious to free themselves from the power of a great lord, secured from the King, usually in return for a money payment, privileges which were set out in a charter. Such privileges included the right to send two members to Parliament, to provide for their own government, and to have local courts. These boroughs had a small governing body, usually formed from the merchant guilds, which generally conducted its business in the guild hall. Both parishes and boroughs came under the close supervision of the Privy Council and the Court of Star Chamber.

Local government fell apart during the Civil War and central control by the Privy Council was not restored in 1660. Instead, government was divided into two parts, parliamentary and local. The latter, left entirely to itself, was administered by the parishes, supervised by the J.P.s, and the borough corporations, which were mostly corrupt and shirked their duties. The only form of control was through the courts; that is, it was judicial and not administrative. When a parishioner failed to carry out the Overseer's directions, he could be sued in the courts, a costly and lengthy procedure.

THE EFFECTS OF THE INDUSTRIAL REVOLUTION

At the end of the 18th century, therefore, local government was still based on ancient divisions and on the principle that service should be compulsory and unpaid. This gave useful training in the work of government, but it led to avoidance of duties. The mixture of judicial and administrative control through the J.P.s, while emphasising that all government is based on law, led to the bare legal minimum being performed and to laxity in enforcement on account of the trouble and expense involved. The result was inefficiency and corruption. The vestries of the parishes often became 'closed' bodies, permanently controlled by a local oligarchy which filled vacancies by co-option. Profits were made out of the commuted payments of the local inhabitants who wished to avoid unpaid parish duties. The corporations of the boroughs were no better. They too were often closed bodies, and sometimes the mayor did not attend even to be sworn into office. Jobbery was rife, and membership of the corporation was regarded solely as a source of illegal gain.

Not surprisingly, the system broke down under the stresses of the Industrial Revolution. Apart from its corrupt nature, it had been designed solely for a simple agrarian society. Large industrial cities, such as Manchester, Leeds, Birmingham, Bradford and Halifax, still had the old feudal form of government based on the parish and J.P. The local councils were either indifferent to or incapable of dealing with the squalor around them. Charles Dickens portrayed the harsh conditions of an England that was rapidly being industrialised. In his *Sketches by Boz*, 1833, he writes: 'How much is conveyed in those two short words — "The Parish!" And with how many tales of distress and misery, of broken fortune and ruined hopes, too often of unrelieved wretchedness and successful knavery, are they associated!' Furthermore, local deficiencies were not made good by the central government. Indeed, throughout the 18th century, the problem was avoided. New *ad hoc* bodies, local 'Improvement Commissioners', were appointed to deal with such problems as water supply, sewers, street paving and lighting. Both these and the Turnpike Trusts, which were responsible for certain stretches of road, were established by Act of Parliament and, although they were semi-private bodies, they had the power to levy a rate and make charges, and included some elected representatives.

Although economic factors produced a breakdown of local government, nothing was done until the political climate changed in the 1830s. Even then, enthusiasm died out after the passing of two Acts, the Poor Law Amendment Act, 1834, and the Municipal Corporations Act, 1835. The first was a logical attack on a specific problem — the vast increase in poor relief which had followed the adoption of the 'Speenhamland system'. It was based on the ideas of Jeremy Bentham, who had long advocated the introduction of a coherent local government system, and its driving force was Edwin Chadwick. The Act applied three great principles to English local government: (1) an *ad hoc* authority, the local Boards of Guardians, responsible within a given area for a single service, the relief of the poor; (2) an area, the Union of Parishes, appropriate to the function to be performed; (3) central control, through the three Poor Law Commissioners. 'The Poor Law Commission initiated that system of partnership between Whitehall and the local authorities which with varying fortunes has survived as the essence of the system to the present day' (Professor Smellie). Poor relief was now made more stringent. The able-bodied pauper had to be less favourably placed than the lowest-paid labourer, and people were to be deterred from pauperism by the 'workhouse test'. But when the system was attacked, the Commission had no representative in Parliament to defend it. Consequently, in 1847 it was replaced by the Poor Law Board, whose President sat in the House of Commons.

The Municipal Corporations Act, 1835, reorganised government in the towns and initiated a system of *elected* councils for all purposes of town government. While a high property qualification for councillors was inserted into the Act, all ratepayers with three years' residence in the town were qualified to vote. Provision was made for the co-option of aldermen, the proper appointment of the Mayor, Town Clerk and Treasurer, the regular audit of accounts, and the admission of the public to council meetings. Magistrates were separated from municipal administration and their appointment was transferred to the Crown. A process was also laid down by which towns could achieve municipal borough status. Thus ended the privilege and corruption of 19th-century local government.

But in many ways the Act suffered from serious defects which laid up trouble for the future. Unlike the Poor Law Amendment Act, it was inspired by no general principles. Since it perpetuated obsolete areas, the size of boroughs varied from the new large industrial area to the small market town. Such disparity made it difficult to frame general functions and powers, and so these were limited to establishing a Watch Committee for control of the police, providing street lighting, regulating licensed premises, and making by-laws for securing order. No functions of the independent bodies, such as the Improvement Commissioners, were transferred to the new municipal councils, and no definite provision was made for adding to their powers later. Additional functions came piece-meal (as when the borough councils were made urban health authorities in 1872) or by the promotion of private bills (as in Birmingham under the leadership of Joseph Chamberlain). Above all, there was no central control, except in a few minor details.

THE SETTING-UP OF HEALTH AUTHORITIES

The rapid increase in the population and the growth of large towns aggravated the problem of water supply and sanitation, the lack of which was undermining the health of the urban communities. Chadwick, when secretary of the Poor Law Commission, showed that ill-health was one of the main causes of poverty and, with Dr. Southwood Smith and William Farr, he agitated for reform. But it was not until the cholera epidemic, 1847, had taken its toll of 55,000 people that anything was really done. The Public Health Act, 1848, created Boards of Health for local health districts, either on the petition of local ratepayers or compulsorily where the death rate was over 23 per 1,000 of the population. (The national average was 21.) Where a municipal borough adopted the Act, its town council became the local sanitary authority. But, outside the boroughs, completely new authorities had to be created. Two years previously, the responsibility for removing nuisances had been imposed on the Boards of Guardians and, in practice, the areas of these new sanitary authorities were closely related to them. The urban part of a union area was made an urban sanitary district and the remaining rural part became a rural sanitary district. Altogether some 670 local Boards of Health were created and these came under the control of a new central authority, the General Board of Health. The Act, however, was a failure. The new authorities had no real knowledge of the cause of disease, while the central Board of Health could exercise little control since it provided no funds to the local authorities. Hence, in 1858 it was scrapped.

The Reform Act, 1867, was followed by the appointment of a Royal Sanitary Commission, which reported in 1871. It condemned the many varieties of local authorities, and their inefficiency, and recommended a simplified structure, a universal code of health, and a strong central authority. These recommendations were implemented in three stages. In 1871 Disraeli set up a Local Government Board combining the functions of the Poor Law Board and the residual powers of the General Board of Health. In practice, the two elements did not mix, and the deterrent attitude of the poor law section dominated the more enlightened approach of the health representatives. The next year, a Public Health Act renamed the existing health authorities. Local borough councils, local Boards of Health and Improvement Commissioners became Urban Sanitary Authorities; the remainder, which were the rural parts of the Unions of the Boards of Guardians, were termed Rural Sanitary Authorities. Provisions for public health became compulsory throughout the country, and each Sanitary Authority had to have a medical officer of health and a nuisance inspector. The Public Health Act, 1875, codified and revised the various health laws and applied them to all health authorities.

STEPS TOWARDS MORE UNIFORM AUTHORITIES

After 1834, new subjects of local administration had been provided for either by delegating the responsibility to J.P.s or by the creation of additional *ad hoc* authorities. Thus, when in 1856 every county was given the duty of organising a police force, the J.P.s in Quarter Sessions became the police authority. Other duties for which they were responsible concerned the inspection of food and drink, the provision of asylums, and the licensing of public houses and slaughter houses. The Education Act, 1870, on the other hand, provided for another elected *ad hoc* authority. Where voluntary bodies were not providing adequate elementary education in any School District (or did not do so within six months), School Boards were to be elected to establish schools out of the proceeds of a rate which they were empowered to raise. The School Districts were the areas of either municipal corporations or groups of parishes.

By 1880 a chaotic system existed. Separate *ad hoc* authorities, each raising its own rate, looked after the poor law, health, and education. Outside the towns, other services were provided under the old system of supervision by the J.P.s. Moreover, further subjects for local action were being pressed upon Parliament, and there was a prospect of additional *ad hoc* bodies being created. It was decided, therefore, to construct a more uniform system of local authorities covering the whole country.

The major step was taken by the Local Government Act, 1888. This created sixty-one elected county councils, and transferred to them many of the powers exercised by the J.P.s in Quarter

Sessions — highways, asylums, food adulteration, etc. The police, however, were reserved for the control of a Joint Committee of the county and the J.P.s. Unfortunately, the area of each county (except for Yorkshire, Lincolnshire, Suffolk, and Sussex, which were divided) was based on the old shire, with the result that there was no planned relationship between the size and resources of the authority and its duties (see page 459).

The larger boroughs had resisted incorporation in the new counties. Many had followed a progressive policy, and they were afraid of being dominated by the rural interests. Hence fifty-seven municipal boroughs with a population of over 50,000, together with Canterbury, Chester, Worcester and Burton-on-Trent, which were smaller, were made 'county boroughs', self-contained units with both county and borough functions. In London, a new administrative County of London was formed with an elected Council which took over the duties of the Metropolitan Board of Works (established in 1855). But the metropolitan borough councils were not set up to replace the old vestries until 1899.

The Local Government Act, 1894, further simplified the structure. Elected Urban District Councils replaced the old Urban Sanitary Authorities, and similar Rural District Councils took over from Rural Sanitary Authorities. The latter had represented districts formed from the residue of the areas of a Union of Parishes, often cutting across county boundaries. This was amended by the Act. The new Rural District Councils, in addition to carrying out sanitary duties, became the poor law authority, each councillor representing his parish on the Board of Guardians, which henceforth was not elected separately. Rural Districts were still divided into parishes. Although its powers are small, the parish proved to be a useful device for helping the Rural District Council to look after a relatively large area and in encouraging people to take part in local administration.

This 19th-century structure (summarised in Fig. 12) lasted until 1974 (except for London, which was reorganised in 1965). Instead of being based on carefully thought-out principles, it had developed piecemeal on traditional boundaries. Nor did it provide for a systematic revision of boundaries or redistribution of functions. Thus, in the face of new discoveries in medical science, the development of road transport, the growth in importance of light industry at the expense of the older trades, and the consequent movement of population to the Midlands and the South of England, the structure proved extremely rigid.

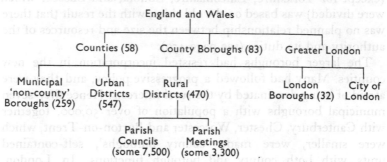

FıG. 12. *The pre-1974 structure of local government in England and Wales.*

III. THE NEW STRUCTURE OF LOCAL GOVERNMENT

EARLY 20TH-CENTURY DEVELOPMENTS

For a large part of the 20th century, adjustments to these new factors were purely marginal. Some responsibilities were redistributed, chiefly towards the county councils. Thus, in 1902 the Education Act abolished the School Boards and made the county and county borough councils responsible for elementary and secondary education. But it was not until 1929 that the county councils took over the duties of the Boards of Guardians.

In contrast, with the development of the Welfare State, some powers, e.g. for health and the relief of poverty, were transferred to the central government. For the functions which local authorities retained, there has been a new conception in standards, reflected in the vast increase in expenditure. This has been accompanied by increased help and supervision from the central government. In 1919 the old Local Government Board was abolished, and the Ministry of Health created, with general powers of supervising local authorities. Present central–local arrangements for England date from 1970 when a unified Department of the Environment assumed control. While the Secretary of State carries the responsibility to the Cabinet, he is supported by a Minister for Planning and Local Government. In Scotland and

Wales, supervisory functions are undertaken by the Scottish and Welsh Offices respectively.

THE PRESSURE FOR REFORM

Between 1958 and 1972, local government came under intensive examination. The blunt reason was that it was proving inadequate to deal with the extra services being imposed on it by the central government, the increasing size of the population and the greater mobility provided by modern transport.

The Local Government Acts of 1888 and 1894 had been based on two basic principles: local democracy and the separate government of towns and rural areas.

As regards the first, the degree of participation by the ordinary person was disappointing. Only a third of the electorate troubled to vote, and in the counties and rural districts over one-half of the councillors were returned unopposed. Attempts were made to combat this apathy by the appointment of the Maud Committee on Management (1964), the creation of a local ombudsman (1972) and provision for the public and Press to have access to committee meetings of local authorities (Local Government Act, 1972).

But it was the second principle — the distinction between urban and rural areas — which proved to be local government's main weakness, for it produced undesirable results:

(a) many small authorities;

(b) conflict between boroughs and counties and rural districts when boundary extensions were proposed to meet the overflow of urban areas beyond the town boundaries;

(c) a static structure of local government as services continued to expand, e.g. housing, planning, secondary and technical education, maternity and child welfare, when there should have been a movement towards larger areas in order to secure greater uniformity and a more economical use of financial resources;

(d) through improved mobility, people increasingly lived in the area of one authority and worked in that of another;

(e) efficiency of administration was impaired because there was little relationship between size of area and the division of function, many important local government services being conducted over quite different areas.

Added to the above was the pressure on the structure arising from changes in the distribution of the population. Here the significant feature was the rapid growth of urban populations — London, the West Midlands, West Yorkshire, Tyneside, Merseyside, S. E. Lancashire, and Glasgow. Many of these conurbations were divided between a number of authorities, although economically they are one unit. Thus in the 1930s depression Tyneside, one of the worst-hit areas, consisted of two counties, four county boroughs, two boroughs and eight urban district councils, a division which made more difficult the planning of relief measures.

PROPOSALS FOR REFORM

For the country as a whole, opinion differed as to what form the new structure should take, and suggestions for reorganisation inevitably ran up against certain fundamental difficulties. In the first place, any solution was bound to hurt and therefore to be opposed by some local authorities. The slow development of local government had helped to foster civic pride, and some authorities were bound to fight for amendments to the reforming legislation. For example, the Isle of Wight, which, although having a population less than half the 250,000 considered by the Government to be the minimum for county status, successfully preserved its independence from Hampshire County Council after spending £5,000 on publicising its case. Above all, however, reorganisation is difficult because the optimum size for a local authority is not the same for all its functions. It cannot be assumed that the provision of fire services, libraries, schools and transport all require the same area of administration.

In essence, reforms can be judged only in the light of the vital purpose of local government. If local government is merely an administrative device to avoid excessive centralisation, then the main concern is efficiency, and the structure should produce this regardless of its complexity or remoteness. On the other hand, if authorities are important as units of representation, the structure must be as simple as possible, make the most use of existing community interests and contain small and really local units. Interest in local government can be aroused and sustained only if the units of administration possess independent and interesting powers for which the electors feel they are responsible.

The first step towards a modernisation of the whole structure was the setting-up of a Royal Commission under the chairmanship of Lord Redcliffe-Maud. This reported in 1969 and recommended that, outside London and the conurbations around Birmingham, Liverpool and Manchester, England should be governed by 58 large all-purpose authorities working directly under Parliament.

This scheme would have had several advantages. First, it would have provided a direct and efficient form of administration, obviating the friction and delay which may occur with a two-tier division of functions. Second, a single authority possessing all local government powers is easy for the citizen to understand and engenders more interest than one which has to share powers with another authority. Third, the large authorities envisaged would have reunited town and country, particularly as many of the proposed authorities would have covered an area which has a principal town as its natural geographic and economic centre. It was recognised that whatever reform was finally decided upon, it should reflect today's manner of living; for instance, the practice of working in town and travelling at the end of the day to a house situated in a suburban or more rural area. Fourth, supporters of the scheme hoped that it might have halted the growing central influence over local affairs, larger and more powerful local authorities being able 'to look Ministers in the face'. On the other hand, it could be argued that Whitehall might find it easier to handle a small number of authorities rather than a great many. Finally, only such big authorities could afford to employ the experts needed to provide an efficient service in such fields as town planning and education.

However, the scheme had its critics who argued that size does not necessarily bring efficiency. Councillors, for instance, cannot have local knowledge of large areas. While the proposal would have been suitable for compact urban areas, many areas would be too extensive for certain services. The two-tier system has the advantage that some services can be planned over wider areas than others. Furthermore, the scheme would have limited the opportunities for real service at the 'grass roots' of our democratic system by reducing the number of councillors directly concerned with main services. Above all, in rural areas, an all-purpose authority would have had to cover quite a large area and it might thus have tended to neglect the minor (but not unimportant) problems of communities away from its centre.

THE NEW STRUCTURE

Although the Labour Government favoured the Redcliffe-Maud proposals, they were succeeded in 1970 by the Conservatives who placed more weight on the objections to the plans and instead introduced, under the 1972 Local Government Act, the present arrangements for local government, which retain a two-tier system, but with a reduced number of units and more logical boundaries than before (Fig. 13).

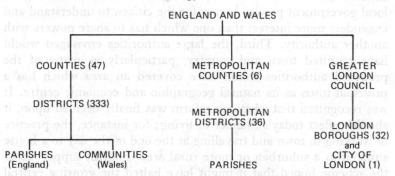

FIG. 13. *The present structure of local government in England and Wales.*

The general scheme is two-tier. The County Boroughs have disappeared, often absorbed into their surrounding counties. However, in six conurbations — complexes of towns centred on Liverpool ('Merseyside'), Manchester, Birmingham ('West Midlands'), Leeds–Bradford ('West Yorkshire'), Sheffield ('South Yorkshire') and Newcastle–Sunderland ('Tyne and Wear')— there is a special Metropolitan system whereby the districts have greater powers than elsewhere.

Outside the conurbations, England and Wales are divided into 'new counties'. The names of some of these new counties are, like Essex and Leicestershire, traditional, but others have unfamiliar titles like 'Avon' and 'Cleveland'. Wales has been divided into 8 new counties.

The new counties are, in turn, sub-divided into 'County Districts', pure and simple, in contrast to the variety of the old county districts. Parishes still exist, but the former parishes have been joined by several new ones. These were small boroughs or urban districts which successfully applied for parish status within enlarged county districts. A parish council can provide local

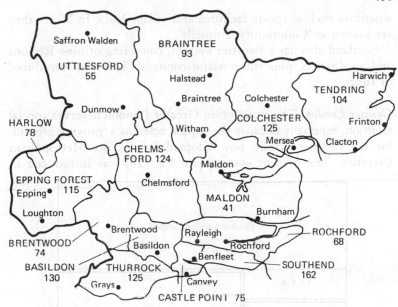

Fig. 14. *A typical new County: Essex. The 14 Districts include a former County Borough, Southend. Populations (to the nearest thousand) are given.*

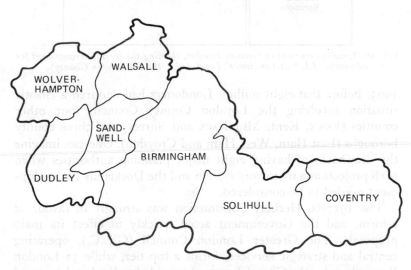

Fig. 15. *A typical Metropolitan County: West Midlands. The 7 Metropolitan Districts are all based on former County Boroughs.*

amenities such as sports facilities and village halls. In Wales they are known as 'Community Councils'.

Scotland also has a two-tier system, consisting of nine Regions and 49 districts, plus three island-councils. This was introduced in 1975.

Greater London. The situation in Greater London deserves special mention, especially because the capital acted as a 'proving ground' for the two-tier system now adopted for the six Metropolitan Counties. The present system (see Fig. 16) was introduced in

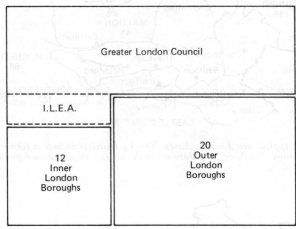

FIG. 16. *Local government in Greater London, showing the special arrangement for education (I.L.E.A.) in 'inner' London (i.e. the old London County).*

1965. Before that eight million Londoners had endured a chaotic situation involving the London County Council, four other counties (Essex, Kent, Middlesex and Surrey) and three county boroughs (East Ham, West Ham and Croydon). One can imagine the drawbacks of having eight major planning authorities when such projects as a motorway system and the Docklands Redevelopment needed to be considered.

The 1957–60 Herbert Commission was strongly in favour of reform, and the Government acted quickly to effect its main proposals. The Greater London Council (G.L.C.), operating central and strategic services, forms a top tier, while 32 London Boroughs (plus the City of London) provide localised and personal services.

One complication in the otherwise simple pattern concerns the Inner London Education Authority (I.L.E.A.) which carries on the work of the highly-regarded education department of the former L.C.C. 'Inner London' means the area previously controlled by the L.C.C. and now contains 12 London Boroughs. In 'outer London', the 20 Boroughs run their own education service — as do the new Metropolitan District Councils.

AN ASSESSMENT OF THE NEW STRUCTURE

How far does this structure satisfy the two tests of making provision for both local democracy and reasonable efficiency? Certainly the change, although large-scale, has been more evolutionary and less revolutionary than the Redcliffe-Maud proposals, which, instead of 422 new local authorities, would have left only 81. In order to keep existing loyalties as far as possible and to minimise administrative problems, most changes were made by merging the district council areas which previously existed, and county boundaries were retained wherever possible so that cities and towns kept their identities, the boundaries of the Metropolitan District of Liverpool, for example, being identical with those of the former City Council. Indeed, in the event, over 700 of the old district councils raised no formal objections at all to the change.

Nevertheless the reorganisation of 1974 was the most dramatic change in local government since 1888, and the benefits and disadvantages cannot be accurately assessed until the new system has been in operation for a number of years. At first, one of the most strongly expressed criticisms concerned 'remoteness'; for example, the Wirral District Council had only been operating for two months when some one-time councillors on the former County Borough of Wallasey formed a Wallasey Residents' Association to protect the town's interests against 'faceless administration', to preserve its traditions and to improve communication. If apathy at election time is to be reduced, councillors on the larger authorities of today must find ways to come into as close a contact as possible with the people they represent. Another early criticism of the administration concerned the effect on the rates of the creation of extra jobs at the town hall at higher rates of pay. However, the management structure has been defended on the grounds that the district councils now undertake a greater volume of work, higher salaries reward men in more demanding posts and serve to attract people of high calibre, and work previously farmed out by small local authorities to solicitors, architects, consultant engineers and similar experts is now undertaken by district councils able to employ their own professional staff. Finally, there have been criticisms regarding functions. Some hold that the Metropolitan District Councils are too small to provide education effectively. Others consider that making District Councils responsible for collecting refuse and the County Councils responsible for disposing of it will give rise to difficulties.

IV. Functions of the different Local Authorities

Parliament, as the supreme legislative body, has in the Local Government Act, 1972 defined and limited the work of local bodies. It has set up county and district councils which are quite distinct from each other, each with its own statutory duties and obligations, neither answerable to the other. Local councils may be given both obligatory or permissive powers, but most of the duties allocated under the 1972 Act are of the former kind, e.g. education, the enforcement of the Shops Acts, health and sanitation arrangements. Examples of the less extensive permissive powers are the provision of libraries and local entertainment.

The work of local authorities can be classified into five main groups:

(1) *protection:* e.g. the police and fire services;
(2) *regulation and control:* e.g. the licensing of motor vehicles and cinemas, the inspection of weights and measures and of food and drugs, consumer protection;
(3) *personal:* services for individuals directly, e.g. education, housing, the care of children and old people;
(4) *environmental:* to maintain and improve people's surroundings by providing public health and sanitary services (e.g. refuse disposal), roads, street lighting, parks, museums, libraries, community centres, etc.
(5) *trading:* services provided on a commercial basis, e.g. passenger transport, entertainments, etc.

One of the drawbacks of the two-tier system is that it raises the difficult problem of what powers should be allocated to each level.

In broad terms the Act requires district councils to deal with more strictly local affairs (such as most housing development, refuse collection, food safety and hygiene), while county authorities have responsibility for functions which nowadays really need planning over big areas and which are most economically provided for on a large scale (such as police, fire and education services and town and country planning at the strategic level). There are other services, marked (c) in the list below, which do not obviously fall into either category and county and district councils have been given concurrent powers to provide these. Examples are the clearance of derelict land and the provision of museums and art galleries. Indeed, one object of the new system of local authorities is that, by having fewer of them, co-operation in providing services is easier. Thus the counties can delegate certain functions to some of their county districts.

In the six metropolitan areas — Greater Manchester, Merseyside, South Yorkshire, Tyne and Wear, West Midlands and West Yorkshire — the main difference is that the metropolitan district councils can run their own schools, libraries, consumer protection and personal social services, functions which elsewhere are the responsibility of the top-tier county council. A separate table of functions for metropolitan areas need not therefore be provided here.

A. NON-METROPOLITAN COUNTY COUNCILS
(1) *Protection*
   (a) Police (tendency to amalgamation of neighbouring forces, to form joint forces responsible to joint committees comprising local authority representatives and magistrates)
   (b) Fire services
   (c) Civil defence (c)
   (d) Consumer protection (weights and measures, food and drugs, trade description)
   (e) Road safety
   (f) Traffic regulation
(2) *Environmental*
   (a) Town and country planning (structure plans, some special local plans, strategic development control, provision of gipsy sites)
   (b) Parks, recreation grounds and open spaces (c)

    (c) Country parks, conservation areas, clearance of derelict land, tree preservation (c)
    (d) Highways
    (e) Refuse disposal
    (f) Litter prevention (c)
    (g) Street lighting (c)
    (h) Swimming baths (c)
    (i) Public lavatories (c)

(3) *Personal*
    (a) Education
    (b) Youth Employment services
    (c) Social and personal health services, covering domiciliary services, services for mentally ill and handicapped, services for physically handicapped, registration of births, marriages and deaths
    (d) Libraries
    (e) Museums and art galleries (c)
    (f) Small holdings, to enable a start to be made in farming
    (g) Transport planning and the co-ordination of public transport undertakings

B. NON-METROPOLITAN DISTRICT COUNCILS

(1) *Regulation and control*
    (a) Building regulations
    (b) Dog licences
    (c) Control over food safety and hygiene
    (d) Licensing of premises for public entertainment
    (e) Control of markets
    (f) Off-street parking

(2) *Environmental*
    (a) Planning (most local plans, most development control, caravan sites and management of gipsy sites)
    (b) Swimming baths (c)
    (c) Cemeteries and crematoria
    (d) Parks, recreation grounds and open spaces (c)
    (e) Country parks, conservation areas, clearance of derelict land, tree preservation (c)
    (f) Allotments
    (g) Refuse collection

(*h*) Street lighting (c)
(*i*) Street cleansing
(3) *Personal*
    (*a*) Housing
    (*b*) Museums and art galleries (c)
    (*c*) Responsibility for housing homeless people
(4) *Miscellaneous*
    (*a*) Levying and collection of rates
    (*b*) Registration of electors

C. PARISH COUNCILS

A parish council has powers on small matters such as allotments, burial grounds, off-street parking, public conveniences, footway lighting, the management of civil parish property such as the village green, recreation grounds and open spaces, war memorials, etc. A parish council also has the right to be consulted over any planning application concerning land in its area. About 300 small towns of about 20,000 population, having lost their former local government powers, were allowed under the 1972 Act to set up parish councils. These have been referred to as 'successor councils' and their creation shows the new importance that parish government has today as a result of the much larger size of the higher level authorities.

D. LONDON

London broadly follows the 'Metropolitan' pattern. *The Greater London Council* is responsible for powers and duties which require uniformity of action throughout the whole of the Greater London area. These are: metropolitan highways, traffic management, the preparation and revision of development plans, main sewerage, main drainage, the fire and ambulance services, some housing (chiefly overspill), education (Inner London only), the probation service, approved schools and remand homes, coroners, licensing of entertainments, legal aid, motor vehicle and driving licences, some parks, etc.

The *London Borough Councils* are responsible for those services which do not require such large-scale administration or unified control — mostly the personal and social services administered elsewhere by the county districts, together with accommodation and welfare for the aged, handicapped or infirm, the registration of births, deaths and marriages, children's welfare, day nurseries, education (Outer London), some road construction, weights and measures inspection, and the Youth Employment Services.

In addition to the above, many councils provide entertainments

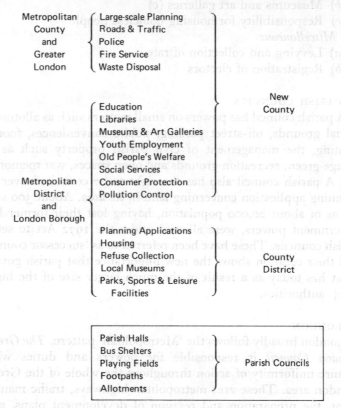

FIG. 17. *The main services of local government and their allocation between the various authorities.*

and run municipal trading activities, such as road passenger transport and ferries.

This impressive list merely indicates the wide range and importance of local government activities. They are not all provided in the same way, for the whole case for local government rests on the need for variety and experiment. But, wherever the citizen lives, he comes into close contact with the work of the local authorities many times during his daily life. As he steps from his house in the morning, the refuse is being collected and grit and salt are being thrown on the icy pavements. His children leave for the local school, and are safely conducted across the main road by a police patrol. The book he reads on the train has been borrowed from the local library. And so on — though rarely is a thought given to such things!

The allocation of the main services between the different local authorities is summarised in Fig. 17.

V. REGIONALISM

ARGUMENTS IN FAVOUR OF REGIONAL GOVERNMENT

In terms of area, population and finance, the local government structure is now better suited to present-day needs. However, there are those who argue that reform should be taken a step further by the creation of large, strong regions which would become the main units of local government, able to give stronger expression to local sentiments perhaps by exercising many of the powers which at present are the responsibility of central departments of government. Thus the Redcliffe-Maud Report suggested replacing the Regional Economic Planning Councils by eight Provincial Councils for England which would exercise the key function of settling for the province the strategy and planning framework within which local authorities would operate. While the Royal Commission on the Constitution (the Kilbrandon Report, 1973) recommended greater regional autonomy for Scotland and Wales, a Memorandum of Dissent prepared by two of its members, Lord Crowther-Hunt and Professor A. T. Peacock, went much further and proposed a scheme of devolution for all parts of the United Kingdom.

Arguments in favour of this further major change in the structure of local government are:

(1) More functions will be lost to local government unless some form of larger authority is instituted. The reorganisation of the National Health Service in 1974 provides evidence in support of this view. When the National Health Service was set up in 1948, it assumed control of the local hospitals but left local authorities responsible for a range of health services. However, to coincide with the 1974 local government changes, the N.H.S. was reorgan-

ised on a two-tier basis consisting of 14 Regional Health Authorities and 90 Area Health Authorities. Generally, the Area Health Authority, which is the key operational and planning body, coincides geographically with the local authority areas, and it has taken over from local government a wide range of services exercised under the National Health Service Act, 1946, including health visiting, midwifery, preventive medicine, immunisation, the provision of health centres, ambulance services and the schools' medical and dental services. Management and popular representation were clearly separated, the latter being entrusted to Community Health Councils. But critics argue that the reorganised National Health Service is too orientated towards management and not sufficiently linked to local opinion. At the same time, water services were similarly reorganised on an *ad hoc* basis with the setting up of a National Water Council with Regional Water Authorities under it to take charge of the supply and conservation of water, prevention of river pollution, sewerage and sewage disposal, land drainage and the provision of water-borne recreation. Thus, although local government has been reformed, its new structure is evidently considered inadequate to carry out all these responsibilities.

(2) Regional government would revitalise local government which might then be expected to regain control over services lost under an earlier and weaker system, thus bringing them more firmly under local democratic control.

(3) It would permit different parts of the country to have different approaches to the problems created by their own special circumstances. Some critics argue that government has become so centralised that the quality of decisions at Westminster and Whitehall is at times adversely affected, for inevitably attention cannot be given to many matters in the way that would be possible under a regional administration. This was the reasoning behind the creation in 1965 of the *Regional Economic Planning Councils* (eight for England, and one each for Scotland and Wales) whose task is to advise on the needs and long-term planning strategy of the region and to co-ordinate the work of the government departments in developing the region. However, the influence of these bodies has proved to be limited. Economic and social priorities, e.g. how much to spend on education, roads or hospitals, continues to be decided by the Cabinet, which in effect determines the

balance between services for the country as a whole by its decisions over the allocation of expenditure.

(4) In a situation where the regions have no strong political and administrative influence, their political life is impoverished. This is because potentially outstanding politicians and administrators feel that they can best develop their talents either in London, the centre of political power, or by going outside the world of government altogether.

(5) The local government reforms of 1974 are unlikely to reduce to any great extent the degree of uniformity imposed nationally, because the system retains all the means of central control which existed before (see Chapter 27). On the other hand, under a system of regional government, not only local government officers but civil servants administering regional affairs could be made answerable to the regional, instead of to the national authority.

DIFFICULTIES OF REGIONAL GOVERNMENT

In spite of the above arguments, it is far from certain that any reform towards regional government will be, or should be, introduced.

First, it is not clear what would be a satisfactory division of powers or allocation of functions between central, regional and local authorities, nor who would control taxation or borrowing. Modern social, technical and economic developments have all tended towards the integration of the country and have made the issues of government so complex and inter-related that the trend may have to be towards wider, rather than more local, planning and control (as Britain's decision to enter the European Economic Community suggests).

Secondly, it is unlikely that such a change could come about without considerable political opposition. Neither Parliament itself, nor national interest groups, such as trade unions and employers' organisations, which are well organised to influence Westminster and Whitehall, would wish to relinquish their power to influence the nationwide direction of public affairs. Moreover public opinion itself may be hostile when it contemplates the variations in standards of provision that might result. As a note of reservation in the Kilbrandon Report puts it: 'The greater the regional discretion, the less guarantee there will be that citizens will be treated alike in all parts of the country in matters which affect their daily lives.' Such variations are unlikely to be acceptable in view of the mobility of the population and the ease of communications today.

Thirdly, even if public opinion came to accept regional authorities, there is a risk that, in England at any rate, people might not support them in the large numbers which are necessary in a democracy — by voting in elections, studying debates and approaching regional councillors with their views and problems. Not only would the remoteness of large provincial authorities tend to discourage such participation, but a proliferation of elected institutions is hardly likely to strengthen political interest and understanding.

Fourthly, if the regions had considerable powers and standing, but were controlled by a political party different from the majority at Westminster, regionalism might make government less efficient, while further political party bickering would not be helpful to the reputation of British democratic institutions. If members of the regional authority were nominated rather than elected, they would seem even more remote from the man in the street and be even less likely to gain his support.

Fifthly, there are no natural political divisions into which England, at least, can be divided.

Lastly, it might be difficult to find an adequate supply of politicians and administrators to service the system.

It is therefore open to doubt whether devolution would really achieve its aims. In a small country such as Britain, there must be some consistency in legislation and taxation through the whole country, and most electors wish to hold the Government at Westminster responsible for dealing with the major problems of the day. Any devolution of powers, therefore, would tend to be quite limited.

DEVOLUTION FOR SCOTLAND AND WALES

Although the Kilbrandon Report, 1973, proposed only a series of regional advisory councils for England, it recommended (though not unanimously) some form of parliament for both Scotland and Wales. The advantages of giving a large measure of self-government to Scotland and Wales are that it would relieve the Westminster Parliament of a considerable weight of business and do much to appease nationalist sentiment in those countries. The

Labour Government has promised that proposals for such devolution will be announced in the 1975–6 session.

It must be admitted, however, that all the difficulties outlined above apply to such devolution. Indeed, since it goes much further than the usual concept of regionalism as applicable to England, there are additional considerations which have to be borne in mind.

First, if there is no system of regionalism throughout Britain, it simply removes Scotland and Wales from the mainstream of United Kingdom politics and administration. This would be true even if devolution was confined to education, social affairs and the environment. Moreover, it would have serious repercussions on Westminster. How many Scottish and Welsh M.P.s should be at Westminster? Would they be excluded from speaking and voting on the devolved subjects? Such changes would have profound effects on party government in the United Kingdom as a whole, particularly as regards the Labour Party, which draws much of its strength from Scotland and Wales.

Secondly, would the move be a once-for-all compromise between the 'nationalist' and 'unionist' view of the constitution? The Nationalists seem to regard it as only a first instalment. If so, the new Assemblies are hardly likely to play a constructive role in harmony with Westminster. This will be divisive for the communities, as many of their members do not wish an enforced separation from Westminster. Regionalism for the whole of Britain would avoid this lack of uniformity.

Thirdly, devolution would affect, often disadvantageously, the present administration at Whitehall. Would it be possible in the event to retain the present Scottish Office and Welsh Office when many of their functions have been transferred? Could the Secretaries of State for Scotland and Wales still command a seat in the Cabinet, especially when most of their civil servants had gone to the new executive bodies? Furthermore, the present arrangement by which Scottish and Welsh civil servants participate in the key Cabinet and inter-departments committees would cease. Nor would civil servants be likely to welcome a detachment from the present integrated British Civil Service, and many might transfer to Whitehall departments, with a loss of quality in the administration of the new Scottish and Welsh governments.

SUGGESTED READING

K. B. Smellie, *History of Local Government* (2nd Ed., Allen and Unwin, 1968).

Lord Redcliffe-Maud and B. Wood, *English Local Government Reformed* (O.U.P., 1974), Chapters 1, 2, 3, 4 and 11.

P. G. Richards, *The Reformed Local Government System* (Allen and Unwin, 1973), Chapters 1, 2, 3, and 8.

25

The Constitution of Local Authorities

'We have never believed that the Gentleman-in-Whitehall knows best.'

LORD HAILSHAM — Conservative Conference on Local Government, 1957

I. THE COUNCIL

With the exception of the parish meeting, the local authorities of England and Wales are the elected councils of the Counties, Districts, Parishes and Towns. While they may appoint committees and officials to discharge their responsibilities, the councils are still, legally and politically, responsible for their acts. In order to facilitate the management of its affairs, the local authority usually becomes a 'body corporate' — 'an artificial person having continuity of life, a continuing identity notwithstanding changes in its component personnel, and the power to hold property as though it were an individual' (J. H. Warren). It can also sue, and be sued, in the courts. In a parish having no parish council, the body corporate is the chairman of the parish meeting, together with the councillor who represents the parish on the rural district council. Elections, qualifications of electors and candidates, the composition of the council and its committees and the appointment of officials are largely provided for by Parliament.

ELECTIONS

Elections for local councils take place on the first Thursday in May. County Councils, the Greater London Council, the London Borough Councils and parish councils have a general election of all members once every four years. But voting for metropolitan district councils takes place each year (except in the years of county elections), one-third of the councillors retiring each year in rotation.

For the purposes of local elections, counties are divided into 'electoral divisions', each returning a single member. Metropolitan districts are divided into 'wards', each returning three councillors. Non-metropolitan districts vary according to the system of election opted for.

The Greater London Council consists of 92 councillors, with no aldermen after 1977. For the election of councillors, the boroughs are at present the electoral division, each sending two, three or four members according to their population. London Borough Councils themselves may have up to 60 councillors.

Non-metropolitan boroughs can choose either for whole council

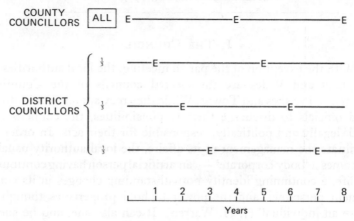

FIG. 18. *Local Government elections.*

elections (as the counties have) or elections by thirds (as in the metropolitan districts). The complete system is illustrated in Fig. 18.

Any person, including a peer, is entitled to vote at a local government election provided he or she is over eighteen years of age, a British subject or a citizen of the Irish Republic and registered as a local government elector for the area. A person is qualified for registration by residence on the qualifying date. Thus the local electorate is much the same as for parliamentary elections, and procedure at elections is similar.

On average, less than 50% of local electors record their votes. This lower poll in comparison with parliamentary elections does indicate that local affairs excite less interest than national affairs, though it must be remembered that local elections may suffer because they are more frequent. The poll is also lower in the south-west of the country than in the north and north-west, while counties record a lower percentage than the boroughs and rural districts. Yet it seems that distance is not a major influence for in elections for the Greater London Council the poll is only about 40%. It may be that here a constantly changing population reduces the poll. In the counties, too, half the councillors are returned unopposed, compared with only a sixth in the county boroughs. This comparative apathy of the counties probably arises because the county town seems remote or because the council's activities receive little publicity compared with the real centre of local interest and loyalty, the town or village. Low polls tend to benefit the Conservative Party who appear more successful in getting their supporters to turn out even in safe constituencies. Publicity, it seems, can do something to overcome apathy. In 1967 the Local Government Information Office ran a 'Go to the Polls' campaign in which 300 councils participated, and about one-third had increased polls.

While party politics plays a considerable part in local government, it may operate differently from place to place. In some areas, it follows parliamentary lines. Thus in London, elections have been highly political contests ever since the old County Council was formed in 1888, with both parties contesting each seat. Even between elections, strict party discipline is observed. There is a Leader of the Council and a Leader of the Opposition and both sides have a Chief Whip and Junior Whips. Each party has a policy committee, and party meetings are held before meetings of the council or of its standing committees. Not only does the largest party keep its majority on all committees, but it appoints the chairman and vice-chairman.

Again, J. G. Bulpitt in his study of four local authorities in the Manchester area found considerable differences in the extent to which party politics entered into council decision-making. On the one hand, the Labour group of the Middleton Borough Council applied the 'whip' to most matters coming before the caucus unless it decided otherwise. On the other, in the county boroughs of Salford, Manchester and Rochdale, no matter was a 'whip' matter unless the caucus voted it so. In both Manchester and Rochdale there was an absence of numerous political controversies in the Council. In all four authorities the two items which gave rise to greatest party controversy were housing and the distribution of patronage.

But this close reflection of the political organisation at Westminster does not exist everywhere. Prof. A. H. Birch, for instance, in his study of political life in Glossop, described debates in the Glossop Council as more like a free-for-all than a battle between organised rival armies, and he found that only 14% of the local electorate thought that party decisions had much effect in local affairs. In places, parties may function at the elections only, discipline subsequently being almost non-existent. Sometimes parties exist which are primarily the result of local issues. Liverpool, for example, contains 'Protestant Party' members, while in Crewe in 1957 the Ratepayers' Association won support for two Independents after a campaign attacking the Council for purchasing a town clock for £12,000 and a theatre for £20,000. Elsewhere, the party system, if it exists, may not be indicated at the election. Thus in Cornwall, Devonshire and Westmorland, all the seats are usually held by Independents, though of course councillors act together both at elections and afterwards without ostensibly forming a party.

The intrusion of party politics into local elections is in some ways unfortunate. A candidate should be someone well-known locally, and his personality should play a large part. But, as with national elections, the 'party ticket' tends to discount these attributes. Moreover, reluctance to engage in political dog-fights may deter the best men and women from standing. Often, too, local issues are obscured in elections by the slogans of national politicians. Above all, the critics of local party politics fear that power is drifting into the hands of a few political leaders who, by calling together the party caucus, can effectively decide the issues of local government before the council has even met. For many local services, such as swimming baths and public libraries, party decisions are mostly irrelevant, while with others, such as public health, the work of councils is fairly closely defined by statutes or departmental regulations.

Nevertheless, parties, even in local politics, can fulfil important functions. First, they awaken interest in local affairs and stimulate local councils to vigorous action. Although the voting figures for London show that the mere existence of parties does not remove apathy, special factors contribute to the low poll — which would probably be even lower without organised local party committee rooms to get people to the polling booths. Secondly, parties provide a link between the elector and the council; as in national affairs, a person, by voting for a particular party, has a definite say in the kind of programme to be carried out. Thirdly, parties bring coherence to the work of the council. Through the party, councillors can agree on a line of policy and, in the council meeting, decisions may be reached more quickly because compromises can be arrived at between the different leaders. In contact with the public, too, the party organisation also serves to introduce the leaders to the various local groups interested in the decisions to be made and authoritative opinions can often be given when political support is assured. Finally, where the council is divided into two distinct groups, the majority party holds a clear responsibility to the electorate for governing, while the other provides machinery for drawing attention to inefficiency.

The truth is that party politics in local government, although not an unmixed blessing, is inevitable. On the one hand, ratepayers do not lay aside their views when they are asked to make decisions about the government of their towns. An ardent Conservative, for instance, would probably not want an enthusiastic Socialist for his representative and hence he would like to know the candidate's political views. On the other, many people able and willing to take part in local affairs have strong political ideas and will naturally organise themselves accordingly.

COUNCILLORS

Candidates must be British subjects over twenty-one years of age and either: (a) be on the local register of electors; or (b) have occupied, as owner or tenant, land or premises within the local authority area for the twelve months preceding nomination; or (c) have had their principal place of work in that area for the twelve months. These qualifications were laid down in the Local Authorities (Qualification of Members) Act, 1971, which replaced more restrictive rules introduced two years previously, when it had been argued that only people who actually live in an area should decide the services to be provided there. However, many people live outside the boundaries of the district where they spend their working lives and acceptance of the narrower view would exclude men and women, such as shop-keepers, solicitors and garage-owners, who pay rates in the area and feel vitally concerned in its affairs.

In addition to the usual disqualifications, there are: failure without good reason to attend council meetings for six months; holding paid office under the council; having been surcharged by the District Auditor for a sum exceeding £2000 within five years of the election.

A sample survey of 4,000 councillors undertaken in 1964 for the Maud Committee found that councillors do not constitute a fair cross-section of the community. Only 12% are women, and the average age of all councillors was 55 years. Of male councillors, 20% were retired, whereas only 5% were under 35 years. Certain categories of occupation predominate — employers, managers, professional workers and farmers — because these can adjust their hours of work to fit in with council business. That they tend to be immobile is shown by the fact that two-thirds had lived within the area they represent for over 25 years. Judged by the test of examination success, councillors tend to be better educated than the average voter. They are also among the most active participants in local affairs, with a high membership rate of political parties and local bodies of all kinds.

Since 1974 a local authority can pay councillors a fixed attendance allowance, but the maximum figure is laid down by the central government. In total this will represent a much larger sum than the old expenses and loss of earnings allowance, and as a result more people may be able to come forward as candidates.

THE CHAIRMAN OR MAYOR

All councils are required by law to elect every year someone to preside over their meetings and enforce the rules of debate. In the counties, districts and parishes, this person is known as the Chairman; but in Districts having 'Borough' status, he is the Mayor or Lord Mayor. He is usually a member of the council, but he may be elected from outside provided he is qualified to be a member.

A Mayor, in particular, fills an important office, for apart from his duties as chairman he carries great prestige and dignity. As the chief citizen of the borough he promotes the town's civic sense and is the representative of the borough to the world outside. He refrains from engaging in party politics during his term of office and takes no part in the work of a councillor. By this neutrality, he can present the views of the council and town to each other when the roll of a mediator is needed and be the confidant of committee chairmen seeking advice.

An important feature of English local government is that the elected representatives of the ratepayers are amateurs who voluntarily perform valuable work for the local community. Any financial interest which they may have in a matter discussed by the council or its committees must be disclosed. The duties of a Chairman or Mayor, however, involve most of his time, and a decision has to be made, therefore, as to how he shall be recompensed and his expenses met. Usually he is given a salary to provide for his everyday needs and out-of-pocket expenses.

II. Organisation of a Council:
The Committee System

Councils, unlike Parliament, meet intermittently; county councils usually meet quarterly, others monthly. Moreover, the council may be large, containing well over a hundred members Hence almost all the work is delegated to committees, and the business at council meetings arises chiefly on the reports and recommendations of these committees.

Other factors have also led to the adoption of the committee system. Councillors have no equivalent to full-time ministers appointed from among their ranks to take charge of departments. Unlike M.P.s, their contact with permanent officials is direct. Yet, as part-time amateurs, their interests and, most certainly, their knowledge cannot extend over the whole range of local government functions. The committee system allows a councillor to specialise in those council activities in which he has most interest or knowledge. Regular contact with such subjects increases his understanding and enables him to assess the ability of officials. Again, committee procedure is more appropriate to the discussion of details and recommendations for action than that of the council meeting, and members can speak informally. The committee is free to conduct its own enquiries, works in smaller numbers and how and when it pleases, and maintains close contact with the official. Moreover, a council, unlike Parliament, has no provision for second thoughts by being divided into two chambers. This, however, is allowed for by the committee system, since, after discussion in committee, the matter can be further considered in the full council. Above all, committees effectively link the council — the elected body — with the official — the expert. Control of the department by the committee is achieved through the departmental head, for he has to report regularly to it and at other times to seek guidance from the chairman.

The functions of a committee of a council, therefore, are: (1) to consider the details of business allotted to it, make recommendations where necessary, and report to the council; (2) to decide and act in those matters where power has been delegated by the council (though this cannot include raising a loan or levying a rate); (3) to supervise the departments on the council's behalf; (4) indirectly, to give councillors intimate experience of some branch of local government work.

The chairman of a committee occupies a key position, for his functions go further than merely controlling debate. He is in close contact with the departmental head, who usually goes through the business with him before a committee meeting and seeks his opinion whenever a quick or particularly difficult decision is required. The committee looks to the chairman to keep it informed of outside views, and it is he who explains the resolutions and recommendations to the full council.

KINDS OF COMMITTEE

Committees may be either statutory or permissive. Statutory committees are those which local authorities are compelled to set up and they include the Finance, Education, Health, and Fire Brigade Committees, when those matters fall within their functions. Sometimes the Act may even prescribe the composition of the Committee. There can be no co-option to the Finance Committee, for instance, while it may be required that a committee includes members with appropriate qualifications and experience. Thus education committees and agriculture committees must contain members who have special knowledge.

Permissive committees are formed at the discretion of the local authority, which also decides the composition, the extent of the powers delegated and whether it shall be a standing or special committee. Sometimes joint committees with other authorities are established. Thus, in London there is a London Boroughs' Association to discuss matters of mutual interest.

Standing committees are appointed to manage a particular service, such as baths and libraries, or for a continuing function, such as control of finance or staff, and are reappointed at each annual meeting. Special committees, on the other hand, deal with a specific problem or a passing need which does not fall conveniently within the province of a standing committee. Like the Mayoralty Committee which advises on the choice of Mayor, and the Selection Committee which makes recommendations for membership of standing committees, they may be appointed regularly.

CO-OPTION TO COMMITTEES

Persons from outside the council may be co-opted to all committees except the Finance Committee. Insufficient time for full membership of a council or a desire to remain outside party politics may have deterred them from seeking election. Yet such people might have much to offer, either by expert knowledge, breadth of experience or by their active interest in certain groups of the community. Thus a place on the Education Committee can be found for a teacher or professor from a nearby university. This partly offsets one of the disadvantages of election through parties — that persons are chosen for their popularity rather than for their ability to deal with specific problems. Moreover, since the co-opted members are not usually strong party men, their presence helps to keep discussion away from party slogans. Finally, co-option allows more people to participate in local government. Indeed, unlike councillors, who often lack the time to attend all committee meetings, co-opted members are likely to be present because they have a definite interest.

Nevertheless, little use is made of the ability to co-opt. Not only is expert knowledge best provided by the official, but co-option gives power to experts having no responsibility for raising the money. Moreover, the tendency has sometimes been to co-opt persons, not because they possess special qualifications, but as a compensation for defeat at the polls. Generally speaking, in a democracy it is felt that the right to exercise public responsibilities should be granted through elections.

PROBLEMS OF THE COMMITTEE ORGANISATION

Although essential, the committee system raises certain difficulties. Many of these cannot be completely overcome, but the council must constantly recognise that they exist so that necessary revisions can be made from time to time. The major problems are:

(1) *How can the council retain ultimate control over committees?*

Committees have been established in order to save the time of the council. Hence, they are given considerable powers to act, subject to a report being made to the council. Often these reports are submitted after the event, and they are seldom complete. Indeed, the great majority are accepted at council meetings without comment. Usually the title of each committee's business and the numbers on the agenda which it covers are simply read and moved by the chairman of the committee and the items go through unopposed. Hence the monthly council meeting of some authorities may last for only about half an hour. Such a procedure is hardly calculated to stimulate a lively interest in local government. The Press has the statutory right to attend meetings of the Council (unless expressly excluded by a resolution stating why the matter should remain confidential) and of committees, but not sub-committees. Even so, it is often doubtful whether the council retains overall control. While the use of committees permits specialisation, broad general matters should be brought before all councillors, for some assurance is needed that committees do not exceed their authority and by-pass the council on matters of principle. In comparison with Parliament, which debates matters before referring them to a committee, the local government committee has more scope for initiative because it often considers business before the council.

(2) *How can the work of the different committees be co-ordinated?*

The splitting of the council's work among a number of committees raises the difficulty of how to co-ordinate their various activities. The problem is far more formidable than in central government, where a large measure of co-ordination is achieved through the leadership of the Prime Minister, the Cabinet, the Treasury and the Chancellor of the Exchequer. The permanent head of each department, too, is not merely an expert but an administrator, trained in appreciating the relationship of his own

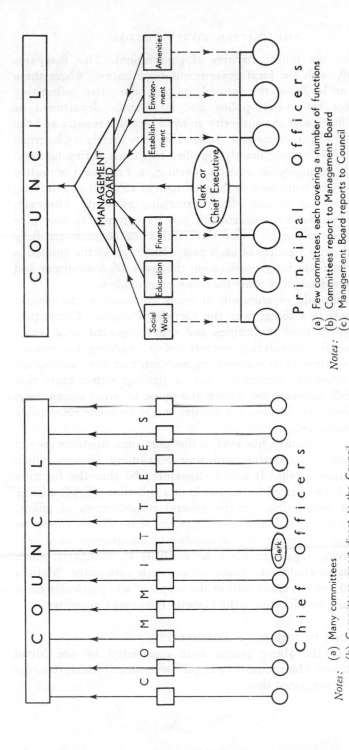

Notes:
(a) Many committees
(b) Committees report direct to the Council
(c) Committees are both deliberative and administrative

Notes:
(a) Few committees, each covering a number of functions
(b) Committees report to Management Board
(c) Management Board reports to Council
(d) Principal Officers head a number of departments
(e) Principal Officers form a team under the Clerk

FIG. 19. Council organisation: (a) Traditional   (b) Maud Committee.

work with the other activities of government. This compares favourably with the local government organisation, where there may be no leader of the council, no one committee collectively responsible for overall policy and no finance department or finance officer with the authority enjoyed by the Treasury and the Chancellor of the Exchequer. Instead there is merely a Chairman or Mayor (performing mainly dignified functions during his term of office), a spasmodic council meeting, a Finance Committee (which may be composed of the chairmen of all other committees) and certainly no finance officer exercising authority. However, political groupings in the council and its committees may give members some sense of direction, and some councils are fully organised, with Leaders of each party. But even so the council is too large a body for co-ordinating the work of committees and some other machinery must therefore be provided.

Under the old organisation of many committees, the nearest approach to a Cabinet was the General Purposes Committee, appointed by most authorities and often regarded as a senior committee for considering general policy, advising the council on such matters as its internal organisation and the distribution of work amongst committees, and for dealing with matters that do not fall conveniently within the scope of other committees. Alternatively the Finance Committee might be made responsible for co-ordination.

The main difficulty, however, is that part-time amateurs are not suitable for the exacting and time-consuming labours which co-ordination entails. It could, therefore, be that the function might be better placed in the hands of a full-time official, a Chief Executive, responsible for the general co-ordination of policy, chiefly by giving directions to the permanent officials sitting on committees. Moreover, if the number of committees were kept small (having regard to the time available to members), much co-ordination could take place within each committee. Matters which did not fall easily within the scope of any particular committee could be allocated to the General Purposes Committee.

THE REPORT OF THE MAUD COMMITTEE

Many of the above points were considered by the Maud Committee on Management in Local Government which reported in 1967. It suggested that:

(*a*) there should be greater co-ordination between the many disparate activities of local authorities;

(*b*) Council members should be freed from detailed administration so that they can concentrate on the major questions and the broad issues of policy.

The Committee therefore recommended:

(1) *The setting up of a Management Board in all local authorities*

This Management Board would be composed of between five and nine councillors. Wide powers should be delegated to them and they should be the sole channel through which business done in committee would reach the Council. The Council would debate and decide questions put to it by the Management Board, which would sometimes circulate before the meeting 'white papers' on important issues of policy. Councillors would have full opportunity to ask questions and table motions for debate.

The Management Board, therefore, would be a sort of Cabinet of the local authority, supervising the work of the authority as a whole. But, if the Council were organised on political lines, then minority parties should be represented on the Board. It was recommended that members of the Management Board be paid a part-time salary.

(2) *A streamlining of the committee system*

Committees should become deliberative not administrative bodies. There should be as few committees as possible, perhaps not more than half a dozen even in large authorities. Subjects should be grouped together and dealt with by one committee: child care, personal health and welfare, for example, might be the concern of a 'social work committee'.

This organisation would be reflected in that of the officials. For each group of departments, there would be a principal officer, a Chief Executive. The chief officers would form a team under his leadership. The Chief Executive would be the undisputed head of the whole paid service of the Council. He should not necessarily be a qualified lawyer, but should be chosen for qualities of leadership and managerial ability. He would be the chief officer to the Management Board.

(3) *There should be a clear distinction between the roles of officers and elected members*

Having settled policy, committees must delegate to officers the taking of all but the most important decisions, and officers should be allowed to exploit their powers of initiative and expert skill more fully.

The above were radical proposals and, as such, they invited criticism. First, it was argued that with fewer committees and a smaller membership, councillors would be limited to serving on one, or perhaps two, committees. Would those backbenchers who were not members of the management board therefore have sufficient information to scrutinise effectively its decisions? In any case, they would tend to be separated from financial administration. Secondly, if backbench members were limited to a minor advisory role, able people could hardly be expected to offer themselves at local elections. Finally, an autocratic management board remote from the other members of the council could damage local democracy.

Nevertheless, many local authorities did recognise the need to stream their committee system, and carried out some modification of it. The principle was thus accepted when the Bains Committee sat.

The Bains Report, 1972, was less radical in its recommendations. A central Policy and Resources Committee should be established to formulate policy on major issues and generally watch over all the authorities' activities, especially as regards a comprehensive plan for expenditure. There would also be four sub-committees to deal with staff, finance, land and a general review of performance; these would concentrate on major issues rather than trivial questions of expenditure. The Policy Committee would not have a monopoly of policy-making because some decisions would be left with other functional committees. Nor would the central committee consist entirely of chairmen of other committees, but should include backbenchers and some drawn from political minorities. Thus, compared with the Maud recommendations, there would be less distinction between inner-group councillors who serve on the Policy Committee and those who do not.

When the councils were reorganised in 1974, most adopted some form of the Bains Report recommendations (Fig. 20).

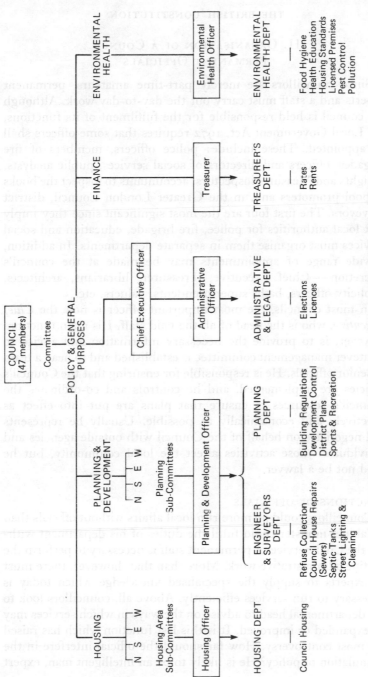

FIG. 20. *The structure of a District Council: the Committees, Chief Officers, and Departments of the Forest of Dean District, Gloucestershire (pop. 55,000), April 1974.*

III. Organisation of a Council: Permanent Officials

Since councillors are merely part-time amateurs, permanent experts and a staff must carry out the day-to-day work. Although the council is held responsible for the fulfilment of its functions, the Local Government Act, 1972 requires that some officers shall be appointed. These include: police officers, members of fire brigades, officers and directors of social services, public analysts, Weights and Measures inspectors, accountants to inspect the books of pool promoters and, in the Greater London Council, district surveyors. The first four are the most significant since they imply that local authorities for police, fire brigade, education and social services must organise them in separate departments. In addition, a wide range of appointments may be made at the council's discretion — Chief Executive, Treasurer, librarians, architects, publicity officers, baths superintendents, valuers, etc.

In most councils, the most important officer is now the *Chief Executive*, who is the head of all the paid staff. His main function, however, is to provide the necessary information and advice to whatever management committee is established and to head a team of senior officials. He is responsible for ensuring that the Council's policies are implemented, and he controls and co-ordinates the Council's resources to ensure that plans are put into effect as effectively and economically as possible. Usually he represents and negotiates on behalf of the Council with outside agencies and individuals whose activities affect the local community, but he need not be a lawyer.

FUNCTIONS OF OFFICIALS

Councillors could no more run local affairs without officials than a Cabinet minister could fulfil the duties of his department without the Civil Service. A permanent staff is necessary to perform the routine administrative work. More than that, however, there must be experts to supply the specialised knowledge which today is necessary to run services efficiently. Above all, councillors look to the departmental head to advise on the ways in which services may be expanded or improved. It is this last function which has raised the most controversy. How far should the official interfere in the formulation of policy? He is likely to be an intelligent man, expert

in his special field. Moreover, unlike the councillors, local government to him is a full-time occupation, and a profession in which he
is deeply interested. Probably, therefore, he has definite ideas, and
through his experience is much better placed to suggest policy than
the councillor. He can foresee the effect of policies, judge their
adequacy in relation to changing conditions and forecast future
developments.

Moreover, unlike the Permanent Secretary at Whitehall, the
local government official, through his committee, is in direct
contact with the elected representatives, and a closer liaison should
therefore exist. On the other hand, there is no experienced minister
to assess the weight which should be given to his opinions and
to relate them to general policy. The chairman of the committee is
the nearest equivalent to the minister. The official in local government, therefore, exerts more influence than a Permanent Secretary.
This, as Lord Stamp suggests, must be accepted. 'The official
must be the mainspring of the new society; suggesting, promoting,
advising, at every stage. The time when the amateur control is all-
wise for either seeing or saying what ought to be done, and the
official's job is merely to do what he is told, is now completely
past. . . . Only the skilled and trained official can really be relied
upon to keep continuity, system, impartial interpretation, tradition,
and disinterested impetus.'

But the official is merely the agent of a freely elected council.
Nor is the expert always right. His relationship with the committee
is similar to that generally prevailing between the directors of a
firm and its managers. The official makes his contact with the
council chiefly through the committee. He informs them on the
work of his department, points out matters requiring their attention or decision, and makes suggestions and recommendations.
Like a civil servant, he must be able to distinguish between those
items upon which he can use his own discretion and those which,
since they raise a matter of principle, must be submitted to the
committee for a decision. Before a committee meeting his reports
are usually circulated with the agenda, a practice which makes him
define his proposals clearly. The key to the relationship between
the official and the committee often lies with the chairman of the
committee, who is responsible for maintaining contact between
meetings. If the chairman is weak and lacking in vigour, too much
leadership may come from the official. Such a situation is more

likely to arise where chairmanships are awarded on the basis of seniority, or where a chairman is retained indefinitely, or where he is in charge of several committees. A committee which is so under the influence of the official that he is able to decide for them makes a mockery of self-government. The aim, therefore, is to permit the wishes of the electorate to bear on the permanent administration, while allowing expert knowledge to play its full part. Winifred Holtby sums up the position of the official as follows:

'He knows that we — all of us, aldermen, councillors, chairmen of committees, we come and go; but the permanent officials stay on. The experts — they are the people who really matter, and in the end they mostly get their own way.'

'Isn't that what you call bureaucracy, Mrs. Beddows?'

'I don't know what you call it. It seems to me common sense. Those men spend their lives on the job of local government, and have little to gain from any particular vote.'

(*South Riding*)

SUGGESTED READING

J. G. Bulpitt, *Party Politics in English Local Government* (Longman, 1967).

Lord Redcliffe-Maud and B. Wood, *English Local Government Reformed* (O.U.P., 1974), Chapters 5, 6, 7.

Report of the Bains Committee, *The New Local Authorities: Management and Structure* (H.M.S.O., 1972).

Report of the Maud Committee on Management of Local Government (H.M.S.O., 1967).

P. G. Richards, *The Reformed Local Government System* (Allen and Unwin, 1973), Chapters 3, 6 and 7.

H. V. Wiseman, *Local Government at Work* (Routledge and Kegan Paul, 1967).

26

The Finance of Local Authorities

'The historical development of British local government has resulted in a present central/local financial arrangement which is so singular that it hardly seems possible that it should work satisfactorily.'

URSULA HICKS: *Public Finance*

The work performed by the local authorities in the United Kingdom involves expenditure of over 16% of the Gross National Product. Thus, in 1974 their total spending on current account amounted to £9,289 million and on capital account to £4,014 million. The annual budget of the Greater London Council alone is greater than that of many sovereign states. Obviously, expenditure on such a scale has to be carefully watched by the Government and capital programmes in particular tailored to the prevailing condition of the national economy. Yet, once it has been decided that local authorities shall provide certain services, the necessary expenditure must be allowed. Naturally, some watch must be kept to ensure that spending is economic, for there always exists the possibility that the authority may carry its permissive powers too far or that the services could be provided more satisfactorily by private enterprise. In this section, the income of the local authorities — its sources and suitability — is the main study.

I. CURRENT INCOME

The sources of the local authorities' income are shown in Table 3.

(1) *Trading income, rents, interests, etc.*

For certain services, such as housing, entertainment, water supply, burial grounds and crematoria, allotments, baths and wash-houses, local authorities may levy charges to meet some of the cost. Roughly the principle is that the persons making use of such services should contribute more towards providing them than those who do not.

TABLE 3: *Current income of the local authorities of the U.K., 1974*

	£ mln.	%
Trading and miscellaneous income:		
Rent - - - - - - - 1,678		
Trading activities - - - - 90		
Miscellaneous (fees, interest, etc.) - 347		
	2,115	21
2. Rates - - - - - - - -	2,991	30
3. Central government grants - - - -	4,819	49
TOTAL	9,925	100

SOURCE: *National Income and Expenditure Blue Book*

This source of income raises few problems. Usually charges do not meet the full economic cost. Thus, council houses and flats have to be subsidised from the rates and by government grants. But some services may make small profits, which contribute to the general rate fund. At times the relief of the rates in this way is objected to on the grounds that profits should be ploughed back into the scheme itself, either to extend it or to lower prices to consumers.

(2) *Rates*

The rate is a tax which is levied by the local authority on the occupiers of buildings and land within its area. Such buildings and land are given a 'rateable value' which, in order to ensure uniformity throughout the country, is assessed by the valuation officers of the Board of Inland Revenue. It is based upon the sum at which the property might reasonably be expected to be rented, less the cost of repairs, insurance and other expenses. Councils can now levy rates on buildings unoccupied for three months.

By totalling all the rateable values of buildings and land within its area, the local authority can arrive at its own rateable value. It must then decide on a rate poundage according to its estimated expenditure and its other sources of income. Thus, in 1976–7 the London Borough of Wandsworth had to raise £3.3 million in rates. As its total rateable value was £49.5 million, the rate poundage was fixed at 67.5p. Hence a person occupying housing in Wandsworth rated at £400 had to pay £196 rates for the year (a rate of 18.5p being deducted for a dwelling-house — see page 494). Any ratepayer may appeal against an assessment and argue his case against a local valuation court. A further appeal from a decision of this body lies to a Lands Tribunal. To succeed, an appeal must show that there is some injustice in the valuation, e.g. that similar properties have a lower assessment. The second-tier authorities, the Districts and London Boroughs levy the rate. The county council receives its income by issuing a 'precept' on the collecting authority, either the borough, district or London Borough councils, and this is included when fixing the rate poundage. Parish councils and meetings are allowed to levy a small rate for all purposes, which can be exceeded if the Government approves.

As a method of financing local government, the rating system has certain advantages. First, by giving councils their own separate source of income (upon which, so far, the Chancellor of the Exchequer has refrained from 'poaching'), it strengthens the independence of local government. Were all their funds provided by Westminster, central control would be increased, and councillors and officials might consider it more important to please Whitehall than local electors. In any case, local people would object whenever the Government withheld revenue needed for services.

Secondly, rates provide a steady flow of income which does not fluctuate with the state of trade or movements of the population. Since expenditure on most services recurs almost automatically each year, it is important that revenue itself should be fairly constant.

Thirdly, the system of rate assessment and collection is relatively simple and cheap to administer. There is less scope for evasion than with income tax.

Finally, unlike income tax, every occupier makes some contribution, thereby encouraging a sense of responsibility for local affairs.

On the other hand, a system which had its origins 400 years ago when most wealth was held in real estate, is bound to have weaknesses for providing finance on today's scale.

First, unlike most other taxes, the yield does not automatically increase with inflation or greater prosperity. Instead the rate poundage has to be increased, and the unpopularity of this deters Councils from improving services by spending more on them. The deterrent effect is heightened by the fact that elections tend to be held soon after the rate is fixed each year.

Secondly, psychologically the rates are a particularly obnoxious form of tax. With indirect taxes, the tax element becomes absorbed in the minds of the people with the price of the goods. Income tax is collected through P.A.Y.E. and is thus accepted. But rates are not hidden in any way. They fall directly on disposable income, a substantial sum having to be paid directly to the rates office usually twice a year. Nor in the interests of social equality is there any connection between the use a rate-payer makes of local services and the size of his rates bill. As a result of this antipathy to rates, the costs of collection are increased by appeals against rate increases.

Thirdly, assessments of rateable value cannot be completely objective, while the shortage of skilled valuers means that quinquennial revaluations are always postponed. Thus rate poundages do not keep pace with inflation.

Fourthly, rates are often regressive; that is, they take a larger proportion of the poorer person's income. It is not always the richer person who lives in the large house. A man may do so, for example, because he has a big family, and he may thus be in a greatly inferior financial position to the bachelor who lives in a small flat and who spends a good income on such luxuries as foreign travel and expensive motor cars. Similarly, no differentiation is made between a business doing well and one doing badly. To some extent, therefore, the rating system negatives the Government's efforts to distribute wealth more equally. In an attempt to alleviate this disadvantage, rating authorities are now empowered to give rebates to poorer persons (see page 491) and to collect rates by instalments.

Fifthly, the regressive nature of rates adds to the natural reluctance of councils to raise them. They are not, therefore, an expansive source of income and operate against go-ahead authorities, who would prefer a more progressive form of tax.

Sixthly, rates have been made all the more insufficient as a result of agricultural land being exempted from payment since 1929. Some other premises, too, are relieved because they are used for valuable work for the community. An Act of 1955 exempted churches and church halls and other premises used for religious purposes, and gave authorities power to remit or reduce rates on premises occupied for charitable, educational or philanthropic purposes, alms houses held on trust, and playing-fields of non-profit-making societies.

Seventhly, the rating system produces in unequal distribution of the burden of local services over the country. It is precisely those areas where the rateable value is low and few people have high incomes that have the greatest need for local authority expenditure. Slums have to be replaced by new houses, and large families mean high expenditure on education. Compare the county borough of Bournemouth with the London Borough of Tower Hamlets.

Eighthly, many people, such as lodgers and others who are not 'occupiers', do not pay rates directly. Yet everyone living in a locality should be conscious of directly contributing to its upkeep, for this encourages responsibility when voting and a lively interest in local affairs.

Lastly, rates tend to act as a tax on better housing and on improvements to shop and hotel premises. Thus, the rateable value of an old house can be raised if a bathroom is installed, while at a time when the Government wishes to prevent cars from being parked on the road, a person who builds a garage in his garden suffers the penalty of having to pay higher rates.

Nevertheless, rates continue to be a fruitful source of revenue, and it is generally accepted that they must remain an essential part of local government finance. But various expediencies have had to be adopted to offset the disadvantages. Thus Inner London has its own rate equalisation scheme whereby the richer boroughs help the poorer. In 1964, rating authorities were empowered to remit part of the rates to householders who had suffered financial hardship because of steep increases in rates since the last valuation, and in 1966 rate rebates were made available to all residential occupiers on low incomes. The central government also pays 75% of such rent rebates.

Thus today the rates provide only a third of the total revenue of local authorities, the tendency being to shift more of the burden on to central taxation.

(3) Exchequer grants

The reasons why the central government makes grants are:

(a) to provide an additional source of revenue in order to offset the rigidity and regressive nature of the rating system;

(b) to assist and encourage local authorities in providing adequate services considered to be of national or semi-national importance, e.g. education, fire brigades, police, housing, highways and bridges;

(c) to exercise some control, through the power to refuse money grants, over the standard of efficiency of such services;

(d) to help the poorer authorities by relating needs and grants, thereby remedying a major defect in the rating system;

(e) to stimulate reluctant authorities to provide for other services beyond the bare minimum;

(f) to give assistance in special emergencies, e.g. floods.

The fundamental problem is to devise a system of government grants which will fulfil these objectives but not weaken local powers of initiative and decision. A grant may be calculated and distributed in alternative ways; but there are two broad groups, 'specific' and 'general'. A *specific grant* is allocated to a particular service. It can be a 'percentage grant' (where a given percentage of the expenditure is guaranteed), or a 'unit grant' (calculated by reference to units, e.g. so much per house erected). A *general or block grant* is a fixed sum, usually calculated on a formula basis, covering a whole group of services.

The main services financed by percentage grants are the police and principal roads, 50% and 75% respectively of approved expenditure. This form of aid is particularly effective in stimulating experiments and the expansion of services. On the other hand, the grant bears no relationship to the necessity of different areas, though to some extent this can be overcome by introducing percentage grants as part of a formula which takes other factors into account. Thus, when education was financed in this way under the Education Act, 1944, the amount given to an authority was based on a capitation grant for each full-time pupil and a payment of a percentage of authorised expenditure less the product of a $12\frac{1}{2}$p rate. From the Exchequer's point of view, the great disadvantage of the percentage grant is the difficulty of estimating future expenditure, since commitments depend on the local authorities' spending decisions. But the main criticism is that it leads to excessive central control over the details of local expenditure, for a careful audit has to be carried out to ensure that each item qualifies for help and spending is not wasteful.

Housing was traditionally financed by unit grants, with possible supplementary payments — for the type of dwelling, the rate of interest paid above 4%, and so on. The chief advantage of this method is that it limits the commitments of the central government. The cost of higher standards of housing had to be borne by the local authority itself. There was thus less need for an Exchequer audit check, and the amount of the grant could be easily calculated. As opposed to this, the payment was not closely related to need, and expenditure varied according to factors other than the number of units. In rural areas, for example, transport costs are high, while in towns, land is dear. Nor is it always possible to find a suitable unit upon which to base grants for some services. Consequently, many grants have had to be based on a formula which often combines the percentage and unit principles. The Housing Rents and Subsidies Act, 1975, accepted the percentage principle, providing a 66% government subsidy of the cost by which a housing unit adds to the housing account debt.

Suggestions for a fixed block grant were first put forward in a minority report of a Royal Commission at the beginning of the century, but not until the Local Government Act, 1929, was the method introduced, and then education was excluded rather than face the opposition which a similar proposal had aroused some four years previously. It came in gradually over a five-year period and was paid according to a formula designed to give additional help to poorer authorities — though no formula can deal with all the factors affecting local needs and ability to pay. But the main criticism of the block grant system is that it tends to discourage local councils from spending beyond the minimum.

The block grant was replaced in 1948 by the Exchequer Equalisation Grant, based on a new and intricate formula covering the number of children under fifteen years of age, the population per mile of road in country areas and the rateable value. Percentage grants, however, covered such subjects as police, fire brigades, highways and, to some extent, education.

In 1957 a Government White Paper attacked percentage grants on the grounds that they led to too much control of detail and gave 'an indiscriminate incentive to further expenditure'. Hence a new 'General Grant' was introduced in 1959 covering nearly two-thirds of all Exchequer assistance. It was calculated according to a formula which took local needs into account. Also introduced at the same time was a Rate Deficiency Grant to help those authorities whose rateable resources in relation to population were below the average for their class.

Both these grants were replaced in 1966 by the Rate Support Grant which contained new provisions to protect the domestic ratepayer. There are now three elements taken into account in the formula used when the grant is calculated:

(a) *the needs element*, a general grant composed of a basic payment related to total population and the number of children of school age, together with supplementary payments based on the number of children under 5 years old and of people over 65, the cost of various stages of education, density of population and road mileage;

(b) *the resources element*, a payment to authorities whose rateable resources are below the average for all authorities in relation to population;

(c) *the domestic element*, a payment designed to shield the domestic ratepayer from the increasing burden of rates. Each year the Minister decides on a rate rebate for dwellings and this is paid by grant, thereby shifting still further the burden of householders' rates to the general taxpayer.

Present arrangements for financing local government are not entirely satisfactory. The ratio of grants to rates is increasing, largely because rates are not a buoyant source of income (see page 489). Could not, therefore, the present income of local authorities be augmented by some other form of tax which would not involve government interference?

One proposal is for a tax on business profits or turnover — though this would raise costs sharply and fail to produce revenue in the residential areas where it was most needed. Another suggestion is the expansion of the 'assigned revenue' system, under which the proceeds of certain national taxes are handed over to local authorities. They already receive the revenue from dog and game licences and the licence fees for hawkers, pawnbrokers, money-lenders and refreshment houses. The history of the 'Road Fund', however, suggests that the contribution to local needs from assigned revenues is likely to be limited. When, in 1888, counties and county boroughs took over the building and upkeep of roads, they were assigned the revenue from vehicle licence duties and driving licences. With the great increase in vehicles between the wars, the Road Fund set up to receive these revenues became so large that successive Chancellors of the Exchequer could not resist the temptation of 'raiding it'. Hence, after 1935 the 'Fund' was financed by an ordinary parliamentary vote, and in 1955 the pretence that a special Road Fund existed was dropped.

The main tax which authorities could impose themselves would be a local income tax, but it raises several difficulties. Where the tax is assessed and collected by the central authority, it amounts to little more than a government grant. Yet if it were entirely administered locally, such costs as inspectors' salaries and evasion detection would be excessive in relation to the yield. Moreover, income tax is used by the central authority for redistributive purposes and as a weapon in controlling the economy. Care would be necessary to ensure that authorities did not negative Government policy when exercising their powers. Finally, there is the objection that the yield would depend upon the prosperity of local inhabitants, thereby leading to still greater disparity between the rich and poor areas. Yet, despite these difficulties, the Royal Institute of Public Administration's investigations led them to recommend that local authorities should be allowed revenue from a limited local income tax, and that the levying of entertainment tax and motor vehicle duties should be transferred to them.

II. CAPITAL EXPENDITURE AND BORROWING

As a general rule, current expenditure, that is regular expenditure on everyday needs, should be financed out of yearly income. On the other hand, capital expenditure (that is, on such projects as schools, housing estates, roads and bridges, land and machinery) affords benefits far into the future, and it would be both unjust and economically disastrous to throw the whole financial burden on the ratepayers of one particular year. Hence it is desirable to furnish such expenditure by long-term borrowing, spreading the cost of the project over the years when benefits are received.

Local authorities, therefore, have been given power to raise loans for any project authorised by statute or approved by the appropriate Minister. The power of loan sanction enables the Minister to check that the scheme is sound both technically and financially, to encourage co-operation with neighbouring authorities if a joint scheme would be more efficient, and to ensure that the proposed expenditure is consistent with government plans for national spending over the period.

Authorities who find it difficult to borrow by issuing their own stock or by private mortgage can turn to the Public Works Loan Board, which is financed by the Exchequer. In fact, between 1945 and 1952 this was the only method permitted, and loans were secured on very favourable terms. Since 1955, however, interest charged has been brought into line with the market rates, and authorities have been expected to raise finance whenever possible on their own credit on the open market. How much local authorities should pay for their loans is largely a political decision. Favourable treatment keeps down the cost of developing services, but to give councils priority in the allocation of scarce capital may encourage them to expand so quickly that private industry may be starved of capital, with dire consequences to exports and the economy in general. In any case, the Government must be able to determine how much capital should be invested in any particular service. Authorities contemplating big programmes not infrequently find restraint irksome.

Finally, capital grants are made by the Government for such basic services as roads, public lighting and housing, though the total amount is small in comparison with that raised on the open market.

III. Control of Local Finance

The financial operations of a local authority are controlled both internally by the council itself and externally by the Government. The latter form of control (for example, by approving borrowing, audit, stipulating conditions for grants, and requiring statistical returns) is described in the following chapter.

The Finance Committee is responsible for the financial co-ordination of the council's work. It considers estimates of expenditure and plans for raising revenue and floating loans. If necessary it can confer with other committees and require them to produce relevant documents. Each March, the Finance Committee submits to the full council an estimate of income and expenditure for the ensuing financial year and recommends a general rate poundage. After each financial year, it also submits an abstract of accounts to the council.

The composition of the committee varies. Sometimes any councillor can sit on it, the argument being that no councillor ought to be debarred from discussing such financial matters. On other councils, it consists either of all other committee chairmen or of councillors particularly interested or qualified in finance. This has the advantage of confining the committee to a size more suitable to the discussion of details.

The council has a Treasurer or chief financial officer and a finance department. The Treasurer acts as financial adviser to the Council and Finance Committee and is responsible for raising, receiving and investing money, making payments, preparing financial statistics and conducting an internal audit and inspection. When money is borrowed on the open market by the issue of stock, he is the Registrar.

SUGGESTED READING

N. P. Hepworth, *The Finance of Local Government* (Allen and Unwin, 1970).

Lord Redcliffe-Maud and B. Wood, *English Local Government Reformed* (O.U.P., 1974), Chapter 8.

P. G. Richards, *The Reformed Local Government System* (Allen and Unwin, 1973), Chapter 5.

27

The Control of Local Authorities

'The objective should be to leave as much as possible
of the detailed management of a scheme or service to
the Local Authority and to concentrate the Department's control at the key points at which it can most
effectively discharge its responsibilities for Government
policy and financial administration.'
*Report of Local Government Manpower Com-
mittee,* 1950. Cmd. 7870

REASONS FOR CONTROL

Although local authorities enjoy a large measure of independence,
they are not sovereign bodies, and for various reasons are subject
to control by the central government.

In the first place, many of the services they perform are of
national importance. Standards of education and health, for
instance, are part of the country's well-being. While there is some
control through the local electorate, it is not easy for persons to
obtain facts and make comparisons with other localities. Thus the
people of Birmingham would find difficulty in comparing their
police service with Liverpool's and in deciding whether they enjoy
equal educational facilities in terms of the number of secondary
school places, the size of classes, the state of buildings, the number
of university awards, etc. Moreover, there is in some areas a
repugnance to self-taxation, and such parsimony is reflected in the
standard of services provided. For both reasons, therefore, the
central government prescribes minimum standards for the obligatory services, although each individual authority decides for itself
how it will implement these standards.

Secondly, local authorities are nowadays such large spenders
that the Government must retain control for planning the national
economy. Frequently this involves applying a brake to the invest
ment projects of the more ambitious councils in order to prevent

inflation and to ensure that resources reach those services which have been promised priority.

Thirdly, since the central government gives financial help to local authorities, it must have some guarantee that the money is well spent.

Fourthly, central control is desirable to ensure standards of probity. While corruption on the scale of the 18th century would be impossible today, it could take a different form. Pressure might be exerted by vested interests, especially on the small authorities, to avoid the controls which a modern State has to impose. Supervision by the central government makes this more difficult, especially when officials, such as policemen, surveyors, public health inspectors, and welfare officers, have not only the support of the local authority but the backing of the national government.

Lastly, the central government can encourage the local authorities to take a broad view in exercising their powers and provide resources to help them. The continuity of the central authority offsets the transitory nature of councillors, and when disputes arise between different authorities, the minister can arbitrate in the national interest. Local authorities themselves need to be informed of what is being done in other areas if successful experiments carried out by enterprising authorities are to be the inspiration of others. Information on such developments is spread by the department, and thus new ideas become part of the code of government. In addition, experts, whom local authorities could not afford, are always available to advise. Thus central control, far from weakening local authorities, can encourage them to extend their range of functions. While councillors and their officials have local knowledge and experience, their vision would become narrow if there were no contact with the central government.

FORMS OF CENTRAL CONTROL

Control over the local authorities is exercised by all three branches of the central government — the legislature, the judiciary and the executive. *Parliament* both compels the local authorities to exercise certain functions and, as a protection to the individual, defines the limits of their powers; the courts interpret the intentions of Parliament when powers of authorities are disputed; departments are mainly concerned with ensuring that the local authorities administer efficiently.

Parliamentary sovereignty means that the constitution and

powers of all local authorities are derived from Parliament. It is Parliament which determines the structure of the electorate, the size and life of the council and the ways in which finance is raised. Powers, both obligatory and permissive, may be derived from general statutes, private Acts, ministerial orders and regulations, or from Provisional and Special Orders. In granting powers, Parliament may enable the central department to influence the way in which they are exercised. For example, Acts often require local authorities to prepare schemes which the minister must approve before they can act. Although it is sometimes said that such arrangements have an inhibiting effect on initiative, the central government cannot allow a local authority to make costly mistakes.

Generally speaking, Parliament does not restrict progressive local authorities. But it has to study the welfare of the community and to ensure that where a proposal affects private interests there is ample scope for objections to be lodged. If a local authority wishes to undertake work outside the obligatory and permissive powers already laid down by Parliament, it has to promote a private bill. By this means, some local authorities have secured powers which are unusual in England. Thus Birmingham owns a municipal bank, while Hull runs its own telephone system. On the other hand, where a local authority does not approve of the obligations laid upon it by Parliament and declines to carry them out, the Government can discharge these functions itself and charge the full cost to the authority. This occurred, for example, in 1973 when Clay Cross Council, Derbyshire, refused to implement the Conservative Government's Housing Finance Act, 1972.

But, having once given powers, to what extent should Parliament supervise local affairs? Obviously control must be exercised where national policy is affected, though this should not be narrow and crippling. However, since members have responsibilities for what are comparatively small constituencies, Parliament will often take a lively interest even in local matters. The extent to which a minister will answer questions on such services depends on how far Parliament has delegated powers. The minister can answer questions only when he is personally responsible, as we saw when considering the nationalised industries. Sharing functions with the local authorities may lead to difficulties. Thus, some dissatisfaction has been felt over the Government's responsibility for police forces. The Home Secretary is generally responsible for the co-ordination and supervision of police matters, and the Commissioner of the Metropolitan Police comes under his direct control. As regards the latter, therefore, the Home Secretary can obviously be questioned in the House. Outside this area, however, police forces come under local Police Committees and Watch Committees, so that the Home Secretary does not enjoy full responsibility, and in the late 1950s members expressed concern because they were unable to raise questions in the House over crimes of violence outside the metropolitan police area, or the photographing of anti-H-bomb marchers in certain northern towns. Control of the police is obviously of crucial importance in a democracy, although a centralised police force would place too much potential power in the hands of the national executive to be desirable. But there must be opportunities, where local control is ineffective or the police abuse their powers, for Parliament to investigate. The problem is to find the relationship between Parliament and local government which gives the right balance between control and independence. While the powerful searchlight of parliamentary question-time is a valuable device, councils must retain real powers over their services if the feeling of local responsibility is to be strong. Thus Government control over the police should only go so far as to ensure that officers feel answerable to the public for the means by which they maintain law and order.

At the citizen's level, Parliament provides, in the Local Government Act, 1974, for a *Commission for Local Administration* (local ombudsman) to investigate complaints of maladministration by local government officials. A person must first contact a councillor, but if he will not act, the complainant can approach the local ombudsman direct.

The *courts* may exercise control over a local authority when: (*a*) it has acted *ultra vires*, by exceeding its power, spending without authority, or failing to observe the rules of natural justice; (*b*) it is not performing the duties imposed on it by statute; (*c*) its actions are, by the statute, subject to appeal in the courts. Either a private person or the Attorney-General may proceed against the authority. The action may take the form of a claim for damages (as, for instance, when there has been negligence in maintaining an old sewer or pavement); an injunction to restrain an authority from committing an *ultra vires* act or to compel it to carry out a legal obligation; a declaration as to the law on a particular subject of dispute; a prerogative order of mandamus, prohibition or certiorari. In 1955, for example, it was held that Birmingham Corporation were exceeding their powers in allowing free travel on buses to persons over sixty-five years of age. Since other authorities had similar schemes in view, Parliament passed an Act the same year permitting them and retrospectively authorising existing schemes.

EXECUTIVE CONTROL

Parliament, which only legislates in outline, has little actual control over the way duties are performed unless it lays down specific requirements. Judicial action, too, apart from the odd occasion when it compels an authority to fulfil its duties, is mainly negative, preventing powers from being used illegally. Hence a comprehensive and effective control has to be exercised by departments to see that authorities comply with Parliament's wishes. They do this by supervising finance, administrative action, vetting the authority's legislative proposals and sometimes acting in a judicial capacity.

(1) *Finance*

Since local authorities are limited to one tax, which is neither buoyant nor progressive, grants have to be made by the Exchequer. But 'he who pays the piper, calls the tune' and the Government makes financial help conditional upon minimum standards of performance.

Except where loan powers have been obtained direct from Parliament, the sanction of the department is also required for capital expenditure. When permission is given, the exact sum which can be borrowed will be specified, together with the purposes for which it must be used. In effect, this allows the minister, who is advised by his own specialists, to pass judgment on proposed developments. Not only can he check ill-advised schemes, but he may insist on co-operation between authorities where this would provide a more efficient service. The control also enables the Government to relate the timing and scale of local activity to national policy.

Ratepayers and taxpayers must be given some assurance that their money is being spent as authorised by their elected councillors and by Parliament. Provision has, therefore, to be made in auditing accounts. In addition to the authority's own audit, the Minister appoints district auditors who examine annually the accounts of authorities, unless they opt to submit their accounts to an approved private auditor. District auditors hold a powerful position. Where, as a result of their own investigations or the representations of a ratepayer, they discover expenditure which is contrary to law, the responsible councillors may be surcharged and required to meet the bill out of their own pockets. Thus, in 1973, 11 Clay Cross councillors were surcharged £6,985 for loss of rents caused by their failure to implement the Housing Finance Act, 1972. Councillors always have the right to appeal to the minister and, for sums of over £2,000 (which disqualify from membership), to the High Court. The minister can remit a surcharge if he thinks the councillor acted reasonably. Although this makes the system less harsh, local authorities still have to bear in mind the district auditor when deciding on policy.

(2) *Administrative action*

Various administrative powers conferred on the central department enable it to influence the local authorities directly. It can specify the qualifications of certain officials, e.g. Public Health Inspectors, chiefly to ensure that parsimonious authorities employ efficient servants. The minister's approval may be required for appointments and dismissals, the former in the interest of the service provided, the latter to protect the official where his duties may conflict with the local authority's views. In 1958, for instance, the Home Secretary supported Captain Popkess, the Chief Constable of Nottingham, and a year later would not approve the promotion of the Deputy Chief Constable when Popkess retired because he considered that, in the circumstances and without any reflection on the deputy, a man from outside the local force should be appointed.

Usually the local authority acts upon suggestions from the department. When they are ignored, however, the minister may issue a directive. Should this not be obeyed, he can withhold the grant and even appoint persons to administer the service and charge the local authority concerned. But such powers of coercion are seldom used; they exist mainly as a threat to persuade recalcitrant authorities.

Generally, the department acts in friendly co-operation with the local authority, exerting influence for the most part by continuously providing advice and information. Model schemes and bye-laws are drawn up, new legislation or the recommendations of Royal Commissions are explained in circulars, and departmental committees and experts are always available for consultation. Inspectors with wide experience (e.g. in education) visit the various authorities, partly to ensure minimum standards of efficiency, but chiefly to encourage them to improve their services. In these ways, local authorities absorb new ideas and learn about developments elsewhere. Only the Government can properly disseminate this broader knowledge, for it can call for reports, make enquiries, and require authorities to provide statistics.

(3) Legislative powers and advice

The minister can often control authorities through his rules, orders and regulations. In addition, the minister advises on private bills and confirms bye-laws to ensure that they conform to national policy. In the Provisional and Special Procedure Order systems too, the minister occupies the key position (see chapter 11).

Circulars issued by ministers may make requests to local authorities, and even though such requests have no legal backing they may be almost as effective. Thus the Labour Governments of 1964–70 pursued their election promise of reorganising schools on comprehensive lines, not by introducing legislation into Parliament, but largely through Circular 10/65 which asked local authorities to draw up plans for such a reorganisation. The authorities generally complied, even when they lacked both the desire to reorganise and adequate buildings, for they realised that approval of plans could be a condition of the central government's financial support upon which they depended.

(4) Judicial power

The minister makes decisions of a judicial nature on a variety of matters. Largely to protect individuals from arbitrary action, compulsory purchase orders and restrictions on development are subject to his over-riding authority. When there is a dispute between one authority and another, the minister's decision may be final. Thus the Secretary of State for the Environment decides any differences regarding the communication of sewers. Above all, recent statutes such as the Education Act, 1944, the National Health Service Act, 1946, and the Town and Country Planning Acts have required local authorities to prepare outlines of their future plans for developing these nationally important services. Such schemes need the approval of the minister, and this allows him to co-ordinate the work of the various authorities and ensure that plans are adequate and technically efficient.

PRINCIPLES TO BE OBSERVED IN CENTRAL CONTROL

Since local authorities enjoy no independent source of legislative power, they have not even a federal relationship with the centre. Yet they are far from being mere agents of the central government. Freely elected bodies, deeply rooted in our political life, they exercise initiative in administration and, within limits, frame policy. But if a harmonious relationship between the central and local bodies is to be preserved, control must not become dictatorial, and grievances must be listened to both in Westminster and Whitehall. Today the government usually consults with the various local authority associations on local government proposals.

It is not easy to lay down precisely the principles which should govern central control. In fact, the present system of control has grown up almost as haphazardly as the areas and functions. Clearly the object cannot be to seek uniformity, for the whole case for local government rests upon the need for diversity. Moreover, if local government is to have any value as an integral part of a democratic system, the central authority must not remove the essential features of local democracy. Hence certain conditions have to be observed: (*a*) no restriction must be placed on the elector's right to choose local councillors; (*b*) within the limitations imposed by Parliament, the council must decide how the rates shall be spent. Only if the object of expenditure is *ultra vires* is there a clear case for disallowance, though local citizens should be given some outside protection against inefficient spending; (*c*) councils must be able to choose their own officials, although the central government may lay down the minimum qualifications; (*d*) even more important, the officials must feel that the local authority is their employer and that they have a primary loyalty to it. Observance of such conditions preserves a system of local government which is the antithesis of State government organised from the centre by an all-powerful Ministry of the Interior.

Yet because the central government has been elected to follow a particular policy, it must have the final say in matters affecting its programme. But the problem is to distinguish between broad control over matters of national concern and niggling interference with a local service. Will restriction of expenditure, for instance, unfairly penalise progressive authorities? How far should a Government whose electoral programme for education adopted the comprehensive principle allow authorities to make different arrangements? And to what extent should the Government lay down what is 'comprehensive'?

The ideal relationship between the central and local bodies is one of friendly co-operation. Both have, after all, the same interest — to provide an efficient service — and each must recognise the other's role in this process. The more efficient the system of government, both central and local, the less the possibility of serious conflict.

Where antagonism occurs it is usually from one of two causes. First, either side may feel that the other is obstructing the solution of an urgent problem. An example may be taken from the depression following World War I. In Poplar, an area which suffered considerably, the councillors endeavoured to pay higher wages than the normal to their employees and to give poor relief in excess of that approved by the Minister of Health. Eventually, in 1921, thirty councillors, including the mayor, were imprisoned for contempt of court when they refused to levy rates for outside authorities, the London County Council and the Metropolitan Police. Secondly, there may exist strong political differences between the local council and the Government. Thus, in 1954 the Coventry City Council, and in 1957 the St. Pancras Borough Council, both objected to the Government's defence policy, which was based on the nuclear deterrent. In both cases, when they refused to carry out their obligatory civil defence functions, the Home Secretary used his default powers. A Commission was appointed to take charge of the local civil defence organisation and its costs were charged to the council. Fortunately, conflicts serious enough to lead to such breakdowns rarely occur.

The central problem raised in all three instances is that of Government responsibility to the electorate for national policy. If local authorities can sabotage Government policy on such matters as unemployment and defence, this responsibility becomes impossible. Hence local councils must accept the broad policy of a freely elected Government.

As regards the actual administration of the service, Whitehall would be misguided in believing that centralisation is basically more efficient. Indeed, some of the main arguments for local government are that services are more likely to be adapted to local needs and that local enthusiasm will be harnessed. On the other hand, some efficiency will be lost if local areas of administration are ill-adapted to needs. Since local authorities are naturally reluctant to surrender area or population or to suffer any adverse change of status, it must be the duty of the central government, in consultation with local units, to modify the structure as necessary.

The strength of local government is a good indication of how far a society holds to the principle that citizens should determine their own affairs. Where people are prepared to be governed in detail by professional administrators from a remote national department of state, the very spirit of democracy has been lost.

SUGGESTED READING

Lord Redcliffe-Maud and B. Wood, *English Local Government Reformed* (O.U.P., 1974), Chapters 9 and 10.
P. G. Richards, *The Reformed Local Government System* (Allen and Unwin, 1973), Chapters 4 and 8.

VI

THE COMMONWEALTH

28

The Commonwealth

> 'It has frequently struck me . . . that when people start talking about the Commonwealth or the Empire — when the word was still in use — they immediately become grossly sentimental, tremendously patriotic or wholly vague'.
>
> H.R.H. Prince Philip, May, 1960

I. HISTORICAL BACKGROUND

While in part the British Commonwealth of Nations is the result of historical accident, to a far greater degree it represents the response of real statesmanship to changing conditions and new ideas. It is these which the following brief historical survey seeks to underline.

EARLY BEGINNINGS

The story began in the days of Elizabeth I, when a few brave men, in search of wealth and adventure, sailed in tiny boats to unknown lands. During the Stuart period the desire for greater economic opportunity, the longing for a more acceptable religious environment, or the wish to escape from political oppression, provided motives for seeking a new life abroad, and the first permanent settlements were made.

Colonies were recognised as important sources of raw materials and as markets for manufactured goods. Despite the loss of the American colonies, it was in the 18th century that Britain acquired an extensive empire. Created for purposes of trade, it was consolidated by war, particularly with France. During the 19th century, the British settled abroad in great numbers — in Canada, New Zealand, Australia, in large parts of Africa and in Hong Kong and Singapore in the Far East. They farmed, dug for precious metals, traded, built cities and spread slowly over the continents where they had made their homes.

The late years of the century marked the height of British imperialism. This was the age of expansion. With the steamship carrying men and goods to all parts of the world and the railways opening up the interior of continents, Britain's influence seemed to be growing everywhere. The Englishman's pride was symbolised by Disraeli's decision to proclaim Queen Victoria 'Empress of India' in 1877.

Typical of the spirit of the times was Cecil Rhodes, with his schemes for expansion in South Africa. His imperialist aims, however, finally culminated in the Boer War, 1899, and it was only after an unexpectedly long and bitter struggle that the Boers accepted British sovereignty under the Treaty of Vereeniging, 1902. But more important, the Boer War led to a reappraisal of the old 'jingo imperialism' and henceforth British enterprise developed along a new line.

THE GROWTH OF THE 'COMMONWEALTH'

By the time Britain entered World War 1, many colonies were already self-governing, and in those countries where large numbers of English people had settled — Canada, Australia, New Zealand and South Africa — even the paternal relationship with Britain had largely disappeared. All had gained considerable experience in looking after their own affairs. That they had moved towards independence was evident at the Paris Peace Conference, 1919, when each occupied its own seat. Hence a new constitutional relationship was recognised — that they enjoyed equal and independent status within the Empire. Ultimately the word 'Empire' was abandoned in favour of the word 'Commonwealth'.

After World War II, several factors contributed to accelerate independence for colonial territories. First, as each country gained its sovereignty, demands were strengthened elsewhere. Secondly, colonial peoples, educated in the West, were now capable of managing their country's affairs. Thirdly, modern propaganda techniques could be used by nationalist leaders, while air travel made meetings between them easier. Fourthly, economic and other aid was available outside the United Kingdom, from the World Bank, United Nations agencies, the U.S.A., and even from the U.S.S.R. Above all, there was less resistance to nationalist aspirations. The ruling powers, urged on by the U.S.A. and the U.S.S.R., recognised that they should help colonial territories to achieve independence as quickly as possible.

With Indian and African nations after the war being admitted as independent countries having a fully responsible status as 'members of the Commonwealth', the Commonwealth incorporated for the first time sovereign countries whose inhabitants were not of European origin. The association, a unique development of colonial imperialism, was now becoming of far greater significance as a dynamic, expanding institution. Not only did it represent a remarkable experiment in inter-racial relations, but it provided an important link between the older Western countries and the growing Afro-Asian groups. At the same time, the likelihood that member countries would pursue divergent policies was increased and some changes in the institutions of the Commonwealth were required.

The position of the Crown in the Commonwealth, in particular, raised a constitutional problem. Hitherto in each country the British monarch had been the Head of State, a Governor-General carrying out this function in the sovereign's absence. It had been affirmed that Commonwealth countries were united by a common allegiance to the Crown, but such a declaration was not acceptable to the new Asian nations for whom the Crown symbolised an imperial rather than a free relationship. Hence, when the question of India's becoming a republic arose, it was agreed that she could remain in the Commonwealth. This set a pattern for many other new member countries which, as republics, have no Governor-General, the Head of State being the President. While they do not owe allegiance to the Crown, the British sovereign is recognised as the Head of the Commonwealth. In addition, Malaysia, Lesotho, Swaziland, Tonga and Western Samoa have their own monarchs.

Hence today (1976) the Commonwealth consists of 35 independent members — Britain, Canada, Australia, New Zealand, India, Bangladesh, Sri Lanka, Ghana, Malaysia, Nigeria, Cyprus, Sierra Leone, Tanzania, Jamaica, Trinidad and Tobago, Uganda, Kenya, Malawi, Zambia, The Gambia, Singapore, Guyana, Botswana, Lesotho, Barbados, Mauritius, Swaziland, Tonga, Western Samoa, Fiji, Grenada, Malta, Bahamas, Papua New Guinea and Nauru.

This then is the background to the Commonwealth of Nations. The countries represented have been gathered together in many different ways. They are separated by thousands of miles of land and ocean and contain a rich variety of races. Their peoples are conditioned by widely different histories, climates, economic standards, social customs and religions. Whilst some have fairly homogeneous populations, in others different races live side by side. Hence, each has its own individual problems to solve. Yet a common historical experience has produced common bonds and developed a feeling of affinity.

II. LINKS OF THE COMMONWEALTH

Why is it that former British colonies, having gained independence, still wish to preserve an association with each other? The answer is that they are drawn together by many ties, some tangible, others nebulous but none the less real.

(1) *Emotional and cultural*

(a) *Common ideals.* Members have inherited through their connection with Britain the fundamental philosophy which believes that the individual should be allowed as much freedom as possible in ordering his own life. Although the British pattern of rule of law and parliamentary democracy is no longer always closely followed, the Commonwealth Prime Ministers declared at the 1965 Conference that 'the Commonwealth should be able to exercise constructive leadership in the application of democratic principles in a manner which will enable the people of each country of different racial and cultural groups to exist and develop as free and equal citizens.' Where policies are rigidly followed in contradiction of these ideals, it may be necessary, as with South Africa, for nations to leave the Commonwealth.

(b) *A feeling of brotherhood.* With the older members a large proportion of the people have close ties with Britain. Some may be recent emigrants, while others still feel a deep affection for the country of their forefathers. Even with the newer nations, although the relationship may be of a love-hate nature, a long history of working together has earned mutual respect and trust.

Yet this should not be misinterpreted. As Margery Perham writes: 'Nothing could be more misleading than to imagine that any of the old sentiment which still, lingeringly, binds the three old white members of the Commonwealth to Britain and each other, has communicated itself to the new members, though there may be a trace of such sentiment in India and the West Indies. The link today is not a single general sentiment, but more a multiplicity of bonds, economic, educational, cultural, as numerous and complex as a spider's web, and perhaps as easy to break by a single rough gesture' (*African Outline*).

Nevertheless, one of the strengths of the Commonwealth is recognition of the need to make it work for the good of all. This feeling is expressed by the Indian leader, Mrs. Pandit: 'It is an experiment in co-existence ... I believe the Commonwealth is already a fairly firm thing. That it is a nebulous thing is true but so is your unwritten constitution ... A strong Commonwealth can be a greater force for good than any other in the world. You have all these blocs — the neutralists, the Asians, the Europeans, the big Powers. But the Commonwealth has everything — Asians, Africans, Europeans — the lot. What a force to contend with! Only the greatest good can come from such an association of *unlike* people' (quoted by D. Ingram, *Commonwealth for a Colour-Blind World*). It is worth remembering that these are the words of someone who was imprisoned three times by the British during the movement for independence.

(c) *Language*. Although in many countries English is not the mother tongue, its wide use has had important results. Throughout the Commonwealth its use has opened up a common field, rich in thought and literature. Through it, for example, India received her modern education and it was a unifying force after independence. Indeed, the plan of Indian nationalists to replace English with Hindi was eventually abandoned, so that English remains as an associate official language of the Union Government for an indefinite period. India's experience suggests that English is likely to remain as a Commonwealth medium.

(d) *Educational exchanges*. The wide knowledge of English has facilitated education and the exchange of ideas. Each year there are tens of thousands of Commonwealth students being trained at universities, colleges and professionally in Britain. From their own countries, many sit for the External Degrees and G.C.E. examinations of the University of London, and take professional examinations through correspondence colleges. Under the Commonwealth Scholarship and Fellowship Plan, certain governments provide awards at their own institutions of higher education to men and women from other Commonwealth countries. Britain also affords training facilities for teachers from overseas, and makes grants to encourage British teachers to serve abroad. Official schemes are supplemented by the work of the Rhodes Trust, the Nuffield Foundation, the English-Speaking Union of the Commonwealth, and the Association of Universities of the Commonwealth. In science, there are strong contacts through the Royal Society, the British Commonwealth Scientific Organisation, which maintains a standing committee and offices in London, and the Commonwealth Agricultural Bureau, which disseminates information on agricultural research.

(e) *Common interests.* In sport, religion, politics, trade-union activities, and the professions, numerous contacts are fostered with the Commonwealth through societies and periodic meetings. Cricket tours and test matches, for instance, are frequently staged between Commonwealth countries.

(2) *Economic*

(a) *Trade.* Over one-fifth of the United Kingdom's trade is with the Commonwealth. The main reason for this is the complementary nature of their economies, British manufactured goods being exchanged for foodstuffs and raw materials. But it has also been fostered by emotional links, the use of common trade practices and, above all, by the system of Imperial Preference which operated from 1932 until Britain joined the E.E.C. in 1973. The present tendency, however, is for the fastest increase to occur in trade with industrial countries and for the proportionate share of Commonwealth trade to decline.

(b) *Capital investment.* Commonwealth countries have looked to Britain as the major source of their long-term capital. Indeed, since World War II they have been the only overseas governments permitted to raise loans in Britain.

Other sources are the Export Credits Guarantee Department and the Commonwealth Development Finance Company. There is also important economic co-operation under the Colombo Plan, a scheme originally proposed by the Australian Minister of External Affairs to help both Commonwealth and non-member countries which could not attract enough private capital in the normal way.

(c) *Technical co-operation.* The Commonwealth, with its mixture of developed and under-developed countries, has special concern with providing this type of assistance. Britain, for instance, gives technical help by recruiting experts to work overseas, providing training places in Britain and undertaking research. In 1968 a Commonwealth Programme of Technical Co-operation was created within the Secretariat, a step which has been particularly helpful to smaller member countries.

(d) *Migration.* The continual movement of people between Commonwealth countries is a major factor in binding them together. Some settle permanently, while others travel on behalf of firms with international connections, e.g. Unilever, I.C.I., the Bowater Corporation. Since it is usually young and skilled persons who emigrate, this represents a large capital investment in Commonwealth countries. Many persons also visit Britain on holiday.

Although Commonwealth countries have often distinguished between citizens of other Commonwealth countries and aliens, rules on migration vary from one country to another. Britain did not control immigration of Commonwealth citizens until 1962 when a voucher system was set up. Subsequent restrictions stemmed largely from the fear that the inflow from certain countries, e.g. Kenya and Pakistan, would be greater than could be absorbed. The latest measure, the Immigration Act, 1971, established a single system of immigration control for both Commonwealth citizens and aliens but made a legal distinction between 'patrials' and 'non-patrials'. Those in the former category, which includes Commonwealth immigrants already established in Britain, naturalised aliens and United Kingdom citizens with family connections in Britain, were given the right to settlement with their families, whereas 'non-patrials', like aliens, require work permits for a stay longer than six months and can only apply for citizenship after a stay of five years. Nevertheless, despite restrictions on settlement, it is likely that the Commonwealth will continue its strong connection through the movement of its citizens.

(3) *Constitutional*

(a) *Law.* Wherever they went, English settlers took with them the principles of common law. Hence, apart from the Province of Quebec, which has French law, there is a fundamental similarity in law throughout the Commonwealth.

(b) *The Judicial Committee of the Privy Council.* Overseas subjects had always enjoyed the common law right of appealing to the King in Council, and in 1833 a Judicial Committee was created by statute. Although in form it is part of an executive body, in practice it is an independent court, with judges from the Commonwealth occasionally sitting in it. Appeals are heard on cases authorised from the courts of the remaining dependencies and of those independent members which have retained the right (see page 252). While the Court's future importance may decrease, many member countries still recognise the value of such an independent authority. Not only does it see that the rules of natural justice are applied, but it is the ultimate arbitrator on the constitution.

(c) *The Monarch.* The British monarch is recognised by all members as the symbolic Head of the Commonwealth. Indeed, except in Malaysia, Lesotho, Swaziland, Tonga, Western Samoa, and the republics, she is also the Head of State, as in Britain, her functions being performed by a Governor-General.

It may seem unlikely that a distant Queen of another race should mean much to a peasant in Ceylon or to a merchant in the West Indies, yet royal tours are always a great success. The 1966 tour of the West Indies included an hour's visit to the Island of Nevis, a change in the royal itinerary made in response to a letter written to *The Times* by leaders of important local bodies. Afterwards, they wrote again to *The Times* saying 'Nevisians are still moving about their daily duties somewhat dazed with the wonder of it all . . . the Royal visit to our island was a great success. Many thousands of our people saw the Queen and the Duke and felt a thrill at their presence on our soil . . . and many persons will continue for many years to say that February 22nd, 1966, was the most exciting day of their lives.'

Rhodesia, in its Declaration of Independence, 1965, proclaimed that its people 'have always shown unswerving loyalty and devotion to Her Majesty the Queen' and the Declaration ends with the words 'God Save the Queen'. However, the Queen did not respond to a request to appoint a Governor-General under the 1965 Constitution and indeed the Governor, Sir Humphrey Gibbs, was later rewarded with the honour of K.C.V.O., which lies in the Queen's personal gift. Later, on her Jamaican tour, when opening a new session of Parliament, her speech from the throne, made on the advice of the Jamaican Prime Minister, was thought to contemplate the possibility that force might be used in Rhodesia, whose Prime Minister angrily replied that they might reluctantly consider becoming a republic if 'the Queen is to be used continually and blatantly as a cog in the Labour Party machine'. Thus the monarch was brought momentarily into the centre of Commonwealth political controversy, but as Head of the Commonwealth she has no political powers or functions and could do nothing to heal the breach in Commonwealth relations.

(d) *High Commissioners.* Ambassadorial duties to governments are performed by High Commissioners, who are now appointed by most members to the other Commonwealth countries.

(e) *The Commonwealth Secretariat.* Until the mid-sixties the main channel of communication between Britain and the member nations was the Commonwealth Relations Office. There was no permanent Commonwealth council. In 1964 the Commonwealth Prime Ministers decided, on the initiative of African states and of Trinidad and Tobago, that a Commonwealth Secretariat should be set up, and a Canadian diplomat, Mr. Arnold Smith, became its first Secretary-General. Its duties include making the conference arrangements for heads of government in co-operation with the host country and the dissemination of factual information to all member countries on matters of common concern. Thus information can now come from a joint Commonwealth source, an application of the principle of 'equality of status' to Commonwealth institutions.

(f) *Prime Ministers' conferences.* From time to time, the leaders of the member nations meet together to discuss Commonwealth, international and economic affairs. While such meetings demonstrate to the rest of the world that the Commonwealth is a living reality, they typify the nature of the association. They have no power to make decisions which are binding on member governments and indeed it is a convention that internal affairs are not discussed, although South Africa voluntarily waived this in 1961, and the Nigerians held private talks in 1969 about their civil war problems with the leaders of Tanzania and Zambia, the two Commonwealth countries which had recognised the seceding state of Biafra. Another convention is that disputes between one Commonwealth country and another are not discussed except with the consent of the parties concerned.

The truth is that the Commonwealth is too diverse in interest to formulate constructive policies. Its conferences seek to reach 'the highest measure of understanding not the lowest measure of agreement'. It is the feeling of the brotherhood discussed on page 491 that gives them an especial value. The British Prime Minister at the 1971 Conference summed up in the following words the nature of the Commonwealth and the part that meetings of leaders play within it: 'To me it is a body of friends brought together by history, free to come and go as they wish, to contribute as much or as little as they can but always concerned, as all friends are, with one another's welfare. The fact that so many leaders have made such a long journey to meet in spite of domestic urgent problems, shows that they find in this conclave what they could not find in any comparable assembly — simple, unfettered friendship and unqualified goodwill. The world needs those qualities which the enemies of freedom would gladly destroy. There is nothing more vital that the Commonwealth can contribute to combat the tensions and discords we are to discuss in the next few days. The Commonwealth contribution is unique and irreplaceable'.

(g) *Meetings of other officials*. Other ministers or officials meet from time to time to discuss specific topics. Such meetings, however, do not necessarily take place in London, that of the finance ministers in 1966, for instance, being held in Montreal.

(h) *Other informal consultations*. Consultation and co-operation take place informally on a scale unknown outside the Commonwealth. Patrick Keatley illustrated this in an article in *The Guardian*, July 8th, 1964, as follows: 'Suppose that one of the smaller African or Asian States of the Commonwealth is co-opted at the United Nations onto a committee to do with nuclear energy. Let us say that military and civilian aspects are involved. The practical thing is to turn to Commonwealth States which have nuclear knowledge — Britain, India, Canada, Australia — and ask for a confidential briefing.

When Uganda was setting up her diplomatic service, with the approach of independence, it seemed quite natural that the Canadians should offer a place on their U.N. team. And so, for six months, a young Ugandan served as a member of the Canadian delegation.'

III. Political Problems of the Commonwealth

An association embracing such diverse peoples in political equality faces far greater problems than the old British Commonwealth of only six self-governing nations each of European, and mostly British, origin. At the present time there are three main problems.

(1) *How can political stability be maintained in some of the newer member countries?*

Each of the newer countries started independence with a constitution designed to follow the basic principles of democratic government. But these countries are immature politically, underdeveloped economically, and divided in language, race, culture, and religion. Thus Malaysia's population consists of 4 million Malays, $3\frac{1}{2}$ million Chinese, nearly 1 million Indians and 1 million others (mostly indigenous races of Sarawak). Nigeria's people speak some 250 different languages, but are divided mainly between the Yoruba in the south-west, the Ibo in the south-east and the Hausa conservative Muslims in the north. Tribal feeling is particularly strong, too, in Uganda, where the relatively rich and better educated constituent kingdom of Buganda had in colonial days sought progress for its people in separate independence, a claim that forced the British in 1953 to withdraw recognition of their Kabaka or King.

The scale of the problem is illustrated by the fact that Prime Ministers of Pakistan, Ceylon and Nigeria have been assassinated, governments have been forcibly swept from power in Zanzibar, Ghana, Uganda and Nigeria, and prolonged civil war has occurred in Nigeria and Pakistan.

These upheavals in Africa and Asia make it clear that the 'Westminster model' of the two-party system and a strong official Opposition can hardly be expected to operate unchanged in countries with such different histories, geographical structures and social systems. Unfortunately, alternative constitutional experiments in terms of federalism or of the one-party state, have not always succeeded in providing government which is both stable and acceptable.

Federalism has been the favoured technique where whole territories have distinct communities which need to be safeguarded (e.g. Nigeria and Malaysia) or where there are several scattered communities (e.g. the West Indies).

Yet, for a variety of reasons, federation has in practice often failed to provide an alternative to unitary government or complete separation.

Geographical obstacles were too great in the West Indies where some of the islands were separated by a thousand miles of ocean and the richer communities were uncertain of their obligation to support poorer members. Thus it was Jamaica, the largest island, which took the initiative in dissolving the three-year-old West Indies Federation in 1961.

In Central Africa, it was hoped that a Federation of Southern Rhodesia, Northern Rhodesia (now Zambia) and Nyasaland (now Malawi) would, by joining their naturally-linked economies, produce a strong economic and political unit which could engage in an experiment in racial partnership. But in 1963, after only ten years, the Central African Federation collapsed as a result of the bitter hostility of the black Africans. In the words of Margery Perham: 'It failed to measure the deeper forces — irrational forces, if you will — against it. Its shock awoke the still politically somnolent Africans' (*The Colonial Reckoning*).

Mutual suspicion has also dealt heavy blows at federalism in Malaysia and Nigeria. In 1965 Singapore seceded from the two-year-old Federation of Malaysia because of the antagonism between the Chinese who make up 80% of Singapore's two million people and the Malay races. The secession of the Eastern Province (calling itself Biafra) from the Federation of Nigeria produced civil war in 1967.

Nor has federalism proved strong in other emergent nations. The Uganda Parliament in 1966, after the defeat and flight of the Kabaka of Buganda, adopted a new constitution introducing a centralised government. And attempts to form an East African Federation of Kenya, Uganda and Tanzania (itself a union of Tanganyika and Zanzibar) have proved abortive.

Thus, while it can be argued that peoples who have wide differences can be brought together successfully as a single nation only in a federal framework, there is strong evidence that where there are sharp divisions and little experience of working together, the federal system cannot, in itself, be relied upon as a device to remove fear and suspicion, to encourage obedience to the law and spirit of the constitution, and to safeguard individual liberty during the uncertainties of newly-acquired political independence.

The *one-party state* is an alternative constitutional device which has been turned to, for example in Ghana and Tanzania, in the search for political stability. Many arguments are advanced in its favour. It is said that political warfare is too dangerous where there are deep and traditional hostilities between different communities. Neither politicians nor a public which is mostly uneducated have experienced or can fully understand the British parliamentary system. Thus President Nyerere of Tanzania argues that 'to try and import the idea of a parliamentary opposition in Africa may very likely lead to violence—because the opposition parties will tend to be regarded as traitors by the majority of our people, or at best, it will lead to the trivial manoeuvrings of "opposing" groups whose time is spent in the inflation of artificial differences into some semblance of reality for the sake of preserving democracy' (quoted by B. Davidson, *Which way Africa?*). In contrast, a single party can cut across tribalism and help build the nation. In the poorer African nations there is one dominant problem—the urgent needs of economic advance. Not only might one-party government provide the decisive leadership needed to grapple with it, but where there is a shortage of educated, experienced politicians, two competing teams tends to be a luxury that they cannot afford.

Yet the one-party state is at best a risky constitutional device. Indeed, in the first instance, it may not in fact be introduced in response to the genuine wish of a free electorate. In Ghana, for instance, its introduction followed a referendum in which there was a favourable majority of over 99·9% of the votes cast out of a 96·5% poll of the total electorate. But two English journalists, invited by the Ghanaian High Commissioner in London to observe the campaign, concluded that the Government's success was due to 'a mixture of intimidation and ballot-rigging, which ranged from the brutal to the farcical'. Thus Ashanti, regarded as the stronghold of opposition to Dr. Nkrumah, did not record a single 'no' vote!

In Zambia, too, the introduction of the one-party state by an amendment to the constitution in 1972 followed the outlawing of one of the opposition parties and the detention without trial of over 100 of its leading members.

Once introduced, although free discussion and competition for office are possible within a single party, the absence of opposition does provide the ideal environment for tyranny. After the referendum in Ghana, the *Ghanaian Times* wrote: 'In this referendum we have mounted our vigilance to find those who are with us and those who are against us. Those who think they can hide under the so-called "secrecy" of the polling booth to fool us must know that the days when we could be fooled are gone. And those fence sitters who prefer to stay at home must likewise know that the people's wrath is apt to descend without mercy upon those who are not with us.' In the following years the independence of Press, universities and courts was undermined, the Chief Justice, for example, being dismissed after the acquittal of two former Cabinet ministers on a treason charge.

Moreover, far from resolving regional and other differences, a single party may encourage instability, for under such a system a government can be changed only by unconstitutional action, as it was in Ghana by the army coup in 1966.

Finally, where outside criticism is not allowed and criticism within the party is either stifled by fear or the hope of office, there is always the danger of inefficiency, waste, nepotism and corruption.

Thus there is little reason to suppose that the advantages of the party system described in chapter 8 are irrelevant even in the very different circumstances of many of the Commonwealth countries.

(2) *Can the differences of outlook and interest of members be resolved?*

As we have seen, there is now a wide variety of political practices and British ideas of democracy and judicial independence no longer always set the pattern. Members sometimes favour the American presidential pattern rather than that of Westminster. Indeed there is now a possibility that a Communist model may also be followed. The events after the 1964 revolution in Zanzibar, for instance, could indicate the gradual establishment of such a type of regime—the setting up of a one-party state, the dismissal of British civil servants, the appointment of an East German as aide to the President, and the adoption of the power to confiscate property without compensation. Could the Commonwealth survive if it contained within itself a group of Communist countries? Patrick Gordon Walker argues that in the Commonwealth 'like institutions produce ways and attitudes that penetrate into a nation's being' and that 'a parliamentary democracy creates throughout the Commonwealth a similar pattern of authority and an atmosphere that affects the manner in which political problems arise and are tackled' (*The Commonwealth*). But if this means that the customary co-operation and feeling of closeness among members depends to a large degree on the maintenance of a certain kind of governmental system, then the Commonwealth's survival is in doubt.

Yet however different their internal political institutions, it could be expected that an international association such as the Commonwealth might have a common defence policy. But this is not so. Thus Australia and New Zealand have joined with the U.S.A. in the ANZUS Pact, from which Britain is excluded, while certain central African states look to Russia or China for armaments. Indeed, Britain's membership of NATO and SEATO and her H-Bomb defensive strategy clash with the views of neutralist members, such as India. Australia, with her special concern over Asia, sent troops to fight with the Americans in Vietnam.

Even in foreign matters, there is no common viewpoint. Members of the Commonwealth may be diametrically opposed in their policies at the United Nations. When the 1965 Prime Ministers Conference set up a peace mission to help end the war in Vietnam, Tanzania advocated a policy of complete non-alignment, while Kenya supported the initiative, but opposed the inclusion of Britain or any country which had committed itself on the issue. And, in times of crisis, members may even abandon the practice of prior consultation on major decisions, as happened over Suez in 1956, which according to Canada's Foreign Minister, brought the Commonwealth to the 'verge of dissolution'.

Above all, there is now no certainty that peace can be maintained within the Commonwealth. For long it could be argued that the spirit of the Commonwealth was expressed in words spoken by Stanley Baldwin in 1929. 'We deem it no small thing in the ordering of the world, that between great communities covering a quarter of the surface of the globe the possibility of war is banished; and instead of devoting our counsels and our energies to the prevention of war between us, we devote them wholly to co-operation in the arts of peace.' Yet membership of the Commonwealth did not prevent or resolve war between India and Pakistan over Kashmir and Bangladesh while certain African members are strong advocates of military action against Rhodesia.

(3) *What shall be the purposes of the Commonwealth?*

Neither the qualifications for membership nor the purposes of the Commonwealth have been legally defined. Membership is open to all former British dependencies upon gaining sovereignty. Republics have been admitted; acceptance of the Queen as Head of the Commonwealth is the only common symbol and co-operation 'in the pursuit of peace, liberty, and progress' (The Declaration of London, 1949) the nearest approach to a statement of aims.

Care must be taken, however, to see that the links which induce nations to join the Commonwealth do not become the only justification for its existence. That the Commonwealth is real is not disputed — each nation knows who the other members are, and all are treated differently from outsiders. Moreover, it has the same reason for association as other clubs — that mutual benefits accrue when those having interests in common meet together to pool ideas, talk over difficulties and plan unity of action.

But are there sufficient common interests? Is there any value in continuing an association whose members no longer have similar political institutions and practices and which has no common military strategy or identity of outlook in international affairs?

The truth is that, with such divergencies of outlook, the basis of membership cannot be more precise than, in Mr. Macmillan's words, 'a common idealism'. And when it comes to translating that 'common idealism' into positive action, we cannot, now that the Commonwealth is a meeting not of like but of unlike peoples, expect it to function as an action group in the sense that it can take decisions binding all its members. But it fulfils an important role even as a sounding place of views for it is generally free of the Power Blocs which bedevil the United Nations' discussions. Indeed, in this role one of its strengths is its broad representation of all colours, continents, religions and economic development. Policies are influenced through the consensus of opinion, though usually this influence is confined to preventing members doing things of which others disapprove. That members do allow some give and take can be seen by studying their deliberations on Rhodesia and South Africa.

The history of the Rhodesian problem is one of protracted efforts to find an agreed solution within the Commonwealth. After the break-up of the Central African Federation, Rhodesia asked for independent status. This the British government was unwilling to grant except under certain conditions largely aimed at securing uninterrupted progress towards majority rule. Rhodesia would not agree to the necessary conditions, and the matter became one, not for British decision alone (the strictly legal position) but for Commonwealth discussion.

Mr. Ian Smith made his Unilateral Declaration of Independence on November 11th, 1965. Britain immediately imposed economic sanctions, but many African Commonwealth countries called for the immediate use of force, and when this was not forthcoming, Tanzania and Ghana broke off diplomatic relations with Britain although they remained within the Commonwealth.

At the Commonwealth Conference in Lagos in January, 1966, Britain's desire to rely solely on the effectiveness of economic sanctions in bringing the rebellion to an end was upheld in spite of Sierra Leone's demand for action by force. It was however agreed that if the rebellion had not ended by July another Conference would be called.

This met in September, 1966, in London. Once again, in deference to the wishes of Britain and the older members, the Afro-Asian members agreed to postpone further action on the condition that if Mr. Smith had not handed over power to the Governor within three months, a resolution in which Britain would join would be put before the United Nations' Security Council asking for selective and mandatory sanctions against Rhodesia. In December, Mr. Wilson, the British Prime Minister, made one final effort to reach agreement with Mr. Smith aboard H.M.S. *Tiger*, and when this failed the sanction resolution went to the United Nations. Throughout the whole proceedings, each Commonwealth member, especially Britain on the one hand and the African countries on the other, had, with two exceptions, shown tolerance in appreciating each other's difficulties.

The 1971 Singapore conference was dominated by Britain's

proposal to resume arms sales to South Africa. On the one hand, Britain viewed with alarm the build-up of Russian sea power in the Indian Ocean; on the other, the African and Asian members considered that the resumption of sales would afford a degree of respectability to a government which they abhorred. Mr. Heath, while asserting Britain's right to follow a policy which she deemed necessary, appears to have been influenced by the views expressed, for actual sales were limited to replacement parts for arms already supplied.

IV. The Strength of the Commonwealth

While it must be recognised that the Commonwealth could be fatally weakened by internal dissension, there are good grounds for expecting it to continue as an important institution in world affairs. First, it has shown in the past such a capacity for change that there seems little danger that rigidity to new conditions and opinions will be allowed to cause its collapse. Thus the setting up of the Commonwealth Secretariat has allowed Britain to withdraw from her old dominant role in Commonwealth affairs, although her unique experience within the association is likely to give her a special responsibility for some time.

Secondly, the Commonwealth is unlikely to be abandoned because it is more than an international political power group. 'People who talk about the deterioration in the health of the Commonwealth are thinking of the political difficulties and are often quite unaware of the organisations whose strength rests largely in the fact that they are run by people, not by governments. There are about 250 of these organisations, varying from the agricultural bureaux with a staff of 350, including more than 200 scientists and technicians and an annual expenditure of just under £1m., down to societies that do little more than meet once a year or organise an occasional conference.' (Hugh Noyes, *The Times*, August, 1967.)

Thirdly, although the proliferation of links with non-member countries may diminish the relative importance of the Commonwealth association, the new relationships should enrich the political experience of members and strengthen their economic position. Indeed, an inward-looking Commonwealth would be a less influential institution in world affairs.

Finally, despite the political controversy, the Commonwealth inspires intense loyalty among those who believe that it provides a unique opportunity to bring together rich and poor nations and eventually to create a genuinely non-racial international community. The fact that it is composed of unlike peoples can be one of its strengths, for it provides a forum for the expression of opinion and a chance of reaching a consensus of views. People of different races, rich and poor countries, one-party and multi-party systems, aligned and non-aligned, and even states locked in bitter dispute can still confer together simply because Commonwealth conferences do not bind or impose any great strain. And, so long as there is evidence of some give-and-take, it is a good thing for them to meet together. Unlike the United Nations, Commonwealth conferences are free from members taking up positions in order to further a particular political ideology.

Mr. Trudeau, the Prime Minister of Canada, expressed the modern spirit of the Commonwealth in his opening address to the 1973 Ottawa Conference: 'Within the Commonwealth we have the opportunity and the means for both communication and understanding. In this forum of discussion, each member is equal. None is senior, none is superior. None is distinguished by economic self-sufficiency; none is possessed of all political virtue. In our discussions during the next few days, I have no doubt that we will be able to demonstrate, to one another and the World, the advantage of our dissimilarity, the richness of our diversity, and the excitement of our variety. We will be able to do so because we are members of an association, not an institution. In the Commonwealth, there is no structure to contain us. The Commonwealth is a reflection of its 33 members and of their desire to consult and co-operate with one another. There is no artificial adhesive. Nor is there any voting, any constitution, any flag, any headquarters. This association is neither regional in nature, nor specialised in its interests. The Commonwealth is an organisation, and this fact guarantees both its vitality and its flexibility.'

The nature of the Commonwealth may have changed, but its basic aim remains as the greater enjoyment of life for people generally through peace, liberty and economic progress. The more advanced countries, with the exception of South Africa, have not found their position undermined by the criticism of the newer members; the newcomers have welcomed the influence they can exert, both inside and outside the Commonwealth, by virtue of membership. Britain in particular values the contact with diverse peoples which the Commonwealth provides, a type of contact envied both by the U.S.A. and Russia. It seems, therefore, that nobody is likely to take the lead in dismantling the Commonwealth.

SUGGESTED READING

E. M. Forster, *A Passage to India* (Edward Arnold, 1924; Penguin Books).
Margery Perham, *African Outline* (O.U.P., 1966).
M. Stewart, *Modern Forms of Government* (Allen and Unwin, 1959), Chapters 3, 4 and 5.
P. Gordon Walker, *The Commonwealth* (Secker and Warburg, 1962).
H. V. Wiseman, *Britain and the Commonwealth* (Allen and Unwin, 1965).

VII

REFLECTIONS ON
THE BRITISH CONSTITUTION

29

The Nature of the British Constitution

> 'An ancient and ever-altering constitution is like an old
> man who still wears with attached fondness clothes in
> the fashion of his youth: what you see of him is the
> same; what you do not see is wholly altered.'
>
> WALTER BAGEHOT: *The English Constitution*

I. CLASSIFICATION OF CONSTITUTIONS

The essential nature of the British constitution can best be
examined by considering its salient features in relation to a broad
classification of constitutions. Comparisons will be mainly with the
constitutions of other Commonwealth countries.

(1) *Written and unwritten*

Unlike Britain, most countries with advanced constitutions
have a document which can be referred to as 'the Constitution' —
a specifically enacted set of rules providing for the government.
The most famous of such documents is that framed by the
Founding Fathers in 1787 which, with a few important amendments, is still in force as the Constitution of the U.S.A.

Written constitutions usually contain three kinds of provisions.
Their principal object is to describe the main political institutions,
the powers they possess, and their relationship with each other.
Thus the 1949 Constitution of India provided, among other
matters, for an elected President, a Federal Legislature comprising
a House of the People and a Council of States, and for Governors
and Legislatures in twenty-eight states. The matters over which
each body had authority were laid down in three lists — a Union
list, a state list, and a concurrent list, which contained the subjects
within the province of both the Union and state legislatures.

Secondly, a constitution may guarantee certain rights. For
example, Ghana's requires her President on assuming office to

declare certain fundamental principles. These include 'that subject to such restrictions as may be necessary for preserving public order, morality or health, no person should be deprived of freedom of religion or speech, of the right to move and assemble without hindrance or of the right of access to the courts of law.' But if such provisions are to be an effective safeguard for the individual, they must be worded with exceptional care. The rules they contain have to be applied in different circumstances and subjected to judicial interpretation. The Government, for instance, can exercise wide powers in 'preserving public order'.

Finally, a constitution may include a general statement on basic attitudes. The South African constitution, for instance, begins with the words, 'The people of the Union acknowledge the sovereignty and guidance of Almighty God. . . . .' While such an expression of belief provides an impressive opening, it serves little practical purpose.

Why have countries found it necessary to draw up these special instruments of government? Three reasons can be advanced. First, they are needed when nations make a fresh start with their institutions, as when India, Pakistan, Ceylon, etc. gained their independence after World War II. Secondly, the country may contain groups of people distinct from each other through race, religion or language. In order to incorporate all people within the nation, each group must be given some guarantee that its identity will be maintained. Thirdly, in large countries, people in different parts may have particular interests and needs which they feel cannot be adequately provided for by a government in a remote capital. Here some form of federalism is likely, the division of powers between federal and state authorities being laid down in a written constitution.

None of these considerations applies to Britain. For nearly 900 years, no invasion of her borders has interrupted the slow evolution of her political institutions. Only once, during the Commonwealth period, was there a complete break with the past, Cromwell's Instrument of Government being Britain's nearest approach to a written constitution. Moreover, Britain has a relatively homogeneous population. While some special provisions are made for Wales, Scotland and Northern Ireland, the protection of a written constitution has never been felt to be necessary. Finally, Britain is a small country. From the earliest times the King's writ could cover the whole realm and in most parts people sensed some contact with the government at Westminster.

Hence, when the British speak of their constitution, they are using the word in a wider sense than other peoples to refer generally to the legal and non-legal rules which regulate their government. The British approach has been purely empirical and no attempt has been made to gather together the most fundamental constitutional laws. Indeed, an unwritten constitution is generally regarded as being advantageous, as the French writer, Emile Boutmy, recognised. 'By this means only', he says, 'can you preserve the happy incoherences, the useful incongruities, the protecting contradictions which have such good reason for existing in institutions, viz. that they exist in the nature of things, and which, while they allow free play to all social forces, never allow any one of these forces room to work out of its allotted line, or to shake the foundations and walls of the whole fabric. This is the result which the English flatter themselves they have arrived at by the extraordinary dispersion of their constitutional texts, and they have always taken good care not to compromise the result in any way by attempting to form a code' (quoted by J. A. R. Marriott: *English Political Institutions*).

The differences between the unwritten constitution of Britain and the constitutions of other countries should not, however, be exaggerated. In the first place, no single document could describe all the rules and principles which determine how the country is governed without running to the length of an encyclopaedia and becoming too involved for the ordinary citizen to understand. Written constitutions are, in fact, only a few pages long, and all have to be supplemented by many other rules. Secondly, many of the basic principles and rules of the British constitution are written down, though not in a single document. They are to be found in statutes, judicial decisions, and the utterances of politicians and constitutional lawyers. Indeed, probably more has been written about the British constitution than any other for, not only has it had a long history, but numerous countries have used it as a model. It is therfore more accurate to say that Britain has 'no written constitution' than to say she has an unwritten one.

(2) *Rigid and flexible*

Provisions must be made for changing the constitution so that it can keep in step with new ideas or provide for needs which could not possibly have been foreseen by its founders. It may, for instance, be desirable for the federal authority to be given more power to control a greatly increased flow of inter-state trade or to promote social welfare and full employment. Yet, special provisions are valueless if a constitution can be changed too easily. The individual states of a federation would have no guarantee of their entrenched rights; the basic freedoms of citizens could be whittled away; sweeping changes in government could be made by a party gaining a small majority perhaps on a different issue. It was such possibilities that the constitution was designed to prevent. The result is that almost all written constitutions are rigid; that is, they contain clauses allowing them to be amended only by some procedure which is distinct from that of ordinary legislation. In contrast, a flexible constitution can be amended by the ordinary process of law making, there being no formal distinction between constitutional and ordinary law.

In practice, there are degrees of rigidity. The legislature itself may be allowed to change the constitution, but only under certain conditions. In South Africa, agreement to change 'entrenched' clauses must be reached by a two-thirds majority of the total membership of the two Chambers. India guarantees the position of the states by stipulating that many of the articles of the constitution can only be amended after affirmative resolutions have been passed in the legislatures of a majority of the states. The procedure in Australia is even more difficult. After an amendment has passed both Houses of Parliament, it must be submitted to a referendum and approved by the majority of the electors. Furthermore, assent must be given by a majority of electors in a majority of the six states. Finally, although it is not usual, the approval of a special convention may be necessary. Thus, the Federation of Malaya's constitution provided that articles concerning the Rulers of the nine Malay states or the special position of the Malays can only be altered with the consent of the Conference of Rulers.

The disadvantage of a rigid constitution is that some time must usually elapse before it can be amended to comply with new philosophies or changed economic circumstances. In fact, however, adjustments often take place informally, either as a result of judicial interpretation or by convention. A rigid constitution necessitates some form of Supreme Court which can decide whether the terms of the constitution are being observed or whether a new proposal represents an amendment. While the judges must apply the text as it is enacted, they can often exercise some discretion by adopting a fairly liberal interpretation. Such an approach may have considerable practical significance as, for example, when the High Court of Australia in 1942 upheld legislation which obliged the states to relinquish their powers to impose income tax and to accept in their place grants from the Commonwealth Parliament. Hardly less important are the changes which come about through usage and convention. In this way, for example, the Governor-General's right to veto bills was gradually modified in Canada, Australia and New Zealand.

But the flexibility of a constitution, even if formal adjustment is necessary, depends largely on the wishes of the country's citizens. A change is usually not difficult when they realise that the constitution embodies outdated ideas or is an obstacle to economic benefits. On the other hand, the people often have a fine appreciation of what is fundamental to political freedom, as, for example, when the referendum in Australia in 1953 rejected the government's proposal to ban the Communist party.

Britain's constitution is essentially flexible. In part, this is a result of the country's steady development to political maturity, for the people have never been forced to gather together basic laws and give them an entrenched position. But chiefly it follows from the acceptance of the legal sovereignty of Parliament and the unwillingness to make the legislature subordinate to a supreme court. Parliament is checked instead by prevailing political opinion, expressed through many institutions. Yet the British Government is much less likely to change the constitution in its own favour than the government of countries having a written constitution but under single-party, totalitarian rule. Indeed, fundamental changes, would probably, as in 1911, be made only after a general election, though the latter is not essential.

(3) *Federal and Unitary*

Unlike a unitary constitution, in which sovereign power is vested in a single legislative body, a federal constitution distributes the ordinary powers of sovereignty among different bodies, each co-ordinate with and independent of the others. Such bodies are usually the legislature of the federal government and the legislatures of the individual states. A federation must be a definite organ of government, not simply a form of co-operation between separate governments, as in the British Commonwealth, or merely a permanent conference, as with the United Nations. It entails a definite sacrifice of some sovereignty by the participating states to the federal authority, although they retain their own legislatures and governments for certain matters. Thus, while in a unitary constitution the legislature may delegate some of its law-making authority and sanction other bodies for local government, states in a federation retain their separate identities but renounce powers which were once their own in favour of the federal body.

In practice, the absence of complete sovereignty in one body may prove a weakness. The division of powers may be interpreted by judges too narrowly, while the constitution suffers from all the defects of rigidity. On the other hand, the distinction between federal and unitary States is not quite so sharp as might appear. In the first place, considerable devolution may occur in a unitary State. In South Africa, for example, the four provinces are able to make laws on a wide range of subjects, though the Union Parliament can change their powers if it wishes. Secondly, some constitutions are more strongly federal in their rules than others. Thus, while all six Australian states are equally represented in the Senate, in Canada Ontario and Quebec have more senators than the other eight provinces. Thirdly, some constitutions (like Australia's) define federal powers, leaving residual powers to the states, while others (like Canada's) limit state powers and give the residual to the central government. Fourthly, the degree of federalism, as we have seen, may change without any formal alteration in the constitution. This has happened in Australia, where the strength of the federal government has grown considerably during the 20th century.

It is even possible to discern some elements of federalism in the United Kingdom. The Government of Ireland Act, 1920, gave Northern Ireland a wide measure of home rule under her own two-chamber legislature and executive, although she is still represented at Westminster (see page 283). In addition, many functions, concerning particularly education and the environment, are performed for Scotland and Wales by the Scottish and Welsh Offices respectively. Scotland has its own Secretary of State, assisted by three Parliamentary Under-Secretaries, in charge of four administrative departments with headquarters in Scotland (see chapter 16). Each is completely independent of its corresponding English department and is subject only to the control of the Treasury. Scotland also retains its own judicial system and law officers. Somewhat less control over its own affairs is enjoyed by Wales, which is judicially part of 'England'. But it now has its own Secretary of State, assisted by a Minister of State and a Parliamentary Under-Secretary. Since 1969, responsibility for health and welfare services in Wales has been entrusted to him, and he has a shared responsibility for agricultural affairs in Wales. Nevertheless, despite this devolution, the United Kingdom's government is essentially unitary, for all its various parts are subject to the legislative supremacy of the Parliament at Westminster, and this will continue if and when the Kilbrandon recommendations are implemented.

(4) *Presidential and Parliamentary*

Where the executive is co-ordinate in power with the legislature, the constitution is presidential. In the United States, for instance, the President is elected separately and has his own particular authority. Where, however, the executive is subordinate to the legislature, the constitution is classified as parliamentary.

Since the legislative authority of Parliament is not restricted by a written constitution, the British system can be regarded as the highest form of parliamentary constitution. On the other hand, although the Civil War was fought to decide the supremacy of Parliament, the practice of having a Prime Minister and Cabinet drawn from an elected chamber and responsible to it depends mainly upon convention. Moreover, the growing importance today of the Prime Minister's position has made such observers as Professor Max Beloff and Lord Boothby assert that we are moving towards a presidential form of government. This is particularly noticeable in foreign affairs. The tendency of other leading powers, especially the U.S.S.R., the U.S.A., and France, is now to work through their heads of government when discussing important issues, and the British Prime Minister has had to reciprocate. Hence, the appointment in 1960 of a peer, Lord Home, as Foreign Secretary appeared to many as a break with convention that this post should be filled from the House of Commons, and an indication that ministers are becoming increasingly responsible to the Prime Minister at the expense of the elected chamber.

II. Components of the British Constitution

Because the British cannot point to a specific document as their 'Constitution', it does not mean, as de Tocqueville asserted, that the British constitution does not exist. A constitution consists of the whole body of rules and practices determining the structure and powers of government. Hence, in Britain, the only difference is that, instead of concentrating on a single document, we have to discover those rules in a number of sources. In point of fact, no formal constitution could describe completely how government is carried on; attention would have to be drawn to the conventions which come into being to work it.

(1) *Historic documents*

Magna Carta, the Petition of Right, and the Bill of Rights, although having no special legal position, contain or imply such fundamental constitutional principles that particular importance must be attached to them.

The Magna Carta, 1215, drew together some of the most important customs of the land in its attempt to guarantee certain rights in the feudal society of the time. Among other things, the King had to promise not to levy scutage or aid, outside of three customary feudal dues, without the consent of the Common Council. Furthermore, no freeman could be seized, imprisoned, dispossessed of his land or outlawed except by lawful judgment of his peers. The important part which these two provisions in particular have played in the development of our constitution has already been shown. But by the 17th century Magna Carta was deemed to possess an even greater significance — seeming to show that there is a law which must be obeyed by the King as much as anyone else and that, if he disregards this law, he can be compelled.

The Petition of Right, 1628, was another stage in the attack on Divine Right, for Charles I had to yield to the protests of the House of Commons against the levying of taxation other than by Act of Parliament, the imprisonment of persons 'by special order of the King', the use of martial law in time of peace and the billeting of soldiers upon private persons.

The Bill of Rights, 1689, removed once and for all the King's claim to certain important prerogatives and contained other declarations basic to our constitution. The King's power to suspend or dispense with laws, to levy money by pretence of the prerogative and without grant of Parliament, and to raise or keep an army in times of peace was henceforth abolished. Freedom of speech and of proceedings in Parliament and the right of subjects to petition the King were all re-asserted.

It will be observed that these documents are concerned almost entirely with the necessities of the moment; they make no attempt to lay down a general code of government.

(2) *Statutes*

Important developments in the British constitution have often been brought about by Acts of Parliament. Thus, statutes create a Parliament for the United Kingdom, thereby determining the territorial boundaries within which the constitution operates (Act of Union with Scotland, 1707), provide for the life of Parliament (Parliament Act, 1911), govern the relationship between the two Houses (Parliament Acts, 1911 and 1949), regulate the suffrage (Reform Acts, 1832–1884), determine the succession to the throne (Act of Settlement, 1701), grant salaries to Cabinet ministers (Ministers of the Crown Act, 1937), create government machinery (Education Act, 1944), guarantee the independence of judges (Judicature (Consolidation) Act, 1925), reform the judiciary (Judicature Act, 1873), establish federations in the Commonwealth (Commonwealth of Australia Constitution Act, 1900), end legal control over the Dominions (Statute of Westminister, 1931), and establish new areas and authorities for local government (Local Government Act, 1972). These are but a few examples illustrating the extent of 'parliamentary sovereignty'.

(3) *Rules of common law*

Parts of our constitutional law have not been enacted by Parliament, but are simply based on ancient custom. Thus our fundamental freedoms are essentially common law rights, though often, as with the Habeas Corpus Act, 1679, they have been further guaranteed by statute. The importance of these common law principles is two-fold. Their emphasis on the rights of the individual has contributed to the essential philosophy of our constitution (see page 434); their application by the judges from the reign of Henry II determined the development of the constitution, for it established the supremacy of law and prevented any extension of the King's powers.

It seems unlikely, however, that all the prerogative powers have been given legal definition by being challenged in the courts. Some must be sought, therefore, in the works of constitutional lawyers, such as Ranulf de Glanville (*Treatises on the Laws of England*, 1189) and Sir William Blackstone (*Commentaries on the Laws of England*, 1765), or in the writings of commentators, such as Walter Bagehot (*The English Constitution*, 1867).

(4) *Case Law*

Rules of both statute and common law have to be interpreted by the courts whenever there is a dispute over their application to a particular case. Because Parliament is sovereign, statute law takes precedence over every other form of law, and judges are restricted to interpreting the texts of statutes. But sometimes the meaning of an Act is ambiguous, and then the judge must apply acknowledged principles to the new set of facts. Such decisions become accepted as part of the law of the land and are followed in subsequent cases.

Many of the rulings of the courts have been of great constitutional importance, and reference to some of them has already been made (see pages 410–11). Other examples are: the *Case of Proclamations* (1611), in which Lord Chief Justice Coke, by ruling that the prerogative was limited by the law of the land, prevented the King from creating any new offence by Proclamation; *Bushell's Case* (1670), which gave immunity against legal action for words spoken by parties, counsel and witnesses in judicial proceedings.

(5) *The law and custom of Parliament*

The privileges enjoyed by both Houses, protecting their freedom, security, dignity and independence, are enforced by the High Court of Parliament and form part of the constitution (see pages 160–2).

Similarly, the procedure of both Houses is based on rules which have been designed to enable government to function efficiently. Most of these rules are to be found in the standing orders and Journals. Thus standing orders require that a bill shall be read three times and a finance bill introduced by a minister of the

Crown. But such procedure, unlike privilege, is not law in the strictest sense. Standing orders, for instance, can be suspended on the resolution of either House.

(6) *Conventions*

In practice, no legal rules, whether of a written or unwritten constitution, could completely provide for the working of government. They have to be supplemented by 'conventions' — practices, regarded as binding, which experience has shown to be necessary for developing within the law existing institutions. Of course, such conventions vary in importance. Some, such as choosing the Government from the majority party in the House of Commons, are obviously fundamental. Others, like appointing a member of the Opposition as Chairman of the Public Accounts Committee, while not indispensable, help government to be carried on in the true spirit of the constitution. Conventions arise because politics is essentially a matter of human relations; as in our everyday life, customs are observed which promote the common good. How they work can best be seen by considering the main institutions in which they play a prominent part.

In the first place, the way in which the prerogative powers of the Crown are used is now decided by conventions (see chapter 13). Such conventions are necessary for two reasons. (*a*) Although the supremacy of Parliament had been established by the struggles of the 17th century, the Revolutionary Settlement of 1689 still left many legal powers in the hands of the King. Conventions, therefore, had to come into being to ensure that such powers were exercised in accordance with the legal supremacy of Parliament. Hence, today, the Sovereign's assent to legislation is purely formal, Parliament must be convoked at least once a year, ministers must be chosen from the party supported by the House of Commons, and so on. (*b*) The Reform Act, 1832, carried the development of the constitution a stage further. Now the powers of the Crown had to be exercised to conform with the political sovereignty of the electorate as expressed through the party system. This can even be discerned in the 19th-century struggles between the Lords and Commons, for the Sovereign showed then that the prerogative of creating peers would be used to support the elected Chamber.

Secondly, the rules governing the Cabinet system are based entirely on convention. While many of them are connected with the prerogative, others have developed independently as needed. Thus, the dominant position of the Prime Minister, the individual responsibility of ministers for their civil servants, the doctrine of collective responsibility, the opportunity for a resigning minister to present his reasons to the House, and the resignation of the Government without meeting Parliament when defeated at the polls, all rest on convention.

Thirdly, while much of the procedure of the two Houses is embodied in standing orders and is, therefore, part of the law and custom of Parliament, many important practices regularly observed rest merely on convention. Examples are: agreements on business 'through the usual channels'; pairing; the understanding that the Government will always find time for a vote of censure; the occupation of the front benches by leading members of the Government and Opposition; the requirement that a member sits when the Speaker stands; and, in the Lords, the non-participation of lay peers in judicial proceedings.

Lastly, Commonwealth relations have been moulded by convention. While many of these conventions were given legal form by the Statute of Westminster, the Act limited itself to removing certain anomalies which they had created. Hence the informal basis upon which the whole Commonwealth idea has developed still remains. Thus, in the preamble, the non-operative part of the Act, it is simply recorded that 'it would be in accord with the established constitutional position' if any alteration of the law touching the succession to the throne or the royal style and titles were to require the assent of the Parliaments of the Dominions as well as of the United Kingdom. The regular meetings of Prime Ministers and the form they take are likewise based on convention.

Conventions, therefore, fulfil a special role in the constitution. First, they help the machinery to run smoothly. For example, 'arrangements behind the Speaker's chair', the selection of standing committees to reflect the composition of the House, pairing, and the fair allocation of the limited debating time between parties, all represent positive contributions to the efficient working of Parliament. Secondly, conventions, being less rigid than law, allow flexibility in government institutions. While it is a recognised rule that certain ministerial posts should be filled from the House of Commons, there is sufficient elasticity to allow the Prime Minister to depart from it when circumstances require. Mr. Harold

Macmillan found it convenient to appoint Lord Home as Foreign Secretary in 1960 although many had assumed that such a key post would not again be held by a peer. Above all, conventions are the means by which the constitution is made adaptable. As new needs arise, so old conventions can be easily modified or fresh ones developed. Some may even be dropped. The Home Secretary did not attend the birth of Prince Charles in 1948, thereby ending a practice first established in Charles II's reign. On the other hand, it can now be recognised as a convention that 'interests' are consulted over legislation which concerns them. In extreme cases, conventions may be given the force of law, as, for instance, when the Parliament Act formalised the power of the Lords with regard to money bills. The part played by conventions is summed up by Sir Ivor Jennings: 'They provide the flesh which clothes the dry bones of the law; they make the legal constitution work; they keep it in touch with the growth of ideas' (*The Law and the Constitution*).

Unlike strict rules of law, conventions are not enforceable in the courts, and we have to look for them outside Acts of Parliament or the rulings of judges. There is a variety of sources — letters and leading articles in the Press, the observations of writers on the constitution, the letters and diaries of monarchs, pronouncements of politicians, memoirs of retired Cabinet ministers and statements in parliamentary debates. Often, too, conventions are more imprecise than rules of law.

Nevertheless, such differences do not mean that conventions are any less binding or important. Often, as Dicey points out, failure to observe them may eventually lead to a breach of the law. Thus, if the monarch neglected to summon Parliament at least once during the year, the Government would soon be involved in illegal expenditure, since the Appropriation Act would not have been approved. Not that this is a complete explanation of why conventions are obeyed. The appointment of a Prime Minister from the House of Lords, for instance, would not lead to a breach of the law.

Ultimately, the answer cannot be found in terms of law. Conventions are not enforced, either directly or indirectly, by the courts, but by the weight of public opinion, which expects politicians to behave in the true spirit of the constitution. Thus, it is a moral, not a legal, imperative upon which conventions depend.

If the Prime Minister were chosen from the Lords, it could easily be represented as undemocratic, and a Government supporting it would lose votes at the next election for offending public opinion. Indeed, law itself is only obeyed when it is in tune with the beliefs of the people. In the final analysis, both conventions and law are a product of the philosophy and character of the British people.

SUGGESTED READING

A. V. Dicey, *Introduction to the Law of the Constitution* (10th Ed., Macmillan, 1961), Introduction by E. C. S. Wade and Part III.

Sir Ivor Jennings, *The Law and the Constitution* (5th Ed., University of London, 1955), Chapter II, Sections 2 and 3; Chapter III.

J. A. R. Marriott, *English Political Institutions* (3rd Ed., O.U.P., 1925), Introduction and Chapters 1 and 2.

C. F. Strong, *Modern Political Constitutions* (8th Ed., Sidgwick and Jackson, 1972).

E. C. S. Wade and G. G. Phillips, *Constitutional Law* (8th Ed., Longmans, 1970), Part II, Chapter 4.

K. C. Wheare, *Modern Constitutions* (O.U.P., 1966); *Federal Government* (4th Ed., O.U.P., 1963).

30

Democracy in the United Kingdom

'Democracy is a most difficult form of government —
difficult, because it requires for its perfect functioning
the participation of all the people in the country. It
cannot function — not function well — unless everyone, men and women alike, feel their responsibility to
their State, do their own duty, and try and choose the
men who will do theirs. It is not a matter of party: it is
common to all of us, because Democracy wants constant
guarding.'

LORD BALDWIN: *Broadcast to Schools*, March, 1934

Most countries describe themselves as 'democratic'. In practice,
however, this means little. There are, for instance, no political
systems in Europe more obviously dissimilar than those of the
communist Eastern countries and the non-Communist West, with
the dividing line drawn dramatically through Germany. Yet
East Germany describes herself as 'an indivisible democratic
republic' (Article I of the constitution), while West Germany is
'a democratic and social federal state' (Article 20 of the constitution). Indeed, it is reported that when a political refugee arrived in
West Berlin and was greeted with the words, 'Welcome to the
West German Democratic Republic', he exclaimed: 'Democratic!
But I have just been escaping from democracy!'

However, there is little mystery about the basic meaning of the
word in its application to the British constitution. It implies that
government rests on consent, public opinion ultimately determining the Government and its policy. Nevertheless, although this is
the final aim, many practical questions have to be answered. What
do we mean by 'public opinion'? How is it formed and influenced?
To what extent does it manage to make itself felt? What are the
main difficulties in bringing about popular participation in political
affairs? It is these questions which we shall attempt to answer in
this chapter.

I. THE MEANING OF PUBLIC OPINION

Democracy must produce a Government which is voluntarily accepted by the majority of the people. To do this, it is necessary to effect a compromise between the wishes of the forty million people who make up the electorate. But although British society is compact and relatively homogeneous in comparison with the populations of the U.S.A. or the U.S.S.R., it clearly contains a rich variety of electors — retired field marshals, London barrow boys, city business men, Scottish crofters, suburban housewives, and so on. To talk generally of 'public opinion' is thus a considerable over-simplification. A democratic system has, in fact, to satisfy four kinds of opinion — majority opinion, minority opinion, informed opinion and group opinion, though the same people may be found in more than one category.

(1) *Majority and minority opinion*

Where political organisations fight each other in an uncompromising life and death struggle, eventually the party in power will be driven by fear to introduce repressive measures against its opponents. They in their turn will find their only means of expression in the illegal use of force. A degree of moderation is thus necessary to democracy. Differences are talked over, not fought over; open debate, not violence, is the means of determining policy.

Hence the relationship between the majority and the minority is one of the best tests of democracy, for each must play a constructive part. Although the majority governs, it has to recognise that there are limits to the restraints it can impose on the minority, and that beyond a certain point (as, for example, when fundamental liberties are threatened) people are not prepared to submit to majority rule. The task of the minority is to make the majority justify its views and policies. To suppress dissenting views is, as J. S. Mill argued, 'to assume infallibility in public affairs.' In a healthy democracy, the arguments of opponents are tolerated. They may be correct; but even when they are not, or only partially so, they provide that controversy without which the ideas of the majority become stale. The absence of challenge engenders a mental laziness which causes people to lose 'the clearer perception and livelier impression of truth, produced by its collision with error' (J. S. Mill, *Essay on Liberty*).

Opposition groups accept majority decisions for both moral and practical reasons. Not only would it be thought wrong to resist the greater opinion and to impose policy on a reluctant public, but, under a democratic constitution, the Opposition hopes that one day it will become the majority. Should it do so, it will then have the power to implement its own policy, and in its turn will be dependent upon the tolerance of its rivals. A wise Opposition party, therefore, sets a good precedent.

We have already seen how the respective roles of Her Majesty's Government and Her Majesty's Opposition are played out in practice. The mutual confidence and respect between majority and minority is symbolised at the opening of Parliament, when Government and Opposition members walk side by side from their own Chamber to the House of Lords to hear the Queen's speech. In doing so, they demonstrate that, at a level deeper than the party struggle, both sides accept the basic rules of parliamentary democracy.

(2) Informed opinion

While the majority decide the Government, the impact of different opinions on political action cannot be estimated simply by counting heads. That section of the community which comprises 'informed opinion' has an influence out of all proportion to its size. Those who are acquainted with all the main facts and arguments, skilled in presenting a case, and accustomed to acting in concert with people of like mind, are naturally more influential than those who are ignorant, inarticulate and apathetic. If it were not so, democracy would be unworkable. There are, of course, many degrees of knowledge, interest and influence, so that there is no sharp division between 'informed' and 'uninformed' opinion. The greater the proportion of the people who can be included in the former category, the more truly democratic is the country, but the need for leadership will remain.

(3) Group opinion

The Industrial Revolution, by increasing the division of labour, split the community into sections concerned with different interests. Yet only the more fortunate part of the country was politically articulate. 'Our democracy was, from an early period, the most aristocratic, and our aristocracy the most democratic in the world', writes Lord Macaulay during the first half of the 19th century (*History of England*). Agricultural labourers scattered over the countryside, and factory workers spending long hours at the bench, lacked the time, energy, ability and financial resources to secure political advance. Moreover, poorly educated, they had few effective leaders within their own group. On those occasions when they failed to attract leaders from other classes, movements, such as Chartism, collapsed.

Yet, in the long run, economic growth encouraged the development of democracy. Once men had become assembled in factories and congregated in large towns, it was easier to canvass their support for political demands. The very abuses of the Industrial Revolution stimulated political thought and action, for the numerous reports of commissions and enquiries into social problems, together with the agitation of philanthropic reformers, helped to create 'a social conscience'. Moreover, industrialisation gradually knit the nation more closely together. The development of communications made people more mobile, and men's horizons widened beyond the family and parish. They found new loyalties in organisations, often nationwide in scope, formed especially to further their own interests in an increasingly complex society.

Above all, public ethics, religion, and the technical needs of industrialisation, demanded a high degree of literacy. And, once the workers had got the vote, the rulers of the country recognised the need to 'educate their masters'. The more educated the working class became, the less easy it was to ignore politically.

Today, therefore, people are organised in a large number of groups based on their common interests, many of which can be wholly or partly furthered by political action. Examples of these bodies are trade unions, employers' organisations, professional associations, and propagandist societies of many kinds. The political initiative exercised by organised groups plays a vital part in the functioning of British democracy, and it will be discussed at greater length later in this chapter.

II. Formation of Public Opinion

The political views of the electorate are the result of two kinds of forces — natural, spontaneous influences, and deliberate attempts to influence people's minds.

(1) The spontaneous formation of opinion

Among the most potent natural influences on opinion are occupation, education, and family upbringing. The effect of these is often shown in the way people vote. There is thus a tendency for business and professional people to vote Conservative and for industrial workers to support the Labour Party. In the latter relationship, however, there is much less consistency. The National Opinion Poll's researches in 1970 indicate that 30% of the wage-earning working groups voted Conservative, accounting for over 40% of the Party's total poll.

It is difficult to determine the influence of education on opinion, though certain effects may be noted. Improved educational facilities increase social mobility and enable children from poor homes to enter managerial and professional occupations. Geographical mobility is also encouraged, educated youths often moving to other parts of the country in order to make the best use of their training. This takes them away from family influences and traditional regional concentrations of opinion.

Above all, the ideas and prejudices generally accepted by family and other social contacts help to condition a person's thinking. Thus, dispassionate views are more easily formed in a different age or outside the country. An Englishman today, for instance, can decide on the morality of the slave trade or South African apartheid fairly objectively. But only a person of independent mind and strong character questions the most deeply held views of friends, family and elders and takes the risk of possible social ostracism for his ideas. J. S. Mill argued that society acting collectively could impose a worse tyranny than that of governments who punish citizens for their politics. 'Society', he wrote, 'can and does execute its own mandates; and if it issues wrong mandates instead of right, or any mandates at all in things with which it ought not to meddle, it practises a social tyranny more formidable than many kinds of political oppression, since, though not usually upheld by such extreme penalties, it leaves fewer means of escape, penetrating much more deeply into the details of life, and enslaving the soul itself' (*Essay on Liberty*).

(2) The deliberate creation of opinion

While economic difficulties or an international crisis may cause people to look for an alternative policy, no party can afford to wait upon the fortuitous turn of events to gain power. Solid and sustained efforts must be made to convert the electorate.

Since 1945, both main parties have paid considerable attention to the section of their organisation concerned with political education. Conferences, lectures and discussion groups are arranged and books, pamphlets and periodicals published. The Bow Group and the Fabian Society, on the Conservative and Labour sides respectively, both carry out research and contribute original ideas for discussion.

But newspapers, television and the radio have a much wider influence. According to an analysis made by the Hulton Readership Survey in 1956, 88% of the adult population reads at least one morning newspaper. Of course, the popular newspapers are not solely concerned with forming political opinion, and the serious dailies, *The Times*, *The Guardian*, and *The Daily Telegraph*, account for only 12% of national newspaper sales. Yet although the mass circulation newspapers may sometimes be inaccurate in their facts and appeal to emotion rather than to thought, they nevertheless present easily understandable accounts and views of the major political issues. It is left to the serious papers and periodicals (such as *The Economist, New Society, Spectator* and *New Statesman*) to thrash out the great issues of the day. Their influence is far-reaching, for they are read by those exercising authority in the community.

Although newspapers have a wide readership, it is doubtful whether they sway voters during an election. People tend to read those journals which appeal to their own political prejudices, and newspapers are probably more effective in confirming the views of the convinced party supporter than in determining those of the floating voter. Television and the radio may have more influence on people's thoughts. Although not having the permanence of the printed word (except for talks published in *The Listener*), they present different views and stimulate discussion. How influential they can be was shown in 1960 when an item about small investors in a B.B.C. television programme did much to cause price falls on the Stock Exchange the following day.

Since the mass media of communication are the main means of influencing opinion, no party or section of the community should have a monopoly of them. Both the B.B.C. and the I.T.A. are required by statute to be politically neutral. While newspapers are usually committed to particular political views, they nevertheless cover a wide range of opinion, although certain minorities, such as Scottish republicans and to some extent the Liberal Party, have comparatively few outlets for expression. And, at their best, British newspapers live up to the maxim of C. P. Scott, a former editor of the *Manchester Guardian*, that 'comment is free, but facts are sacred'.

III. INFLUENCE OF PUBLIC OPINION

THE MANDATE

According to the theory of our constitution, Parliament's legal supremacy is restrained by the political sovereignty of the electorate. But is this so in practice? Can the electorate control the policies of a Government when in power?

During the 19th century, the idea slowly evolved that the electorate gives the Government a 'mandate' to govern along certain broad lines. The general election of May, 1831, fought on the issue of parliamentary reform, was the first in which the electorate chose a clearly defined policy, and it gradually came to be accepted that political reform meant that the electorate could not only choose a Government but indicate a policy. When, in 1885, Gladstone announced his intention of granting Irish home rule, the reactions of his opponents within the Party showed the mandate to be an accepted principle of the constitution. They argued that he could not initiate such a policy without instructions from the electorate, condemning him all the more strongly because an election had been held only a few months previously. Within a year, Gladstone had to dissolve Parliament and place the issue squarely before the electorate.

Nevertheless, the idea of the mandate is, in practice, necessarily imprecise. A party's programme at an election includes many items, and it is difficult to discover which of them has secured support. Hardly more than three elections have been fought on clear issues. The 1831 election has already been mentioned. At the 1868 election, the proposal to disestablish the Irish Church was dominant, while the second election of 1910 was to decide the position of the House of Lords. At a typical election, however, many issues are debated. In February, 1974, for instance, although

Mr. Heath had called the general election in particular to seek the electorate's support for his industrial relations and wage restraint policy, in addition renegotiation of the Common Market treaty, food prices, housing, rents and education were all discussed. Nor is it possible to determine whether people are voting for a policy or merely against a Government. Thus many electors in 1951 may have voted Conservative purely on the negative grounds that they did not want any more nationalisation.

Secondly, the doctrine is difficult to apply when there are more than two parties with none having an absolute majority. What kind of mandate, for instance, could be claimed after the February, 1974 election when 301 Labour, 296 Conservative, 14 Liberal, 11 Ulster Unionist, 7 Scottish Nationalist and 2 Welsh Nationalist members were returned?

A third weakness is that the mandate cannot distinguish between ends and means. Mr. Balfour, the Conservative Leader in 1911, opposed the Parliament Bill on the grounds that, while in the previous December the electorate had clearly shown that they wanted the constitutional relationship of the two Houses to be determined, they could hardly have given a mandate for the Government's particular solution, since the bill had not been previously discussed in the House of Commons. But, of course, no mandate can be so precise, for it would mean holding a general election after the introduction of each major bill. On the other hand, the term does imply that Government action should be subject to certain limitations. Only in times of crisis would a Prime Minister ask, as Ramsay MacDonald did in 1931, for a 'doctor's mandate' to take whatever steps were desirable to solve the country's economic problems.

Fourthly, the mandate cannot be applied to unforeseen problems. Consequently, it has only the most general application to foreign policy. The British Government, for instance, had received no instructions from the electorate as to the policy it should support at the United Nations when South Korea was invaded in 1950.

Fifthly, it is impossible for the electorate to give precise directions on complicated and technical matters. This applies particularly to economic policy, such as the decision to 'float' the pound sterling in June, 1972. Here measures often have to be introduced so swiftly that no reference to the electorate is possible.

Finally, can the doctrine be applied with equal force throughout the whole of the Government's tenure of office? Circumstances and opinions may change considerably. Thus, when the Labour Government introduced the Iron and Steel Bill in the 1948-9 session, the Conservatives argued that the mandate given in 1945 was no longer valid, since the Government had no assurance of support in the country.

But although imprecise, the concept of the mandate is important, for it expresses the basic requirement of democracy that persons chosen to govern must keep to the broad policies of their election statements. If they do not (and subsequent events may make it difficult), the Opposition will ensure that some explanation is given to the electorate in Parliament — and at the polls.

PRESSURE GROUPS

While the Government is accountable to the electorate as a whole, it must also consider group opinion. In fact, many of the great reforms in modern history have resulted largely from the agitation of associations specifically formed for a given purpose. The Anti-Slavery League, the Political Unions, the Anti-Corn Law League, and the Suffragettes, are but a few examples of such movements.

Pressure groups, however, normally work unobtrusively. Far from leading to turmoil, their existence helps to make the constitution work smoothly. Indeed, Professor S. E. Finer considers the phrase 'pressure group' to be misleading, since groups rarely exert pressure by applying sanctions, or if they do so, not continuously.

(1) *Kinds of groups*

Important groups have been formed to protect the economic interests of their members. Thus trade unions and many professional organisations are concerned with wages and salaries. Both on the workers' and employers' sides, these associations may be large. The Transport and General Workers' Union has over $1\frac{1}{4}$ million members, while the National Farmers' Union represents about 90% of the farmers in England and Wales, and the Confederation of British Industry approximately 12,000 firms. Economic groups, of course, are not only concerned with wages and salaries but consider the whole range of economic and political problems. Before Britain entered the Common Market, for instance, all the associations mentioned above had given their views on the subject.

The non-economic groups are of five main kinds. Some, such as the Howard League for Penal Reform and the Royal Society for the Prevention of Cruelty to Animals, further an ideal of social behaviour. Others, like the Lord's Day Observance Society and the Student Christian Movement, are devoted to religious and moral issues. All the churches are well organised to express their particular views. Thirdly, there are groups covering a wide range of educational, recreational and cultural matters, such as the Council for the Protection of Rural England and the Royal Institute of British Architects. In addition, sections of the community have formed bodies to protect special interests. Thus motorists are represented by the Automobile Association and ex-Servicemen by the British Legion. Finally, there are groups concerned with governing — the Association of Metropolitan Authorities, the County Councils' Association and the Magistrates' Association being three typical examples.

Sometimes associations are temporary, formed to achieve one special purpose, and it is not uncommon for various organisations to join together in the fight for a common objective. They can even on occasions persuade a Government to change its mind on a policy to which it appeared to be firmly committed, as in the case of the Government's final abandonment in 1968 of its decision that the third London airport must be situated at Stanstead, Essex, though it must be added that, according to the M.P. for Saffron Walden, this long and vigorous public campaign cost local people some £35,000 and the two county councils involved well over £100,000.

(2) *How groups conduct their activities*

In their everyday work, pressure groups co-operate closely with government departments and other public bodies. The convention is now accepted that recognised interests should be consulted both in preparing a bill and in implementing the Act. Consultation may even be made a statutory duty. Thus the Agriculture Act, 1947, obliges the Minister of Agriculture and Fisheries to consult 'with such bodies and persons as appear to him to represent the interests of producers in the agricultural industry'. In this way, the department draws upon the detailed technical information presented by the group and secures the maximum support from those affected by the policy. Friendly contacts have been built up at all levels of administration, though sometimes the relationship is made formal, as in the representation of the Trades Union Congress on the National Economic Development Council.

When campaigning for a change in policy, groups usually exert pressure through the House of Commons. To show the widespread support for the groups' policy M.P.s may be lobbied, either personally or by letter. The former, while it may not succeed in persuading the M.P., brings the matter to his notice more forcibly than the latter. As J. D. Stewart puts it: 'There are two tactics — the mass assault and the steady trickle. It is a little difficult to say which is the more infuriating.' As an example of the former, he cites the practice of the National Federation of Old Age Pensioners' Associations of holding mass meetings in the Central Hall, Westminster, after which delegates cross Parliament Square to lobby their M.P.s.

Even the 'steady trickle' may result in a member's receiving thirty letters a day, some written entirely on the initiative of a constituent, others inspired by a pressure group. To many he gives but scant attention, a duplicated communication from the headquarters of an association being read only by his secretary. But a personal communication, such as a letter from the local branch secretary, will probably receive serious consideration.

Above all, the views of the principal groups never go unheard in the House because one or more M.P.s are always prepared to speak on their behalf. Members table questions, move amendments and even entertain in order to publicise the interest's views. Quite often a group is associated with a particular party. The National Union of Mineworkers has over thirty Labour members, while even more Conservative M.P.s are associated with the National Chamber of Trade. Other groups, such as the local government and teachers' associations, can count on members from both sides.

The Labour Party's constitution allows trade unions to sponsor candidates at general elections, and rather more than one-fifth are supported in this way. Unions can contribute to expenses at a parliamentary election and towards constituency organisational expenses. The Trade Union Act, 1913, stipulates that a trade union may only adopt 'political objects' after a ballot of members, and a separate fund, from which members can contract out, must be established.

No similar system has been laid down in the Conservative Party, though some associations such as the N.F.U., the N.U.T. and the British Medical Association have contributed to the expenses of Conservative candidates. It is more usual merely to invite an M.P. to take an interest in the group's work. Often the member is given some position of honour, such as vice-president of the association, and contact is maintained with him through his post and by inviting him to conferences and dinners.

In any case, it is doubtful whether Labour's practice makes much difference to the loyalty which the M.P. feels towards his group. A miner M.P. would probably be just as loyal to the National Union of Mineworkers even if he were not sponsored, while other M.P.s, both Conservative and Labour, represent interests because they sympathise with their objects.

Members sometimes introduce a private members' bill on behalf of the group, which in its turn assists in its preparation and passage. Thus the Protection of Animals Anaesthetics Bill, 1954, was promoted by the British Veterinary Association. Other bills, as we have seen, may be introduced for publicity. This kind of activity, however, is less important than the routine work of securing amendments to legislation and gaining sympathy in Parliament.

(3) *The importance of pressure groups in the constitution*

The name 'pressure group' is unfortunate, suggesting a backstage influence by people who place their own advantage above the general good. But the system does not work in this unhealthy manner. Members are expected to reveal any personal financial interest in matters under discussion by the House and they often disclose positions held in outside groups. Professor S. E. Finer suggests that such declarations should be made obligatory.

When members speak with the backing of an important organisation, such as the B.M.A. or a trade union, they are listened to with added respect, and it is the task of the House to balance this expert knowledge with the member's natural bias towards the interest. Moreover, the system of lobbying ensures that the opinions of the most important groups in the community are heard in Parliament. It spreads knowledge, creates a public opinion and produces practical legislation. Above all, by drawing people together for political action, pressure groups are a powerful check to bureaucracy. Thus, far from weakening democratic government, they play an essential part in it, providing a channel of communication between those responsible for policy and the people most affected by it.

Yet, to what extent is the community protected against groups, such as the N.F.U., which carry great weight with government departments? The answer lies in the publicity given to their activities and in the action which the electorate can take. Where fundamental decisions affecting the 'national interest' are being made, widespread discussion by political parties and newspapers is likely. Pressure groups are called upon to justify their reasoning in open debate. On most issues, this is the only way of determining the 'national interest'. Moreover, any failure of the Government to reconcile the claims of competing pressure groups will cause discontent, expressed later at the polls. While Governments may have certain natural sympathies (for instance, Labour Governments with the trade unions), their ultimate appeal must be to the electorate as a whole and to the floating vote in particular.

IV. DIFFICULTIES FACING DEMOCRACY

THE DETERMINATION AND PROTECTION OF CIVIL LIBERTIES

Although citizens in the United Kingdom consider themselves entitled to certain 'fundamental 'liberties — freedom of expression, freedom of the person, freedom of meeting, freedom of religion and freedom from racial discrimination — the constitution provides, in fact, no consistent procedure for checking that these liberties are not being infringed. The Courts are concerned with them, but in applying the law they rightly avoid becoming involved in matters which might bring them into the arena of political debate. Pressure groups, too, exist to draw attention to what is considered to be any undue interference with such freedoms. But the most effective control is the vigilance exercised by back-benchers. Not that this is free from difficulties. In the first place, backbenchers are subject to party discipline. Secondly, they share with society generally the difficulty of defining what is essential to such liberties.

Freedom of expression, for instance, cannot be unlimited. There must be protection against libel, slander, sedition, obscenity and contempt of court. But are the remedies of the law sufficient? To what extent should living persons be pilloried in public? How far should criticism of such established institutions as the monarchy or the armed forces be allowed to go? Should there be some prevention of obscenity rather than the mere judicial punishment after the event?

In the United Kingdom it has been felt that there should be some form of censorship as regards these matters, though for the stage this has been relaxed by the Theatres Act, 1968, which abolished censorship of plays by the Lord Cnamberlain. For licensing the showing of films, the Local Authorities are responsible, but over half of them have delegated their powers to justices of the peace. Usually the licensing authorities follow the advice of the British Board of Film Censors, an independent board set up on the initiative of the cinema industry. The Board may require cuts to be made before it will grant a certificate of showing, or it may refuse a certificate. Films passed by the Board are classified 'U' (suitable for universal exhibition), 'A' (parents are warned that the film may be unsuitable for children under 14), 'AA' (barred to children under 14 years of age) or 'X' (barred to children under 18 years of age).

Such censorship is unlikely to have any political significance, though in 1938 the Foreign Secretary is said to have been able to suppress a newsreel showing interviews with opponents of appeasement. But in his duties a censor has to determine what may be said in public, deciding whether it offends morality or public feeling or whether it might lead to a breach of the public peace. This is always a matter of judgment. Some persons may think he is too strict, others that he is not strict enough. A recent Lord Chamberlain has suggested that he favoured little censorship, merely leaving it to the Courts to decide whether a play had gone so far as to be a breach of the law. Local authorities, too, may vary in their decisions regarding the same film, some local authorities granting a licence, others refusing one.

Television and radio have such a powerful influence on large audiences that any rules restricting them are of particular importance. There is wide agreement on the objects of control — the balanced, impartial reporting of public affairs, the preservation of a standard of good taste, and the avoidance of any encouragement to crime and disorder. But here political pressure, which may come from several sources, has to be resisted. Leaders of parties may limit the opportunities for minor parties or even for their own backbenchers. In 1968 the Labour M.P. Mr. Christopher Mayhew, complained that the Chief Whip had on at least two occasions during the previous two years protested, without effect, to the B.B.C. against M.P.s such as himself appearing so often without taking the strict party line. Again, Mr. Wilson's refusal to be interviewed by the B.B.C. at the end of the 1964 election campaign raises the question of the possibility of pressure on the issues chosen and the interviewers. Even local authorities may hinder free comment. Thus Salford City Council refused to allow broadcasts about the city without its permission because of a television programme about its health services. Sometimes the origin of pressure, or even its existence, is uncertain, as it was over the decision of the B.B.C. in 1965 not to televise 'The War Game', a programme showing the effect of nuclear war. But after complaints in the Commons, 'The War Game' did get a limited showing in certain cinemas. Thus Parliamentary debate is a safeguard against abuse, but it may be that further constitutional guarantees are needed. There have been increasing complaints in the House of Commons in recent years that television and radio programmes are at times presented in a way which reflects the personal outlook on social and political matters of those in charge of them. Another criticism is that in a search for lively treatment, television (quoting the words of Mr. Richard Crossman) 'trivialises great issues by snippety treatment and personalises politics into a vulgar gladiatorial show between men who are constantly treated as though they were criminals or liars.' Mr. Crossman complained that viewers were only likely to be shown a couple of sentences of a fifty-minute speech on a serious issue before the cameras turned to a heckler and that the rest of the 'news' item would be devoted to a procession with banners which took place after the meeting. Such treatment, if followed regularly, could well influence public attitudes and might help to undermine the serious, tolerant and informed approach to current affairs upon which democracy ultimately depends. Yet it is difficult for Parliament to ensure that the B.B.C. and I.T.A. carry out their duty to produce properly balanced programmes, for direction from a minister over the content of programmes would destroy the independence of the broadcasting authorities.

A free Press is considered fundamental. Even during the war, control was kept to a minimum and was largely self-imposed. In any case, rivalry between newspapers makes them less susceptible to pressure — hence the concern felt over the decline in the number of national and local papers. But there may be subtle pressure. Dependence on advertising revenue, which can only be earned by large sales, may tempt editors to present mainly the news and opinions which will please readers. On the other hand, direct political pressure seems to be unusual, though it did occur in the case of Edward VIII's friendship with Mrs. Simpson. Generally, however, newspapers and magazines cover opinion throughout the whole political spectrum. Thus any concern is more over the methods of obtaining information and the standard of reporting than freedom of expression. In 1953, after the report of a Royal Commission, the newspaper industry itself set up a press Council to encourage a sense of public responsibility among journalists. Ten years later, following criticism, Lord Devlin was appointed its first lay chairman.

Although today television, radio and newspapers are the main means of communicating public opinion, the right to hold public meetings and demonstrations is still important. This is because broadcasting and the Press may give only limited scope to those holding minority views. Thus the C.N.D. movement succeeded in arousing public debate because its demonstrations and meetings created so much interest that they were widely reported. Naturally, when there are public meetings, the police have to be given discretionary powers to prevent disorder, but the Courts and Parliament would not sanction any attempt to stifle minority views or to arrest demonstrators unlawfully. Normally political groups are allowed to use public buildings, though local authorities are not legally obliged to grant facilities, and indeed may withhold them from persons opposing their policies. In 1966, for example, the Mayor of Godalming banned a picture from an exhibition held in the public library by the local Trust Society, observing 'we decided it should come down because it was detrimental to the Council'.

Penalties for religious belief hardly exist today, though perhaps a few laws arising from such beliefs are restrictive, for example, over the opening of shops on Sundays.

In post-war years racial discrimination became such a problem that the Race Relations Act, 1965, was passed, making the incitement of racial hatred a criminal offence. Under it, the Home Secretary appoints a Central Race Relations Board, and local conciliation committees look into complaints of discrimination. If settlement of a complaint cannot be reached, the matter is reported to the Board which may refer it to the Attorney General for legal action. The Board's annual reports to the Home Secretary are laid before Parliament. A second Race Relations Act, 1968, greatly widened the scope of the 1965 measure, making unlawful any discrimination in the provision of goods, facilities or services, in employment, in membership of employers' or workers' organisations, or in the disposal of housing accommodation. While such legislation cannot enforce goodwill, and sometimes may even be resented, it serves to influence public attitudes and helps to ensure that public rights are independent of race or national origin.

SOCIAL PRIVILEGE

Democracy is limited if leaders are drawn from a narrow and closed class. Although social privilege finds few defenders today, environmental influences still restrict social mobility. This affects the composition of our government institutions. Top-ranking politicians, civil servants, judges and bishops still tend to be drawn from a somewhat narrow range of society. Thus, it is usual for about three-quarters of Conservative M.P.s, and even about one-fifth of Labour M.P.s, to have been educated at public schools.

Every country, of course, must have some sort of élite, people who know each other and who are involved in major decisions governing public affairs. It is sometimes argued that such people constitute an 'establishment', by which is meant a permanent body of influential persons who are neither democratically elected or controlled, nor even selected by merit. Does such a group in practice control Parliament, the law, the Press, finance and industry, the professions, the administration, the Armed Forces and so on? Anthony Sampson in his *Anatomy of Britain* concludes that 'the rulers are not at all close-knit or united. They are not so much in the centre of a solar system as in a cluster of interlocking circles, each one largely preoccupied with its own professionalism and expertise, and touching others only at the edge . . . they are not a single Establishment but a ring of Establishments, with slender connections. The friction and balances between the different circles are the supreme safeguard of democracy. No one man can stand in the centre, for there is no centre.'

Moreover, able men who have received only an elementary education have reached the highest posts, particularly in Labour Governments. Herbert Morrison, Ernest Bevin, Aneurin Bevan and George Brown are four notable examples. In any case, with the development throughout the 20th century of new ideas regarding society, people no longer accept the old rigid class structure which enabled a narrow group to govern the country. Above all, the foundations of privilege have been undermined by economic and social forces. Progressive taxation has equalised the distribution of wealth and leisure. Educational opportunities have been widened and increased so that today ability, leadership and organising skill can be fully trained wherever they exist. The effect of such developments is that M.P.s and higher civil servants are now drawn from a wider section of society.

THE DISTRIBUTION OF POWER WITHIN THE PARTIES

Since policies are largely worked out by the political parties, the degree of democracy within them is important. Where does power really lie?

The most important right of the local association is to choose a candidate. Applications are first considered by a selection committee consisting of some half a dozen party members. For a safe seat, a hundred names may be put forward, from which the committee draws up a short list of five or six. These persons are invited to address the executive council of the association, a body of about forty party officers, and this makes the final choice.

While party headquarters may suggest names (and, in the case of the Labour Party and for by-elections only, can add names to short lists that offer too narrow a choice), they cannot dictate the selection of a candidate. Thus, in 1958 when Sir Hartley Shawcross left the Commons, the executive committee of the Constituency Labour Party at St. Helens did not short-list Tom Driberg, the Chairman of the Labour Party, although his nomination was entered on behalf on the National Executive Committee as well as by local affiliated organisations. In the event, the General Management Committee of the Constituency Labour Party (a larger body than the local executive) chose the nominee of the National Union of Railwaymen in preference to the candidate, a leading Roman Catholic layman, thought to be favoured by the executive.

Prospective candidates, therefore, are selected, subject to the veto of National Headquarters, by a small group of party enthusiasts who need not necessarily be a cross-section of the people voting for the party at the election. In contrast, the United States holds primary elections where, in the early summer of election years, parties choose candidates both for Congress and local state offices. But whether the adoption or such a system in Britain would lead to either a wiser of more representative choice is doubtful.

At both constituency and national levels, policy tends to be controlled, for both technical and psychological reasons, by even fewer persons. Most party members do little more than pay their subscriptions, and leadership is exercised by the few people who are prepared to devote most of their spare time to the work. In the Labour Party, the tendency towards oligarchy is intensified by increased centralisation of the affiliated trade unions, which have found full-time officials necessary for collective bargaining. The result is that the relationship of the individual to his trade union and to the Labour Party is, in the words of G. D. H. Cole, 'almost infinitely remote.' The problems which apathy gives rise to will be discussed later.

Psychologically, the tendency towards oligarchy comes from the need of mass members for guidance and from their gratitude to those who have led them through tribulation to triumph. Moreover, parties themselves often endeavour to create a popular image of the Leader's personality, characterising it if possible in some easily recognisable feature — Lloyd George's mane of hair, Churchill's 'V' sign and cigar and Wilson's pipe.

In both parties, the Leader is very influential, but more so in the Conservative than the Labour Party, where the stress is on the Annual Conference. Once elected, a Leader can be abandoned only at the cost of severe damage to the party's prestige. George Lansbury, the Labour Leader in 1935, and Neville Chamberlain, the Conservative Prime Minister in 1940, were overthrown only because they were quite out of step with the views of members. But the Leader likewise finds it difficult to ignore the wishes of the constituency organisations. It is they who keep him in touch with popular opinion and give him that confidence which comes from having a massive following.

Nor would democracy be increased by allowing more direction of policy at the 'grass roots' level of the party organisation. Such a step would raise serious constitutional difficulties. Governments must be responsible, not to their party supporters, but to a House of Commons freely elected by the whole adult population. Were parliamentary leaders dictated to by a national party organisation representing the constituencies, this true democratic chain of responsibility would be broken. Democracy reasserts itself at a general election because leaders must win the support, not only of their influential followers, but even of those who owe no party allegiance.

THE POLICE

Whereas in many countries the armed forces and the police are powerful, in the United Kingdom their activities are critically watched by the House of Commons.

The position of the police often indicates the spirit in which a country is governed. In Britain, the high regard in which the police are generally held is shown by the popularity of such fictional television personalities as Dixon of Dock Green. Even the carrying of arms by the police in the United States strikes an Englishman as somewhat odd. The system of joint police committees comprising local authority representatives and magistrates has, for the most part, removed the police from central government control and policemen do not take part in political activities other than voting. Policemen were reminded of this principle in an article in the *Police Review* in 1973 which criticised a few Chief Constables who had 'made the error' of attending county council meetings with county council staff or regular meetings of council chief officers.

Nevertheless, the position of the police in the Constitution is particularly important today as they now regularly question and check not only the criminal, but also the ordinary citizen, as, for example, when he drives a car or takes part in a political demonstration. While there have been expressions of public sympathy with the police, as after the murder of three policemen at Acton in 1966, there has also been evidence of lack of support and even hostility, as when, in the same month a crowd of over a hundred threatened four policemen when they tried to arrest a youth in Newcastle-upon-Tyne.

If the police are to maintain the confidence of the public, certain principles must be observed. First, policemen must respect the ordinary rights of the individual. In 1957, a barrister was disbarred largely on the evidence of transcripts of a telephone conversation between him and a criminal suspect which were given to the Bar Council by the police. Concern was expressed in the House of Commons and, as a result, a Committee of Privy Councillors was set up. While this committee accepted that the Home Secretary should be able to authorise the police to tap telephones — an interference with the normal right to freedom of speech — it considered that telephone-tapping should only be resorted to if there seemed to be little chance of solving a serious crime in any other way and that information obtained should not be given to members of the public.

Secondly, local Watch and Police Committees, although they are the police authorities, must not influence the enforcement of the law. This principle was applied in 1958 when the Home Secretary would not allow the Nottingham Watch Committee to suspend Captain Popkess, the Chief Constable, for refusing to give a report to the Watch Committee on his manner of enquiring into matters involving councillors, including the claiming of expenses.

Thirdly, there must be faith in the procedure for investigating complaints against policemen. Present arrangements allow for internal enquiries to be made by officers of forces other than the one directly concerned and compel a Chief Constable to consult the Director of Public Prosecutions whenever he is in doubt about the instigation of proceedings against a member of his force. But critics point out that, especially as the system of local police forces makes it almost impossible to raise questions in the House of Commons (see page 501), it is bad public relations for investigations against policemen to be undertaken by other policemen even if they are from a different force. 'Justice', the British section of the International Commission of Jurists, has suggested that people whose complaints are rejected should be able to appeal to legally qualified independent investigators and that policemen criticised by the investigators should have the right to appeal to a review tribunal.

Events such as the Thurso case (1959) and the Challenor case (1964) have at any rate shown the strength of public vigilance. Abuses of their power are likely to be few while the police are restrained by their own traditions and training, the guidance of the Courts, Parliamentary debate, public opinion, and a free press.

THE MAINTENANCE OF PUBLIC ORDER

Although the law rightly protects the freedom of association, experience in Germany in the thirties showed that the processes of democracy can be undermined with the help of the mob in the streets. Similar violent and provocative action in England led to the passing of the Public Order Act, 1936, which makes it an offence to carry any offensive or unauthorised weapon at any public meeting or procession, bans political uniforms, and gives the chief of police power to re-route a procession or to lay down certain conditions if he has reasonable grounds for thinking that the procession can lead to serious public disorder.

Demonstrations by very large numbers such as those organised in London against the Vietnam War, in March 1967 and October, 1968 are occasions when citizens are exercising their constitutional right to dissent from certain political policies and to urge that these be changed, but constitutional safeguards do need to be strong enough to ensure that militant groups do not establish anarchy by using violence and brute force. How strong the threats of the demonstrators may be was shown in 1970 when the Home Secretary, Mr. Callaghan, was induced by fears of disorder to request the Cricket Council to withdraw their perfectly lawful invitation to the South African cricket team.

Mass picketing by trade unionists, too, may go beyond peaceful demonstration and lead to intimidation. In 1973 three building workers were imprisoned following the activities of 300 pickets who had visited various sites in Shropshire during the previous year's building strike. On the one hand, people must be allowed as much opportunity as possible to attract the attention of others and persuade them peacefully; on the other hand, citizens also expect the civil right to move freely about their business without being forcibly stopped and possibly intimidated by other private citizens. When, in 1974, the Government suggested that new laws should allow pickets to force people to stop and listen to their arguments, the Chairman of the Road Haulage Association argued that drivers should not be compelled to stop for anyone except a policeman in uniform and that it would be a 'dangerous doctrine that an armband should give a striker power which is not even extended to government officials carrying out legitimate inspection of vehicles'.

At the universities, too, vocal groups have used displays of force. In 1970 some Cambridge University students were sentenced to imprisonment for their part in a riot outside a hotel which was holding a Greek evening to promote interest in Greece. Dismissing most of the appeals, the Appeal judge, Lord Justice Sachs, drew attention to the gravity of the crime of disturbing the peace and intimidating the police. 'Any suggestion', he said, 'that a section of the community strongly holding one set of views is justified in banding together to disrupt the lawful activities of a section whose views are different or less strongly held cannot be tolerated. Those who take part do so at their peril. When there is wanton and vicious violence of a gross degree the court is not concerned whether it comes from gang rivalry or from political motivations. It is the degree of mob violence which matters and the extent to which the public peace is broken.'

Intimidation at universities has also taken the form of driving guest speakers away from meetings unheard. Indeed, at the National Union of Students' Conference in 1974 a national ban was placed on speakers described by militants themselves as 'racist and fascist' being allowed to speak on university premises and soon afterwards Mr. Harold Soref, vice-chairman of the Conservative Monday Club, was chased by a 'howling mob' at Oxford University where he had tried to speak, and was forced to escape by scaling a six-foot wall. However, within a month about 30 student unions affiliated to the N.U.S. had voted against the ban, thus recognising the importance of freedom of speech and that democracy depends upon a willingness to reach decisions after discussion based on a degree of respect for different beliefs. Fortunately, this is a widely held view in Britain, but a tolerant attitude, without which democracy would collapse, can only survive within the framework of good order.

THE EXTENT OF THE STATE'S PROTECTIVE FUNCTION

A framework of public order is one form of protection which the State can provide for the citizen. There are demands, however, that the State should take an increasingly positive role in protecting individuals from many sorts of possible harm.

One protection desired by some has already been mentioned,

the call for censorship to preserve public morals by halting the intrusion of obscene or violent matter on private individuals, especially the young. The tendency recently has been to relax all forms of censorship because many resent the view that persons in positions of authority know what is good for people better than they do themselves. However, the issue remains a controversial one. A bill to control the deliberate display of indecent material in public places where the passer-by cannot exercise a personal choice whether or not to allow himself to be exposed to such material was being considered by Parliament in 1974, but was lost when the Prime Minister called an election. There is also some support for the view that film violence can lead to imitation and that the public interest therefore justifies some intrusion on the filmgoer's liberty. How far should the State limit the freedom of all in order to reduce the risk of harm to a small number of mentally unstable people? In a successful prosecution in 1970 under the Children and Young Persons (Harmful Publications) Act, 1955, a psychiatrist from the Maudsley Hospital, London, told the magistrates that he had patients whose disturbed condition could be traced back to reading the horror-comic type of publication. On the other hand, there is criticism that existing control is still unnecessarily restrictive; for example, councils, under local provisional orders, have wider powers over the sale of published material than is often realised.

Licensing laws are retained partly to protect children and young persons. In 1972 the Erroll Committee's recommendations for a relaxation of the restrictions included the suggestion that children under 14 should be allowed into licensed premises if accompanied by older people. This would allow families on a day out to follow customs of eating and drinking together which are normal on the continent, but most licensees opposed the change and the *Police Review* thought that the adult atmosphere was wrong for children and that there would be fears of a re-enactment of the Dickensian scene of children asleep in the corner and, worse still, children being exposed to 'punch-ups' and other spectacles.

Technical and scientific advance has led to many new demands both for the State to protect citizens and at the same time provided the means of protection. Widespread use of fast private transport, for instance, raises the question how far individuals should have their freedom restricted to reduce the risk of harm to others and to themselves. In 1973 Parliament debated the compulsory wearing of seat belts. It was realised that this proposal raised issues of personal liberty as well as the obvious problems of enforcement, but the counter argument was that if the proportion of people wearing seat belts could be raised from 30% to 90%, nearly 1,000 people would not die on the roads annually and over 10,000 serious injuries would be prevented. However, this result could be achieved only by compulsion. Such regulations have not yet been brought into force, but under the Motor Cycles (Wearing of Helmets) Regulations, 1973, motor cyclists are forbidden to ride without crash helmets. Critics argue that some motor cyclists may feel less safe when not wearing a crash helmet and may therefore drive more carefully; and, in the case of an accident only the motor cyclist himself is harmed by the absence of a crash helmet. More fundamentally, the critics ask whether it is the duty of the State to protect citizens against every danger. If so, they say there are strong arguments for severe State restrictions on the freedom to smoke and drink alcohol.

State action to protect the health of the citizens whether they like it or not has been taken by those local authorities which have decided to add fluoride to the water supply on the grounds that this will supplement the fluoride intake of children so that their teeth will be more resistant to decay. Health advisers to the Government, and bodies such as the British Dental Association, support a pro-fluoridation campaign, but as a result of local opposition during the sixties and seventies only a minority of water undertakings added fluoride to their supplies. Objectors were less concerned with the expert scientific evidence on the effects of fluoride than with the principle of compulsory State medication—deliberately adding a chemical to the public water supplies to influence the development of a part of the human body without the consent, and even against the will of, many water consumers.

Health is also affected by the general environment in which we live and people have become increasingly aware of the deterioration in the environment. Demands for greater protection under the law led to the Control of Pollution Act, 1974, which gives powers to deal with industrial waste from factories, noise abatement, and the pollution of the atmosphere caused by a dangerous level of lead in petrol, restricting the freedom of industrial concerns, but giving citizens a better guarantee of the right to live in an unpolluted environment.

How far should the State protect the privacy of the individual? Complaints have been made about unwarranted intrusions by the Press into private lives, 'bugging' by electronic devices and the use of computers to store information about private citizens, in particular their credit-worthiness. A committee under the chairmanship of Sir Kenneth Younger was appointed to look into the question of privacy and its Report in 1972 included recommendations of prison sentences for bugging and a strengthening of the lay membership of the Press Council. A Minority Report favoured a general right to privacy, but the majority thought that this might hamper the Press in exercising their right to expose scandals and reveal the truth. In the same year a Private Member's Bill to establish a data bank tribunal which would licence all stores of information failed to get a second reading.

Now that public affairs have become more complex and harder to control, a mass of State regulations has been introduced to provide for the safety and health of individuals and to protect citizens' rights. While many feel that still more laws are needed to protect the citizen, the counter view is that too many regulations may weaken the almost instinctive regard for freedom which has been an important part of the British political tradition. This danger in a democracy was foreseen nearly 150 years ago by de Tocqueville when he wrote of government covering 'the whole of social life with a network of petty, complicated rules that are both minute and uniform' and of government, which without being tyrannical, 'hinders, restrains, enervates, stifles, and stultifies so much that in the end each nation is no more than a flock of timid and hard-working animals with the government as its shepherd' (*Democracy in America*).

APATHY

The maintenance of democracy is dependent, not only upon people having the opportunity to participate, but upon their willingness to do so. Certain factors today make for indifference to political issues.

In some ways, prosperity is a major adverse influence. The attraction of such luxuries as the motor car, television set, and household appliances, tends to distract attention from the serious, though somewhat dull, matters of public concern. Similarly, welfare services and full employment both weaken the impulse towards political action.

Secondly, many current issues lack the personal impact of earlier struggles. Whereas the right to vote, the legality of strike picketing, or a bill to limit the power of the Lords were matters easily understood, many modern political problems, such as disarmament or economic ties, often appear so complicated that interest evaporates.

Fortunately, in Britain the roots of democracy go deep, and though people may seem to take their system of government for granted, the political parties rarely fail to evoke a response at a general election. When we allow for the people who find it impossible to get to the poll and the time lag in bringing the register up to date, the percentage of the electorate who vote is almost as high as that in Australia, where voting is compulsory. Nor is there a shortage of important issues today. Demonstrations over such matters as housing and rents, wages, and injustices in foreign countries are frequent. Finally, organised pressure groups, with better opportunities for publicising their views, are more numerous than ever. Yet there should be no complacency. Casting a vote is the minimum of democratic participation, but less than half the electorate trouble to do so in local government elections. Moreover a public which shows insufficient interest may tolerate too much secrecy in local government. Most of the real work is done by the committees which may be closed to the press and public. So the question is raised 'How far should a publicly elected body operate in private in a democratic society?'

In trade-union activities, apathy has often enabled the Communists to gain an influence completely out of proportion with their popularity as measured by their support at general elections or by the readership of the *Morning Star*. A former Communist, Bob Darke, has described how a small group of Communists have waited at trade-union branch meetings until some members have drifted away, particularly at 'closing time', and then pushed through resolutions reported next day by the *Daily Worker* as majority decisions. Indeed, the case of *Byrne and Chapple v. Foulkes and others*, 1961, showed that some Communists will go further than this for the large and important Electrical Trades Union was kept in Communist hands by means of fraudulent election practices. To those who cherish democratic freedoms, 'the price of liberty is eternal vigilance'.

V. Degrees of Democracy

Athenian democracy of the 5th and 4th centuries B.C. allowed people to participate directly in the State's affairs. All citizens above eighteen years of age were able to vote in the popular assembly which met about four times a month to decide the most important domestic and foreign issues. Policy was initiated by a council of 500, for which any citizen over thirty years of age could stand. Councillors were chosen by lot, but no member was allowed to serve for more than two years and there were rules to prevent any tribe or faction from gaining control.

Such a form of government, however, is possible only in a small State. Attica, centred on Athens, was about the same size as the county of Cheshire, just over 1,000 square miles. Its population was a mere 316,000, of which only 180,000 were full citizens. The rest (save for 28,000 resident aliens) were slaves who had no voice in government.

Thus Athens achieved a direct form of democracy. But in a large complex State, democracy must always be a matter of degree. Not only must representation be indirect, but some people will participate more in political affairs than others. Moreover, since leadership comes from groups and individuals, at some stage hard to define, popular influence may be so reduced that oligarchy replaces democracy.

At the other extreme, it is difficult to imagine a State, even a dictatorship, in which citizens have no influence whatsoever over the way the country is governed. To some extent, all governments must be tolerated by at least a part of their subjects, for rulers do not want to drive people to the point where they turn to assassination, revolt and civil war. Moreover, the army, police and civil servants must be sufficiently conciliated for them to remain loyal and to work with tolerable efficiency. Even in the most autocratic country, therefore, some trace of the democratic idea may be discerned.

No two democracies are alike, nor does any democratic constitution work in the same way today as twenty years back. All we can do, therefore, is to indicate tests for determining whether a nation can be justly described as 'a democracy'.

(1) Ample opportunities must be available for expressing opinions. Freedom of speech, freedom of the person and freedom of public meeting are therefore essential.

(2) Opinions and policies must be formed by appeal to reason in open debate.

(3) In selecting their government, people must be free to choose between rivals in secret ballot. Democracy cannot be reconciled with one-party government, for the electorate then loses the ultimate sanction of being able to change its rulers and their policies.

(4) People must feel that they are able to influence policy if only in a small way.

(5) The administration must be accountable to the people.

(6) A spirit of tolerance must prevail between the majority and minorities.

(7) There must be no punishment for political views; but the law must be so framed as to prevent violence and sedition, and to protect individuals from libel and slander.

(8) No group must be unduly privileged politically. Any considerable degree of democracy is probably irreconcilable with extreme inequality in the distribution of wealth or with a very rigid class structure.

The attitude and way of life of the British people provide an environment in which democratic principles and practice can flourish. But society is constantly changing, and democracy in Britain is therefore dependent upon the invention of new checks and balances. Adaptation, however, will only come about if our leaders are critical of political institutions and vigilant against abuse. It is upon the maintenance of this spirit that the preservation of our democracy depends.

SUGGESTED READING

J. Blondel, *Voters, Parties and Leaders* (Pelican, 1968), Chapters 6–10.

N. H. Brasher, *Studies in British Government* (2nd Ed., Macmillan, 1971), Chapter 12.

S. E. Finer, *Anonymous Empire* (2nd Ed., Pall Mall, 1966).

P. Goodhart, *Referendum* (Tom Stacey, 1971).

G. Marshall, *Police and Government* (Methuen, 1965).

G. C. Moodie, *The Government of Britain* (2nd Ed., Crowell, 1964), Chapter 11.

C. H. Rolph, *All Those in Favour? The E.T.U. Trial* (Deutsch, 1962).
A. Sampson, *The New Anatomy of Britain Today* (Hodder and Stroughton, 1971).
S. A. de Smith, *Constitutional and Administrative Law* (Penguin, 1971), Part V.
F. Stacey, *A New Bill of Rights for Britain* (David and Charles, 1973).
J. D. Stewart, *British Pressure Groups* (O.U.P., 1958).
H. Street, *Freedom, the Individual and the Law* (3rd Ed., Pelican, 1972).

31

Power and Politics

'To make the real decisions, one's got to have the real power'

C. P. SNOW: *Corridors of Power*

I. DECISION-MAKING

THE NATURE OF DECISION-MAKING

Political activity becomes necessary because some decision must finally be reached when there are conflicting opinions and irreconcilable interests. This is essentially what politics is about. To the British Steel Corporation, the future of Shelton Works in North Staffordshire must be decided in the light of its responsibility as a nationalised firm to promote the efficient development of steel-making in Britain; but, to the 10,000 men, women and children of the district, 'Shelton Bar is its people, a deep-rooted, living and richly successful human community' dependent on the works. To the motorist, Britain's longest elevated motorway, the four-kilometre Western Avenue extension in London, is a welcome means of fast travel; but familes living a stone's throw away in Acklam Road have described it as 'Hell'.

There are various distinctive features common to much decision-making in contemporary politics. One is the conflict between benefit to the community as a whole and real harm to a smaller group who are very directly affected.

Secondly, each large project decided upon competes with all other schemes for scarce money, resources and manpower. The four-kilometre elevated motorway mentioned above cost £30 million which could have been spent on schools, hospitals or improving the police force. Decision-makers should know the costs of what they are giving up in order to achieve one object, but little decision-making is probably really taken in that way.

A third characteristic is the complexity of so much modern

decision-making and this means that it is not always easy to decide which factors are the most important when a choice has to be made. For instance, selecting a route for a new motorway is likely to involve a decision on the relative importance to be attached to the effect on agriculture, on landscape and recreation, minimising cost, the demolition of buildings (whether historic ones or ordinary houses), the visual effect on property close to the motorway and noise and pollution. Cost-benefit analysis may help, but the choice still involves irreconcilable conflicting interests. Even such an ordinary matter as a council's decision to build a new housing estate is a much more involved process of policy-making than might at first be thought. At some stage a number of people will become aware that a housing problem is developing and that a decision must be made whether to build an estate, and if so where, when and of what size and nature. Once the decision to build has been made, complicated design work on roads, sewers, shops, schools and other facilities must follow, and planning permission and even compulsory purchase orders obtained, and central government approval sought, especially for loan sanction.

Some decisions are on simple, easily-identifiable matters; for instance, whether a local authority under its planning powers should allow a man to cause a certain amount of nuisance over a few months by building a large boat in the garden of his house which is situated in a quiet residential area. Other decisions involve more than simple administration. Whether to build a Channel Tunnel combines a purely administrative element with technical questions (e.g. on the cost and manner, of construction), quasi-judicial decisions (e.g. about the degree of harm some people will suffer by having roads or railways driven through their homes and property) and political judgement (e.g. about relations with European countries).

Some decisions, such as one to build a sewer, involve no more than carrying out a statutory obligation; but others, such as whether to abandon censorship of films in London, have mainly moral implications.

Another feature of most complex decisions is that there can be no clear distinction between policy and execution. Means almost always interact with ends. Relatively few decisions are so purely technical that they have no implications for policy. Thus Parliament may decide to raise the school-leaving age. But after the bill has been passed, many further decisions in implementing that policy have to be taken by administrators, local authorities and members of the teaching profession, and it will be the combination of all these decisions made during the implementation of Parliament's legislation which will determine whether the objectives of the measure are achieved or not. All along the line, decision-making involves aspects of the policy.

INVOLVEMENT IN DECISION-MAKING

Involvement in the decision-making process may take various forms. Quite large numbers of people may participate indirectly by either electing or appointing the people who eventually are going to make the decisions. Another indirect form of involvement is widely open. A free society gives good opportunities to people concerned about public affairs to try to influence the climate of opinion which forms the background to decision-making. What the general public expects and supports must frequently have a persuasive effect on policy-makers. Sir Keith Joseph directed the minds of members of the National Viewers' and Listeners' Association in this direction when he spoke to them in 1975 about 'cleaning-up' television. 'The key', he said, 'lies with public opinion, invisible, inaudible, hard to measure, and yet so powerful, so difficult to resist. So if we are to bring about a change, it will not be done primarily by urging the government, central or local. It is the climate of opinion which we must work on. If that comes right, the rest follows.'

The likelihood that groups or individuals can make the climate of opinion 'come right' depends on many factors, including the strength of their motivation, their personality and experience, their organisation, the sources of information available to them, their skill and education, their financial backing, their access to the media of communication, their contacts with people in politically important positions, the sanctions available to them, whether they are geographically isolated or at the heart of political affairs and the strength and determination of opposing factions.

There is a more direct involvement on the part of those whose role is to advise and submit information and ideas. Eventually a single individual or a relatively small number of people must make each final decision. It should not be thought that people are necessarily restricted to working in only one of these categories. In addition to taking a direct part in the administration of affairs by giving advice, for instance, the same people may also be acting indirectly on decision-making by trying to exert a formative influence on society's values.

It is inherent in the concept of democracy that the power to make decisions should not be reserved to the few, that the decision-makers must be responsive to the views and attitudes of citizens, and must in a real sense be accountable to them. In deciding the basic question of how far conflicts over a decision have been settled in a democratic way, many other questions need to be raised about the procedure. Who initiated the political action? Who advised those with final authority? What compromises were made and why? What were the relationships between those involved, and why did some give way while others were able to enforce their opinion? What effect, if any, did the social background of those involved have on the final outcome? What restraints were placed on those in positions of authority and power?

II. WHO ARE THE DECISION-MAKERS?

THE UNEVEN DISTRIBUTION OF POLITICAL POWER

At the October 1974 general election an extremist group put up posters bearing a simple message for the electorate: 'Don't vote — it only encourages them!' Fortunately in Britain such an exhortation is certain to fall on deaf ears. Participation in free elections is a vital condition of democracy. Elections are the only peaceful means by which governments can be made ultimately answerable to all the community, and by voting people are showing that they do wish to have at least some say in public policy.

Voting at general elections, however, is such a limited form of political participation that it only takes us a fairly small way along the road to democracy. In the first place, elections normally take place only every four or five years, while decision-making is a continuous process. Secondly, voting at an election is a simple action, involving no more than putting a cross against a single name. Decision-making, on the other hand, is often a most complex operation involving the initiation of specific policies on complicated subjects, the resolution of conflicting views and the implementation of involved measures. Topics such as defence and foreign relations, economic policy, industrial relations, social welfare, local government, law and order and so on, call for the application of specialist knowledge. In addition, there are complicated inter-relationships between the different spheres of policy, so that the broad framework of public planning becomes very complex indeed. Even people who become more involved than the ordinary voter often find it easier to put their efforts into the simpler individual decisions than into working out overall plans involving whole series of related decisions. Lord Simon once complained that the old Manchester City Council would let new schemes worth several millions of pounds through 'on the nod' and yet spend hours discussing the location of a public lavatory in the suburbs.

So complex is policy-making and such is the size and social diversity of Britain that it would simply not be possible to disperse decision-making equally among the mass of citizens — nor to go to the other extreme and concentrate it effectively in one single place. There must be some specialisation of political functions, just as there is of economic ones. Probably no more than a few hundred people are members of a fluctuating group of top decision-makers and a few thousand others occupy an important but less prominent role in policy-making. All these people are well placed to exert pressure and make proposals, but they are also continuously subjected to pressures and proposals coming from the many groups which involve themselves in the nation's affairs.

This uneven involvement in policy-making might seem to offend against the ideals of democracy, but it is an inevitable consequence of the fact that not all voters possess the political interest and skill, the intelligence and energy, the powers of advocacy and the ability to command the confidence of others that are required when policy is being formed and decisions taken.

ELECTION AND APPOINTMENT TO OFFICE

Positions of influence may be reached through two quite different processes, election or appointment. At times the two may overlap, as with a minister who is both elected (if an M.P.) and appointed by the Prime Minister. For places in Parliament and the council chamber, politicians compete through the party system and those who reach the top decision-making positions in this way are always subject to dismissal by the voters. They are, therefore, likely to be the best policy-makers from the point of view of democratic, representative government.

In contrast, other institutions, such as the civil service, local government administration, the nationalised and private industries, are staffed by men and women who have been appointed to the posts where they can make decisions and they are not subject to direct popular control. Appointment through advertisement and interview is the best method of arranging for decisions to be taken by those who are most equipped by their education, character, training and skill to cope with specialist and complex tasks at the highest level.

Most political decisions involve to some extent both kinds of policy-maker, but sometimes one will be more predominant than the other. How satisfactorily they work together is one of the important considerations of modern politics. The other relationship which is particularly significant is that between both those elected and those appointed to official positions and the public, either in the form of consultation with spokesmen of organised groups or with individuals who have grievances or through the electoral system.

III. THE POWER OF DECISION-MAKERS

THE PRIME MINISTER AND THE CABINET

Great problems of state — such as whether to belong to the E.E.C. or to nationalise an industry — must be determined at least in principle by elected representatives. This gives primacy to the party system and especially to the politicians who rise through it to the highest decision-making posts, the Prime Minister and the Cabinet.

Although the Prime Minister has a position of superiority, there is no uniformity in the method of decision-making. Some executive decisions are made by him on his own. Attention has already been drawn to the increased concentration of power in his hands (Chapter 14). Other decisions are made after consultation with senior Cabinet Ministers, or in the Cabinet, or in Cabinet committees or by Ministers after consultation with their senior civil servants. Naturally only a small amount of government business actually reaches prime ministerial and Cabinet level. Politically important as such decisions obviously are, it is worth remembering that it is not necessarily the occasional headline-hitting policies that have the most significance for the daily life of the citizen. He may well be affected even more by the impact of the continuous output of decisions reached at much lower levels.

The combination of the theoretical concepts of political and legal sovereignty with the practical effects of a relatively well-disciplined two-party system appears to concentrate much authority in the hands of the Prime Minister and Cabinet. Certainly, with the help of party discipline, the Government takes up so much of the time of the Commons that Parliament has to concentrate on passing Government bills and can devote much less time to making its own decisions on a non-party basis. In practice legislation is only occasionally debated on non-party lines, although on such matters as the abolition of capital punishment and changes in the divorce laws, for instance, it was felt by all parties that voting should be decided by individual decision without the enforced conformity to the Government whip. Yet although the Government is in a strong position to push its measures through Parliament, it is constrained by principles such as the rule of law, with its emphasis on equality before the law and on no punishment except for a breach of the law as established before an ordinary court, and by the importance attached to basic freedoms such as those of expression, publication and assembly, not to mention the final sanction provided by free elections based on universal suffrage. Sometimes, also, Parliament does itself become a top decision-making body and compel the Government to change its plans as, for example, its sanction on the Labour Government's move in 1968 to reform the House of Lords (see page 48).

Although the Prime Minister and Cabinet can be thought of as being at the centre of decision-making, this idea of a single centre of political power is at most times open to question and major decision-making is likely to involve not only the Prime Minister and Cabinet, but also Parliament, political parties, top civil servants from several ministries, pressure groups, specialist advisers (such as senior military officers or experts brought in from universities to advise on economic questions), the Treasury, specialist institutions such as the Bank of England, the boards of nationalised industries, Regional Planning Boards, and the E.E.C. if its regulations and policies are involved, not to mention the politicians' assessment of what importance to attach to views expressed by the Press and the public generally. In the rest of this chapter we shall look more closely at some of the groups who contribute to decision-making.

POLITICAL PARTIES

Parties channel power into the hands of political leaders. Electors must necessarily remain remote from most decision-making, but through the party system they can have a say in deciding to which party leaders — central and local — authority may be transferred. Under the party system, competition for office ensures that leaders pursue objectives which are important to the electorate.

This is the first constraint upon the considerable powers of the main political parties when they are in office, for their effectiveness in decision-making will depend in part upon the active co-operation of the public in general, and of important groups in particular, especially in the case of policies which affect the mass of the public, such as wages, prices and industrial relations. When large sections of the public have serious doubts about the wisdom of such policies, the execution of them, whatever their merits, can run into formidable difficulties. Mr. Heath discovered this during 1970–4 with his industrial relations and anti-inflationary measures. As the anonymous author of the 1974 Preface to *Crockford's Directory* put it: 'A majority in Parliament could make a law that all blue-eyed babies are to be killed at birth, but it is more than doubtful whether such a law can be enforced. A majority in Parliament is unwise to make laws which are deeply resented and whose moral basis is repudiated by significant sections of the population.'

Another restraint upon the parties is that, because the Conservative and Labour Parties are so large (approximately 6 million) and therefore so diverse in membership, from time to time leading party members may disagree on important issues, not only on the determination of priorities, but even on the wisdom of certain policies, such as how to tackle inflation or whether to belong to the Common Market. This provokes wide discussion on the decisions that have to be made. When important party leaders are divided or unsure, the backbenchers and the party outside Parliament are likely to have more influence on the course of action. A dramatic example of this occurred during the Labour Government of 1966–70 when, faced with discontent especially from trade unionists both within and outside the Parliamentary Party, the

Government decided not to proceed with the industrial relations policy outlined in the White Paper *In Place of Strife*.

Generally, however, the party outside Parliament has a limited role in decision-making. Although its leaders have to rely on loyal party support at future elections, and while an openly divided party may sap the confidence of the electorate the Government is, nevertheless, responsible to the whole electorate, not just to its own paid-up party members. It is significant that leading trade unionists seem to regard a seat on the National Executive of the Labour Party — or on the backbenches of Parliament for that matter — as a less attractive power base than membership of the General Council of the T.U.C. Few leading trade unionists have gone through the party system to membership of a Labour Government. Moreover, when the Labour Party held a special conference on membership of the E.E.C., prior to the referendum in 1975, the vote of two to one against the Labour Prime Minister's recommendation that Britain should remain inside the Market had no affect whatsoever on the policy of Mr. Wilson and his pro-Market colleagues. On the Conservative side, too, the fact that the parties in the constituencies do not have a decisive say was made clear at the time of the leadership change in 1975 when constituency support on the first ballot was said to have been firmly behind the unsuccessful Mr. Heath.

In local government, where there is no equivalent to the Prime Minister and Cabinet, the power structure is different. If local authorities have an important discretion in decision-making, as they have on education and housing, for instance, the local political parties may have a big say in policy-making through the local government system. Especially on the larger councils, where the party system is most entrenched, the practice is for each party to lay down its policy at its own group meeting held before the council meets, and although there are occasional rebellions, councillors are expected to follow the party line.

Group meetings tend to be dominated by leaders of the local party who are usually best informed on the policies under discussion. If the reorganisation of secondary schools is being reviewed, for instance, councillors who have not served on the Education Committee are at a considerable disadvantage in forming and expressing a view.

Committee chairmen, too, have usually had the benefit of

advice from the authority's permanent officials. One of the important questions of local government is how influence in policy-making should be distributed between the elected councillor, usually a layman, and the professional official, who can offer expert knowledge and advice on the functions of his department. Now that councils are larger and called upon to perform more complex tasks, the balance may have moved towards the officials on all but the broadest issues. On matters of education, for instance, the Director of Education, who is in charge of a large department of professional officers, would be in a strong position to show whether local conditions favoured schooling on comprehensive lines and, if so, which particular scheme of organisation would be most suitable. Nevertheless, a switch of local party control can make a crucial difference to the principles behind local decision-making on such issues as education and housing.

DEVICES FOR REFLECTING PUBLIC OPINION IN THE DECISION-MAKING PROCESS

One of the difficulties in applying the ideals of representative and responsible government is that, on the one hand, the issues to be determined are so great in number and often so complex in character, while, on the other, the millions of adults who make up the public are not only divided in outlook but composed of every sort of person from the inarticulate, ignorant and totally uninterested, to the vocal, well-informed and passionately committed.

The public as a whole may be able to do little more than elect M.P.s; yet if the system of government is to remain basically democratic in character, public opinion must be effectively heard during the decision-making process. In addition to the *ballot box* at election time and the not necessarily undistorted reflection of views through *the media*, three devices have been developed especially to enable the decision-makers to hear the voice of collective public opinion. These are *pressure groups*, *public opinion polls* and *the referendum* (used only on one occasion in Britain so far).

Pressure groups are vital to modern systems of indirect democracy. Until it has been organised in some way a collective public opinion can hardly be said to exist. Only when people have been brought together in groups, can they discover what views they have in common and press them upon the politicians. An important result of the formation of groups is a much wider participation in public affairs. Political decision-makers reach positions of influence through the party system and pressure groups ensure that they hear a wider diversity of views than they would get from their own party activists who may be narrow and doctrinaire in outlook.

Much decision-making has little to do with party conflict. Pressure groups have become involved in the routine consultative process. An interested group, for instance, may have a spokesman on an Advisory Committee set up in a Government department to make recommendations to the Minister. Governments nowadays have to make so many decisions on questions of social welfare and economic control that they have become increasingly dependent upon groups for information and advice during the formulation of policy, and often for co-operation over its execution. Representatives of interested organisations might, for example, make recommendations during the drawing up of regulations affecting hygiene in shops, the sale of drugs or safety in factories.

On higher policy matters, such as whether to build a 'motorway box' around London, the number of interested parties is much greater, the issues more complex, the decision-making process necessarily much more complicated and drawn out and the outcome more uncertain. Concerned groups need to win the support not only of top civil servants, but also of local government officials, councillors, Parliament and public opinion generally.

In any controversy, a group is likely to have greater influence if it is broadly in sympathy with the Government's objectives. Sometimes opposing sides in a dispute are supported by rival groups, as in education where the Campaign for the Advancement of State Education, which favours a completely comprehensive system, can hope to make greater headway under a Labour Government, while the National Educational Association, which wants to retain grammar and direct-grant schools, is likely to be listened to more attentively when the Conservatives are in power. Where there is controversy, the existence of opposing groups reduces the danger that spokesmen for one sectional group will have too much say over decision-making, although the groups will not necessarily be evenly balanced.

When the Government and a group have sympathetic relations with each other, the Government, too, can hope for the group's co-operation over the execution of policy. Thus the Labour Government in 1974 relied upon trade union support when it decided to base its anti-inflationary policy on a 'Social Contract' between itself and the trade unions. Under this the Government promised to pass various measures desired by the trade unions, such as the repeal of the Industrial Relations Act, 1971, in return for which the trade unions were expected to exercise certain broadly specified self-restraints in wage demands.

Pressure groups which successfully identify their case with the national interest or which are working in harmony with the cherished cultural values of society have an advantage in winning favourable decisions over those pursuing ends which may be interpreted as purely sectional or those supporting causes considered too unorthodox. Thus the National Union of Mineworkers made progress over increasing wages in the mid-1970s by arguing that such increases were necessary both to ensure an increased output of coal to meet Britain's fuel needs and to apply widely approved standards of social justice. Groups such as 'Help the Aged', the 'Child Poverty Action Group' and the R.S.P.C.A. can more easily attract both public and official sympathy than supporters of such causes as euthanasia.

Modern techniques of making *surveys of public opinion* might at first appear to provide a rival form of pressure on decision-makers, but they have not diminished the effectiveness of the network of interest groups which are now linked to Westminster and Whitehall in the decision-making process. Partly this is because opinion polls necessarily reflect opinions which may be prejudiced, oversimplified and changeable, whereas pressure group spokesmen, although possibly prejudiced, do speak for a vitally affected group with knowledge and authority. In any case when coming to a decision on a particular issue, public opinion in general usually seems to be only one of the factors that is taken into account. Neither entry into the E.E.C. nor the abolition of capital punishment was initially decided upon in response to the popular will.

There is evidence of growing support for the view that the wider public should have a greater say in determining policy on particular issues. In 1975 the Government took the unprecedented step of holding *a referendum* on whether Britain should stay in the E.E.C., a problem of such complexity that many ordinary people thought it should be decided by those with some expert knowledge. Support for more public involvement in decision-making was also given in the Report of the Committee on Public Participation in

Planning (the Skeffington Report, 1969) which recommended that much more stress should be laid on trying to establish the state of public opinion (for example, by the use of surveys) before policy is decided over planning matters.

CIVIL SERVANTS AND LOCAL GOVERNMENT OFFICERS

An important political development in modern times has been the vast increase in the number of professional administrators appointed. This large growth of 'the bureaucracy' has been an inevitable consequence of the developing social and economic responsibilities of government. It is an important question whether this leviathan is compatible with and necessary to democratic decision-making.

At the highest level, the Minister is responsible for providing the framework of overall policy within which decisions will be made. But civil servants continually make a positive contribution to decision-making through their involvement in the processes of initiation, co-ordination, consultation and execution. In reaching decisions, there is a constant interaction between ministers and administrators, the latter advising and warning. Civil servants may encourage their ministers to support new policies. How far the minister is influenced will depend upon such factors as the extent to which he is politically committed on the issue, the attitude of his political colleagues and perhaps upon the extent of his own knowledge.

An example of the way civil servants gather together various kinds of expertise needed in fulfilling their duty to look ahead and offer advice is the small Fuel Policy Planning Unit which the Department of Industry has set up to look into such questions as the fuelling of power stations. A senior civil servant is in charge of the unit which includes an engineer, an economist, an administrator and the necessary supporting staff. When formulating their advice, which may become the starting point for later decision-making, these civil servants can not only draw upon their own practical experience but they consult other experts from large companies who are dealing with similar planning problems in private industry.

In the work of co-ordinating policy formation, top civil servants, like the politicians, are organised into committees. Parallel to each Cabinet committee, for instance, there is another committee of civil servants drawn from the same departments. As far as possible, all different viewpoints have to be reconciled.

Much of the decision-making at Whitehall takes the form of a process of bargaining, consulting and negotiating in which politicians, administrators and spokesmen for interest groups all take part. Civil servants from their professional experience in carrying out past policy have some precise knowledge of the practical problems that are likely to arise and of how policy-making may be modified so that objectives can be achieved more effectively. Politicians, even when they are clear about the overall objective, may not be so well prepared to decide how it is to be reached. Professor R. Rose quotes Emanuel Shinwell, who was given responsibility after World War II for nationalising the coal mines. Shinwell confessed: 'We are about to take over the mining industry. That is not as easy as it looks. I have been talking of nationalisation for forty years, but the complications of the transfer of property had never occurred to me' (*Politics in England Today*). In such circumstances, it is possible, as Richard Crossman shows in his diaries, for civil servants to exert influence when they are unwilling to implement certain decisions.

Because resources are always limited, policy-making will depend partly on what funds can be made available for carrying out proposals. Hence the importance often attached to the Treasury as an influence in both national and local affairs. Civil servants in particular departments will know their colleagues in the Treasury and will enter into lengthy negotiations with them, but if agreement on major policies cannot be reached, the minister, aided by a few advisers, may well have to press the matter with a Treasury minister, who will also have his own expert official advising him. The outcome will depend on the strength of the arguments — and the civil servants will have played a big part in the presentation of these — and also on the vigour, determination and political standing of the minister involved.

Similarly in local government it cannot simply be said that councillors decide upon the policy and officers carry it out. The most important matters in the hands of a local authority will in the end be decided at a full council meeting, but this vote will have followed not only decisions in committee, sub-committee and probably a majority party group meeting, but also a whole process of investigation, argument and consultation. Involved in this as well as the councillors and the officers, are on the one hand the central government which confers powers, gives grants, approves expenditure and so on, and on the other, local pressure groups and individual citizens. Local residents mainly take up detailed administrative matters, such as why a particular child has not been given a place at a certain school. Sometimes — but not very often — there is an attempt to bring to bear on the Council the full force of local opinion on such matters as secondary school organisation or the fluoridation of water, but in practice such campaigns rarely seem to change the Council's decision.

The influence of the officers will depend upon the particular issue, the political circumstances and the personalities of everyone involved. Traditions of party government and internal organisation vary widely between the different councils and while some issues are controversial, complicated and related to party politics, others are not. It is not possible to describe a simple policy-making pattern which applies everywhere and to every issue.

Officers are often more than passive advisers to the Council. Frequently the initial source of information to the Council will be the chief officer and his staff. Over such matters as a building programme, the fluoridation of water supplies or the reorganisation of secondary schools, they are as likely as the councillors to initiate discussions, and they put forward recommendations for action to be taken in the light of the information which they have placed before the councillors. The ability of the councillors to assess this information and these recommendations depends on how far they come into contact with other information, perhaps conflicting opinions from pressure groups, national or local, and from the public, including professional people involved in the proposed schemes, people whose views and knowledge may not necessarily be in line with the leaders of a local pressure group, and whose spokesmen may claim to possess a greater monopoly of expert opinion than is in fact the case. The wider the sources of advice available to the councillor, the less he is dependent upon the initiative of the officer.

Where parties are strongly organised, the ability of officers to influence important decisions will depend in part upon their personal relationships with committee chairmen. There are quite big differences between councils as regards the ways in which officers and councillors see their own roles in policy-making. Now that local government units are larger than in the past, the position of the chief officers may have been enhanced. The greater range and complexity of decision-making today also strengthens the position of the full-time professional officer relative to that of the part-time amateur politician. Naturally, good officials will always wish to make some positive contribution to decision-making, and no one would want to employ a Director of Housing who was indifferent to the quality and quantity of houses provided in his borough. But democracy requires that officers should not be allowed to have a predominant position for they do not have to submit to the political sanctions which the electorate can impose upon the politicians.

Normally councillors and officers recognise each other's position and there is no conflict over powers and status, but at times the relationship can be an uneasy one, and open clashes, though rare, have taken place. In 1970 some councillors in the London Borough of Barnet openly blamed their Council for 'allowing the officers to dictate to them'. This caused the Town Clerk to attack those councillors at a full council meeting with a declaration that 'the chief officers have a duty and responsibility to offer their professional advice. The fact that the majority of members may from time to time accept that advice is, of course, no fault of the chief officers'. In 1974 Somerset County Council actually dismissed its Chief Executive because of a clash of personality with some of the council members.

In both central and local government, therefore, officers make a large contribution to decision-making, but there are many important restraints upon them which have been referred to in various sections of this book; for example, the existence of opposition parties with competing policies, Question-Time, the Parliamentary Commissioner for Administration and the Commissioner for Local Administration for England and Wales, the various parliamentary committees and so on. Another safeguard is the stability of the political system. At the highest level, for instance, the Minister has behind him solid support in Cabinet and Parliament through the party system. If politicians, through any kind of weakness in the political system, were unable to give a lead in decision-making, then the gap would be filled by the 'bureaucrats'.

IV. Decision-making and Democracy

Elitist and Democratic Strands in Decision-making

How far is a share in the decision-making process open to the public in general? Some political theorists believe that political systems always tend to be run by a ruling élite whose members hold the key decision-making positions in the dominant institutions of society. Members of such an élite share a similar social background, have the advantages of an élite education and there is a pattern of inter-marriage and friendship among their families.

It is indeed still the case that a significant number of ministers, top civil servants, military leaders and directors of the Bank of England, commercial banks, city firms and insurance companies have been educated at Oxford and Cambridge and at one of the six great public schools, Eton, Harrow, Winchester, Rugby, Charterhouse and Marlborough. Many also belong to the same clubs and there is some tradition of inter-marriage, for instance among banking families. This is a social structure which encourages the sharing of values and beliefs and provides a basis for a close informal relationship between decision-makers.

Yet the argument that Britain is governed by a small ruling clique, a self-perpetuating 'Establishment', cannot be sustained. There is no single 'Establishment' based on social privilege (pages 563-4) and significantly none of the three politicians elected to the leadership of the two main parties since the mid-sixties — Mr. Wilson, Mr. Heath and Mrs. Thatcher — have come from exclusive sections of society. When it comes to realities, it is difficult to pinpoint an 'Establishment'. To a large degree, the term is merely a reflection of the general conservative attitude of the British people to change, especially as regards matters of government. This attitude has simply been given a label by the more 'progressive' thinkers who object to the slowness of change towards their ideas.

Policy-making, as we have seen, is not so much a unified process as a continuous involvement of separate and diverse groups of people in reaching decisions on different kinds of issues. In effect there can be said to be various separate élites in such different spheres as politics, finance, trade unionism, administration and so on. People generally only attain a commanding position in their own field. Only rarely, for instance, do distinguished trade union leaders, financiers or scientific experts become political leaders at either a national or local level. Public policy is influenced by the leaders in these different sectors as they either compete against or co-operate with each other.

Democracy cannot be realistically defined as a system under which every citizen can play an equal part in determining the policies of government. It would not do to decide everything simply by counting heads because some of the heads are not well equipped to understand the more difficult problems and moreover, on any particular issue, some people are much more personally involved or committed than others. People with interests in common therefore are best served if some of the most able of their number can be put in positions where they are able to further those interests. The result is leadership in policy-making by various élite groups, but this does not mean that the political system must be dismissed as undemocratic. There are different degrees of political involvement and modern trends have widened participation in decision-making and allowed for top positions to be filled by people drawn from broader sections of society. Not only is popular opinion tested at general elections, but opinion polls, letters to the newspapers, deputations and demonstrations between elections can guide those who make decisions at Westminster, Whitehall and Town Hall. Anyone can join a political party or a pressure group, and entry by open competition into the Civil Service has been the rule since the reforms of the 19th century.

Nevertheless, it has been widely recognised in recent years that in the interests of greater democracy means should be found for increased public involvement in policy formation, especially by citizens who will be directly affected by schemes under consideration. Local planning procedures, for example over a new motorway, today provide for a democratic element in the resolution of the inevitable conflicts. The first step in involving local people is the announcement informing them that a plan is to be prepared. In order that effective local discussions and meetings can take place, the choices which are open to the community must then be put before the people. Local residents are provided by the Department of the Environment with maps showing various alternative proposed routes and with questionnaires, the answers to which can be taken into account when the Minister, advised by his civil servants, publishes a draft proposal under the Highways Acts. After this there are statutory rights of objection and a public enquiry may be held.

Such procedures are in line with the ideas in the Skeffington Report on Public Participation in Planning, 1969. This Report recognised that participation, if it is to be real, must involve an effort not only to consider the submissions of spokesmen of organised groups who may be regarded as the customary leaders of opinion, but also to seek the opinions of those who do not join societies or even attend meetings, and it must allow the people affected the opportunity and the time to come forward with a further alternative proposal different from those officially put to them. Consultation is not real unless options are genuinely open, yet it has not been a customary feature of policy-making in Britain for either central departments or local authorities to invite public discussion before the policy-makers themselves have formed an opinion as to which scheme should be prepared.

Indeed officials may go further than merely adopting a prior view as to what will be the best course of action. It is possible for a commitment to a particular line of action to be incurred before consultation takes place. A few chief officers and committee chairmen in a local authority have considerable opportunities to cause commitment by going so far with the drawing up of provisional plans by architects, making costings, negotiating with the ministry where approval is needed and so on, that the cost and delay involved in changing the proposals are generally accepted as formidable.

Even Members of Parliament may find themselves at some disadvantage if they are brought into the consultative process after an inner group has reached a conclusion on what should be done. Thus it is an admirable practice for spokesmen of interested pressure groups to consult with civil servants either informally or on consultative committees when policy proposals are being formulated. But when the matter reaches Parliament and legislation is being discussed, it can lead to M.P.s being urged not to press amendments which would upset agreements already reached with such bodies as the T.U.C. and the trade unions. One of the problems of consultation therefore is to ensure that it is both genuine and well-timed.

CONCLUSION

It cannot be said that decision-making in modern times has always satisfactorily met both the needs of democracy and technical efficiency by giving proper weight at the right stages to both expert and professional opinion and to the general public. One major controversy over which the decision-making process can only be regarded as spectacularly unsatisfactory was the siting of a third London airport, a problem which involved particularly complex technical, administrative and political decisions.

The necessity for such an airport was agreed in a report which a committee composed of staff from several government departments prepared in 1963. This committee's recommendation that Stansted should be chosen was approved by the Government. Public discussion followed and the Government appointed an independent inspector to hold a public enquiry into local objections. When the inspector finally reported in 1966, he said that the airport would be a calamity for the neighbourhood and, for further consideration of the problem, he recommended setting up a committee equally interested in traffic in the air, on the ground, regional planning and national planning. The Government did set up another interdepartmental committee to review the matter, but it also announced that 'after careful consideration' it had decided to proceed at Stansted. Against a background of a growing public campaign against the decision, the Government in 1968 set up a special Commission under the chairmanship of Mr. Justice Roskill. Local hearings were held, evidence from organisations was taken, and an investigation was made by a research team. Starting with a list of 78 possible sites, the commission considered cost of surface access, defence, noise, air traffic control and site preparation. Eventually in 1970 Cublington (Northamptonshire) was recommended, but the Government finally chose instead Maplin (Foulness, Essex), the minority recommendation of one member of the commission, Professor Colin Buchanan. In October 1973, ten years after the first report from government departments, the Maplin Development Bill authorising the establishment of a development authority to reclaim land from the sea at Foulness was passed. However, this was not the end of the saga because in 1974 the Labour Government rescinded the Maplin plans and, at least for the time being, has abandoned plans to build a new airport anywhere.

This long controversy illustrates some of the main problems of large-scale policy-making. Its lessons are many. The right people must be consulted and at the right stage. All alternatives should be identified at the outset. Effective procedures for enquiry and research must be chosen and the membership of any investigating body must be well selected. Clear thinking is needed over the weight to be given in a cost-benefit analysis to the different criteria of judgment, in this instance, for example, to the firm economic calculations as against the basically immeasurable environmental considerations. Finally there must be close scrutiny by relevant Ministers, the Treasury and by Members of Parliament, who must in turn be sufficiently responsive to public feeling.

The story of the third London airport shows how complex policy-making on major issues can be. Perfection in the process of policy formation will never be reached, but the main steps towards it seem to lie partly in improving the procedures and partly in informing and educating the citizens. Information and understanding must be as widely distributed among the people as possible if decision-making is to become both more effective and also more compatible with the ideals of democracy.

SUGGESTED READING

R. M. Punnett, *British Government and Politics* (Heinemann, 1968), Chapter 5.

R. Rose, *Politics in England Today* (Faber, 1974).

A. Sampson, *The Anatomy of Britain Today* (Hodder and Stoughton, 1965).

C. P. Snow, *Corridors of Power* (Macmillan, 1964).

VIII
INTERNATIONAL POLITICAL
INSTITUTIONS

32

Towards World Government?

'It is only now that we begin to realise the real scale
and profundity of the changes in the conditions of
human life that are in progress. ... The scale of
distances has been so altered, the physical power
available has become so vast, that the separate
sovereignty of existing states has become impossible.'

H. G. WELLS: *A Short History of the World*

I. CAN COMPLETE NATIONAL SOVEREIGNTY BE RETAINED?

The concept of separate national states possessing sovereign
powers over their citizens has long been taken for granted. In fact,
during this century, the prestige of national political institutions
has been strengthened. Not only do people make unprecedented
demands on their governments for defence, material prosperity and
welfare services but, through improvements in communications
and the development of modern administrative and statistical
techniques, governments are better placed to satisfy the community's needs.

But after World War I people began to wonder whether
independent sovereign States were consistent with the maintenance
of world peace, for nationalism had often found expression in
military pride and selfish economic policies. Hence the Peace
Conference of 1919 decided to set up an international body, the
League of Nations, to prevent further war. Although the League
ultimately failed, it did create a precedent for international
organisation and provided valuable experience. During the same
period, too, a body of international law was being built up by the
International Court.

The old form of nationalism and the failure of countries to co-
operate during the trade depression of the 1930s contributed
largely to World War II. It was now obvious that strategic,

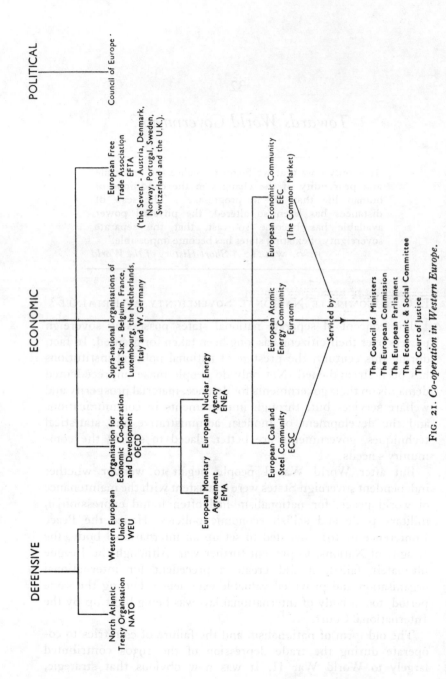

FIG. 21. Co-operation in Western Europe.

POLITICAL

Council of Europe

ECONOMIC

European Free
Trade Association
EFTA
('the Seven' - Austria, Denmark,
Norway, Portugal, Sweden,
Switzerland and the U.K.).

Supra-national organisations of
'the Six' - Belgium, France,
Luxembourg, the Netherlands,
Italy and W. Germany

European Economic
Community
EEC
(The Common Market)

Organisation for
Economic Co-operation
and Development
OECD

European Monetary
Agreement
EMA

European Nuclear Energy
Agency
ENEA

European Atomic
Energy Community
Euratom

European Coal and
Steel Community
ECSC

Serviced by

The Council of Ministers
The European Commission
The European Parliament
The Economic & Social Committee
The Court of Justice

DEFENSIVE

North Atlantic
Treaty Organisation
NATO

Western European
Union
WEU

political and economic forces had made it impossible for isolated States to guarantee their citizens either adequate defence or increased welfare. Even to fight the war effectively, the West had to give General Eisenhower supreme control over national forces and, in the post-war reconstruction, international co-operation played a large part.

Aided by the development of communications, international co-operation has, since 1945, taken positive forms. There has been 'a coming together in Europe', an extension of the body and practice of international law, and attempts by the United Nations to promote mutual help on the widest possible scale. Britain herself has been drawn into many of these international bodies, a consequence which has important constitutional implications. While in theory parliamentary sovereignty is retained and legally Britain could always decide to renounce her membership, in practice, for the reasons mentioned above, she would find such withdrawal exceedingly difficult. Moreover, present-day international agreements go much further than the old traditional trade and military treaties, and often involve the surrender of autonomous control to an international body. Already, for instance, British army units have fought under the United Nations' command. Since 1973, the United Kingdom has been a member of the European Economic Community. Our constitution can no longer be viewed as an isolated organism, but instead it has to adapt itself to function in harmony with world institutions.

II. EUROPEAN CO-OPERATION

Schemes for a common action in Europe have drawn States into two kinds of organisation, which may be termed 'inter-governmental' and 'supra-national'. The first is based on the principle that nations are sovereign States and that there should be no interference in their domestic affairs. The second, on the other hand, involves a transfer of some sovereignty to the new multi-national organisation.

(1) *Inter-governmental organisations*

The 'European idea' found expression in 1949 when the Council of Europe was created to achieve 'a greater unity between its members for the purpose of safeguarding and realising the ideals and principles which are their common heritage and facilitating their economic and social progress'. Institutions, centred in Strasbourg, provide for discussions between ministers in a Committee of Ministers, and among members of the national parliaments in a Consultative Assembly. Although supporters of European integration hope that this Council might form the basis of a European Parliament, countries have not yet shown readiness to hand over sovereign powers to it. But the United Kingdom has, by membership, signified her recognition of belonging to a wider community.

In terms of actual achievement, however, the common organisations having definite functions have proved more fruitful than the Council of Europe with its broad aims. In the economic field, the first real co-operative effort was the Organisation for European Economic Co-operation (OEEC), originally set up in 1948 to administer American aid. Re-constituted in 1961 as the Organisation for Economic Co-operation and Development (OECD), its aims are to liberalise trade (through the European Monetary Agreement), to study the joint development of nuclear energy for peaceful purposes (through the European Nuclear Energy Agency), to stimulate industrial efficiency, and to co-ordinate aid to developing countries. Regular discussions take place at ministerial level, and at times its Council meets under the chairmanship of the Chancellor of the Exchequer — a significant extension of his role in government.

Co-operation has also been considered imperative in defence. When, after World War II, Europe became split into two mutually-suspicious political groups, the majority of non-communist European countries joined with the United States and Canada in the North Atlantic Treaty Organisation (1949). Plans by the original six members of the E.E.C. to set up a supra-national authority, the European Defence Community, broke down when France refused to join, but a defensive alliance, the Western European Union, was formed in 1954 and both the United Kingdom and West Germany are members.

Military planning is co-ordinated at all levels. At the top, the British Cabinet is represented in NATO and WEU where the Foreign Secretary may act as the quarterly chairman. The Defence Minister and the Chancellor of the Exchequer also take part in inter-ministerial discussions associated with NATO meetings. Lower down, the Chiefs of Staff Committee forms part of the joint planning machinery, while in the field there is a concession to the supra-national idea in that forces operate under the Supreme Commander.

An interesting extension of NATO has been the widening of its interests beyond defence matters through the realisation that defence could not be separated from problems of political policy. For instance, disagreement between three members — Greece, Turkey and the United Kingdom — over Cyprus, has continually threatened the efficiency of the organisation. Since 1955, therefore, NATO has held an Annual Parliamentarians' Conference.

The Suez invasion in 1956 provided further evidence of disunity within NATO. Hence, a committee was set up to consider the situation and this recommended:

(1) countries should inform the North Atlantic Council of developments which affect the alliance;

(2) member governments and the Secretary-General should be able to raise matters of common NATO concern for discussion in the Council;

(3) member countries should not adopt firm policies or make major political announcements without advance consultation;

(4) the interests and views of other governments should be taken into account in the development of national policies.

These strongly-worded recommendations were significant because they revealed that some modification of the concept of national sovereignty was desirable. Nevertheless, although the Secretary-General reports regularly on major political problems, NATO has not become a consultative political assembly.

(2) *Supra-national organisations*

The first supra-national organisation, the European Coal and Steel Community, was created in 1951. Its object is to make coal and steel freely available from the member countries — at the time, France, West Germany, Italy, Holland, Belgium and Luxembourg — and to arrange for the rational expansion of both industries.

The success of ECSC led to the formation in 1958 of the European Atomic Energy Community, a similar organisation for the peaceful use of atomic energy, and the European Economic Community, a customs union usually referred to as 'The Common Market'.

Since 1967 these three Communities have all had common institutions and in 1973 membership grew to nine countries with the addition of the United Kingdom, the Republic of Ireland and Denmark.

The most important organ is the *European Commission*, a truly supra-national body. Its 13 members (two each from France, Germany, Italy and the U.K., one each from the other five countries) are nominated by their respective governments, but once chosen, the Commission acts as an independent body in the interests of the Community as a whole, and its members are instructed neither to solicit nor to accept instructions from governments or from outside agencies. Its task is to initiate policy and draft the detailed measures required to carry it out. Members of the Commission are put in charge of particular departments and the first two British members in 1973, Sir Christopher Soames and Mr. George Thomson, were given responsibilities for external affairs and regional policy respectively. Decisions are taken by a simple majority vote and, as in the case of the British Government at home, are preceded by consultation with affected interest groups such as trade unions, employers and farmers. The Commission has a staff of permanent officials, contributed by member countries, but owing a loyalty to the Commission itself, and this is in effect the civil service of the Community.

The *Council of Ministers*, containing one representative from the Cabinet of each member country, is the supreme decision-making body. Most Council decisions are taken on the basis of a proposal by the European Commission, the Council's task being to ensure that the policy of the Commission is harmonised with the wishes of the Governments concerned. While the Commission drafts and implements the Community policies, they have to be approved by the Council. Certain decisions have to be taken by unanimous vote, thus allowing one member to veto a proposal affecting vital interests. Other voting is on a weighted basis with the United Kingdom, Germany, France, and Italy each having 10 votes, the Netherlands and Belgium 5 votes, Denmark and Eire 3 votes and Luxemburg 2 votes. Some important issues cannot be agreed unless at least 40 out of the possible 58 votes are cast in favour. The Council meets several times each month and, between meetings, a Committee of Permanent Representatives in Brussels, made up of ambassadors of the nine member countries, prepares and co-ordinates its work. In practice Community decision-making has been very successful. This has been achieved by the system by which proposals and compromise plans are exchanged between the Council and the Commission. If the Council becomes deadlocked, the Commission breaks the deadlock by changing the proposal so that it meets some or all of the demands of the countries which caused the impasse.

The *European Parliament* at Strasburg, a body of 198 members drawn from the nine National parliaments, can dismiss the Commission on a motion of censure by a two-thirds majority, but its present role is largely consultative. Britain may send 36 members drawn from both Houses of Parliament and representing proportionately the different parties in the House of Commons. Meetings are held for some five days each month, and there are also twelve standing committees which work closely with the relevant departments within the Commission and indeed some committee meetings are held in Brussels.

For hearing complaints on the application of the Treaty, whether from member States, private enterprises or the organs themselves, there is a *Court of Justice*. Its nine judges, appointed for a six-year term by agreement among member governments, can only be removed if all the other judges agree unanimously. While a national court cannot consider actions of the European Commission, these may be annulled by the Court of Justice if they cause 'fundamental and persistent disturbances' in the economy of a member state. The Court also has the power to rule on questions arising in national courts on the interpretation of the Treaties and of subordinate legislation flowing from them. These powers are no more than one would expect from an international court. The Court simply establishes the breach, but it does not impose legal sanctions. The enforcement of sanctions (which the Court may define) against firms or individuals is left to national courts.

III. The Impact of E.E.C. membership on the British Constitution

It will take a number of years before firm conclusions can be drawn on how the British system of government has been changed as a result of entry into the E.E.C. Among the many possible

influences upon the working of the Constitution the following
deserve close examination.

(a) *The sovereignty of Parliament*

Critics of entry argued that membership of the Community
involves a clear and explicit surrender of the sovereignty of the
United Kingdom Parliament and that, as a consequence of joining,
Parliament can no longer be free and unfettered in its power to
make decisions and thus be the sole law-making agency. Various
arguments are put forward against the simplicity of this view.
Under the British constitution, one Parliament cannot bind its
successors, and, it is argued under international law, treaties
which violate constitutional restrictions do not bind the state
concerned. Apart from such complex legal theories, it is said that,
from a common-sense point of view, there is now such economic
and political interdependence between states that, in practice, no
fundamental change has been made in abandoning, in certain
specified areas, the power to make unilateral decisions as part of
the acceptance of the obligations and rights of membership and the
receipt of the attendant benefits, both economic and political,which
follow. This view envisages a 'sharing of sovereignty' rather than
the unwilling submission to policies imposed by a supra-national
body. In other words, a quite new form of government has
emerged, a grouping of European sovereign states quite unlike
any federal system such as that of the United States of America.

(b) *British M.P.s' powers in the European Parliament*

Because the European Parliament's role is largely consultative,
British M.P.s who serve in it find that it has not the same power
as the Westminster Parliament as regards safeguarding citizens'
rights and shaping policy. As a result, it cannot do nearly as much
as they are used to in keeping the decision-making body, in this
case the Council of Ministers, in line, although it must be remembered that each member of the Council is responsible to his
own national parliament. Another danger, too, is that of inadequate
control over the European Commission and its staff of international
civil servants. Hence, at present, British M.P.s are seeking to
extend the powers of the European Parliament, using weapons
well tried at home, such as the introduction of question-time.
Peter Kirk, in the first speech made at Strasburg by a British
M.P., said that through the European Parliament there can be a

relationship between the people of Europe and the Community and he argued that 'the Community cannot function unless it has a base in the hearts and minds of the peoples, and Parliament is the only body which can provide that base'.

However, if national parliaments, representing the electorates of member countries, are to become more involved in the process of European legislation, new institutional arrangements will be required. Andrew Shonfield recommends that a network of parallel committees be set up in the various parliaments concerned with European matters and that they act in liaison with one another. European M.P.s could arrange joint meetings of parliamentary groups and committees drawn from the different countries and provide for parallel moves to be made in the different parliaments to put simultaneous pressure on several members of the Council of Ministers.

Perhaps even more fundamental changes are required if there is to be a sufficiently strong link between public opinion in the member countries and the determination of policy at the power centres of the Community. Critics argue that as long as the European Parliament is a body nominated by national parliaments, it will be subordinate to the larger national governments and cannot have the true independence and standing of a directly-elected body. There would, however, be considerable difficulties in moving towards direct election. Many people feel that it is important that European parliamentarians should also be members of their own sovereign parliaments. A European parliament with the same ratio of M.P.s to voters as Westminster would have more than 2,500 members; so in practice there would probably have to be one M.P. for about every half a million people. Maintaining accountability to such an electorate and the planning of election campaigns would raise problems. Probably, too, some form of proportional representation would have to be used; and perhaps elections would have to take place throughout Europe on the same day, making it impossible to fit in with national dates for general elections.

There is little likelihood of these changes in the near future, but the issue of democracy within the Community is important if it is to inspire the loyalty of ordinary people in member countries and if the E.E.C. is to be accepted as being in tune with the basic principles of the British system of government.

(c) The British Parliament's powers of scrutiny

The European Commission enacts some 2,000 regulations a year and Parliament may not find it easy to ensure that, in addition to the considerable task of watching the delegated legislation made under British statutes, there is adequate scrutiny of the regulations coming out of Brussels. The subject-matter of directives can be very varied and may touch upon controversial matters, ranging from the length and weight of lorries (an important environmental issue as well as a factor affecting the economics of international transport), to directions on mutual recognition of professional qualifications intended to allow professional persons to practice outside their own country, but raising the danger that courses of education might have to be forced into a common European pattern. This could clash with the view in Britain that one guarantee of freedom is that governments do not interfere with the content and make-up of education.

Where instruments are of particular importance, Parliament needs to be able to have its say before they reach the stage of becoming Community law. A House of Commons Select Committee reported on these matters in 1973 and recommended the setting up of a new Committee reflecting the party balance in the Commons, which would be served by an expert staff and would receive reports from the minister responsible for E.E.C. co-ordination and from a new law officer, who would inform Parliament of the legal consequences of proposals. The object of the Committee would be to inform the House about proposals of legal and political importance, to make recommendations about their further consideration, to point out the principles or policies they affect and the changes in United Kingdom law involved. The Select Committee also recommended that Parliament find adequate time to debate E.E.C. matters, that S.O.9 be used when urgent debate was required, and that a special place at Question Time be allotted to E.E.C. matters.

(d) The effect on English Law

For 700 years, courts in England have operated the English common law (page 357). Especially during the 20th century, political, economic and social factors have led to a trend away from this judge-made law towards laws found in parliamentary statutes and regulations enacted under them. With entry into the E.E.C., another form of enacted law, Community law, has had to be introduced into the framework of English law. English courts may decide at what stage to refer to the European Court of Justice for preliminary rulings on the application of Community law in cases where there is a European element, though matters of fact and interpretations of English law are likely to be determined before any reference is made in order to prevent any unnecessary expense and delay. The first reference came in 1974 when the European Court was asked to rule whether a Home Office refusal to allow a Dutch scientologist into Britain conflicted with obligations under the Treaty of Rome to allow free movement of workers between member States.

Critics fear that in time European Community law will supplant English law, but against this it is argued that there will still be a vast field where English common law and statute law will prevail as it did before the United Kingdom entered the Community and that two legal systems can flourish harmoniously side by side as have the English and Scottish systems for some 250 years.

(e) *The effect on Commonwealth relations*

Entry into the E.E.C. may be expected to encourage a greater proportionate share of United Kingdom trade to be with members of the Community, and cultural relations with Europe are likely to be strengthened also. However, it is argued that the new links with Europe will not replace Britain's historical links with the Commonwealth, but rather Britain's world-wide association with the Commonwealth countries will be an invaluable and unique contribution to the Community.

Future developments

Britain's membership of the E.E.C. remains at home a matter of controversy and if the British people are to be prepared to see an increasing range of decisions affecting such important matters as economic growth, employment and price levels taken through common European institutions rather than at Westminster, then critics will need to be satisfied that the institutions of the Community operate efficiently and that decision-making can be brought increasingly under democratic control.

IV. THE INTERNATIONAL COURT OF JUSTICE

The belief that nations, like individuals, are subject to some common fundamental law is traditional, but the present body of international law has resulted chiefly from comparatively recent recognition that States cannot live in isolation from one another. Hence, countries have entered into treaties covering a wide range of subjects, e.g. air routes, fishery conservation, the rule of the road at sea, and tele-communications, and their observance is the main concern of international law.

In 1899 a special court — the International Court — was set up at The Hague. Its fifteen judges are today elected by the Security Council and the General Assembly of the United Nations for a term of nine years. Selection is based on qualifications, not nationality, though no two judges may come from the same country and representation must be secured for the principal legal systems of the world.

The Court carries out two main functions — it hears disputes between States and gives advisory opinions to United Nations bodies and inter-governmental agencies. Such opinions, unlike the Court's judgements, are not legally binding on the organisation or agency requesting them. In arriving at its decisions, the International Court follows the usual judicial procedure. It applies the rules contained in treaties recognised by the disputing States, legal principles and practices accepted internationally, and those rules of law found in the judicial decisions and the teachings of legal authorities in the various States.

But the International Court is very different from the courts described in Chapter 19. First, it will not consider cases submitted by individuals, who must seek redress in the courts of their own country. Secondly, it can only consider disputes which parties agree to submit to it, for international justice is still optional. Thus, when Britain submitted objections to the Court against Iceland's unilateral decision in 1972 to extend its fishing rights from 12 to 50 nautical miles, Iceland refused to recognise the court's jurisdiction in the case.

Thirdly, the International Court has no bodies comparable with police and prisons, so the acceptance of its authority is purely voluntary. Thus Albania refused to pay damages awarded against her in 1947 for the loss of life and damage to United Kingdom warships and when the Court in 1974 upheld Britain's fishing rights in the zone between 12 and 50 miles from the Icelandic coast, Iceland rejected the verdict and said that it had plans to extend its limits eventually to 200 miles.

Does the Court affect the sovereignty of individual States? A government will not usually accept the jurisdiction of the Court when political issues are involved, even though such a refusal may weaken its position in the eyes of other nations. Indeed, it is because legal questions are not always distinguishable from the political and economic interests of disputing nations that the observance of international law is not made obligatory. In the dispute with Albania, Britain had tried to establish its case before the Security Council, but Russia's use of the veto rendered this procedure abortive and so recourse was made to the International Court. The political nature of the case meant that the Court could only function imperfectly, proving that, in such circumstances, it is no substitute for the usual channels of diplomacy. But when legal principles can be applied to a dispute, its decisions are usually accepted. In any case, appeal to it allows time for tempers to cool and alternatives to the use of force to be found. For instance, in the dispute between Britain and Iceland mentioned earlier, the Court also ruled that the two countries were obliged to negotiate a settlement of their differences, paying regard to the legal rights of each other, to the facts of the particular situation and to the interests of other states with established rights in the area.

V. THE UNITED NATIONS ORGANISATION

The United Nations was set up in 1945 at a time of achievement and of hopeful looking forward. Its purposes are:

(1) to take effective collective measures for maintaining international peace;

(2) to develop friendly relations among nations, based on respect for the principle of equal rights and self-determination;

(3) to achieve co-operation in solving international problems of an economic, social, cultural or humanitarian character, and in promoting respect for human rights and the fundamental freedoms without distinction as to race, sex, language or religion;

(4) to be a centre for harmonising the actions of nations in attaining these common ends.

The machinery established is shown in Fig. 22. The chief organs are the General Assembly and the Security Council.

The General Assembly, the chief deliberative organ, meets once a year but can be called in an emergency. Each member country

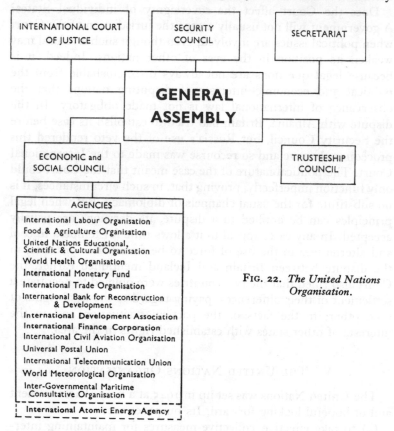

FIG. 22. *The United Nations Organisation.*

has one vote, but any recommendations upon which action is necessary must be referred to the Security Council.

The Security Council, as its name suggests, is intended to play the major part in maintaining peace. Five of its members (Britain, the U.S.A., the U.S.S.R., The People's Republic of China and France) are permanent, but the other ten are elected for two-year terms by the General Assembly. Each member has one vote, and decisions are made by an affirmative vote of nine members which must include the votes of the five permanent members (though in practice an abstention does not count as a veto). In theory, the Council occupies a position somewhat similar to that of the executive in domestic politics and sits continuously. Its two functions are: (1) to promote the peaceful settlement of disputes; (2) to stop aggression. Where it decides that a nation has broken, or appears likely to break the peace, it may take action by diplomatic boycott, economic embargo or, ultimately, military measures, but such sanctions may be vetoed by the negative vote of one of the five great powers. If military action is decided upon, member States are obliged to provide the Council with armed forces.

THE IMPACT OF THE UNITED NATIONS ON NATIONAL GOVERNMENTS

Some form of world government is now a permanent feature of modern civilisation. As André Maurois prophetically said of the League of Nations: 'Whether people want it or not, their destinies are now so closely intertwined that . . . if tomorrow some catastrophe destroyed it, it would come to life again under another name.' No country today can live in isolation from world events and, recognising this, all independent States, with the major exceptions of Switzerland, North Vietnam, South Vietnam, North Korea and South Korea, are now members of the United Nations. Such wide recognition invests an international body with a moral authority which cannot be entirely ignored even by sovereign States. This can be appreciated by studying its most important functions.

(1) The maintenance of peace

Since its formation, the United Nations has had to consider several serious disputes — the Arab-Israel wars, the disagreement over Kashmir, the Korean war, the Hungarian uprising, the Anglo-French invasion of Egypt, Turkey's invasion of Cyprus, disorders in the Congo, the Vietnam war and the occupation of Czechoslovakia. To what extent can it influence sovereign nations in such matters?

In the first place, since discussion is the only alternative to force, the United Nations, by providing such a forum, helps towards a peaceful solution, even though nations may try to use it as a platform for propaganda.

Secondly, nations are now placed in a position where they have to justify their actions before the bar of world opinion. In the

United Nations such opinion can be swiftly expressed with force and clarity, as it was, for instance, over the invasion of North Korea (1950), Russian intervention in Hungary (1956), the Anglo-French invasion of Egypt (1956), the action of the U.S.A. in Vietnam (1965) and the Russian occupation of Czechoslovakia (1968). Thus, the United Nations may be looked upon as the most important international 'pressure group'. The response of a nation to United Nations' resolutions will depend on how much it values world opinion, how essential a part of its policy is under discussion, and how deeply its prestige is involved. Thus, Russia did not withdraw her troops from Hungary after an overwhelming condemnation by the General Assembly, since she regarded the maintenance of a satellite government in Hungary as indispensable. Britain and France, on the other hand, did respond to United Nations' pressure over Suez. No country is entirely unheeding of world sentiment, and the importance of having an institution which can express it should not be underestimated. In Britain, the major deliberations of the United Nations are widely reported, and they may have a notable influence on the formation of opinion. No democratically-elected government would wish to strengthen the arguments of its opponents at home by acting against world opinion.

Thirdly, the United Nations may take physical action in a crisis. In the Korean war, seventeen nations, including the United Kingdom, responded to the appeal of the Security Council to send troops, and United Nations forces have since operated in the Gaza strip, the Congo and Cyprus.

Finally, although the United Nations has little power to change the domestic policies of member nations, it can outline ideals of political behaviour, criticise if those ideals are not being followed in particular countries, and make recommendations to the government concerned. Its Commission on Human Rights has studied the repatriation of prisoners of war, compensation for Nazi victims, and racial policy in South Africa and Rhodesia, and in each case made recommendations.

(2) Colonial administration

Although the United Nations can have no strong claim to supervise the development of ordinary colonies, Chapter XI of the Charter describes colonies as 'a sacred trust'. Article 73, however, requests colonial powers to send regularly to the Secretary-General 'statistical and other information of a technical nature relating to economic, social and educational conditions'. It is thus recognised that poverty, ignorance and the welfare of dependent peoples are problems of world concern.

The Colonial Office in 1948 pointed out that Article 73 did not require colonial powers to submit information on political and constitutional subjects. The British Government later protested that the inclusion of Cyprus on the agenda of the United Nations was an infringement of its sovereignty. While such arguments may have legal force, they have little practical importance. World opinion now clearly takes account of colonial matters, and any criticism it makes is disadvantageous to the standing of the colonial power.

(3) *Economic and social policy*

The work of the Economic and Social Council and of the fourteen inter-government agencies whose activities it co-ordinates (Figure 22) rarely offends national sovereignty. Its task is the conquest of disease, ignorance and poverty. While there is no power to enforce its recommendations, countries usually find it in their own interest to take action.

(4) *Administration of international affairs*

The United Nations' Secretariat consists of the Secretary-General, appointed by the General Assembly upon the recommendation of the Security Council, and such staff as the organisation may require. The Secretary-General has three functions — to act as the chief administrative officer of the United Nations; to bring to the attention of the Security Council any matters which threaten international peace; to report to the General Assembly on the work of the Organisation.

The administration of the United Nations raises interesting questions relating to State sovereignty, for many thousands of nationals from member countries now form an international civil service scattered throughout the world, in the headquarters at New York, at the International Labour Office in Geneva, with the Food and Agriculture Organisation in Rome, and so on. What, for instance, is the position of British civil servants who are transferred to these organisations? While they have a personal loyalty to their own country, they are paid by U.N.O. and are expected to carry out its policy. An oath is taken not to accept instructions from any authority other than the organisation for which they work and to 'refrain from any action which might reflect on their position as international officials responsible only to the Organisation'. National governments, for their part, are enjoined to respect the international nature of the work of the Secretariat and not to seek to influence those who administer it.

The creation of the Secretariat is a notable development in international collaboration, but it is not, of course, entrusted with vital information concerning the security of member States. One of the most difficult obstacles to be overcome in a system of world government would be the creation of a body of administrators with standards of integrity so high that they could handle secret matters.

THE BRITISH CONSTITUTION AND WORLD GOVERNMENT

When the United Nations was set up, many people envisaged the General Assembly as the embryo of world government. It seemed that Tennyson's vision might be realised:

'The war-drum throbb'd no longer, and the battle-flags were furled
In the Parliament of man, the Federation of the world.'

(Locksley Hall)

But it soon became clear that such a development was remote. Even within a single country, responsible government does not flourish easily. As we have seen, the success of the British constitution is dependent upon tolerance, trust, mutual respect and identity of view regarding fundamentals — qualities conspicuously lacking at the international level.

Nevertheless, the growth of international institutions is important to the British constitution. More than ever before, its functioning depends, not only upon how it harmonises conflicting interests within its own geographical boundaries, but upon the extent to which it can reconcile national policies with the political, military and economic plans of other peoples. No constitution in the modern world can be self-contained. In the words of C. F. Strong, writing on the United Nations: 'It is a moral certainty that, if in this Atomic Age the nations do not make this world constitution work, no national constitution can survive' (*Modern Political Constitutions*).

SUGGESTED READING

Max Beloff, *Europe and the Europeans* (Chatto and Windus, 1957).
Central Office of Information, *Britain: an Official Handbook* (H.M.S.O., 1975), Section 3.
S. Holt, *The Common Market* (Hamilton, 1967).
Bernard Moore, *The Second Lesson* (Macmillan, 1957).
H. G. Nicholas, *The United Nations as a Political Institution* (4th Ed., O.U.P., 1971).
C. F. Strong, *Modern Political Constitutions* (8th Ed., Sidgwick and Jackson, 1972), Chapter 16.

Index